Civil War in the
North Carolina Quaker Belt

Civil War in the North Carolina Quaker Belt

The Confederate Campaign Against Peace Agitators, Deserters and Draft Dodgers

WILLIAM T. AUMAN

McFarland & Company, Inc., Publishers
Jefferson, North Carolina

LIBRARY OF CONGRESS CATALOGUING-IN-PUBLICATION DATA

Auman, William T.
Civil War in the North Carolina Quaker belt :
the Confederate campaign against peace agitators,
deserters and draft dodgers / William T. Auman.
p.   cm.
Includes bibliographical references and index.

ISBN 978-0-7864-7663-3
softcover : acid free paper ∞

1. North Carolina—History—Civil War, 1861–1865—Protest movements.
2. North Carolina—History—Civil War, 1861–1865—Social aspects.
3. North Carolina—History—Civil War, 1861–1865—Campaigns.
4. United States—History—Civil War, 1861–1865—Protest movements.
5. United States—History—Civil War, 1861–1865—Social aspects.
6. Military deserters—North Carolina—History—19th century.
7. Quakers—North Carolina—History—19th century.
8. Copperhead movement. I. Title.

E573.A96 2014   973.7'456—dc23   2013046988

BRITISH LIBRARY CATALOGUING DATA ARE AVAILABLE

© 2014 Anne Auman Brown. All rights reserved

*No part of this book may be reproduced or transmitted in any form
or by any means, electronic or mechanical, including photocopying
or recording, or by any information storage and retrieval system,
without permission in writing from the publisher.*

On the cover: Secret Meeting of Southern Unionists, sketched by A.R. Waud,
August 4, 1866, *Harper's Weekly* (courtesy of harpersweekly.com);
background © 2013 Shutterstock; flags and NC State seal clipart.com.

Manufactured in the United States of America

*McFarland & Company, Inc., Publishers
Box 611, Jefferson, North Carolina 28640
www.mcfarlandpub.com*

To the memory of

Sergeant John Slack, who served six years in the Maryland Continental Line, Artillery. He fought at Monmouth under the command of General George Washington and at Eutaw Springs under the command of General Nathanael Greene.

Private Dempsey Auman, who served in Company K of the 2nd North Carolina Regiment, Confederate States Army. He died of disease at Harrisonburg, Virginia, on October 29, 1862.

Private Riley Luther, regimental blacksmith, Company F, 46th North Carolina Regiment, Confederate States Army, who was captured at Hatcher's Run, Virginia, March 31, 1865, and confined at Point Lookout prisoner of war camp where he died on April 30.

Private Ira Slack, Company I, 85th Indiana Regiment, Sherman's Army, who was mortally wounded at the Battle of Resaca, Georgia, in May 1864.

1st Lt. John B. Crisp, navigator on a B-24 Liberator, Squadron 325 of the 93rd Bomber Group, Heavy, United States Army Air Corps, who died when his Liberator went down in the North Atlantic while crossing to England on September 9, 1942, with the loss of all on board.

Fireman First Class Thomas Auman, United States Navy, who died in Honolulu, Hawaii, on June 13, 1945, and was buried at sea.

Private Max Cornelius Auman, 24th Cavalry Reconnaissance Squad, U.S. Army, who was killed in combat during the Normandy Invasion on July 18, 1944. He was buried at the St. Mère Église Cemetery, No. 2, Normandy, France.

Ronald Gale Trogdon, U.S. Army 1st Air Cavalry MediVac Unit, who was the first soldier from Randolph County killed in Vietnam. He was mortally wounded in combat on June 19, 1967, and was posthumously awarded the Purple Heart, the Distinguished Flying Cross, and the Bronze Star.

Acknowledgments

I am indebted to James M. Woods and Gordon B. McKinney for reading and critiquing early versions of my manuscript for this book. I thank David D. Scarboro and Mac Whatley for their recent labors on my behalf analyzing my revisions of the text. Mac also brought to my attention several important historical items such as the William Burson book that I have incorporated into my narrative. I owe a special debt to Marie D. Moore, who, while editor of *The North Carolina Historical Review*, directed me through the publication of three articles. Likewise to Paul D. Escott, who perused my chapters on the peace and convention movements.

About thirty-five years ago, Buren Garner related to me his memories of the William Owens deserter gang and other Red String actors in the inner civil war in the Quaker Belt told to him by his parents and grandparents and others. For that I am most grateful. I thank Larry Parks for prodding me over the years to get this book published. Kudos go to Joe R. Covington for producing the maps of North Carolina and the Quaker Belt that are used in this book. Thanks to Tiffany Auman for the assistance she has given me. I am beholden to my sister, Anne Brown, for the support she has rendered to me over the years. Without her aid, this book could not have been published.

Contents

Acknowledgments vi

Preface 1

Introduction 5

ONE. The Antislavery Impulse and the Quaker Belt   9

TWO. The Secession Crisis and the Militant Unionists   26

THREE. The Inner Civil War   42

FOUR. The Copperhead Insurgency, Phase One: The Peace Movement   78

FIVE. General Hoke's Great Deserter Hunt in Late 1863   103

SIX. The Copperhead Insurgency, Phase Two: The Convention Movement and the Gubernatorial Election of 1864   126

SEVEN. The 1864 Election Uprising and the Vance Repression   155

EIGHT. The Last Hunt and the Conclusion of the Inner Civil War   180

Summary and Conclusions 199

Notes 215

Bibliography 247

Index 257

Preface

This book gives an account of the war conducted by the Confederacy and Governor Zebulon Baird Vance against deserters and disloyalists in the Quaker Belt of North Carolina. It also discusses the internal war that raged in the region from the spring of 1861 until war's end between militant Unionists (those who remained loyal to the United States after secession) and their deserter and draft-dodger allies on the one hand and the secessionists on the other. Fifteen counties in the central piedmont of North Carolina settled by antislavery, pacifist Quakers and Moravians in the mid-eighteenth century comprised the Quaker Belt. I describe the seven military campaigns conducted by Confederate authorities against the deserters, draft-dodgers, and disloyal militant Unionists in the district during the war. I explain how the "outliers" (deserters and draft-dodgers) managed to elude capture and survive despite extensive efforts by Confederate authorities to hunt them down and return them to the army. I discuss the development of the secret, underground pro–Union organization the Heroes of America in the area and how its members utilized the Underground Railroad, dug-out caves, and an elaborate system of secret signals and communications to elude the "hunters." I devote a chapter to each of the great deserter hunts conducted by Confederate and state authorities in the summers of 1863 and 1864. The internal war was vicious and bloody; I provide numerous instances of murder, rape, torture, assault and battery, intimidation, house and barn burning, house demolition, theft, plunder, and the destruction of crops and household items. I present many accounts of skirmishes between gangs of deserters and Confederate and state troops.

In 1861, Zeb Vance, a Whig politician from the western mountains, ardently opposed secession. Nevertheless, upon taking the reins of power as governor in the summer of 1862, he morphed into a champion of the Confederacy. He was unrelenting in his repression of deserters, draft-dodgers, and disloyal militant Unionists to the end of the war. When he won reelection as governor in August 1864, an insurrection of dissidents who had championed his opponent William Holden erupted in the Quaker Belt. Vance reacted swiftly and viciously. Determined to eliminate the threat posed to Confederate power in the west, he ordered a massive force composed of Home Guards, Militia, Senior Reserves, and Confederate troops to the area with orders to arrest and detain in military camps anyone who aided or abetted the dissidents. As a result, women (many of them pregnant), children, and the elderly were confined without adequate food and water or shelter for days in makeshift prisons until the deserter hunt was over. Women were tortured and children frightened in an effort to force them to disclose the hiding places of their husbands, sons, fathers and brothers. The troops tore down the homes of many of the deserters and otherwise destroyed their property and provisions. Vance's actions in this campaign amounted to a declaration of martial law and the suspension of the writ of habeas corpus, powers he did not have under the law at the time. Vance clearly exceeded his legal powers as governor in this deserter hunt; yet, despite efforts by Quaker Belt politicians to impeach him, he was never brought to task for his transgressions. Chapter Seven, "The 1864 Election Uprising and the Vance Repression," relates the details of this bloody deserter hunt.

A secondary goal of the book is to present a revisionist interpretation of the wartime Tar Heel peace movement that originated in the Quaker Belt in 1862 during the peace demonstrations held in Randolph and Davidson counties, and with the publications of Bryan Tyson, a pro-reunion Whig political activist from Moore County who had Quaker antecedents. I present evidence that the North Carolina peace leaders launched their peace movement in response to the one initiated by the "Peace Democrats," or "Copperheads," in the north in the winter of 1863. The Copperheads clamored for the return of the Southern states to the Union on a Constitutional basis, that is, with the institution of slavery protected by the Constitution. Most of the leaders of the North Carolina peace movement, including their head, William Holden — editor of the largest and most influential newspaper in the state, the *North Carolina Standard* — worked for a return of the Tar Heel state (and the Confederacy) to the Union on the Copperhead basis to save slavery and avoid the humiliation of defeat and the social revolution in race relations emancipation would incur. The standard view is that Holden, motivated by disloyal sentiments, initiated the peace movement in an effort to return the state to the Union presumably on the Lincoln basis, that is, with emancipation. Or alternately, as some historians believe, the peace movement was foremost a rant against the centralizing efforts on the part of the Davis administration such as the draft and tax laws.

This narrative introduces the reader to Bryan Tyson and Lewis Hanes, individuals who have received scant attention from historians but played critical roles in the founding of the Copperhead insurgency in 1863 and in the internal war that raged on the home front between the reunionist faction in society and the secessionists. Traditionally, historians have credited William Holden as being the founder of the Tar Heel peace movement. In this book I demonstrate that in the summer of 1862, Bryan Tyson in his book *A Ray of Light* and his "reunion circular" broadside emerged as the first North Carolinian to advocate returning to the Union on the Copperhead basis. Tyson's call for reunion on the Copperhead basis fell on deaf ears in 1862, but this idea reemerged in the summer of 1863 as the central tenet of William Holden's peace movement. Holden made clear his Copperhead leanings and reunionist intentions in an essay printed in the *Semi-Weekly Standard* in July entitled "The Secessionists — their Promises and their Performances — the Condition into which they have brought the Country — the Remedy, etc." Historians have overlooked this essay. It was written by Lewis Hanes, an editor from Davidson County who used the pen name "Davidson." About three weeks after he published Hanes' treatise, Holden wrote an editorial in the *Standard* (August 25, 1863) in which he argued for a "restoration of the old government ... with all our rights guaranteed." By printing Hanes' pro–Copperhead essay and this editorial,

Holden made it obvious that he favored reunion on the Copperhead basis. At the time, everyone realized this, but for some reason this fact has eluded historians. As a result, none of the studies of the Tar Heel peace movement or the biographies of William Woods Holden mention Lewis Hanes, his treatise, or the writings of Bryan Tyson. Neither have any of them viewed Holden's peace movement as a Copperhead insurgency. Hopefully, this historical oversight stands corrected and Lewis Hanes and Bryan Tyson will take their places as central figures in the Civil War drama known as the North Carolina peace movement, in which they passionately argued for a return to the Union on the Copperhead basis.

Introduction

The purpose of this study is to document the war against deserters promulgated by state and national Confederate authorities, to investigate the causes and extent of disaffection and disloyalty to the Confederacy in the central piedmont of Confederate North Carolina — referred to in this study as the "Quaker Belt" — to detail the resulting fratricidal "inner civil war" between supporters and opponents of the Confederacy in the area, and to analyze the agitation for peace and reunion based on the Copperhead plan for reconstruction widely advocated in the district. The central piedmont counties of Randolph, Chatham, Moore, Davidson, Guilford, Forsyth, Yadkin, Davie, Surry, Wilkes, Montgomery, Orange, Alamance, Stokes, and Iredell comprised the Quaker Belt.[1] (See map below.)

It has been more than seventy-five years since historians first alerted the historical profession to the extent and seriousness of the interrelated problems of dissent, disaffection, desertion, and disloyalty in the Confederacy.[2] Many historians over the decades since then have contributed to the subject, including a recent synthesis of the topic by David Williams.[3] Of the many reasons given for opposition to the Confederacy by white Southerners, the more important advanced were persistent Unionism, lingering Whiggery, rampant inflation, poverty, hunger, opposition to the conscription laws, class antagonisms, persistent inter–South sectionalism, states' rights ideology, fear of a "central military despotism" in Richmond, and

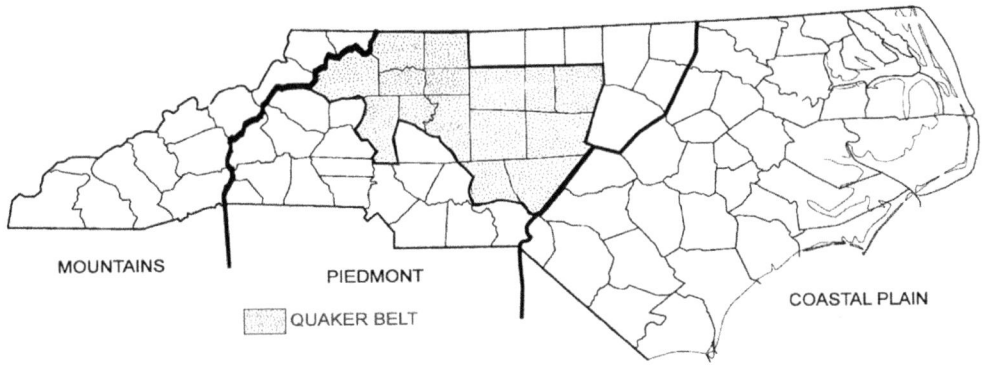

The Three Geographic Regions of North Carolina and the Quaker Belt

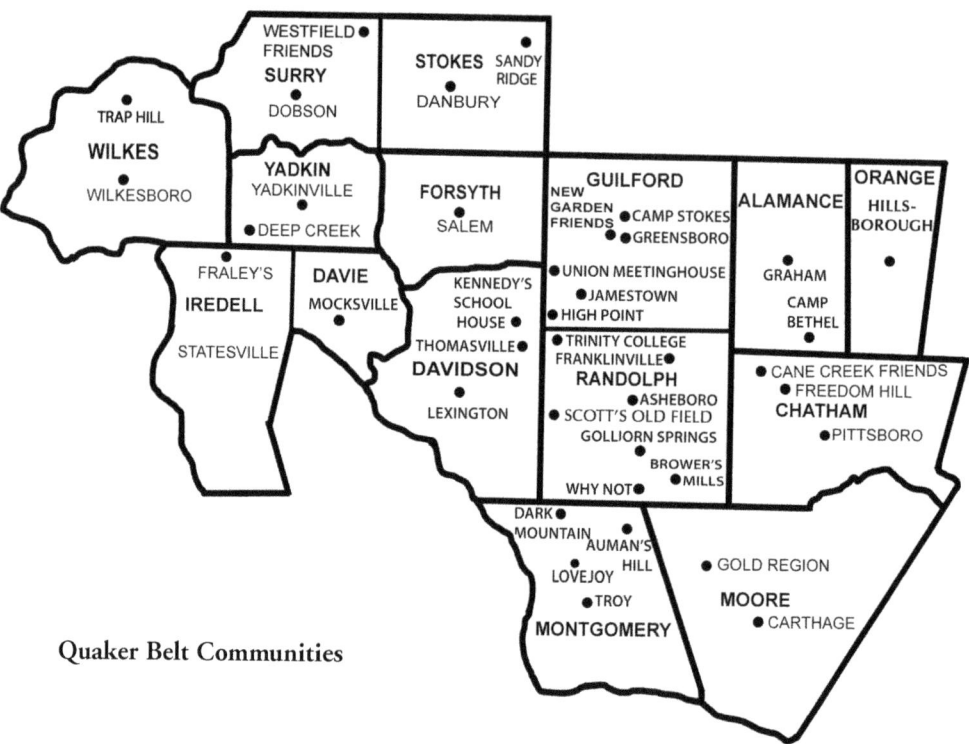

Quaker Belt Communities

defeatism. Studies done by historians in recent years have led some scholars of the Civil War to conclude that Southern whites opposed the Confederacy far more strongly than hitherto believed. Disloyalty, persistent Unionism and desertion were so widespread that state and Confederate authorities in fact fought two wars: one against the hated Yankees and another against internal enemies.[4] In the first two years of the war, the major loci of disaffection and disloyalty to the Confederacy were northern Arkansas, eastern Tennessee, and northern Alabama.[5]

As the war progressed, pockets of discontent appeared in all the other states of the Confederacy, but most notably in the Appalachian Mountains and bordering uplands of Virginia, North Carolina, South Carolina, and Georgia.[6] Serious centers of disaffection and disloyalty appeared in three areas of Confederate North Carolina: in the Appalachian Mountains of the far west, in the sound region of the northeastern coastal plain, and in the central piedmont. The piedmont was a large area of rocky red clay uplands situated between the mountainous west and the near-level, sandy-soiled coastal plain that dominated the eastern half of the state. (See map of the three geographic regions of North Carolina and the Quaker Belt.)

Diehard Unionists of disloyal East Tennessee launched an uprising against Confederate authority as early as the fall of 1861. The actions of these disloyalists affected Appalachian North Carolina, especially the counties bordering Tennessee.[7] The influence of the militant Tennessee Unionists, enhanced by impending famine, rampant inflation, defeatism, and the growing disaffection with the policies of the Davis government as the war progressed, made Appalachian North Carolina a center of discontent in the Confederacy.[8] The Appalachian and adjacent foothill counties of Confederate North Carolina furnished two North

Carolina regiments to the Union army as well as numerous troops to various Union regiments from other states.[9]

In December 1861, Union naval and army forces captured Roanoke Island in the sound region of northeastern North Carolina. By the summer of 1862, the Federals had occupied New Bern and Beaufort to the south. Thousands of poor whites, free blacks, and slaves fled to the Union lines.[10] Once under the protection of Federal troops, many Unionist whites, mostly former Whigs, proclaimed their loyalty to the United States. A lot of them organized "free labor" associations and congratulated President Abraham Lincoln on his emancipation policy.[11] Encouraged by the display of loyalty to the Union by the local populace, the Lincoln administration attempted to organize a loyal North Carolina government in the occupied sound region, but the effort collapsed due to political bickering among the North Carolina loyalists and to the failure of the new provisional governor to accept many of Lincoln's policies, especially emancipation.[12] Two white and four black regiments recruited from eastern North Carolina mustered into the Union army before the war ended; many others joined the Federal navy.[13] Armed bands called "buffaloes"— made up of poor whites, free blacks, and former slaves — roamed the grey area between the Union and Confederate lines robbing, murdering, and otherwise terrifying whites loyal to the Confederacy.[14]

The Quaker Belt of the central piedmont constituted the third center of disaffection and disloyalty to the Confederacy in North Carolina. Historians have written little about wartime disaffection there, probably because they have not been attracted to an area that remained remote from the battlefields until the last days of the war. Georgia Lee Tatum, in her pioneering study of disloyalty in the Confederacy, briefly noted that the piedmont counties of Iredell, Guilford, Davidson, Chatham, Randolph, Forsyth, Yadkin, and Wilkes were centers of anti–Confederate unrest, but she made no extended analysis of the situation in the area.[15] Historians have repeated Tatum's charge that disloyalty was strong in the central piedmont of North Carolina, but with few exceptions, none has made a detailed examination of the discontent.[16]

The Quaker Belt was culturally unique in the antebellum South; it defined the boundaries of the largest settlements of Quakers, Moravians, and Wesleyan Methodists in the region. The Moravians were antislavery and pacifistic; the Quakers were more ardently so; the Wesleyans were outright abolitionists. The Quaker Belt included, besides the Quakers, Wesleyan Methodists, and Moravians, a miscellany of religious sects including Lutheran, German Reformed, Presbyterian, Methodist Protestant, Methodist Episcopal, Christian, Episcopal, and Baptist denominations.[17]

In addition to being a center of pacifism and abolitionism, diehard anti-secessionist Whigs composed a majority of the populace of the Quaker Belt. They opted for the Constitutional Union ticket in the presidential election of 1860, and voted down by large majorities in February 1861 a proposal to hold a state convention to consider secession.[18] When war erupted, the Quaker Belt became a breeding ground for dissent and disloyalty to the Confederacy due to the influences of the Quakers, Moravians, Wesleyans, and Whigs.

As early as the spring of 1861, diehard Unionists under the leadership of John Hilton formed a secret, underground, anti–Confederate group that evolved into an organization called the Heroes of America. This armed band of pro–Union disloyalists originated in Davidson, Randolph, Forsyth, and Guilford counties but soon spread throughout the Quaker Belt. Authorities sent Confederate and state troops to the area in August 1861 to quell a pro–Union uprising of the Hilton band—the first of seven times Confederate commanders rushed troops into the Quaker Belt during the war to suppress armed insurrection. With the passage of the conscription laws in the spring of 1862, hundreds of area draft-dodgers fled to the woods to escape conscription authorities. In March, the governor ordered troops into the Randolph-Davidson area to repress "peace demonstrations" and open hostility to Confederate power. Encouraged and assisted by their families and the disloyal Heroes of America underground organization, numerous deserters joined the draft-dodgers in the woods in the summer. These developments led to an inner civil war in the Quaker Belt between the deserters, draft-dodgers, and militant Unionists on the one hand, and the loyal Confederate citizens, the militia, the Home Guards, and Confederate troops on the other. Murder, torture, arson, assault and battery, rape, robbery, and larceny characterized this internal war.[19]

In the summer of 1862, Bryan Tyson of Moore County emerged as a leader of reunionist forces in the region. His writings encouraged Tar Heels and Southerners to abandon the Confederacy and return to the Union on the basis offered by the Northern peace Democrats, that is, with the institution of slavery protected by the Constitution for returning states. In 1862, Tyson's efforts at reunion fell on deaf ears, but in the summer of 1863, William Holden, editor of the largest newspaper in the state, rejuvenated Tyson's movement for peace and reunion on the Copperhead basis. The movement spread across North Carolina, but most of the peace sentiment came from the Quaker Belt where disaffected citizens held numerous peace rallies. The peace movement sparked an insurrection of deserters, draft-dodgers, and militant Unionists across the Quaker Belt in August 1863 that presented a serious threat to Confederate power and control in the area. It took large numbers of Confederate troops deployed into the region over a five-month period to quell the uprising. Another revolt of dissidents occurred in August 1864, when the leader of the Peace Party, William Woods Holden, was defeated in his bid for the governorship. Again, Confederate leaders ordered large numbers of troops into the Quaker Belt to pacify discontent. A final rebellion by anti-Confederate disloyalists occurred in March 1865, when pro–Holden deserters and draftees deserted from the Army of Northern Virginia and returned home to terrorize their pro–Confederate neighbors through arson, murder, assault, battery, and robbery. General Lee ordered from the trenches at Petersburg two regiments and a detachment of ten companies pulled from various regiments into the Quaker Belt to pacify the uprising.

By the end of the war, the internecine conflict between neighbors in the Quaker Belt had led to scores of deaths and the torture and wounding of many more. Overzealous troops and marauding bands of deserters had destroyed an uncounted number of homes, barns, crops, and other properties. Thousands of people of all ages and stations in life suffered murder, torture, abuse, rape, intimidation, threats, and deprivation. The deep physical and psychological scars inflicted during the inner civil war led to hatreds that resurfaced after the war in numerous court battles between wartime antagonists, and between Scalawags and their former Confederate tormentors in the vicious politics of the Reconstruction era.

What follows is a detailed account of the origin, progress, and conclusion of the Confederate war against deserters, the internal war of neighbor against neighbor, and the agitation for peace and reunion on the Copperhead basis that occurred in the Quaker Belt of Confederate North Carolina. We shall begin with an investigation of the antebellum history of this region.

CHAPTER ONE

The Antislavery Impulse and the Quaker Belt

Historian Carl Degler argued that the South was never the monolithic "solid South" that historians have traditionally depicted. Rather, noted Degler, the South has had a strong tradition of dissent, especially when heterodox Southerners opposed slavery before the Civil War, supported the Union during the war, became Republicans during Reconstruction, and joined the People's party in the Gilded Age.[1] The Quaker Belt — the focus of this study of dissent in Confederate North Carolina — was a microcosm of Degler's "Other South," where a tradition of alienation from the Southern status quo held sway in the nineteenth century. (See the map Quaker Belt Communities in the introduction for the location of towns and other places mentioned in this study.)

Immigrants from Pennsylvania and Maryland settled the area beginning in the 1740s, though a few came from colonies farther north, including New Jersey and Massachusetts. Palatine Germans, Moravians, Scots-Irish, and English Quakers composed the major ethnocultural groups among these immigrants. Motivated by the desire for cheaper lands and the need to get beyond the range of attacking Indians, settlers traveled down the "Great Wagon Road" in the Shenandoah Valley of Virginia and fanned out into the piedmont of North Carolina. They were independent yeoman farmers and artisans who were unaccustomed to the system of slave labor and the cash crop agriculture that dominated society in the coastal plain region of the state.[2]

The ethnic and religious groups of immigrants from the North who settled the central piedmont had long suffered persecution in their former homelands. While they were nearly all white and Protestant, they nonetheless formed part of a pluralistic society where the ardently pacifistic and antislavery Quaker rubbed shoulders only grudgingly with the truculent Scots-Irish Presbyterian; where German-speaking Calvinists of the Reformed faith rarely mixed with fellow Calvinists from Ulster who spoke English with a Scottish brogue; and where language and culture divided the German-speaking Moravians and Lutherans from the English-speaking majority around them.

While the Scots-Irish settled throughout the piedmont, they were concentrated in the central and western counties. The Germans of the Lutheran and Reformed faiths settled primarily in the counties of Guilford, Randolph, Davidson, Davie, Stanly, Rowan, Iredell, and Cabarrus. German-speaking Moravians established several communities in Forsyth County in the mid-eighteenth century; by the time of the Civil War, Moravians had established congregations in some of the adjoining counties. The Quakers settled in Alamance, Chatham, Orange, Guilford, Randolph, Forsyth, Yadkin, Surry, and Stokes. These Quaker counties, which comprised a contiguous line of counties from Surry and Yadkin in the west to Orange, Alamance, and Chatham in the east, formed the core of the Quaker Belt. The Quaker settlements in Orange, Forsyth, Surry, and Stokes were small, and in general were in decline by the time of the Civil War. Yadkin, Randolph, Chatham, and Guilford were by far the strongest Quaker counties. With the founding of Guilford College in 1833, New Garden (located in central Guilford County) became the center of southern Quakerism.[3]

Two major immigrant types settled in the North Carolina piedmont in the colonial period: one group, as discussed above, was the yeoman farmers and artisans from the North who arrived in the area via the Great Wagon Road. The other was the slave-owning "planter culture" immigrants who came from south side Virginia, eastern North Carolina, and, to a lesser extent, from South Carolina. These people were mostly Anglicans of English descent. After 1770, a few Highland Scots moved into the Quaker Belt from the Cape Fear Valley via the Haw and Deep River valleys. Most immigrants from the coastal plain had lived in a society that had long accepted black slavery as a norm. They settled throughout the piedmont but were strongest in the eastern one-third of the region and became weaker in numbers and influence as one traveled west.[4]

The Quaker Belt was a hotbed of dissent and disorder in the eighteenth century.[5] Armed farmers known as Regulators ended by open revolt a decade-long protest against unfair taxes and unscrupulous, exploitative county officials. Governor Tryon's army defeated them at the Battle of Alamance in 1771. Their leader, Herman Husband, a Quaker resident of the Sandy Creek section of Randolph County (then western Orange County), fled to western Pennsylvania where in 1793 he was condemned to death for his leadership in the Whiskey Rebellion. Hundreds of his Regulator followers likewise abandoned their farms in central North Carolina and fled to Tennessee and Kentucky to avoid prosecution for "rebellion."[6]

Historians have characterized the Revolutionary War in North Carolina, as elsewhere in the South, as a civil war between partisan bands of Whigs and Tories. Nowhere was this truer than in the old Regulator counties of central North Carolina.[7] Murder, torture, house and barn burning, assassination, and assault and battery committed by Whig and Tory alike defined the nature of the Revolutionary experience in the Quaker Belt of North Carolina — a scenario that was to repeat itself in the Civil War of the next century.[8]

The Quaker Phase

Dissent took a new direction in the antebellum decades when the Quaker Belt became a center of antislavery activity in the South. Antislavery agitation went through two phases prior to the Civil War: first the Quaker phase, then the Wesleyan phase.

The Quaker faith was the first organized religion to take root in North Carolina. Friends dominated the political scene in the colony during the last decade of the seventeenth century, when Quaker John Archdale became governor. With the influx of Pennsylvania

Quakers into the backcountry in the mid-eighteenth century, the center of Quaker power and population shifted to the piedmont from the tidewater region.[9] Quaker settlers came mostly from Pennsylvania, though a few arrived from Nantucket Island — places influenced by the antislavery agitation of John Woolman and other northern and British Quaker activists. In 1768, Quaker leaders began to admonish their congregants to not buy, sell, or own slaves. After a decade of discussing the matter, the North Carolina Yearly Meeting ruled in 1778 that Quakers could no longer buy or sell slaves. Taking action on their antislavery sentiments, Quakers began manumitting their slaves on a large scale in the 1770s. The proslavery majority in the state, viewing free blacks as a threat to the security of both whites and slave property, responded by passing laws that forced many of the newly freed slaves back into slavery and, further, made it difficult thereafter to manumit slaves legally in the state.[10]

In 1816, the Tar Heel Quakers organized the North Carolina Manumission Society as a vehicle to spread the antislavery cause and to find ways and means to colonize freed blacks to Haiti and Africa, or send them to the free states of the North. Non-Quakers, including a few planters, joined the society, but Friends comprised the great majority of the membership. The society met semiannually at a Quaker meetinghouse in either Randolph or Guilford County. Over the years delegates attended from Yadkin, Surry, Stokes, Davidson, Orange, Alamance, and Chatham counties, but the majority of attendees came from Randolph and Guilford. The Manumission Society encouraged North Carolina slaveholders, Quaker and non–Quaker, to free their slaves, and helped them with the cost and logistics of transporting them out of the state.[11]

The actions of Benjamin Lundy and William Swaim highlighted the antislavery impulse sparked by the activities of the Manumission Society in the Quaker Belt. In 1824, Benjamin Lundy (1789–1839), abolitionist editor of *The Genius of Universal Emancipation* and future mentor of the prominent northern abolitionist William Lloyd Garrison, gave a series of antislavery speeches in the area, the first of which he delivered at a rally at the Deep Creek Quaker meetinghouse in Yadkin County.[12] In 1830, the General Association of the Manumission Society of North Carolina published the vehemently antislavery document *An Address to the People of North Carolina on the Evils of Slavery*. William Swaim (reputed author of the tract), basing his arguments on the Holy Scriptures, the Declaration of Independence, the Bill of Rights, the federal and state constitutions, and the laws of nature and reason, denounced slavery as "radically evil" and "founded on injustice and cruelty." Recognizing that slavery rested on a foundation of racial prejudice, the author declared that the color of one's skin was a false basis for putting a human in bondage and depriving him or her of natural rights. Swain believed in educating slaves to the extent that each could read the scriptures. He advocated a system of gradual emancipation instituted by the state and ultimately by the nation.[13]

William Swaim was born and raised in south-central Guilford County in the Centre community, a Quaker settlement near the Randolph County line. The Swaims were not members of the Society of Friends. Nevertheless, as in the case of so many non–Quakers living in the Quaker Belt, the pacifist and antislavery beliefs of their Quaker neighbors deeply influenced them. William served as secretary of the General Association of the Manumission Society of North Carolina from 1826 to 1832, and his cousin, Benjamin Swaim, who lived in the north-central Randolph County community of New Salem, served as president of the society for several terms. In 1829, William worked in Baltimore as an assistant editor of the abolitionist newspaper owned by Benjamin Lundy. After working only about six months with Lundy, William went back to North Carolina to settle his father's estate. Rather than return to Baltimore, William bought the Greensboro *Patriot*, which he edited with distinction until his premature death at the age of thirty-three in 1835. Under his editorship, the *Patriot* served as a moderate yet firm voice for the antislavery cause in central North Carolina.[14]

An ardent follower of Henry Clay and his American System, William Swaim championed in his editorials the economic development of the piedmont region of North Carolina through state support of banks, railroads, turnpikes, canals, and other forms of internal improvements. He also advocated public education, penal reform, and the humane care of the deaf, dumb, blind, and mentally retarded. As a bold and outspoken promoter of progress, Swaim anticipated the direction North Carolina's Whig party would take when political leaders founded it in 1834 in the state. Thereafter, a majority of the people in the Quaker Belt advocated the Whig cause from then until the coming of the Civil War.

Soon after the establishment of the Manumission Society, two of its members, Levi and Vestal Coffin, founded the Underground Railroad. Both were Quakers and natives of Guilford County. The Coffins and other Friends and antislavery supporters throughout the Quaker Belt provided food, shelter, and guidance to runaway slaves who sought their aid in fleeing north to freedom. The Carolina Quakers, in cooperation with Quakers and antislavery sympathizers in Virginia, Kentucky, and Ohio, spirited the runaways to free soil through a secret network of "stations" spaced a few miles apart. In the 1820s, Levi Coffin moved from North Carolina to Newport, Indiana, where his house became an important station on the Underground Railroad. In the late 1840s, he relocated to Cincinnati, Ohio, where he became celebrated as the "President of the Underground Railroad."[15]

David Walker, a former slave who had escaped to the North from Wilmington, North Carolina, added a radical tinge to the Tar Heel voices decrying the evils of slavery. In 1830, he published an abolitionist tract titled *Appeal in Four Articles*. Walker advocated immediate emancipation and encouraged slaves to revolt. The next year, insurgent slaves slaughtered 56 whites during the Nat Turner slave rebellion in Southampton County, Virginia. With the Turner revolt, the center of antislavery activity in the United States moved from the upper South to the North. State legislatures across the South made laws more strictly regulating free blacks and slaves, and society no longer tolerated the open expression of antislavery sentiments.[16] A victim of the growing repression of free speech on the slavery issue, the North Carolina Manumission Society declined from a peak of nearly 1,600 members in 1827 to but a handful in 1834, when it held its last meeting at Marlborough Friends Meetinghouse in northern Randolph County.[17]

With the death of William Swaim in 1835 and the demise of the North Carolina Manumission Society the year before, the antislavery impulse in North Carolina declined greatly. The Quakers remained antislavery advocates, but their influence dwindled with the advent of the militant proslavery upsurge following the Turner rebellion. Of equal importance was the numerical decline of the state's Quaker population that had been in progress since the turn of the century. In the first three decades of the nineteenth century, hundreds of North Carolina Quakers, attracted by richer soil and the absence of slavery, had immigrated to the states of Ohio and Indiana, especially to the latter. Hundreds of others followed them after 1830, some in reaction to a discriminatory militia law that required Quakers to swear to an oath, a practice against their religious scruples, or face criminal charges.[18]

The practice of "disowning" members who did not strictly follow the religious precepts laid down by the religious community also led to the decline of Quaker influence. Quakers disowned congregants most commonly for "marrying out of unity," that is, marrying non–Quakers. Other causes included failure to use "Quaker pronouns" such as "thee" and "thou" in daily speech, using tobacco or alcohol, owning slaves, and refusing to conform to the Quaker dress code of "plainness."[19] When the Civil War erupted, many non–Quakers in the central piedmont had blood ties to the Quakers, but whose parents, grandparents, or other ancestors had been disowned by the Society of Friends. Many of these people favored pacifism and the antislavery cause. Most former Quakers and their offspring became Baptists or Methodists. They were an important factor in the continuation of antislavery sentiment in the district after 1830, when Quaker numbers and influence began to decline in the area.

At the time of the Civil War, the Methodists had the largest religious denomination in the Quaker Belt.[20] Religious leaders introduced Methodism into the colonies during the Revolution, and it quickly spread across North Carolina after the war. Following the antislavery example of its founders John and Charles Wesley and Francis Asbury, the early Methodist church welcomed blacks into its ranks—both free and slave. However, as the eighteenth century ebbed and as the church absorbed more and more slave owners into its ranks, Methodism in the South increasingly turned proslavery.[21] Yet in central North Carolina, antislavery sentiment never completely died out in the Methodist ranks.

The Wesleyan Methodist Phase

In the 1840s, all of the major Protestant denominations in the United States split into North and South factions over the slavery issue. But a remarkable event occurred in 1845 among the Methodists in the Guilford/Randolph area of the Quaker Belt. Due to its antislavery sentiments, a congregation of the Methodist Episcopal Church located in the southwestern Guilford County community of Jamestown refused to join the Methodist Episcopal Church, South. Instead, they called themselves the Free Methodist Church and remained an independent congregation until 1847, when they applied to the Wesleyan Methodist Church in Ohio to accept them as a member congregation. They asked the Wesleyan Methodists to send them a minister to serve the needs and champion the cause of antislavery Methodists in their area. Abolitionist zealots who did not think that the Methodist Episcopal Church in the North had gone far enough in its stand against slavery founded the Wesleyan Methodist Connection in 1843.[22] The Wesleyans favored immediate emancipation and actively sought black congregants.[23] With the arrival of Wesleyan Methodism at Jamestown, the antislavery cause underwent a remarkable rejuvenation in central North Carolina.

When Wesleyan minister Adams Crooks arrived in Jamestown from Ohio in 1847, he roomed at the home of Richard Mendenhall, a former Quaker and onetime head of the North Carolina Manumission Society. The Quakers permitted the Wesleyans to use their meetinghouses for services in the early years of Wesleyan growth in the state. When Crooks began his ministry, the North Carolina Wesleyans numbered about forty souls divided into four congregations, none of which had a church building of its own. Within a year, Crooks

Columbia Manufacturing Company, Ramseur, North Carolina, 1885. Established in the 1850s, Columbia was one of five cotton mills active along the Deep River in Randolph County during the Civil War (courtesy Mac Whatley and Randolph County Public Library's Historical Photograph Collection).

had expanded his following to eight congregations and 140 members.[24] Remarking upon his success at mixing abolition and religion in slave country, Crooks said: "Calls for me to preach are numerous — Congregations generally large. I seldom preach without denouncing the peculiar institution; mostly I have Slave-holders to hear."[25] Crooks added: "There is much more antislavery sentiment in this part of North Carolina than I had supposed. This is owing, in great measure, to the influence of the society of Friends."[26] As the following quotation demonstrates, the young abolitionist proved to be a bit too optimistic in his hopes for the future of his sect in the Tar Heel State: "It is the opinion of some of the most intelligent men of North Carolina that she will be a free State before many years; and that in the event of a dissolution of the Union, North Carolina will go with the North. The great spirit of liberty is beginning to breathe upon the people."[27]

In 1848, church leaders constructed the first Wesleyan abolitionist church built in the South at Freedom's Hill in the Snow Camp community of Chatham County (now in Alamance County). The Freedom's Hill church was located about one mile south of the Cane Creek Meetinghouse, the first Quaker church built (1752) in central North Carolina.[28] Next, Crooks founded a church at Flint Hill in west-central Randolph County, where "long sermons seemed to be the order of the day, as Crooks speaks of preaching for two hours, while more than half his congregation had to stand, there being no room in the house where he preached. To accommodate the crowds he would stand in the door so that those within and without might hear the life-giving message."[29]

Crooks also established Wesleyan congregations in Grayson County, Virginia, during his first year in the South. (Grayson County, Virginia, is located about sixty miles northwest of Guilford County, North Carolina.) In late 1848, church authorities sent Wesleyan missionary Jarvis C. Bacon to aid Crooks; Bacon took over the Grayson County, Virginia, charge. Jesse McBride, a third Wesleyan missionary and a former Quaker, arrived in Jamestown in October 1849. Crooks relinquished the Guilford Circuit to McBride and moved to the southwestern Randolph County community of Hill's Store to open up new territory in Randolph, Davidson, Montgomery, and Stanly counties. The abolitionist missionaries experienced little opposition during their first two years in the Tar Heel State, though Bacon early on got into legal difficulties with proslavery opponents in Virginia.[30]

Then in 1849 trouble erupted between Wesleyans and the owners of the Randolph Manufacturing Company when managers fired several workers for attending Wesleyan services.[31] Randolph Manufacturing Company was one of two cotton mills located in Franklinsville, a village located in east-central Randolph County.[32] In the preamble to a series of resolutions decrying the baleful influence of the Wesleyans, the stockholders of the company declared, "It is understood that an emissary of the Abolitionists, under the guise of the True Wesleyan Church, has been covertly and insidiously instilling the mischievous doctrines of Abolitionism and amalgamation in our community, and has received countenance, encouragement and support in the village of Franklinsville." Such conduct, claimed the management, has brought "reproach and discredit" upon the people of the village and the company that threatens injury and financial loss.[33] A few months later, the stockholders met and endorsed a resolution stating they would no longer dismiss employees from their jobs because of their religious or political convictions.[34] Despite their efforts at reconciliation with the Wesleyan workers, the management of the Randolph Manufacturing Company may have provoked someone into an act of arson, for on the night of April 19, 1851, the cotton mill burned to the ground "in an unaccountable and very mysterious manner."[35]

The other cotton mill in Franklinsville, the Island Ford Manufacturing Company, also opposed Wesleyan influences in their workplace, but there is no evidence that the company suffered reprisals at the hands of dismissed or disaffected workers. On January 8, 1850, the stockholders of the Island Ford Manufacturing Company resolved at their annual meeting that they would no longer employ anyone, including Wesleyans or Free Soilers, who advocated the abolition of slavery. A year and a half later when the conflict between the Wesleyan preachers and their proslavery antagonists peaked in North Carolina, the Island Ford stockholders fired three employees "for going to hear Crooks preach."[36]

The Wesleyan ministers' advocacy of the antislavery cause got them into serious trouble with state authorities in April 1850. While Crooks and McBride were holding services in Forsyth County, McBride handed an antislavery pamphlet to a young daughter of his host. Titled *The Ten Commandments*, the tract showed how slavery violated each commandment. McBride's host was not a slave owner; yet authorities charged McBride and Crooks in the Forsyth County courts with bringing into the state and circulating a printed pamphlet that incited insurrection, conspiracy, and resistance among the slaves—a felony under North Carolina law. The jury acquitted Crooks but convicted and sentenced McBride to an hour in the pillory, 20 lashes, and one year in jail. Upon the appeal of his case to the state supreme court, the sheriff released McBride on bond.[37]

A hostile North Carolina press eagerly followed McBride's trial, coming as it did when passions over the slavery issue raged at a fever pitch on the national scene. A Charlotte newspaper accused the residents of Guilford County of Free-Soilism for harboring so many people who sympathized with the Wesleyans.[38] McBride noted that the charge of Free-Soilism would have held equally true for Randolph, Alamance, Chatham, and Montgomery counties.[39] The notoriety attending his arrest and trial renewed old passions over the slavery issue in the Quaker Belt: "Excitement runs high in this country on the question of slavery, Wesleyanism, etc. My [McBride's] trial and conviction have caused more excitement on the question than any thing else, ... It has caused almost every man, woman and child to take sides. Slavery is the common theme of conversation in all circles, among all parties and on all occasions."[40]

As 1851 opened, slaveowners feared Wesleyanism as a threat to their power and influence. Its congregations ranked among the largest of any denomination in the counties its missionaries worked; slaves, influenced by the spirit of abolitionism spread by the Wesleyan preachers, became insubordinate and often ran away; and increasingly whites divided over the slavery issue as the Wesleyans gained more and more converts. McBride wrote in August 1851 that the rapid growth and popularity of antislavery sentiments in the Guilford area caused alarm among the proslavery element: "Slave-holders, knowing that a majority of the freemen of Guilford and of the whole State, are opposed to the peculiar institution — that Anti-Slavery sentiments are gaining ground and likely to triumph unless speedy, vigilant and violent means are resorted to ... that if the present effort [to drive the Wesleyan preachers from the state] proves a failure all is over, that it is *now* or never."[41]

Violent proslavery vigilantes began to dog McBride and Crooks on their rounds about their circuits. Armed proslavery mobs, often numbering in the hundreds, warned the Wesleyan ministers that they must either leave the state or face the consequences.[42] In May 1851, a crowd estimated to be between 300 and 500 in number, and "all armed with pistols, bowie-knives and clubs," overtook McBride while on his way to the Sandy Ridge Wesleyan Church in northeastern Stokes County and forced him to agree to leave the state forever, which he did.[43]

Meanwhile Adam Crooks had his problems in Randolph, Davidson, Montgomery, and Stanly counties. A committee of men appointed at a meeting of proslavery citizens from Montgomery and surrounding counties approached Crooks and warned him to leave the area or face their wrath.[44] Undaunted, Crooks remained at his post. On Sunday morning, June 15, 1851, a proslavery mob of about 175 men led by Samuel H. Christian,[45] a magistrate and one of the richest men and largest slaveholders in Montgomery County, forced Crooks from the pulpit of his church at Lovejoy (located in north-central Montgomery) and took him to Troy, the county seat, and put him in jail. Two days later, Crooks signed a bond agreeing never to preach in Montgomery County again, and the county authorities released him.[46] Thereafter, Crooks limited his preaching to Randolph, Chatham, Guilford, and Davidson, where he continued to face threats from proslavery mobs.

A remarkable reaction against the excesses of the vigilantes began to take place among members of the populace who favored the antislavery cause and those repulsed by the unconstitutional and extralegal methods used by the proslavery advocates to force their way on society. Upon his release from the Montgomery County jail Crooks discovered that some of his supporters had raised "a company" to free him forcibly from jail if peaceful measures failed. Soon thereafter, a vigilante committee in southern Davidson County threatened to return him to jail if he preached there. In reaction, Crooks's supporters threatened to shoot anyone who laid a hand on him. In another instance, a follower in Guilford County offered to raise and lead an armed, mounted band of men who would escort the Wesleyan preacher on his rounds and provide him with protection from the proslavery mob. Crooks rejected the offer.[47] As the pro- and antislavery factions organized into armed camps, the threat of a violent outbreak between the two factions loomed.

The threatened showdown occurred on July 27, 1851, at Union Meetinghouse about four miles above Jamestown in Guilford County. John Gilmer, William H. Hill, and Francis Fries, the leaders of the proslavery vigilantes, sent out word for supporters from surrounding counties to congregate at the Union Meetinghouse where they expected Crooks to preach.[48] Several hundred of Crooks's supporters, many of them members of the local militia, also assembled at Union. They vowed to prevent the proslavery mob from arresting or harming him. The militia men's muster day happened to fall on the same day as the meeting at Union. Since their muster ground was nearby, many of them showed up in the crowd with their muskets in hand.[49] Crooks decided not to go to Union that day for fear his presence would lead to bloodshed. Crooks observed that many of his supporters that day at Union were not Wesleyans, but rather were citizens who "looked upon the conduct of the mob as contrary to law, in violation of the Constitution and their rights as citizens, which the Constitution and those laws were designed to protect, and who were determined to die in their defense."[50] Crooks's decision not to appear at Union proved to be a wise one, because by ten in the morning, about 300 proslavery advocates had arrived on the scene "armed with clubs, pistols, dirks, etc." They were determined to prevent Bacon or any "Northern Abolitionist" from preaching that day. At about the same time, a large antislavery crowd had assembled in support of Bacon and the Wesleyans.[51]

While someone from the proslavery side made a speech, a fight broke out between two men from the opposing factions. As one of the combatants called for help from sympathizers, the situation threatened to explode into a general bloodbath:

"The cry of order, peace, and murder," rent the air. Some are swinging their clubs, some preparing to discharge fire arms, the sister begs her brother, and the son his father, to flee for their lives. Here and there, three or four men are employed in taking one out of the company to keep him from shooting. Others are pushing and pulling with all their might to separate the contending parties, a line is now drawn, and the first who crosses from either side is to be killed. Had a single blow been struck then, it might have cost a hundred lives. So great was the excitement that many who were looking on thought they were doing the work of death. The confusion having partially subsided, search was made for [Daniel] Wilson [a Wesleyan minister] who had been present, but stepped aside. Some said if they got him they would hang him. He was not found.[52]

In another account of what happened at Union that day, a witness suggested that one life might have been lost: "There is still much excitement in re gard to Crooks, Bacon etc[.] Last Saturday they had a meeting appointed in Guilford. Large numbers of both parties attended all armed *thirsting for battle*, ... Crooks did not appear; one of his party was supposed to be mortaly wounded by a blow on the head, from a Mr. Stone of Forsythe; no one else was hurt."[53]

The proslavery force won the day at Union Meetinghouse when they forced the Wesleyan abolitionist preachers to stand down and leave the field. They offered a reward of

$200 for the apprehension of Jarvis C. Bacon or Adam Crooks, or $100 for either of them, if found in the state of North Carolina after August 6. Both missionaries fled the state rather than place their lives, or the lives of their followers, in further jeopardy.[54] One historian of Wesleyanism in the South concluded: "The scene that was enacted that day [at Union Meetinghouse] was but a foreshadowing of the enlarged battle line that was to be drawn a few years later between friends and foes of slavery."[55]

The standoff at Union indicated that the Wesleyan preachers brought to the surface hostility to slavery among the populace that theretofore had not been widely expressed. As Crooks wrote, "Wherever these Wesleyans have obtained the foothold that they now have in Guilford, the peace and quiet of the slaveholding community is at an end." After leaving the state, Crooks commented: "Never did the Carolinians think as much on the subject as they do now, and never did they hate Slavery as they now do."[56] McBride reported in 1852 that six hundred antislavery families had left North Carolina and Virginia since proslavery leaders had him, Bacon, and Crooks expelled.[57] They departed "in disgust at the outrage committed, not only on their religious privileges, but also on their political rights." Many of the most ardent antislavery advocates emigrated from the Quaker Belt with this exodus, and controversy over the slavery issue slackened for about five years.[58]

The Reverend Daniel Wilson — Tar Heel Wesleyan Abolitionist Leader

With the departure of the northern missionaries, the Reverend Daniel Wilson became leader of the Wesleyan Church in North Carolina.[59] Wilson, whom the proslavery mob had sought to hang at Union Meetinghouse, was one of the original founders of the Wesleyan Church in the state.[60] Since he was a native North Carolinian, the proslavery element tolerated Wilson. This is surprising, because he was no moderate; in 1852, Wilson wrote, "Reformation is the word. Let us have it on Temperance, on Slavery, on Secret Societies, on War, on Capital Punishment, and everything else that should be reformed."[61] During most of his tenure as head of the Wesleyans in the state, Daniel Wilson lived in New Market, where he worked part-time as a carpenter.[62] New Market was a small community on the plank road in northwestern Randolph County, just a few miles below the Guilford County line, near the Marlborough Friends Meetinghouse and the Caraway Wesleyan Church.[63] When proslavery vigilantes forced Crooks, McBride, and Bacon from the state in mid–1851, there were nearly 600 members in the Wesleyan church.[64] A year later, Wilson reported that he had eleven churches in four counties (five in Guilford, one in Chatham, three in Randolph, and two in Montgomery), with a total membership of 350.[65]

At the request of Jesse McBride, the Reverend Wilson, a poor man with a large family, received financial support from the American Missionary Association, a nonsectarian organization of evangelical Christian abolitionists based in the state of New York.[66] Wilson's connection with the American Missionary Association remained a secret, because public disclosure of the fact likely would have precipitated riots against him by the proslavery element.[67] Under Wilson's leadership, the abolitionist cause remained alive in the Quaker Belt. Indeed, in a letter to the treasurer of the American Missionary Association, Wilson noted that antislavery advocates in central North Carolina boldly supported the Free Soil Party in elections despite the absence of an official ballot: "Such Is the Influence of the Slave Power that the Editors would not print [ballots] for us but there is Some Prominet Politicians here that are advocating the Free Soil principles here and In fact there Is a great deal of that Sentiment In this country —"[68]

In the election of 1848, several Quakers and Wesleyans supported the Free Soil cause under the leadership of John Stafford.[69] He led a Free Soil party rally at Jamestown on October 13 in which adherents opposed the extension of slavery into lands won in the Mexican War and supported Van Buren for president. Since there were no Free Soil tickets allowed in North Carolina, diehard advocates placed write-in tickets in the ballot boxes. Records indicate that 47 Free Soilers voted in Guilford, 17 in Orange, 13 in Chatham, and 9 in Surry. Clearly, most Quakers and Wesleyans voted Whig in this election.[70] The Free Soil Party (officially called the Free Democratic Party) supported John P. Hale of New Hampshire as the presidential candidate in 1852. Members opposed slavery in the territories, the admission to the Union of any new slave states, and the Fugitive Slave Law. Plank VI of the party platform read: "That slavery is a sin against God and a crime against man, which no human enactment nor usage can make right; and that Christianity, humanity, and patriotism, alike demand its abolition."[71]

Wilson's remarks on Free-Soilism indicated not only that antislavery sentiment remained strong in the Quaker Belt, even after the exodus of hundreds of Wesleyans following the forced departure of Crooks, McBride, and Bacon, but that its adherents had taken their cause into the political arena. The advent of political antislavery, though a political faction small in numbers and never powerful, heralded a new wave of antislavery activity in the Quaker Belt that centered on the lives and activities of three men: Benjamin Sherwood Hedrick, Hinton Rowan Helper, and Daniel Worth.

Benjamin Sherwood Hedrick — Antislavery Republican

Benjamin Sherwood Hedrick was born and raised in Davidson County. His German ancestors emigrated from Pennsylvania to the central piedmont of North Carolina in the middle of the eighteenth century.[72] The Germans, mostly yeoman farmers and artisans, did not adapt readily to the slave labor system. Large numbers of them migrated from North Carolina in the early decades of the nineteenth century to the free states carved from the Old Northwest Territory. They believed slave labor to be a permanent bar to the economic advancement of the non-slaveholders. In 1856, Hedrick wrote: "Of my neighbors, friends, and kindred, nearly one-half left the State since

Benjamin Sherwood Hedrick (1827–1886) around 1860. University officials dismissed him in 1856 from his professorship in chemistry at the University of North Carolina for openly expressing pro–Republican, antislavery views. In 1861, President Lincoln appointed him to a high position in the Patent Office in Washington, D.C. Hedrick was from the Quaker Belt county of Davidson (courtesy the North Carolina Collection, University of North Carolina at Chapel Hill Library).

I was old enough to remember. Many is the time I have stood by the loaded emigrant wagon, and given the parting hand to those whose face I was never to look upon again. They were going to seek homes in the free West, knowing, as they did, that free and slave labor could not both exist and prosper in the same community."[73]

Hedrick's father, a farmer and a brick mason, earned enough income to send all of his children to a local academy for a secondary education. Benjamin, a bright student, entered the University of North Carolina in 1847. Four years later, he graduated with highest honors in chemistry and mathematics. Recommended by fellow Tar Heel William A. Graham, secretary of the navy, and David Swain, president of the university, Hedrick received an appointment as a clerk in the office of the National Almanac in Cambridge, Massachusetts. While working in Cambridge, Hedrick attended classes at Harvard. In 1854, he accepted the Chair of Analytical and Agricultural Chemistry at the University of North Carolina.[74]

After antislavery advocates organized the Republican Party in 1856, Hedrick — a longtime Democrat — openly stated that he would vote Republican if polling officials allowed a Republican ticket in North Carolina. Since professor Hedrick's friends and acquaintances knew of his antislavery views, his pro–Republican remarks caused no sensation when made. But a few weeks later, articles appeared in the leading Democratic newspaper of the day, the *Standard*, calling for his immediate dismissal from the university for poisoning the minds of students with "Black Republican" values.[75] William Woods Holden, editor of the *Standard* and a strong proponent of secession, initiated the attack against Hedrick in hopes of raising an issue that would help propel the Democrats to victory in the fall elections. Hedrick responded with a lengthy letter explaining why he supported Fremont and the antislavery cause. The letter, which Holden published in the *Standard*, led to such a powerful public outcry against Hedrick that the University trustees felt compelled to dismiss him.[76]

Facing unemployment and threatened by mobs in North Carolina, Hedrick sought a university position in the North. Though unsuccessful at getting a teaching position at a major university, he did manage to land a position teaching mathematics and chemistry at the Cooper Union in New York for two years. In 1861 Lincoln appointed Hedrick to a high position in the Patent Office.[77] As the war progressed, Hedrick became a recognized leader of the political dissidents who fled to the North from North Carolina, or who deserted to the Union side from Tar Heel regiments.[78]

Hinton Rowan Helper — Abolitionist

At the same time that Hedrick was making national headlines with his ouster from the University of North Carolina for harboring "Black Republican" sentiments, Hinton Rowan Helper roamed the North trying to get his book *The Impending Crisis of the South; How to Meet It* published. Helper, like Hedrick, descended from German immigrants. He grew up in Davie County, which bordered Hedrick's home county of Davidson to the west. In the mid–1850s, Helper lived and worked in New York and California. He returned home to North Carolina impressed by the higher standard of living the North enjoyed over that of the South that he grew up in. Helper attributed the North's economic superiority to its free labor system and the South's comparative poverty to its slave labor system. In his *Impending Crisis*, Helper urged nonslaveholders, who made up about 80 percent of the registered voters in the South, to vote slaveholders out of office and slavery out of existence. He warned slaveholders that their continued exploitation of both the black slaves and the white nonslaveholders would eventually end in an uprising in which the two oppressed groups would unite and exterminate the master class.[79]

When first published in 1857, Helper's *Impending Crisis* attracted little public attention, other than from proslavery advocates in the South denouncing it as an "incendiary document." The book did achieve enduring fame in early 1860 when the Republican Party adopted and published it as a campaign document. It then became the centerpiece in a struggle for the speakership of the House of Representatives. The fact that its publication followed closely on the heels of the John Brown Raid at Harpers Ferry compounded the popularity of *The Impending Crisis* in the North.[80] For North Carolinians, Helper's book served as a catalyst for another show-

Hinton Rowan Helper (1829–1909) around 1860. The Republican Party promoted his book, *The Impending Crisis*, an abolitionist tract, as a campaign document in the 1860 elections. In his book, Helper urged nonslaveowning southern whites to vote slavery out of existence. Helper was a native of David County, a Quaker Belt county (courtesy the North Carolina Collection, University of North Carolina at Chapel Hill Library).

down between pro- and antislavery forces in the state. A Wesleyan minister by the name of Daniel Worth emerged as the chief protagonist this time.

Daniel Worth—Wesleyan Abolitionist

Daniel Worth, born in 1795, grew up a Quaker in the Centre community of south-central Guilford County. In 1822, he moved with his family to Indiana, where he became a Methodist minister. Worth was elected the first president of the Anti-Slavery Society of Indiana in 1840, and he was one of the founders of the Wesleyan Methodist Church in 1843. In 1856, he became president of the Wesleyan's Indiana Conference.[81] Described as "mono-maniacal" by his cousin Jonathan Worth (Randolph County resident and governor of North Carolina, 1865–1866), the Reverend Worth did not compromise principles, especially those in his favorite cause, abolitionism.[82] The Indiana Conference selected Worth, age 62, to go to his native North Carolina in 1857 to serve as a Wesleyan missionary.[83] That summer, a power struggle divided the Wesleyan community between the followers of Alfred Vestal,[84] a self-proclaimed Wesleyan minister from Chatham County, and supporters of Daniel Wilson, the officially recognized leader.[85] Daniel Worth, church leaders hoped,

Reverend Daniel Worth (1795–1862) around 1858. This Wesleyan Methodist leader was sentenced to a year in jail in 1860 for distributing copies of Hinton Rowan Helper's *The Impending Crisis*, an abolitionist tract, in Randolph and Guilford counties. He was a native of Guilford County, a Quaker Belt county (courtesy the North Carolina Collection, University of North Carolina at Chapel Hill Library).

would be able to reunite the Wesleyans.

The American Missionary Association assisted Worth financially just as it had Bacon, McBride, Crooks, and Wilson before him. It also kept him supplied with copies of Helper's *Impending Crisis* for distribution in North Carolina.[86] Worth made New Salem, a village in north-central Randolph County, his home and headquarters. He traveled a two-hundred-fifty-mile circuit serving twenty churches or chapels in five counties.[87] After serving his circuit for two months, a confident Worth wrote a friend: "The ministers here almost universally defend slavery from the Bible.... Such preachers are regarded as hypocrites by a large portion of the common people with whom I converse. Their 'purblind mental vision' seems utterly to have failed to reconcile 'love & good will to men' with whips and thumb screws. *I am induced to believe there is no point within the limits of slavery so open to an antislavery gospel as this section of N.C.*"[88] (emphasis added).

Daniel Worth, a native Tar Heel and an elderly gentleman, had numerous wealthy and powerful relatives in the state. As a result, legal authorities winked at his illegal distribution of abolitionist literature, and proslavery leaders made but little protest against his abolitionist preaching. All that changed with John Brown's raid on Harpers Ferry. The state's press, especially William Holden's *North Carolina Standard*, demanded Worth's arrest and trial for the crime of distributing incendiary literature. In addition, the editors often hinted that mob justice would be appropriate in his case. In December 1859, legal authorities issued warrants for the arrest of Daniel Worth in Alamance, Chatham, Guilford, and Randolph counties. Anticipating that his friends there would help him, he surrendered to the sheriff in Guilford County. Authorities charged him with circulating Helper's writings and "speaking in such a manner as to excite Negroes to insurrection and rebellion."[89]

In December, Governor Ellis received a letter from John T. Harris,[90] who lived in Eden, a post office located in western Randolph County. Harris charged Daniel Worth with circulating copies of *The Impending Crisis* in his community. Implying that Worth led an abolitionist conspiracy to arm the slaves in preparation for a revolt, Harris accused him of secretly stockpiling arms at the home of one Jacob Briles.[91] The panic resulting from John Brown's recent raid at Harpers Ferry doubtless inspired this latter charge. Governor Ellis sent a copy of Harris's letter to Judge John M. Dick in Greensboro. Ellis warned Judge Dick that "the local magistrates of Randolph County have been up to this time wholly remiss in suppressing the most flagrant violations of Law — the circulation of incendiary books and papers, and the use of language calculated to incite slaves to insurrection.... The people of that section of the country must look elsewhere for a preservation of the public peace." Ellis requested that Judge Dick investigate the situation and search for arms and incendiary books.[92] Governor Ellis's distrust and sidestepping of the civil and legal authorities of Randolph County at this time suggests that sympathy and support for Daniel Worth and his abolitionist activities indeed must have been widespread there.

On January 6, Judge Dick informed Governor Ellis that "Col. Boon, sheriff of this County ... will leave this morning for Randolph and Davidson [suggesting that the supposed abolitionist conspiracy extended from Randolph into Davidson County]. He is also authorized to search the house of Briles for books, etc." Dick also mentioned that legal authorities had bound one Jesse Wheeler over to the superior court at Jamestown with bail set at $4,000, and charged him with circulating fifty-six copies of *The Impending Crisis*. Judge Dick referred to Wheeler as "one of the ring leaders."[93] Jesse Wheeler, a middle-aged man of some distinction, prospered as a farmer in Guilford County.[94] He had been a firm opponent of slavery ever since he had joined the Manumission Society at the age of nineteen. In 1851, he had befriended the Wesleyan preachers. In September 1859, Wheeler had ordered 100 copies of *The Impending Crisis* from Helper sent to his home address in Jamestown. Helper mailed the tracts as merchandise, not as books, in an effort to hoodwink postal authorities. In spite of his social prominence and lifelong residence in Guilford County, Wheeler had to flee North Carolina to avoid conviction and a prison sentence for circulating Helper's book.[95] He and his family settled in Indiana.

In the spring of 1860, legal authorities tried and convicted Worth in the superior courts of Randolph and Guilford counties for distributing copies of Helper's *Impending Crisis*. Each court sentenced him to twelve months in jail. Freed on bond pending appeal of his case to the state supreme court, Worth fled north where he received a hero's welcome among antislavery enthusiasts. He died in Richmond, Indiana, in December 1862.[96]

The Quaker Belt: Center of Antislavery and Abolitionist Sentiment in the Antebellum South

What would have come of the antislavery movement in the Quaker Belt if there had been no John Brown's Raid on Harpers Ferry, no firing on Fort Sumter, no Civil War? Some have argued that, unfortunate though it may have been, the war was necessary to the ending of slavery on the North American continent, that without the force of war and defeat, white Southerners would have tried to maintain their peculiar institution into the twentieth century. Two chroniclers of North Carolina history, one writing at the end of the nineteenth century and the other soon thereafter, argued otherwise for the Tar Heel state. J.G. de Roulhac Hamilton in the preface to an article on Benjamin Sherwood Hedrick wrote: "But for John Brown's raid and the rapid progress of the States to civil war, North Carolina of the sixties would probably have been interesting as the scene of a fierce internal contest over slavery with the odds in favor of its gradual emancipation."[97] John Spencer Bassett in his *Anti-Slavery Leaders of North Carolina* concluded: "Indeed, if we consider the righteousness of anti-slavery in the abstract, and the superior strength of the vigorous west [that is, the piedmont and mountain counties], it cannot be doubted that, had the question been left to be determined in a peaceful struggle, the west would finally have removed the stain of slavery from the State."[98]

Writing in 1864, Bryan Tyson — a wartime pro–Union activist from Moore County — expressed views similar to those of Professors Bassett and Hamilton on the question of the viability of slavery in North Carolina: "I know the nonslaveholders south are much incensed against their slave holding brethren, for having been drawn by them into this wicked and unnatural war, and the probability is, that when times will admit of their having a fair sweep at the ballot-box, they will attack and do away with this institution of themselves."[99] Were Tyson, Bassett, and Hamilton accurate prognosticators on the slavery issue? Indeed, had disputants settled the matter of slavery in the territories amicably, perhaps antislavery leaders like Hinton Rowan Helper, Benjamin Hedrick, Daniel Worth, and Jesse Wheeler would have led the Free-Soil cause to victory in North Carolina in their lifetimes. Perhaps, but one must remain skeptical of the possibility of such a triumph if one remembers that when these men did make their stand against slavery in the state, they were overwhelmed quickly and easily by a determined proslavery opposition just as had been the Reverends Bacon, McBride, and Crooks before them.

If one examines the historical sources on which Professors Bassett and Hamilton based their optimistic theses, it becomes clear that the antislavery spirit in North Carolina that they referred to came — with but one or two important exceptions — from individuals and religious institutions indigenous not to the state as a whole or to the piedmont as a whole or to the "west" as a whole, but solely to the Quaker Belt. Bassett recognized Randolph, Guilford, and surrounding counties as the center of antislavery sentiment in the state, but then he referred to this area as the "western counties" as opposed to the "eastern counties," thereby confounding the Randolph-Guilford area with all of the counties west of the fall line, the geological divide between the piedmont and the coastal plain.[100] Hamilton implied that the antislavery sentiments common to Benjamin Hedrick, who was from Davidson, a Quaker Belt county, were common to whites from the yeoman class all over the state. Each historian drew his conclusion that antislavery sentiment would eventually triumph in the state from studies of Benjamin Hedrick, Hinton Rowan Helper, Daniel Worth, the Wesleyans, and the Quakers — all of whom lived in the Quaker Belt, a subsection of the piedmont, of the "west," and of the state.[101] The professors failed to appreciate that the Quaker Belt, with the exception of a few counties in the northeastern sound region that contained a small number of Quaker settlements, harbored the only strong local antislavery tradition in the state. The professors incorrectly assumed the antislavery values common to the Quaker Belt to be normative for the rest of the state.

The Quaker Belt became one of the most disaffected regions in the new Confederacy. In 1861 it gave rise to the militant Unionists (or Tories) and their secret, underground, pro–Union organization, the Heroes of America; in 1862, the area became a haven for deserters and draft-dodgers; in the summers of 1863 and 1864, hundreds of Confederate troops had to be rushed into the area to suppress massive revolts by powerful armed deserter gangs; in

1863 and 1864, the Quaker Belt provided most of the support in the state for the pro–Copperhead reunionist peace and convention movements. In March 1865, Quaker Belt dissidents made a desperate last-ditch stand against two Confederate regiments and ten companies detached from various units sent into the area to destroy them. This bent toward disaffection in the Quaker Belt during the war was but a continuation in new guises of the area's alienation and rebellion against the slave system in the antebellum years.

Chapter Two

The Secession Crisis and the Militant Unionists

Between 1836 and 1850, the Whig Party controlled the governorship and the state legislature in North Carolina and elected the majority of the state's delegates to Congress. The Whigs favored an activist government that promoted internal improvements, banks, public schools, asylums, industry, and other progressive measures. Whig strength prevailed in the Quaker Belt, in the western mountains, and in the sound area of the northeastern coastal plain. (During the nineteenth century, observers usually referred to the mountain and piedmont sections collectively as "the west.") Of these three Whig strongholds, the Quaker Belt ranked foremost in terms of numerical strength and persistent party loyalty.[1]

The heart of Whig power in the west came from the small farmer class, mostly non-slaveholding yeomen who favored government financing and building of railroads, turnpikes, canals, and plank roads needed to open their isolated, economically backward region to statewide, national, and international markets. (Yeoman farmers owned their own land as opposed to tenant farmers, who did not own the land they worked.) Though rooted in the yeoman, tenant, and artisan common folk, a wealthy planter, business, and professional class led the Whig party. They sought to expand their investments in industry, manufacturing, mining, commercial agriculture, commerce, and real estate.[2]

Democratic strength lay in the central and western coastal plain, especially in the Neuse and Tar River basins where staple agriculture and plantation slavery prevailed. The Democrats also reigned in the tier of piedmont counties on the Virginia border where tobacco plantations flourished, and along the South Carolina border where cotton thrived.[3] In 1850, the Democrats wrested control of the state government from the Whigs on a platform of liberalization of the franchise and the advocacy of internal improvements and humanitarian reform. Democrats remained in power until 1862, but the Whigs ran them a close race in nearly all elections in the 1850s and in the 1860 campaign. Despite their adoption of certain progressive measures, the Democratic Party remained under the control of the eastern planter class, who led the state into secession under Governor John W. Ellis in 1861.[4]

The center of Whig strength in western North Carolina lay in the Quaker Belt.[5] Mountain counties generally supported the Whigs until the mid–1850s, when many turned Democratic. With the exception of a handful of loyal Whig outposts, the Democrats remained strong in the piedmont outside the perimeter of the Quaker Belt.[6] With the demise of the national Whig Party in 1854 over the issue of slavery in the territories, most North Carolina Whigs turned to the American Party for political leadership. The American or Know-Nothing Party proved to be a poor substitute for the old Whig Party; it declined rapidly in North Carolina after the 1856 election, which it lost 57,698 to 44,970 in the gubernatorial contest, and 48,242 to 36,720 in the presidential race. With the threat of disunion again in the air, the Whigs of North Carolina reorganized themselves as a political party in 1859, with the aim of electing congressional representatives and state officials who would oppose secession. The Whigs ran a close race in 1860, losing the governorship to the Democrats 53,123 to 59,463, but winning half of the state's congressional seats.[7]

The Quaker Belt formed the largest single bloc of Whig (or Opposition Party as the Whigs then called themselves) voting strength in the state in the 1860 gubernatorial race. All the Quaker Belt counties but two[8] gave majorities to John Pool, the Opposition (Whig) candidate. Outside the Quaker Belt, the Whigs carried one county in the lower coastal plain, three in the piedmont, four in the mountains, and several in the northeastern sound region.[9] In the 1860 presidential election, Democrats split into northern and southern wings. Southern Democrats, who supported John C. Breckinridge of Kentucky for president, advocated a federal slave law that would guarantee the right of slave owners to carry their chattels into the territories. Northern Democrats, who championed Stephen A. Douglas of Illinois, balked at the idea. The Republican Party, which contained a strong abolitionist contingent, opposed the creation of any new slave states. It nominated Abraham Lincoln of Illinois as its champion. A fourth party, the Constitutional Unionists, viewed both secessionists and abolitionists as dangerous radicals; they advocated defending the Constitution and preservation of the Union. John Bell of Tennessee led that faction. The North Carolina Whigs supported the latter party. The Constitutional Union Party devoted itself to the single issue of preserving the Union. It appealed primarily to the border-state South, where most people viewed the "black Republicans" of the North and the "fire-eating secessionists" in the Deep South with equal repugnance. The North Carolina Constitutional Union Party, composed mostly of old-line Whigs, made the question of Union or disunion their main issue. They claimed that a vote for John C. Breckinridge, the champion of the southern Democrats, would be a vote for disunion.

The Breckinridge Democrats carried North Carolina, but only by the small majority of 48,539 over Bell's 44,990. The Douglas Democrats, who were Unionists, won only 2,701 votes.[10] The Republicans did not have an electoral ticket in North Carolina in the 1860 election. In the presidential election, as in the gubernatorial election, the Quaker Belt proved to be the area of greatest Whig (Constitutional Union) strength. All but two Quaker Belt counties gave Whig majorities.[11] The Whigs also did well in the northeastern sound region and in several mountain counties.[12] A majority of North Carolinians, including most Breckinridge Democrats, opposed secession in 1860. They did not feel the election of Lincoln to be a sufficient cause for disunion. However, a group of radicals, mostly Breckinridge Democrats from the large slaveholding counties in the east, favored secession upon the election of Lincoln. Governor John W. Ellis, a large slaveholder from the piedmont county of Rowan, assumed the leadership of the radicals after his election in August. In November and December 1860, the radicals held meetings across the state advocating the call of a convention to address the secession issue.[13] Secessionist leaders at this time resorted to lurid rhetoric to frighten the populace into supporting their cause. For example, a Randolph County militia officer explained how he was persuaded to support secession: "Our preacher on this circuit, the Rev. T.C. Moses, for the year 1861, told me that old Abe was after our land, our negroes, our women and our babies. That our land was to be confiscated, our negroes stolen, our pretty women appropriated and our ugly women made slaves of and our babies brains knocked out against rocks. I then believed this to be the true programme of the war, and, Mr. Editor, I did get mad and felt like fighting."[14]

At this point (the fall of 1860), a fundamental restructuring of political parties occurred in North Carolina. The secessionists, consisting of about 30,000 Democrats and about 10,000 former Whigs, united under the Democratic leadership of Governor Ellis. The Unionists, made up of about 40,000 old-line Whigs and about 30,000 former Democrats called themselves the Union or Conservative Party.[15] William Woods Holden — editor of the *North Carolina Standard* and a secessionist before 1860 — turned Unionist and led the Union Democrats in the gubernatorial and presidential elections that year.[16] The new Union (Conservative) Party, which drew most of its leaders and members from the old-line Whigs, took up the Democratic challenge and held their own meetings across the state in November, December, and January. They passed resolutions declaring that the election of Lincoln provided insufficient cause for leaving the Union, and that secession would lead to civil war, anarchy, military despotism, and the destruction of slavery.[17] Many Conservatives attached conditions to their Unionism. These "conditionalists" supported North Carolina remaining in the Union, but only as long as Republicans respected the rights of the South and as long as the new Lincoln government did not try by military force to coerce the states of the lower South back into the Union. Several Union Party meetings in the central and western counties passed resolutions in favor of an unconditional attachment to the Union.[18]

Union meetings held in Randolph, Moore, and Wilkes counties provide good examples of the anti-secession feelings aloft in communities that became radically anti–Confederate during the war. Between 500 and 1,000 citizens attended a meeting led by Jonathan Worth and his brother John Milton Worth in Asheboro, the seat of Randolph County, in December 1860. The

Jonathan Worth (1802–1869) around 1865. Attorney, businessman, Whig politician and legislator, he served as state treasurer under Governor Vance and as governor of North Carolina from 1865 to 1868. Ardently opposed to secession, he never warmed up to the Confederacy though he held high political office. In his private correspondence, he championed the Copperhead plan of reunion (courtesy Randolph County Public Library's Historical Photograph Collection).

assemblage resolved that it would be unwise, even suicidal, for North Carolina to secede from the Union for any reason now existing. Yet the South should stand up for its rights, especially in regard to slavery. If the country is dissolved, North Carolina should not associate either with the extremists of the North or the South, but should form a "Central Confederacy" composed of the Conservative states North and South. The people of Randolph opposed calling a convention to consider secession. A better plan would be to call a national convention of all the states North and South to iron out their difficulties. The people of Randolph stood by the Union and the Constitution.[19] Another Union meeting was held in Randolph County at Bush Hill (present-day Trinity), a community located in the northwest corner of the county. About 500 voters from Randolph, Guilford, and Davidson counties assembled there and resolved to use every effort to preserve the Federal government — in their view the best government ever established. They opposed calling a state convention to consider secession; rather, they favored calling a convention of all the states of the Union to settle their disputes. If secession were forced on North Carolina, the assemblage favored creating a new nation in cooperation with the conservatives in the "middle States."[20]

The call by staunch Quaker Belt Unionists to react to secession by forming a new nation composed of "Conservatives" in the upper South and the old Northwest had profound implications for the future course the area would take in the peace and convention movement controversies of 1863 and 1864. Both groups — the Midwestern Democrats and the Quaker Belt Unionists — denounced and loathed the extremist factions North and South, that is, the fire-eating secessionists and the abolitionists. The antiwar faction in the Ohio River Valley of the Northwest opposed the war and later emancipation, policies they blamed on the abolitionists, capitalists, bankers, and railroad magnates in the Northeast, especially New England, who exploited them economically. Antiwar proponents in the Northwest early on threatened to form a "Central Confederacy" with states in the upper South if the war continued. This western opposition faction became known during the war as the "Copperheads."[21] Just as the Midwestern Democrats felt exploited by the radicals and capitalists in New England, Quaker Belt Whigs felt exploited by the planters and politicians of the eastern coastal plain and Richmond during the war. Efforts would be made to politically unite these two alienated groups under the Copperhead banner in the peace and convention movements as the war progressed.

A Union meeting in Moore County, held at John R. Ritter's property, featured a speech by Bryan Tyson, a soon-to-be leader of the area anti–Confederate faction. The symposium of dedicated Unionists passed a resolution condemning South Carolina for seceding and for its seizure of United States property at Charleston, which they termed "reprehensible" and in violation of the Constitution. The Federal government had a right to use force against law breakers, including those in the Palmetto State. The people of Moore County stood by the Constitution. Nevertheless, they agreed to fight the United States if it invaded North Carolina to abolish slavery or tried to interfere with any right guaranteed by the Constitution.[22]

In January and February, antisecession activists held two Unionist meetings in Wilkes County. Calvin J. Cowles, a merchant in Wilkesboro, served as secretary at one of the meetings; he would be a leader in the peace faction in the county during the war. Participants urged everyone to stand by the Union and the Constitution. No one in the North in their opinion had committed sufficient offenses to justify secession — an act that surely would lead to a horrible civil war. They opposed calling a convention to consider the question of secession.[23]

Most Unionists supported calling a state convention on the secession issue because they held a solid majority over the Democrats among the electorate. They believed that they easily could control the convention and stay any move for secession. A minority of Unionists opposed a convention because they believed that wily secessionists might somehow manage to utilize it to manipulate the state out of the Union. Most of the politicians in the Quaker Belt fell into the latter category. This was especially true for Randolph, Wilkes, Chatham, Alamance, Moore, and Montgomery counties.[24]

The state legislature passed the convention bill on January 29. "The bill provided that the election of delegates should be held on February 28, 1861, each county electing a number of delegates equal to its representation in the commons, and at the same time the people were to vote for or against a convention."[25] Were the convention approved by a majority vote, the governor could call one after March 10. Senators and representatives from twelve of the fifteen Quaker Belt counties voted against the bill.[26] Representatives from ten other counties in the state also voted against the measure; seven of them were traditional Whig counties in the sound region.[27] (There were eighty-five counties in the state at that time.)

The voters rejected the convention issue on February 28, 1861, in a statewide referendum by the narrow margin of 47,323 to 46,672. Because Unionists cast much of the pro-convention vote believing that a Unionist majority of convention delegates could prevent secession, one should not interpret this close vote as indicating that nearly half the people favored secession. The delegate selection results provide a better gauge of Union strength in the referendum. Of the 120 delegates elected, secessionists got 39, and the Unionists 91—giving the Unionists nearly a two-thirds majority in the convention.[28] When the electorate cast ballots for or against a convention on February 28, all of the counties in the Quaker Belt voted large majorities in opposition to the convention. Voters in nine of them opposed holding a convention by majorities of 90 percent or more: Iredell (90), Moore (90), Montgomery (92), Guilford (96), Wilkes (97), Randolph (98), and Yadkin (98). These counties became the most disaffected Quaker Belt counties during the war.[29]

North Carolina Unionism proved to be no match for the centrifugal forces then pulling the United States apart along sectional seams. With the secession of the Deep South, the failure of one sectional compromise effort after another, the secession of Virginia, the firing on Fort Sumter, and the call by Lincoln on each state for troops to force the seceded states back into the Union, most Tar Heel Unionists—including those in the Quaker Belt—felt compelled to choose between what they viewed as the lesser of two evils and take their stand with their native section. North Carolina seceded on April 20, 1861.

Demographic and Economic Factors Influencing the Quaker Belt

Factors other than antislavery and anti-secession tendencies contributed to making the Quaker Belt an "Other South" enclave in antebellum Dixie. Demographic and economic factors also played an important part. Because of its rocky, less fertile soil, the Quaker Belt had not become part of the staple crop plantation culture that was the norm by 1860 in the state's eastern and piedmont border counties. Rather, the independent yeoman farmer who typically owned no slaves and engaged primarily in subsistence farming characterized the area. Upon completion in 1856 of the North Carolina Railroad, the counties of Chatham, Guilford, Randolph, Davidson, and Rowan became centers for the commercial production of grains, mainly corn and wheat. Grains were not labor-intensive crops, and thus their production created little demand for slaves; they were the ideal commercial crops for the nonslaveholding yeomanry.[30]

Population statistics show that the Quaker Belt contained 20.5 percent of the state's total population, and 25 percent of its white population.[31] The latter figure is important, because it indicates that one-fourth of the white male population of North Carolina liable for service in the Confederate army resided in the fifteen Quaker Belt counties. Political, economic, social, religious, and cultural factors often alienated much of this white male population from the Confederacy. In near conformity with their one-fourth share of the state's white population, the Quaker Belt contained 24.2 percent of the state's free families and 26.3 percent of its farms.[32] Of the four counties in the state containing 2,500 or more families, three — Davidson, Guilford, and Randolph — were in the Quaker Belt, and nine of the state's 17 counties containing 2,000 or more families were located there.[33] Four of the five counties in the state containing 1,500 or more farms — Davidson, Guilford, Randolph, and Chatham — were in the Quaker Belt, and ten of the 19 counties in the state containing 1,000 or more farms were located there.[34] This high concentration of farms and families shows that yeoman farmers, tenant farmers, artisans, mechanics, and laborers made up a large percentage of the population of the Quaker Belt. Since the Confederacy had to draw from this class most of the recruits needed to flesh out its regiments, whether they became loyal to the Confederacy was of first importance to its chances of success.

While landholding yeoman farmers headed most Quaker Belt households, in 1860 a "permanent class of poor whites existed in the central Piedmont"[35]; landless farmers and laborers, most of whom were tenants, headed between 26 and 30 percent of the households. Three factors contributed to the making of this underclass: slavery, the commercialization of agriculture, and an oppressive credit system. Slavery curbed the development of industrial wage jobs and the need for white farm labor. The construction of railroads through the area in the 1850s led to a doubling of land prices, which made it nearly impossible for landless farmers to afford land. Moreover, few farmers had the means to grow commercial crops such as cotton and tobacco to take advantage of the new rail system. The increase in wheat and corn production did benefit the small producer. The system of debt and credit in antebellum North Carolina worked against the interests of poor and landless whites. North Carolina did not have a homestead law to exempt the sale of farms for debt. Cases against debtors, many of whom lost their land, filled the courts. This landless debtor underclass had little incentive to support the new Confederacy.[36]

In 1860, about 97 percent of the people in North Carolina made their living in agriculture. Artisans and mechanics, working almost exclusively at the handicraft stage, supplied the backbone of industrial production in the Quaker Belt, as in the rest of the state and the South. No large urban centers existed in the state to provide markets for manufactured goods, and roads remained impassable much of the year, thereby limiting access to the markets that did exist.[37] The leading industries in North Carolina in 1860 were (in descending order of importance): turpentine, flour and meal, tobacco, lumber, and cotton textiles. The southern coastal plain region led in turpentine production. Among the Quaker Belt counties only Chatham and Moore (especially the latter) produced turpentine. Flour and meal production and cotton textiles were the leading industries in the Quaker Belt. Nearly one-half of the state's cotton mills were located there: Randolph and Alamance counties each contained five cotton mills; Surry and Iredell, two; and Forsyth, Montgomery, and Orange, one.[38] The Tar Heel counties leading in the commercial production of meal and flour stretched across the midsection of the Quaker Belt.[39] Small factories throughout the region produced snuff, cigarette tobacco, and chewing tobacco.[40] Iron works, mostly small concerns, existed across the Quaker Belt. Several gold mines operated in the southern part of the area, but only rarely did they prove profitable. Other products produced widely in the Quaker Belt, usually on a small scale, included leather, boots and shoes, lumber, furniture, woolen goods, wagons, carriages, and staves.[41]

North Carolina, a large slaveholding state, had one-third of its population slave in 1860. In the coastal plain, the location of most of the large plantations in the state, slaves comprised 44 percent of the population; in the piedmont section, 24 percent; and in the mountain region, 10 percent.[42] The Quaker Belt counties, which for the most part lay outside the cotton- and tobacco-producing areas of the piedmont, were 21 percent slave.[43] All of them but Chatham and Orange were less than 30 percent slave. (Chatham and Orange were 33 and 30 percent slave, respectively.) Slavery was strongest in the eastern part of the region and declined in strength as one moved westward. This relatively low commitment to the slave system in the Quaker Belt proved to be an important factor in the area's alienation from the Confederacy. Randolph County had a slave population of slightly less than 10 percent in 1860. By way of comparison, the counties adjoining Randolph had slave populations from one and one-half to three times greater. The low slave presence in Randolph reflected the influence of the Quakers and Wesleyans and its relatively poor soil. Randolph had eight Quaker meetinghouses and six Wesleyan churches within its borders in 1860—far more of each than any other Quaker Belt county. Little wonder that Randolph became central North Carolina's most persistently anti–Confederate county.[44]

A study of the geographical origins of the enlistment of soldiers into the Confederate army from North Carolina concluded that areas of the state that had a low slave population, Quaker settlements, strong Union sentiment during the secession crisis, and large numbers of deserters during the war had low enlistment rates. Referring to the Quaker Belt, the study concluded: "The location of Quaker settlements in the central section of the state influenced the secession sentiment there, as well as the rate of enlistment into Confederate service. These people were against slavery, secession, and the war, and, as a consequence had low enlistment rates."[45] In 1861, Davidson had the lowest enlistment rate of any Quaker Belt county (9.5%); the next lowest were Guilford (11.8%), Randolph (14.2%) and Wilkes (15.3%). The uprising of the John Hilton band of militant Unionists in the summer (discussed below) explains in some measure the unusually low enlistment rate in 1861 for Davidson County, as well as for Randolph and Guilford counties. The enlistment rate for the Quaker Belt as a whole in 1861 was 18.9%, whereas it was 23.8% for the state.[46] For the period 1861–1865, the enlistment rate for the Quaker Belt was 50.8%, whereas for the state it was 58%.[47] The unusually high rate of the conscription of troops from the Quaker Belt explains why the figures for the enlistment rates of Quaker Belt and state troops for the years 1861–1865 were so close.[48]

For the year ending July 16, 1863, 11,874 conscripts passed through the Camp of Instruction at Raleigh. The Quaker Belt counties furnished 4,617, or 39 percent of these draftees. Containing about 25 percent of the state's white population, the Quaker Belt supplied nearly 40 percent of the state's Confederate draftees that year — a rate that reflected the unwillingness of many Quaker Belt men to volunteer for the Confederate army. Davidson County, which had one of the state's lowest enlistment rates, furnished 5% of its population as conscripts — the largest percentage of any county in the state. Other Quaker Belt counties contributing a high percentage of their population as conscripts were Chatham (2.7%), Forsyth (3.2%), Guilford (2.2%), Iredell (3.0%), Orange (2.7%), Randolph (2.7%), Stokes (4.1%), and Wilkes (3.1%). Two non–Quaker Belt counties, Johnson (4.0%) and Wake (3.3%), the residences of the Peace Party leaders Dr. J.L. Johnson and William Holden respectively, also had large conscription numbers. By contrast, leading secessionist counties such as Mecklenburg (1.9%), New Hanover (1.2%), Caswell (1.5%), Cumberland (0.9%) and Anson (1.5%) tended to supply fewer numbers of conscripts as a percentage of their population, presumably because more of their military age men volunteered.[49]

Containing about one-ninth of the Confederacy's population, North Carolina furnished between one-sixth and one-seventh of its military manpower. It provided about 103,400 enlisted men to the Confederate army — more troops than any other state. Of them, about 23,694 deserted, resulting in a desertion rate of 22.9%.[50] North Carolina troops had about one-fourth of all Confederate desertions. A recent study on desertion in the Confederate army suggests that correct figures on the desertion of Confederate troops are impossible to determine because the Confederacy did not maintain accurate records on desertion, and those they did keep are incomplete.[51] The statistics on North Carolina's troops in the Confederacy seem paradoxical: the fact that it furnished more troops than any other state suggests that its people were loyal Confederates; yet its desertion rate was about double, or many times greater than, the rate of any other Southern state — a detail that forces one to question the loyalty of its people.[52]

The Militant Unionists

In May 1861, Jesse Wheeler wrote from exile in Schuyler County, Illinois, to Benjamin Hedrick in Washington, D.C. Wheeler noted that he received a letter from a friend in Greensboro "who says that the people in the counties of Guilford, Randolph, and the adjoining counties are unshaken in their devotion to the Stars and Stripes and I believe that some thing ought to be done for the relief of those true but oppressed people."[53] As the Wheeler letter suggests, the wave of enthusiasm for the new Confederacy that swept the state with secession was not universal. Many North Carolinians, especially those in the Quaker Belt, remained loyal to the United States and worked, either overtly or covertly, for the overthrow of the Confederacy and the return of North Carolina and the South to the Union. These "militant Unionists" (or Tories, as their detractors often called them during the war) believed that the old Union offered the best example of free republican government on earth, and that any effort at secession would lead to a civil war that would force the new Confederate government to become a military despotism in order to survive. By its very nature, a military despotism would extirpate civil liberties and free republican government, thereby destroying the very goals for which secession ostensibly stood.

In a commentary on disaffection in Confederate North Carolina, an historian writing in 1914 noted that in 1862 "the assertion was constantly made that extreme disloyalty existed in Davidson, Forsyth, Randolph and Guilford counties. As early as July 1861, Gov. Clark was notified of treasonable utterances and actions in Davidson, but was powerless to do more than appeal to the people to assist him by their influence."[54] A close look at the record reveals that indeed "extreme disloyalty" existed in central North Carolina in the summer of 1861, and that "treasonable utterances and actions" stemmed not only from people in Davidson County, but also from persons in Randolph, Guilford, Montgomery, Moore, Wilkes, and Yadkin counties. Governor Clark, far from being powerless to counter treason in Davidson County, ordered Confederate and state troops into the area in August 1861, to quell rebellion.

In April 1861, a soldier stationed at Fort Caswell on the North Carolina coast wrote to his brother in Montgomery County: "The people of Montgomery seem to be such union men at all hazards that I fear some of you will be fighting against me though I hope not. Old Huli [Hulin] is such an abolitionist (or unionist which is almost the same) that I am afraid he does not post you correctly in the news of the day." "Old Huli" was probably Hiram Hulin, Wesleyan abolitionist and father of three sons who became draft-dodgers rather than fight for the Confederacy.[55] Citizens from Yadkin County wrote Governor Ellis in April that their head militia officer, Colonel Cabal Bohanan, had urged his men not to support the Confederacy, but if Lincoln made a call for troops, for them "to come foreward." He also told them that every secessionist ought to be hung.[56]

From Wilkes County came word that the secession Democrats had organized a "Vigilance Committee" to harass "disloyal" former Whigs and other Unionists and coerce them into the ranks. A member of the committee tried to force a free black man to serve as a cook in a company in the Confederate army that authorities were then recruiting in Wilkes County. The black refused, and when forced, he resisted, killing one white man. The vigilance committee captured and hanged the black man. The committee next directed its venom at white militant Unionists:

> Soon after this [that is, the hanging of the black man] the Committee arrested[,] tried & condemnd O. Sprinkle & Milton Speaks Union men of the Co. [county]—tied them to a tree & whiped them on their bear backs, shaved their heads and brought them to our jail [in Wilkesboro] & threw them into the Dungeon.... The red handed party resolved to compel these prisoners to avow themselves favorable to the Southern cause & go to the war [and] on they refusing[,] to take them from the jail & Hang them ... and one of the Men O.S. [that is, O. Sprinkle] steadily refusing to retreat & volunteer[,] a rope was procured & the knot arranged for hanging ... which was only prevented by the Whig friends of these men who were Whigs rising against the leaders of the Vig. Committee whose leaders were Democrats.... Soon thereafter the jail was entered at mid-night by armed men—these poor defenceless men were hand cuffed taken out placed in a Wagon & carried off under guard and thrown into the service being compelled to serve in some one of the Forts then being seized by the Confdt. forces[.][57]

In May, a loyal Wilkes County Confederate and member of the vigilance committee bemoaned that only 96 men had volunteered for the army, and there was little hope of any more doing so. He hoped that the draft would soon force the dawdlers in Wilkes into the ranks. He noted that O. Sprinkle, Lindsey Sprinkle, and Milton Speaks—the Unionists mentioned in the block quotation above—had been convicted of setting the woods on fire and sentenced to 39 lashes and jail.[58]

Secessionists in the Randolph area, panicked by the aggressive activities of the militant Unionists, organized paramilitary units called "Home Guards," a local variation of the vigilance committee. (Do not confuse these Home Guards with the state forces by the same name organized in July 1863.) Confederate enthusiasts organized the Home Guard units soon after the war started to suppress sedition and disloyalty among both blacks and whites.[59] A man trying to raise a Home Guard unit in the Centre community — a Quaker settlement on the Randolph-Guilford County border — complained: "The truth is we have but 4 or 5 persons in this district (that is land holders) but are Lincoln men or they say they are Union men now they hold up for the republican Party, and the north, the result to my call was not noticed by any of them.... They say we must keep on the good side of the negroes and there will be no danger from them and that they are not going to form a guard to protect the homes of those who go to fight against the Union." He added that the local postmaster, A.C. Murrow, "is a regular Lincoln man." He and other members of the community "keep up correspondence with those Northern fanatics such as Daniel Worth."[60] The numerous complaints about disloyalty in the state, many of them emanating from the Quaker Belt, led the legislature to pass a treason law on May 11, 1861, that prescribed death for anyone professing allegiance or fidelity to an enemy of the state.[61]

Pro-Confederates organized a Home Guard unit in the eastern Randolph County mill village of Franklinsville in June 1861. Several of its members informed Governor Ellis that their mission was "to protect the homes, lives and property of this county, for we have Abolitionist and Lincolnite among us who defy the home guards to molest them, they say they have as many armed men as we can raise." In a statement pregnant with implications for the future, the loyalists added that the dissidents "have made their threats what they will do, as soon as our venteers [volunteers] leave the county."[62] The foregoing testimony indicates that by June 1861, militant elements of the pro–Union segment of society in Randolph County had armed and organized themselves into anti–Confederate paramilitary units in a determined effort to defy their pro–Confederate neighbors and relatives.

Militant Unionists also organized themselves in neighboring Davidson County. In July, one J.H. Moore wrote Governor Henry Toole Clark (Governor Ellis died in June) a remarkable letter charging that in the northeastern corner of the county a combination of persons opposed the Confederacy and openly advocated the coercion policy of Lincoln; they held secret meetings where they mustered under the United States flag. One of its leaders "openly declared it to be the design of the band to fight in support of the Lincoln government whenever an opportunity shall present — declaring that the State was unconstitutionally carried out of the Union, and that they will never submit to the Southern Confederacy." Moore identified the leader of this group as John Helton (the correct spelling was "Hilton").[63] According to Moore, Hilton "stated that there are five hundred men in Davidson and other counties around ready to strike for the Old Union ... [and] that there were certain secessionists in the neighborhood that would 'feel the rope' in a short time." Moore complained that ordinary criminal proceedings against the dissidents proved useless since the citizens of the disaffected area not involved with the troublemakers remained neutral and in the past had conducted only "*mock trials*" for incendiaries.[64]

During the first week in August 1861, Governor Henry Clark ordered troops into the Quaker Belt to pacify the militant Unionists.[65] One observer wrote in his diary on August 6: "there is some rebellious disturbance in part of Davidson and Randolph Counties, where there are a good many Quakers and yankees. Our Governor has sent several companies to 'High Point' station to overawe any such feeling."[66] A young Confederate soldier who was a member of the 160-man detachment sent to quell the insurgents informed a friend: "It appears some of the good citizens of our adjoining county Davidson have not forgotten their once great love for the Union of all the States, and have been taken to especial devotion to that prince of baboons—Abe Lincoln. They have endeavored to resist the laws of the state, and even permitted themselves to proceed in their rebellious course until the Sheriff had to call for assistance."[67] The Fayetteville *Observer* reported on August 5 that the sheriff of Davidson County arrested John Hilton near Thomasville for "using incendiary language, and making many violent threats of violence." Authorities sentenced Hilton to twelve months in prison for resisting an officer. They jailed him when he proved unable to post $5,000 bond to assure his appearance at the next superior court.[68]

State authorities in May 1861 organized the Trinity Guards, a military unit composed of the students and faculty of Trinity College, a small liberal arts school located in northwestern Randolph County. Its mission was to serve as an armed state force for the suppression of disloyalty and sedition in the area. Quakers and Methodists founded Trinity College in 1839. The state commissioned Braxton Craven, president of the college, captain of the Trinity Guards.[69] Craven had organized the Guards in an effort to deter his faculty and student body from volunteering for Confederate service, thereby preventing the dissolution of his college.[70] The Trinity Guards played a prominent role in quelling the "rebellious disturbance." Braxton Craven wrote Governor Clark that his company "very promptly responded to the call of Davidson [county authorities] for help. In two hours after receiving the notice we were on the way. I stationed a strong guard in Thomasville ... and with the remainder of the Company marched throughout the country ... and visited nearly all the houses. That country will be perfectly quiet." Craven added that troops needed to be sent into the lower part of Randolph County and into Montgomery.[71]

The arrest of John Hilton suppressed only temporarily the activities of the militant Unionist underground. In August a secessionist wrote a friend, "there are many abolitionist[s] in Randolph, some of which have had to leave for their large talking in favor of Lincoln, others keep quiet and are let alone."[72] Threats by secessionists did not cow everyone. For example, Confederates charged Thomas Dougan in the Randolph County Courts with using "language in favor of the Federal government." One witness swore that Dougan said: "Sessessions are rascals and traitors and would be whipped." Another alleged Dougan claimed Lincoln was correct in his war policy and was only doing his duty as president.[73] In neighboring Chatham County, secessionists had Martine Wilson arrested for "treasonable talk and incendiary language and for fear of private injury done to his neighbors." Two justices of the peace ordered Wilson to jail in June.[74]

In January 1862, the Quaker Belt achieved national notoriety in the Confederacy when the *Richmond Examiner* printed an expose of disloyalty in the district in an article entitled "The Demand for Vigilance," written by someone using the pen name "A Traveler," warning that "there is a strip of country in North Carolina which is largely disloyal. Beginning with Randolph and Guilford, it extends through Davidson, Forsyth, Davie, Yadkin, into Wilkes." "A Traveler" claimed that the disloyal element had a secret organization and that an informant in the Salem area of Forsyth County confided to him that "he knew of persons in the community who were in correspondence with the Lincoln government." The author added, "I

The Trinity Guards, assembled in 1861 before "Old Main," the most important building on the campus of Trinity College, a liberal arts school located in northwestern Randolph County, founded by Methodists and Quakers in 1839. The Trinity Guards was a state military force created in May 1861 and commanded by Braxton Craven, president of Trinity College. The primary mission of the Guards was the suppression of disloyalty and sedition in the Davidson-Randolph County area. It played a key role in the subjugation of the insurrection of militant Unionists led by John Hilton in the summer of 1861 (courtesy the University Archives Photograph Collection, Rubenstein Rare Book and Manuscript Library, Duke University).

believe that this same correspondence is still going on, and at the proper time some sort of demonstration will be made to further the interests of the enemy.... Let a detachment be sent to Salem or Winston and arrest all suspected persons at once; and then scour the whole of this disloyal region."[75]

The editor of the Greensboro *Patriot* strongly denounced the claims of "A Traveler" as false. Yet, in light of the disloyal utterances and actions that occurred in Randolph, Guilford, Chatham, and Davidson counties in 1861, it would appear that "A Traveler" was on firm ground in his charges. It is noteworthy that his list of disloyal counties — Randolph, Guilford, Davidson, Davie, Forsyth, Yadkin, and Wilkes — formed the very heart of the Quaker Belt. W.L. Scott, a prominent Greensboro attorney, added credence to the charges of "A Traveler" when he informed a friend in January 1862, "I will say to you (confidentially) that in my opinion ... there is more disaffection in our particular section of the state than you or even many people here suppose."[76]

In early 1862, another observer of the home front in the Quaker Belt wrote to his father about the issue of disloyalty: "It may be very imprudent to make public that there is *any* disappointment [over secession] among our people, but persons who deny it in private are either totally ignorant of the State of feeling in this region of the State or are themselves unsound." The correspondent, writing from Alamance County, then gave a remarkable example of militant Unionists defying Confederate authority: "At a recent constable election, one of the candidates announced himself as still devoted to the union and his supporters voted for him with ballots having on them the [American] Eagle, as emblematic of their attachment to the Union. And still later, we hear that in the same part of the county some of the militia have on the field refused to muster under the Flag of the Confederate States and have defended themselves from arrest with arms in their hands."[77]

At about the time of the report of dissidence in Alamance County, word reached Governor Clark that a "traitorous spirit" flourished in certain areas of Surry County. Loyal men there hesitated to volunteer for army service, because they feared that their disloyal neighbors would be a threat to their families and property if they absented themselves from home.[78]

The State Draft

By February 1862, Federal forces in eastern North Carolina had captured Roanoke Island and threatened New Bern. Governor Clark, in an effort to raise troops to repel the invaders, ordered one-third of the state militia drafted and organized into state regiments.[79] Thus did state authorities subject the citizens of North Carolina to a draft one month before the Confederate Congress passed its first national conscription act. The state draft provoked serious opposition across the Quaker Belt, notably in Moore, Yadkin, Forsyth, Surry, Chatham, Iredell, Randolph, and Davidson counties. A witness to the state draft in Moore County reported: "I never saw people in so great a state of excitement. All that was lacking was for the stars and stripes to have been planted there, with a force sufficient to defend them. They [the draftees] would have enlisted under the banner almost unanimously."[80] The state adjutant general ordered about thirty troops into neighboring Chatham County to arrest draftees who refused to go to camp as ordered. Were any of the draft-dodgers to resist arrest, the adjutant general ordered the commanding officer to "fire [on them] without any hesitation."[81] In March and April, the adjutant general ordered militia officers in Iredell, Guilford, and Surry counties to arrest draft resisters and disloyalists.[82] On the eve of the state draft in Forsyth County, a resident wrote: "Tomorrow our county is drafted & I fear the result will not be auspicious to the southern cause." Another Forsyth citizen observed, "great dissatisfaction is ex pressed among the people—and I fear it will be difficult to get many of the drafted ones to go with out an outbreak. Many declare they will die at home first. They may however change their minds."[83]

Opposition to the state draft in Randolph and Davidson counties took the form of so-called "peace meetings," the earliest on record in the Confederacy. Demonstrators held the Randolph County peace meeting in "Scott's Old Field," Captain's District, located in present-day Tabernacle Township in the west-central part of the county. A brief description of the peace meeting reads as follows: "Week before last we had a little excitement—a precinct 10 miles from here [that is, from Asheboro], in a community where there were very few men with any education, they had a kind of prayer meeting where some 50 men raised a white flag and said they were for peace. The Captain of that district, John C. Hill, a rather illiterate man, gave the command for all who were in favor of peace to follow in the procession; over 50 persons obeyed, and they marched after the white flag, had prayer for peace, and then dispersed."[84] This peace meeting, along with a meeting held in Davidson County at about the same time, were the first manifestations of the "peace movement" (see chapter four) that swept through the Confederacy in the last two years of the war, which had as its goal the cessation of hostilities and reunion.[85]

From the foregoing account, one could hardly conclude that North Carolina or the Confederacy had much to fear from fifty peace demonstrators; yet more serious matters must have been going forward in Randolph, for on March 4, 1862, Governor Clark issued a proclamation against disaffection and disloyalty in the county. He received communications from Randolph that persons had conspired to resist, by force if necessary, efforts by the state to draft members of the militia into state military service. Further, "they denounce our State and Confederacy, and openly approve the conduct of the public enemy, and desire to effect a union with a government at war with us now invading our soil; and in various ways, by word and deed, and giving aid and comfort to the enemy."[86] The governor sent one of his aides, Colonel Spier Whitaker, to Randolph to investigate the situation. He ordered the sheriff to arrest all guilty parties. If the disloyalists proved recalcitrant, the governor promised the sheriff "a sufficient force" with which to subdue them.[87]

Governor Clark's description of an anti–Confederate organization of militant Unionists that sought reunion offers evidence that by March 1862 the Heroes of America was active and entrenched in Randolph County. The Heroes of America, also referred to as the "Red Strings," was a secret, underground, anti–Confederate organization of militant Unionists. Confederate officials knew of the existence of the Heroes of America as early as 1863, but authorities first brought them to the public's attention in North Carolina during the gubernatorial campaign in the summer of 1864. The anti–Confederate activities of the secret organization included espionage and sabotage; aiding deserters, draft-dodgers, and escaped Federal prisoners; operating Underground Railroad routes to the Federal lines; and protecting its members from the Home Guards, the militia, Confederate troops, and loyal Confederate citizens. The HOA also supported the reunionist-oriented Peace Party that was active in state politics in 1863 and 1864.[88]

An old Davidson County Confederate soldier recounted in his reminiscences published in 1909 the peace meeting held in Davidson County in early March 1862 — apparently in conjunction with the meeting held in Randolph County at Scott's Old Field. He recalled that "a peace movement was inaugurated and attained to some prominence in the state, especially among the original union men and parties dissatisfied with the existing state of affairs." He said peace activists held a meeting near Thomasville at Kennedy Schoolhouse. The people attending the meeting, he explained, were "prompted by honorable motives, merely wishing to hear discussed or explained the plan proposed by the leaders of the movement." The authorities, warned in advance of the meeting, ordered troops to the gathering. The soldiers arrived unnoticed and charged into the crowd, capturing many prisoners, several of whom were old men whom the authorities jailed. Most of the young men captured in the surprise raid volunteered for the Confederate army — apparently to avoid prison.[89]

In March 1867, many of the participants of the wartime Kennedy Schoolhouse meeting had a "Union Meeting — Celebration" at the schoolhouse to commemorate their ordeal that day. They recalled the occasion not as a "peace meeting," but as a "Union meeting." "We cherish with fond recollections, the unswerving fidelity of our Union friends of this district, who were betrayed and captured by rebel troops, whilst holding a Union meeting at this place, the 6th of March 1862, and carried to Raleigh, and confined in Confederate prisons, for their Union sentiments. Some of whom were eighty years of age, but who are with us ... to-day, living monuments of loyalty, and protected by that government and flag which they never deserted." The celebrants then proceeded to thank "the honorable members of the thirty-ninth Congress, for their indefatigable efforts in behalf of Union men South, in passing the Stevens and Sherman military and reconstruction bill." These Southern Unionists — soon to be known as Scalawags for endorsing the Republican Reconstruction plan — were voicing support for the Congressional or Radical plan of Reconstruction against the presidential plan advocated by Andrew Johnson.[90]

On the day of the Kennedy Schoolhouse meeting, Governor Clark informed Colonel Whitaker that informers had reported "treasonable conduct and threatened violence" in Davidson County "as serious as the threatened outbreak in Randolph County." He told the colonel that three hundred troops under the command of a Captain Ross had left for High Point the day before to aid the sheriff of Randolph County, and that Colonel Hoke's Thirty-third Regiment had been ordered up and would arrive shortly. Colonel Whitaker, who was in High Point, was to take command of the troops when they arrived. The governor advised Whitaker to detach two companies to send to the aid of the sheriff of Davidson County if the need arose.[91] On March 8, military authorities ordered "John Hitton, Jr." and others arrested and sent to the camp for conscripts in Raleigh.[92] "Hitton" was a misspelling of Hilton, the militant Unionist leader arrested near Thomasville the preceding August. On March 14, Colonel Whitaker reported: "Holton has probably escaped to Tennessee."[93] John Hilton fled to the Union lines and joined the United States Army, where he attained the rank of captain by war's end.[94]

On March 14, Colonel Whitaker noted that all the dissidents from Randolph County had been rounded up, including three of their leaders by the names of Rush, Kindly, and Hill, who had either been drafted or had "volunteered." He coldly added, "their families and farms are sureties against [their] desertion." He continued, "two-thirds of the drafted men from Randolph have volunteered; more will volunteer."[95] And so ended the rebellion led by militant Unionists in Randolph and Davidson counties against the military draft levied by North Carolina state authorities on its militia in March 1862. The reunionist sentiments that underlay these protests resurfaced more forcefully in the peace and convention movements in the state in 1863 and 1864.

Despite his bold use of military force against the Unionists, warnings of disloyalty in central North Carolina continued to reach Governor Clark in the first half of 1862. In March, Braxton Craven, commander of the Trinity Guards, wrote: "Deep, inveterate hate to this government abounds and the authorities of the County [Randolph] will never crush it."[96] In the same month, the governor received "important information, and some very serious charges against some of the citizens" of Moore County.[97] In April, he got word that, in the area between Jamestown (in Guilford County) and Gladesboro (in Randolph County), Union men clandestinely manufactured and stored powder and arms.[98] On July 14, Lt.

Coble of the Guilford County Militia charged that Thomas Stafford headed "Several Night Meetings. And would like to see and welcome the yankees."[99]

Widespread opposition to the draft levied by the state in March appeared across the Quaker Belt, especially in Randolph and Davidson counties where political activists held pro–Union peace demonstrations. The next month, the Confederate Congress passed its first national conscription act obliging all males between 18 and 35 to stand for the draft. Its enforcement led to bloodshed between Confederate loyalists and militant Unionists; thereafter, the inner civil war waxed ever more severe in the area as time went by.

Chapter Three

The Inner Civil War

Between the passage of the state draft law in March 1862 and the accession of Zebulon Baird Vance to the governorship in September, disloyalty and disaffection increased in the Quaker Belt. The faction advocating reunion formed a common front with those disaffected by the hardships brought on by a long and bloody war and those disenchanted with the policies and direction of the Davis administration. The main factors contributing to this sense of alienation included spiraling inflation, a growing shortage of food and other necessities, opposition to the draft laws, and the prospect of a long, costly war. As the summer progressed, hundreds of deserters opted to return home rather than to continue to fight for Confederate independence. They joined the draft-dodgers and militant Unionists in the woods, and — under the aegis of the Heroes of America — they organized themselves into armed, disciplined guerrilla bands and squared off against Confederate and state troops and their loyal Confederate neighbors. Thus did the inner civil war between neighbors that had been smoldering for over a year begin to wax dead serious when conflict led to bloodshed. From that time until war's end, a cycle of spiraling violence characterized society in the Quaker Belt as terrorism, murder, arson, rape, pillage, and torture impelled the actors in the internal war to ever greater heights of hatred and acts of vengeance.

In April 1862, the Confederate Congress passed the first conscription act — the single most volatile cause of the inner civil war. It made all white men between the ages of eighteen and thirty-five liable for military service. Congress increased the age to forty-five in October of that year and to fifty in early 1864. Widespread opposition to the conscription acts appeared in North Carolina and the Confederacy.[1] The nonslaveholding farmers in the western half of North Carolina considered the draft law especially odious, because they had to depend upon their own labor for a livelihood. They felt that they had already contributed their fair share of men to the army and that any further drain of labor from their area, which, for the most part, contained few slaves, would perforce reduce their families to starvation and destitution.[2] For example, the wife of a nonslaveholding farmer and mother of eight children (all under the age of fifteen) living in Randolph County urged Governor Vance "to look to the white cultivators as strickly as congress has to the slaveholders." She warned him that if the men between the ages of thirty-five and forty-five were drafted, "it is bound to leave a thousand families in a starving condition in our county."[3] Another Randolph County citizen writing to the editor of the *Standard* complained: "If the conscripts, who are the stay of the people, are taken from our county, ruin and devastation must soon follow, for it will be impossible for those that are left to sustain themselves."[4]

Holden often expressed sympathy in his newspaper for the plight of the needy small farmers of North Carolina. He chastised planters and wealthy farmers for charging the families of poor soldiers extortionate prices for grain and other foodstuffs: "Every one who has anything to spare should cheerfully part with it to the destitute families of soldiers, and thus encourage the soldiers to stand by the flag and fight on.... Your negroes will have meat as well as bread, and they will have shoes next winter. Who will shoe the families of our soldiers, and furnish them with meat, or a taste of it once a day?"[5] The editor of the Salem *People's Press* gave the high cost of food charged by speculators as the main cause of desertion. Only the reduction of food prices for soldiers' families, he argued, would decrease desertion.[6]

As the concerned mother from Randolph County implied in her letter to the governor cited above, the nonslaveholding farmers resented the favoritism shown by the Confederate Congress toward the wealthy slaveholders over them in the conscription acts. The substitution and exemption clauses strikingly manifested this favoritism. The substitution clause allowed those liable for service to substitute in their place someone not liable for service. This favored those who could afford to hire a substitute, an option few draftees — most of whom were artisans, laborers, and yeoman and tenant farmers — could afford. An assemblage of conscripts from Orange County at Camp Holmes near Raleigh registered their resentment of allowing the wealthy to buy their way out of the draft in the following resolution: "That we do not approve of that feature in the act of conscription which tolerates substitutes. In the fight for freedom all should fight, as all will be free."[7]

The exemption clauses gave draft exemptions to, among others, militia officers, teachers, ministers, state and Confederate civil servants (which included selected local government officials such as justices of the peace and sheriffs), skilled artisans, and certain manufacturers and industrialists. Except for the laborers needed to work on the railroads, at the state salt works, or at state ordinance facilities, few persons in the artisan, yeoman, and tenant farmer category had the education and economic means to qualify for exclusion. This led to bitter class resentments against those fortunate enough to receive a deferment, especially the militia officers whose duty it was to arrest draft-dodgers and deserters and escort them to the conscript camp in Raleigh.[8] Bryan Tyson, a militant Unionist and anti–Confederate political activist from Moore County, aptly referred to these exempt militia officers as the "mainstay of the rebellion." He explained: "These officers being liable to be conscripted and forced into the army in case of dereliction of duty, were, generally speaking, very zealous in the discharge of the same, in order that they might thus screen themselves."[9] Rather than submit to the perceived injustice of being forced into the ranks by one of the "better sort" who had been deferred from military service primarily because of his wealth, education, and social position, many a poor man took to the woods to avoid the draft.[10]

Old political animosities also contributed to the popular outcry against the exemption of militia officers from the Confederate draft. For example, in Forsyth County where the Democrats had been strong before the war, and thus held most of the militia commissions, Whigs found themselves drafted into the ranks at the hands of their old Democratic political enemies. As one victim wrote: "All the parties that are conspicuous in arresting conscripts, are members of the old & much hated Dem. party, & consequently very obnoxious to the great majority."¹¹ The resentment of the draft-eligible citizens toward the exemption of militia officers had another side to it. The main responsibility assigned militia officers during the war involved hunting down truant conscripts and deserters and taking them to the Camp of Instruction in Raleigh, where all draftees were processed before assigning them to regiments. This activity soon led to bloodshed. In September 1862, a citizen of Randolph County observed: "Some mischief is occasionally done by outlyers, one gets shot once in a while."¹²

By October 1863, about 21,558 men had received exemptions in North Carolina. This figure does not include totals from the First Congressional District that was largely occupied by Federal forces. Those exempted included 2,346 militia officers and 407 magistrates — individuals involved in hunting and prosecuting deserters and disloyalists.¹³ The most controversial draft deferment went to owners of twenty or more slaves. Confederates intended the "twenty slave clause" to provide a permanent force of armed white males among the slaves to supervise their work, police their activities, and prevent possible slave insurrections.¹⁴ The twenty slave and the substitution clauses led to the charge that the War for Southern Independence had become "a rich man's war, and a poor man's fight." Holden gave wide publicity to this sentiment in his newspaper, the *Standard*. By the summer of 1862, Holden had taken a strong political stand against the Confederate leadership both in Raleigh and in Richmond.¹⁵

Under Holden's leadership, the Union Party, created by old-line Whigs and Union Democrats to oppose secession in 1861, metamorphosed into the Conservative Party in 1862. In addition to old Whigs and Unionist Democrats, the new Conservative Party attracted those who, for whatever reasons, opposed the Jefferson Davis administration, the conscription acts, or were dissatisfied with conditions in general. The Conservatives never denied that they had opposed secession and the war. However, once the general assembly approved secession, they claimed then to be loyal Confederates who supported the war effort and Confederate independence. Nonetheless, the Conservatives announced that they would never allow the Davis administration (that is, the old Democrats) to use military necessity as an excuse to establish a "military despotism." The military and the Confederate government must always respect the civil liberties of free speech, free press, and habeas corpus. The traditional republican rights and liberties of individuals and the states must remain inviolate no matter what.¹⁶

Governor Zebulon Baird Vance's Crackdown on Deserters, Draft-dodgers and Disloyalists

In the gubernatorial contest held in the summer of 1862, the Conservative party chose Zebulon Baird Vance — colonel of the Twenty-sixth Regiment North Carolina troops, former Whig congressional representative, and anti-secession Unionist from the mountain county of Buncombe — to be its standard bearer. The old secession Democrats and Whigs, reincarnated as the Confederate party, nominated William L. Johnston, a railroad official, Davis supporter, and former secessionist Whig from Mecklenburg County.¹⁷

Vance beat Johnston by a landslide vote of 55,282 to 20,813 (73 percent of the vote). Officials inaugurated Vance as governor of North Carolina on September 8, 1862.¹⁸ Vance carried all of the Quaker Belt counties, garnering 89.8 percent of their total vote. Seven of them gave him 90 percent or more of their vote.[19] Of the 55,282 votes cast by Conservatives in the 1862 gubernatorial election, 18,177, or 32.9 percent, came from the Quaker Belt, whereas only 10 percent of the Confederate Party vote originated there. In addition, of all the votes cast in 1862, Conservative and Confederate combined, 20,235 out of 76,095 votes, or 26.6 percent, came from there.[20] These statistics indicate that almost 27 percent of the state's voting electorate in this election lived in the fifteen counties of the Quaker Belt. In addition, they show that the Quaker Belt was the backbone of the wartime Conservative Party, just as it had been the mainstay of the antebellum Whig Party and the Union Party during the secession crisis.

The near solid support of Vance by a region viewed by most leaders in Richmond as one of questionable loyalty to the Confederacy caused many Confederates to look askance at the new Tar Heel governor. Many had feared that were Vance elected, his Unionist following would manipulate North Carolina back into the old Union. One hostile newspaper editor accused Vance of being the "Massachusetts candidate" for governor.[21] Soon after taking office, Vance's actions proved his political opponent's fears unfounded. In his inaugural address, Vance promised all-out support of the war effort. Moreover, much to the chagrin of the Unionists, he announced that there would be a spirited enforcement of the conscription laws in North Carolina.[22] One observer reported that Vance had the audacity to proclaim before an audience of mountain folks: "If there is any in North Carolina who ought to be in the army, and who is not there, I will make the state too hot to hold him."[23] Vance kept his word. Using every means available to him, he relentlessly pursued the deserters and draft-dodgers in the Quaker Belt and in the rest of the state to the last days of the war. The governor heartily endorsed using the North Carolina militia as an adjunct to the Confederate Conscript Bureau for rounding up draft-dodgers, deserters, and absentees, and enforcing the conscript laws generally.[24] The second conscription act added men between thirty-five and forty-five to the conscription rolls. This reduced Vance's militia to a skeleton force of officers whom the conscription law had exempted from the draft.[25]

Zebulon Baird Vance (1830–1894) about 1875. As governor of North Carolina, 1862–1865, he relentlessly pursued the deserters, draft-dodgers, and disloyal militant Unionists in the Quaker Belt with his state troops until the last days of the war. In his massive deserter hunt conducted in the summer of 1864, his troops under his orders illegally arrested and confined the wives, children, and elderly parents of deserters in makeshift prisons where they were held and sometimes tortured until the deserters surrendered to the military authorities. Vance successfully opposed and defeated the Copperhead insurgency conducted by William Holden's Peace Party in 1863 and 1864 (courtesy the North Carolina Collection, University of North Carolina at Chapel Hill Library).

Quakers and Conscription

The pacifist Quakers opposed the conscription acts for religious reasons. The state passed a law granting them an exemption from service in the state forces upon payment of a $100 fee. Another law passed in October 1862 allowed Friends an exemption from the Confederate military upon the payment of a $500 fee.[26] Some few Quakers — holding strict religious scruples — refused to pay the fee. On occasion, overzealous and cruel military officers tortured, imprisoned, or even killed recalcitrant Friends. Though sensational, such actions were exceptional. They violated the policies of both the Jefferson Davis administration and the wartime governors of North Carolina.[27] Due to the special efforts of John Milton Worth,[28] who had been appointed state salt commissioner in early 1862, state authorities allowed Quakers to work at the state salt works near Wilmington in lieu of military service. This law proved helpful to Quakers who could not afford to pay the exemption charge.[29] Due to the influence of Worth, authorities detailed numerous Randolph County area residents — including many non–Quakers — to work at the state salt works rather than serve in the army. According to General Whiting, the Confederate military commander for the lower Cape Fear area of North Carolina, most of these "salt hands" were members of the Heroes of America, and were in communication with the Federal naval forces patrolling the coast.[30]

J.M. Worth and his brother, Jonathan, the State Treasurer, were born into a Quaker family living in the Centre community in southern Guilford County. In 1860, both were residents of Asheboro, the seat of Randolph County. Neither remained members of the Society of Friends as adults, but both worked to promote tolerance of the pacifist principles of the Quakers by the Confederate and state governments during the war. Before the war, J.M. Worth was an ardent anti-secessionist Whig, but during the conflict, he became one of Randolph County's most outspoken champions of the Confederate cause.

"War Quakers" proved to be a special problem for conscription authorities. They were Quakers disowned by their congregation for some offense, or

John Milton Worth (1811–1900) around 1850. A wealthy businessman, state salt commissioner under Governor Vance, a state senator, and a colonel in the Randolph County militia, he played a leading role in the deserter hunt in the Quaker Belt in the fall of 1862. An ardent opponent of secession, by 1862 he had become a champion of Confederate independence. After the war, he served as state treasurer (courtesy Randolph County Public Library's Historical Photograph Collection).

individuals who had attended meetings and believed Quaker doctrine, but had never bothered formally to enter the fold. The law exempting Quakers disallowed the exemption of anyone who joined the Society of Friends after the passage of the law. Thus, many of the people in the Quaker Belt who held genuine and deeply felt pacifist and antislavery principles, but who had not been long-standing members of a Quaker congregation or had been disowned, found themselves conscripted. Many of these "fellow travelers" of the Quaker faith became draft-dodgers and took to the woods to avoid conscription.[31] After the war, William Holden, editor of the *Standard*, praised the Quakers for their loyalty to the Union and efforts on behalf of peace during the conflict. "The rebel officials," commented Holden, "were aware of the sentiments and character of the Quakers — of their peaceful disposition and yet of their fidelity to the Union. The latter was unpardonable, and many of the Friends were made to feel the heavy hand of despotism."[32]

Militant Unionists, Draft-Dodgers, Deserters and Red Strings

In the summer of 1862, a volatile mixture of six elements combined to set the stage for an inner civil war between white Southerners. Three of them were already present: the militant Unionists, the draft-dodgers, and the conscription laws. The militant Unionists and draft-dodgers had united in the spring and rebelled against the state and Confederate draft measures. The fourth element was the deserters. When the deserters arrived in the summer, the militant Unionists and draft-dodgers welcomed them to join the Heroes of America, their secret, underground organization that could offer the absconders a means of obtaining food and shelter and a well-organized system of defense against state and Confederate forces sent in to hunt them down. The fifth element was Governor Vance, who upon his inauguration promised to prosecute unflaggingly desertion, draft-dodging, and disloyalty in the state. The sixth element was the increasing hunger and destitution the yeoman and landless tenant and laboring classes faced because of rampant inflation, short crops, lack of adequate labor to produce their crops, and shortages of life's necessities.[33]

In the summer of 1862, the desertion rate of North Carolina troops increased markedly, a development that inflamed the internal war between neighbors. This negative development can be attributed primarily to one issue: the resentment of the twelve-month volunteers at being forced by the conscription acts to reenlist for the duration of the war, or suffer the indignity of being drafted. When their one-year enlistment expired, and commanders denied them a furlough home, many soldiers deserted.[34]

Complaints against the draft continued through the summer in the Quaker Belt from Yadkin in the west to Moore in the east. A soldier serving in a company from Yadkin County wrote to his wife about the trouble in the ranks caused by the forced reenlistment of the twelve-month volunteers: "There is some dissatisfaction in the co. among those who did not reenlist about having to remain in the service under the conscript law after their time is out, and I would not be surprised if they dont give Tom [the company commander] a good deal of trouble; they are already raising bickerings in the company ... and if they continue he will have no control over them in less than a month."[35] The extreme disaffection displayed in Yadkin prompted Confederate authorities in June to order a unit of Confederate troops from Georgia, described as "select men," into the county to hunt down deserters. In one action, the troops wounded three skulkers, and in another, they captured eighteen.[36] In Moore County an observer noted in September that some local draft-dodgers proclaimed that what fighting they would do would be at home. They declared that like-minded deserters were joining them.[37] Randolph County soldiers abandoned the ranks for home in such large numbers that in August Governor Clark issued a proclamation warning them to return to duty "without delay" or face being captured and punished as the law provides.[38]

On September 11, just three days after taking office, Governor Vance issued the first of his many proclamations against dissidents. The governor vowed to suppress the actions of disloyal persons who were organizing open resistance to the draft law by encouraging men to defy its execution. He warned that the law will be enforced and encouraged loyal citizens to support those officials charged with its implementation.[39] In his war against the disloyalists, the governor had the hearty support of Major Peter Mallett, head of the Confederate Conscript Bureau in North Carolina.[40] Just one month before the governor issued his proclamation, Mallett reported to his superior in Richmond that he was having "the disaffected sections of the Western portion of the State thoroughly patrolled for the purpose of getting up the delinquent conscripts and *arresting the leading disloyalists*" (emphasis added).[41] The threat posed to national authority by deserters and disloyalists in central North Carolina deeply concerned both the head of the Confederate Conscript Bureau in Richmond and Governor Vance as the summer of 1862 came to a close. Both vowed to break their power.

Bryan Tyson — Militant Unionist

A militant Unionist from Moore County named Bryan Tyson played an important role in convincing Confederate and state authorities through his writings and political activism that the disloyalists in the Quaker Belt posed a threat to reckon with. He was born in 1830 in southeastern Randolph County in the Brower's Mills community. His father, Aaron Tyson, was a prosperous farmer, physician, owner of twelve slaves, and former Quaker whom the Society of Friends had disowned for marrying out of unity.[42] Bryan Tyson clandestinely published two anti–Confederate tracts in 1862 in which he pressured Southerners to abandon the cause of Confederate independence and opt for reunion. Confederate authorities limited Tyson's influence by suppressing his writings before they could be widely circulated. The press did not mention Bryan Tyson's name and writings during the war for security reasons. As a result, historians until recently have failed to notice Tyson, his political career, and his writings.[43] Nevertheless, his activities as an anti–Confederate political protester shed a great deal of light on why disloyalty in central North Carolina concerned Vance and Confederate conscription authorities in the summer of 1862. In addition, his writings and political activism both in North Carolina and in the North in 1863 and 1864 influenced the advent and course of the reunionist peace movement that swept the state in those years. They also offer unique insight into the mind and anti–Confederate activities of a Quaker Belt militant Unionist.

Bryan Tyson received a classical education at a private academy in Carthage — the seat of Moore County — where he studied Greek, Latin, grammar, geography, geometry, and arithmetic.[44] On inheriting a farm and four slaves from his mother, he settled down to a career as a farm implement manufacturer and "experimental" farmer in the "Gold Region"

Three. The Inner Civil War 49

Bryan Tyson (1830–1909) around 1864. Author, Whig political activist, and Copperhead crusader, he laid the foundation for the Tar Heel peace movement in his 1862 book *A Ray of Light*, in which he advocated the return of the South to the Union on the Copperhead basis, that is, with slavery protection by the Constitution. Tyson's call for a return to the Union on the Copperhead basis became the central tenet of William Holden's 1863 peace movement. Tyson tried to unite Southern peace agitators and Northern Copperheads into a political coalition to create a Copperhead America that would replace both the Confederacy and the version of America envisioned by the Republicans (courtesy the Bryan Tyson Papers, Rubenstein Rare Book and Manuscript Library, Duke University).

of northwestern Moore County.⁴⁵ During the secession crisis, Tyson wrote several Unionist tracts, but he was unable to get them published because they "savored too strongly of Union sentiments."⁴⁶ Nevertheless, in March 1862, when Governor Clark issued his order drafting one-third of the state militia to repel the Federal invasion of the sound region of eastern North Carolina, Tyson joined with many others in the Quaker Belt in expressing disloyal sentiments toward the Confederacy. Referring to the public reaction to the draft in Moore County, Tyson declared: "I never saw people in so great a state of excitement. All that was lacking was for the stars and stripes to have been planted there, with a force sufficient to defend them. They [the draftees] would have enlisted under the banner almost unanimously. I was urged to start an opposition movement, some of the boys telling me they would die by me if it were necessary. This I had already resolved to do were I drafted or appointed to go."⁴⁷

Repelled by the conscription acts, Tyson in the spring of 1862 began writing an anti–Confederate tract entitled *A Ray of Light; or, a Treatise on the Sectional Troubles Religiously and Morally Considered*. In August, F.K. Strother, a Raleigh printer, clandestinely published Tyson's 168-page book.⁴⁸ While conscription was the immediate cause of Tyson writing *A Ray of*

A Ray of Light, published by Bryan Tyson in August 1862, is the founding document of the Tar Heel Copperhead insurgency. In it, Tyson first called for the South to return to the Union on the Copperhead basis, that is, with the institution of slavery in the returning states protected by the Constitution. Tyson's call for a return to the Union on the Copperhead basis fell on deaf ears in 1862, but that policy became the central tenet of the peace movement launched by William Holden in the summer of 1863 (courtesy HathiTrust).

Light, an underlying reason for his passionate activism lay in a "profession of religion" that occurred in 1848. He then was a student at a private academy in Carthage, where he fell deeply in love with a young woman who took no interest in him. Tyson became so distraught that his parents believed he had gone mad, so they confined him to his room for several days. While thus restricted, Tyson had multiple visions and theophanies that he relates in fascinating detail in his book, but they depart too far from our topic here to recount now.[49] Suffice it to say, Tyson was thereafter a marked man bent on a mission to relieve human suffering.

In *A Ray of Light*, Tyson argued that there had been no adequate cause for secession and that the Confederacy was an illegal usurpation of political power, because the seceding states had not held plebiscites to approve the ordinances of secession.[50] He warned his readers that the North, with its enormous advantages in manpower, naval strength, and industrial output, could not be defeated or held at bay by the South. Union armies and naval forces now occupied about one-half of the Confederacy, and the South had no hope of amassing enough power to retake the lost provinces. The Confederacy must negotiate a return to the Union while it still had enough clout to do so, or the South surely would be defeated and subjected to Republican rule. Tyson pointed out that while the Northern Democrats opposed Confederate nationhood, the antiwar or peace wing of the party was willing to compromise with the South and work for reunion on a Constitutional basis, that is, with the institution of slavery left intact in the returning Southern states.[51]

Throughout the war, the Northern Democrats adhered to a platform of strict construction of the Constitution and states' rights. They strongly opposed Lincoln's Emancipation Proclamation as a blatant violation of the constitutional guarantee of the right to own slaves. Historians have divided the Democrats in the North during the Civil War into two groups: the "War Democrats" and the "Peace Democrats." The War Democrats, who grudgingly supported the war policies of Lincoln, composed a majority of the party during the war. In opposition to Lincoln's war measures, the Peace Democrats advocated peace, compromise, and reunion. Republicans derisively called the Peace Democrats "Copperheads," a term implying traitor.[52] They were especially strong in Ohio, Indiana, New Jersey, and Illinois, and a fair number of them existed in Pennsylvania, New York, and other states.[53] During the war, the War Democrats dominated the party, but at times, as in the summer of 1864, the Copperhead faction was powerful enough to threaten a takeover of the party.[54]

Tyson thought his readers should take the Peace Democrats in the North at their word and cooperate with them in a drive to reconstruct the Union peacefully and by means of compromise.[55] Tyson's call in mid–1862 for Southern moderates and Unionists to affect a return to the Union based on the Constitution by cooperating with the Copperheads proved premature, but his scheme resurfaced a year later in the peace movement led by William Woods Holden. (Tyson did not use the terms "Copperheads" or "Peace Democrats" in his writings; rather, he used the broader appellation of "Democrats." Since historians have widely used the terms to refer to the Northern peace wing of the Democracy — the faction of Democrats that Tyson chose to work with and support — I use the terms interchangeably when discussing references by Tyson to the Northern Democrats. I refer to the demand by Peace Democrats that reunion be based on a Constitutional guarantee of the right to own slaves in the returning Southern states as the "Copperhead basis (or plan) for reunion." Moreover, I refer to the Southern political activists in William Holden's Peace Party in 1863 and 1864 who advocated a return of North Carolina and the South to the Union on the Copperhead basis as Copperheads.

Not long after the publication of *A Ray of Light*, military conscription authorities arrested Tyson as a draft-dodger and incarcerated him in the Moore County jail at Carthage for four days. While in jail, he wrote a circular that he later used in his anti–Confederate activities.[56] In this reunion circular, Tyson appealed to Southern leaders to arrange a two- to three-month armistice with the North, and — provided Federal negotiators respected Southern rights — to return to the Union. Tyson noted that the Confederacy had no hope of building a navy capable of lifting the blockade of Southern ports by the U.S. Navy. Unless the blockade were lifted, land victories by the Confederate army would be worthless. Thus, it was imperative that the Confederacy negotiate a settlement of the war before defeat became inevitable. Perhaps, Tyson reasoned, Northerners would impeach and replace Abraham Lincoln with a president acceptable to both the North and South. If Lincoln remained in office, he should be required to guarantee the constitutional rights, including the right to own slaves, of the citizens of the readmitted states. If the North under Lincoln insisted on abolishing slavery, then the South should abandon all efforts at reunion. Tyson believed that a bona fide proposal by Southern leaders to restore the Union on terms fair and equitable to both sections would have one of two results: the Union would be reestablished, or, if the Republican Party balked at compromise, a strong opposition party would arise in the North and sow "discord among the Northern people," forcing the Republicans to come to terms with the South. Tyson's reunion circular, as was his book *A Ray of Light*, was a pro–Copperhead tract that laid the foundation for the Copperhead insurgency that underlay the peace and convention movements of 1863 and 1864 in the Tar Heel state.

With the help of influential friends, Tyson gained an exemption from military service on the ground that he would be more valuable to the Confederacy as a manufacturer of agricultural implements than as a soldier.[57] Nevertheless, Tyson had no intention of becoming a loyal Confederate. When he returned home to his farm implement business, he joined the Heroes of America in their strategic campaign to sabotage the Confederate war effort by inducing Confederate soldiers to desert, return home (or if home on furlough, to stay there), and hide in the woods as "outliers" for the remainder of the war. Tyson vividly depicted how he helped to implement this strategy:

> I ... availed myself of every opportunity to stab the confederacy.... I, with others, visited the Southern army, and I co-operated with said persons in influencing desertions. Soon after we arrived home, a squad of some eight or ten deserters arrived from the army. (I don't think that persons who remained true to the United States flag should be called deserters, but this is the usual term applied.) I was informed of it and requested to write to certain others, as another squad would leave if the others arrived safely. I wrote the letter, holding out all possible inducements for them to come.... After a nucleus was formed of the resident Unionists and deserters from the army the Union element in this section [the central piedmont] rapidly increased and soon became the dominant party. If a man could be induced to remain in the woods a week he was never after that worth anything to the Confederacy. I regret that I have not space to give some incidents illustrative of the great privations these people endured through devotion to the Union. The advent of a Union army to this section would have been hailed with the utmost joy.[58]

In October 1862, Tyson had copies of his reunion circular printed in Raleigh and recklessly resumed his anti–Confederate propaganda efforts. He took forty copies of *A Ray of*

Light and the circular to Richmond and posted them to President Jefferson Davis, Vice President Alexander H. Stephens, and selected members of the Confederate Congress. Then he returned to Raleigh.[59] Still not content, Tyson once again boarded the train to Richmond and distributed his reunion circular to passengers. Authorities arrested Tyson and imprisoned him in Raleigh. Three days later, Tyson met with Governor Vance, who released him after the dissident agreed not to circulate his writings anymore.[60] Vance warned Tyson that he would be tried for treason were he arrested again.[61]

The vehement opposition by Democrats to the Preliminary Emancipation Proclamation created a political crisis in the North in the fall of 1862. Fearing that the Democrats might stop supporting the war effort, thereby opening the way for Confederate independence, Tyson decided to renew his efforts at urging the Confederate leaders to compromise with the North and negotiate a sectional reunion. He broke his pledge to Vance and distributed 150 copies of his publications among the members of the General Assembly in Raleigh. By so doing, Tyson hoped that "our public men might be brought to see the error of their ways, retrace their steps, and thus put a stop to the further effusion of blood." "My effort," he claimed, "elicited a secret meeting on the part of the members of the legislature, but with no known practical results."[62]

Because he had broken his pledge to Governor Vance not to distribute his anti–Confederate tracts, Tyson knew that he faced harsh treatment were he arrested again, so he decided to flee to the North.[63] Anticipating a warm welcome among Northern dissenters whose political sentiments he believed were closely akin to his own, Tyson decided to join the peace Democrats in the struggle to break the Republican hold on government and to restore the Union to its prewar condition. Joshua Moon, a Quaker from Snow Camp in Chatham County and a Unionist guide on the Underground Railroad, conducted Tyson incognito 200 miles eastward to the Federal lines in New Bern, North Carolina.[64] When he crossed the lines, Tyson "had no difficulty in finding friends in the eastern part of the State who gave him information as to the best route to pursue. He received such advice from a Confederate captain, who, with nearly his whole company, is for the Union. He also received aid and comfort from negroes, and the last night he spent in the rebel lines was in the house of a negro slave who the next morning ferried him across the river."[65] After clearing himself with Federal authorities, Tyson made his way to New York City and thence to Washington, D.C., arriving on April 14, 1863.[66] Fellow Tar Heel Benjamin Sherwood Hedrick, chief of the Division of Chemistry, Metallurgy, and Electricity in the United States Patent Office, befriended Tyson. He lent him money and helped him find a place to live.[67] Tyson received a clerkship in the Treasury Department and soon made friends both with Democrats and moderate Republicans.[68]

Tyson began to implement his mission to save the Union and reunite the sections as quickly and with as little bloodshed as possible. He issued a circular to 288 newspapers alerting the North and England to the existence of a strong pro–Union element in the South. The North Carolinian then advised the United States ministers in Paris and London on the best ways to undermine Confederate attempts at gaining diplomatic recognition by European countries, and he offered the secretary of war his thoughts on the proper strategy to adopt for a rapid military subjugation of the Confederacy.[69] Tyson's reserved his boldest stroke for the one person whom he perceived could best aid him in the achievement of his goals — Abraham Lincoln. He sent copies of his book and reunion circular to Lincoln and asked the president to assist him in publishing a pro–Union propaganda tract that he planned to distribute to Confederate prisoners of war in the North.[70] Lincoln ignored the importunate Tyson. It is likely that Lincoln's failure to assist Tyson and other Southern Unionists such as Benjamin Hedrick and Dr. J.L. Johnson (discussed below) resulted from a fear that Southern Unionists, being mostly proslavery, would stand in the way of emancipation.[71]

During his war years in Washington, Tyson made visits to the Old Capitol and Point Lookout prisoner-of-war facilities and took food, clothing, and blankets to relatives and friends from central North Carolina interned there. Tyson also proselytized among the Confederate prisoners on behalf of the Union cause, beseeching them to forsake the Confederacy and to take the oath of allegiance to the United States. He received numerous letters from Tar Heel prisoners asking for aid. Many of them were Unionists who sought Tyson's help in gaining a release from prison so they could join relatives in a midwestern state (usually Indiana) or join the Union army.[72]

In 1862, Bryan Tyson emerged as an important leader of the Quaker Belt militant Unionists. His book *A Ray of Light* and his "reunion circular" broadside first advocated the policies of peace, compromise, and reunion on the Copperhead basis in the Tar Heel state. In the peace and convention movements that followed in 1863 and 1864, William Holden and other politicians tried to end the war by implementing these measures. His political activism alerted Confederate leaders in Raleigh and Richmond that potentially powerful anti–Confederate forces had surfaced in the central part of the state.

The Fall 1862 Deserter Hunt

On September 11, 1862, the day that Governor Vance issued his first proclamation against deserters and disloyalists, the head of the Confederate Conscript Bureau in North Carolina asked the chief executive for permission to use the state's militia officers to enroll conscripts. Major Peter Mallett made this request at the behest of the Confederate secretary of war.[73] Vance immediately agreed and ordered his militia officers "to enroll & bring in the Conscripts." When necessary, they could apply to Major Mallett for assistance. Major Mallett ordered his troops to serve under the command of the local militia officers who requested their help.[74] Mallett had about 750 troops under his command, mostly conscripts from North Carolina. Observers referred to Mallett's troops either as the Raleigh Guards or as Mallett's Battalion. Mallett divided them into six companies, with four stationed at Camp Holmes in Raleigh and two at Camp Hill in Statesville, the seat of Iredell County. (Camp Hill was disbanded in Septembers 1862.)[75] Prior to this, the state militia had been used unofficially in helping the Confederacy enforce the conscript acts; now they were under standing orders from their commander, Governor Vance, to do so.

In December of 1862, the Confederate Conscript Bureau ordered an "enrolling officer" (commonly abbreviated "EO") assigned to each congressional district in North Carolina to oversee the enforcement of the conscription laws.[76] The bureau usually referred to them as district or chief enrolling officers. In the seventh district, which included the Quaker Belt counties of Randolph, Davidson, Moore, Montgomery, and Chatham, the chief enrolling officer made his headquarters first in Wadesboro (seat of Anson County) and later in Lexington (seat of Davidson County). The district enrolling officer had subordinates in each county of the district, officially referred to as "sub-enrolling" officers, but commonly called county enrolling officers. They enforced the conscription laws in their county and served as liaisons between the district enrolling officer and the local militia, Home Guard, and Reserve (Junior and Senior) units whose duty it was to arrest draft-dodgers, delinquents, and deserters and transport them to the Camp of Instruction in Raleigh.[77]

The Camp of Instruction at Camp Holmes was the main processing center for the recruitment of conscripts into the Confederate military from North Carolina. Upon arrival, a recruit received a physical examination and was assigned either to the navy, infantry, artillery, or cavalry. Next the quartermaster issued the draftee a uniform and basic equipment. Then a squad of guards transported the enrollee to a regiment in the field where he received a rifle and drill instruction. Draftees were at the Camp of Instruction for only a few days.[78] In August 1863, Mallett ordered two companies of his troops to staff Camp Vance in Morganton (Burke County), which served as a Camp of Instruction for the western part of the state. Due to a reduction of troops assigned to him, Mallett dismantled Camp Vance in August 1864 and moved its personnel to Greensboro (Guilford County) where he established Camp Stokes. To counter the power of the deserter bands in the eastern part of the Quaker Belt, Mallett in November 1863 ordered a company of his infantry and a squad of cavalry to staff Camp Bethel, in Alamance County near the Quaker settlement of Snow Camp, to serve as a base from which to hunt deserters and draft-dodgers.[79] From the winter of 1863 until the end of the war the troops in Mallett's Battalion spent the bulk of their time hunting and capturing deserters and draft-dodgers and transporting them, often shackled and chained, to Camp Holmes in Raleigh, where they remained under guard until escorted to a regiment in the field. They did this duty with the assistance of local militia, Home Guard, and, after February 1864, Senior Reserve units.

Soon after his September 11 proclamation, Governor Vance initiated the first of his four major campaigns made during the war to hunt down and arrest deserters, draft-dodgers, and militant Unionists in the state — most of whom were in the Quaker Belt — and either return them to the ranks or send them to prison. This first campaign, which lasted from the early fall of 1862 into December, included sending troops into the Quaker Belt from Wilkes in the west to Chatham in the east and down into Moore and Montgomery counties. Army officers conducted deserter hunts in the fall and winter because the absence of foliage made the search easier. Furthermore, with the summer's campaigning over, the army had troops to spare for the job. Working with his commander of the state militia, Adjutant General J.G. Martin, and the Confederate commandant of conscripts for North Carolina, Major Peter Mallett, Vance ordered militia officers in Chatham, Montgomery, Moore, Randolph, Yadkin, and other counties to cooperate with detachments from the Raleigh Guards in ridding their areas of deserters and draft-dodgers. This was the third time during the war that Confederate authorities ordered troops in conjunction with state troops into the Quaker Belt to hunt deserters.

On September 22, Colonel J.F. Revis, commander of the Fiftieth Regiment North Carolina Militia at Pittsboro (county seat of Chatham), ordered out his entire command to handle problems caused by deserters and draft-dodgers. The adjutant general told him that if his militia found the task too great, he would send troops to his aid.[80] Colonel J.M. Worth of Randolph and Colonel W.B. Richardson of Moore received similar orders to join forces and arrest all dissidents breaking the law in the areas of their commands, but especially those reported making "disturbances in the corner of Randolph adjoining Moore and Montgomery."[81] By October 24, Colonel Revis was operating in the Peddlar's Hill area of southwestern Chatham County. The adjutant general issued him twenty-five pounds of powder and one hundred pounds of buckshot and stated that Governor Vance felt that the colonel ought to be able to pacify the deserters and draft-dodgers in Chatham without any help from the army.[82]

Governor Vance misjudged the ability of his militia to quell the dissidents. Consequently, in early November, he ordered two companies of the Raleigh Guards into Chatham to assist his state militia to arrest deserters and delinquent conscripts.[83] One company, commanded by Lieutenant T.S. Robards, swept down into central Chatham from Alamance County. The other company, commanded by Captain John McRae, embarked from Durham's Station in Orange County (now in Durham County) and entered Chatham at its northeast corner. The two companies planned to drive forward and meet somewhere in the center of the county.[84]

Meanwhile, Colonel J.M. Worth wrote Governor Vance that he was having a "successful expedition" in Randolph County. "The authority to arrest all suspected persons," he noted, "brought out the hidden parties like a charm." Worth then told the governor of "a shooting affair that took place by a party of outlaws at a squad of men" under the command of Major Provo, one of his subordinates.[85] Note that Colonel Worth here used the term "outlaws" rather than "deserters" or "draft-dodgers" or "Unionists," inferring that criminal, rather than political, ideological, or rebellious intent was the underlying motivation for their behavior. Thus did staunch Confederates throughout the war and into the Reconstruction years libel and denigrate their militantly anti–Confederate neighbors.

In Chatham County, some militia officers refused to aid Captain McRae in the capture of deserters and draft-dodgers. Colonel Mallett ordered McRae to arrest and send them to the Camp of Instruction in Raleigh. He further ordered the Captain to "be particular in reporting to these Headquarters every disloyal citizen, man, woman or child interfering in any manner with the execution of your orders, and warn them they will be severely punished. Deserters and recusant conscripts [that is, draft-dodgers] *must* be taken and brought to these Headquarters."[86] Mallett ordered Captain McRae to return one of his companies of the Raleigh Guards to headquarters. Commanders decided to retain the other company in Chatham, because they feared that the "loyal citizens would be subjected to annoyance" if they withdrew all the troops at once. Mallett ordered McRae to "proceed to Randolph and Moore" as soon as he had the situation in Chatham under control.[87]

Dissidents also caused trouble in the western part of the Quaker Belt. A resident of Wilkes County wrote a friend that "the Conscript Law is very unpopular here & many threaten its resistance."[88] By late September, a company of the Raleigh Guards was hunting deserters and draft-dodgers in Wilkes. They stumbled on a party of 25 draft evaders from Guilford County. The Guards shot one absconder while the remainder escaped.[89] From Germantown, a Stokes County village located just above the Forsyth County line, a militia officer reported that the draft-dodgers in his district vowed that they would die at home rather than go into the service. He had orders to take them dead or alive. The officer found it "a very unpleasant business to have to treat neighbors in that way."[90]

Vance believed that the "disagreeable spectacle" of Confederate troops traversing the state arresting citizens would alienate the people from Confederate authority. Therefore, as noted already, he chose the less offensive tactic of using his militia force to arrest deserters and draft-dodgers.[91] Nevertheless, Vance's insistence on using state militia officers to enforce national conscription laws placed his citizen-soldiers in a nearly hopeless predicament. If they obeyed the governor's orders, they had to perform the arduous and dangerous duty of hunting down desperate armed men — men who happened to be their neighbors, and often their relatives or close friends — and turn them over, often shackled and chained, to Confederate authorities. If they failed to obey the governor's orders, military commanders arrested them and forced them into the ranks for refusing to do their duty.

A report to Governor Vance on affairs in Yadkin County illustrates the dilemmas militia officers faced. A man over the draft age rescued one of his brothers from conscript officers by force of arms. Rather than attempt to arrest the rescuer, the militia officer decided the better part of valor was to let him be. "The Capt says he could have shot him down or at the risk of his life have attempted to arrest him but as he was a man of most desperate character and has 5 other brothers as bad as himself, the better plan he thought was to let him alone." The informant added, "This man ... has said that he would rather join the Federal army than ours."[92]

In October, Governor Vance received a letter decrying the predicament of militia officers from a man who lived in the west-central Randolph County community of Caraway. "On Saturday night last an officer that lives within a mile of me arrested a conscript a nighbour of His. The Next Night the officers Barn with all its Contents Except His Horses was Burned to the ground." Describing the growing anarchy, chaos, and violence that surrounded him, the informant continued:

> Men Have Been shot in this county in the Day Time a citizens Horse Has Been shot while He was driving Him in His Buggy. Out of some 500 conscripts on this side of the [Deep] River ... I have no thought 150 Has gone to the War.... Men May disguise the Fact as much as They Please about Randolph But she Has any amount of Lincolnites and Abolitionists within Her Borders the Reasons for not wishing My Name used in this Matter is that I am certain that My Property and Perhaps My Life would [illegible word] for this, for My life Has Been threatened again and again ... for the position I Have Taken since this War Broke Out.[93]

Another observer wrote on October 25 that within the past two weeks "renegade" conscripts and deserters burned five barns in Randolph and Chatham counties, and that a "number of persons have been shot at ... and in every instance, the party suffering was one who had been engaged in trying to catch these miscreants."[94]

Two of the victims of the "miscreants" were W.R. McMasters and B.B. Marley, both captains in the Randolph County militia. When McMasters arrested two draft-dodgers, the female companions of the arrested men threatened to burn the captain's "premises." That night (January 4, 1863), someone torched McMasters's barn.[95] On January 17, miscreants burned Captain Marley's barn at a loss of between eight and nine hundred dollars. He reported to Vance that about 60 draft-dodgers recently fired into the militia officers' camp, wounding a captured deserter and a black servant. "It is getting wors times here than it is in the army," he complained. "The people about here is so [a]frade of Private injury they ar[e] all most affrad to draw a long Breath."[96]

A deserter in Moore County wrote a letter to a friend in the Twenty-sixth Regiment North Carolina Troops, which fell into the hands of Sergeant G.B. Jordan. The undated letter refers to a crisis precipitated by the enrollment of men up to forty years of age for conscription. The absconder probably wrote the letter around December 20, 1862, for, on that date commanders ordered the militia officers in North Carolina to enroll all men subject to conscription between the ages of eighteen and forty.[97] The editor of a newspaper sent the following excerpt from the letter to Governor Vance:

> It looks like there will be bad times in this county, Moore[,] from the way things are working, the men are called out to forty, and they say they will die at home, They were to meet at Carthage to be examined and prepare to go to Raleigh. I can't tell what the consequences will be I look for a revolution in these parts shortly if the war continues, there are a majority of union men hear and they are going to have *union* or die, the conscripts and deserters number prety strong and they keep coming, col. W. Owines and his company are taking the secesh prisoners and making them take the oath as union men, they took Peter Shamber [Shamburger — a militia officer] and Kupt him a day or two and paroled him and sent him home he wont tell any thing about it at all. If he does death is his portion. You cant get a man to say he is a secessionist hear now. You want to know who was lying out and who was going into the service. I cunot tell you there is so many, I asur you there are many and more of them are going unless they are exempt and carried. I tell you Lincoln has lots of agents through hear, Even those who come home on furlough tak thir guns and lay [out] they will do their next fighting at home.
>
> My fulugh is out, but I have got another that will last during the war.[98]

The "Col. W. Owines" to whom this letter makes reference was Bill (or William) Owens, a deserter from Company B of the Fifty-second Regiment North Carolina Troops, a Randolph County company.[99] The reference to Owens as "Colonel" suggests that he led an organized and disciplined guerrilla unit. His "taking the secesh prisoners and making them take the oath as union men" indicates that politics rather than criminality motivated his actions. Further, his "paroling" of militia officers implies that he looked upon himself and his men as a legitimate guerrilla military force fighting for the United States in North Carolina.

A letter to the editor of the Fayetteville *Observer* offers additional evidence that supports the contention that the William Owens band was a pro–Union guerrilla unit and not merely a gang of outlaws. The letter written by the correspondent was postmarked Why Not, Randolph County.[100] (Why Not was located about three miles north of Christian Union on the plank road.) In the letter, the author said that deserters, who forcefully seized weapons from loyal citizens in the area, took possession of a "Smith Shop" and set "to work repairing guns etc — and tis quite current reported that the [Confederate] arsnel in F[ayetteville] is to be the first attacked after they get there force concentrated." Owens's scheme to capture the arms stored at the Confederate arsenal at Fayetteville implied that he planned to use them to equip a large insurrectionary guerrilla force. The "Smith Shop" belonged to Pleasant Simmons — a silversmith and owner of four slaves who lived in northeast Montgomery County, a few miles south of Auman's Hill. The Owens gang forced Simmons, a loyal Confederate, to repair guns they stole from secessionists in the Randolph, Montgomery, and Moore County area.[101]

The writer of the letter accused Moore and Montgomery counties of being as "Corrupt and Treasonable" as Guilford, Davidson, and Randolph counties. He impassionedly added:

> But oh if you knew our Condition here you would say may the good Lord Deliver them men have been shot some Beat that Life has been Dispaired of property taken Barnes and Fences Burned and we tak[en] from our Familys as Prisoners and Compeled by threats not to talk nor act in now way against the out Laws and Murders it would take days to give you all but sufice it to say it all abounds here in this named section of our old N.[orth] State where Crooks

McBride and Daniel Worth ... have been and with the Quaker influence they have strengthened and grown ... a way with such unprincaled men. I say they are not fit to live or die.

Then, in a remarkable exposition of the depredations by deserters upon militia officers and other loyal citizens, the author continued:

> One object I have is to let you know some of the outrages Committed here ... some of our [militia] officers [were] shot some [were] Beat and so it goes[.] Leiut B. Prissly was Beat till Life was Despaired of for several days three weeks ago and Last week his house [was] attacked the windows Broken his wife maimed by a rock thrown and he shot at in his escape[.] Capt Presslys Barn and ... grain [were] Burned and his house Plundered[.] Capt Peter Shamberger was taken on the 30th Last Month Bare headed and made to go all day through the rain till they viseted several Familys and secured 9 guns and other Property[.] [T]he Widow Cole and Daughters Living on the Plank Road who has a son in the army was most shamefully treated and Robed of various Household Property[.] [They] Kill[ed] her Cow ... [dressed] it [and] taken the meat and left the Head and Hide at her door. One Felow Put Down her Water Buckett and Jumpt booth Feet on it and Smacked it to the ground and all such Pitiful conduct. This is only what come under my Notice and tis a very Small Part of what is going on. I will now give you my own case. On Monday last 18 men armed Came to my house threatened my wife and Mrs. Harriss my Daughter ... — they demanded me to give it [his gun] up I Declined to do so as it was my own property[.] Four of them cocked there guns and haeled them at my Brest my Wife and Daughter screaming[.] [O]ne advanced and seized the gun and I gave it up.... *They cursed me and said if I behaved my self they would before two months restore me to the Bosom of Abe Lincon ... but if they herd from me any more they would send me to the Devil where the Secession Came from and my age only saved my Life* [emphasis added].
>
> The deserters went to a Poor widows House close by whose Husband died in the Army leaving her with 5 small Children and not much else but a few Pewter Spoon[s] which the merceless vilians caried of[f].[102]

Clearly, William Owens's deserter band unleashed a reign of terror in the name of the Union cause against their secessionist enemies, especially the militia officers, in the fall of 1862.

According to local historian Buren Garner, the deserter leader William Owens lived in Moore County less than a quarter mile south of the Randolph County line, and about as far west of the Fayetteville and Western Plank Road.[103] Historian Victoria E. Bynum questions Garner's belief that Owens lived in Moore County. According to her research, the noted deserter leader was probably the William Owens who, as listed in the 1860 census, lived near the Moore County line in northeastern Montgomery County. At that time, this community was known as Auman's Hill. (According to the census, Owens lived four households away from William Auman,[104] merchant, who operated the Auman's Hill Post Office in his store. Today, the Auman's Hill community is called Asbury[105] and is the location of the Asbury Baptist Church.) Owens was 32 years old and had a wife, Adeline, age 22.[106] Bynum was correct that Owens lived in Montgomery County in 1860; the William Owens that Garner referenced was the "William B. Owens" listed in the 1860 Moore County federal census as living in the Good Spring community, which was located somewhere in northwest Moore.[107] He survived the war to be listed in the 1870 census as Bailey Owens, who then lived in the northwestern corner of Moore County in Sheffield Township, but his post office was Auman's Hill in neighboring Montgomery County.[108] Vigilantes murdered William Owens, the deserter leader from Montgomery County, in 1865. William Owens of Montgomery County and William B. Owens (or Bailey Owens) of Moore County lived within about four miles of each other, and both men had the same post office address — factors that have contributed to the confusion over their identities. William Owens became the most noted of the guerrilla deserter leaders in the Randolph-Moore-Chatham-Montgomery County area. Suggesting the immediate cause of William Owens's resort to violence against Confederate authority, one Moore County resident wrote that Owens ordered his followers to kill "them [militia officers] and burn ... [their] property for hunting him and his crowd and a huring [hurting] his wife."[109]

Partisan bitterness peaked in Randolph County on January 5, when militia officers reportedly caught and hanged a twenty-year-old draft-dodger by the name of Alson Allred. Since draft dodging was not a crime under North Carolina law, militia officers had no authority to hang captured conscripts. It is possible that personal enemies murdered Allred for reasons unrelated to the war.[110]

The Winter 1863 Deserter Hunt

In January 1863, Confederate congressman J.R. McLean, representative of the Sixth Congressional District (which included the Quaker Belt counties of Guilford, Alamance, and Orange), informed a friend in Greensboro (seat of Guilford County) that the desertion rate of North Carolina troops was "alarming." He blamed the situation on members of the disloyal Unionist underground and their practice of writing letters to soldiers prompting them to desert and return home. The pro–Union activists were especially strong in Randolph County. "These men ought to be promptly arrested and the ring leaders immediately hung," asserted the congressional representative.[111] Congressman McLean's letter indicated that desertion and disloyalty remained a serious problem in the winter of 1863 in the Quaker Belt, especially in Randolph, despite Governor Vance's strenuous efforts in the fall of 1862 to rid the area of dissidents. The redoubtable governor decided to try once again. In early January 1863, he issued orders to his local militias and magistrates to arrest deserters and draft-dodgers in cooperation with a regiment of Confederate troops whom Confederate authorities had ordered into "Wilkes and other counties." His adjutant general ordered the commanders of the combined forces to arrest all persons who assisted the deserters and draft-dodgers to evade capture or resisted the execution of their orders. He further enjoined the troops to release all those arrested as soon as they had achieved their objectives.[112] Indicating a respect for the civil liberties of his citizens, Vance instructed his militia officers not to "enter forcibly into any house to search for deserters without a warrant from a magistrate, nor to arrest any body on mere suspicion, but only on plain proof of their aiding deserters to escape or offering resistance."[113] Well aware that any irresponsible or undisciplined behavior by these troops would reflect negatively upon himself and the Confederate government, Vance cautioned them "to execute the [conscription] law of Congress firmly and respectfully," but to take special care "to respect the feelings of good citizens, to commit no act of violence nor make any insulting or unseemly show of force towards any body."[114] The Fifty-sixth Regiment North Carolina Troops, probably supported by several companies from the Raleigh Guards, ranged through the Quaker Belt from Wilkes to Chatham hunting deserters and draft-dodgers during the second and third weeks of January 1863 in this fourth sweep by Confederate forces into the Quaker Belt during the war.[115]

As Confederate troops scoured the Quaker Belt for dissidents, Vance delivered a special message to the General Assembly concerning "the alarming increase of desertion in the Army." "The consequence is that numbers of deserters are concealed in many parts of the State, and banding together for company and mutual protection, depredate upon the citizens near them, thus forming a kind of outlawed population in the midst of our quiet and orderly people." The governor requested the General Assembly to pass an act making aiding and abetting deserters a crime. He also asked the assembly members to empower him "summarily to drop from the rolls [militia] officers guilty of gross and willful neglect of duty." Vance stated his intention to issue a proclamation giving deserters thirty days to return to duty without punishment; after the deadline, captured deserters would receive the "severest penalties of the law."[116]

On January 26, 1863, the governor issued his promised proclamation in which he warned all deserters and absentees to return to their regiments by February 10. In a statement implying that North Carolina troops were subject to an inadequate furlough system, Vance indicated that he believed that most of the men absented themselves due to "a natural and almost irresistible desire to see their friends and homes once more after so long an absence," and not because of cowardice. Thus, those who would voluntarily return by the February 10 deadline would suffer no more punishment than loss of pay for time absent. He warned, however, that authorities would try those captured after refusing to surrender voluntarily and, upon conviction, sentence them to death. "There shall be no rest for the deserter in the borders of North Carolina," he threatened.[117] In an effort to shame the deserters into surrendering, Vance added the following admonition: "And let none excuse their desertion by declaring that they go home to take care of their families; they will add nothing to the comforts of their families by hiding like guilty men in the woods by day and by plundering their neighbors by night; they only bring shame and suffering upon the heads of the innocent, and their little children, when gray-headed old men, will have the finger of scorn pointed at them and the bitter taunt will ring in their ears, 'Your father skulked in the woods to keep from fighting for his country.'"[118]

The nonslaveholding Confederate soldier often ignored Vance's appeal to him to place his loyalty to the Confederate government above his loyalty to his starving and destitute parents, wives, and children. The following petition to the governor from over fifty mothers, wives, and daughters of Confederate soldiers in Iredell, Wilkes, and Yadkin counties, written the day after Vance issued his proclamation against desertion, reveals the pressures placed on the conscience of Confederate soldiers from the yeoman and artisan class: "Last Fall our Husbands brothers & sons were carried from their Farms [as conscripts] into the Army. Consequently there was very little small grain sowed. And as you very well know we have very few slaves in Western North Carolina. Therefore Famine is stareing us in the face. There is nothing so heart rending to a mother as to have her children crying round her for bread and she have none to give them which is, and will be the case if more men are taken from this Section." The petitioners asked the governor to allow "us to retain what few laboring hands we have to help us make corn that we perish not."[119] As the pleas to the Governor from the mothers of hungry children attest, by early 1863, thousands of families in the Quaker Belt faced starvation due to a lack of labor to plant, tend, and harvest food crops. Though state authorities tried to feed the families of soldiers and needy citizens, their efforts proved woefully inadequate. When the war started, government leaders and public opinion pressured planters to use their large slave labor force to produce needed food crops for the army and public. Unfortunately, most planters continued growing commercial crops such as cotton, tobacco, and sugar for easy profit rather than sacrifice their lands to growing food for needy families. This contributed mightily to the shortage of food on the home front and to Confederate defeat.[120]

In *A Ray of Light*, Bryan Tyson warned that the people of central North Carolina faced a "grievous famine," because "the major part of our working class is now in the army; so that there are but comparatively few left behind to raise the necessaries of life." To avoid this impending food crisis, Tyson advised his readers to support the return of North Carolina and the south to the Union.[121] Due primarily to the privations faced by families on the home front, the desertion of North Carolina troops continued at an increasing rate through the winter, spring, and into the summer of 1863.

The Buxton Investigation

Governor Vance sent Superior Court Judge Ralph P. Buxton of Fayetteville into Randolph and Moore counties to investigate the validity of the many reports from the area complaining about the depredations by deserters and disloyalists. In January Judge Buxton advised Vance that the reports were true, and that matters probably were worse than suspected. He reported the existence of a "thoroughly organized gang, consisting at present of some fifty men, but their number augmenting constantly by deserters and others.... Most of their operations have hitherto been carried on in Randolph Co — to which County the members of the gang principally belong."[122] Buxton reported that many of the militia officers did not do their duty. Those that did try to obey orders "have been hunted, captured, and *parolled* (!) with the distinct threat that any further effort on their part to enforce the law, or any disclosure of what had occurred, would be punished with death."[123] Since the deserters operated within the border area of four counties (Randolph, Chatham, Moore, and Montgomery), the civil authorities, noted Buxton, were hamstrung in making arrests, for "they [the deserters] have accomplices and places of rendezvous in several counties, and when hunted from one, will take refuge in another."[124] The deserter band led by William Owens had its main camp located within yards of the intersection of three counties — Randolph, Montgomery, and Moore — near the juncture of Old Gap and Cagle Roads, situated about three miles south of Seagrove. The outliers would have positioned their camp around a nearby spring. If a sheriff's posse approached this camp, the deserters simply ran a few yards to one of the other two counties to escape the jurisdiction of the pursuing law officers. Buxton suggested that a cavalry company made up of men familiar with the terrain of the disaffected area, in cooperation with the sheriffs of the four counties, should form a force sufficiently mobile to apprehend the offenders. He added that he had deposited warrants for the arrest of fifteen of the leading members of the gang with the sheriff of Moore County.[125] All of them were members of the William Owens deserter band.[126]

Lt. William A. Pugh to the Rescue

Acting on the advice of Judge Buxton, Vance ordered a company of Confederate cavalry into the four-county region to cooperate with area militia in a major campaign to eradicate the offending dissidents. On January 29, 1863, the adjutant general ordered Colonel Henry Steed, commander of Randolph County's Sixty-third Militia Regiment, to assist the sheriff of Montgomery County in executing warrants against certain individuals. In addition, he instructed Steed to command a concerted effort on the part of the militia forces of Randolph, Chatham, Montgomery, and Moore counties to arrest all deserters, conscripts, and absentees in the area. In conducting this arduous undertaking, Colonel Steed had the assistance of a cavalry detachment under the command of a Lieutenant William A. Pugh.[127] The adjutant general told Steed that the governor expected him to "make a clean sweep" and "thus convince every deserter or conscript and their aiders and abettors that he is determined to execute his orders and to enforce the Conscript Law."[128]

Lieutenant William A. Pugh arrived in Asheboro with his troops on February 1, after a tiring seventy-mile ride from Raleigh through a snowstorm. Due to the inclement weather, Lieutenant Pugh quartered his sixty troops at the Hamlin and Hoover Hotels and their outbuildings for four days. Showing initiative, Pugh during that time dispatched several squads with local guides to hunt deserters on foot. They captured eighteen men and sent them to Camp Holmes in Raleigh, where military authorities assigned them to regiments. Later, Pugh bemoaned that "before I got back to Raleigh on my return [several weeks later], two-thirds of those men had [deserted and] returned to their homes, this was refreshing!"[129] The trials and frustrations experienced by Lieutenant Pugh on this difficult and dangerous mission illustrate the problems faced by army and militia officers ordered to hunt and capture armed deserters and draft-dodgers in a region where a majority of the populace sympathized with the dissidents. Such missions often proved thankless and placed the commanding officers in jeopardy of civil lawsuits and courts-martial.

To expedite the capture of deserters and draft-dodgers, Lieutenant Pugh appropriated their horses from their farms and held them as ransom to be returned if the delinquents surrendered. He justified his actions in this manner: "The deserters and conscripts under a man named Wm. Owens began to get too sharp for me, as they knew the mountain paths better than I. So I supposed by taking their Horses, on the promise of pardon when they returned to their allegiance, also to return their horses that I might be able to get through quicker I did so. I took Eighteen Horses the owners Came in and the Horses were delivered."[130]

On March 18, the adjutant general ordered Colonel Steed to call off the hunt and disband the troops under his command.[131] As late as March 22, an observer in Moore County reported cavalry and infantry operating against Bill Owens, who, it was stated, was down to about twelve followers. Reflecting the partisan bitterness that had by then developed, the Moore County resident wrote that the troops "say [they] will halt them [deserters and draft-dodgers] if they see them and if they do not halt they will Shoot them down and if they ketch them they meane to appoint a day for thir execution and for all the [people to] come in out of the neighbourhood that has any thing Stole from them and See them whoop them desrters to death and make them tell all they hav Stole from [them]."[132] Both Colonel Steed's and Lieutenant Pugh's troops resorted to illegal, strong-arm tactics against the deserters and draft-dodgers and their families and sympathizers in direct contradiction to Governor Vance's orders issued on January 6. They often conducted themselves in as barbaric a manner as any attributed to the deserters. Before long, the victims of military abuse flooded the governor with bitter complaints.

John W. Hunt of the Hoover Hill community in west-central Randolph had a son who had been absent without leave, but had recently returned to his regiment. On March 6, he questioned Vance if he had ordered the militia troops to search citizens' homes and take property from fathers, because their sons are in the woods. Or did the governor order his troops to sneak up on deserters and fire on them before giving them a chance to surrender? Just such a situation as that occurred recently in his community, in which a detail of militia "killed one of the deserters and wonded two or three others and the deserters say the[y] did not know ther was any body about tell the guns fired[.] [T]hey was giting Breakfast and the[y] was sorouned."[133] Hunt said that a member of the militia shot at his son, but he escaped unharmed. He then related how army or militia officers tortured their captives by burning their genitals: "When the[y] was out in camp the head officers wold give orders for some of the men to take others up and strip ther pants and hold them to the fire baby fashion tell the[y] wdd bern and then have a Doctor to examine them to see if the[y] had warmed them enough."[134] The militia, complained Hunt, was more troublesome and dangerous than the outliers. Implying rape, Hunt said that members of the militia went "to lone [illegible word] houses of a night and calling them up and makes them open the dors and lets them in but wont let her make no lite and a buse them [to] ther on sattesfaction."[135] Reflecting the resentment prevalent in Randolph County against the exempted militia officers, Hunt suggested to the governor that they be drafted into the army "for they dont do any good at home only drink liquor."[136]

A complaint of torture by militia officers reached Governor Vance from one Jeremiah Phillips of Moore County. Phillips swore before a justice of the peace that, on March 17, Lieutenant Colonel B.G. Campbell of Randolph County's Sixty-fourth Militia Regiment took his horses. The next night Campbell's troops arrested him and put him in the militia guardhouse at a militia camp in Randolph County, where "a man by the name of Thomas tied a rope round his neck threw it over the joist drew him up and chocked him hurting his neck very bad[.] What after letting him down they abused him bad with a lightwood knot."[137] A few weeks later, a militia unit operating in southwest Chatham County shot into a group of deserters, killing one boy (no age given) by the last name of Phillips. His father, described as a "Linconite" that "harbors outliers," threatened to swear out a warrant against his son's killers.[138] In April "Many Citizens," residents living in Auman's Hill, a community located in the northeast corner of Montgomery County, sent Vance a letter. They complained that the cavalry and infantry took property from them, including over nine horses, a colt, corn and fodder, guns, leather and rawhide, and a "band" from a thrashing machine. "Nearly all of the citizens have been injured more or less and some nearly Brookup," complained the anonymous writer, who said he was the father of "16 helpless children."[139]

One woman, probably the wife of a deserter, wrote a letter to the governor detailing an incredible amount of abuse by militia officers and army troops. She gave her address as Salem Church in southwest Randolph, but she lived just across the county line in Davidson. The troops pulled up her onions and destroyed her garden; they entered her house, broke into her chest of drawers, threw out her clothes, and tore up her bed; they went through her fields destroying her wheat and corn, and broke into her two smokehouses. The troops, she wrote,

> are using ever efort they can to scear the woman [women] to death and using such language to them that a decende woman is a fraid to travil alone — they went into a corn field where a

neighbor's girl was plowing by herself and using vulgar language threatened to shoot her and pointed their guns at her threatening to bayonet her and firing off their guns eight at a time. [She thought it] ... very harsh that often my Brothers and Kindreds and friends had Spilt ther Blood for the Sake of the Southern confederacy ... and in the cause of our country ... not with Sanding [standing] all of this that i must Suffer abuse and Starvation on the account of the Militia oficers who has just as Much to fight for as my husband.... Send me a few lines ... and point me to some place where i may find Shelter as i have Bin poorley for nine month[s] and i want a place of refuge thy from.[140]

As this letter indicates, the bulk of the heavy-duty farmwork such as plowing had to be done by the women of the family, since the great majority of the able-bodied males under age forty-five were in the army, dead, disabled by wounds, or prisoners of war. As Holden commented, "Hundreds of white women in this State have been brought to the plow by this war." As a result, families could not sufficiently feed or school their children.[141]

Many of the letters sent to Governor Vance in the spring of 1863 from the Randolph area complaining of depredations by the militia and army troops singled out Lieutenant Pugh for condemnation, largely because his troops managed to raise the ire of some of the area's most prominent and influential citizens. On March 10, Vance received a letter complaining that Lieutenant Pugh burned the distilleries of Clark Spencer, Loton Williams, and a man named Kagle [Cagle]. Pugh believed that these parties had been distilling whiskey to sell to conscripts and deserters. In the process, the troops made illegal searches of the victims' houses and, in one case, stole some tobacco. The author wrote that, of the three victims, he knew Loton Williams to be innocent of making and selling liquor. Pugh's troops, he continued, "also burnt the Little Powder mill of Solomon Hendricks — They sent two or three men to act as deserters and try to get some powder, and as soon as Hedrick showed a willingness to sell to them in that capacity, they destroyed his works —.... They shot a hog belonging to Harris York, and cooked it at Esquire [Issac H.] Foust's house — he being absent and his daughter protesting against their stopping there."[142] The writer also accused Pugh's men of taking four blankets and a quilt from Mrs. Hoover's Hotel and of cutting "a new apron off of the buggy of Mr. Alfred Brower." In conclusion, the correspondent, who was not a resident of Randolph County, said that "the people of Randolph where these acts were committed are rather indignant, say the deserters and conscripts do them less injury — than those sent to take them do — and they would rather be troubled with the former than the latter."[143]

Issac H. Foust, a wealthy cotton mill owner from the east-central Randolph County community of Reed Creek (present-day Ramseur), wrote Governor Vance complaining that Lieutenant Pugh took horses and fodder from farmers.[144] Randolph citizens had elected Foust to the House of Commons to fill the vacancy created by the resignation of Jonathan Worth, who became state treasurer in the Vance administration.[145] Foust told Vance that he has received numerous complaints from old men whose horses were seized by the militia because their sons were lying out in the woods to avoid military service. Foust pointed to one victim, Jacob Craven, who had one son in the woods and another one in the army. "Tho' an old man, a loyal citizen, ... his horses were taken from him leaving him nothing to cultivate his farm with. Such cases are of daily occurance whether a parent can control his son or not until it is growing intolerable to the community."[146]

Foust's letter points out just how divided in their loyalties many families were in the Randolph area. Since many of the men who became deserters or draft-dodgers were beyond the control of their parents, was it fair to punish the latter for the misdeeds of the former?

Likewise, was it fair to punish wives and children for the crimes of their spouses or parents? As Squire Foust's letter and the letter from the deserter's wife at Salem Church point out, many of the people accused of being related to deserters were just as likely to be guilty of being related to Confederate soldiers, living and dead.

Lieutenant Pugh's superior officers sent papers to Vance defending Pugh's conduct in the Randolph-Moore area. After reviewing them, the governor wrote to General D.H. Hill that he found Lieutenant Pugh's explanations for his conduct unsatisfactory. Vance questioned the general: "It is exceedingly strange that 15 or 20 horses should be taken and the officers not know who they are taken from or who they belong to! This being so, in all conscience how did he know them to be disloyal. What right had Lt. Pugh to plunder the citizens? By whose authority did he undertake to try these people and decide upon their loyalty, and proceed to confiscate their property? And more especially who authorized him to burn the still houses of the citizens?" He assured the general that he had not. Vance concluded that, in light of his confessions, the lieutenant had made a case sufficient to dismiss him from the service. While the governor did not seek the discharge of Lieutenant Pugh, he felt he should return the horses to their owners or pay for them.[147]

In July, Lieutenant Pugh wrote an invective-filled letter to his superior officer defending himself from the many charges of thievery made by Randolph citizens. About Randolph County he commented: "The whole neighborhood is related in some way and I can very well see how it is that so many letters came from there, denouncing us as not fit to live. If it is necessary to send troops there to quell open mutiny[,] Is it right to believe the Statements gotten up by the relatives of the men who were engaged in it against the Officers and men who were sent to punish them. Justice says *NO*."[148] Pugh admitted that he had taken eighteen horses from citizens, but he explained that his men had returned six of them to the owners, and the Quartermaster's Department paid for twelve of them. Concerning all other charges leveled at him and his men, Pugh, apparently unaware that Vance had declared him unfit for command, said that the governor "knows the character of these people too well to place too much credit on them."[149] In a parting shot laden with sarcasm, Pugh indirectly complimented the anti–Confederate faction in the Randolph County area on its military prowess: "Confederate troops would do well in that Country, *the people are so very kind*. Gov. Vance sent a company of Infantry up there and they were Completely Whipped out. These people should be pittied. They are of such amiable dispositions."[150]

Chief Justice Pearson and the Schoolhouse Shoot-Out in Yadkin County

In the second week of February 1863, a skirmish in Yadkin County between a band of draft-dodgers and deserters holed up in a schoolhouse and a squad of attacking militia officers left two men dead on each side. The militia officers, "James West, a magistrate, and John Williams, a most excellent man[,] ... were shot dead in their tracks." The leaders of the deserter gang were William Dobbins, Jesse Dobbins, Benjamin Willard, and Lee Willard. All but three of the approximately 25 desperadoes escaped.[151] The legal issues raised in the aftermath of this confrontation became a major cause of the high desertion rate of North Carolina troops the following spring.

In mid–February, Governor Vance received two reports on the shoot-out, each offering valuable insight as to why Yadkin County had so many militant draft-dodgers, and how they managed to survive and grow stronger over time. The first report came from "Confederate Friends" who told the governor that the conscription laws caused most of the disaffection in the county. A majority of the citizens considered them unfair to the nonslaveholders. The small farmers and artisans could not at the same time both fight for the Confederacy and feed and clothe their families. Another cause of draft dodging in Yadkin County centered on race: many white men feared that, with so many of them out of the county in service, their wives and daughters would be at the "mercy" of free blacks. "Confederate Friends" stated their case this way:

> Second destrees [distress] if the white men is taken & the mulaters or free cullard men is left[.] [W]e the Sitazons of this cunty wish you to order them to Bee taken in Camp for wating Boys for we cant put up with ther maners here[.] [T]hey have Beecome pilphering & Sasey to white women[.] We Just ask you to make this order & doo it quick or we will Bee Ablige to put Some of them to deth for this is wone cause of the con Scrips dooing the way they have[.] [I]f you had of had them taken from this county I dont think they [the] Battel wood a Bin fought on Deep Creek the 13 of February With the con Scripts & desers ... and the men Swars they will fight til they dy Be fore they will go and leave ther wives and daughters here and they free negros & mulatters not gon ... they Sware they will die Be four they will go with out you will have them taken first.[152]

In 1860, Yadkin County had 172 free blacks and 1,436 slaves in a total population of 10,714. Free blacks comprised 1.6 percent and slaves 13.4 percent of the total population.[153]

The second communication explaining the causes of the shootout in Yadkin County came from R.F. Armfield of Yadkinville, the county seat. Armfield attributed the unfortunate event to an "uninformed" class of citizens in the county who "swore they would die at home" rather than obey the conscription laws. When pressed by draft authorities, about 100 of them fled to the woods. Since these "skulkers" had more "active friends" than the militia, "they could always get timely information of every movement to arrest them and so avoid it." Encouraged by this state of affairs, other dissidents from Yadkin deserted the army, returned home, and joined the outliers. Emboldened by their growing numbers and the failure of the militia to arrest them, the deserters and draft-dodgers organized themselves into armed bands and "openly defied the law.... They ... even sent menacing messages to the militia officers, threatening death to the most obnoxious of them and all who assist them."[154]

Armfield feared that, were the four captives involved in the schoolhouse shoot-out tried for murder, the state Supreme Court might declare the conscription act unconstitutional and free the defendants. Such a scenario, he thought, would lead to "a mutiny in the army of the Rappahannock" by draftees and threaten the cause of Southern independence. At the best, he wondered, "how would you get another conscript to the field or keep those there who have already gone."[155] Armfield's fears came true. The draft-dodgers whom state authorities had arrested and imprisoned for the slaying of the militia officers at the schoolhouse shoot-out applied for writs of habeas corpus. They appeared before Judge Richmond M. Pearson, chief justice of the North Carolina Supreme Court, who performed his legal duties at his plantation in central Yadkin County. Judge Pearson discharged the prisoners by ruling that, according to North Carolina law, the governor had no authority to arrest deserters or conscripts. Such power "pertained to the Confederate authorities alone."[156]

The Confederate Constitution provided for a Confederate supreme court and inferior federal courts, but Congress failed to establish them during the war. Thus, the rulings of the various state supreme courts defined the law of the land.[157] In North Carolina, Governor Vance, champion of states' rights and civil liberties, upheld and defended the decisions of his chief justice and other judges, whether he agreed with them or not.[158] In November 1862 and January 1863, Governor Vance urged the state legislature to pass laws giving him the right to arrest deserters and draft-dodgers and making it a crime to aid and abet them, but to no avail. The members of the legislature told him that Congress should provide for the enforcement of its own laws. Vance then, through a North Carolina senator, asked Congress to pass the legislation. The Confederate Congress rebuffed Vance on the issue. The governor, rather than "risking my militia to be shot down with impunity," revoked his orders to the militia commanding them to enforce the Confederate conscript laws; rather, he ordered them to "aid Confederate officers as a posse when requested." Unfortunately, noted Vance, "news of Judge Pearson's decision went abroad to the army in a very exaggerated and ridiculous form. Soldiers were induced to believe that it declared the conscript law unconstitutional, and that they were entitled, if they came home, to the protection of their civil authorities. Desertion, which had been temporarily checked, broke out again worse than before."[159]

According to a report from the adjutant general's office, the state legislature in February 1863, passed a law granting the governor the wartime power to use the militia to arrest deserters and recusant conscripts. The state's Supreme Court judges remained unaware of this act for some time after its passage, because the state printer inadvertently failed to publish it on a timely basis. When the justices became cognizant of it, they concurred that the governor had the right to use the militia to arrest deserters and draft-dodgers.[160] By May, the governor was stationing squads of militia officers at bridges, ferries, and at points on the roads to apprehend deserters returning home from the front.[161]

Knowledge of the governor's authority to arrest deserters moved slowly through the populace. Throughout the spring, the general population continued to believe that state authorities had no legal right to arrest deserters. Brigadier General W.D. Pender wrote the Confederate Adjutant General's Department on April 23 complaining of the recent rapid rise in the desertion of North Carolina troops in his brigade. He noted that about 200 men from the Twenty-fourth Regiment North Carolina Troops had deserted in the past month. The general explained that the troops deserted because they believed that Chief Justice Pearson ruled the conscription law unconstitutional. "Hence they draw the conclusion, that Enrolled conscripts will not only be justified in resisting the Law, but that those who have been held in service by the law, will not be arrested when they desert." The general stated that the militia officers in Yadkin County no longer felt comfortable arresting deserters or draft-dodgers in light of Judge Pearson's ruling unless protected by the government. He related that "letters are received by the men, urging them to leave, that [they] will not be troubled when they get home.... *What I have stated concerning Yadkin, I fear holds good elsewhere and unless some check is put upon it, will work great & serious injury to the cause. I would suggest that a Regt. be sent to that section of the State*" (emphasis added).[162]

In August, a citizen writing from Yadkin County confirmed the general's assessment of conditions in the area when he complained that since the skirmish between the deserters and militia in February, the militia had stopped arresting conscripts. Indeed, "the conscripts and deserters go about openly and in defiance of the officers; in fact, in some cases they are together. Most of the deserters that have been arrested are now back at home. The same situation exists in Wilkes County." The writer concluded: "I am told that not another man will go and when we enroll up to 45 I think there will be between eight hundred and one thousand between 18 and 45 [avoiding the draft] in the county."[163]

In April, Colonel Mallett ordered a company of his Raleigh Guards into Wilkes and Alexander counties to hunt deserters. The Guards were regular army troops from outside the area whose families, unlike those of the militia officers, were not subject to vengeance at the hands of deserters. A Confederate soldier serving in that unit wrote to his mother describing his frustrations and disappointments: "I suppose you would be glad to know what we are doing up here with the deserters well I think we are doing nothing, and we never will catch them, for there are too many hiding places in these mountains we have not caught any deserters yet, but have shot at several running, we have taken up several conscripts and old men for harboring There was a squad of twelve started to camp this morning ... but we have been among worse enemies than the Yankees for the last fortnight, for two-thirds of Wilkes County are tories."[164]

Vance issued yet another proclamation denouncing deserters and their aiders and abettors on May 11. The great cause of desertion, lamented Vance, was "the many persons in the country who incite and encourage these desertions and harbor and conceal these misguided men at home." Vance commanded "all such evil disposed persons to desist from such base, cowardly, and treasonable conduct." He warned the deserters and their aiders and abettors that "observing and never-failing eyes have marked you, every one. When the war ends and the victorious Confederate veterans return home, their wrath will make you regret, in the bitterness of your cowardly terror, that you were ever born."[165]

The dissidents largely ignored Vance's threats and his plea for them to be good Confederates. Desertion of North Carolina troops continued apace despite Vance's edict. For example, in a little more than a week after the issuance of the proclamation, Lee complained to the secretary of war that "the desertion of No Caro. troops from this army is becoming so serious an evil that unless it can be promptly arrested I fear the troops from that state will become greatly reduced."[166]

The Spring 1863 Resurgence of Deserter Depredations

As spring advanced into summer, Governor Vance received numerous complaints about the depredations of deserters from the Randolph-Moore-Montgomery-Chatham County area. Apparently the winter deserter hunt by Lieutenant Pugh and his cavalry company in conjunction with the militia of that district had failed in its mission to rid the area of the deserter gangs infesting the region. In April, a citizen of the Moore County community of Pharr's Mill (located near the junction of Moore, Randolph, and Chatham counties) complained to the governor that the deserters resumed their depredations as soon as he dismissed the militia. The author estimated that there were about one hundred deserters within a fifteen-mile radius of his house. For example, he said, "A few nights ago twenty or thirty entered on the premises of an aged and respectable citizen of this County roused him from his slumbers presented guns at his door and windows and said they would blow his brains out if he put his head out, forced the locks of his smoke house and corn crib, and robbed him of nearly all his bacon and a quantity of corn."[167]

Deserters and draft-dodgers could not raise crops to properly feed their livestock and families since militia or soldiers detailed from the army to hunt them often watched their homes. Denied the opportunity to earn a livelihood by ordinary means, they looked elsewhere for food, clothing, and other provisions. They sought no further than the smokehouses, grain bins, and cupboards of their secessionist neighbors. The outliers undoubtedly justified their plundering of their loyal fellow citizens as revenge against those who supported the Confederacy, which "hunted [them] down like wild beast[s]."[168] The stealing of grain, provisions, livestock, and crops growing in the field discouraged farmers from planting crops and caring for young animals. This spoke ill for the future well-being of an area already grievously stricken with a shortage of food and other necessities such as salt and cloth. As a Randolph County citizen noted: "If this state of affairs continues, there will be little grain raised this year, and most of that will be stolen before it is matured. Then every hog, cow and sheep will be devoured, and women and children will suffer."[169]

The resident of Pharr's Mills next informed the governor that the deserters in the Moore County area had little to fear from the militia or army troops: "If a company is raised to apprehend them they scatter off to their hiding places to return more desperate [than] when they are dismissed. They threaten vengeance on every man who takes an active part in apprehending them. A citizen of this neighborhood who has rendered himself obnoxious to them is compelled to guard his property at night to prevent them from destroying it."[170] Before his election as governor, Vance had been the commander of the Twenty-sixth Regiment North Carolina Troops. The correspondent, suggesting that he had served with Vance in the army, indicated a preference for the relative safety of the battlefield over the dangers faced at home. "God Bless you I hope you may never be in as great danger of yankee bullets as you were at Newbern and Malvern Hill. I confess that I feel in more danger at home than I did at either of those places."[171]

Dismayed at learning that his winter campaign against the deserters and draft-dodgers in the Randolph, Moore, Chatham, Montgomery County area had been of little benefit to the Confederate loyalists, especially those in Moore, the governor asked Major General Daniel Harvey Hill to send troops into the latter county. "That county," lamented Vance, "*certainly harbors more deserters than any other in the state. They can lick my militia in a fair fight* [emphasis added] and something *must* be done."[172] The general responded to Vance with the comment: "I would order a company of Cavalry there, if I thought the governor would not order it back, infantry cannot operate rapidly enough."[173] One wonders what prompted the terse reply by the general to Vance's request. It was probably in reaction by the general to Vance's chastisement of Lieutenant Pugh and the resulting embarrassment of the military at being "slapped on the wrist" by Vance for not respecting the civil liberties and property rights of his citizens.

The failure of Vance to recruit additional Confederate troops to assist his militia left the loyal citizens of Moore County to the mercy of the deserters. According to a correspondent from Prosperity (located in northwest Moore), the deserters entered upon a new level of boldness in April: "Until recently stealing was done under the old plan secretly, but now they go to our houses soon after dark, place an armed gard around our doors. dare you to walk out. and with axes batter down the doors where meat and grains is kept. and in many instances carry off all the meat and salt a man has.—I have twelve in [my] family and they have left me twice in the last 6 *mo* without a mouthful of meat or grain of salt."[174] Then, claiming that some of the deserters and draft-dodgers crossed the line from outlier to outlaw, the writer exclaimed: "It is a notorious fact that certain men [who] never were worth $25 in their lives, since lying in the woods have become quite lousy with money." In addition, in their moment of success, the deserters became cocky. "On last sabbath there was quite an excitement produced, by an armed company of deserters entering the church during service. they stacked their guns and assumed conspicious seats." Alluding to a reign of terror of neighbor against neighbor, the writer continued: "It is supposed that your Exc is hardly aware of the extent and frequency of the acts of robery to which a portion of us are subjected at the hands of those who were our neighbors—we are afraid to make complaints or seek redress for fear worse evils befall us. *to offend is followed by the burning of our houses or being waylayed and shot*" (emphasis added).[175]

In July the governor received a letter from three loyal citizens in Montgomery County detailing the depredations of the Bill Owens gang, who, they complained, was "Runing us as fast as time can move." The correspondents charged that many of the deserters enriched themselves by their plunder: "Some of them has said to our knowing that this war has bin a blessing to them[.] [T]hey say they live better than they ever did and without work and they say when the yankees takes the confederacy they will be well paid for it to some [sum] up their outrageous acts."[176] This statement indicates that Owens's men justified their plundering by believing that, when the United States defeated the Confederacy, the Federal government would endorse their acts of crime against the laws of the Confederacy as legitimate acts of guerrilla warfare. The trio writing from Montgomery County told the governor that many of the loyal men in the community found ways to avoid going into the service, not because they were unwilling to fight for the Confederacy, but because they refused to leave their families to the mercies of the deserter bands. They pled for Vance, therefore, to send them ammunition and weapons so they could "subdue thease Vandels."[177] In May, a concerned citizen asked the governor to authorize a Court of Oyer and Terminer in Moore County for two "criminals" held in the local jail.[178] Courts of Oyer and Terminer were special sessions of the courts called by the governor to try cases too important to hold over until the next scheduled court session. The governor's failure to sanction the special court proved injudicious. In July, 25 to 30 armed deserters and draft-dodgers entered the jail in Carthage and forced the release of "two conscripts of the very worst character."[179]

A company from the Seventeenth Regiment North Carolina Troops hunted deserters and draft-dodgers in Randolph and Moore counties in late April under the orders of General Ransom. A soldier in that company boasted in a letter to the *Standard* that his company enjoyed a successful hunt. The hunter related that the citizens of Asheboro provided "many acts of kindness to us poor soldiers." He added: "There are people, Mr. Editor, who believe them to be a perfect nest of Yankee sympathizers, and untrue to the cause in every sense of the word. To such I would say, ye know nothing. Come and try the good, the noble, glorious people of Randolph as we have, and if you do not go away a wiser and more charitable man, then *I'll desert.*"[180] This report contrasts so strongly with the numerous reports to the contrary from soldiers serving in the area, one wonders if perhaps the animus behind it derived from Holden's desire to make his peace Conservative followers in the district look good.

Outlier Culture

One may wonder how the dissidents in the Quaker Belt managed to successfully elude capture and conceal themselves from Confederate and state authorities, and how these men provided themselves with food and shelter while being hunted and under surveillance. The numerous accounts of their robbery and pilferage of loyal Confederates recounted above explained how they acquired provisions. How they remained undetected for months and, in some cases, years at a time requires greater explanation. Unlike outliers in the Appalachian portion of the state, who had the fastnesses of the mountains in which to roam, or those in the eastern swamps, which provided a maze of virtually inaccessible terrain, the men in the piedmont wishing to avoid service in the Confederate military, with a few exceptions, could not rely on the lay of the land for assistance. The warm weather foliage provided the only protection nature afforded outliers in the central piedmont. However, it was available no more than half the year. Outliers in Wilkes and Surry counties, which were located partially in the Appalachian Mountains, did enjoy easy access to mountain hideouts in times of emergency.

There were three small mountain ranges located in the Quaker Belt: the Brushy Mountains ranged in parts of Wilkes, Alexander, Iredell, Yadkin, and Caldwell counties; the Sauratown Mountains situated in Stokes and Surry counties; and the Uwharrie Mountains located in southern Randolph, northern Montgomery, and parts of southeastern Davidson and northeastern Stanley counties. The Uwharrie and Sauratown Mountains, along with most of the higher elevations in the piedmont section, are not mountains at all; rather, they originated as a result of the erosion of the ancient Schooley peneplain dating to Miocene times. However, the rocks that make up these hills date to Precambrian times. They range in elevation from several hundred feet to a little over one thousand feet. Because of the rocky soil and steep slopes, the Uwharrie region was thinly populated. Nevertheless, the area, because of its remoteness and inaccessibility, proved a popular haven for outliers. The same held true for the Sauratown and Brushy Mountains. Keep in mind that while these small mountain ranges were difficult territory for troops to maneuver in, they were nowhere as extensive or as rugged as the Appalachian Mountains to the west.[181]

Outliers in the eastern half of the Quaker Belt, on average, were but seventy miles from Raleigh, the state capitol, and were as near or nearer to several other relatively large population centers such as Fayetteville, Charlotte, Greensboro and Salisbury. Further, three railroads passed through the area. The North Carolina Railroad bisected the central piedmont. Running from Raleigh to Charlotte, it passed through Durham's Station (present-day Durham), Hillsborough, Company Shops (present-day Burlington), Greensboro, Jamestown, High Point, Lexington, and Salisbury. The Western North Carolina Railroad ran from Salisbury west to a point near the base of the Blue Ridge Mountains. About a year before the war ended, civil engineers completed a short line running from Greensboro, North Carolina, to Danville, Virginia. Telegraph service, available in the railroad towns, provided local officials with rapid communication with Confederate and state authorities.[182] Railroads ran through all of the Quaker Belt counties but Surry, or adjoined a county that did.

A plank road, although in decline by 1861 due to competition from the railroads, passed diagonally across Randolph and Moore counties, running from Salem in Forsyth County to Fayetteville in Cumberland County. Fayetteville, the main trading center for the eastern piedmont of North Carolina in the eighteenth and early nineteenth centuries, had steamship connections on the Cape Fear River to the seaport of Wilmington. The presence of railroads, telegraph services, and a plank road, coupled with the relative absence of imposing natural features such as large swamps and high, remote mountain ranges, made the Quaker Belt an unlikely area for widespread opposition to the Confederacy to occur. In addition, these factors made it even more likely that, in the off chance that strong resistance did develop there, it would have had but little chance of success. The outliers in the Quaker Belt succeeded against such great odds because a large percentage of the population — probably a majority by the summer of 1863 — preferred reunion to any continuation of the war. The discussions in previous chapters of the Quakers, Moravians, Wesleyans, abolitionists, nonslaveholding yeomen, and tenant farmers, Whigs, and militant Unionists explained the source of this antipathy to the Confederacy in the Quaker Belt.[183] Without the sympathy and wholehearted support of many of the members of this large segment of the population, it is unlikely that the outliers could have subsisted for long or eluded capture.

The Cave Dwellers

In February 1865, Mrs. Benjamin Sherwood Hedrick wrote an account of two Unionists from Randolph County who decamped from Confederate ranks to the Union army. Soon after proving their loyalty to the United States, military authorities released them from Point Lookout, a large Federal prisoner of war camp located in Maryland.[184] The story, possibly intended for a newspaper or magazine, throws light upon how the outliers in the Quaker Belt survived. She related:

> These men lay [out] 18 and 21 consecutive months and had been occasionally in the woods for two and three months at a time before but at this [time — the summer of 1864 —] the conscripting became more cruel so that it was not safe to be at home at all. Sometimes especially during harvest they would come in and work in squads but always with their muskets within twenty rods and with the women and children stationed around to give the alarm if an unknown person or persons approached.... They [the outliers] forbade shooting in general in the neighborhood of their camps lest it might lead to discovery. They dug themselves houses underground [in] the side of the hill with a trap-door covered with sticks brush and leaves and looking exactly like the face of the land around it. In this but little fire was needed to keep warm and much of the time none at all. Their food was usually cooked at home, excepting wild game, and brought to certain places at certain times. signals[—]sometimes a whistle, sometimes a shout[—]were used to give notice of apprehended danger. When driven far from their homes as occasionally happened, as once they were ten miles, they always found those who would befriend them. They have a secret society formed for mutual protection [The Heroes of America] for all lovers of law and order and there signs are so plain that though entire strangers it is sufficient to gain protection and food so far as possible.[185]

One of the intriguing aspects of outlier life in the piedmont area was the extensive use of underground caves as mentioned in the above story, a technique long used by runaway slaves in the area to conceal themselves.[186] Without the caves, the outliers would not have survived as well as they did. It is ironic indeed that Confederate draft-dodgers and deserters adopted the idea of building and hiding in dug-out caves from practices devised by runaway slaves to elude capture and live free. The classic exposition of how outliers utilized caves to elude the hunters is David Dodge's essay "Cave-Dwellers of the Confederacy." Dodge detailed the criteria used in selecting cave sites and explained how the outliers constructed their hideouts. Were a cave site judiciously selected and the cave properly built, about the only chance the authorities had of finding it was to inadvertently step onto its roof and fall into it, which, of course, was a misfortune for hunter and cave dweller alike. The outliers only used the caves in case of emergency, and thus they remained unoccupied most of the time. The outlier needed the caves only during daylight hours. At night, they rendezvoused with some member of their family to get food and other necessities, or, if surveillance were intense, they picked up food that family members secretly deposited at some prearranged location, as mentioned in the Hedrick account.[187]

In her description of cave dwelling, Mrs. Hedrick noted that accomplices used signals such as whistles or shouts to give the outliers warning of approaching danger. David Dodge added that different colored or patterned bed quilts hung out on the clothesline constituted a system of signals between family and outlier. In addition, different songs and even hog calls formed a part of their secret communications repertoire.[188] Indicating that some areas had elaborate neighborhood warning systems, Jesse Wheeler wrote: "When soldiers are sent to hunt conscripts the blast from trumpet[s] will set an underground telegraph in operation by which information necessary was imparted to all parties concerned in short order."[189]

Though correspondents only rarely mentioned caves, there can be little doubt as to their extensive use in the Quaker Belt, and especially in the Randolph area, as suggested by the Hedrick story. For example, Governor Vance was informed by a Randolph County resident of the existence of caves in the Brower's Mills community, as follows: "6 caves perhaps not more than 3 miles apart[,] 1 near Browers[,] 1 near Black and moons[,] 1 near Palmers etc. about 20 men in a cave."[190] A letter from a citizen of the Good Springs community in Moore County suggested that the hunters, in order to locate them, burned over wooded areas suspected of containing caves.[191]

The Underground Railroad

Militant Unionists used the prewar "underground railroad" that area antislavery activists established to spirit runaway slaves northward to clandestinely transport outliers and others seeking to flee the Confederacy to the Federal lines. As in the case of the caves, there is considerable irony that deserters and delinquent conscripts fleeing from the Confederate army benefited from a system originally designed to assist runaway slaves. The case of John Carter, superintendent of the New Garden Boarding School (a Quaker institution in Guilford County), provides a good example of the Underground Railroad activity that occurred in the Quaker Belt during the war. Carter "labored incessantly to keep young men out of the Confederate army by either concealing them, or passing them north via the 'Underground R.R.'" Referring to the demands placed on him by this activity, he stated: "There was often a week at a time that I did not take my clothes off to go to bed."[192] Jesse Wheeler provided further evidence of Underground Railroad operations between the Tar Heel State and the North. In November 1862, in a reference to the North Carolina refugees then arriving in Indiana, he wrote: "They say that there is a perfect underground rail road through the mountains of Kentucky by which hundreds escape."[193]

An account of the escape of a Captain Hock of the Twelfth New York Cavalry from the Salisbury prisoner of war camp in 1864 contains vivid testimony of the existence of the Underground Railroad and cave dwelling in the Tar Heel State. Upon escaping the prison confines, Captain Hock

> found in North Carolina an underground railway, as systematic and as well arranged as that which existed in Ohio before the war. From the time that Captain Hock by accident, happened upon one of the stations of this road, his sufferings and trouble were, in large measure, over. He found food and resting places, stations in secure spots, guides over intricate mountain paths and a hostility to rebellion which the north, bitter as it was, hardly knew. Sometimes he would spend the night at the house of a prosperous farmer, sometimes in a cave with two or three young fellows who were seeking to baffle conscripting parties, and sometimes alone in the forest. But wherever he was, he was sure to find either explicit and unmistakable directions for the next stage, or a conductor, alert, active and cautious, who accompanied him over the more dangerous part of his way. Nor was this help withdrawn until from a mountain peak near the Tennessee border he was shown the federal flag floating over an outpost of our army.[194]

Conductors instructed escapees from the Salisbury prison to follow the Yadkin River (which flowed a few miles northeast of the prison) north to Wilkes County, where militant Unionist pilots would guide them across the mountains to the Union lines.[195]

There can be little doubt that hundreds — probably thousands — of North Carolinians, many from the Quaker Belt, fled North, especially to Indiana. In January 1862, Jesse Wheeler wrote from Dublin, Indiana: "Some hundreds of Carolineans have arrived in Indiana and hundreds of others are serious to come when opportunity offers. In this section [Wayne County] of Indiana the Carolineans and their descendents preponderate over the emigrants from ... other States ... and in nine cases out of ten are anti slavery [and] out and out firm supporters of the Administration [Lincoln's]."[196] The exodus of Unionists from the Quaker Belt to the United States continued unabated until the end of 1864. Writing from Spring Town, Indiana, Wheeler reported in December 1863 that "a number of N.C. refugees reached Indiana this fall. I have knowledge of over forty from Guilford and Randolph[.] Some of them had been on the road nearly a year."[197] In May 1864, he noted that many refugees and deserters had recently arrived from Guilford, Alamance, Randolph, Chatham, and Forsyth counties.[198]

Reflecting the reaction of the Unionists and outliers to the February 1864 conscription act, which enrolled all able bodied men between the ages of 17 and 50 into Confederate military service, and that summer's deserter hunt, Wheeler noted that in November "the number of refugees from North Carolina who have arrived in Indiana is much larger this season than at any other period since the commencement of the war. Over a hundred have arrived in this month mostly from Guilford, Forsyth and Davidson, more than five hundred have escaped from Guilford and the counties adjoining since the 1st of march last mostly young men to escape being drafted and forced into the rebel army."[199] Wheeler contended that, according to reports, Guilford County had almost one thousand outliers consisting of draft-dodgers, deserters, and "escaped Yankee prisoners."[200] Indicating that the notoriety of the lower Randolph border area reached far and wide, he wrote: "The counties of Randolph, Moore and Montgomery are all famous for outliers, and it is said very few are captured through that portion of the State and that any [that] are captured ... mostly get away or are released by their friends before they get to any military post."[201]

Correspondence of local citizens provides a few references to Randolph area people fleeing the state. For example, one correspondent noted: "Linday Leonard says he was 15 miles from the Yankee line and going to the Yankes as fast as he could get there, he says they will not be mealy mouthed about it any longer."[202] An excellent example is Jesse A. Miller, a deserter from Randolph County.[203] Miller, a member of the Heroes of America, wrote a letter on November 15 in which he announced that he had made the decision that hundreds of other citizens in the Quaker Belt had made during the war — to go to the "Yanks": "I have tried camp life [i.e. the army] a little and i dont like it at tall and I am on my way to the other side.... I want you all to come as Soon as you can if I get threw Safe and the Prosket [prospect] is good tell all the folks good by and right to Jo that I am gon to the Yanks and tell him goodby and all the rest I dont Never expect to see any of you any more good by to all.... Mother says Shee is bound to go in thee Spring if Not Before to the yankes it is only a Bout 100 Miles [to] the Nearist place in the Mountains."[204]

As indicated previously in the example of A.K. Pearce, militant Unionists unfortunate enough to be drafted or captured and forced into the ranks often decamped to the Union side at the first opportunity. Others, captured in combat before a favorable situation to desert arose, found themselves inmates in Federal prisoner of war camps. Many, with the aid of Bryan Tyson, Benjamin Sherwood Hedrick, or other sponsors who would vouch for their Unionist sentiments, took the oath of allegiance and went to live with relatives in Indiana or some other Northern state.[205] Thus capture, as well as decamping and the Underground Railroad, provided the militant Unionist with a ticket out of the Confederacy to the United States.

Black Heroes

There is some evidence that blacks, free and slave, cooperated with white militant Unionists in the operation of the Underground Railroad and in the anti–Confederate cause in general. We have already seen that a slave ferried Bryan Tyson across a river in eastern North Carolina to the Federal lines in 1863 during his escape to the North, and that a slave assisted Federal army private Burson in his escape from the Confederate prisoner of war camp at Florence, South Carolina, to the Quaker settlements in central North Carolina. George Clark, a free black carpenter living in Davidson County and a member of the Heroes of America, served as a Unionist pilot to help guide Union general George Stoneman's cavalry when it invaded the western and central parts of the state in April, 1865.[206] Near the end of the war, a loyal Confederate from Randolph County informed Vance: "Our negroes are nearly all in league with the deserters."[207] In 1864, Vance was warned by another loyal Confederate that the deserters in Chatham County "intend arming the slaves."[208] The same year, authorities arrested a "free woman of color" in Montgomery County for "aiding deserters, etc."[209] A year earlier, a Confederate soldier, writing to his sister in Randolph County, speculated: "more than two thirds of those 'slaves' around Father's are tories. I talked very plain to them and told them I wished the last tory was hung sixty thousand feet high!"[210]

Unable to obtain large numbers of Confederate troops to assist his intimidated and weak militia force, Governor Vance had to sit by in the summer of 1863 and watch as deserters gathered into armed bands in the Quaker Belt and defied his militia officers, magistrates, and sheriffs. Due to their clever system of communications and concealment, the deserter bands controlled the countryside in most of the Quaker Belt. Only when large numbers of Confederate and state troops were in their communities was their power seriously challenged. But as soon as the troops left, they resumed control of their areas. By July, the deserters and draft-dodgers roamed at will throughout the Quaker Belt, the authorities either unwilling or unable to stop them. That set the stage for the next act in the drama of the inner civil war: the insurrection of deserters, draft-dodgers, and militant Unionists in conjunction with the movement for reunion and peace that swept the political scene in North Carolina in the summer and fall of 1863.

CHAPTER FOUR

The Copperhead Insurgency, Phase One: The Peace Movement

Scholars have agreed that most of the popular support for the peace movement that swept across North Carolina in the summer of 1863 came from the "west."[1] A closer look at the voices behind the peace protests reveals that a majority of the Peace Party rallies held in the state that summer occurred in the Quaker Belt. Furthermore, much of the reunionist sentiment behind the peace agitation came from two residents of the Quaker Belt — Bryan Tyson and Lewis Hanes — whose writings and protests provoked sharp dissent in the state, but whose careers have received scant attention in historical accounts of the period. Moreover, students of the Confederacy have failed to realize that the peace movement that flashed across the state in the summer of 1863 ended not with a whimper, but with a bang. In the summer, hundreds of dissidents grouped themselves into armed bands, especially in the Quaker Belt, and defied local, state, and national authorities. At the behest of Governor Vance, Confederate leaders rushed two regiments of infantry and a squadron of cavalry under the command of Brigadier General Robert Hoke into the Quaker Belt to restore order. Only after five months of continuous operations were

Brigadier General Robert F. Hoke (1837–1912) around 1864. He commanded a brigade of troops in the Army of Northern Virginia. In the late summer of 1863, General Lee ordered him into the Quaker Belt of North Carolina with two infantry regiments and a squadron of cavalry to quell a massive deserter uprising and to intimidate the Copperhead insurgency led by Holden's Peace Party agitators. Peace advocates held more than half of the peace meetings carried out in North Carolina in 1863 in the Quaker Belt, the epicenter of the Copperhead insurgency. Over a period of five months, Hoke's troops captured and returned about 3,000 deserters to the ranks (courtesy the North Carolina Collection, University of North Carolina at Chapel Hill Library).

the combined state and national military forces able to overawe the dissidents and quell the uprising.

The peace movement that burst on the political scene in the Tar Heel State in July 1863 had its roots in the strong defeatist and antiwar spirit that arose in the North in the first half of 1863. The defeats and heavy losses suffered by Union forces at Fredericksburg (December 1862), Chancellorsville (May 1863), and in other battles contributed to this declension of the martial élan of the Northern people. Other factors included opposition to the Emancipation Proclamation, the draft, the use of black troops in the army, and the violation of civil liberties by the Lincoln administration and military authorities. The antiwar Democrats in the North — usually referred to by historians as "Peace Democrats" or "Copperheads"— took full political advantage of the disaffection by initiating a peace movement in January that lasted into the summer months. Clement L. Vallandigham of Ohio, who emerged as the leader of the peace faction of the Democrats, demanded that Lincoln stop the bloodletting by arranging an armistice and negotiating an "honorable peace" that would bring the South back into the Union. Vallandigham's partisans expressed their political agenda of compromise and reunion in the slogan "The Constitution as It Is, the Union as It Was."[2] In advocating "the Constitution as It Is" the Peace Democrats denied the constitutionality of the Emancipation Proclamation and opposed the passage of an amendment to the Constitution abolishing slavery. The desire to return to "the Union as It Was" reflected the Copperheads' ambition to restore the seceded states to the Union as it was before the war started. They believed that the key to ending the war rested in assuring the Southern states that, were they to agree to return to the Union, the institution of slavery would continue under the protection of the Constitution in the South just as it had in the antebellum years. Vallandigham invited Southern peace men to cooperate with Northern peace men "in giving reality to the slogan 'The Constitution as It Is, the Union as It Was.'"[3] While holding numerous peace rallies throughout the Northern states, Democrat political activists concentrated their efforts in the strongly Democratic Midwest. They demanded peace, compromise, and reunion.[4]

The peace activities in the North had a profound effect on the thinking of certain North Carolinians. In 1862, Bryan Tyson, in his book *A Ray of Light* and "reunion circular," had urged the people in the South and Confederate leaders in Raleigh and Richmond to return to the Union on the basis of the constitutional guarantee of slavery in the returning states offered by the Northern peace Democrats. Few takers responded to Tyson's pleadings in 1862, but all that changed in the wake of the movement for peace initiated by the Northern Peace Democrats in early 1863. Vallandigham's suggestion that Southern peace men cooperate with Northern peace men stimulated the founders and leaders of the Tar Heel peace movement into action. They decided to launch a peace movement of their own.

William Woods Holden, editor of the *North Carolina Standard* in Raleigh, the most influential newspaper of its day in the state, emerged as the movement's leader.[5] Only three other newspapers supported Holden in his peace crusade: the *Daily Progress* (Raleigh), the *Times* (Hendersonville), and the *People's Press* (Salem).[6] In the first six months of 1863, all four newspapers publicized the growing strength of the Northern peace movement and praised the Copperheads as a positive influence. For example, in January Holden published an article on Senator William A. Richardson of Illinois who denounced Lincoln for his "perversion of the war into a war of abolition." Richardson called for a speedy restoration of peace between the sections through a convention of commissioners from the legislatures of all the states to meet at Louisville to iron out a compromise for the "maintenance for the Union as it was, under the Constitution as it is."[7] Holden published a commentary in June titled "The Peace Movement at the North," in which he noted that the peace faction at the North, which was made up mostly of Democrats, was "growing stronger daily." He reported that peace activists in New York City passed a resolution "recommending a speedy suspension of hostilities and a general Convention of the States with a view to reconciliation or other pacific settlement of the controversy."[8] In August, the Salem *People's Press* published an editorial advising Southerners to form a peace party to cooperate with the Northern peace men: "If we rejoice at the formation of peace parties at the North, and live in expectation of help from that great body of citizens there who look on the war as wicked and unnecessary, and who want it stopped, why not create a peace party at the South to encourage and cooperate with them in their efforts to arrest the progress of the war?"[9]

The first indication that Holden may have entertained disloyal thoughts and collaborated with others in a move to obtain reunion on the basis offered by the Peace Democrats occurred on May 27, 1863, when he published a letter to the editor in the *Weekly Standard* from Dr. J.T. Leach. Leach believed that Southern leaders could terminate the sectional conflict favorably if only they would "offer the olive branch of peace to those who are arrayed against us, with the inscription upon our banner the Constitution as it is, the Union as it was." Within six months of such a peace initiative, exulted Leach, "Abraham Lincoln's grand army will be demoralized, Jefferson Davis will not only be President of the Southern Confederacy, but he will be President of the United States." Leach optimistically added: "There are thousands of good and true men of the North that will flock to our standard. The great Northwest will come as one man; it is in her interest to preserve and perpetuate the Constitution and institutions of the country, as they were before Abraham Lincoln laid his parasitical hands upon them." Leach's use of the political slogan of the Northern Peace Democrats—"The Constitution as it is, The Union as it was"—alerted the readers of his letter that he was advocating reunion on the basis offered by the Copperheads. About a year later, Dr. Leach was serving in the Confederate House of Representatives. When asked by a fellow congressman, "Is he for peace on any

William Woods Holden (1818–1892) around 1868. Newspaper editor, leader of the Tar Heel peace and convention movements (a.k.a. the Copperhead insurgency) in 1863 and 1864, he was appointed provisional governor in 1865, and elected Republican Governor of North Carolina in 1868. He was impeached and removed from office in 1871 for the illegal measures he used to suppress the Ku Klux Klan (courtesy the North Carolina Collection, University of North Carolina at Chapel Hill Library).

other terms than the independence of the Confederate States?" Dr. Leach replied, "I am for peace on the terms of independence, if I can get it; otherwise, I am for peace on the best terms I can get, short of subjugation." To the savvy listener, Dr. Leach was saying here that while he was for Confederate independence, if he could not get that, he would settle for reunion on the Copperhead basis, which offered peace "short of subjugation."[10]

James Thomas Leach, age 58 in 1863, owned a plantation in Johnston County. A physician and owner of 47 slaves, he was an anti-secession Whig before the war. In the congressional elections held in the fall of 1863, he won a seat in the House of Representatives on a platform of "a just, honorable and lasting peace." In Congress, he opposed the centralizing measures advocated by President Davis. When Davis refused to initiate peace negotiations with the North, Leach "urged separate state action for the best terms available." Second only to W.W. Holden, Dr. J.T. Leach was the most noted leader of the peace crusade in North Carolina. He and Holden cooperated in launching and pushing forth the movement.[11]

A week before Holden printed Dr. Leach's letter praising the peace plan of the Northern Democrats, the editor issued a piece in which he noted that while they were for peace, the Copperheads demanded that any peace had to be based on a restoration of the Union. "Not one in a thousand of them, perhaps, advocate it on any other grounds."[12] Here, Holden seemed to find the Northern Democracy's rejection of Confederate independence distasteful. But just three weeks after he published the doctor's letter, he issued an article in which he expressed satisfaction that the Northern peace faction was growing stronger daily. Holden proclaimed that the "advocates of peace, both North and South, are the best friends of humanity and the best patriots."[13] Evidently, Holden was trimming his sails for a change in political direction.

1863 Peace Meetings by Region and County

Mountain Region counties held 7, or 9.3 percent, of the meetings

| Alleghany | 1 | Henderson | 1 |
| Buncombe | 4 | Watauga | 1 |

Coastal Plain Region held 8, or 10.6 percent, of the meetings

Greene	1	Sampson	1
Harnett	2	Wayne	2
Johnston	2		

Piedmont Region held 60, or 80 percent, of the meetings as follows:
Piedmont Counties outside the Quaker Belt held 14, or 18 percent, of the meetings

Cabarrus	1	Rutherford	2
Gaston	1	Stanly	1
Lincoln	1	Wake	6
Rowan	2		

Piedmont Counties in the Quaker Belt held 46, or 61.3 percent, of the meetings

Alamance	1	Montgomery	2
Chatham	6	Moore	5
Davidson	4	Orange	1
Davie	1	Randolph	2
Forsyth	2	Surry	1
Guilford	4	Wilkes	8
Iredell	5	Yadkin	4

Holden's peace movement flourished between mid–July and early September. In those weeks, Holden printed in the *Semi-Weekly Standard* the accounts of seventy-five peace meetings (that is, Peace Party political rallies) held in North Carolina.[14] (See chart of 1863 peace meetings by region and county.) He gave the date, the location (community and county), the leaders, and the resolutions passed at each meeting. The resolutions passed at the gatherings fell into two categories. First, the peace men denounced the Davis administration for violating states' rights and civil liberties. They argued that the conscription, tax-in-kind, and impressment laws unfairly burdened North Carolinians. North Carolina had already furnished more than its fair share of soldiers to the Confederacy; thus, before conscripting any more Tar Heels, the other Confederate states must first supply their just proportion of troops. The peace activists charged Confederate authorities with enforcing the tax-in-kind and impressment laws more strongly in North Carolina than elsewhere. They denounced those laws as unfair taxes on the poor nonslaveholding class who were already shouldering a disproportionate share of the cost of the war. The peace men especially disliked the political proscription of the former anti-secession Unionists from North Carolina by the Davis administration. Davis had appointed no North Carolinian to a cabinet post, and he had systematically overlooked old Whigs both for civil service and for high-ranking military appointments. To compound the injury, Davis appointed nonresidents to administer the tax-in-kind and conscription laws in North Carolina in 1863. Moreover, conscript officials ignored the rulings of the North Carolina courts by refusing to release draftees from military custody who had secured writs of habeas corpus. To the peace men, the Confederacy had become the central military despotism they had predicted it would become during the secession crisis.[15]

The second category of resolutions passed at the peace rallies concerned the question of a negotiated peace. Peace proponents suggested several peace plans. The simplest plan was a blunt demand to stop the fighting "forthwith" and make a peace settlement — the implication being, the best settlement one could get. Other plans involved the demand that an armistice be arranged between the armies, and one of five moves be made: have the president and Congress negotiate a settlement based on Confederate independence; call a convention of the Southern states and empower it to negotiate a peace; call a state convention and have North Carolina negotiate a separate peace (implying secession from the Confederacy by the Tar Heel State); hold a national convention of all the states, North and South, to settle the war; opt for reunion based on the compromise offered by the Northern peace Democrats, that is, a return to the status quo antebellum.[16]

The Northern peace Democrats and the North Carolina peace advocates shared similar political goals: each demanded an immediate negotiated peace, and each supported slavery in the Southern states as a constitutional right. The Copperheads' insisted upon a return of the Confederate States to the Union as a condition of compromise. Most of the Tar Heel peace activists concurred with the Copperhead stipulation that the South should return to the Union so long as the institution of slavery would be protected by the Constitution in the returning states. Only a handful of the Peace Democrats in the North favored peace at any price. Most, like their leader Vallandigham, were for "compromise *and* reunion."[17]

Of the seventy-five peace meetings reported in the *Semi-Weekly Standard* between July 21 and October 13, 1863, activists conducted only 8 (10.6 percent) in the planter-dominated coastal plain in the east, and only 7 (9.3 percent) in the mountain section in the far west.

The piedmont, the heartland of the state's artisans and yeomen, fathered 60 (80 percent) of the meetings. The populace in the Quaker Belt sponsored 46 (61.3 percent) of the peace rallies. It produced fourteen of the state's thirty-three counties that held peace meetings, and seven of the nine counties that sponsored large numbers (between four and eight) of rallies. Clearly, the Quaker Belt was the epicenter of the peace movement. As the focal point of the peace crusade, the Quaker Belt gave voice to the discontent with the Confederacy and the war by the artisan and small farmer class, the anti-secession Whigs, and "Other South" malcontents such as the antislavery Quakers and Moravians, Wesleyan abolitionists, and Heroes of America.

The peace issue split the Conservative Party—the party of Governor Vance—into a "war" wing led by Vance and a "peace" wing led by Holden. At this point, the War Conservatives and the old "original secessionists" merged into one political pro–Confederate bloc. The two factions became bitter enemies, as the following account of fistfights between champions of each side illustrates:

> There was a [peace] meeting in Concord [the seat of Cabarrus County] last week and the Destructives [that is, the war Conservatives and secessionists] under took to mob Doc Fink a [peace] Conservative[.] [T]hey got him pened up in [a] back lot and about to get him But his friends found it out and Come to his help and they got to using Brick bats and the Doctors party beet them Badly and broke Some of there Bones[.] Wilson overcash is at home and he was in Concord last week and one of the Secesinest give him Some Slack talk and he knocked him down three times as fast as he Rose[.] D. Corrikier and A. Henry Seckler Come nearly to a fite last week[.] I will inform you that [there is] to be a meeting [at] Jno litakers (?) Shop on tensday the 8th of Sept next[.] [I]t is [to] be a [peace] Conservative meeting[.] [T]hey Say they are Determined to not yeald to the Destructives [i.e., secessionists] I heard Some Say yesterday at church that they intended to Die at Reighly [Raleigh] Before holden Should be molested[.][18]

A third political faction was the moribund Confederate Party, an uncompromising supporter of the war but largely ineffective after 1862.[19]

When charged with disloyalty and reunionism, Holden and the peace leaders retorted that they were loyal Confederates and supported Southern independence. Nevertheless, they claimed, independence would be meaningless if Davis turned the new nation into a military despotism, and victory would be pyrrhic if it cost the Confederacy its last man and its last dollar to achieve. Most people doubted the fidelity of the peace men to the Confederacy despite their claims to the contrary.

Governor Vance opposed the peace movement but at first avoided a break with Holden over the issue. When the editor insisted on promoting the peace cause after repeated pleas by the governor for him to do otherwise, Vance severed his ties with his old political ally.[20] In 1866 in a letter to Bartholomew F. Moore,[21] a prominent Raleigh attorney, Holden wrote of this break with Vance over the peace issue. The editor related that he and Vance in the summer of 1863 had had a heated conversation in which he asked Vance "to reconsider his determination to urge the further prosecution of the war, and unite with his real friends [the peace advocates] in taking such steps as would lead to restoration, as an alternative infinitely preferable to subjugation."[22] While admitting in this letter that he advocated reconstruction during his 1863 peace movement, Holden failed to define the kind of "restoration" he had in mind. Did he want to restore the Union on the Lincoln basis of emancipation or on the Copperhead basis with slavery preserved? Or did he have something else in mind?

Holden answered that question twice in the winter of 1865 when he made it clear in remarks in his newspaper that he had urged Vance in 1863 to forgo independence and cooperate with him in a push to restore North Carolina and the South to the Union on the Copperhead basis. In March 1865, in a commentary published in the *Standard*, Holden — still reluctant to unequivocally state that he had advocated reunion on the basis offered by the Northern Peace Democracy — obliquely affirmed that he had promoted the peace movement for that purpose in the summer of 1863 in an effort to save slavery. Holden credited the loss of slavery to the actions of his political enemies, Jefferson Davis and Zeb Vance: "If our humble advice had been heeded and taken eighteen months ago [that is, during the peace movement]," wrote Holden, "the State could have secured the privilege to themselves of perpetuating slavery as long as they pleased. But our advice was rejected, we were denounced as a traitor, and at last in the hope of silencing us, we were mobbed, if not by the order, with the connivance of the Richmond and Raleigh authorities." An angry Holden followed his condemnation of his political enemies with this threat of revolution: "We trust the day is near at hand when the people of Western Carolina will rise up *en masse* and demand a Convention, so as to close speedily this unhappy struggle."[23] "Eighteen months ago" was a reference to September 1863 — a time when the peace movement was waning. In 1864 Holden wrote about a bitter confrontation he had had that month with Vance over the peace issue: "In a conversation I had with him [Vance] on the 22nd of September [1863] ... he declared to me, after having labored in vain to induce me to change my course, so fixed and bitter was his repugnance to the peace movement, that if I persisted in publishing the peace meetings and encouraging the peace movement in the South, my property would be laid in ashes by an armed mob, and I would meet a violent death."[24] Perhaps the "heated conversation" mentioned in his 1866 letter to Bartholomew Moore that Holden had with Vance in the summer of 1863 happened to be the same as the one that occurred on September 22.

Holden revealed his Copperhead proclivities a second time in his newspaper in the winter of 1865, when he blamed Governor Vance for the loss of slavery by his insisting that peace be based upon independence. Holden avowed that, had Vance supported his peace efforts, slavery could have been saved by a "restoration" of the Union: "Beyond all question, if Gov. Vance had gone with the Editor of this paper in August 1863, when he began to advocate peace on the independence and sovereignty of the States, 'our property and slaves' could have been saved, either by a temporary separation, or a restoration of the old government; and not only could have our slaves been saved, but hundreds of thousands of precious lives would have been preserved. But the Governor hardened his heart and stiffened his neck, and urged *war* as the only means for saving slavery, and now behold the result!"[25] The only avenue open to Southerners to preserve slavery in 1863 — other than a total defeat of United States military forces — would have been a negotiated peace and reunion on the Copperhead basis. So, according to his own testimony, that is what Holden ultimately must have been promoting in his 1863 peace movement. Given the preservation of slavery as the prime objective of his advocating a "restoration of the old government," Holden tacitly admitted that he then was a Copperhead partisan.

Between July 17 and August 25, Holden printed four pieces in his newspaper that suggested that he leaned towards Copperheadism: his July 17 editorial entitled "Peace — When shall we have Peace!" launching the peace movement, his publication of Lewis Hanes's Copperhead Manifesto, his printing of the pro–Copperhead resolutions passed at peace meetings in Surry and other counties, and his August 25 editorial entitled "North-Carolina Politics," in which he first endorsed the "restoration of the old government."

"Peace — When shall we have Peace?"

On July 17 in an editorial in his *Semi-Weekly Standard* entitled "Peace — When shall we have Peace?" Holden laid forth the rationale behind his peace crusade. In this perspective, Holden stated its central premise: "What the great mass of our people desire is a cessation of hostilities and negotiations. If they could reach that point they would feel that the conflict of arms would not be renewed, and that some settlement would be effected which would leave them in the future in the enjoyment of 'life, liberty, and happiness.'" Many peace leaders agreed with Holden that if only an armistice were arranged and hostilities stopped, the great mass of the people North and South would never let politicians renew the war. Among his arguments for peace, Holden made the following additional points: As did Bryan Tyson a year earlier, the editor maintained that the Confederacy was too weak militarily to prevent defeat by the Union forces, and defeat meant emancipation. Holden pointed out that Union armies now occupied about half of the Confederacy, and President Lincoln has just issued a call for 300,000 more troops — and he will get them. He noted that the South's fighting population is limited and exhausted, and the North knows this. The only way to save slavery, Holden concluded, would be to arrange an armistice and negotiate a peace before the North conquered the Confederacy. The recent military reverses at Gettysburg and Vicksburg indicated that the Confederacy could never achieve independence through military means alone. Indeed, the recent Federal victories hushed the clamor for peace in the North and united its people in their determination to defeat the South. Plainly, the editor added, the war will continue until one side conquers the other. It is time for Southerners to face the truth. "Our people must look at and act upon things as they are, and not as they would have them." In conclusion, Holden asked his readers: Can five million Southerners hope to defeat twenty million Northerners? While not stated, the answer to that question had to be no. Here Holden makes it clear to his readers that the war for independence advocated by Vance and Davis would inevitably lead to defeat and disaster for the Confederacy, and that a negotiated peace that would guarantee property rights was the only viable option open to reasonable Southerners.

If defeated, Holden asked his readers, what was the worst the South faced? "It would be the condition of provincial dependence on the federal government, each State being ruled by a military Governor as Tennessee is, and the emancipation and arming of our slaves in our midst. That would be the worst. If the war continues is it not likely that this will happen? Judging the future by the past — and we have no other means of judging — we fear it will. What then? Must we rush on to our doom?" At this point, Holden gets to the crux of the peace movement: "If the worst is destined to overtake us, would it not be wise and prudent to take less than the worst, provided we could do so compatibly with honor?" Holden implied here that a peace short of independence might be acceptable as long as the South's "rights" (that is, slavery) were respected. And it is on this point that Holden's critics accused him of being a traitor who was for reconstruction. That was because everyone knew that the only peace option proffered at the time that would assure the preservation of slavery was reunion on the Copperhead basis. In this editorial Holden first made clear to the public his Copperhead intentions.

Holden chided his readers to not be shy about freely expressing their opinions. "If they want continued, wasting, bloody war, let them say so; if they want peace, let them say so, and let them state the terms on which they would have it. That peace cannot be attained by fighting merely is now apparent to all." Holden then advised his readers on a plan designed to achieve peace: "Let our next Congressional elections turn on the proposition that Congress shall appoint commissioners to meet others on the part of Lincoln, to make an honest effort to stay the effusion of blood by an honorable adjustment. Let what these commissioners may do be submitted to the people. If they approve it, peace will be the result; if they reject it, the war will be renewed and continued indefinitely." At no point in his arguments did Holden specify that the independence of the Confederacy be recognized.

Lewis Hanes's Copperhead Manifesto

On July 31, Holden printed in his newspaper the most important pro–Copperhead work by a militant Unionist from the Quaker Belt — and indeed in the state — since the publications of Bryan Tyson's *A Ray of Light* and reunion circular in August and September 1862. Lewis Hanes wrote the tract, which he titled "The Secessionists — their Promises and their Performances — the Condition into which they have brought the Country — the Remedy, etc."[26] Hanes, a Davidson County farmer and editor, used "Davidson" as his nom de plume. Historians have overlooked Lewis Hanes and his "Copperhead Manifesto" in their writings on the peace movement.[27]

Lewis Hanes, a Whig and an ardent opponent of secession in 1861, ran for a seat in the United States House of Representatives from North Carolina's Seventh Congressional District in October 1865. In that campaign, he explained to the voters why he had turned to reunionism in 1863:

> But in the summer of 1863, I saw or thought I saw that the Confederacy had passed the culminating point of its power and its glory and that sooner or later, if we persisted in the struggle, we would be a subjugated — or at least a conquered people. I, therefore, commenced, in my humble way, advocating negotions for peace upon the basis of restoration of the Union and of the national authority — To accomplish this end, I wrote a number of articles for the different news papers in the State in many of which I openly and boldly took grounds for "reconstruction." Some of these you may perhaps remember published in the *Standard* over the signature of "Davidson."[28]

Republicans refused to seat Hanes in the United States Congress. Despite his Unionist credentials, Hanes, in the eyes of the Republicans, committed the "crime" of serving in the "rebel" state legislature of Confederate North Carolina. In 1860, voters elected Lewis Hanes to the lower house of the state legislature; in 1864, supporters reelected him to the House of Commons on a "reconstruction platform." Hanes's Davidson articles so enraged his political opponents that they charged him with being a "Convention agitator," "premature peace brawler," and "reconstruction shrieker."[29] After the war, he served briefly as private secretary to Provisional Governor William Woods Holden, a Republican. He broke with Holden politically, joined the Democratic Party, and became editor of *The Old North State*, a newspaper published in Salisbury. In 1870, party stalwarts drummed him out of the Democratic Party for his opposition to a state convention favored by the Democrats. He then joined the Republicans and became editor of *The Raleigh Era*, the party organ. In 1880, voters again elected Hanes to the state legislature, and when he died in 1882, he was a trustee of the University of North Carolina.[30]

In his Copperhead Manifesto, Lewis Hanes articulated the political views championed by most Peace Conservatives in the Quaker Belt in the summer of 1863. Nearly all of them had been anti-secession Whigs or Unionist Democrats who had never been able privately to accept secession or the new Confederate government. Encouraged by the peace activities of the Copperheads in the North, and innerved by the Confederate defeats at Gettysburg and Vicksburg, these covert reunionists came out of the closet and for the first time boldly and publicly expressed their true political feelings. Hanes accused the secessionists of deliberately setting out to destroy the Union, first over the tariff issue and then over the issue of slavery in the territories. The secessionists charged that Lincoln and the Republicans would turn the Federal government against slave interest in the territories. Yet President Lincoln, when he entered office, faced both a Supreme Court and a Congress solidly controlled by proslavery forces. Thus, argued Hanes, in light of the power advantage enjoyed by Southerners, secession as it was carried out in the winter of 1861 was unjustified.

In spite of the protests of the Unionists to the contrary, the secessionists had their way due to the "long list of magnificent *promises* which looked so splendid as almost to dazzle the mind with their brilliancy." The secessionists promised, "first and foremost that secession should be *peaceable*." They promised that if a war should ensue, it would be a very short war, and that England and France would grant diplomatic recognition to the Confederacy and come to its aid militarily in case of a war with the United States. They promised that all the slave states save Delaware would join the Confederacy, and "that slave property should be established upon a basis as safe as that of landed property." They promised, Hanes wrote, "that the new government should be a mere Confederacy of States of absolute sovereignty and equal rights; that the States should be tyrannized over by *no* such '*central despotism*' as the old government at Washington; that the glorious doctrine of States rights and nullification as taught by Mr. Jefferson and Mr. Calhoun, should prevail in the new Confederacy — that the *sovereignty* of the States and their judicial decisions should be sacredly respected." They promised "the early and permanent establishment of the wealthiest and best government on the earth, whose *credit* should be better than that of any other nation; whose prosperity and happiness should be the envy of the civilized world." They pledged, "that if a war *should* ensue, *they* would go to the battle field and spill, if necessary, the *last* drop of their blood in the cause of their beloved South."

"While such have been their *promises*," noted Hanes, "what have been their *performances*?" Secession was not peaceable; rather, the secessionists plunged the Confederacy into a devastating war. England and France have not recognized the Confederacy nor helped raise the blockade. The slave states of Maryland, Kentucky, and Missouri proved unable to make an effective union with the Confederacy, and "more slaves have been lost to the South forever since secession was inaugurated, than would have escaped from their masters *in* the union in five centuries." Secessionists, declared Hanes, have not kept their promise that they would respect the sovereignty and rights of the states: "Whatever the government may be in *theory*, in *fact* we have a grand military *consolidation*, which almost entirely ignores the existence of the States, and disregards the decisions of their highest judicial tribunals." Hanes viewed the government at Washington to be "a most mild and beneficent government compared with the *central despotism* at Richmond, under which we are now living."

Instead of establishing the "wealthiest and best government in the world with unbounded credit," the Confederacy has lost the states of Missouri, Arkansas, Kentucky, Tennessee, Texas, Louisiana, and Mississippi. Moreover, its monetary credit among the nations of the world has declined. "And as regards their promise 'to go to the war and spill the last drop of their blood in the cause of their beloved South,' I will say nothing. Every body knows how the Secessionists of North-Carolina have kept that promise. Every body knows that the leaders, with a few honorable exceptions, will neither fight nor negotiate."

Hanes concluded that "all calm and dispassionate men every where" would now admit that the South would have been better off to have compromised with Lincoln and the Republicans. Before hostilities broke out, they had offered to support a constitutional amendment guaranteeing the right to slave property in the traditional Southern slave states if Southerners would agree to stop agitating for the right to carry their slaves into other states and the territories. But rather than accept a fair compromise, the secessionists thrust Southerners into a terrible, devastating war "which has spread a pall over the whole land—has brought mourning into every family—has rendered hundreds of thousands of hearthstones desolate—has filled the land with the maimed and disabled, with widows and orphans, and squalid poverty—has crowded our poor-houses and almhouses—has sported away many hundreds of thousands of lives, and many hundreds of millions of treasure only to find the institution for which they profess to have gone to war, in a thousand times as greater jeopardy than ever before."

This being the condition to which the secessionists have brought the country, Hanes asked: "Is there any remedy?" Answering in the positive, Hanes said the remedy would be a "speedy peace." The people of North Carolina, especially those in the central part of the state, wanted "*peace* upon any terms that will not enslave and degrade us. They may, perhaps, prefer that the independence of the South should be acknowledged, but this they believe can not now be obtained, nor in viewing the situation of affairs, do they see much hope of it in the future." If the South could not obtain independence, Hanes continued, the people of North Carolina would be willing to compromise based on an amendment to the Constitution of the United States permitting slavery in a readmitted Southern state. Perhaps the warring parties could inaugurate a movement for sectional reconciliation by calling an armistice and then "submitting all matters in dispute to a convention of delegates from all the states North and South, *the delegates to be elected by the people themselves,* in such manner as may be agreed upon by the two parties." Hanes restated in his manifesto points advocated by Bryan Tyson in 1862 in *A Ray of Light* and his reunion circular, and by the Northern Peace Democrats—that a reunion of the states could be achieved by negotiating an armistice and then hammering out a peace agreement through a convention of all the states, North and South, based on a Constitution that protects slavery in the returning states. In other words, Hanes advocated a return to the Union on the Copperhead basis. And by implication, so did Holden, who published the essay.

Jonathan Worth in August 1863, suggested that many North Carolinians had come to the same conclusion that Holden, Tyson, and Hanes had arrived at regarding reunion on the plan offered by the Northern Peace Democrats. In a letter to his brother John M.

Worth in Asheboro, he wrote: "Many believe, among whom is Holden, that we will be vanquished, and that now, with a large army in the field and a large peace party at the North, anxious for reconstruction on the basis of the present Constitution protecting our property in slaves, a treaty could be made, avoiding emancipation and confiscation which must ensue if our arms fail,...."[31]

Editors reprinted Hanes's Copperhead Manifesto in several Northern newspapers as proof that anti–Confederate sentiment was rife in some parts of the South. Anson D.F. Randolph, probably a Peace Democrat, published the article in New York in 1863 under the title *A Voice from North Carolina*.[32] The 1870 federal census lists A.D.F. Randolph, age 49 and father of four school-age children, as a retired stationer living in Yonkers, New York. (In the mid-nineteenth century, "stationer" could mean bookseller or publisher as well as seller of stationery.) In a prefatory note on page 3, the publisher noted that *A Voice from North Carolina* was a reprint of an article that had appeared in the *North Carolina Standard* on July 31, 1863. He added that it was "reported to have been written by Hon. R.S. Donnell Speaker of the House of Commons of North-Carolina, aided by F.D. Satterthwaite, president of the Governor's Council, and to have been published with the approval of Gov. Vance." Donnell and Satterthwaite were Raleigh Peace Conservatives. The publisher was incorrect in attributing the authorship to them, and Vance never approved the publication of Hanes's Copperhead Manifesto.

According to the editor of the Fayetteville *Observer*, Northern editors reprinted many articles, such as Davidson's Copperhead Manifesto, from Holden's *Standard* as "evidence that the Standard and the people of North Carolina were hostile to the Confederacy and in favor of reconstruction." The Federals ensconced in the sound region of eastern North Carolina felt likewise. The editor noted "that the Yankees at Washington, N.C. were so thoroughly satisfied by the Standard's publications that it and the state were for 'the constitution as it is and the Union as it was,' that they held a meeting calling for reinforcements to march into the interior of the state for the purpose of developing the Union sentiment." It is plain that these Federal authorities believed that Holden and his followers were Copperhead sympathizers. The editor then drew attention to the speech made by Edward Everett[33] at Gettysburg just prior to the famous address given by President Lincoln there in November 1863. In his two-hour oration, Everett, without mentioning Holden's name or the name of his newspaper, implied that he believed that Holden promoted reunion sentiments through his paper: "The heart of the people North and South are for the Union. Indications, too plain to be mistaken, announce the fact ... [in] the States in rebellion. In North Carolina ... the fatal charm at length is broken. At Raleigh ... the lips of honest and brave men are unsealed, and an independent press is unlimbering its artillery. The weary masses of the people are yearning to see the dear old flag floating again upon the capitals, and they sigh for the return of peace, prosperity and happiness which they enjoyed under a Government whose power was felt only in its blessings."[34]

After Holden published "Davidson's" Copperhead Manifesto, no one ever took seriously his claim that he was a loyal Confederate.[35] During the 1864 gubernatorial contest, the editor of Vance's political organ, the *Daily Conservative*, cited Holden's publication of the manifesto in the summer of 1863 as proof that Holden was "notoriously in favor of reconstruction."[36] Largely because of the Davidson article, Holden's political enemies relentlessly accused him of being a traitor. For example, the editor of the pro–Vance Fayetteville *Observer* quizzed its readers: "Is there in the State a deserter, a disaffected man, a reconstructionist, a traitor, who is not Mr. Holden's friend? No — emphatically no. All such persons believe that Mr. Holden is the deserter's friend, and Lincoln's friend, and will vote for him accordingly."[37] In another article, he stated: "If Mr. Holden expects to make peace otherwise than as the constitution provides, he must expect to do it by a base and cowardly *submission—submission to Lincoln and his abolition hordes.*"[38]

In the first issue of his newspaper printed since the sacking of the *Standard* office by Confederate soldiers on September 9, Holden stoutly denied being for reconstruction himself, though the proceedings of many of the peace meetings called for reunion or hinted strongly in that direction.[39] Holden, a covert Copperhead, could not afford to openly admit his reunionist leanings, because to do so would have led to the shutting down of his press and his arrest and imprisonment for treason. His enemies knew this, and constantly egged him on by accusing him of being a Lincolnite in hopes that he would break under the pressure and reveal his Copperhead intentions. On September 7, Governor Vance issued a proclamation in which he denounced the peace meetings. Two days later, Alabama troops mobbed and severely damaged Holden's printing office. It was about a month before Holden was able to resume printing the *Standard*.[40] The 1863 phase of the peace movement was over.

In his proclamation opposing the peace meetings, especially those that passed resolutions threatening resistance to the execution of the conscription and tax laws, Vance's wording indicated that he viewed the peace meetings in the summer of 1863 to be counterrevolutionary proceedings: "Let no one be deceived. So long as these laws remain on the statute book they shall be executed. Surely, my countrymen, you would not seek to cure the evils of one revolution by plunging the country into another.... Attempts suddenly to change the existing order of things would only result in bloodshed and ruin." He implored the peace activists "to abstain from assembling together for the purpose of denouncing each other ... and to avoid seeking any remedy for the evils of the times by other than legal means and through the properly constituted authorities."[41] Thereafter, Vance and his War Conservative wing of the party, as well as Confederate Party members, accused Holden and his Peace Conservative followers of being traitors to the South. The peace movement, they charged, was but a subterfuge masking reconstruction schemes and disloyal sentiments; indeed, it was a plot to secede from the Confederacy.[42] The editor of the Salem *People's Press* admitted that perchance some of the peace advocates were reconstructionists: "This is perhaps true of some of them, who think that our prospects of ultimate success are slender, and that any peace that would secure to us our lives, our liberties, and our property would be preferable to the longer continuance of this war under such circumstances. But *who* among them ever expressed himself a Unionist *per se*?"[43] It is clear that the editor, when he referred to a peace that would secure "our property," alluded to "reconstructionists" that favored reunion on the Copperhead basis, which would preserve slavery.

The Surry County Copperhead Resolution

Vance was further convinced of Holden's disloyalty when the editor published the resolutions passed by a Peace Party rally in Surry County, one of which proclaimed: "That in our opinion, under the circumstances, the best thing the people of North-Carolina could do would be to go in for the 'Constitution as it is, and the Union as it was.'"[44] Readers recognized this brandishing of the Copperheads' slogan as a blatant call for reunion on the terms offered by the Northern Peace Democrats. In addition to the Surry County peace activists, advocates passed resolutions endorsing reunion on the Copperhead basis at Peace Party rallies in Guilford, Iredell, Alamance, Stanly, and Rowan counties — the first three counties were in the Quaker Belt; the latter two bordered it.[45] In the gubernatorial contest in 1864 between Holden and Vance, the governor charged Holden with being "untrue to his country" for printing the resolutions advocating reunion on the basis advocated by the Northern Peace Democrats in his newspaper during the 1863 peace movement.[46] The Fayetteville *Observer*, a staunchly pro–Vance newspaper, declared the Surry peace activists guilty of "treason" and "subversion of the government by resolving that they are 'for the Union as it was.'"[47] On the day Holden's *Standard* printed the Surry County reunionist resolution, an angry Vance wrote a friend that Holden "is for submission, reconstruction or any thing else that will put him back under Lincoln and stop the war."[48] Here Vance deceitfully charged Holden and his Surry County peace followers with wanting reunion on the Lincoln and Republican basis — with emancipation — rather than on the Copperhead basis of continued slavery. Vance and his Confederate political allies would continue to charge Holden and his followers throughout the peace and convention movements of advocating reconstruction on the Lincoln basis despite their claims to the contrary.

At meetings in Wilkes, Montgomery, Randolph, Alamance, Orange, and Alleghany counties — all but the latter located in the Quaker Belt — advocates passed resolutions implying support for reunion on the Copperhead basis.[49] For example, peace advocates in Wilkes resolved that "we are fully convinced that the great body of the people, both North and South, are anxious and desirous that peace should be restored between the two countries; and we fully believe that every honest and just person in the Northern government is heartily opposed to the prosecution of the war against the South, in its present form and for its present purposes."[50] In Orange, peace activists urged peace men in both the North and South to meet in conventions and work together to make peace.[51] Colonel Oliver H. Dockery, a wealthy planter and Holden supporter from Richmond County, gave a speech at a peace meeting in Montgomery County in July in which he implied that he was for reunion on the Copperhead basis. He stated: "That we would hail with joy any movement by the great body of the people, North and South, which might promise to lead to an honorable and lasting peace." He preferred independence but warned that if the war continued, the South faced defeat and annihilation. It would be better to accept voluntary reconstruction with parity and protection of assets guaranteed than suffer extermination at the hands of our enemy. He added that if the government submitted proposals to the people for approval or disapproval for reunion with equality and property safeguarded, he would, as their representative in the state legislature, abide by their decision.[52]

Vance and the War Conservatives were not entirely without merit when they accused Holden of Lincolnism. Holden occasionally printed opinions in the *Standard* that fueled suspicions that his peace activities tended toward a Lincoln reconstruction. For example, in July, Holden printed a letter to the editor endorsing his peace efforts entitled "Let Us Have a Peace Convention." "Patriota"— a Quaker Belt Peace Conservative with "reconstructionist" tendencies — penned the missive. He noted that the people were tired of the war that produced only death, destruction, starvation, and widows and orphans, and wholeheartedly supported Holden's call for a peace convention to negotiate a "speedy peace." Revealing "Lincolnite" proclivities, he declared secession to be not only evil but tantamount to "rebellion."[53] Another instance of Holden kindling suspicions that his supporters were "Lincolnites" occurred when the editor printed a resolution passed at a peace rally in Chatham County. It read: "That we are in favor of any and every means that can be employed to bring about an honorable peace between the parties engaged as speedily as possible, without the shedding of any more blood, even if we must concede a part of that which we claim as our rights." These peace advocates were willing to yield the emancipation issue to Lincoln and the Republicans in return for peace.[54] No doubt, many Holden supporters preferred reunion on the Lincoln basis. They chose Holden over Vance as the lesser of two evils. At least Holden was anti–Confederate and maneuvered in the direction of a return to the Union.

For Vance, the War Conservatives and Confederate Party members to have charged Holden and the Peace Conservatives with desiring reunion on the Copperhead basis would have been counterproductive. Most North Carolinians after the defeats at Vicksburg and Gettysburg entertained few hopes of winning the war. They would have looked favorably on a sectional compromise in which the Southern states could return to the Union with their dignity intact and the institution of slavery protected by the Constitution, thus allaying their fears of emancipation and its ensuing revolution in race relations. Hence, for the War Conservatives to have advertised the Copperhead cause by loudly and continually denouncing it in the press likely would have benefited the cause of the peace men and retarded the cause of Confederate independence. They feared that the dangling of the Copperhead issue before the public would backfire with the populace reacting to their efforts by endorsing Holden and the Copperhead plan of reunion. If that happened, they feared support for the Confederacy would disappear overnight. Instead, they chose to play upon racial fears by charging Holden with favoring a Lincoln reconstruction that would result in equality for blacks with whites and encourage amalgamation of the races.

The peace activists in North Carolina's Quaker Belt were not the only Southerners promoting reunion on the Copperhead basis. On August 11, Holden printed a letter from a Confederate army officer who was a combat veteran from Columbus, Mississippi, who advocated the same scheme: "As for myself, I am not willing to submit to Lincoln, but my plan is to join hands with the great peace party of the north, with the view of overthrowing Lincolnism, and then to establish the government with slavery guarantees settled to our satisfaction. The true interests of slavery require the country to be one, not two."[55] Holden's printing of this statement advocating reunion on the Copperhead basis by an experienced Confederate army officer could be interpreted as tacit approval of that policy by Holden himself. Activists in Alabama, Tennessee, and West Virginia also advocated the Copperhead cause.[56]

Holden Boldly Endorses "Restoration" to Save Slavery

While many of his supporters, such as Dr. J.T. Leach, Bryan Tyson, and the Surry County peace activists, openly called for reunion on the Copperhead basis, Holden never did because he feared military authorities would shut down his press and arrest him as a traitor. Nonetheless, on August 25, 1863, Holden strongly suggested in an editorial titled "North-Carolina Politics" that reunion on the Copperhead basis was the only *practical* choice open to the South if Southerners wanted to save the institution of slavery and avoid a societal revolution in race relations. As Holden had warned in his July 17 editorial on peace, he cautioned that half the South was already in Federal hands, and the Confederacy had not the power ever to retake its lost territories. The South's only hope was a negotiated peace; the alternative was subjugation, which meant emancipation and an unthinkable social revolution. However, neither President Davis nor Congress could ever achieve a negotiated peace, because for Lincoln "to treat with the Confederate government for peace *is* to recognize that government." Lincoln would never do that because in doing so, "he would surrender the whole question of the war" by recognizing the Confederacy as a legitimate government. "What then?" asked Holden. "If the federal government will not hear the Confederate government, it may hear the sovereign States. The people of the States, north and south, by mutual co-operation, *may obtain an armistice.*"[57]

Holden's suggestion that "the people" of all the states North and South settle the war was, in effect, a call for a convention of the states, North and South, which would bypass both the Lincoln and Davis governments, declare an armistice, and negotiate a peace. This was a plan for reconstruction borrowed straight from the peace Democrats in the North, and his readers recognized it as such.[58] Holden's insinuation that a convention of all the states, North and South, arrange a sectional settlement was not only an idea derived from the Copperheads, it went all the way back to the Union meetings in the Quaker Belt held in January 1861, when anti-secession supporters advocated the same policy to settle the secession issue.[59] Then Holden, having alerted his readers to the possibility of working with the Northern Peace Democrats for an armistice and peace, frankly stated, in so many words, that reunion on the Copperhead basis would be a lesser evil than military defeat and subjugation by Lincoln: "We are opposed to reconstructing the old government ... [but] before we would see our State permanently subjugated and trodden down as Mississippi is, we would consent to a restoration of the old government, or the establishment of a new common government, with all our rights [that is, slavery] guaranteed, as the lesser evil. But we would avoid this by all the means in our power, as a great political and sectional humiliation; .... If *forced* to choose between the two evils, we would rather live *with* than *under* the Northern people."[60] The editor's idea for "the establishment of a new common government," just as his idea for a convention of all the states, North and South, to arrange a sectional settlement, can also be traced back to the 1861 Quaker Belt Union advocates. Protesters at two Randolph County meetings suggested the creation of a new "Central Confederacy" in cooperation with the Conservatives (that is, Democrats) in the "middle States."[61]

In earlier discussions of the peace issue, Holden had implied that perhaps he would accept reunion on the Copperhead basis if no better alternative existed other than subjugation, but in this article he boldly spoke of the "restoration" of the old government or the creation of a new common government provided all property and civil rights were assured. In effect, Holden daringly endorsed reconstruction on the Copperhead basis. This approval came less than a month after he had printed Lewis Hanes's Copperhead Manifesto in his newspaper. In the eyes of President Davis, endorsement of reunion on the Copperhead basis, or talk implying support of it, was treasonous.[62] Nevertheless, an audacious move towards reunion on the Copperhead basis underlay Holden's peace movement of 1863.

By August 1863, Holden had spoken frankly to his readers about the condition of the country and the prospects for peace: Confederate independence through military victory was impossible. Confederate independence through negotiations with the Lincoln government was unattainable. Military defeat would mean subjugation and emancipation of the slaves. A negotiated reunion on the Lincoln basis of emancipation would be little different from military subjugation. The only *practical* move for the South to make was to opt for reunion on the Copperhead basis, which would preserve slavery and end the bloodletting. The only way to do that was for the states to wrestle the power to negotiate from the existing governments: Lincoln would never compromise on the slavery issue, and Davis would never compromise on Confederate independence. The best way to overcome Davis and Lincoln was to bypass the national governments in both sections through the calling of state conventions, and later a convention of all the states North and South. In addition, since only the states under the Confederate Constitution had the right to legislate on the subject of slavery, only a convention of the Southern states had the legal power to negotiate a peace that dealt with the issue of slavery — hence the necessity of calling a convention.[63] Thus was the rationale behind the peace movement led by Holden in 1863.

In the issue of the *Weekly Standard* printed on the day Alabama troops ransacked his newspaper office, Holden wrote a defense of his peace movement in which he listed the causes that underlay it. First and foremost, the political maltreatment by the Davis administration of anti-secession Democrats and Whigs fueled the peace agitation. These pre-war Unionists resented "the repeated course insults and injuries which had been heaped upon our State, and especially that portion of our citizens known as Conservatives."[64] This sense of grievance must have been strong, because Governor Vance warned President Davis that his proscription of "old Union men" provoked the anger behind the Tar Heel peace movement.[65] The military prison at Salisbury ranked as one of the Conservatives' major complaints. There "citizens were dragged, without rightful authority, and without having charges regularly preferred against them, or when so preferred, not having due notice thereof; and when they sought relief through the duly constituted authorities of the country, the military refused them the opportunity of obtaining remedial writs, or refused obedience to the writs when obtained; and there in the loathsome prisonhouse they were suffered to languish and die, without lawful warrant of arrest, and without lawful charge to detain them." In addition, "some of our people were seized and dragged to prisons without the State, and forced to stand trial before unauthorized and irresponsible tribunals." Here Holden primarily refers to the victims of military arrest for disloyalty made in 1861 and early 1862 in the Quaker Belt. Those arrested then included many peace demonstrators in Randolph and Davidson counties and members of the John Hilton band. What's more, military authorities disregarded the decisions of the state courts, "and thus the military overrides the civil authority, and North Carolina receives not only another gross insult, but the liberties of the people are stabbed in the most vital part." Besides the above-listed outrages against the people of North Carolina, Confederate authorities further insulted Tar Heels by appointing citizens from other states to head the Camp of Instruction in Raleigh and to enforce the tithing laws across the state. Holden concluded that the desire to end the indignities that the Confederate authorities imposed on them led the people of North Carolina to initiate the peace meetings: "As the repeated insults and injuries to the State were the prime cause, so the avoidance of them was the main object of these meetings, and people considered that a speedy and honorable peace was the most direct method of accomplishing this result."[66] In this rationale for the peace movement, Holden portrayed the peace crusade as an uprising of disgruntled old anti-secession Conservatives protesting their maltreatment by the secessionists, most of whom were Democrats. Holden viewed the peace crusade as the climatic battle in which the anti-secession Unionists strove to vanquish their secessionist oppressors. The ultimate goal of Holden's peace movement was the replacement of the world the secessionists created with a Copperhead America.

Counter to what his political opponents charged, Holden denied that most of the men holding the peace meetings sought reconstruction or submission: "While acting in these conventions [that is, peace meetings], there may be a few who favor reconstruction, a great majority of those who compose them are as free from desiring peace upon terms dishonorable or inconsistent with the independence of the South, as the most rabid, 'fight to the bitter end, last man and last dollar' partisan of them all." Holden noted that, as best as he could remember, only the Surry County peace enthusiasts suggested reconstruction.[67] Holden failed to recollect that activists passed resolutions favoring the Copperhead plan of reconstruction at public meetings not only in Surry County, but also in Rowan, Stanly, Alamance, and Iredell counties, and soon would be passed in Guilford County.[68] In addition, six other public meetings passed resolutions implying approval of the Northern Democracy's call for reunion on the basis of the Constitution.[69] Holden was not candid when he denied being for "reconstruction."

Examples of Disloyal Peace Men

Holden's political opponents constantly denounced the peace movement as traitorous. Deserters and disloyal reunionists, they charged, organized and led the peace meetings. For example, the editor of the Fayetteville *Observer* claimed that some of the "prime movers" of the peace meetings were men between the ages of forty and forty-five who were "thus muddying the waters for the purpose of devising some mode of screening themselves from obedience to their country's call." Others, stated the editor, were nonslaveholders who argued "that peace and reconstruction would only result in the abolition of slavery, and as ... many ... owned no slaves, they need not care — their property would be safe." The *Observer* went on to state: "We have reason to believe that in at least one case a meeting was in great part composed of the immediate relations and friends of a number of deserters who are prowling about the woods in that neighborhood, and that its main object was to countenance the dastardly conduct of the deserters."[70] A citizen of Fair Haven, a community in Moore County, wrote Governor Vance that the men holding the peace meetings in his area had never been for the South and were mostly outliers and deserters.[71]

An analysis of peace meetings held in Randolph and Moore counties offers proof that those charging that pro–Union elements were behind the meetings were correct, at least in part. At a meeting held on August 15 in the Little River Captain's District of south-central Randolph, activists passed resolutions calling for an end to the war and for "any Peace that will secure our rights, and which will not tend to enslave us." Obviously not advocates of Confederate independence, their call for "any Peace" implied that a peace based on reunion would be acceptable. And their demand for a peace that would "secure our rights" implied that a satisfactory peace had to be based on the U.S. Constitution to protect slavery in the returning states. In a roundabout way, they made it clear that they advocated the Copperhead plan of reunion. They endorsed Holden's stance on the peace question and urged the people to vote in the upcoming congressional elections only for a candidate who supported a speedy peace. Members of the local gentry — Colonel J.D. Cox, W.M. Smith, Dr. E. Phillips, and "William Gollahorn, Esq"— led the meeting.[72]

The last-mentioned leader, William Gollahorn (usually spelled Gollihorn), was a militant Unionist. Gollihorn was a justice of the peace who lived on a farm in the Christian Union settlement about one-fourth of a mile north of the Randolph-Moore line adjacent to the plank road.[73] The Minute Dockets of the Randolph County Court of Pleas and Quarter Sessions and the Superior Court reveal that until the fall of 1862 William Gollihorn served as a judge on the former and as a juror on the latter.[74] Yet, in the spring of 1864, the Randolph Superior Court indicted him for harboring deserters when a captured deserter admitted publicly that Gollihorn provided him with free "rations."[75] Two of his sons, Alpheus and Milton, earned the reputation of being "notorious outlaws" in the southern Randolph area during the last two years of the war.[76]

On January 30, 1864, peace men held a meeting at Carthage, the seat of Moore County. (This meeting was part of the "convention movement," the second phase of the peace movement that occurred in 1864, which will be covered in chapter six.) The Moore convention activists passed resolutions condemning the tax-in-kind law and the suspension of the writ of habeas corpus. They resolved that civil leaders should always hold the military subservient to their authority and approved the "patriotic course" of the Supreme Court of North Carolina in maintaining the civil rights of its citizens. They urged the Confederate Congress to take steps towards making a just and lasting peace and asked Governor Vance to convene the legislature to consider the calling of a state convention "to consult the greatest good of the greatest number of people." According to states' rights theory, the peace men maintained, each state had the right to call a convention that, when assembled, could call upon Congress and the president to initiate moves toward peace.[77]

The meeting was sponsored by members of the social and economic elite of Moore County, including Cornelius Dunlop, J.A. Barrett, Captain T.W. Ritter (member of the House of Commons), John K. McLean, Esq., Colonel A.A. Seawell, Captain Thomas Brown, Major S.W. Seawell, Lieutenant Colonel S.C. Barrett, and Colonel W.B. Richardson. The latter three were the top-ranking members of Moore County's Fifty-first Regiment North Carolina Militia.[78] Colonel Richardson,[79] who commanded the regiment, had been a Unionist during the secession crisis. In March 1862, when Governor Clark ordered the state militia to stand for a draft, Bryan Tyson, who was a militia officer himself, implored Colonel Richardson to "stand by his former principles" and disobey the orders to hold a draft. In a reply laden with disloyal inferences, the colonel, Tyson reported, said, "were he to do that the authorities would be upon him. He further said that our time had not yet come, thus intimating that at a proper time we [that is, covert militant Unionists] would come out in defense of our principles."[80] Colonel Richardson's discretion enabled him to use his position to aid covertly the reunion cause. In August 1863, the pro–Confederate editor of the Fayetteville *Observer*, wrote Vance "that it is understood by the true men in Moore County that its colonel of the Militia Regt there, W.B. Richardson, is not only unfaithful to the cause of the country, [he] has [illegible word] to some of the men of his Regt, who were unionists under 45, certificates of exemption from militia duty on the ground that they were over that age. Further, that he lives in the very midst of the gang of prowling deserters, and makes no effort to arrest them."[81]

During Reconstruction, a Moore County resident wrote Governor William Woods Holden (elected in 1868 as a Republican) a letter in which he claimed that Colonel Richardson had used his influence in 1863 while commander of the county militia to get him appointed constable "for the purpose of keeping me out of the Service." Then, using Richardson — who had been elected to the North Carolina Senate from Moore County as a Republican in 1868 — as a reference to prove that he was a Union man during the war, the correspondent added: "He [Richardson] can tell you all about my *Loyalty* etc, when you see him."[82]

William Gollihorn and Colonel W.B. Richardson serve as case studies that validate the loyal Confederate's oft-repeated claim that Holden's followers in the peace movement were disloyal.[83]

Peace Candidates Win in Seventy Percent of the Fall Congressional Elections

Peace sentiment was so strong in the piedmont and mountain areas in 1863 that every district in the west but one elected peace candidates to congress. The westerners elected to congress on a peace platform were Josiah Turner, Jr. (resident of Orange County) of the fifth district, John A. Gilmer (Guilford) of the sixth, Samuel H. Christian (Montgomery) of the seventh, George G. Ramsey (Rowan) of the eighth, and George W. Logan (Rutherford) of the tenth. All of the western congressmen but Logan and Ramsey lived in the Quaker Belt. There were ten congressional representatives elected from North Carolina in all. Only three of the peace men supported Holden: Dr. James T. Leach (resident of Johnston County) of the third district, Samuel H. Christian, and George W. Logan. The other peace congressmen — Josiah Turner, Jr., John A. Gilmer, and James G. Ramsey — advocated an "honorable peace" but either disliked Holden or opposed holding the peace meetings.[84]

The most interesting race in the fall congressional elections of 1863 took place in the Seventh Congressional District, which contained five Quaker Belt counties.[85] Samuel H. Christian of Montgomery opposed the incumbent Thomas Ashe of Anson.[86] Ashe, a prominent lawyer, was pro–Confederate and outspokenly against the peace meetings.[87] "Colonel" Christian, a textile industrialist, planter, owner of forty-two slaves, and immensely wealthy by Montgomery County standards, came out strongly in favor of the peace movement.[88] Everyone in the state kept their eye on this election because it tested the comparative strength of Holden and Vance in central North Carolina. As the Fayetteville *Observer* put it, "There is perhaps no election in the state in which so general an interest is felt."[89]

While claiming to be a loyal Southerner, Christian believed the Yankee army to be invincible and further resistance hopeless. He noted that the enemy held half of the Confederacy's territory and nearly all of its ports, and Richmond had little hope of regaining any of them.[90] Christian favored holding a convention of all the Southern states to consider peace and urged the Northern states to do likewise. He noted that the Peace Party in the north was on the move, and Southern peace men "ought to meet them." The Montgomery

County peacemaker hoped that an armistice of three to six months might be arranged to negotiate a peace. Stating that he opposed unconditional surrender, Christian said that he favored continuing the war if the North refused Southern peace overtures. He approved of the peace meetings because he believed that they encouraged the peace element in the North and gave cheer to Confederate soldiers. Christian warned that if the South did not soon negotiate a settlement of the war, the Confederacy would decline in power to the point that it could not demand an honorable peace.[91] At a speech in Troy, seat of Montgomery County, Christian boldly stated that while he opposed reconstruction, he preferred it to subjugation.[92] In his preference for reconstruction above subjugation, Christian echoed a stance previously advocated by Holden and Dr. Leach — a position that suggested that the bearer probably harbored a Copperhead bent.[93]

Bryan Tyson, William Holden, Lewis Hanes, Dr. J.T. Leach, and the Northern peace Democrats influenced Christian in his political thinking. He echoed Tyson, Holden, Hanes, and Leach when he warned that the South must negotiate a peace while it still had the power to do so. He reflected the sway of the Northern Democrats in his advocating an armistice followed by a negotiated peace hammered out by conventions of states, North and South. In a reference to the influence of Lewis Hanes, he asserted: "My sentiments in relation to the origin of our troubles, and as to our present condition, may be found in a communication recently published in the *Standard* over the signature of 'Davidson.'"[94] Christian suggested that if the Federal government refused to negotiate a peace with a convention of the Southern states, "then we can call upon the peace party at the North to put Lincoln out of power, and place men in power who will make an honorable peace with us." Christian concluded with a sentiment widespread among Tar Heel peace men: "The people North and South are clamorous for peace, and if they had a chance they would make it."[95]

Ashe declared that the peace agitation weakened the South and encouraged the enemy. Southerners must fight until they won independence. He denounced the movement for peace as a disguised maneuver for submission and reconstruction. Ashe chided the die-hard Unionists that the old government no longer existed and the old Constitution was a "dead letter."[96] Near the end of the campaign, Ashe yielded somewhat on the peace issue when he stated that if the Confederacy should have another great victory, it ought to make a proposal of peace to the Federals.[97]

Christian won the election, 3,631 to 2,126, and became one of six peace men elected from North Carolina in the fall of 1863 to serve in the Confederate Congress.[98] This turn of events encouraged Holden, who, in the winter of 1864, felt strong enough to challenge Vance directly for the governorship. S.H. Christian died of typhoid fever on March 5, 1864, before taking his seat in Congress, and officials called a by-election in the seventh district to replace him.[99]

The Gentry Versus the Plain Folk: A Class Analysis of the Peace Movement

Historian David D. Scarboro viewed the peace movement as rooted in class antagonisms between the state's gentry (the planters and county ruling elite, which included lawyers, ministers, teachers, editors, business leaders), the squirearchy (that is, militia officers, justices of the peace, sheriffs, and magistrates) and the rural, less well-informed, poor, and socially unrefined small farmers, artisans, and laborers. The former owned most of the slaves in the state and the bulk of the rich farmlands; the latter possessed very few slaves and worked small holdings on the subsistence level or held no land or slaves at all. When the great deserter uprising swept across the Quaker Belt in the summer of 1863 and rendered local justices of the peace, magistrates, sheriffs, and militia officers powerless to enforce the law or protect loyal citizens and their property (discussed in detail in the next chapter), the gentry of all political parties in the state feared that a radical, pro–Lincoln, reconstructionist revolution was afoot that would sweep them from power and replace them with a new ruling class composed of the unlettered, socially backward, rural hoi polloi. To avoid this debacle, the Peace Conservative gentry under the leadership of William Holden, Dr. J.T. Leach, and Quaker Belt leaders such as Bryan Tyson, Samuel H. Christian, James M. Leach, Lewis Hanes, and Calvin Cowles choose to co-opt the radical unconditional reconstructionism of the rural proletariat with the gentry-led Copperhead plan of reconstruction. The Peace Conservatives hoped to use racism to annul the class consciousness of the nonslaveholders. Scarboro viewed the proslavery language of the Peace Conservatives as an appeal to racism. If successful, the traditional gentry and squirearchy, who based their power on the institution of slavery, would remain in authority and control the political and social order as usual.[100]

Scarboro cites remarks made by Peace Conservative leaders in 1863 such as Alfred and Oliver Dockery, Calvin and Andrew Cowles, Lewis Hanes, Dr. J.T. Leach, Samuel H. Christian, and J.M. Leach, among others, expressing fear that the rise of armed, pro–Union deserter bands and radical reunionist activists across the Quaker Belt and in other areas of the west would lead to social and political disaster.[101] In this study, examples of deserter leaders such as William Owens, John Quincy Adams Bryan, the Dial brothers, Granville Smoot, John Templeton, and Harrison Church — to mention a few — are discussed who expressed such radical views or implied them by their actions.[102] A number of the nonslaveholding citizens in the west, most of whom had opposed secession, concluded that they had nothing to lose by a Union victory because they owned no slave property.[103] Class resentments fueled the bitterness of the yeoman, artisan, and laboring classes at the draft exemptions granted to planters and the county squirearchy, especially the militia officers. This led to the widespread view that the gentry had perverted the war for independence into "a rich man's war and a poor man's fight." The Peace Conservative leaders, according to Scarboro, decided to counter the rising tide in favor of a Lincoln radical reconstruction evident among the yeomanry and laboring classes. To achieve this goal, they initiated a campaign designed to co-opt the agenda of the radical agrarians by advocating immediate negotiations for peace on the Copperhead basis, which would stop the war, save slavery, prevent a racial and social revolution, and preserve traditional Conservative rule in North Carolina.[104]

Scarboro's theory that the gentry's fear of a social revolution from below would lead to the disestablishment of traditional Conservative rule in North Carolina has validity. No doubt, class resentments fueled the inner civil war and contributed to the launching of the peace crusade. Nevertheless, the desire to end a costly and bloody war that the yeomanry and laboring poor and many others believed could not be won also underlay the peace movement. But the main thrust behind the peace crusade came from the political war between the old anti-secession Whig Unionists and the "original secessionists" that largely remained hidden underground after secession until the summer of 1863. The love for the old Union of the peace wing of the Conservative Party remained dormant for two years after secession. The peace movement launched by the Copperheads in Congress in the winter of 1863, followed by the devastating defeats at Gettysburg and Vicksburg, caused them to thrust aside their latent Unionism and boldly make a bid for reunion. For two years they had been humiliated by Confederate authorities who overlooked them for high-ranking positions in the army and the Richmond government. Ardent Confederates always had viewed them as less than loyal and as unreliable supporters of the cause of independence. In effect, their own government treated them as second-class citizens. Under Holden's leadership, their pent-up anger exploded into the peace crusade for reunion on the Copperhead basis.[105] They then vied for a new Copperhead America at the expense of their old secessionist enemies.

Another factor influencing the peace movement also can be traced back to the secession crisis. Then, both antiwar Peace Democrat leaders in the North and anti-secession conservative Tar Heel Whig political activists proposed that the two groups unite and form a front against their political enemies, the abolitionists of the Northeast and the fire-eating secessionists of the Deep South. Some of them went so far as to advocate the creation of a new "common government" composed of the disaffected elements in the Midwest and the upper South.[106] The peace crusade unleashed constrained political feelings held at bay since secession that resurfaced in the summer of 1863. The Peace Conservatives under Holden — following the example established by their anti-secession political predecessors — endeavored to unite politically with their Northern counterparts, the Northern Peace Democrats, and defy the Southern secessionist Democrats and the Northern abolitionist Republicans by achieving reunion on the Copperhead basis. Perhaps some of them envisioned the creation of a new "common government" that excluded the abolitionist New England states and the fire-eating secessionists of the Deep South. The mind-set that Northern and Southern Conservatives should unite politically against common enemies preceded the class resentments and fears that became manifest in 1863. That attitude was an important cause of the peace movement.

The Peace Conservatives' worst fears came true during Reconstruction, when Congress passed the Military Reconstruction Act of 1867 and Republican William Holden won the governorship in 1868. The Republicans under Governor Holden, largely a coalition of poor whites and blacks, passed many democratic reforms that eliminated the rule of the old Conservative squirearchy in North Carolina. Holden always showed a strong concern for the small farmers and artisans of western North Carolina, especially for those in the Quaker Belt. This reflects his origins as an illegitimate child whose father — a man of moderate means — apprenticed him around the age of ten as an assistant to the editor of the Hillsborough *Recorder*. Holden, a man who knew the life of the working man, grew up to adulthood in the Quaker Belt county of Orange before moving to Raleigh at the age of eighteen to pursue a career in the newspaper trade.[107] By 1860, Holden was the foremost Tar Heel editor; more people read his *Standard* than any other newspaper in the state.

Between 1868 and 1872, Klu Klux Klan terror reduced the black vote in many areas of the state, and in 1870, the Conservatives (or Democrats) regained power and voided many of the democratic reforms made by the Republicans, and restored old-fashioned Conservative rule across the state. They also impeached and removed Holden from office in March 1871 for illegal measures he used to suppress Klan activity in Caswell and Alamance counties.[108] It was ironic to witness William Holden, leader of the pro–Copperhead peace insurgency during the war that sought to preserve slavery in order to safeguard, as Scarboro argued, traditional conservative rule and privilege, direct the Republican Party while governor during Reconstruction in the destruction of the old Conservative power structure. The restoration of Conservative rule under the Democrats after 1870 proved the Peace Conservatives' wartime fear unfounded that Conservative control of the state would vanish with slavery.

Bryan Tyson's Day-Star Circular and *The Institution of Slavery in the Southern States, Religiously and Morally Considered in Connection with Our Sectional Troubles*

The political developments occurring in North Carolina in the summer of 1863 delighted Bryan Tyson. His suggestion, first made in 1862 in *A Ray of Light*, that moderate Southerners cooperate with Northern Democrats in working for compromise and reunion, was finally bearing fruit. Tyson sent a circular to the Tar Heel peace activists for them to copy and distribute among the electorate. Tyson dated this "Day-Star Circular" August 28, 1863, and signed it "A Union War Democrat." It contained a counterrevolutionary call for reunion: "The day-star of the Union is looming up in the distance. Old North Carolina will soon take her position under the stars and stripes; and, one star plucked from the Confederacy, the remaining States would soon follow. Yes, if we will pull together, pull steadily, and pull long enough, just as certain as there is a God in Heaven and that to-morrow's sun will rise upon us, just so certain will the stars and stripes wave triumphantly throughout the entire length and breadth of the land."[109] It is clear that Tyson viewed Holden's 1863 peace movement as a plot of Southern Copperheads to return North Carolina and all the Southern states to the Union. According to Richard L. Zuber, Jonathan Worth's biographer, Worth "had copies [of this Day-Star Circular] published and circulated them anonymously."[110]

Tyson published a sixty-page Democratic political tract entitled *The Institution of Slavery in the Southern States, Religiously and Morally Considered in Connection with Our Sectional Troubles* in October 1863. The work addresses the question of whether slavery was morally justified. Tyson, a man of his times, believed blacks to be inferior to whites; therefore, they would be at a great disadvantage in society were they emancipated. Illiterate and without property, how could they possibly feed, house, and clothe themselves and not become a great social liability? Better that they remain in the custody of their white masters who provided them with shelter, food, clothing, and other necessities. In time, they can be taught to read and improve themselves. If the blacks progressed socially and intellectually, then emancipation might be appropriate.[111] While a slave owner, Tyson was not inflexibly proslavery. His Quaker heritage moderated his views on the subject. He wrote that he was "by no means prepossessed in favor of slavery." Indeed, he had resolved never to acquire money through the sale of human beings. He ordered his overseer in North Carolina to allow his slaves to go to the Union army if one was near and they wanted to go. Tyson wrote: "I am for consulting exclusively the interests of the servants [slaves] in this matter and am for freeing them, or not, according as their interests require."[112]

In *The Institution of Slavery*, Tyson appealed for Southerners to abandon the Confederacy. He advised Confederate soldiers to "speedily desert and flee from them [that is, Confederate authorities] like rats from a sinking ship, and let the structure founder, and go down with the sesch only on board...." He pled with his Northern readers to encourage the Unionist-led peace movement in the South by passing resolutions in each Northern state that assured Southerners that they supported the war only to defend the Constitution and to preserve the Union, and that the conflict would cease once negotiators had achieved those aims. With the passage of such resolutions by the Northern electorate, Tyson predicted that Southern reunionism would blossom and become strong enough to expel Confederate diehards and effect reconciliation with the North. Tyson no doubt intended to time the issuance of *The Institution of Slavery* with the peace agitation in North Carolina, but Confederate authorities repressed the peace meetings before he could publish the pamphlet.[113]

Republicans took a dim view of Tyson's publication. The flier advertising *The Institution of Slavery* had at its top in boldface the political slogan and rallying cry of the Northern Democratic Party: "The Union as It Was — The Constitution as It Is!" Influential Republicans had Tyson dismissed from his job as a clerk in the Treasury Department for publishing the pamphlet.[114]

William Holden, Bryan Tyson, Lewis Hanes, Jonathan Worth, and many others saw that the South did not have the power to prevail against the North, and defeat meant humiliation, emancipation, and a revolution in race relations. The Northern peace Democrats' offer of reunion upon the basis of a Constitutional protection of slavery to any returning slave state had an enormous appeal to war-weary and destitute Carolinians, most of whom had opposed secession. The Copperhead plan of reunion seemed to many Tar Heels as infinitely preferable to defeat, emancipation, a revolution in race relations, and a Lincoln reconstruction through military force. As the evidence demonstrates in this chapter and in chapter six on the convention movement, pro–Copperhead sentiment underlay and propelled the agitation for peace in both iterations of the Tar Heel peace crusade.

CHAPTER FIVE

General Hoke's Great Deserter Hunt in Late 1863

The peace meetings, along with the feeling of futility engendered by the defeats at Gettysburg and Vicksburg, led to increased desertions and disaffection in the summer of 1863.[1] By August, many new deserters had poured into the Randolph County area, and depredations upon the loyal citizens increased. In that month, a woman wrote Governor Vance from Asheboro: "Nearly all the deserters taken up during the spring and summer are here in the woods again, and there is a great number of them — most of whom have deserted two or three times. They are growing so bold and reckless, it is dangerous for a loyal man or woman to travel even a short distance, alone." She had an "afflicted" father and two sisters who had husbands in the army. She complained: "We have a good crop of growing corn, which, if it could remain unmolested, would probabley make bread for us all. I have plowed and worked in the field all the spring and summer, to make the crop, that my sisters' little children should not suffer for bread; but now the green corn is being torn down nightly and carried off to supply the families of these cowardly tories and deserters, who prefer the fame of the highway robber, to that of the honest patriot who lays his life upon his country's altar." Unless he restrained the deserters, she warned the governor, the loyal citizens — and especially the wives and children of soldiers — would soon face starvation.[2]

Another distraught citizen, writing from the northern Moore County community of Prosperity, informed Vance: "We could not be worsted from a direct raid of the Yankee Vandals, our enemies at home are fully as unprincipaled and as much to be dreaded." Upon returning from church the preceding Sunday, lamented the correspondent, "we found our house broken open, every Bureau, Trunk, and drawer broken open and smashed to pieces, money, clothing, and almost every thing of value carried off or torn up, destroyed." The deserters, claiming "that they intended to make the dammed war men suffer," threatened to return when the wheat was harvested to get their share.[3] The correspondent — charging that the militia was ineffective, unreliable, and useless — informed Vance that unless he stopped such depredations, the faithful citizens would be facing starvation. On the back of the letter, Vance wrote the following comment: "I sympathize with them etc and intend organizing ... the Home guards for their defence as soon as possible."[4]

The state legislature passed a law in July creating a state military force called the Guard for Home Defense. The law inducted all the able-bodied men between the ages of eighteen and fifty exempted from the Confederate service into the "Home Guards." This included all militia officers (except commanding officers of regiments and generals) who were to serve as privates, unless commanders selected them to serve as officers in the Home Guards.[5] The Home Guards had the dual assignment of enforcing the conscript laws and arresting deserters on the one hand and, on the other, protecting loyal citizens from the disloyal ones. As one Home Guard officer put it, his "officers and men had specific duties to perform in guarding bridges, arresting deserters and returning them to the army, [and] protecting the people against deserters, robbers and traitors."[6] On the same day that it created the Home Guards, the legislature enacted a law entitled "an act to Punish Aiders and Abettors of Deserters." Persons convicted under it would be subject to fines up to $500 and to imprisonment up to four months.[7]

Despite the new laws, desertion continued to increase, and in the Randolph area the deserters attained a new level of boldness. For example, an informant wrote Vance in late August, "The Deserters and Conscripts are banding to gether in squads and companys in Randolph Co. and the upper edge of Chatham Co. they have the Stage Road leading from Pittsboro to Ashboro guarded and halt evry man that pases and demand his arms."[8] A gang of Randolph deserters, acting on a tip from an informer in High Point (located in southwestern Guilford County), robbed an ordinance wagon while on its way from the small railhead town to the Home Guard commander in Asheboro.[9] The organization of deserters and draft-dodgers into squads and companies, and their concomitant efforts at stockpiling weapons and ammunition, indicated that disloyal leaders in the Randolph area had set an armed rebellion in motion by August 1863. The success and popularity of the many peace meetings held throughout the Quaker Belt at the time no doubt inspired their plot to foment armed rebellion against Confederate authority.

On September 2, a woman writing to her husband in the army reported that observers had seen thirty-one armed deserters that recently killed a member of the Raleigh Guards hunting them in Randolph on the plank road.[10] A letter from the Carbonton community near the Chatham-Moore line revealed that the deserters and draft-dodgers—"boasting that they numbered now eleven hundred men"—were kidnapping loyal men and liberating draft-dodgers confined in local jails, and stealing provisions, horses, and guns. The Moore-Randolph-Chatham-Montgomery area had earned a widespread reputation as a region sympathetic to deserters: "The region is getting so notorious that deserters from other states make their way thither and often stop along the road to enquire the directions."[11]

Randolph County was especially famous as a haven for deserters. Lieutenant Colonel S.G. Worth (son of J.M. Worth), commander of Randolph's Fifth Home Guard Battalion, informed the governor that about half the deserters in the county were natives of the adjoining counties of Moore, Chatham, Montgomery, and Davidson. "They find more men in this county who sympathise with them," he noted. "Hence they collect here from all the above-mentioned counties." "There are so many men here who sympathise with the deserters," lamented Worth, "that it is almost impossible to get any information, or to conseal [sic] any plans, for their arrest." The commander complained that his Home Guard battalion, acting alone, was not strong enough to challenge effectively the powerful deserter bands present in Randolph. He urged Governor Vance to order the Home Guard Battalions of surrounding counties to unite with his in a combined campaign against the disloyal element.[12] In an effort to strengthen the local Home Guard forces, the Confederate Conscript

Bureau in September detailed all men between the ages of forty and forty-five enrolled as conscripts in Randolph County to serve with the county Home Guard until further orders. This decision indicated the extremity of the situation in Randolph and the degree to which Confederate authorities were willing to go in their efforts to discourage desertion and disloyalty in central North Carolina.[13]

Issac H. Foust confirmed in a letter to Governor Vance that Randolph County soldiers deserted on a large scale in the summer of 1863. Foust wrote, "The fact is notorious that the desertions from the army from companies sent from this county, recently have multiplied until several hundred are now here." Foust opined that any effort on the part of the Home Guards to arrest the deserters would be futile and result only in the destruction of private property unless regular army troops reinforced and supported them.[14] Foust buttressed his argument with an analysis of the "classes" of people residing in the county that offered insight into how the war divided their loyalties: "Our people are of three classes — the most dangerous sympathise with them [the deserters] — the second fear to do any thing for fear of destruction both of life and property and if forced out will effect nothing the third class would aid in arresting them but are too weak to hope for success."[15] Then, in a statement, which marks the summer of 1863 as the turning point in which the disloyal and disaffected elements in Randolph County gained the upper hand over local and state authorities, Foust remarked: "Our people I mean the loyal portion of them are perfectly overawed — the deserters have taken a bold position. Stalking about publicly and the loyal element here perfectly insufficient to arrest it indeed I may as well admit the fact that I greatly fear a majority of those whose duty it should be to arrest them [meaning the militia and Home Guards] sympathise with them and encourage them — the condition of things here can only be realized by actual observation — The citizens have to a great extent been disarmed." Foust pleaded with Vance to send aid immediately.[16]

Dissenters in the western part of the Quaker Belt — especially those in Yadkin, Iredell, and Wilkes counties — also proved to be troublesome in the summer of 1863. As early as June 11, a loyal Confederate reported that "in the disloyal counties formerly Unionist — as Yadkin and Wilkes — they [the deserters and draft-dodgers] number hundreds and are committing depredations on persons and property."[17] A loyalist wrote Governor Vance from Wilkes County in July that between 200 and 300 well-armed deserters, mostly draftees, were abroad in the county threatening militia officers and loyal citizens.[18] Another Wilkes County resident reported to her uncle, "I am sorry to tell you of the Union sentiment existing in this county among the women as well as the men. The women write to their husbands to leave the army and come home and that's the reason that so many of them are deserting. The[y] have a regular union company up at Trap Hill! march under an old dirty United States rag!" In closing, she lamented, "Some of the people about here have actually rejoiced at the death of Genl. [Stonewall] Jackson! Oh! it makes me so mad to think about it I just want to fight, and I wish the Yankees had the last one of them."[19]

A citizen writing from Iredell County offered a vivid description of the "Union Company" at Trap Hill, a highly disaffected rural community in the north-central part of the county, situated at the foot of the Blue Ridge Mountains. He portrayed it "as an organized band of deserters and tories..., composed of deserters from that section, from several of the States South of us, and some citizens who have never been in the army. They are said to number about 600, have regularly elected officers and have all taken the oath to support the Lincoln government. They are armed and express a determination to resist all State and Confederate authority."[20] A Confederate soldier in the Army of Northern Virginia, informed of the disloyal events taking place back home, complained to his sister that "the people of Wilkes are badly whipped and willing for our patriotic old State to return to the pretended Union, and claim Abraham Lincoln as their chief magistrate."[21]

The high tide of militant Unionist power and display in Wilkes County occurred at a "Union Meeting" held at Wilkesboro, the county seat, on August 30. One citizen recounted the event as follows: "Bad state of affairs in our county — they had a Union Meeting at Wilkesboro last Sat, gotton up by the diserters & the citizens in Trap Hill & Mulbury & R [Roaring] River Country to the number of 300 or upwards, Marched into Town ... to gether (some of the Company being Mounted) sent out pickets upon all the roads leading to Town — & then raised the Union flag, a Very large one besides other Smaller ones of the Same kind, made Union or peace speeches, etc. Bad affair, they will rue the day I guess before Very long[.]"[22] A loyal citizen of Wilkes County informed Governor Vance that the leaders of the Union meeting in Wilkesboro were Granville Smoot[23] and John Quincy Adams Bryan,[24] both citizens of Trap Hill. The informant also alerted the governor to another assembly of Unionists held at "Covington meeting house" in Wilkes, where a United States flag was hoisted.[25]

John Quincy Adams Bryan (1833–1905), a farmer, was the most noted anti–Confederate leader in the Wilkes County area during the war. In 1861 he married Martha Ann Bryan, age 20 (the daughter of Thomas Bryan), of Trap Hill. Over the next seventeen years they had seven children, one of whom they named America, and two others — Thomas Sherman and John Grant — they named after famous Union generals.[26] The insurrection of deserters, draft-dodgers, and militant Unionists that Bryan led in the Wilkes area reached its climax on September 8. On that day, Bryan's deserter band skirmished with a detail of fifty-six of the Raleigh Guards commanded by Lieutenant Robert S. Robards at Fraley's in northern Iredell County.[27] Military commanders had ordered the lieutenant into the area from the Camp of Instruction in Raleigh to hunt deserters.[28] The fighting took place near the home of Jacob Fraley, a militant Unionist and merchant who lived at present-day Union Grove, a rural community located in northern Iredell County.[29]

A deserter, who was privy to the councils of the deserter bands near Fraley's just before the skirmish, reported that the insurgents came from Yadkin, Wilkes, and Iredell counties. He described the situation thusly: "for a short time at a place in the woods near Templetons or Warrens Bridge where four or five hundred armed men were assembled that they were advised by a man named Bryant [J.Q.A. Bryan] who told them that the State guard was in the neighborhood that it was the intention of the deserters to assist the guard by bushwhacking and that they were to retreat to Wilkes for a stronger position[.]"[30]

Another account of the affray at Fraley's appeared in the *Iredell Express*. According to that version, meeting organizers issued a call for a "Union meeting" at Fraley's on an appointed day. They extended an invitation to the deserters and skulkers in the area to attend the proceedings. Home Guard and militia troops, warned of the meeting, marched overnight from Statesville to Fraley's (about twenty miles) and surrounded the building in which the activists met. They arrested the ringleaders but released the women and other citizens. The troops put five deserters who attended the meeting under guard. When they heard about the presence of the Home Guards, about one hundred and sixty deserters on their way to the Union meeting stopped three miles from Fraley's at Warren's Bridge. "The supposition was that they were waiting for reinforcements from Trap Hill in Wilkes County and intended attacking the next day but the Guard were disappointed on reaching the place of an anticipated battle the following morning, the deserters having skedaddled to the mountains of Wilkes." The Confederate troops arrested two militia officers for aiding and abetting deserters.[31]

Outnumbered and outgunned by the Confederate forces under General Hoke sent into North Carolina to hunt down and destroy him, Bryan and many of his followers fled to the Union lines in Tennessee and joined the Federal army. Serving in Company H of the Tenth Tennessee Cavalry, he attained the rank of captain before war's end. Bryan received a shell wound at the Battle of Franklin that left him partially disabled for the rest of his life. After the war, he served in the state legislature as a Republican from 1876 to 1883 and helped found the Trap Hill Seminary (Methodist), which leaders later chartered as Fair View College. He also served as a major general in the North Carolina Militia.[32]

Rampant disaffection also occurred in Yadkin County (adjoining Wilkes to the east), where a Confederate woman complained to her husband that "the tories term every southerner Secessionist, and call them in addressing them 'you secessionist' etc. I do wish that something could be done to stop this miserable increase in tory feeling." She wrote that she dared not go to East Bend, a nearby community, "for they are such unloyal citizens, I would fear for my life."[33] On another occasion, she wrote that an "incendiary" had burned a neighbor's barn. In closing, she commented: "Sam Davis is now capt[.] of a crowd of tories and conscripts and threatening vengeance on Joe Bitting. He has turned out to be a miserable wretch."[34] Joe Bitting was a captain in the Yadkin County Home Guards.[35] One of Bitting's fellow officers, Captain Quill Hunter, received a threatening letter from the Dial brothers, who comprised a family of "tories" that had spread terror among the "secesh" in Yadkin and Forsyth counties. The letter, which had a menacing drawing of a pistol in its upper left-hand corner, illustrates dramatically the danger loyal militia and Home Guard officers faced from their deserter, draft-dodger, and militant Unionist neighbors:

> Capt Quill Hunter if yo ever hunt for us a gin i will put lead in yo god dam your hell fired soll[.] Yo have give the people orders to shoot us down when they find us and if yo dont take your orders back i will shoot yo[.] If sutch men as yo are is Christians of heaven i want to know who is the hippocrits of hell[.] [W]e have never done yo any harm for yo to hunt for us[.] [W]e will give yo something to hunt for here after ... the secessions neednet to begrudge what we steel for we are the United States Regulars ... we ... dare yo to go and Abuse Mother or talk about tying them[.] When the Yankees comes we will go and show them some secesh to kill[.] If this dont give yo warning enough the next warning we will give yo with powder and lead[.] [T]ake the hint intince[.] We are the old United States Regulars[.][36]

Evidently, the Dial brothers and their allies viewed themselves as a guerrilla force fighting for the United States. The "secesh" beat the Dial brothers in their row with them. On October 29, a citizen of Yadkin County wrote a relative: "The 3 Dials had been Caught one of [them] was shot and so badly wounded that he has since died[.] [There are] so many losing their lives at home and in the Army it is awful to think about it[.] [W]hen will such things have an end[?] ... the Colberts has not been Caught yet[.] Calvin Norman has died from his wound[.]"[37] Near the end of the war, the Home Guards wounded and captured one of the Dial brothers—described as an "artful deserter, well known throughout this community [Forsyth County]"—and killed his companion.[38] An observer described the incident this way: "The party was closed upon while in the house, both the parties sprung forward, one towards the door, the other the staircase, but instantly Captain Williams, an officer on recruiting service in the community, who was in command of the guard, fired upon Dial, the ball taking effect in his left hip, and penetrating, it is supposed, around the bone and passing out near the groin, instantly turning he fired upon the other man, Fann, the ball penetrating his bowels, and is believed to have inflicted a mortal wound."[39]

Confederate soldiers plundered citizens in Yadkin County as severely as did the deserters in the summer of 1863. In a letter printed in the *Standard*, "A citizen" complained that troops under the command of a Lieutenant Maroney, under the orders of General D.H. Hill, wrought havoc in the county, stealing food, guns, brandy, clothing, tobacco, honey, and anything they wanted from families suspected of harboring or feeding deserters. These soldiers, complained the informer, "would take bacon, flour, chickens, etc., from families and carry them to houses of *ill fame* and give to them." Many of the victims of abuse had husbands or sons in the army. "A Citizen" explained that class resentments fueled desertion in Yadkin County. He related that soldiers from the county deserted because most of the original secessionists were still at home and not in the army. Among them were militia officers, preachers, lawyers, and doctors. He added that the deserters said "they have no property at stake that the war is about, and but few men that have property are in service as privates."[40]

Matters were also red-hot in Iredell County, which bordered Wilkes and Yadkin counties on the south. In August 1863, radical Iredell peace men passed resolutions at a public meeting held at Jenning's Mill, calling for "a speedy and lasting peace" and "a State Convention forthwith for the purpose of effecting a peace." Their final resolution was a blatant cry for reunion on the basis offered by the Northern Peace Democrats. It read: "That in our opinion, under the circumstances, the best thing the people of North-Carolina could do would be to go in for the Constitution as it is and the Union as it was." The leaders of the meeting were Thomas and John Templeton, the latter a captain in the militia.[41] Both were militant Unionists who would play leading roles in the deserter insurrection. The commander of the Iredell County Home Guards reported to a Confederate officer that "I consider Capt John Templeton one of the most disloyal men in this vicinity [north-central Iredell County] & I think he is responsible to a good degree for all this disloyalty in the neighborhood[.]"[42]

Encouraged by the news of the successful flouting of reunionist sentiments back home, a young Confederate soldier stationed near Orange Court House in Virginia wrote home threatening to desert. He told a cousin: "You know the folks [in Iredell County] is gathering feathers and burning tarr for the Secession men[.] [T]hey are all for the union at home and half of the army is the Same way[.]"[43] Another Confederate soldier serving in a company from Iredell County and stationed in Virginia wrote home: "i can tell you the soldiers are most all for the union they are runin a way every day[.] [T]har is lots of them ben at me to goo with them i cdd name 150[.]"[44]

Lieutenant Colonel Lay's Report

Confederate leaders in Richmond, alarmed by the numerous reports they had been receiving about disloyalty and the depredations of armed deserter bands in central North

Carolina, sent Lieutenant Colonel George W. Lay to the state in August to inspect and report to them on the conditions there. In his report, dated September 2, 1863, Lay wrote that in the central and western portions of North Carolina, "desertion has assumed ... a very different and more formidable shape and development than could have been anticipated.... The unquestionable facts are these: Deserters now leave the Army with arms and ammunition in hand. They act in concert to force by superior numbers a passage against bridge or ferry guards, if such are encountered. Arriving at their selected localities of refuge, they organize in bands, variously estimated at from fifty up to hundreds at various points."[45]

Lay reported five hundred deserters and draft-dodgers entrenched, organized, and drilling regularly in Wilkes County. He wrote that "the reports of our patrols indicate three or four hundred organized in Randolph County, and they are said to be in large numbers in Catawba and Yadkin, and not a few in ... Iredell."[46] It is noteworthy that all of the counties mentioned by Lay, with the exception of Catawba, were Quaker Belt counties. Lay continued: "These men are not only determined to kill in avoiding apprehension ... but their esprit de corps extends to killing in revenge as well as in prevention of the capture of each other.... While the disaffected feed them from sympathy, the loyal do so from fear. The latter class (and the militia) is afraid to aid the conscript service lest they draw revenge upon themselves and their property." Lay added that disloyalists sent letters "to the Army stimulating desertion and inviting the men home, promising them aid and comforts. County meetings [peace meetings] are declaring in the same spirit and to hold back conscripts."[47] Lay concluded, "There is danger of marked political division and something like civil war if the military evils reported be not at once met by strong measures of military repression." He recommended that a strong force "should proceed to occupy the infected districts, surround the traitors, bring the disloyal to punishment, fortify the loyal, and decide the wavering."[48]

In his report, Lay made the erroneous claim that "all this trouble is of very rapid, recent growth."[49] He believed that the disaffection in North Carolina was "intimately connected with — indeed, mainly originates in and has been fostered by — the newly developed but active intrigues of political malcontents, having the Raleigh Standard for their leader."[50] Lay's contention that "the newly developed ... intrigues of political malcontents" caused the disaffection manifested in the Tar Heel State in the summer of 1863 was at best only half-true for the Quaker Belt. In August 1861, that area witnessed the "active intrigues of political malcontents"; in March 1862, under the guidance of John Hilton, John C. Hill, and others; and in the fall of 1862, under the direction of Bryan Tyson, William Owens, and others. None of the protests led by Tyson, Hill, Owens, or Hilton "originated" in the peace movement that began in the summer of 1863. In addition, wives and relatives of soldiers, at the prompting of the Heroes of America, had long been sending letters to the army urging soldiers to desert and come home. Though the peace meetings staged by Holden and his supporters certainly encouraged desertion, disaffection, and disloyalty, it was incorrect for Lay to blame Holden or the peace meetings entirely for these problems, since they all existed in the Quaker Belt on a large scale prior to the summer of 1863.

Governor Vance wrote on August 26 to Secretary of War John Seddon that powerful bands of deserters had rendered local authorities ineffective in the western part of his state. "The vast numbers of deserters in the western counties of this State," he noted, "have so accumulated lately to set the local militia at defiance and exert a very injurious effect upon the community in many respects. My home guards are poorly armed, inefficient, and rendered timid by fear of secret vengeance from the deserters." Vance beseeched Richmond authorities immediately to send him a force sufficient to crush the deserter uprising. "If General Lee would send me one of our diminished brigades or a good strong regiment to North Carolina, with orders to report to me," claimed the governor, "I could make it increase his ranks far more than the temporary loss of his brigade, in a very short time. Something of this kind must be done."[51]

Seddon referred the letter to General Lee, who endorsed it as follows: "General Hoke, with two regiments and a squadron of cavalry, has been sent to Governor Vance."[52]

The Deserter Hunt in the Wilkes Area

On arriving in North Carolina with his troops, General Hoke reported to Vance for instructions. The governor ordered him into Wilkes County "to capture the deserters and conscripts, and break up and disperse any organized bands of lawless men to be found there, resisting the authority of the Government." He told Hoke to arrest all persons "guilty of harboring, feeding, aiding or abetting deserters" and charge them in the civil courts according to the law. Militia officers and justices of the peace guilty of the same offences, or who "have willfully failed or neglected to execute my orders for the arrest of deserters, you will arrest & place in [the] camp of instruction."[53] Vance ordered the Home Guards in all counties entered by Hoke's troops to assist the Confederate regulars in rounding up the dissidents.[54]

General Hoke led the Twenty-first Regiment North Carolina Troops into the Iredell, Wilkes, and Yadkin County area from High Point, and ordered the Fifty-sixth Regiment North Carolina Troops commanded by Colonel Paul F. Faison into Randolph and surrounding counties. The adjutant general placed the Home Guards in Chatham, Randolph, Moore, and Montgomery counties under the command of Colonel Faison. Faison ordered a company of his troops into Union and Stanly counties.[55]

On September 8, General Hoke encamped the Twenty-first Regiment near Salem, a Moravian community in Forsyth County. The next day a resident wrote her husband: "Their place of destination I know not, but I think their business is to arrest deserters, & if possible quell the union feeling in the western part of the state." She met General Hoke at a party held for the officers of the regiment the night before. The general, she reported, "is a gallant officer" who had "very pleasant manners, fine conversational powers, & is very handsome[.]"[56]

Two days after leaving Salem, Hoke's troops reached Yadkin County.[57] On the 15th several hundred of them entered Wilkes County and marched toward Trap Hill.[58] By the 17th, Wilkes County was "full of Soldiers."[59] Calvin J. Cowles, a merchant in Wilkesboro and a covert reunionist, reported to a friend on September 22 that "a fight with Deserters was expected but [now] we think there will be none[.]"[60] General Hoke, remarked Cowles, encamped his regiment at Trap Hill (the home of John Q.A. Bryan, the chief leader of the area insurgents), where the General "has waited several days for an attack but no enemy has thus far shown himself."[61]

On October 1, the *People's Press* printed a letter titled "N.C. Troops in the Mountains," dated September 22, from one of Hoke's troopers posted at Trap Hill in Wilkes County, describing how the deserter hunt was coming along. He reported that during his first foray against the area deserters, they "ambushed us in the mountain gorges and fired at us but no one was hit.... We have caught some 80 or more deserters and conscripts; but the mountains are full of them and it is impossible to catch them as they can move from mountain to mountain as we approach.— Gen. Hoke has been with us for a week. He had great success in Yadkin — nearly all the deserters and conscripts came in. The country there is more level, and hence they are not so safe." He noted that troops caught several of the deserter leaders, including a man by the name of Smoot and another named Brewer. This may have been Granville Smoot, a leader — along with John Quincy Adams Bryan — of the Trap Hill insurrectionists.

A few days later, a citizen reported that Hoke had ordered his troops to Wilkesboro to give the citizens of Trap Hill time "to reflect & Come in & behave themselves." If they refused, the general vowed to go back and "sweep the Country." Feeling compassion for the outliers and their families, the writer noted that the crops in the Trap Hill community "were very poor ... I understand & what they make will be destroyed I fear; & what they are to do for provisions next winter and spring I do not know[.]"[62] According to one report, Confederate troops plundered and harassed the Trap Hill community: "The ladies of Wilkes County complain that a detachment of troops in the neighborhood of Trap Hill, instead of arresting deserters in a proper way, are plundering houses, taking stock, grain, and provisions from women and children, getting drunk, fiddling, dancing, etc." In addition, a group of soldiers rustled thirty-five to forty-five cattle from Wilkes to neighboring Ashe County, where they sold them and kept the money.[63] Another observer complained: "There has been a great deal of property destroyed or taken in Wilkes by the troops employed to catch deserters, such as horses, saddles, wagons, work steers, etc. Horses have been taken from helpless women, and they have to carry their corn on their hips to mill."[64]

Calvin Cowles's brother Josiah, a merchant and militia officer who lived in Hamptonville in southwestern Yadkin County, advised Calvin to be moderate in expressing his views about the events then transpiring in the area. He warned, "There is great trouble in store for all of us and it is best for every one to preserve silence on the political affairs of the day.... The guard [are] in heavy force and are determine to go to Trap Hill & arrest every rebel to the southern cause take every sympathizer that they can get hold of. Should they succeed in getting hold of any of the leaders they will be hung like dogs this is no idle talk they will be subjected to the severest treatment[.]" He cautioned his brother "to be very careful of what you say[.] [Y]ou have enemies that will exagerate & expose you ... & seize upon any word you utter & report it."[65]

Josiah's fear that political proscription would follow the military repression proved well founded. Two weeks later, Calvin wrote from Wilkesboro, "arrests of citizens as well as conscripts and deserters is of daily occurrence in the co. [county]."[66] Soldiers arrested Cowles "upon the representations of my old enemies [that is, the Democrats] but am allowed the freedom of the town[.]"[67] They charged him with "selling powder to deserters, managing Union meetings & disloyalty ... [and] for not performing Home Guard service!" Authorities soon dropped all the charges. Disgusted, Cowles exclaimed, "Why not arrest everybody?" In a fit of anger, he wrote Governor Vance a letter in which he revealed just what a deep role old political animosities played in dividing the people into hostile camps during the war:

Today a part of our population with guns in hand are hunting up another portion and the Military from our own & from our sister states are scouring our Valley & our Mountains & arresting not deserters and Conscripts alone but many of those very old men who delighted to vote for you & to listen to your speeches [that is, old line Whigs who had become militant Unionists]. Yes Governor we have a "Castle Thunder" in our once quiet little village and it is [word unintelligible] to you that I acknowledge the fact that I have been an inmate of it. I was arrested at the instance of old political enemies to gratify old political animosities. Many of the same old "squad" are still here who used to denounce us all as unsound who wouldn't vote for & with them & they are true to their instincts — they never forgive nor forget nor do they neglect an opportunity to vent their spite especially ... when they can use an organized force for the purpose & shirk the responsibility. So much for our harmony — now as to our safety — it is nowhere — every man should make his will & prepare to die for who can tell what a day may bring forth.[68]

During the peace movement, activists passed resolutions at several peace meetings in the Quaker Belt decrying the "arbitrary" arrests of citizens by the military and the incarceration of the victims in military prisons without charges. For example, at a Guilford County meeting, protesters resolved that "we look upon the proceedings at the Confederate prison in Salisbury, as a stain upon our good old State — the conduct practiced there finding a parallel only in a French Bastile or a Spanish Inquisition."[69] Authorities sent many of the ringleaders of the resistance captured by General Hoke's men to Castle Thunder prison in Richmond, including several men military officers promised could return to their companies in the army if they voluntarily surrendered.[70] After the war, John Pool — Republican senator and supporter of Radical Reconstruction — reflected on the harsh treatment meted out to Unionists in North Carolina by state and national authorities who arrested them and sent them to prison in Richmond, Salisbury, and other locations. The Confederacy established the prison at Salisbury, noted Pool, to "overawe the struggling Union sentiment of our people." Salisbury became the scene "of horrors, at the recollection of which the blood still runs cold.— Hundreds of our private citizens, exempt from conscription, were there, and at Castle Thunder in Richmond, incarcerated upon mere suspicion of Unionism, and met their death by starvation and other indescribable cruelties."[71]

General Hoke established his headquarters at Wilkesboro and deployed his troops mainly in Wilkes and Yadkin counties, but he often ordered detachments into the surrounding counties.[72] The North Carolina adjutant general ordered the Home Guard battalions in all the area counties to support Hoke's troops. He organized the Home Guards of Iredell and Alexander counties into a regiment under the able command of Colonel S.A. Sharpe of Statesville, the seat of Iredell County.[73] Colonel Sharpe established his headquarters in northern Iredell at Fraley's and from there fanned his 300 troops into southern Wilkes (south of the Yadkin River), and into northern Alexander County. Over the next four months his troops, Home Guard battalions in other counties, and General Hoke's troops scoured the Quaker Belt and captured many, perhaps most, of the insurgents and their leaders.[74]

A trooper assigned to the Fifty-sixth Regiment hunting deserters in the Wilkesboro area wrote the editor of the Fayetteville *Observer* on October 10: "We will send off about 130 deserters and conscripts to-morrow, which will make over 700. They have come in and surrendered themselves by dozens. 32 reported in one day."[75] On October 21, a Confederate officer reported that troops captured and sent into the ranks to date more than 500 deserters and draft-dodgers from Wilkes County alone.[76] An enterprising enrolling officer in Forsyth

County — a Captain D. Barrow — captured 150 deserters and draft-dodgers in October and sent them back to the army.[77] The next month, General Hoke claimed that his troops captured and returned 3,000 deserters and draft-dodgers to the ranks, and that they induced many others to return voluntarily. The Twenty-First Regiment North Carolina Troops, having been under the command of General Hoke in the state for over two months hunting deserters, embarked from High Point for Richmond on November 19. A regimental officer boasted that his men "have returned to the service at least five deserters or recusant conscripts to each man in the regiment."[78] Near the end of November, Hoke told a friend "Wilkes is now the truest and most loyal county in the State."[79]

General Hoke, like so many others who hunted deserters and draft-dodgers in the Quaker Belt both before and after his foray into the area, was unduly optimistic about his successes. For example, on November 16, a Wilkes County citizen wrote Governor Vance complaining that there were "no less than 150" deserters and draft-dodgers "still in this co. [county]."[80] S.E. Love was a member of a detail left behind to hunt the few "tories" remaining in the Wilkes area after the majority of Hoke's troops had departed. On November 26, he wrote his father of his successes as a hunter: "We killed one man yesterday he was in the Wader and started to run he was Shot thru the head his name was Blackburn thare Was 4 of them in a gang We got them all We Still git a few of them."[81]

On December 8, commanders ordered the Wilkes County Home Guards into the field against deserters; a company of Confederate troops joined them on the 16th.[82] On January 4, 1864, Colonel Faison wrote, "The deserters of Wilkes ... killed one of [my] men last week & wounded one or two of the home guard." Faison, who was in Randolph County at the time, wrote Vance that he was sending a full company back to Wilkes to aid the fifty beleaguered troops still operating there. To his chagrin, the colonel noted, "the deserters sent from Wilkes were rapidly returning [home] thinking our force withdrawn."[83] Evidently, General Hoke's lengthy effort to quash the insurgents in the Wilkes area enjoyed only a brief and limited success.

The Deserter Hunt in the Randolph Area

General Hoke, upon arriving in the Quaker Belt, established two foci of operations: one centering in Wilkes County under his command, and the other one in the Randolph County area directed by Colonel Faison. General Hoke soon ordered Colonel Faison and the Fifty-sixth Regiment out of Randolph into the Wilkes theatre of operations. He did this because the skirmish at Fraley's in Iredell County on September 8 led him to believe that a full-scale battle with the deserter army commanded by John Q.A. Bryan and Granville Smoot was imminent, and that Faison's troops would be necessary to assure Confederate success.[84] Consequently, the loyal citizens in the Randolph area had to depend on themselves to contain the insurrectionists for a while longer. One observer noted that the Randolph County militia made an inglorious attempt to intimidate the deserters at this time. They placed "small squads in ambush on roads frequented by the avowed deserters ... [to] shoot them down. They succeeded in shooting down three of them — two killed — one seriously wounded. The men shot were not leaders and were shot from ambush, the whole of the militia running immediately after they fired."[85]

On October 3, the adjutant general, confident that he had his troops sufficiently organized and armed, ordered the Home Guard battalions in Chatham, Moore, Montgomery, and Randolph counties into the field after the deserters and draft-dodgers that were "in a state of insurrection against the laws."[86] An example of the depredations suffered by loyalists at this time occurred at Fair Haven in Moore County. A band of "vile outlaws, deserters and cowardly conscripts" burned the barn and schoolhouse of Harris Tysor, destroying most of his winter feed for his livestock and stealing most of the leather from his tannery.[87] Despite the threat imposed by marauding deserters, within two weeks the guardsmen muted the uprising so well that the adjutant general complimented their commander for restoring order in the area.[88]

When General Hoke left the state on November 19 with his Twenty-first Regiment to return to duty in Virginia, he left Colonel Faison with his Fifty-sixth Regiment in North Carolina to continue the deserter hunt, especially in the Randolph County area. Prior to Colonel Faison's return to the Randolph area from Wilkes County, one of his officers advised "the friends of the misguided men in parts of Chatham, Randolph and Moore to come in. Gen. Hoke will soon be there and no man caught with arms in his hands will be suffered to live.... These men may suppose that ... they are doomed to execution if they come in, and so may as well remain in the woods. But the 700 taken in Wilksboro have not been executed, neither will they be, except the ring leaders and hardened villans, who amount to perhaps one in a hundred."[89]

By the second week in December, Colonel Faison had established his headquarters in Asheboro with his troops scattered over Randolph and the adjoining counties searching for outliers. He complained that the deserters "had numerous friends which makes it more difficult to catch them."[90] By mid–January 1864, a detachment of the colonel's men had established a base at Christian Union on the Randolph-Moore border hunting deserters in conjunction with the Moore County Home Guards.[91] During the winter of 1863–1864, another force of Confederate troops under Captain N.A. Ramsey, a native of Chatham County, searched for outliers in the Chatham-Moore area. He served under the orders of General William Henry Chase Whiting, headquartered in the southeastern part of the state.[92] In this hunt, Ramsey reported that his company of men of the Sixty-first North Carolina Regiment "scoured" the woods and "cleared up" a "lawless gang of marauders," an action that resulted in the capture of over one hundred deserters. He boasted that his troops "shot to death" the "two leading spirits of the gang" in a skirmish.[93] Faison's and Ramsey's forces totaled some 1,000 then-active troops hunting dissidents in the Randolph, Chatham, Moore county area.[94]

A Confederate soldier taking part in this campaign commented in a letter to his brother about the "claver" outliers there: "I hav left Weldon and come to the Co[mpany]. It is in Randolph County NC taking up dissersters but we don't get many here[.] [T]hey ar too Smart for us.... This is the poreest country I ever Saw. the people is all pore but vary claver to us. aheep of them lying out."[95] In neighboring Guilford County, "incendiaries" prowled the countryside. In the third week in December, arsonists torched the barn of Sheriff Boon. The sheriff lost his barn and all its contents, worth about four thousand dollars.[96] In adjoining Alamance County, "supposed" incendiaries burned the "extensive foundry and machine shops of Dixon, Albright, & Co., Snow Camp, N.C. ... to the ground.... Loss heavy. No insurance."[97]

A Confederate force other than Faison's or Ramsey's operated in the Randolph area at this time. From November 1863 to March 1864, a company of Mallett's Battalion maintained a camp at Bethel Methodist Church in Alamance County—called Camp Bethel— from which they hunted deserters in the eastern Quaker Belt. (Bethel was located about two miles northeast of the Quaker settlement of Snow Camp.) A hunter stationed there expressed regret at the way the troops were treating the families of deserters: "we have a heap of fun[.] [T]he wimans give us sass som times a bout ther sons[.] [I] am sorry for them[,]" He continued: "we press ever thing we eat[.] [W]e take it from disurtors wher tha live[.] [I] dont think it is rite[.]"[98] A month later he reported to his wife: "I git plenty to eat[.] [W]e go to disurtors houses and make them cook for us[.] [T]he folks is good round hear[.] Jane it makes me sorry for som of the folks[.] [T]ha [the soldiers] take what tha want[.]"[99] In March 1864, he noted that Colonel Mallett stated that there were 600 deserters to apprehend; he ordered his troops to remain in the field until they caught all of them.[100] In April, the hunter recorded that some of the companies headquartered at Bethel ranged as far afield as Moore County seeking deserters, and that the troops caught more of them than ever.[101]

During October, November, and December, commanders ordered the Davidson County Home Guards into the field to hunt deserters and conscripts. Troops from the Twenty-first, Forty-second, Forty-ninth, and Fifty-sixth North Carolina Regiments assisted them.[102] A soldier searching for outliers in Silver Valley, a rural community on the Randolph-Davidson border, informed his brother in November that "nearly all" the inhabitants were "union people" and "half of them are deserters[.]"[103] Captain John W. Graham, son of former Whig governor William A. Graham, commanded a detachment of troops searching out deserters in the lower Davidson County community of Healing Springs in late November.[104] In a letter to his father, he noted that a company of the Twenty-first Regiment, which left the area when he arrived, engaged in "indiscriminate plunder" both against deserters' families and against "good citizens." The deserters and draft-dodgers in Davidson County, reported Graham, though very numerous, were largely inoffensive. All the "intelligent people" in Davidson, he claimed, "rejoice at our success in catching deserters, as the Randolph lawlessness was beginning to spread in this County." Randolph, Moore, and Montgomery counties, lamented the captain, "are in a deplorable condition. No loyal man, I understand, can live there unless troops shall soon be sent them."[105] Graham complained that his troops had little chance of capturing deserters in the woods. "The only way to get them," he asserted, "is to seize their property and keep it until they surrender." Experience taught him that "by pressing a horse ... a man who has not been seen or heard of by his family in six months, can be produced in three hours."[106]

Captain Graham's policy of seizing deserters' property and returning it only if they surrendered—as in the case of Lieutenant Pugh—got him into trouble with Governor Vance, who demanded that his men cease their "depredations" upon his citizens and restore property taken from them. The captain defended his seizure of deserters' property as a prerequisite to the capture of outliers. "If after the explanations I have given," retorted Graham, "I am still required to restore every thing that I hold in pawn over these deserters, and to confine my men simply to hunting, I think my occupation will be gone, and would respectfully ask to be relieved from duty of that kind."[107]

The Internal War Turns Vicious

Between September 1863 and February 1864, a vicious inner civil war raged across the Quaker Belt as Confederate hunters scoured the area. The conflict between the hunters and deserters resulted in the assault, injury, death, or torture of hundreds of people. Troops and outliers burned, tore down, or otherwise damaged an untold number of homes and barns and other properties, and stole or destroyed household items, meats stored in smokehouses, and crops in the field. Hunger stalked the land due to the pillaging and short crops.

During the closing months of 1863, Alexander K. Pearce[108] sent Bryan Tyson two letters that presented a vivid account of the internal war in the Quaker Belt. The military incarcerated Pearce, a prisoner of war, in the Old Capitol Prison in Washington, D.C. He had recently deserted from the Confederate army and would soon join the Union forces. The twenty-one-year-old Pearce grew up in Brower's Mills (Bryan Tyson's home community) in southeastern Randolph County. His letters offer rare insight into the mind, emotions, and point of view of the rank-and-file militant Unionists in the Quaker Belt. They describe in poignant detail the pro–Union dissidents' determined resistance to Hoke's troops in the fall of 1863. On November 25, Pearce wrote Tyson of the growing spirit of reunionism in the Randolph area:

> Ther is more union in Randolph then ther was when the war commesed.... The union is not forgotten and all ar waiting for the yankees to come. if they would go through N.C. I believe they would get more men then [Jefferson] Davis has. ther are many lying out to keep from fighting.... Every time the union army whips it make the union [sentiment] that much more in creasing. about the time of the Getysburg battle nearly all the people was union. if a man said he was union his life was threatened and nearly all the men was union but ther was men sent from the army [Hoke's troops] to quell this union sentiments.... But the good old union men stand firm. they believe the union will [be] reestablesed and they have a love for the stars and strips. often have I heard them say how butiful it would be to see the old flag once more floting in the air[109] [punctuation added].

Pearce told Tyson that he did not hear much about his book, *A Ray of Light*, in the army, "as the authoritys would not let them pass through ... but the people at home was glad to get them[.] [A]ll the union people said that all was correct and every one would read them and try to convince others that you was right but the strong cecesh would not believe them and would say you were a traitor to your country[.]"[110] Pearce added: "I left home with the intention of joining the union for I did not believe that the rebellion was right nor I never did and my friends told me to leave [that is, desert] the first chance I got so the first chance I left[.]"[111]

Pearce wrote Tyson another letter that is remarkable for its description of the killing of several Unionists by loyal citizens and soldiers in the Randolph area, and for its passionately partisan point of view:

> Neill McDonnold was killed ... by a party of secesh and soldiers. it was because he was working for the union cause and as he had but one arm he would be nothing lost and they thought it would stop the union cause but alas they were mistaken. the more they kill the more union ther was. John Garner was shot in the arm so that he lost the benifit of it. this was for nothing because he was aiding in the union cause. Another horible murder was commited in Chatham. one Phillips was shot while traveling along the road ... because he was aiding in the union cause.... Another horable act was commited near Ashboro in Randolph by shooting an old

grey headed man. this was for nothing but because he was a union man and would not yield to the cecesh party. Another murder was commited at Ashboro. the man executed was Benjamin Northens. he was well thought of by the union party as he was on[e] that said what he saw would do the union good and because he had much influence over the people he was killed.... Some of them said just befor being killed that they were dying in a good cause that they had rather die at home than to die in the Rebel cause. thes men was fighting for the union cause. more than these would have been [killed] if the union [men] had not been so strong. often would they take a man to kill him but the union men would go and take [rescue] him by force of arms. in one of these actions there was one Rebel officer killed[112] [punctuation added].

According to Pearce, the disloyal reunionist element sponsored the peace meetings held in the Randolph area. "Ther has been many union meetings held in Randolph and adjoining countys and if they could only have help they would soon put down this Rebelion."[113] In conclusion, Pearce warned of a day of reckoning when the "cecech" would pay for their misdeeds committed against the Union men. "When I left home all most all the cecesh," reported Pearce, "said that they were whiped and even I heard some say that they never had been cecesh but alas it is Recorded ther if the union caus succeeds wich ther is no doubt in my mind they will be remembered by the union."[114] Because he believed that it was his duty to "help defen our flag and demolish Slavery," Pearce joined the Union army. Reflecting the strong antislavery influences that he had been exposed to since childhood, Pearce wrote that slavery was "an evile thing, freedom to all man kind, and god will never allow it, let the country be free and united."[115]

The exploits of two men, Peter Garner and Adam Brewer, provide another example of the bitterness engendered in the Quaker Belt between the "secech" and the militant Unionists and outliers. Both men were "professional hunters," well versed in the "philosophy of hunting." Peter Garner, a native of southeastern Randolph, was a conscript. The army detailed him from Mallett's Battalion to hunt deserters. Adam Brewer operated a mill in the Brower's Mills community. He was over the draft age, but having been "completely broken up by ... robbers," he, in revenge, zealously supported the military in their efforts to capture outliers.[116] As one observer put it, "This man Brewer does not belong to the servis. this is just a voluntary act to hunt down his neighbors and kill them."[117] Often acting together, Brewer and Garner served as guides to Confederate troops detailed to hunt deserters. In a few instances, they commanded small detachments of troops on their own.

An eight-page pamphlet published in the North recounted an incident involving Adam Brewer. The author wrote the pamphlet as a Republican propaganda tract to report in lurid detail the "cruelties and atrocities" perpetrated by Confederate troops upon loyal Unionists in the South. Bryan Tyson provided the information on events in North Carolina for the publication. Setting the incident in a broad perspective, the author reported:

> After the battle of Gettysburg, the Unionists of North Carolina began to speak more freely, and revolt was feared; in consequence, a regiment of soldiers was sent to Randolph County to preserve order. The kind of order that was preserved may be known by the following atrocity, one of many committed upon the unprotected loyalists of that region: These soldiers decoyed a one-armed man [Neil McDonald], under pretense of employing him as a guide, into a piece of woodland, where his body was found several days after, completely riddled with bullets; he was heard a long distance begging and imploring for his life. From the marks of blood and footprints, it was believed that he was compelled to run around his tormentors, they shooting at him as he ran to see how many times they [could] hit and not kill him.[118]

Alexander K. Pearce gave an interesting sidelight on this incident in a letter to Bryan Tyson. Pearce said that the troops killed McDonald more because of his "character" than for his political loyalties. Had he been an honest man, noted Pearce, McDonald might still be alive.[119] Pearce's claim that McDonald died because he was dishonest stands in marked contrast to his earlier claim that a "party of secesh and soldiers" killed him "because he was working for the Union cause." Pearce's insight into the matter indicates that some of the atrocities perpetrated by loyal Confederates and militant Unionists alike might have been acts to avenge personal grudges. Pearce confirmed that Adam Brewer and a party of soldiers killed McDonald. According to Pearce, Brewer and his detail of hunters were drunk when they killed McDonald, which perhaps best explains their unusually cruel behavior.[120] Brewer, a bootlegger, forfeited a $3,000 bond for not appearing at his trial at the county court in May 1864, for illegally distilling liquor.[121]

In another incident, Adam Brewer killed a draft-dodger named George Moore described as "a poore man with a large family [who] was conscripted ... and did not choose to go to the war and took [to] the thicket."[122] Thomas W. Ritter, a member of the House of Commons from Moore County and a covert reunionist, described to Governor Vance the ambushing of George Moore and two other outliers, all of whom were unarmed. "Brewer and a man by the name of Peter garner sliped up to Moore and two others and without saying a word presented and fired killing Moore and wounding one of the others."[123] Ritter wrote Vance another letter in which he described several other atrocities committed by Adam Brewer. In one instance, Brewer's men took a young man under the draft age from his home. The boy's mother and several young girls followed the troops.

> The men commenced cursing ... them and told them they had come ... to get the boy to run-away[.] [O]ne of the young ladis spoke and told them they had not come for no such thing. Adam Brewer the randolph man I spoke of ... told the other men to form round her and god dam her; they would take her along. they formed a round her and she told them not to tuch her.... They was ordered ... to put on their Bayonets which was done and one made at her as if he was going to run it through her frighting her very much[.] She made an attempt to climb over the fence to get away and ... one of them caught her by her Dress and attempted to pull her back and tore her Dress very bad.... [She] got loos and run off and Adam Brewer ordered them to shoot her where upon one cocked his gun and aimed as if he was going to shoot but did not, Brewer holowing shoot all the time.

An indignant Ritter added: "this young lady is of a respectable family as any in the country[.] Governor such conduct is two bad and ought not to be allowed[.] [L]et them go ahead and arrest the deserters and conscripts if they can and not destroy property and carry off horses and other property from the poore women who are about to starve any how and to be treating women in such style. The good people are looking to you for protection."

The squad of troops that Brewer led in this incident, Ritter continued, belonged to Captain Ramsey's company. Just a few days before, one of Ramsey's men "shot a young man and kiled him dead who was not a conscript was only seventeen years old." Ritter goaded the governor: "You ought to send an order here to have him [Adam Brewer] arrested and brought to Justice[.] The people are madning at such treatment and say they canot put up with it much longer."[124] Governor Vance, who apparently himself was "madning" from the many complaints received from the victims of military abuse, told Ritter that it "is the duty of the civil magistrates to have men arrested who violate the law in this way." Vance admonished the complainer: "I cannot be Gov[,] Justice of the Peace and Constable at the same time."[125]

Another incident that caused considerable controversy involved the killing of two outliers by some of Captain Ramsey's men.[126] They were Enoch Davis[127] and a man named Brewer. The army insisted that troops shot the captives while trying to escape, but friends of the victims, though admitting the men were guilty of plundering, claimed that the troops deliberately murdered them. Arguing on behalf of the victims' friends, Thomas W. Ritter wrote Vance: "As for their being shot trying to escape from the guard that I do not think is so[.] [T]hey certainly were parted from the other two conscripts that were taken at the same time and carried a different road to the camp and before they got to the camp they[,] Davis and Brewer[,] were parted and found shot and were in fact tied when found and no doubt were seperated on purpose to be shot. Davis I suppose was shot by a log as if he was setting on the log when shot and fell over by the side of the log with his brains shot out."[128] The commander of the Moore County Home Guard Battalion, describing Brewer and Davis as "ring leaders of the worst band of robbers and plunderers that ever infected any community," stoutly denied that his men wantonly murdered them. Alleging that he gathered testimony from a "reliable" witness who was a soldier in the squad that shot the men, the commander insisted that the two men ran, and the soldiers killed them only because they were trying to escape.[129] Brewer and Davis were but two of a number of outliers in Moore County murdered by overzealous and vengeful hunters. Offering proof that the "hunters" had a successful season in the Moore-Randolph area in late 1863, the Fayetteville *Observer* reported on December 21 that "a subscriber writing from Moore County, mentions that a deserter was shot dead on last Tuesday night, (resisting, of course) and that he is the sixth notorious robber that has been executed near there."

In late 1864, Bryan Tyson received word that dissidents shot both Adam Brewer and Peter Garner.[130] Brewer likely survived, for in the spring of 1866 the Randolph Superior Court indicted someone by his name for the murder of one George Moon.[131] A band of deserters, however, killed Peter Garner one morning while he crossed a stream on a foot log on the way to some fish traps. The book *Hoot Owls, Honeysuckle and Halleluyah* by C. Waldo Cox gives an absorbing account of this incident and the events that led up to it. Mr. Cox's father was one of the gang that assassinated Garner.[132] The book offers a sympathetic description of the life of the outliers in Randolph County during the war.

The Capture and Murder of Bill Owens

While Peter Garner and Adam Brewer and their ilk terrorized outliers in the Randolph-Moore area, their counterpart, Bill Owens and his band of pro–Union advocates, paid the secessionists back in kind. On February 17, 1864, an event of great significance in this internal war between the reunionists and the "sesech" occurred when the Owens gang went to the residence of Pleasant Simons in Montgomery County and broke into his smokehouse. Since early 1863, the Owens gang forced Simons — a silversmith and ardent pro–Confederate — to repair guns in his workshop that they stole from area secessionists. Pushed to the brink by the continual harassment of the Owens gang, Simons and a man named Jacob Sanders fired into the group of marauders, wounding two of them, including their leader Bill Owens, before the deserters gunned them down. Both Simons and Sanders were over sixty years of age.[133] Describing the battle scene, one witness wrote: "The yard was strewn with human gore: it stood in some places in puddles where the men lay." As the deserters left, they affirmed their Unionist proclivities by denouncing their victims as "a d — d set of secessionists" who had "sent their sons to the war."[134]

In 1864, legal authorities charged William Owens, Murphy Owens, Riley Cagle, and John Latham with the murders of Jacob Sanders and Pleasant Simons. In court cases after the war, Riley Cagle confessed to shooting Pleasant Simons. Before the war, Cagle worked for Simons. J.M. Leach, lawyer for Murphy Owens, identified John Latham as the shooter of Jacob Sanders.[135] Court authorities tried and convicted Murphy Owens for the murder of Pleasant Simmons, for which he received a pardon from Governor Holden.[136] They then tried him for the slaying of Jacob Saunders. Again, Holden pardoned Owens. Owens's lawyer, in his petition to the governor for a pardon for his client's homicide of Saunders, noted that during the war, Murphy Owens, a self-proclaimed Union man, refused to serve in the Home Guards.[137] Jacob Saunders, charged the attorney,

> was the sole cause of all the trouble & the deaths that ensued, for he rushed out without any provocation, or any authority from Simmons, the proprietor of the house, reached out, & fired on the crowd, which was *returned*, (*not by Murphy Owens* for he was on the other side of [the] house leaving) but by Latham (since killed) — Mr Saunders was a respectable man, but was as is every where in Montgomery Known — a *bitter desperate Secessionist*, & consequently for exterminating all deserters, & it was this feeling, doubtless that prompted him to the daring desperate act, that resulted unfortunately in his death — he having commenced the dreadful affray.[138]

About two months after the shootout at Simons's the sheriff of Randolph, with a posse composed of men from Asheboro, captured Bill Owens at a hideout in the southeastern part of the county. Peter Garner found the deserter leader in the woods near the outlier's camp with his wife. Owens could not elude the posse because of his wound. The sheriff incarcerated the luckless deserter chief in the county jail in Asheboro.[139]

The sheriff discovered the location of Owens's hideout through the exertions of Alfred Pike, one of his deputies.[140] In September, Thomas Settle, a state solicitor and wealthy planter from Rockingham County, wrote Governor Vance about the torture of Bill Owens's wife by troops led by Colonel Alfred Pike. Settle related that "Pike and others jerked Owens wife down by the hair, dragged her a short distance to a fence, laid her on her back and placed her thumbs under the corner of a heavy fence, and tortured her for some time, in order to make her disclose the whereabouts of her husband."[141] On October 4 Settle wrote Vance that while in Asheboro making inquiries about the alleged torture of Owens' wife, Colonel Alfred Pike came to him saying that he need look no further for witnesses, for he would give him the facts himself. Pike proceeded to give Settle a statement of the event that was remarkable for its candor. It provides a singular glimpse into the brutal acts and feelings engendered by the inner civil war in the Quaker Belt:

> I went with my squad to Owins spring where his wife was washing and inquired of her as to Owens whereabouts, she said he was dead and buried, I told her that she must show us the grave, she thereupon began to curse us and abuse us for every thing that was bad, Some of my men told me that if I would hand her over to them they would or could make her tell, I told her to go some twenty steps apart with them, she seized up in her arm her infant not twelve

months old and swore she would not go — I slaped her Jaws till she put down her baby and went with them, they tied her thumbs together behind her back and suspended her with a cord tied to her two thumbs thus fastened behind her to a limb so that her toes could just touch the ground, after remaining in this position a while she said her husband was not dead and that if they would let her down she would tell all she knew, I went up just then and I think she told some truth, but after awhile I thought she commenced lying again and I with another man (one of my squad) took her off some fifty yards to a fence and put her thumbs under a corner of the fence, She soon became quiet and behaved very respectfully, the rails were flat and not sharp between which I placed her thumbs, I don't think she was hurt bad.

Pike, apparently feeling that circumstances warranted such conduct, offered no apologies. He continued: "This is all I have done sir, and now, if I have not the right to treat Bill Owens, his wife and the like in this manner I want to know it, and I will go to the Yankees or any where else before I will live in a country in which I cannot treat such people in this manner."[142]

The reports on Bill Owens remained blank for about five months after his capture. Then, in early September, a source from Moore County revealed a remarkable turn of events when he reported on the success of a deserter hunt. "We learn that Capt. Owens, who has been a sort of a leader among the deserters, is now doing good service, bringing in three and four of his party at a time. In one instance, he is said to have brought two in, in irons. Some of the prisoners are expected to arrive here to-morrow. Moore county will soon be rid of deserters."[143] It is not clear whether the "Capt. Owens" referred to above was the deserter leader William Owens. It is possible that he was a relative, as the Owens name was common in the area at that time. If he were the famous deserter leader captured in April 1864, one must wonder how his captors induced him to turn traitor to his own men. On September 29, the Greensboro *Patriot* reported that the sheriff, due to a change of venue, moved Bill Owens — "that abandoned and desperate outlaw, housebreaker, burner and highway robber,"— from the Randolph jail to the one in Pittsboro, the seat of neighboring Chatham County.[144]

If Bill Owens did betray his men and the militant Unionists' cause, it did him little good. On April 5, 1865, the Raleigh *Weekly Conservative* reported that "Bill Owens, the notorious deserter, house burner, murderer, etc, who some time since moved his trial to Chatham Superior Court, was taken from the jail of that county on Wednesday night the 22d instant, by a party of persons unknown to the jailor, and shot to death — four balls penetrating his body." The mob took Owens from the jail, "carried him some half mile from town [Pittsboro], and shot him," because "the Judge presiding declined to try the case." The imminent approach of Union troops under Sherman may have precipitated the judge's tepidness. Occupying Federals likely would have treated harshly a Confederate judge who tried and sentenced to death a noted Unionist and leader in the Heroes of America.

History has not been kind to William Owens. All that we know of him comes from the pens of his enemies who feared and hated him. There are no legends, songs, or poems keeping alive the memory of him and his Red String band of Heroes and their bold deeds on behalf of the Union cause. During the last three years of the war, newspaper accounts of his actions made the name William Owens well known across the state. Today no one but a few historians has ever heard of him. Was he an American hero who sacrificed his family, his property, and his life on the altar of his country — the United States of America?

Alternatively, was he the villainous murderer, house burner, and thief as depicted by his secessionist enemies?

William Holden mentioned Bill Owens in his newspaper about a year after the war ended. In an article entitled "General Amnesty in this State," Holden complained that court officials charged the Union people across North Carolina in county and state courts for acts of murder, arson, and robbery committed by them during the war, while they gave a pass to former loyal Confederates guilty of similar crimes. He noted that Vance and Davis forces hunted and brutalized hundreds of Union men, women, children, and elderly persons throughout the war. Today, these same men roam free in the state. As an example, he noted that the men who tortured William Owens's wife to make her tell where her husband was hiding were yet unpunished for their crime. Then the editor asked, "Who murdered Bill Owens? Are there no grand juries in Randolph County?" It appears not, for the men who murdered Owens remain anonymous to this day.[145] The capture of their leader did not stop the depredations of the deserters and draft-dodgers in the Randolph area upon the loyal element. For example, on May 23, 1864, Confederate authorities ordered a company of troops to "proceed ... to any convenient point in Moore or Randolph Co's for the purpose of arresting deserters and recusant conscripts." Commanders ordered the soldiers to act in conjunction with the Home Guards of the respective counties.[146]

More Depredations by Confederate and State Troops

Upon the resignation of Shubal G. Worth in December 1863, the adjutant general appointed Isaac H. Foust commander of Randolph County's Fifth Home Guard Battalion. In February 1864, Foust wrote Vance, "I conclud a line giving account of quiet in the most abused county in the state which if not consoling would at least not be considered boring."[147] Although, as Foust claimed, "quiet reigns in Randolph," peace proved costly. Both Colonel Faison's troops and the Raleigh Guards lived "on the country without compensation to our people." He continued: "While they professed to live on the friends and those aiding the deserters, they were often from improper motions misled and deceived."[148] The troops, Foust complained, "were doing no good, or scarcely any, in picking up deserters and giving by their conduct a feeling of hatred and hostility to the Government on the part of the community that is damaging to the cause we profess to be engaged in."[149] In his letter to the governor, Foust implied that he believed that the Confederacy had an ulterior motive in detailing whole regiments of troops to hunt deserters in disaffected districts. By exercising their right of impressment of provisions, fodder, horses, and wagons, the troops could not only save the Confederate government the expense of feeding them, they could also, to a great extent, clothe and equip themselves.[150]

Foust included with his letter to Vance an affidavit sworn to by Samuel Allen of Randolph County. Allen claimed that Sergeant James Pounds of Mallet's Battalion, with seven or eight men, came to his house and told him that they wanted to buy some beef. Allen replied that he had none for sale. Thereupon, Sergeant Pounds stated that he had orders to take provisions from old men who had sons lying out. The sergeant then took one of Allen's cows and came back later to take another, in spite of the fact that Allen claimed that he had no sons lying out. The soldiers took the cattle to their camp near Franklinsville, slaughtered them, and sold the hides for two dollars per pound, realizing a profit of about eighty dollars. The foregoing, said Foust, was just "one of a multitude of similar cases to which our people are quietly submitting."[151]

A new onslaught of complaints to Governor Vance about the abuses of the military followed on the heels of Foust's criticisms. In October, a Davidson County man complained that a detail from the Forty-second Regiment North Carolina Troops not only plundered his property, "they stole chickens and other things all over, even from widows and women who had no children at all and so could not have any sons outlying. They broke into locked houses and stole things if residents were away."[152] A mother of five children, living in the Marley's Mill community near the Chatham-Randolph line, wrote that the militia arrested her husband, who was over the draft age. In addition, the troops "grievously insulted" her with indecent language. She had not heard from her husband in over two weeks.[153]

The wife of an outlier reported from the lower part of Davidson County:

> When my husban had to leav the house he left but little to go upon and i hav three little children to Werke for and i have Werk[ed] for ever thing that i have to eat and Ware and these details has ... taken ever mouth[ful] ... i have got to eat. they have tuck the last hog i had ... wich i ... fed every greain of corn i have got.... They took up My Clothing and tuck My Molases and pord them over the flore and told me they dident Want to ketch all the deserters and conscripts So they couldant git to Stay [at home and out of the army] and What they ketch thay Would pot agard around them So they Could git away.... It ant only Me they air takeing from it is every body. they take the Women[s'] horses out of the plows and Wriding them and beeting them Scanles and destroying every thing they can lay hans up on[.] [T]hese is from the regment NC Troops. pleas answer this and tell me what to do.[154]

Clarinda Hulin and her husband, Nelson, lived on a farm in Montgomery County. She failed to inform the governor in her letter that she belonged to a family of ardently anti–Confederate Wesleyan Methodist abolitionists.[155]

As the year ended and the new year began, the governor received several other letters complaining of abuse by military authorities. In a letter from Davidson County, a man reported that soldiers took his mare and promised to return it if a boy "bound" to him surrendered. The correspondent wrote Vance: "I donte have Any controle over him more ... than Any other man and I want you to Rite to me ... and Let me know how I shall procede to git my Beast."[156] An old man who had a son under the draft age wrote the governor of the abuse he suffered at the hands of the hunters. A detail of "half drunk" militia officers came by his house, tied up him and his son, threatened them, and then "put a roap ... round my neck and swung me up clear of the ground until I was insensible."[157] A woman writing from Jamestown in Guilford County complained to the Governor that a squad of soldiers "entered the house of a respectable honorable woman whose husband is absent, one night this week—searched her house—robbed her smokehouse & set fire to hay in her barn."[158] A man in Iredell County who had two sons in the army wrote Vance: "B.J. Monday one of the home gard went to my hous yester[day] and raised a fuss with my wife in my absence & she was compelled to defend her self with an ax.... I ... have [never] been in favor of the gard imposing on wining [women] and children[.] [T]hey burnt Elizabeth Fortners hous and I heard of some others.... James Davis of Wilkes & Lieutenant Cooly presented their guns at a Lady in Alexander County last week[.] We can not put up with Sutch mutch longer[.]"[159]

War on Women and Children

The five-month-long deserter hunt in the Quaker Belt by Confederate forces was more than a manhunt for deserters, draft-dodgers, and disloyal Unionists. It was also, as one observer put it, a "war on women & children."[160] The army and Home Guards impressed horses, cows, hogs, fodder, wagons, and other items and held them as ransom until the deserter or draft-dodger surrendered himself. This strategy usually worked, and most offenders gave themselves up to save their property so their family would not face destitution and starvation. Nevertheless, many did not. The process proved lengthy, and as the weeks and months passed, the troops stole, pillaged, or ruined most of the household furniture, farm implements, livestock, and grain of the recalcitrant outliers. Shocked at the destitution and the impending starvation of the victims of the hunters, Calvin Cowles wrote: "What is to become of the poor families whom they have despoiled — families of Deserters & outlyers — God only knows — there is no eye to pity no hand to save. Some have not a bushel of corn nor a pound of meat yet neighbor's would think it an indictable offence to furnish them with a days rations or even to aid some of these poor mothers to bury a dead child!"[161]

Confederate troops committed numerous instances of indiscriminate plunder and other outrages during their hunt in the Quaker Belt. They butchered and ate farm animals, or stole and sold them on the black market; they tore down or burned the homes of many outliers; they burned or otherwise destroyed crops growing in the field; they terrified and threatened women and children; they plundered the homes of outliers; they shot innocent men mistaken for outliers; and they illegally made liquor from impressed grain that was desperately needed by the young, the elderly, the sick, and the life-supporting farm animals.[162]

The dissidents in the Wilkes area became the victims of organized theft rings active in the Confederate army. In December 1863, General Hoke corresponded with a Dr. Hackett in Salisbury, asking the physician to be a member of a committee whose duty it would be to investigate the charges of theft and plunder committed by some of his officers and troops in Wilkes County. The general explained in the letter, "it was my custom to temporarily impress the property of deserters in order to cause them to surrender which was cared for and returned upon the presence of the absentee and in case of damage to the said property full remuneration was returned." Unfortunately, lamented Hoke, some of his men violated their power and stole the impressed property. He concluded: "I am exceedingly anxious to ascertain the names of the officers and men who have [been] acting in this manner and also that of the persons who sustained the losses in order that I may have all damages paid for."[163]

The families of dissidents whose fathers, sons, and brothers had been captured and sent back to the ranks or to prison would have starved in the winter of 1864 had not they received support from the secret Heroes of America underground organization. Many Heroes hid out in the mountains or in dug-out underground caves near their homes and evaded capture. With the departure of the majority of Hoke's troops, they emerged from hiding, returned to their families, and proceeded to plunder their loyal Confederate neighbors for food, clothing, and other necessities to sustain their families and the families of fellow Heroes who were unfortunate enough to have their menfolk captured or shot by the Confederates.[164]

The following verse memorialized the courage and suffering of the wives of militant Unionists at the hands of Confederate troops:

> Then Chiear up you union ladies bold
> For of your courige must be told
> How youv withstood abuses
> When your property theyd take
> The witty ancers you would make
> That would vanish thir rude forces[165]

The insurrection of deserters, draft-dodgers, and militant Unionists that took place in North Carolina in the summer and fall of 1863 and early winter of 1864, like the peace movement that preceded it, occurred mainly in the Quaker Belt. General Hoke's troops, along with the state Home Guards and detachments from other Confederate units — in one of the largest and longest continuous operations against dissidents by Confederate forces in the Civil War — likewise confined their exertions almost exclusively to the Quaker Belt.[166] They managed to suppress a dangerous insurrection of pro–United States sympathizers who, had they been successful, would have opted to return North Carolina to the Union.

CHAPTER SIX

The Copperhead Insurgency, Phase Two: The Convention Movement and the Gubernatorial Election of 1864

On the issuance of Governor Vance's proclamation against the peace meetings on September 8, 1863, and the sacking of Holden's newspaper office in Raleigh by a mob of Confederate troops the following day,[1] the 1863 phase of the peace movement in the Tar Heel state ended. By late December, Holden decided to rejuvenate the Peace Party and launch a drive to call a state convention to arrange a peace. As Bryan Tyson argued before him, Holden believed that only negotiations could end the war favorably for Southerners, because the Confederacy was too weak militarily to "conquer a peace." It was imperative that talks be initiated immediately, because in less than a year, the Confederacy would probably be too weak militarily to demand an honorable peace. Indeed, by then, argued Holden, most of the South would almost certainly be subjugated and under the control of Federal military governors as in Tennessee and Mississippi.[2] Since the Davis administration could not or would not negotiate a peace, then, concluded Holden, the sovereign states acting in convention together, or if necessary, in convention alone, must parley a peace.

Holden gave four reasons for calling a convention. One, a convention, being the sovereign power in the land, could demand that the Davis administration conclude a peace with the North; if Davis failed to act, the convention could override the president and Congress and negotiate a peace of its own. Two, a convention could protect the states from the excessive powers exercised by the central government exhibited in the draft laws, tithing laws, and the suspension of the writ of habeas corpus. Three, a convention with its final authority on all issues could provide valuable assistance to the central government in Richmond in carrying on the war and in making a peace. Four, a convention could prevent the extinction of slavery. Slavery existed solely on the basis of state law. Were a state government dismantled by conquest, a state convention constantly in existence would remain in power to negotiate a deal with the conquerors for the preservation of slavery.[3]

Any attempt by a number of Southern states to act in convention jointly to negotiate a peace with the United States would lead to a basic power conflict between it and the duly constituted authorities in Richmond—the president and Congress. Moreover, a move by any single Southern state to negotiate a peace with the North on its own would require the secession of that state from the Confederacy.[4] The Davis administration would have considered either option disloyal and counterrevolutionary and productive of a civil war within a civil war.[5] Despite the risks involved, Holden decided to launch a movement to call a state convention to arrange a convention of the Confederate States to parley an armistice, and negotiate a peace between the sections with the preservation of slavery a fundamental objective. His goal of safeguarding slavery indicated that Holden had reunion on the Copperhead basis in mind. On December 22, Holden wrote to a close political ally: "The future darkens, and I can see no ray of hope. It is now apparent that North-Carolina must soon look to herself. The power that made the war can alone close it — the power of the sovereign states. Our next [gubernatorial] election will turn on the question of a State Convention. You will know where to find me on such a question."[6]

As mandated by the Confederate Constitution in Article V, the conventions of three states acting together could call a convention of all the Confederate States.[7] According to Holden's understanding of states' rights political theory, individual states that created the national government were sovereign over their progeny. A state convention was the sovereign expression of a state's power. Members of a state convention took no oath of allegiance to a state or a national constitution, since they were sovereign to both. A convention of the states of a country was sovereign to the president and government of the country to which it belonged. Thus a convention of the Confederate States had the right to arrange an armistice and negotiate a peace with the enemy as it so chose. The objections of the president or congress had no standing.[8]

Governor Vance soon caught wind of Holden's plans. In January 1864, he wrote a friend of the personal anguish he was going through over the matter:

> The final plunge which I have been dreading and avoiding, that is to separate me from a large number of my political friends [that is, the Peace Conservatives] is about to be made. It is now a fixed policy of W.W. Holden and others to call a Convention in May to take N.C. back to the United States, and the agitation has already begun. Resolutions advocating this course were prepared a few days ago in the Standard office and sent to Johnston County [the home county of Dr. J.T. Leach] to be passed at a public meeting next week: and a series of meetings are to be held all over the state.
>
> For any cause now existing or likely to exist, I can never consent to this course. Never ... believing that it would be ruin alike to state and Confederacy, producing war and devastation at home, and that it would stain the name of North Carolina in infamy and make her memory a reproach among the nations.

Vance, who had a hand on the pulse of public sentiment in the state better than anyone save perhaps Holden, ended his letter on a despondent note: "Still, no great political or moral blessing ever has been or can be attained without suffering. Such is our moral Constitution, that liberty and independence can only be gathered of blood and misery sustained and fostered by devoted patriotism and heroic manhood. This requires a ... hold on the popular heart, *and our people will not pay this price* I am satisfied for their national independence! I am convinced of it."[9] Despite his misgivings about the dedication of his people to the goal of Confederate independence, Vance had by this time become committed to the war effort, a position he maintained until war's end. Thereafter, Vance adamantly opposed making any peace with the Federal government short of Confederate independence.[10] One must wonder how Civil War history would have turned out had Vance — a talented politician and leader — supported Holden and the convention movement. By January 1864 Vance must have known that the Confederacy had little chance of winning the war and that defeat would bring emancipation and a social revolution in race relations. Had he gone along with Holden and the Northern Democrats in advocating reunion on the Copperhead basis, he would have had at least a shot at saving slavery (for a while at least) and ending the devastating war. Vance also made it clear in his letter that he did not believe that the Confederate leaders in Richmond had persuaded the preponderance of the people of North Carolina to support Confederate independence. Indeed, the Confederacy collapsed due in great measure to the failure of the majority of its people to embrace Confederate nationalism.[11] Clearly, enthusiasm for Confederate sovereignty failed to take root in the Quaker Belt, where the bulk of the people directly or indirectly resisted national authority, and many, perhaps most, by mid–1863 yearned to return to the old Union.

John Gilmer, a War Conservative living in Greensboro (seat of Guilford County), wrote Vance in January that he recently conversed with a convention advocate. When asked what good a convention would do, the man replied that it would "propose the terms on which N.C. was willing to agree for peace," and would invite other Southern states "to call Conventions & come into Conference with NC etc." When asked what North Carolina should do in case Lincoln and the United States Congress were to ignore or refuse its peace overtures, the man replied that "he would have N.C. secede from the Confederacy, & then make the very best terms with Lincoln & the Congress of the U.S. that she Could." In closing, Gilmer stated the War Conservatives' main objection to the demand for a state convention: "To attempt to settle this matter by the separate action of N.C. or the separate action of N.C. & other States, will certainly end in civil war among ourselves, & make our state & condition indescribably worse."[12]

Three days after Gilmer penned his letter to Vance, Jefferson Davis expressed to the governor his concern about the reactivation of the Peace Party by Holden. Davis considered the peace movement a treasonous affair that must be "put down at any cost." Then, in a statement that verified the War Conservatives' fear that Richmond would meet any attempt by North Carolina to negotiate its own peace with the Federals with immediate and devastating military repression, Davis warned Vance: "You may count on my aid in every effort to spare your state the scenes of civil warfare which will devastate its homes if the designs of these traitors be suffered to make head [way]."[13] Despite the vocal opposition of Governor Vance and President Davis to his plans, Holden defiantly launched his convention crusade in January.

Historians of the peace movement give two main reasons why Holden decided to initiate the convention movement in January 1864: First, the election of six pro-peace men to the Confederate Congress in the fall of 1863 encouraged Holden to believe that the peace issue had the backing of a large majority of the voters in the Tar Heel State. Second, Holden hoped to ride the peace question into the state house in the 1864 gubernatorial election.[14] But two other possibilities existed. One, perhaps Holden started the convention movement in reaction to alternate proposals for reconstructing the Union made by Lincoln and by Peace Democrats in the Federal Congress in December 1863.[15] Two, in an article titled "Negotiations for Peace," Holden argued that the Confederate Constitution — according to "the 4th paragraph of the 9th section" — did not allow the national government to say or do anything about Negro slavery; only the individual states had that power. Thus, in order to arrange a peace settlement under the Constitution of the United States that would preserve slavery in the returning Southern states, it was necessary to call a convention of the Confederate States to get the job done.[16] This constitutional point underlay, in part, Holden's insistence on holding a state convention and/or a convention of all the states North and South to hammer out a peace. Perhaps it was the determining factor in his decision to launch the convention movement. Holden's insistence upon utilizing a convention to make a peace, because only a convention could negotiate on the issue of slavery, suggests that Holden was jockeying towards a peace and reunion on the Copperhead basis.

On December 8, 1863, President Lincoln issued a proclamation in which he presented his so-called ten percent plan for the readmission of a seceded state to the Union. Lincoln offered "reconstruction" to any state in which "a number of persons, not less than one tenth in the number of votes cast" in the 1860 presidential election "shall reestablish a state government which shall be republican ... such shall be recognized as the true government of the state, and the state shall receive thereunder the benefits of the constitutional provision which declares that the United States shall guaranty to every state in this Union a republican form of government, and shall protect each of them against invasion; and on application of the legislature, or the executive (when the legislature cannot be convened) against domestic violence."[17] Needless to say, Jefferson Davis and Zeb Vance both were adept enough at arithmetic to calculate that the Quaker Belt alone, which contained about one-fourth of the voting population of North Carolina, easily could have mustered the requisite ten percent of the ballots cast in the 1860 presidential election to vote North Carolina back into the Union had the legislature called a state convention and held a referendum on the issue.

Lincoln's pledge to "protect" the newly created governments "against invasion ... [and] domestic violence" was a clear promise that the reunionist forces in the seceded states had the backing of the United States military in any counterrevolutionary enterprise they undertook. On the same day he issued his proclamation announcing his ten percent reconstruction plan, Lincoln delivered his third annual message to Congress. In it, he elaborated on the need to promise military aid to those loyal to the United States in the Confederacy. He noted that reunionists "with-in a [seceded] State favorable to republican government in the Union may be too feeble for an opposite and hostile element external to or even within the State, and such are precisely the cases with which we are now dealing."[18] Lincoln's message to Congress emboldened the North Carolina peace men. Were they to make a stand against their "external" enemies (that is Jefferson Davis and the Confederate army) or their enemies "within the State" (that is, Zeb Vance, the secessionist and War Conservatives, the Home Guards and the militia), they could look to the president of the United States and the Union army to rescue them.

Obviously, Lincoln's ten percent plan for reconstruction of the Union would have appealed to the antislavery advocates in the Quaker Belt. A consideration of greater interest concerned the proslavery majority: How did they react to Lincoln's plan? Some found it appealing. While Lincoln was himself a staunch advocate of the permanent emancipation of the slaves,[19] Congress and the Supreme Court at the time Lincoln issued his ten percent plan had not yet said the last word on the issue. The oath that Lincoln would have pro-reunionist Southerners swear before again becoming eligible to be United States citizens reflected the current uncertainty about the future legal status of slavery in the United States.

It required oath takers to swear to defend the Constitution of the United States and the Union created by it. They also had to obey and support "all acts of congress passed during the existing rebellion with reference to slaves, *so long and so far as not repealed, modified, or held void by congress, or by decision of the supreme court*" (emphasis added). Lastly, they had to obey and support "all proclamations of the President made during the existing rebellion having reference to slaves, *so long and so far as not modified or declared void by decision of the supreme court*"[20] (emphasis added). The wording of the oath encouraged proslavery Southerners to opt for reunion on Lincoln's ten percent plan based on the hope that an act of Congress or a decision of the Supreme Court might retain the peculiar institution. The following comment made by Lincoln in his annual message to Congress further encouraged them in this expectation. "Saying that reconstruction will be accepted if presented in a specified way, it is not said it will never be accepted in any other way."[21]

Lincoln hoped his ten percent plan would trigger reunionist activism in the Confederacy. In his annual message, Lincoln asked rhetorically: "But why any proclamation now upon this subject [reconstruction]?" Lincoln answered his question in words that must have sounded to many North Carolina peace men as if the president were referring directly to them: "In some States the elements for resumption seem ready for action, but remain inactive apparently for want of a rallying point — a plan of action.... By the proclamation a plan is presented which they are assured in advance will not be rejected here. This may bring them to act sooner than they otherwise would."[22]

Soon after Lincoln announced his ten percent plan for reconstruction, Peace Democrats introduced resolutions in the House of Representatives supporting it, but with the proviso that Congress allow Southern states to return to the Union with the institution of slavery left intact. Proponents voiced several such resolutions in the House in December 1863. For example, one of them resolved that when Confederate power is subdued in any one of the seceded states by "Federal arms or *by the voluntary submission of the people of such State to the authority of the Constitution*, then such State will be thereby restored to all its rights and privileges as a State of the Union, under the constitution of such State and the Constitution of the United States, *including the right to regulate, order, and control its own domestic institutions [including slavery] according to the constitution and laws of such State, free from all congressional or executive control or direction*"[23] (emphasis added).

Both the proslavery and the antislavery peace men in North Carolina had reason to rejoice in December 1863. Plans for reconstructing the Union were proposed both in the Federal Congress and by the president of the United States that were in their eyes generous, lenient, practical, and, most of all, attainable.

The Convention Movement

Holden initiated the 1864 convention movement just as he had the 1863 peace movement. Advocates held Peace Party rallies, usually in county seats, where they made speeches and passed resolutions advocating the party platform. Supporters held their first political rally in Johnston County on January 7, where Congressman Dr. J.T. Leach delivered a "spirited and patriotic" speech to the crowd. Convention enthusiasts passed resolutions condemning "military despotism," conscription, impressments, the tax-in-kind law, and any suspension of the writ of habeas corpus. The Peace Conservatives declared that the people had a right to hold a state convention were they "forced to decide between a military despotism and ... sovereignty." They asked Governor Vance to convene the legislature to consider the issues facing the country.[24] War Conservatives recognized the call for Vance to convene the legislature, which did not regularly meet until May, as a maneuver to call a state convention "and make an effort to secede."[25]

In 1864, activists held only about 32 peace meetings in North Carolina.[26] The relatively small number of gatherings, compared to those held in the summer of 1863, reflected the repressive political climate then extant in the state and Confederacy. Peace activists held only eight of the rallies in the Quaker Belt. Moreover, they held none in the highly disaffected counties of Wilkes, Randolph, Iredell, and Yadkin, where they conducted so many the previous summer. Newspapers reported two meetings each in Forsyth and Guilford, and one each for Davidson, Moore, Alamance, and Chatham. Undoubtedly, the great deserter hunt in the Quaker Belt in the fall and winter of 1863-1864 and Davis's suspension of the writ of habeas corpus (discussed below) had produced dividends for the Confederate cause by nearly silencing the voices of dissent in the area.

The adjoining counties of Wake (7) and Johnston (5) held by far the largest concentrations of peace rallies in 1864. Wake and Johnston were the home counties respectively of William Holden and Dr. J.T. Leach, the founders and key leaders of the peace and convention movements, which explains why these counties remained strong centers of protest in 1864. Confederate authorities sent a few troops into Wake and Johnston counties to hunt deserters in 1863. However, neither county experienced the extensive repression that the Quaker Belt counties suffered that year.

In January, Holden printed a letter to the editor written by "Solus," which left little doubt in the reader's mind that Holden's convention movement was a conspiracy of reunionists. Solus complained that, despite three years of war, independence remains elusive. Notwithstanding appalling battlefield losses and dreadful suffering on the home front, there seems to be no end to the war in sight. Obviously, means other than warfare must be sought to terminate the conflict, and for Solus, negotiations provided the best approach to that end. No advocate of Confederate independence, Solus wrote of peace without victory and implied that reunion was an acceptable solution to the war if that was what the "people" wanted: "Now it matters not what propositions are made, or what terms accepted, the great desideratum now is to get the move made, and let the people, to whom the government belongs, decide as to its correctness." "The other [Southern] states," concluded Solus, "are all waiting and watching for the action of North Carolina."[27]

Another letter to the editor, this one by "Observer," appeared in the *Standard* the same day as did the one by "Solus." Observer, arguing that "North-Carolina may as well lead as any other State," urged Governor Vance to convene the legislature "without delay" to call a convention, and "commissioners be sent to the other States for the purpose of preservation of the country and its institutions [that is, slavery]." Such actions, concluded Solus, might lead the Northern peace men to act in coordination with their Southern counterparts and call conventions in their states to apply pressure on the government at Washington to end the war. This letter, with its emphasis upon preserving slavery and working with the Northern Peace Democrats, suggested that Solus had reconstruction on the Copperhead basis in mind.

In February, Holden published a letter to the *Standard* from "Pacificus" that left little doubt among his readers that his convention movement was a starkly radical counterrevolutionary venture. Pacificus declared that a convention had "the right in connection with the other States assembled in Convention, to direct and control their common agent, the government at Richmond. They have the right to demand of that government that it shall at once enter into negotiations for peace upon such terms as they may direct, and if it will not do this, they have a right to *revoke* its powers and *terminate* its existence, and then to initiate negotiations themselves." Pacificus added that if a convention of the Confederate States failed to negotiate a peace, then North Carolina had the right "peacefully to sever her connection with the Confederate government and enter into negotiations for a separate peace."[28]

At the same time the peace meetings were getting underway again, Peace Conservatives in the west, especially in Forsyth and Rutherford counties, initiated a drive to inundate the governor with petitions demanding that he call a state convention to cooperate with other states in stopping the war.[29] Peace Conservative petitioners from Forsyth County concluded that nearly everyone in the county was for a convention, even those who in the past favored secession.[30] Governor Vance's secretary of the treasury, Jonathan Worth — a Randolph County native — became an enthusiastic supporter of Holden's convention movement. He encouraged friends in the Quaker Belt to print and distribute a petition written by him calling for a convention. Worth did not sign his name to the document. He preferred to remain anonymous on the convention issue because he held a high state position and wanted to appear neutral on the matter to Vance and Holden, both of whom were his friends.[31]

Jonathan Worth, an ardent Whig with Quaker antecedents, adamantly opposed secession in 1861 but, like so many others, caved in to the disunionists when Lincoln issued his call for troops. Worth never reconciled himself to the Confederate cause; in fact, he remained a covert reunionist, as did so many of the old Whig politicians. Like Holden and Tyson, he believed that Confederate independence was impossible to achieve by force of arms and defeat would lead to emancipation of the slaves. Like everyone else in North Carolina, he was aware of the call by Northern Peace Democrats for a reconstruction based on the U.S. Constitution, that is, with the maintenance of the institution of slavery in the returning Southern states. Reflecting that the Copperhead plan for reconstruction had many advocates in North Carolina, Worth, in January 1864, reported in a letter to a relative that almost everyone he met along the way on a trip to Wilmington from Raleigh was "openly for reconstruction on the basis of the Constitution of the U.S., if these terms can be obtained."[32] Again, in late January in a letter to another relative, Worth wrote that he was "now certain that a large portion even of those most active in bringing on the war would settle on the basis of the Constitution of the U.S."[33] Indeed, wrote Worth, the great majority of the people of the state believe "that we ought to accept peace on the basis of restoring the Union — and the Constitution of the U.S., provided this can be done without any infraction of our rights under that Constitution." Noting that while Holden contends for peace, he denies being for reconstruction. Worth felt such a position was untenable: "It is idle to talk of peace except on the basis of a restored Union, and I believe an immense majority North and South, would gladly proclaim a universal amnesty and restore the Union —"[34] In his letters, Worth reflected opinions expressed by Bryan Tyson in *A Ray of Light* and his reunion circular, and by the Northern Peace Democrats. Evidently, by early 1864, Worth believed that a majority of Northerners and North Carolinians favored a cessation of the war and a restoration of the old Union, a position he favored above Confederate independence provided slavery were protected by the Constitution.

Robert P. Dick, a Peace Conservative from Guilford County, like Worth, urged Southern peace men to cooperate with their Northern counterparts in ending the war. He believed that a strong Southern Peace Party "would greatly increase the power of the peace party at the North and enable them to overturn the Black Republican dynasty at Washington." With the Northern Democrats in power, Dick held that it would be easy for the South to negotiate a peace to end the war.[35]

On February 13, the Raleigh *Daily Progress* printed the proceedings of a public meeting in Chatham County. The resolutions passed at the meeting revealed the nexus that existed at the time between Northern Copperheads and Tar Heel peace men. The peace activists asked that each Southern state hold a convention so "that we may meet in general convention to propose terms to the United States that this war may be settled." They then resolved: "That the vote upon the resolutions introduced by the Hon. Fernando Wood of New York, to send delegates to our capital to open peace negotiations, show most conclusively that there is a huge peace party at the North, and we consider it our imperative duty to join our wishes with theirs to that end. It will save the lives of many of our gallant boys, who to day are but moving targets for deadly weapons."[36]

Fernando Wood was a representative from New York and one of the leaders of the Peace Democrats.[37] He asked that the negotiators restore the Union "on terms of equity, fraternity, and equality under the Constitution."[38] That is, allow returning Southern states to retain the institution of slavery. Davis and the War Conservatives noticed that Wood's proposal called for negotiations to *return* the Southern states to the Union. Wood did not mention recognizing Confederate independence, an action he opposed. Since everyone knew that Wood and all the leading Peace Democrats in the North opposed Confederate independence, President Davis and loyal Confederates could only interpret the peace men's call to act in concert with the Copperheads to open peace negotiations as a disloyal plot to restore North Carolina and the South to the Union. As an uncompromising proponent of Confederate independence, President Davis rejected the Northern Democrats' offer of a constitutional guarantee of slavery in exchange for the return of the Southern states to the Union. Because of the susceptibility of many Southerners to the siren call of the Copperheads, he feared that the election of a Peace Democrat to the presidency in 1864 would result in "the disintegration of the Confederacy."[39] Davis believed that Holden's convention movement encouraged the peace faction at the North and strengthened the Copperhead's bid for the presidency in the November elections. Worst of all, it was "a plot to restore North Carolina to the Union."[40]

The Convention Movement and the Copperheads

In December 1863, when Holden was still toying with the idea of promoting a convention, he warned his readers that only negotiations for peace could save slavery, implying that continued war for independence would surely lead to the destruction of the peculiar institution. Everyone, especially the slaveholders, should keep in mind, argued Holden, that only the sovereign states acting in convention together had the power and authority to negotiate on the issue of slavery.[41] How could Holden have hoped to have saved slavery through a convention unless he planned to work through it with the Northern Peace Democrats for reunion on the Copperhead basis? By his reference to the slaveholders, Holden seems to have been suggesting to the wise planter that if he wanted to keep his slaves, he would surely be smart enough to support reunion as proffered by the Northern Peace Democrats. This begs the question: Why did not slaveholders in the summer of 1864 — at least a significant number[42] of them — fall in behind Holden and his convention movement? It was the commonsense, practical move to make to preserve slavery under the difficult circumstances then extant. Secessionists precipitated the Civil War primarily as an act to preserve and defend slavery. By 1864, it was clear that the Confederacy only had a remote chance of winning its independence. Defeat meant emancipation and rule by Republican-appointed military governors. Everyone knew that. Apparently, most secessionists, like Davis, chose Confederate independence over the preservation of slavery — but ended with neither.

Historians have charged Holden with treason and favoring secession and reconstruction on the Lincoln basis because that is what Davis, Vance, secessionists, and War Conservatives — that is, his political opposition — accused him of during the war.[43] Nevertheless, at the time, most people knew better. Vance, Davis, and many others were perceptive enough to understand that Holden's peace and convention movements were more reactions to the entreaties for peace and reunion offered by the Copperheads than they were either moves for a Lincoln reconstruction or merely protests against violations of civil liberties or states' rights by the Richmond authorities. But they could not afford to charge Holden with Copperheadism for fear that the populace across the state would flock to the editor's side. If that happened, Richmond and Raleigh leaders feared that the support for the Confederate war effort that remained in the state would vanish overnight.[44]

An article printed in September in Vance's party organ, *The Daily Conservative*, provides proof that Vance and his War Conservative and Confederate Party supporters believed that Holden and his Peace Conservative faction slanted towards the Copperheads. The Northern Democrats, noted the editor, in the summer of 1864 called for an armistice suspending hostilities and a convention of all the states to iron out sectional grievances and make a peace. Further, their party platform demanded that the Union be maintained "in all its territorial integrity" and that those states in rebellion must return to their old allegiance, the United States of America. This the editor pronounced unacceptable. Better that Lincoln wins reelection. The editor continued: "The election of McClellan on such a platform we fear would have a tendency to demoralize our people. It would give courage to the miserable factionists [that is, the Holdenites] that have so recently received so signal a rebuke at the hands of the people. God forbid that we should ever [again] have to go through such a contest as the one from which we but recently emerged.... *The election of McClellan might prove the syren's song luring us to certain destruction*"[45] (emphasis added). Clearly, Vance and his followers considered Holden and his Peace Conservative supporters to be advocates of the Copperhead plan for reunion, even though publicly they almost never charged them with that; rather, they constantly accused Holden and his followers of advocating reconstruction on the Lincoln basis — a change that would lead to social and legal equality for blacks — to divert the public mind away from the lure of Copperheadism. Undoubtedly, Vance and his War Conservative following, as well as Davis and the Confederate Party, feared that the election of McClellan as president would lead to an uprising of Holden's supporters in the

Quaker Belt and throughout the state (and of people all over the Confederacy) in support of the Copperhead demand for peace and reunion on the basis of "the Constitution as it is, the Union as it was."[46]

Amusingly, one leading War Conservative—the editor of the Fayetteville *Observer*—pretended that the Copperheads did not exist, while everyone knew otherwise, when he wrote: "The Standard flatters itself that in some contingency not yet reached, it could secure peace without sudden emancipation. Upon what this strange delusion is based, we are unable to conceive."[47] Perhaps the War Conservative editor was baiting Holden into revealing his Copperhead leanings.

With two exceptions,[48] historians of the North Carolina peace movement have failed to appreciate the nexus between many of the Tar Heel Peace Conservatives and the Northern Peace Democrats,[49] both of whom strove for a reunion based on the Constitution under which slavery in the South would be protected. One such historian was Chandra Manning, who argued that Vance won the 1864 gubernatorial election in great measure because he warned the electorate in his campaign speeches that a Holden victory would result in a peace with the Lincoln government that would lead to reunion, the emancipation of the slaves, and a disastrous social revolution. Freed blacks would be given the vote and civil liberties equal to those of whites; the property of whites would be confiscated and given to freedmen; blacks would serve alongside whites in the military; and other such presumed horrors. Vance's masterful play on nonslaveholding whites' racial fears, argued Manning, drove thousands of voters away from Holden, giving the governor an overwhelming victory at the polls.[50]

While Manning may have been correct, at least in part, about Vance's racial rhetoric frightening many whites into his arms, she failed to realize that many Peace Conservatives at the time did not view Holden as advocating reunion with emancipation;[51] rather, they saw Holden as a champion of reunion on the Copperhead basis, which would preserve slavery and prevent a racial revolution. Reunion did not automatically have to mean emancipation as many historians have assumed. Confederate victory was not necessary to save slavery. Reunion on the Copperhead basis would have avoided emancipation and preserved slavery in the former Confederate states. Confederate defeat would surely end slavery and upset the social and racial order in the south. And as Bryan Tyson, Lewis Hanes, and William Holden convincingly argued, a Confederate victory was all but impossible to achieve on the battlefield. The only viable route open to save slavery was to adopt the strategy of "The Constitution as It Is, The Union as It Was," as advocated by the Northern Peace Democrats in their drive to end the war and save the Union.

On one occasion, the editor of Governor Vance's political newspaper did openly discuss the Copperheads when he condemned advocates of the Copperhead plan of reconstruction as traitors and spies. In a few instances, the War Conservative editor admitted, "there are those in our midst, who are for the 'Constitution, as it is, and the Union, as it was,' [but] ... they do not belong to the Conservative party of North Carolina. Such men may be *with* us, but they are not *of* us.—They are Lincolnites at heart and the sooner they go north the better for themselves and the State.... Indeed, we do not see how a man entertaining such a sentiment can remain in the South, unless his object is to be a traitor and a spy." The charge that peace men who opted for the Copperhead plan of reunion were "Lincolnites" was nonsense and intended to confuse and mislead the uninformed. The War Conservative editor continued: "'The Constitution, as it is,' is well enough, for, as we have shown, the *spirit* of the system of government formed by our fathers constitutes the principles we are contending for. But 'the Union, as it was,' means re construction, the idea of which is not to be tolerated for one moment. A desire to return to the old Union forms no part of the creed of the Conservative party of North Carolina."[52]

To the contrary, a great deal of evidence indicates that many in the peace wing of the Conservative Party heartily advocated returning North Carolina and the Confederacy to the Union based upon the political ideas encapsulated in the slogan "The Constitution as It Is, and the Union as It Was." The most important indicia are Bryan Tyson's reunion circular, Day-Star Circular, *A Ray of Light, The Institution of Slavery in the Southern States, Religiously and Morally Considered in Connection with Our Sectional Troubles* and *Object of the Administration in Prosecuting the War* (discussed below); Lewis Hanes's Copperhead Manifesto[53]; J.M. Leach's postwar testimony that "an honorable peace" was understood to imply reconstruction[54]; Dr. J.T. Leach's advocating reunion on the Copperhead basis in a letter to the *Standard* in May 1863,[55] and in his peace resolutions proposed in the Confederate Congress in December 1864, in which he called for a peace that would protect personal property under the Constitution (discussed below)[56]; University of North Carolina president David L. Swain's remark in a letter to Vance in 1864 that many people that he knew hoped for a McClellan[57] victory in the presidential election and a reconstruction under him[58]; the observation by Jonathan Worth in a letter in January 1864 that most of the people he met along the way on a trip between Raleigh and Wilmington expressed a desire for a reconstruction based on the Constitution.[59] In other letters to friends that year, Worth stated that he believed that the people of North Carolina and the majority of the public in the North preferred an armistice and a negotiated peace rather than a continuation of the war. He made it plain that he preferred reunion on the Copperhead basis to Confederate independence,[60] and the numerous direct and implied demands for reunion on the terms proposed by the Northern Peace Democrats made in the resolutions passed at the peace meetings in 1863.

Davis Suspends the Writ of Habeas Corpus

Alarmed at the rebirth of the peace movement in North Carolina, and at the determined drive by its adherents for a state convention to supersede the president and congress in negotiating a peace with the Federals, Davis urged congress to grant him the authority to suspend the writ of habeas corpus. In a special message to congress, Davis spoke of the need to thwart disloyalty and subversion in several areas of the Confederacy. Though not mentioning North Carolina by name, the president left little room to doubt that the activities of the Tar Heel peace men were the major source of his concern. The disaffected and disloyal, maintained Davis, are holding public meetings in areas of the South advocating the holding of conventions to address grievances, "but with the real design of accomplishing treason under the form of law." These disloyalists have formed secret leagues and associations, and in many instances, their leaders openly avow their hostility to the Confederate cause and advocate "peace on the terms of submission and abolition of slavery."[61] Davis, in an indirect jab at North Carolina's Chief Justice Richmond M. Pearson, complained that a "particular judge" granted release to every draftee or deserter arrested by military authorities who applied to him for a writ of habeas corpus. Arresting officers ordered by the judge to bring the petitioners before his court for trial lost valuable time. For the judge "to temporize with disloyalty in the midst of war," warned Davis, "is but to quicken it to the growth of treason."[62]

In February 1864, the Confederate Congress passed a bill by solid majorities in both houses granting the president authority to suspend the writ in thirteen cases. One case, aimed directly at the peace men in North Carolina, "suspended the privilege of the writ when a person was arrested for 'advising or inciting others to abandon the Confederate cause, or to resist the Confederate States, or to adhere to the enemy.'"[63] The suspension of the writ spread terror through the ranks of the peace men. In their eyes, as most of them were old Whigs, Davis had become the "military dictator" and the Confederacy the "military despotism" they warned about all along. In a letter to Vance written several months after congress suspended the writ, David L. Swain, president of the University of North Carolina, confided: "Have you observed the extent to which the suspension of the Writ of Habeas Corpus paralyzed and stupefied the public mind. It inaugurated a reign of terror, which its expiration has not yet overthrown. Men speak sparingly, cautiously, warily."[64]

On February 24, Holden, intimidated by the suspension of the writ, ceased publication of his newspaper. On regaining his courage, the editor announced on March 3 that he would be a candidate for governor in the election next August. If elected, Holden promised that he would "do everything in my power ... to secure an honorable peace."[65] Holden's use of the term "an honorable peace" caused devoted Confederates to further question his loyalty, because Northern Democrats had been using that term since 1861 in their call for the South's return to the Union with the institution of slavery protected by the Constitution.[66] Remarks made by J.M. Leach after the war confirmed the Confederates' suspicions. He stated that in the fall 1863 elections when he ran for office in the Seventh Congressional District, he called for an "*honorable peace* which everyone knew meant *re-construction*," and that Holden used the term before him in his newspaper.[67]

In his run for governor in the 1864 gubernatorial campaign, Holden defined what he meant by "an honorable peace": "We want Commissioners appointed to treat for peace; and when the Commissioners thus appointed shall have met, deliberated, and agreed upon a treaty, and when that treaty shall have been submitted to the people of the States at the ballot-box and approved by them, we shall call that treaty an honorable one, and the peace that will result from it an honorable peace."[68] Holden failed to affirm that Confederate independence had to be a component of any "honorable peace," and his political opponents considered that tantamount to an admission that the convention movement was a scheme for reconstruction. Indeed, many viewed the call for "an honorable peace" by a Peace Conservative politician in the summer of 1863 as an appeal for reunion. For example, an editorial in the Greensboro *Patriot*, a pro–Vance newspaper, declared those at public meetings calling for "an honorable peace" to be disloyal reconstructionists.[69]

The Execution of Pro-Holden Deserters from the Quaker Belt

Support for Holden's peace policies was widespread among troops from North Carolina in the Army of Northern Virginia, especially among Quaker Belt soldiers. In November 1863 Holden printed a letter in the *Weekly Standard* from a soldier in the Twenty-second Regiment

North Carolina Troops in camp at Orange Court House, Virginia, who stated that a majority of the men in his regiment "are with you in every respect." He reported that officers called a meeting of the regiment "for the purpose of suppressing your paper." Not more than a dozen men attended the convocation, which the writer termed "one of the grandest humbugs ever gotten up." While the meeting was in session, "a certain Captain said that if there were any men in the regiment who endorsed W.W. Holden, he wanted to know who they were, when suddenly someone knocked out the light, and more than a hundred men hurrahed for Holden and the *Standard*."[70] Half of the companies in this regiment came from the Quaker Belt: three from Randolph County, and one each from Guilford and Stokes. All the other companies came from the piedmont, except one from the mountains.[71]

Holden's convention movement rekindled hopes among Tar Heel troops in the Army of Northern Virginia that an armistice would be called and a return to the old Union negotiated. As a result, desertions increased. In January 1864, a Guilford County soldier wrote to his mother from winter quarters near Orange Court House, Virginia, telling her of rampant desertion and reunionist sentiments among the troops of his regiment: "my belief is that the Army is too much disheartened to ever doo much more good all give it up that we are over-powered ... all the N.C. boys wish that old N.C. would go back into the union.... Robert Kirkman says for you to give the secesionist Hell and Rub it in ... the old 21st Regt. got to running aways so bad that they had to move their post up the river to a pond where they couldent wade across the River[.]"[72]

Over half of the 229 men executed for desertion by the Confederate army came from North Carolina, many of them from the Quaker Belt.[73] These executions no doubt intimidated Holden supporters in the ranks and their Peace Conservative relatives and neighbors back home. In January 1864, a medical officer from Forsyth County, serving in the Fourth Regiment North Carolina Troops stationed in Virginia, reported that a firing squad "shot to death with musketry" two Surry County soldiers for desertion. He "pited them very much" because "their crime was instigated by the pernicious teachings of Holden etc., who have much to answer for in the reckoning yet to come."[74] In February, he described the execution of another Holden supporter: "Private King, Co. I, of this Regiment, a conscript from Randolph County, having been convicted of Desertion, was shot to death with musketry agreeable to the sentence of the court. His breast was pierced with seven balls, and he died almost immediately." When asked why he deserted, Private King replied: "I have been led to this by the advice of persons at home, and the teachings of Holden's paper!" The medical officer concluded with: "Next Tuesday private McDaniel, Co. G. of this Regt. from Davie County will be executed, and in a week there-after private Hunnicut, Co. A., from Iredell County, will meet a similar fate."[75]

In April, Shaffner wrote a vivid account of the execution of three deserters from Wilkes County, one the father of nine children, and all more than likely members of the Heroes of America:

> On last Thursday I witnessed a very painful scene. Three members of this Regiment, conscripts from Wilkes County were "shot to death with musketry" agreeable to the findings and sentence of a Court Martial.... All had previously deserted, and been apprehended, but were pardoned. Of course their cases were of an aggravated nature and could not be passed over a second time with leniency. The poor fellows stated that they had been led to believe that N.C. would return to the Union, and that in leaving the Army and going home they would be sustained by the

people. One said *his wife* had influenced him to desert, promising him the protection of the neighborhood if he would come home, and taunting him with his want of nerve, as exhibited by fear of risking consequences! What a miserable woman she now must be! herself and her *nine* children disgraced and dishonored by an act of the husband and father, which he says he was induced to do by his wife's influence![76]

Tar Heels other than Quaker Belt soldiers supported Holden and the peace movement. For example, William F. Wagner, a soldier in the Fifty-seventh Regiment from Catawba County, wrote a letter in August 1863 to his wife from camp near Orange Court House about a poll taken by regimental officers of troops on whether they favored peace. Wagner said that a majority of the men voted for a peace "on some terms," but the officers dishonestly reported that a majority of the men voted against peace and for a continuation of the war. A brave soldier who served in the ranks for two years and in many battles, including Gettysburg, Wagner by the summer of 1863 came to believe that the war was lost and Confederate independence was not worth fighting for any longer. He wrote that "the solegers is nearley all wiling to go back in the union a gain and that is what I think they aut to doo for it is a bout all they way it Ever [will] be setled we aut to staid in the union in the first plase as for my part I want peese...."[77] A firm supporter of Holden's peace movement, Wagner believed that if the question of peace were submitted to the people back home to vote on, they would choose to return to the Union.[78]

A loyal Confederate who viewed Holden's peace agitation as the prime cause of desertion commented: "There has been a good many N. Carolinians shot in this army for Desertion[.] [O]ld traitor Holden is Responsible for most of it.... I think the N.C. Soldiers passing through Raleigh on Furlough ought to stop and hang the old son of a bitch."[79]

By-Election in the Seventh Congressional District

State authorities scheduled a by-election on April 21, 1864, to determine who would replace Samuel H. Christian in Congress for the Seventh Congressional District. The people of the district elected Christian to the House of Representatives on a peace platform in the fall 1863 elections, but he died shortly thereafter. Since March 3, Vance and Holden had been campaigning against each other in the gubernatorial race, and this by-election served as a preliminary test of the protagonists' respective strengths in central North Carolina. Three men ran for the office — James Madison Leach of Davidson County, Alfred G. Foster of Randolph, and Captain N.A. Ramsey of Chatham. It was primarily a contest between Foster and Leach. Though depicted as a pro–Holden man or "Holdenite" by the opposition, Leach was, in fact, an independent peace candidate. Foster had the hearty support of Governor Vance and the War Conservatives.[80]

J.M. Leach was born and raised on a plantation near Trinity in Randolph County. He received his education at the Caldwell Institute in Greensboro and at the United States Military Academy. He read law and established a legal practice in Lexington, North Carolina, the seat of Davidson County. He became a renowned trial lawyer who lost but one (the first) murder case out of twenty-five in his career. Leach helped to found Union Institute Academy in Randolph County, which later became Trinity College and in the twentieth century developed into Duke University. He served as a Whig in the state legislature from

1848 to 1858 and in the United States Congress from 1858 to 1861. Bitterly opposed to secession in the beginning, Leach reacted to Lincoln's call for volunteers by returning home from Washington, raising a company of troops, and serving as a lieutenant-colonel in the Confederate army. He fought at First Manassas but resigned his commission in December 1861. When S.H. Christian died, Leach ran for the newly vacated congressional seat on a peace platform. He was a brilliant lawyer and a talented politician who never lost an election.[81]

Leach, an old-line Whig, found it difficult to accept W.W. Holden as the leader of the Peace Party because, before 1860, Holden had been the chief spokesman for the hated Democratic Party and a staunch secessionist.[82] Holden, before the war, described Leach in the then–Democratic *Standard* as "unscrupulous" and "a demagogue."[83] The consummate politician, Leach realized that only a strong "peace man" could win in the seventh district. He, however, found himself in an awkward position. In order to get the "peace" vote, he could not afford to offend Holden, his old political enemy and a man whom he despised; yet his pro-peace and convention political rhetoric would label him a Holdenite and of necessity offend Vance, whom he admired. In March Leach wrote Vance a letter in which he expressed the opinion that the only real issue dividing them was Leach's siding with the "peace men" in their demand that negotiations for peace must be initiated immediately. Leach pleaded with Vance to come out in a speech or a proclamation with something that would satisfy the peace men, and "you could and would beat Holden and all comers to death! The people do like you personally, and don't like your present competition Holden personally."[84]

On April 5 Leach issued a circular addressed "To the Soldiers of the 7th Congressional District," denying, as his opponents claimed, that he ever expressed disloyal sentiments, denounced Governor Vance, or spoken in favor of a peace being made "on any terms." The former Confederate colonel made it clear that he supported peace based upon Southern independence but at the same time held that "every legitimate and well-directed effort should be made for peace, and kept before the Yankee Government." He added: "I believe that whenever peace Commissioners shall be appointed by the two governments that the last battle will have been fought, and this terrible war will soon be ended."[85]

A.G. Foster was a lawyer and one of the largest slave owners in Randolph County. War Conservatives believed that he could get more votes in the seventh district than any other non–Holdenite man. Foster staunchly favored independence. He wrote Vance that "in truth there are but two parties in the State—the Independence Party and the Submissionists or Lincolnites."[86] The Fayetteville *Observer*, which was pro–Foster, reported speeches made by "Colonel" Foster and "General" Leach in Asheboro on April 11. Striking out at the leaders of the peace movement, Foster claimed that "getting up disaffection to our government, and indulging in threats of taking N.C. out of the Confederacy" diminished chances of gaining recognition as an independent country. He was for peace attempts only through regular and constitutional channels; any other methods would be revolutionary and dangerous.[87]

Leach took a far more radical approach to the peace question. He exclaimed that the people who held all the political power must set aside the politicians who obstructed efforts to attain peace. He did not favor a state convention just now but did support "a Convention of the Confederacy to aid in instituting negotiations, or obtaining peace, or Congress sending

Commissioners to negotiate." According to the *Observer*, Leach claimed that he could not support Vance unless the governor offered more "consolation to the peace men."[88] In a letter to Vance explaining his position on the peace issue, the Confederate congressman expressed the hope that "Davis shall propose and keep before Lincoln and the world propositions for peace, and offer at all times ... commissioners for that purpose." Otherwise, he favored calling a convention of the Confederate States to negotiate a peace. He believed that Davis "would listen to the voice of his countrymen expressed thus through the sovereign states." Leach said that while he was a peace man, he did not support Holden, who had been an "original secessionist." "The miserable Secessionists," added the former Whig congressional representative, "always have hated me."[89]

Leach's letter to Vance denouncing Holden but supporting peace negotiations pointed up the dilemma so many peace men faced, most of whom were old-line Whigs. They were enthusiastic advocates of Holden's peace politics, but despised Holden himself because of his past political record as an "original secessionist" and a leader of the state Democratic Party for over a decade. In addition, Holden had been in the forefront of Democratic leaders who had inflamed public opinion against Benjamin Sherwood Hedrick, Hinton Rowan Helper, and the Wesleyan abolitionist activists Jesse McBride, Adams Crooks, Jarvis Bacon, and Daniel Worth. Had the Peace Party had a less controversial leader, it surely would have been more successful at the polls than was the case. It was strange indeed to witness such a hard-core Whig community as Randolph County, with a strong antislavery and anti-secessionist tradition, unite under his political banner in 1863 and 1864.

In accusing Leach of being a Holdenite, his political opponents labeled him not so much a warm personal supporter of Holden but a reunionist — which he was. After the war, Leach boasted: "I was the first *public man* in the state ... as having taken ground boldly on the *stump* ... for an *honorable peace* which every body knew meant *re-construction* & it was so charged on me. Gov. Holden had taken the same ground, as Editor before me."[90] In late July 1863, Leach gave a two-hour speech at a large Peace Party rally in Forsyth County attended by over 1,500 people — many from surrounding counties — in which he implied he was for reunion on the Copperhead basis. In the speech, Leach called for "an honorable peace through the action of a Convention, or in some other mode, whereby our property [that is, slaves] and rights may be secured."[91] The assemblage concurred with Leach's Copperhead leanings when it passed resolutions denouncing the secessionists' war that must inevitably result in the destruction of slavery unless the conflict is "stayed" by a negotiated peace.[92]

An observer of this by-election described how Vance supporters used their influence to try to defeat Leach and elect Foster. A few days before the election, they spread the rumor that a list of the names of anyone who voted for Leach would be given to the county enrolling officer, "and that at the ensuing enrollment of Conscripts, no man who had thus voted, would be allowed a detail or exemption on any grounds whatsoever." A state contractor for the North Carolina Railroad in Thomasville (Davidson County) warned his detailed employees that any of them who voted for Leach would have their details revoked and would be turned over to the enrolling officer for conscription. The superintendent of the lead works in Davidson County did likewise to his detailed employees.[93]

Governor Vance received the results of the election on April 28. They were as follows, including civilian votes, and state and Confederate military votes[94]:

James M. Leach   4,058
Alfred G. Foster   2,420
Capt. N. A. Ramsey 482

Leach's victory at the polls was important in three respects: It demonstrated that the peace movement had strong grassroots support in the Seventh Congressional District, and that it was not limited in appeal only to disloyal militant Unionists and disgruntled draft-dodgers and deserters. Leach himself represented a class of wealthy men who were not only at odds with the direction and methods of the Davis administration, but were covertly hoping and working for reunion, and he used the peace movement as a vehicle to that end. Finally, the great majority of the citizens in the seventh district wanted negotiations for peace to be initiated immediately — either by the Richmond government, by a state convention, or by a convention of the Southern states — and made their point evident through the ballots cast in this Congressional election.

The Gubernatorial Campaign of 1864

Officials set the polling date for the gubernatorial race between Holden and Vance for August 4, 1864. Vance conducted an aggressive campaign. He stumped across the state and among the North Carolina troops stationed in Virginia. His speeches drew vast crowds, and, being the most gifted and popular orator North Carolina has ever produced, he drew many of the wavering and disaffected into his orbit through his wit and engaging rhetoric.[95]

Vance boldly initiated his campaign by delivering his first public speech at Wilkesborough in the heart of "deserter country"; indeed, throughout his campaign he maintained the policy of stumping extensively in the disaffected (and voter-rich) Quaker Belt.[96] He largely preempted Holden's position, based upon championing states' rights, civil liberties, and peace, by strongly promoting the same principles. The governor advocated timely and repeated negotiations for peace by the proper authorities. Vance, however, made it clear that the peace he spoke of had to be based upon Southern independence. He accused Holden of plotting to use his convention scheme to secede from the Confederacy — a charge that Holden denied.[97] He alleged that the peace Holden called for would lead to a Lincoln reconstruction with emancipation and social and legal equality for blacks. Vance warned Holden and his Peace Conservative followers against counterrevolution, separate state action through a convention, reconstruction, submission, or combined resistance against the Confederate government. He denounced as dangerous the idea of calling a state convention or a convention of the Southern states to make peace. The governor threateningly predicted that if the Holdenites triumphed in the election, North Carolina would be devastated by an internal civil war between Confederate troops sent in from Richmond and the peace advocates. He insisted that only the duly elected congressmen and executive leaders in Richmond should make peace.[98] Vance's threats of North Carolina becoming a center of an internal civil war, and his charges that many of Holden's supporters were unconditional reconstructionists who endorsed emancipation and social and political equality for freedmen, frightened many away from Holden.[99]

Holden conducted his campaign strictly through his newspaper and made no public speeches or appearances. He had the endorsement of only three other papers in the state. Since he had offended at one time or another nearly every prominent person in the state (Whig, Democrat, and Conservative alike), Holden had few adherents among the state's power elite. Thus, he had to depend upon local and relatively obscure grassroots leaders to advance the peace cause.[100] Only three prominent men, all of whom were from the central part of the state, supported him: Alfred Dockery of Richmond County, Robert P. Dick of Guilford, and Thomas Settle of Rockingham. Jonathan Worth, after much soul-searching, finally gave his support to Vance, though he refused to take an active role in the campaign and tried to maintain, at least ostensibly, a neutral position.[101]

In May, Vance asked the General Assembly to devise a plan for peace and instruct North Carolina representatives in Congress to take every opportunity to offer one to the enemy. The governor, however, warned against separate state action or reconstruction.[102] In response, the General Assembly instructed the Confederate government to make an offer of peace to the enemy on the basis of independence and pledged continued support for the Confederacy. Further, the Assembly resolved that President Davis and the Confederate Senate were the only legitimate agents empowered to conduct negotiations with the enemy. The lawmakers expressed confidence in Vance's leadership of the state. Vance's success at winning over the legislature to his viewpoint undermined Holden's support in the government and isolated him from Conservative Whig leadership. This isolation proved fatal for his gubernatorial campaign and convention movement.[103]

Since Holden differed from Vance primarily in the degree to which he denounced the Richmond authorities as violators of states' rights and civil liberties, and in his advocating a state convention or a convention of all the Southern states to negotiate peace rather than seeking peace through the president and Congress, the campaign proved to be primarily a contest of personalities. Vance, with his unique combination of backwoods wit, brilliant oratory, and courage, easily won.[104]

In the election, Vance had the solid support of the Confederate Party. Knowing that Vance was the best friend the Confederacy had in North Carolina, these partisans of the Davis administration sat on the sidelines and winked at Vance's vilification of the "original secessionists" for precipitating the war, and at his denunciation of President Davis for his "dangerous" tendency towards "military despotism."[105] Vance also had the support of the War Conservatives and numerous Peace Conservatives, many of whom feared that the convention movement was a radical move for unconditional reconstruction.[106]

The Heroes of America and the 1864 Elections

Holden received a devastating blow when, on July 2, 1864, the *Conservative*, a newspaper established in Raleigh to express Governor Vance's political viewpoint after his split with Holden, published an expose of the Heroes of America and accused Holden of being a member and leader. The Heroes of America, as related in chapter two, was an underground organization of militant Unionists. The clandestine society furnished information to the Federals, organized all those who opposed the Confederate cause, and used secret signs, signals, and oaths to conceal themselves and their families.[107] The exposure of the Red String organization in the papers suggested "that Holden was the leader of a conspiracy of Unionists and that the convention movement was a façade to cloak treason."[108] Further, a critic charged that the gang leader Bill Owens, his deserter followers, and the Heroes of America supported Holden in the upcoming election.[109] Another complained that scarcely a week passes but what a member of this "association of crime" murders a loyal man somewhere in the state.[110] Though Holden vehemently denied any knowledge of or connection with the "HOA"— and no one ever submitted proof to support the charges made — he doubtless lost many votes on account of his alleged involvement.[111]

A Reverend Orrin Churchill from Chatham County first publicly outed the Red Strings. The *Conservative* based its expose of the Heroes of America in early July on his testimony.[112] About the same time, the editor of the *Daily Confederate* reported that he soon would print important disclosures on HOA activities in Guilford and Randolph counties, implying that he would expose many of its leaders and followers.[113] Lamentably for the historian, the promised revelations did not show up in subsequent issues of the newspaper that have survived. The Fayetteville *Observer* assigned Randolph County a leadership role in the Red String organization when it printed the "confessions" of some Richmond County members who claimed that a Randolph County man named Phillips had introduced the secret society into their area.[114]

The August 1 issue of the *Observer* exposed two justices of the peace and five militia officers in Montgomery County as members of the Heroes of America.[115] One of them was Noah Auman, a justice of the peace who lived in the Auman's Hill community in the northeastern corner of the county. On August 12, Auman wrote Vance asking for a pardon: "Some eight months ago i was over pursuaded to Joine the association caled the Heroes of America. my harts Desire is to git out of it and has Ever Since i got in to it. tha give it to afue others tha air as tired of it as i am. the reaisen that i have not Exposed it before now is this if the Deserters was to find out that i would Expose it the[y] would kill me. i am ... as true to my Country as any man ... and i will pledg my life that i never will be Caught in another Such trape"[116] (punctuation added). Apparently Vance pardoned Auman, for he remained a justice of the peace until the end of the war. There is some question as to just which country Auman had in mind when he wrote Vance, "i am ... as true to my country as any man." In July 1865, he wrote Provisional Governor Holden,[117] "i right you afue lines ... to give you my love and Best Respects and i thank god that we air from under the Rule of Secssion." Auman closed by asking Holden to start mailing him copies of the *Standard*.[118] Indicating that he had been a man of at least moderate pro–Union sentiments, Provisional Governor W.W. Holden, a Republican, reappointed Auman justice of the peace after the war.[119]

Although historians have been uncertain as to just when the Heroes of America first appeared in North Carolina, J.G. deRoulhac Hamilton, the historian who pioneered the study of the secret order, concluded that it was probably some time in 1863.[120] He was uncertain where the HOA originated; perhaps, as some observers speculated, it began in the North, and secret agents carried it to the South. According to the evidence presented in this narrative, a more likely scenario is that native Tar Heel Unionists spawned it in the Quaker Belt. As recounted in chapter two, militant Unionists in the first days of the war in the Randolph-Davidson-Forsyth-Guilford County area went underground under the leadership of John Hilton of Davidson and organized a secret group that resisted Confederate power. It is probable that members of the Hilton band organized the Heroes of America at that time (late spring or early summer of 1861) or, at the latest, at the time of the passage of the state and Confederate draft laws in March and April 1862. It is significant that three of the best-known leaders of the Heroes of America in North Carolina came from that area: Dr. John Lewis Johnson, from southern Forsyth County, and William F. Henderson and Henderson Adams, both from Lexington, the seat of Davidson County.

Dr. J.L. Johnson was a prominent organizer and leader of the Heroes in North Carolina and in the Confederate army during the war. Daniel R. Goodloe[121] testified in 1871 in the Ku Klux Klan trials that Dr. Johnson — after he fled north late in the war — initiated President Lincoln, General Ulysses S. Grant, Benjamin Sherwood Hedrick, Joseph Barrett (the commissioner of pensions), and himself into the order. Other than the testimony of Goodloe, no one else has put forth evidence to indicate that Grant or Lincoln was initiated into the Heroes of America. William F. Henderson was the leader and "Grand Secretary" of the Heroes of America during Reconstruction, when the secret order was composed mostly of Scalawags, and served as an auxiliary to the Republican Party. Henderson was a close personal friend and advisor to Governor William Woods Holden. Henderson Adams was a wealthy merchant in Lexington, owner of eight slaves, successful peace candidate to the state house in 1864, personal friend of Lewis Hanes (author of the Reunionist Manifesto), and acclaimed to be one of the "founders" of the Heroes of America.[122]

A.G. Foster wrote Governor Vance a letter in June describing the political prospects for Vance in the Randolph-Davidson area. In a reference to the Heroes of America, Foster asked Vance to expose a "secret society" known to be widespread in Randolph and surrounding counties. By doing so, he would frighten many of Holden's followers who belonged to the clandestine organization into abandoning their leader. Elaborating upon his point, he continued: "It is to me I confess a mortifying thought that we have in our midst a set of men who only want the aid and backing of Yankee bayonets to murder and destroy ... the true men of the country. I believe there are hundreds such and I believe also that many men who aspire to be public men — who *pretend* to want a Convention *to help the Confederate Govt*— a Govt they have persistently opposed and denounced — would become Andy Johnsons and Brownlows' but for the want of the necessary backing from the Yankees."[123] Both Andrew Johnson and "Parson" Brownlow were outspoken pro–Union leaders in East Tennessee during the war who actively worked for the overthrow of the Confederacy. Johnson, of course, became vice president in 1864 and acceded to the presidency upon Lincoln's assassination.[124]

William Burson — an Ohio infantryman who passed through Randolph County in October 1864 after escaping from the Confederate prisoner of war camp at Florence, South Carolina — wrote a book later in life describing his wartime experiences. In his book, Burson reinforced Foster's contention that many citizens in Randolph County belonged to a disloyal "secret society." A friendly slave directed the fugitive to a pro–Union Home Guard trooper who advised him to head to the "Quaker settlement" in Randolph County, where a secret organization of Unionists existed that would aid him in his trek to the Federal lines in Tennessee.[125] After several arduous days travelling mostly at night, Burson arrived in Franklinsville, a cotton mill village on the banks of the Deep River in Randolph County. There the local "president" of the Heroes of America initiated him into the secret society, an organization that "was doing almost as much injury to the rebel cause as an invading army." The Red String leader boasted "that there were seventy-five thousand of this Order in North Carlina alone." He served as a pilot on the Underground Railroad, which had a station in Franklinsville. After about a week in the village, the HOA chief directed Burson on his way to the Union lines in Tennessee.[126]

The War Conservative press seized every opportunity to intimidate peace candidates in the election by "exposing" them as traitorous Red Strings who welcomed the vote of "highway robbers and house-burners." For example, the Raleigh *Weekly Conservative* charged that the pro–Holden candidates in Chatham and Randolph did not deny, when accused on the stump, that they were members of the Heroes of America, which the editor derisively referred to as "Hiders Out of the Army."[127] The August 1, 1864, issue of the Greensboro *Patriot* contained two articles calculated to cost "Holdenites" votes. One, entitled "Voting in the Woods," declared: "All the deserters and skulkers, house-burners and robbers, all the desperate characters in the land intend to vote for Holden, if they can. No provision having been made for carrying the ballot box to the bushes, Mr. Holden's vote will be more slim and meager than it otherwise would have been." Another article, headed "The Last Desperate Game," related the story that "Holden's friends and followers" in Montgomery County were "a band of deserters" who were spreading a rumor that Governor Vance had been assassinated.

The defamation of Holden as the candidate of disloyal deserters, outlaws, robbers, house burners, and murderers reached its apogee in a letter to the editor printed in the *Daily Conservative*, the political organ of the War Conservatives. The author warned:

> In some sections, Vance stock *is* at a low ebb. Where ever the foliage is so dense or the mountain fastness so inaccessible as to make the pursuit of deserters impracticable to the small force left in the West, Holden stock is far above par. His supporters hold their midnight meetings in undisturbed security, rob hen roosts and smoke-houses, or shoot down such Vance men as have incurred their displeasure by attempts to arrest them or interfere with their nefarious practices. Wherever there is a deserter's camp, there you find a Holden caucus. All army men, who have been in the West, know how populous the woods are in that section and who compose the inhabitants. There is not a Vance man among them. They are all "Conservatives of the straitest sect;" [that is, peace Conservatives] Peace men who hate a line of battle, but glory in lying behind a stump to ambuscade loyal citizens.[128]

The Election Results

The election results revealed Vance to be the overwhelming favorite, for he won by a landslide: 57,873 to 14,432.[129] Holden conceded victory to Vance in an editorial in the August 17 issue of the *Weekly Standard*. He went on to claim that had he won the election, and had Congress adopted and carried out the views advanced by him on the question of peace in the *Standard* in July 1863, commissioners from the two sections would by now have met, declared an armistice, and be sitting in session working on a peace agreement. Holden then pointed to the peace resolutions introduced into the Confederate House by Representative Dr. J.T. Leach in March 1864, which the House rejected. In his resolutions, Leach recommended that the president and Senate appoint commissioners to try to negotiate a ninety-day armistice with the Lincoln government preliminary to peace negotiations. If the Federals agreed to an armistice, then the president and senate, along with the several states, should appoint commissioners to work with Northern commissioners to hammer out a peace between the sections "as will be consistent with the honor, dignity and independence of the States, and compatible with the safety of our social and political rights." Doubtless, Leach, a known Copperhead, meant "compatible with the safety of our social and political rights" to denote that any peace must include the protection of slavery by the Constitution in a returning state. Regarding Leach's peace resolutions, Holden opined that had Congress adopted them at its last session, progress towards a satisfactory solution to the problems between the sections would now be underway. With an armistice and negotiations for peace in the works, Holden believed that the people of the North, who were anxious for peace, would defeat Lincoln's reelection next November, thus clearing the way for a peaceful settlement of sectional difficulties by Conservative leaders from both sides. However, in light of current military and political developments and the attitudes of Lincoln and Davis, a gloomy Holden concluded that he saw no hope that Lincoln would be defeated, or that the war will end until one side conquers the other.[130]

After the defeat of Holden in the gubernatorial contest, Tyson sent a letter to Governor Vance reflecting on the conversation he and the governor had in 1862, when authorities brought him before Vance while under arrest for distributing his pro–Union writings in Richmond and Raleigh. "If I could only see you and converse with you once more as in days of yore. You have my publications with you. Time only convinces me that they should be read more closely." Tyson added: "Words can't express the desire I have to see you. I have had two pamphlets[131] published since I came to Washington, the last of which is just from the press. We have of course heard of the termination of the election in North Carolina. I have regretted that I did not impress certain of my words more when I last saw you. Things must however take their course."[132] Apparently Tyson believed in himself enough to think he could persuade Vance to give up his insistence on Confederate independence and cooperate with Holden in pushing forth the Copperhead plan for reunion.

Vance's massive victory devastated the opposition. Holden carried only three counties—Johnston, Wilkes, and Randolph.[133] Members of the state legislature and sheriffs were up for election on August 4 also. Little has remained to tell the story of these local elections other than their results. Randolph County, reflecting a deep alienation of the majority of its citizens from the Confederacy, elected pro–Holden candidates to every office. Its blanket rejection of such establishment figures as Governor Vance, J.M. Worth (brother to state treasurer Jonathan Worth), and M.S. Robins (an incumbent commoner, university graduate, and future editor of Vance's political organ, *The Conservative*) in favor of mavericks like W.W. Holden, Joel Ashworth (a common school teacher and a Wesleyan abolitionist), Z.F. Rush (son of Zebidee Rush, the chief of the Heroes of America in Randolph County), and Enos T. Blair (a Quaker) shocked many and clearly revealed that its citizens remained stubbornly at odds with the Richmond government. (J.M. Worth and M.S. Robins [War Conservatives] and Joel Asheworth and Enos T. Blair [Peace Conservatives] ran for seats in the House of Commons. Z.F. Rush ran for sheriff as a Peace Conservative.)[134]

Holden, reveling over the defeat of Robins in Randolph, commented in the *Standard* that he lost the election because he abandoned his Conservatism and joined Vance and the secessionists. Holden claimed that the Peace Conservative majorities in Randolph would have been even greater had it not been for the "military terrorism" enforced by Confederate bayonets and instituted by Governor Vance and President Davis "for the sole purpose of carrying the elections." Upon losing the election, Robins became eligible for the draft.

Enos Blair house about 1870, built around 1770. Enos T. Blair, age 38 in 1860, was a Quaker farmer who was elected in 1864 to the House of Commons as a delegate from Randolph County. He was an ardent peace activist (courtesy Randolph County Public Library's Historical Photograph Collection).

Holden charged that the governor, a good friend of Robins, saved him from conscription by appointing him editor of his party newspaper, *The Conservative*.[135]

Accounts of election results in the Fayetteville *Observer* revealed that Chatham, Moore, and Montgomery counties failed to elect a pro–Holden candidate to the House of Commons or state senate by slight to moderate margins. In only one case was the pro–Holden candidate soundly defeated, and that was in the race for the senate in Chatham. While Montgomery County gave 59 percent of its vote to Vance, the Auman's voting precinct, located in the northeastern corner of the county where the deserter leader William Owens and many of his gang members lived, voted 97 percent for Holden. The Bean's precinct, where the Wesleyan abolitionist Hiram Hulin and his three sons lived, reported 83 percent for Holden. Troy, the county seat, gave a surprising 38 percent to the editor.[136] The pro–Holden faction in Davidson achieved considerable success. Henderson Adams, a reputed founder of the Heroes of America, won the senate race, and Lewis Hanes, who authored the Reunionist Manifesto, won a seat in the commons.[137] In a card advertising their candidacies for political office published in the *Standard*, Adams and Hanes revealed themselves to be ardent peace and convention advocates. If elected, they promised to submit the question of convention or no convention to the people if they desire it, and work for a peace on terms acceptable to the people.[138]

A Confederate patriot wrote Vance from Davidson County that, during the election campaign, Henderson Adams deluded the "uninformed" men in the county by arguing that all that was necessary for peace was the election of Holden. He predicted that if Holden won the governorship, the deserters "would have bin Ready to Come forward & resisted the enforcement of the laws & joined northern troops."[139] Peace Conservatives did well in Wilkes County, where the Raleigh editor beat Vance 567 to 534, and Holdenites Phineas T. Horton and A.S. "Tip" Calloway captured the seats in the House of Commons.[140]

In Guilford, Forsyth, and Yadkin counties, Vance beat Holden by slight to solid majorities. However, in Guilford, vilified as "the Massachusetts of North Carolina" by secessionists, Holdenites carried every seat in the legislature: Robert P. Dick in the senate, and David F. Caldwell, Abraham Clapp, and A.S. Holton in the House of Commons.[141] In Forsyth County two ardent convention supporters, W.B. Stipe and William H. Wheeler, carried the two seats in the House.[142] According to an observer writing from Salem, the army vote gave Vance the winning edge in Forsyth County.[143] Yadkin's one seat in the Commons went to Andrew C. Cowles — militia officer, wealthy merchant, and brother of Calvin J. Cowles of Wilkes County. Unlike his brother Calvin, who was an ardent Holdenite, Andrew supported Vance.[144]

Voter Intimidation and Election Irregularities

Some historians have interpreted Vance's smashing victory over Holden in the 1864 gubernatorial election as proof that the vast majority of North Carolinians were loyal if unenthusiastic Confederates, and that all the talk about rampant treason in the state was little more than confounding disaffection for disloyalty.[145] Holden and leading Peace Conservatives denounced the election as a fraud because of voter intimidation and election irregularities. Vance and the War Conservatives denied the charges. But if Holden and his followers were correct in their assessment of the election as essentially fraudulent, then the view that its results proved that the preponderance of the electorate of the state was basically loyal Confederates becomes questionable.

Five factors indicate that the election was biased in favor of the candidacy of Vance. One, it was conducted under the pall of the suspension of the writ of habeas corpus. Peace Conservatives, most of whom favored reunion, could not frankly express their political sentiments for fear of military arrest and imprisonment without benefit of trial. Indeed, informed Confederates such as Vice President Alexander Stephens openly expressed the view that Davis suspended the writ to assure Vance a victory in the election.[146] Two, the Conscription Act of February 1864 made every male between the ages of seventeen and fifty liable to the draft. Thus, the great majority of voters in the state who were not in the army were men either exempted from the draft or detailed from the army or Senior Reserves to work for the government. They were at the mercy of army officers, the vast majority of whom were pro–Vance. These officers could threaten at any time to revoke their men's exemptions or detail assignments and force them into the ranks.[147] As one observer complained: "There are hundreds of honest, hard working poor men, who are now working for the State, *subject to the control of Gov. Vance*— thereby, keeping out of the army, and earning a scant but honorable living for their families," who — if they voted for Holden, and Vance won reelection — would be forced into the army, because they had not voted for Vance.[148] In a like manner, all state officials, including justices of the peace, militia officers, and Home Guard officers, were liable at any time to be cashiered by the governor or adjutant general for disobeying orders, negligence of duty, disloyalty, or incompetence. Dismissal from office for most entailed the loss of their draft exemption — a possibility that perforce made them, ostensibly at least, Vance supporters.[149] For example, a Holdenite from Randolph County charged: "The Conservative party of Randolph was shamefully mistreated. There were strong guards of armed men at nearly all the precincts. The detailed hands and reserves between 45 and 50 took the alarm, and most of them voted for Vance against their previously expressed wishes."[150] Obviously, a free electorate did not go to the polls in North Carolina on August 4, 1864. Three, polling irregularities denied the voters the right to a secret ballot. Traditionally in North Carolina elections, polling officials issued ballots printed on white paper so that a voter could fold and cast a ballot without anyone knowing how he voted. However, on Election Day, the War Conservatives issued Vance tickets printed on yellow paper "so as to detect every citizen that did not vote for him." Thereby, the election procedures intimidated men exempted or detailed from the army into casting yellow tickets or chance exposure as Holden supporters. That disclosure incurred "the fearful risk of being immediately picked up and sent to the front as conscripts." In addition, authorities viewed a refusal to vote as proof that one was against Vance and the Confederacy.[151] Four, Vance ordered troops into many of the Quaker Belt counties to protect the polls from interference by deserters, some of whom threatened to prevent War Conservatives from voting on Election Day. However great the need may have been to guarantee the right to vote at the polls, the presence of armed troops near the ballot boxes frightened large numbers of Holden supporters into remaining at home on Election Day.[152] Five, soldiers were intimidated into voting for Vance by their officers, who threatened pro–Holden privates with unpleasant camp duties, the denial of passes, furloughs, and medical care, and placement in the front ranks in battle.[153] As one observer put it, "Every detailed man and every soldier was free to vote as he pleased, but the distinct understanding was, as a general rule, that if he did not vote for Gov. Vance he would be punished."[154]

Vance routed his opposition in the army as well as among the civilians. The soldier vote was Vance 13,209, Holden 1,824; the civilian vote, 44,856 and 12,647.[155] About four months after the election, an angry Holden commented: "The truth is, it was no election at all, so far as the army and two thirds of the Counties were concerned. Gov. Vance was re elected by the patronage of the Confederate and State governments, and by the bayonet. It was no free election. Every body knows this."[156]

Ill-Timed Efforts for a Copperhead Peace

In October, the *Standard* published a letter from Senator William W. Boyce of South Carolina to Jefferson Davis that introduced a new voice into the Copperhead cause. Boyce urged President Davis to support McClellan's bid for the presidency by declaring his willingness to call an armistice and a convention of all the states to consider a peace agreement. The Chicago platform of the Northern Democratic Party was reasonable, argued Boyce, and the Confederate government should do all it can to enable the Democrats to gain power.[157] Like Boyce, many citizens in North Carolina, especially in the west, hoped for a McClellan victory over Lincoln in November 1864, because they believed it would lead to an armistice, a cessation of hostilities, and a negotiated peace agreement. The editor of the Salem *People's*

Press heartily endorsed Boyce's proposals: "Let the plan be adopted and the men of the South appointed to meet like men of the North in a general Convention or Congress of all the States North and South, and consult for peace."[158]

Following the Boyce letter, a new wave of peace sentiment erupted in the General Assembly under the leadership of John Pool[159] of Bertie County, and in the Confederate Congress by Representative Dr. J.T. Leach. This was a last desperate effort by the Peace Conservatives to avoid the impending military subjugation of North Carolina by Sherman's army and other Federal military forces in east Tennessee, the sound region, and Virginia then encircling North Carolina. In early December, Congressman Dr. J.T. Leach introduced the following resolution in the Confederate Congress: "That whenever the Government of the United States shall signify its willingness to recognize the reserved rights of the States and guarantee to the citizens of the States their rights of property, as provided in the Constitution of the United States and the laws of Congress ... we will agree to treat for peace." Through this resolution the Confederacy, in effect, would have agreed to reunion on the Copperhead basis. Holden endorsed the Leach peace resolutions. The Confederate Congress overwhelmingly defeated the motion.[160] The editor of the Fayetteville *Observer* reported that Dr. Leach's peace resolutions induced the New York *Herald* to inform its readers that North Carolina's representatives are "ready for peace upon the basis of the Constitution of the United States."[161] It is strange to witness Dr. Leach's promotion of the Copperhead plan of reunion after the reelection of Lincoln a month earlier killed forever any reason to believe that Congress might still block the emancipation of the slaves.

At about the same time that Leach presented his peace resolutions into the Confederate House of Representatives, Peace Conservatives — including two from the Quaker Belt — under the leadership of John Pool began introducing peace proposals into the North Carolina General Assembly in Raleigh. In late November, Pool introduced a set of resolutions in the state senate recommending that the general assemblies of all the Confederate states appoint commissioners to cooperate with North Carolina in asking President Davis to establish a conference in the name of the states to negotiate a peace with the United States through the commissioners.[162] In his proposals, Pool made no demand that slavery be protected under the United States Constitution, as did Dr. Leach in his peace resolutions to the Confederate House. Apparently, as he reported after the war, he was willing to make the best deal possible with the Federals to end the sectional conflict.[163] Vance and the War Conservatives managed to table the Pool resolutions and not open them for discussion in the Senate.[164]

In the House of Commons, Leander Q. Sharpe of Iredell County introduced an unusual resolution in which he declared that the sovereign states had the right to address the question of peace or war, "and settle it without consultation with the President of the Southern Confederacy or the *so-called United States*." Sharpe intended this resolution to remove the chief roadblock to peace negotiations that Peace Conservatives faced — Jefferson Davis with his insistence on independence as a precondition to any treaty. No doubt Sharpe aimed the reference to the "*so-called United States*" at President Lincoln, who refused to negotiate with the Confederacy except on the basis of unconditional surrender. The defeat of the Sharpe resolutions by the narrow margin of 51 to 50 indicated a decline in Vance's power in the General Assembly.[165] Holden, who supported the Sharpe proposals, said that they would have passed but for the absence of several members of the House who would have voted for them if present. The editor believed that the great majority of the people of North Carolina, who wanted peace, approved the idea of removing President Davis from the peace negotiation process.[166]

Near the end of January 1865, Lewis Hanes, member of the House of Commons from Davidson County and author of the Reunionist Manifesto (July 1863), introduced peace resolutions into the North Carolina House. Hanes "took grounds boldly and unequivocally in favor of reconciliation with the people of the North 'under the Constitution of our fathers' as the alternative to be preferred to subjection."[167] Here, Hanes clearly called for reunion on the Copperhead basis. He argued that the Confederate states in general convention together had a right to negotiate a peace with the United States. Following on the lead of Leander Sharpe of Iredell, Hanes added that the negotiations should be made "without consultation with the President of the Confederate states, but subject only to the subsequent ratification of the several states in their separate State Conventions." By a vote of 59 to 40, the pro–Davis forces rejected Hanes's peace resolutions.[168] Thus did the last effort by a North Carolina Peace Conservative to belatedly push forward the Copperhead plan for reconstruction end in failure.

Following the introduction of his peace resolutions, Hanes gave a speech before the House of Commons explaining his reasons for calling for a peace convention. The defeat of the Democrats by Lincoln and the Republicans last November doomed the Confederacy. Then why, reasoned Hanes, continue the war? Why not make an immediate peace? Hanes added that quick action now just might save the slavery that remains. Since slavery cannot be abolished except by an amendment to the Constitution requiring the approval of three-fourths of the states, it is apparent "that such an amendment might be prevented by speedy action on our part."[169] Hanes's strategy to save slavery may have been behind—at least in part—Holden's peace and convention movements. If a peace were negotiated with the North and the Confederate states agreed to return to the Union, but the Republicans still controlled the presidency and/or the Congress, the congressmen from the former Confederate states along with the Northern Democrats would likely be able to block any attempt to pass a constitutional amendment to abolish slavery.

After the war, John Pool, leader of the peace insurgents in late 1864 and early 1865 in the General Assembly, made it clear that the peace leaders at that time advocated reunion on the best terms available. Angry that the peace efforts failed due to the opposition of the war Conservatives and Confederates, Pool lamented: "Had the peace movements of 1864 – '65 been allowed, we could have easily stipulated for an immediate return to the Union, the restoration of political rights and representation in Congress."[170]

Bryan Tyson's *Object of the Administration in Prosecuting the War*

After Bryan Tyson settled in Washington, D.C., in May 1863, he began cultivating friendships with leading members of the Peace Democrats in the North. By 1864, Tyson had become acquainted with many of the leading Copperheads, including Samuel F.B. Morse, famous inventor of the telegraph and president of the Society for the Diffusion of Political Knowledge,[171] the main propaganda organization of the Democratic Party; Charles Mason, a prominent Washington patent attorney who had been chief justice of the supreme court in Iowa and the United States commissioner of patents; August Belmont, co-owner with Fernando Wood of the Democratic newspaper the *World* (New York); Manton Marble, editor of the *World*; and George B. McClellan, a celebrated Union general and Democratic Party nominee for the presidency in the fall 1864 election.[172]

Tyson spent the time between the defeat of Holden and the November elections in the North campaigning tirelessly for the election of McClellan to the presidency of the United States. As part of that effort, he published a Democratic campaign tract entitled *Object of the Administration in Prosecuting the War*, which had printed on the title page "Approved by the Democratic Resident Executive Committee." In the tract, Tyson accused Lincoln and the leading Republicans of adopting policies aimed at deliberately discouraging Southern Unionists from abandoning the Confederacy and supporting the Union cause due to the fear that they would unite with Northern Democrats and moderate Republicans and achieve reunion short of emancipation—a policy Tyson denounced as unconstitutional and dangerously disruptive to Northern unity.[173] If Lincoln had adhered to his original constitutional goal of saving the Union, Tyson argued, the war would have long since been won by Union forces.

Examples of Lincoln's efforts to outrage Southern whites and drive them solidly into the Confederate camp, thereby robbing Southern Unionists of mass support, included the Emancipation Proclamation, the dismissals of Generals George B. McClellan and Don Carlos Buell—both proslavery

Object of the Administration in Prosecuting the War was published by Bryan Tyson in 1864. In it, Tyson stated that he was a "Holdenite" and had been working with Holden and the Peace Conservatives in North Carolina to bring the state back into the Union on the Copperhead basis. This was a Democratic campaign tract that had printed on its title page "Approved by the Democratic Resident Executive Committee." It indicates that Bryan Tyson provided a link between the Tar Heel peace advocates and the Northern Copperhead political leadership (courtesy HathiTrust).

Democrats—from high-ranking positions in the Union army; the refusal of Lincoln to allow the vice president of the Confederacy to enter Washington on a mission of peace; and the selection of General Benjamin Butler—hated in the South for his harsh administration of occupied Louisiana—to take charge of the Union military Department of North Carolina and Virginia in late 1863, thus alienating the people in the Tar Heel state from the Union cause and dampening their enthusiasm for the peace movement. Referring to the negative effects of such tactics on the peace advocates and Unionists in North Carolina, Tyson wrote: "Without doubt, we the Conservatives of North Carolina, with that champion, W.W. Holden at our head, would have long and long ago have brought the people of that State in overwhelming force against the Confederate Authorities, had it not been for the adoption of these extreme, unjust, and unconstitutional measures North, by which means much of the Union sentiment South has been dispersed."[174] Tyson urged his readers to support the Democratic Party, vote for McClellan, and promote the return of the South to the Union on a "strictly Constitutional basis." Tyson demanded, however, that any peace or compromise must be preceded by the south agreeing to return to the Union.[175] Tyson's activities on McClellan's behalf, in addition to his writings, included travelling to army camps in the field to distribute McClellan election tickets.[176] But his efforts proved in vain. Lincoln won the election by a large majority in November.

In the *Object of the Administration*, as noted in the quotation above, Tyson admitted that he was a "Holdenite" when he wrote that he and other North Carolina Conservatives had been coordinating their efforts against the Confederacy in the summer of 1864 "with that champion W.W. Holden at our head."[177] Tyson probably first became acquainted with Holden in the summer of 1862, when he was in Raleigh getting his book *A Ray of Light* and his reunion rircular published. About that time, Holden published a letter in the *Weekly Standard* from Tyson. The practical-minded Tyson discussed in the epistle methods on how to cure "camp diseases" common to soldiers in the field.[178] This letter suggests that Holden may have met Tyson in the summer of 1862. Could Holden have had a hand in the publication of Tyson's political tracts that summer? Surely he knew F.K. Strother, the Raleigh printer who published them.[179] In 1870, Tyson sent Governor Holden a letter in which he wrote of missing an appointment to meet with him a few days before. It is unclear whether this incident occurred in Raleigh or Washington, D.C., the place from which Tyson issued this letter. At that time, Governor Holden was engaged in suppressing Klan activity in Alamance and Caswell counties, where Klansmen had recently murdered two Republicans. Tyson tried to console the Governor: "If I could do any thing [in] these perilous times according to my desires it would be to smoth your path and render your labors less arduous and difficult—impossible of course. Our rulers are to a very great extent composed of wicked men, and the people mourn."[180] This letter suggests that Holden and Tyson were acquaintances, perhaps even friends.

The failure of Holden's peace and convention schemes, climaxed by his defeat by a coalition of the War Conservatives and "original secessionists" in an election characterized by voter intimidation and polling irregularities, led to a fierce uprising of deserters, draft-dodgers, and militant Unionists in the Quaker Belt in the summer of 1864. Vance's reaction was swift and vicious.

CHAPTER SEVEN

The 1864 Election Uprising and the Vance Repression

Defeat dashed the hopes and wishes for peace and reunion engendered in the election campaign of 1864—especially in the gubernatorial contest between Vance and Holden—as the War Conservatives with few exceptions trounced the peace men at the polls at every level. Tired of being bullied by national and state authorities and infuriated by the strong-armed tactics and irregularities practiced against them by the War Conservatives and Confederates in the 1864 elections, the dissidents rebelled once again in the Quaker Belt. Faced with a growing threat by the Federals to take Fort Fisher and close the port of Wilmington, Governor Vance swiftly took stern measures against the forces of anarchy, political opposition, and disloyalty in the west. By 1864, the fleet of blockade runners at the port of Wilmington—known as "the life line of the Confederacy"—had become the last link between the Army of Northern Virginia and world markets. Casting aside all civilized restraints of law and decency that he had hitherto respected, Vance unleashed an offensive against the dissidents that rivaled Sherman's march to the sea in its cruelty to civilians. On a much smaller scale, the Tar Heel governor conducted his own version of "total war" against his internal enemies.

The Home Guards and the Junior and Senior Reserves

Before continuing with the main topic of this chapter—the postelection uprising of anti–Confederate dissidents in the Quaker Belt and the Vance reaction—it is necessary to review certain changes and developments in auxiliary military organizations that occurred in the Confederacy beginning in the winter of 1864. In February, Congress modified the conscription law to include all males between the ages of seventeen and fifty. The law authorized the creation of auxiliary armed forces called "Reserves," which the military placed under the command of district enrolling officers. The law assigned males between seventeen and eighteen years of age to the Junior Reserves and those between forty-five and fifty to the Senior Reserves.[1] Commanders organized the Senior Reserves into companies and regiments and detailed them to hunt deserters and draft-dodgers under the control of the district or county enrolling officer. The Reserves replaced the Home Guards as the primary enforcement arm of the Confederate Conscript Bureau. Officials ordered them to duty in case of invasion or insurrection.

In North Carolina, the most important consequence of the creation of the Senior Reserves was the removal of men (mostly those between forty-five and fifty) from the Home Guards, who were under state jurisdiction, and their reassignment to the Senior Reserves, military units controlled by Confederate authority. Thus, many men who had been serving in the disloyalist-prone and usually unreliable Home Guard battalions found themselves serving in the Confederate military establishment, answerable to Richmond rather than to Raleigh for any misconduct. In a letter to the Randolph County enrolling officer, Captain D.C. Pearson (the chief enrolling officer for the Seventh Congressional District) made it clear that he expected more of the Senior Reserves than the Home Guards: "Keep in mind they are not like the H.G. You order & if they dont obey make them."[2]

In the summer of 1864, Confederate authorities created another military organization, the so-called "Supporting Force." It was an elite arm of the Senior Reserves dedicated solely to the hunting of deserters and draft-dodgers. On June 10, Captain Pearson ordered the enrolling officer for Randolph County to recruit a Supporting Force of one hundred men from the counties in the Seventh Congressional District, of which Randolph's quota was fifteen. The enrolling officer should select personally "the very best men" from the Senior Reserves under his command and assign them to the unit.[3] In one case, Senior Reserve commanders ordered some Supporting Force recruits sent to Camp Holmes for two or three months' training and then returned them to their home counties to arrest deserters and draft-dodgers under the orders of the county enrolling officers.[4]

Troubles in Yadkin and Davie Counties

About a month before Election Day, matters began to come to a head in the Randolph, Moore, Montgomery area, and in the Yadkin, Davie area. Reports of serious trouble first came from the latter locality, where, one observer warned, "hells to pay."[5] In mid–July, the adjutant general ordered the Home Guard commanders in Yadkin and Davie counties to assemble their battalions immediately and "capture or destroy all deserters you may find, and break up any Military Organization that may exist in violation of our laws."[6] Indicating that Governor Vance intended to keep his pledge to the voters to always subordinate military law to civil law, the adjutant general wrote Major Harbin, the commander of the expedition, "Your letter of the 16 inst. has been received. I am directed by the governor to reply that the persons referred to must be arrested according to law, i.e., swear out warrants and arrest them on the warrants."[7]

All the excitement centered on the actions of dissidents in Yadkinville. There, a gang of deserters and draft-dodgers, numbering between 100 and 300 men, forcibly released three prisoners from the Yadkin County jail. Rumor had it that they, being Holden supporters, intended to take possession of the polls in the western counties and prevent Vance men from voting. Alexander Johnson and Elkanah Willard led the deserter band.[8] In the past, Johnson had been "charged with housebreaking and Stealing in company with negro Slaves in Davie County."[9] Willard was related (probably a sibling) to Benjamin and Lee

Willard, two of the leaders of the dissidents involved in the schoolhouse shootout the year before who had been incarcerated in the Yadkin jail ever since.[10] A loyal Confederate unflatteringly described the deserter band as a conglomeration of "jail-breakers, escaped murderers, deserters from the Army, recusant Conscripts, Some of them Known to have been lying out for two or three years and desperately bad men, escaped Yankee prisoners, and a few disloyal persons, over and under the military age."[11] It is unclear whether Benjamin and Lee Willard were among the three liberated from the Yadkin jail by the mob. Nevertheless, they, along with William Willard and a man named Enoch Brown, escaped from the Yadkin County jail in January 1865. All had been incarcerated for two years while awaiting trial for resisting and killing militia officers at the Yadkin schoolhouse firefight.[12]

Officials had charged two of the three rescued prisoners with the murder of the two militia officers killed in the Yadkinville schoolhouse shootout. Soon after liberating their comrades in the county jail, the desperados — said to be composed of men from Randolph, Forsyth, and Yadkin counties[13] — re-entered Yadkinville and seized the arms and ammunition belonging to the local Home Guard battalion. They then "left Yadkin County with the avowed purpose of going within the enemy's lines, and enlisting (Some of them at all events) in the Federal army."[14] On their way to Tennessee, the deserters skirmished with members of the Surry County Home Guards; one man on each side "was dangerously wounded."[15] They then proceeded through Wilkesboro into Watauga County, where Confederate and Home Guard troops managed to kill five and capture forty-one of the band. Among the captured were two of the Yadkin jail escapees and "the man who took the keys from the jailer."[16]

Home Guard troopers assigned to hunt deserters often paid a fearful price for doing their duty. Guardsman J.F. Woodward of Alexander County was waylaid and shot at his residence by a gang of ten deserters. "A short time previous, as a member of the Home Guard, he went with his company into Wilkes county in search of deserters, and in the discharge of his duty he shot a notorious desperado and deserter named Jo. Younger." Two days after it became known that Woodard shot Younger, the slain deserter's comrades got their revenge. Friends of Woodard swore they would kill ten deserters in retribution.[17] Deserters murdered another Home Guard officer in Davie County a few days later. The victim was a Mr. Glasscock, who "was shot by some unknown person, or persons, last Sunday, while riding along the public road above Mocksville, near the Yadkin line. His body was penetrated by five balls. It is believed this deed was done by deserters. He was robbed of his pistol."[18]

Vance gave a campaign speech at Yadkinville a few days after the deserter band absconded to Tennessee. In July the *Weekly Conservative* (Vance's political organ) warned citizens that the "tories" and deserters "intend to take possession of the polls in the Western counties — that they intend themselves to vote for Holden, and that no man shall be allowed to vote unless he votes the Holden ticket." The motivation for this intended behavior, thought the editor, was "obvious." If elected, they believed Holden would protect and defend them so they would be free to leave the woods and return home. Further, Holden's election would achieve much towards the collapse and ruin of the Confederacy.[19] On the day before the election, the editor restated his alarmist charge that the "Yadkin tories and deserters" were "making their way to Tennessee, in order to obtain reinforcements with a view of returning to the Western counties of this State and controlling the election in favor of Mr. Holden."[20] The written testimony of four men intimately familiar with the actions and personnel of the Yadkin deserter band made no mention of threats by the deserters to "take possession of the polls." According to Richmond M. Pearson, chief justice of the Supreme Court of North Carolina, and a resident of Yadkin County, and Major J.R. McLean, commander of Camp Vance, who had charge of the Yadkin deserters captured in Watauga County, the purpose of the deserter band was to escape to Tennessee to join the Union army.[21] L.L. Chamberlain, one of the captured deserters and a friend of Alexander Johnson, the band's leader, testified that Johnson planned to go to Indiana, where he said that he could earn wages of $60 per month. Johnson offered to lead others with him to Indiana after he dropped off the main body of the gang in Tennessee.[22] Johnson did not go to Indiana but remained in Tennessee, where he became a recruiting agent for Union regiments stationed in East Tennessee. Johnson did most of his recruiting behind the rebel lines in western North Carolina, where he induced deserters, draft-dodgers, and militant Unionists to flee to the Union lines and join the Federal army.[23] While some of Alexander Johnson's band may have bragged that they planned to link up with Tennessee militant Unionists and raid the polls in North Carolina on Election Day, such a boast hardly would have been credible and did not represent the collective plan of action of the gang.

Calvin Cowles expressed to William Holden the view that the War Conservatives' cry that deserters would take possession of the polls was a "mere pretence ... for putting soldiers at the ballot box." Cowles observed that the deserters' "object seems to be to get away. Now who is afraid of such men as these taking possession of the polls — no one."[24] Cowles was right. The charge that Tar Heel deserters and militant Unionists in cahoots with "tories" from Tennessee could somehow plan and carry out a widespread raid on the "western" counties of North Carolina and disrupt the elections was absurd. Any significant hostile force ordered across the Blue Ridge into piedmont North Carolina would have faced hundreds, probably thousands, of Confederate army regulars. Commanders could easily rush them in by rail from the eastern part of the state and southeastern Virginia to the foot of the Blue Ridge at the railhead in Burke County. It may have been possible for a determined force to disrupt elections in a few of the mountain counties adjoining Tennessee, but that hardly would have been surprising.

Kirk's Raid

The War Conservatives' charge that the disloyalists in western North Carolina, reinforced by "Tories" from East Tennessee, intended to disrupt the polls on Election Day and prevent Vance men from voting, though far-fetched, did have a basis in reality. In mid–June 1864, Colonel George W. Kirk led a raiding party of 130 Federal troops across the mountains into the western piedmont of North Carolina. Kirk was commander of the Third North Carolina Mounted Infantry Volunteers stationed in East Tennessee — a Union army regiment made up mostly of North Carolinians from the western piedmont and Appalachian region. Kirk planned to commandeer a locomotive at the railhead near Morganton (seat of Burke County) and transport his troops to the Confederate prison at Salisbury (seat of Rowan County). He then would liberate the Federal prisoners of war at the prison, burn the railroad bridge across the Yadkin River near Salisbury, and make a hasty retreat back to Tennessee before the Confederates could muster the forces to stop him.[25]

Kirk's proposal to liberate the prison at Salisbury was an implausible scheme. Had he made it into Salisbury with his 130 raiders,[26] hundreds of militia, Home Guard, and Junior and Senior Reserve troops would have confronted him immediately. In addition, since Salisbury was accessible by rail from Raleigh, Greensboro, High Point, Charlotte, and other piedmont railheads — all of which contained telegraph services and some Confederate troops — hundreds of Confederate regulars would have descended on Kirk's force within hours of the first warning of trouble. Salisbury, located near the geographical center of the state, was a hundred miles from the Blue Ridge Mountains. With such a large distance to cover to get to safety, it seems unlikely that Kirk's raiders, burdened with liberated but malnourished and poorly armed POWs, could have fought their way to freedom.

On the morning of the 28th, Kirk's "raiders" captured Camp Vance near Morganton. Camp Vance was a Camp of Instruction established for the western part of the state by Colonel Peter Mallett, commandant of the Confederate Conscript Bureau headquartered at Camp Holmes in Raleigh. At the time of Kirk's raid, the camp contained about 250 unarmed Junior Reservists and a handful of regular army officers. Caught completely by surprise, the post commander surrendered to Kirk without a fight.[27] Confederates at the railhead at Morganton managed to warn the garrison at Salisbury before Kirk's men could cut the telegraph wire. Faced with "a force of home guards and prison guards ... raised to pursue him," the intrepid Kirk and his raiders beat a hasty retreat back to the safety of the western slope of the Blue Ridge Mountains.[28]

Clearly, Kirk and his raiders posed no great threat to the Confederacy or the Tar Heel State in this brief foray into western North Carolina. He got lucky and captured a couple hundred unarmed, untrained, teenage Confederate soldiers, most of whom he released before his retreat back to Tennessee. Any future raid of the polls in western North Carolina on Election Day by Kirk, to be successful, would have required a Union army instead of a company of "mounted infantry." However, the War Conservative press in its propaganda campaign to discredit Holden, preached otherwise. The editors routinely prophesied the imminent second coming of Kirk and his raiders, who would arrive in western North Carolina on Election Day and assure Holden a victory by scaring Vance voters away from the polls.[29]

Troubles in the Randolph Area

Meanwhile, trouble also threatened in the Randolph, Moore, Montgomery, Chatham area in the weeks before the election. On June 29, Lieutenant T.H. Houghton, county enrolling officer for Montgomery, said none of the men conscripted in the last enrollment reported for duty, and about 200 deserters and draft-dodgers were "lying in the woods." He urged Captain D.C. Pearson, chief enrolling officer for the Seventh Congressional District, who was headquartered in Lexington, to send him a company of Supporting Force troops.[30] "The presence of a good active force here," he wrote, "would have a beneficial effect upon the loyalty of the citizens which I must say is not of the most exalted character."[31] "Send me men guns and ammunition," pleaded Houghton, "[and] I will pay you back in deserters and conscripts."[32] Three days later, Houghton wrote his superior: "If you believe me two third[s] of the county are Lincoln men, they would vote to-day for Abe Lincoln." He added that he was "threatened by the deserters in this county in every conceivable way. I get reports every day that they are preparing to attack me here and liberate the few men I have here." "If the devils attack me," resolved the fearless Confederate, "I will fight them to the last."[33]

Lieutenant J.A. Little, enrolling officer for Moore County, reported conditions similar to those in Montgomery County. Thwarted by the disloyalty and disobedience of his subordinates, Little wrote in frustration on July 11: "Neither the men nor the [militia] Captains who were ordered to [duty] ... reported, their seems to be a perfect contempt for orders or anything else." "One of the Captains is a Holden Candidate," he added, "& I have not seen him nor heard from him."[34] In his monthly report for July, he wrote: "Any amount of Deserters in this county, the Home Guards & Militia are too weak for them, & no dependence in them any way, a good force is much needed here, Robberies are of common occurance."[35] Noting that the trouble with the organized dissidents was only just beginning, he said, "they have been holding meetings and planning for the winter Campaign."[36]

Matters must have been equally critical in Randolph County, for Lieutenant E.R. Holt, the Randolph County enrolling officer, wrote Captain Pearson on July 19 to send him as many of the Supporting Force as he could spare. Referring to the actions of the William Owens gang, he added: "The deserters are carrying on at a high rate in the lower part of this co. [county] pressing guns etc. most every day I hear of their depredations.... The M. [militia] Officers are afraid to do anything."[37] On July 13, Lieutenant Holt arrested and sent to Camp Holmes in Raleigh a conscript named B.F. Wheeler, who paid a high price for his defiant conduct when he attempted to break away from the guard house. "Wheeler, who seized the gun of the sentinel nearest the door, intending to wrest it from him, was shot in the breast and fell dead after running off a few steps."[38]

On the day before the election, an article appeared in the *Weekly Conservative* titled "Heroes in Chatham." It claimed that deserters, who had been defying authorities in the county for several months, were members of the Heroes of America. They had recently banded together and begun stealing guns from loyal citizens. The dissidents, the editor claimed, stole the weapons in order "to get to the polls *armed* on the day of the election, as they have been advised to do by their leader, W.W. Holden.... It is very much feared in Chatham that they will overawe the people and take possession of the polls, unless prompt measures are taken to prevent it."[39] The victims of the gun-stealing deserters in Chatham included the households of Captain T.J. Goldston, J.J. Goldston, Sr., A.J. Goldston, and B.N. Watson — two of whom were not at home at the time of the robberies — who lived in the Gulf community in the south-central part of the county. Five deserter marauders escaped with ten guns. The editor advised citizens to start resisting the deserters: "*Use* the guns instead of giving them up. Kill a few of the robbers, and they will be careful how they go upon such a business." Then the editor made an unusual suggestion: "If the men be from home, can't the women show their pluck and skill and shoot the robbers?"[40]

The Vance press, which already had been inflaming fears of a force composed of deserters and Tennessee Tories overrunning the western counties to take control of the polls on Election Day, now charged that deserter gangs in the piedmont under the aegis of the Heroes of America of plotting the same crime. The *Daily Confederate* quizzed its readers: "Shall the risk be run that on Election Day outlaws, subject to the death penalty for crimes already committed, will approach the precincts and take possession of the election?"[41] Apparently Governor Vance thought not, for the adjutant general issued the following order to Lieutenant Colonel I.H. Foust in Randolph: "The Governor directs that you have your command under arms on the day of election in localities where the deserters may be threatening; to protect the polls."[42] The adjutant general sent duplicate orders to the Home Guard commanders in Montgomery, Moore, Chatham, Iredell, Wilkes, Yadkin, Surry, and Henderson counties — all but Henderson were in the Quaker Belt.[43]

At the end of July, the adjutant general ordered Lieutenant Colonel E.L. Yellowly, commander of the Sixty-eighth Regiment North Carolina Troops stationed then at Morganton (seat of Burke County), to send one company of his regiment to Trap Hill in Wilkes County, and another company to Yadkin County to protect the polls from deserters. He instructed Yellowly to select "very discret officers" to command these companies. The troops were to encamp no closer than a mile to the polling stations "and [were] not to go nearer, unless it becomes necessary to do so in order to prevent interference with the Elections." No officer was "to allow his men in any instance to interfere with any Citizen by threat or otherwise."[44]

Captain Pearson directed his enrolling officers (who were also commanders of local Senior Reserve companies) in every county in the Seventh Congressional District to order the Reserves "to report to them on the day before the election, and distribute them at the precincts in their respective counties where they may have cause for thinking the Deserters intend voting." "Discretion should be used," warned the captain, "so that it may not be said that the Polls have been controlled by an armed force."[45] Despite the precautions taken by Vance and the Confederate authorities, armed deserters voted for Holden in several counties, including Moore, Wilkes, Johnston, and Richmond.[46]

A miller in the upper Moore community of Prosperity reported to the governor that all of the militia officers in his area had voted for Holden. He added that a rumor was circulating that the deserters intended to kill all of those who had voted for Vance. In conclusion, he warned Vance to "keep this to your Self as i am in a damed Set of the ... robers."[47] Another Moore County resident warned his brother on August 2 that "the deserters and conscripts is doing a bout the Same[.] [T]here is Some of them at the Sunday School every Sunday[.] [T]hey will Soon take the day unless Something is done[.]"[48]

Insurrection

Moore County teetered on the brink of insurrection in the days immediately after the election. A resident wrote to the editor of the Fayetteville *Observer*: "Ever since the election large groups of armed deserters have been roaming over the Country, inquiring who of the citizens voted for Vance and who for Holden, swearing that they had been deprived of their rights and intended to have revenge." He noted that witnesses reported seeing several large gangs of deserters numbering between 20 and 90 men each on the roads in the county. Fully expecting an armed struggle with the deserter guerrillas, the writer concluded: "Our Home Guard and citizens are under arms acting on the defensive. We are not quite ready yet for an aggressive movement."[49]

Reflecting several years afterward upon the wartime conditions in Carthage, a resident recalled that deserters and "outlyers from among the ignorant classes" in the area had twice threatened "to burn our village, their attempts being frustrated by the constant vigil, day and night, of those who were left among us for our protection." She noted that she had a "faithful servant" named Isam who, armed with a pistol, maintained a watch every night outside her window so that she could feel secure enough to sleep.⁵⁰ It is ironic to consider that her "faithful servant" likely was a slave. Military authorities in Carthage placed pickets around the village to provide warning in case of attack by the deserters.⁵¹

On August 1, the enrolling officer for Moore County reported that a company of Supporting Force commanded by a Lieutenant Mills had arrived in the county to protect the polls. He noted that this elite force of hunters had "arrested three men on their way, and wounded one pretty seriously; Lt Mills received a very heavy blow (from the mother of the man that was shot) on side of his head. The women is bad as the men down here."⁵² After capturing several deserters on August 5 in the upper edge of Moore County, Lieutenant Mills took them to Carthage and jailed them for the night. The next morning, he marched his prisoners eastward on the plank road heading for a railway station.⁵³ About three miles out, a band of deserters, about seventy in number, ambushed his company of forty men. The attackers included many friends and relatives of the prisoners. The deserters killed three of the Supporting Force and wounded eighteen, one mortally. The lieutenant managed to rally his men and drive off the attackers. One or two prisoners escaped, but the Supporting Force captured one of the bushwhackers.⁵⁴ Just two days after the attack on the Supporting Force in Moore, a similar ambush occurred near Franklinsville in Randolph, where the attackers killed four members of the Senior Reserves.⁵⁵

In later years a doctor, who had been a boy living in Carthage at the time of this incident, wrote that the Senior Reservists brought the three dead soldiers back to town and placed their bodies in the "Old Tyson House": "Everybody in town flocked up to see them and, boy-like, I was among them. The men were laid out on what looked like rough work benches. The excitement in the town was great, but feeling was divided between sympathy for the outliers who had killed them, and patriotic feelings for the dead soldiers."⁵⁶ Authorities tried and convicted the deserter captured in the ambush of murder. The state supreme court upheld his conviction. By that time, the war was nearly over, and somehow the defendant managed to escape the gallows.⁵⁷

Excited by the shootout between Lieutenant Mills's company and the ambushing deserter band, a young Confederate loyalist wrote to her brother serving in the army that "it looks like we are geting right in to war at home neaightbour against neaightbour." Indicating just how vicious hatreds between partisan factions had become by 1864 in the Quaker Belt, the Confederate stalwart threatened: "I could nock them in the head with a ax just as fast as they would bring them tow me and never flinch at it[.]" Exasperated, she exclaimed, "I wish the deserters had to dig up Randolph with there teeath and carry it off with there mouths."⁵⁸

In mid–August, sixteen deserters "raided" Troy, the seat of Montgomery County. They "captured" the arms of the Home Guards and a small quantity of "government bacon," both conveniently stored in the same building. Next, they robbed a "gentleman" of his "Confederate Treasury Notes" and sixteen bundles of cotton yarn. The gang capped their chain of successful raids when they "captured a tan yard and 'impressed' ... the leather."⁵⁹

On August 9, H.J. Haughton wrote Governor Vance from Pittsboro (the seat of Chatham County) that there were 800 to 1,000 deserters in Randolph, Moore, Montgomery, and Chatham counties, and that many "Holdenite" deserters were presently leaving General Lee's army and coming into that area. He intimated that "deserters who have been stealing guns in the lower part of this county intend arming the slaves & that this was confessed by slaves of a highly respectable man."⁶⁰ Indicating the level to which the bitterness and hatred of neighbor for neighbor had arrived, Haughton continued: "The feeling of all our best & most prudent citizens so far as I have heard ... is that a war of extermination be waged on deserters, that it is time to cease making captures — that the plan adopted in Alabama ... is the only one that will avail, that is to hang them up to the pine tree[s] & then let them hang. I assure you the most stringent & urgent measures you can adopt will be most acceptable to the loyal people of this section. I doubt not of the whole state."⁶¹

On the same day, J.M. Worth wrote Vance from Asheboro. In terse, deliberate terms, he portrayed conditions that were insurrectionary: "More than half" of Randolph, Moore, and Montgomery counties were "in the hands of the desperatoes." The deserters ranged "in squads all over the Country robbing every Loyal man they can find. The Red Strings are exempt from their depredations." The armed dissidents recently had ambushed militia squads in Randolph twice, wounding several officers, one mortally. "I assure you," wrote Worth, "that nothing but prompt and efficient aid will save us from utter ruin [of] both life and property." "I write under no panic and I assure you that I cannot make the case appear as strong as it is."⁶²

Making note of just how radical political sentiments had become in Randolph, Worth told the governor that state authorities denied the sheriff-elect, Z.F. Rush, a commission in the militia because of "his Abolition sentiments."⁶³ Another source reported that in the recent election campaign, Rush "would not deny on the stump his membership with the H.O.A.'s[.]" His father, Zebedee Rush, "was said to be the High Priest of the concern" in the county.⁶⁴ Indeed, exclaimed Worth, Rush "had nothing in the world to recommend him for the Sheriffs place but his Red String and disloyal sentiments."⁶⁵ The sheriff-elect's brother, Major Noah Rush, commanded Randolph's Fifth Battalion Home Guards.⁶⁶ It is interesting that so much power would be concentrated in one family. With the local sheriff and Home Guard commander in the Red String camp, there was little chance of effective enforcement of the conscript laws or of catching "outlaws" in Randolph County. Major Richard Anderson, who had recently arrived in Asheboro in command of the Fifty-eighth Battalion Home Guards, noted that revolution was afoot in the area: "I assembled my command at Ashboro fully impressed that there was need of men to put down the insurrectionary movement then threatening that vicinity."⁶⁷

Repression

With the deserters in the Quaker Belt again in a state of insurrection, Confederate and state leaders took immediate and drastic action. Governor Vance, in an effort to finally silence the deserters and militant Unionists, launched a massive campaign against them. This was the fourth time he, in cooperation with Confederate authorities, had resorted to repressive measures against dissidents in the Quaker Belt.⁶⁸ And it was the sixth time commanders ordered Confederate forces into the area during the war since the summer of 1861. On August 13, 1864, the adjutant general ordered eleven battalions of the Home Guards into Chatham, Randolph, Montgomery, and Moore counties to "capture or destroy" deserters who were "committing murders, robberies and other depredations upon the peaceful citizens." The state troops were to "be kept in the field for sixty days, or until the deserters are captured, destroyed or driven from the Country." Four of the battalions were ordered into Moore, three into Randolph, two into Chatham, and two into Montgomery.[69] The Confederate Conscript Office in Raleigh ordered Captain Pearson to call out all of the Reserve troops in the seventh congressional district to assist the Home Guards in arresting the deserters. Superiors ordered Pearson to "instruct the county E.O. [enrolling officer] to cooperate with Col. Foust — and report progress from time to time, until every deserter is arrested."[70]

By August 22, Home Guard and Senior Reserve units had begun operations. From Randolph, a Richmond County Reservist wrote "ther is a plenty Desertrs her[e] at this plese we have cot three a redy."[71] From Chatham came the rumor that the deserters threatened to burn Pittsboro as soon as the Home Guard units sent into the county to hunt them returned home.[72] From Moore came the report that "there has been two or three companies ordered to this county from other counties which will add 250 men to our present force. You may look out for Squally times soon. They are going right into plundering and eating out the deserters families & their friends." The writer added that Captain Pearson, the chief enrolling officer for the Seventh Congressional District and commander of the Senior Reserves, had established his headquarters at Asheboro.[73]

Just as the defeat of Holden had precipitated an uprising of deserters and draft-dodgers in the Randolph, Moore, Montgomery, Chatham area, the failure of the Holdenites at the polls created a similar situation in the Forsyth, Yadkin, Wilkes, Iredell area, and in a few other counties, including several in the eastern coastal plain. Two days before the election, Josiah Cowles reported unrest in Yadkin, where "there is a guard down from camp Vance arresting members of the H.O.A."[74] Five days after the election, military commanders ordered the Forsyth County Home Guards into service to arrest "deserters and depridators." The adjutant general ordered their commanding officer to "keep his command in the Field, until the work is completed and report promptly to this office all who fail to perform their duty with alacrity."[75] Troops sent into the Trap Hill area of Wilkes County "had quite a severe skirmish with a large number of ... miscreants." The deserter band killed between six and eight Confederates before the troops retreated, abandoning the field to a body of men described by the press as "worse than Yankees."[76]

Frightened by the deserter uprising and horrified by the gunning down of state and regular army troops in Wilkes, Randolph, and Moore counties, the pro–Confederate press encouraged the governor to lead the loyal citizens of the state in a crackdown against the insurgents, whom the editors portrayed as mostly "ignorant" poor men engaged in a war of annihilation against wealthy secessionists who had forced them and their sons into a war to preserve their slave property. The editors vilified Holden as the primary instigator of this class war against the secessionists. For example, the Fayetteville *Observer*, commenting on the ambush of the Supporting Force in Moore County, laid the blame for the slaughter of the four Confederate troopers on the shoulders of Holden and the Peace Conservatives, who taught that "the poor are forced by unconstitutional laws to fight for the property of the rich; that our Gov't is a despotism and our President a tyrant, and that 'resistance to tyrants is obedience to God.'" The editor noted that the Holdenites proclaimed "that Jeff Davis and his cabinet and Congress ought to be hung; that the only way to settle our difficulty is to kill all the Secessionists." Irate fathers fueled much of the discontent, added the editor, many of them swearing they would not allow Confederate authorities to hunt down their sons and force them into the army. Holden and his minions, he continued, inflamed "the minds of ignorant men" to make them believe that "it is their sacred duty to resist rather than obey the laws of the country." The editor forcefully concluded that "this fire in the rear must be put out." The power of the government must be utilized to quickly crush "these organized, and armed traitors, *their counsellors, aiders and abettors.*"[77] A few days later, the editor of the pro–Davis *Confederate* asked its readers if peace and safety will rule in North Carolina, or will "lawlessness, violence and murder" be allowed "to run riot?" Governor Vance must stand up and "crush out now, at once and forever," demanded the editor, the "pestilential influences" that the majority of voters defeated in the last election. But a word from him "and an armed host will spring to the succor of law and loyalty in the State."[78]

Goaded by the press and infuriated by the killing of Confederate and Home Guard troops in Wilkes, Randolph, and Moore counties, Vance ordered seventeen more Home Guard battalions into the field in the fourth week in August "to destroy the deserters from the Confederate army who are represented as banded together in the Counties of Johnston, Union, Wilkes, Nash, Wilson, Forsyth, and Yadkin, committing murders robberies and other depredations on the peaceful citizens."[79] On September 10, commanders ordered two battalions of Home Guards into Robeson County to hunt deserters.[80] Clearly, the insurrection had spread beyond the Quaker Belt to several eastern counties.

The adjutant general ordered five Home Guard battalions to hunt deserters in Wilkes, three in Yadkin, three in Union, three in Nash, two in Johnston, and one each in Forsyth and Wilson. Just as he had done in the Randolph area, the adjutant general ordered the Home Guard commanders to keep their battalions "in the field for sixty days or until the deserters are either captured destroyed or driven from the county."[81] On September 5, a Wilkes County resident wrote in his diary that there were about 600 Home Guard troops in Wilkesboro from adjoining counties hunting deserters.[82] The adjutant general's office in Raleigh issued one hundred fifty muskets and 6,000 rounds of ammunition to the Home Guard commander in Forsyth County whom it ordered "to call out the full strength of ... [his] Battalion"[83] to "operate against these deserters who were robbing and plundering the peaceable citizens of the county."[84] Confederate authorities ordered the Senior Reserves in Forsyth, Davie, Yadkin, and Wilkes counties to cooperate with the Home Guards in their respective counties.[85]

On August 24, 1864, Vance issued a proclamation offering amnesty to all deserters not guilty of capital felonies who surrendered within thirty days. He warned those who refused to comply with his terms "that the utmost powers of this State will be exerted to capture them or drive them from the borders of ... [the] country ... and that the extremest penalties of the law will be enforced without exception when caught, as well as against their aiders and abettors in the civil courts." Vance also cautioned that justices of the peace, militia, and Home Guard officers would have their draft exemptions revoked if they refused or neglected to perform their duties in this operation. The governor ordered out the entire military arm of the state to enforce the conditions of his proclamation.[86]

Many of the Home Guard battalions and Senior Reserve regiments sent into the Quaker Belt during this hunt came from "secession" counties such as Caswell, Cumberland, and Mecklenburg. For example, a Senior Reservist from Mecklenburg County on his way by rail to help repress the uprising of "deserters and Holdenites" in Guilford and surrounding counties wrote of his opportunity to hunt and kill disloyalists: "We have orders to march to Greensboro fourthwith to meet the Raiders in that vicinity[.] [T]he deserters and the Holdenites are fighting desperately — they have whipt out the home guards and Killed many of the citizens that was loyal to the South[.] They number about two thousand.... If I fall, I fall in the defence of my country. I am anxious to give them a few rounds for they are worse than the yankies.... I expect We will have hard fighting to do in 2 or 3 days[.]"[87]

A family man who served in the "Caswell Cavalry," a Home Guard unit, reflected a more sober attitude towards those Tar Heels who were "worse than the yankies." In late September, he recorded in his diary: "our Company has been 38 days taking up deserters in Randolph & other counties[.] [W]e took up over 300 & returned home [&] found my family well."[88] A few months later, the veteran hunter, grateful to be alive, wrote: "All winter myself & horse was in the Confederate service in the Caswell Cavalry in the counties of Randolph & adjacent counties arresting deserters.... I have lived a hard & dangerous life for a long time[.]"[89]

On January 28, 1865, a woman writing to the editor of the *Standard* from Asheborough (the seat of Randolph County) described depredations by Home Guard Cavalry: "I write to tell you how the cavalry served me on last Friday. They searched my house — said our folks were in the woods — took meat, and salt, and chickens from me and commenced to take my corn. I begged so hard they let my corn alone. They also snapped their pistols at me and Mrs. _____. I have always done my part by the soldiers, and it is hard that I should be treated in this way.... The cavalry stopped at every house and took what they pleased." The writer "was an unmarried lady whose brother, who had been her protector, was wounded at the battle of Gettysburg, and is now a prisoner in the hands of the enemy."[90]

Vance initiated this campaign against the outlier dissidents in the same spirit as he had prior ones — by insisting that his troops respect the civil law of his state and the civil liberties of his people. On August 26, the Home Guard commander at Troy (seat of Montgomery County) received the following orders: "These aiders and abettors of deserters must be proceeded against according to Civil law, We can order no other Course. Let you have Magistrates in the H.G. they can issue warrants upon the Spot and require Such a bail as will keep these people in jail for a time at least."[91]

Observing the procedures of the civil law, however, proved time-consuming and usually provided the delinquent with warning in time to make good his escape. Governor Vance was painfully reminded of this fact by A.G. Foster, who wrote on August 27: "The Home Guards now attempting to arrest deserters are doing little good, The whole County [Randolph] is Tory where they are & the women act as couriers & carry the news of every movement they make in advance of them[.] The Col (Hargrave) says he has no authority to arrest them & keep them in camp — nor disloyal men — hence he never will catch a deserter."[92] Jesse Hargrave, a wealthy planter and commander of the Davidson County Home Guard Battalion, directed Home Guard operations then taking place in Randolph County.[93] Commenting on the frustrations experienced by Hargrave's troops in trying to capture deserters at this time, A.G. Foster made a statement that illustrated the alienation of Randolph County from the mainstream of the Confederacy. "One of the Davidson Home Guard ... said to day the men were talking of recognizing the Independence of Randolph Co & quitting the chase."[94]

As noted above, on August 26 Vance had instructed his Home Guard commander in Troy to respect the procedures of the civil law in his military operations against the deserters and their aiders and abettors.⁹⁵ In dramatic contradistinction to that order, the governor, just three days later, authorized the adjutant general to issue the following command to Lieutenant Colonel Jesse Hargrave at his headquarters at Oak Grove Church in southwestern Randolph County: "The business of your Command is to arrest deserters. All obstacles thrown in the way by Sympathizers & others, must be removed. Arrest all persons Suspected of aiding and abetting deserters and Confine them to your Camp, until their cases can be disposed of by a magistrate, or until the hunt is over, Give these instructions to the Commanders of all detached parties."⁹⁶ The adjutant general, aware that the Randolph Home Guards behaved true to form in this emergency, added: "It is reported that but few of the 5th Battn have turned out, Ascertain why they have not, and let me know."⁹⁷

The next day the adjutant general issued almost identical orders to Home Guard commanders in Moore, Chatham, Mecklenburg, Davie, Wilson, Edgecombe, Wayne, Wilkes, Cumberland, and Montgomery counties.⁹⁸ The wording of the orders indicated that Vance had abdicated his traditional role as defender of civil liberties and had in effect become a "military despot" in his own right. His order to confine all aiders and abettors of deserters in a military prison until the hunt was over was extralegal and amounted in practice to suspending the writ of habeas corpus and establishing martial law — powers Vance did not have the legal authority to exercise.⁹⁹

Heretofore, the best method of capturing outliers had been to impress their horses, livestock, and feed grain and hold them as ransom until their owners surrendered. This worked well in some instances, but the stubborn outlier always had the option of "recovering" his losses from his loyal neighbors when the troops left. That system created more problems than it solved. Vance's authorization to allow the Home Guards to arrest and confine all persons "suspected" of aiding and abetting deserters until the campaign ended added a completely new dimension to the situation. The military commanders, no longer hampered by the necessity of paying obeisance to the niceties of the civil law, could make unlimited arrests, confine their prisoners to the military guardhouse, and use them as ransom to get the outliers to surrender.

No time was lost in utilizing these orders, for on August 29, a soldier wrote from Asheboro: "we marchet 16 miels an back yesterday ... the desrtrs shot in our men an kild one an hit a noter one in the under gaw We ar taking the fathers of the Desertrs to the Camp an trete them as prisners untill thay send for ther suns to relece them we ar taking property too ... we bring wiming to the camp that has husbins In the wodes tell thea send for them an bring them in that is the best way to Cetch them."¹⁰⁰ A day later he wrote: "we cap taking wiming in prison[.] [W]e cep a gard arroud them day an nite."¹⁰¹

A Moore County citizen wrote a friend on August 24 that the governor had ordered state troops from eleven counties to Carthage to hunt deserters, and that many of the outliers were surrendering to the military authorities.¹⁰² A loyal citizen optimistically wrote from Carthage on September 6 that a revolution was taking place in Moore County and that nearly all the deserters will soon surrender. He noted that everyone seems to take an interest in the hunt, and that troops are pressing the horses, wagons, wheat, etc. owned by the families of the deserters and their friends causing those with property to surrender in swarms. The power of the deserter bands, he concluded, is now clearly in decline.¹⁰³

On September 17, a report on the progress of the deserter hunt in Moore County appeared in *The Carolinian*, a Fayetteville newspaper. The article contained interesting comments on the Home Guard's policy of holding women and children as hostages until their deserter spouse, parent, or sibling surrendered: "An old woman and three children were arrested near the front and brought to camp yesterday. They were immediately incarcerated in the Presbyterian church. This was right. It is highly creditable to our troops to have accomplished in 15 days, what was prescribed for sixty.... If we can't catch the men in the woods, take their youngest babies — This was the plan pursued by Hanibal and Jackson in the Indian wars and by our Northern brethren." A week later, a citizen reported to a friend that the troops in Moore County have "began to hunt in earnest now tha taken a great deal of pains to try to get them to come in[.] I saw the cornel the other day he said he reckon tha thought he was a preacher but now tha would Soon find out[.] [T]hay are tarering [tearing down homes of deserters?] all too peaces hawling off every thing they have thare wheat and horses and waggons and taking the women to carthage."[104]

The Chatham Home Guards, using similar methods, prompted a letter to the governor on behalf of their victims that hinted that the troops sexually assaulted outliers' womenfolk: "I umble pray you to heare the cry of the oppressed and over troddon citizens of our County. Col Arie [Lieutenant-Colonel Ihrie, commander of the Chatham County Home Guard Battalion] with a Company of solders are incampt in this neighbourhod and have arrested many of the neighbors Women and took them to camp. some [of] these [the] Col take into the wood to examine the[m] about Deserters the object they say is to *hug them etc.*"[105] Giving an example of the oft-practiced injustice of making the elderly parent suffer for the misconduct of their adult offspring, he related the experience of William McBane and his wife Sarah, both in their seventies. They had been arrested and sent to camp several times because their sons were in the woods. Their sons had long before married and did not live in the same community as their parents. McBane, a veteran of the War of 1812, had urged his sons to serve in the army, but to no avail. The hunters warned that if McBane did not get his sons to surrender to army authorities, they would destroy his property. McBane was too old to be able to work or ride a horse. The correspondent said that he was for driving the enemy from Southern soil, but, he lamented, "we can do it without such measures ... for surely god will not smile on such doings."[106]

In one instance, a determined father stood down a squad of mounted militia officers sent to arrest him, because two of his sons were in the bushes. In a story related by Bryan Tyson, the officers informed Isham Wallace,[107] a resident of Moore County, that he must accompany them to their militia camp. Isham refused. When an officer started to dismount to arrest him, Isham warned him that he would shoot him dead before he touched the ground if that was the last thing he ever did. Rather than risk one of them being killed, the militia officers rode off, abandoning their effort to arrest Isham.[108]

Tyson related another incident of conflict between a father and militia officers. Thomas Macon, a Quaker farmer who lived in the Brower's Mills community of southeastern Randolph County, had five sons ages 12, 13, 22, 24, and 25 in 1860. The latter three were draft-dodgers. The militia officers approached and told Macon that he had to go with them to Asheboro—a distance of about fifteen miles—until his sons gave up. Macon refused to move and forced the officers to carry him to Asheboro in a buggy. They threatened to incarcerate him in the county jail, but he refused to give in. Finally he got a writ of habeas corpus that permitted him to give bail and to be tried according to law for anything he had done wrong. The militia authorities released him because they had no legal charges to try him on. Thereafter, those who could afford bail and the legal fees obtained an attorney and a writ of habeas corpus to gain release.[109]

A young woman whose pro–Union husband had been conscripted into the Confederate army related details of the Vance repression of civilians to an escaped Yankee prisoner of war then hiding in her community (Franklinsville, Randolph County) while enroute on the Underground Railroad to Union lines in Tennessee: "An order had been issued from the Confederate War Department conscripting all able bodied men, from seventeen to fifty years of age, to go to the field immediately; and where men refused to go, and could not be found, the guards were to take their wives, mothers or sisters, and throw them into prison and keep them there until released by the men coming in and giving themselves up."[110] She reported that three of her sisters, the only support for their ninety-year-old mother, had been forced in prison. She added: "Old women from sixty to eighty years of age, and younger women with three or four little children, and young ladies yet single, went to make up the number thus thrown into prison."[111]

One of the imprisoned sisters, after her release, reported to the Union veteran about her suffering during the ordeal. Many of the arrested women "would have starved had they not taken provisions with them [to the prison camp]. She related instances of women who had small children with them, who, having been robbed by the rebels, and having nothing to take to prison with them, almost starved to death. The cries of the children for bread were scarcely ever hushed." When they heard of the imprisonment and suffering of their wives and children, many of the outliers abandoned their hiding places and surrendered to authorities to gain their release. Two of the sisters' brothers fled via the Underground Railroad to Tennessee to join the Union army. As they left, one sister told them "to not come back until secession and the Southern Confederacy were whipped out; and declared that she would rather die in prison than see her brothers go into the army to fight for Jeff-Davis and against the Union."[112]

In late August, hunters in Forsyth County killed two deserters who were members of a "gang of robbers." The deserters in Forsyth, moaned one observer, "spare all persons who voted for Holden, and only take from persons who voted for Vance."[113] In early September, a skirmish occurred in Forsyth between five deserters from Randolph County and the Home Guards, in which no one was injured and the absconders escaped.[114] In neighboring Stokes County, troops killed F. Ellis and wounded a man by the last name of Lawson. Ellis, who had "been a terror to the citizens for a long time," was "regarded as the leader of the deserters."[115] In Wilkes and Watauga counties Home Guard troopers and members of Mallett's Battalion engaged in a series of skirmishes over several days in August with a large band of deserters, mostly from Yadkin County. The Confederates had over 200 men in their ranks, the deserters around 150. Approximately 100 deserters were captured.[116]

On September 1, Vance appointed Brigadier General Collett Leventhorpe supreme commander of the several battalions of the Guard for Home Defense then operating throughout North Carolina hunting deserters.[117] Leventhorpe was free to "establish his Head Quarters at such a point as he may elect."[118] Signifying the importance of the campaign in the Randolph area, the brigadier general established his headquarters at Asheboro by September 14.[119] It is noteworthy that Captain Pearson, senior officer of the Senior and Junior Reserves in the Seventh Congressional District, and Brigadier General Leventhorpe, commander of the state Home Guards, chose Asheboro as their headquarters at this time. This twin concentration of Confederate and state military commanders in Randolph County indicated that the power of the deserters in that area at that time was extraordinary.

Documentation of the deserters and draft-dodgers captured by Senior Reserve troops in the Randolph area during this campaign is recorded in the "Record Book of the Camp of the Senior Reserves," which is on deposit in the Randolph Room, Randolph Public Library, Asheboro, North Carolina. In all, the Record Book indicates that military authorities sent about 283 captured men to either Camp Holmes (Raleigh) or Camp Stokes (Greensboro) between September 1864 and January 1865. Among them were two "Federal Prisoners" (Indiana and New York cavalrymen), free blacks, members of the Junior and Senior Reserves, paroled prisoners who had not returned to their units, "salt hands," and about seventeen Quakers. On one page, the record clerk noted "Deserters shot in January — Noah Williamson and John Jordan."

The Fayetteville *Observer* reported on September 8 that a Major Barringer commanding a force comprised of sixty Montgomery and Richmond County Home Guard troops had a "hard skirmish" with some deserters near the Montgomery-Moore line. Barringer lost one man; the Confederates killed three of the deserters. The *Observer* noted optimistically: "The advantage is to be followed up and it is thought many, if not all will be taken in. The deserters are coming in squads of 4 and 5 every day, and they think all but the ringleaders will soon be in." The *People's Press* reported that 50 deserters surrendered to military authorities in Troy, the seat of Montgomery County, during the first week in September.[120] A few days later, 106 deserters had surrendered to the Home Guard forces in Moore County.[121] On September 24, the *Observer* reported the capture or surrender of about 300 deserters and draft-dodgers to the Home Guards in Randolph, Chatham, Moore, and Montgomery counties since the governor's proclamation.[122]

A letter from Randolph, written on September 25, indicated that troops achieved considerable success in their roundup in that area: "We have quite a calm time of it here now

Brigadier General Collett Leventhrope (1816–1888) around 1865. Supreme commander of North Carolina's Guard for Home Defense, he established his headquarters in Asheboro in September 1864. His troops scoured the Quaker Belt for deserters in this sixth foray by Confederate and state forces into the district during the war. His troops penned the wives, children, and elderly parents of deserters in makeshift prisons, where they remained for days with inadequate food, water, and shelter until the deserters surrendered to military authorities. In several instances, the troops tortured the wives of deserters to force them to reveal the hiding places of their husbands (courtesy the North Carolina Collection, University of North Carolina at Chapel Hill Library).

... the deserters have most of them come in and give up and are gone.... Those who have not give up, have laid down their guns, and ... most of them will give up soon. Some of the bad boys are gone. I learn that they have one chained in camp that they caught yesterday by the name Brown that has been a bad one and no mistake."[123] From Watauga County, a Home Guard trooper wrote, "We captured Granville Smoot and Brooks and 7 others[.] Smoot and Brooks will not Trouble you any more[.] [T]hey went up the Spout[.] When I Come down I can tell you about many things[.]"[124] The phrase "up the spout" meant that someone either died or was killed. The Home Guards executed Smoot and Brooks after their capture because they were recruiting officers for the Union regiments stationed in East Tennessee.[125] The deserters in Stokes County took advantage of the governor's offer of pardon, and by the middle of September, 50 of them had surrendered to authorities.[126] Barn burners were on the prowl in neighboring Forsyth County. Joel Fultin's barn went up with 124 bushels of wheat and other grains. Insurrectionists ignited William Fulp's barn, but "the wind fortunately being unfavorable, the barn was unharmed." The incendiaries also set ablaze Jasper Raper's barn. The arsonists were a gang of dissidents who had publicly posted an advertisement in which they threatened vengeance against the men named therein.[127]

On September 19, the adjutant general notified General Leventhorpe in Asheboro that he would order the Home Guard troops under the general's command home about the 30th of the month.[128] The Home Guard commanders in Moore County requested an extension of this deadline.[129] Military authorities denied their request, and by October 1 they had disbanded and sent home all the Home Guard battalions.[130]

Outrage Against Vance's Severe Repressive Measures

Some officers interpreted Governor Vance's order allowing the arrest and imprisonment of suspected aiders and abettors of deserters and draft-dodgers for the duration of the hunt as carte blanche to do whatever they felt was necessary to capture the delinquents. The victims of military abuse found champions in Congressman J.M. Leach and state solicitor Thomas Settle, but their most poignant advocate was a young woman from lower Davidson County who wrote to Vance on September 15:

> I will now inform you of some of the conduct of our Militia oficers and Magistrats of this county thir imployment is hunting Deserters they say and the way they Manage to find them is taking up poor old grey headed fathers who has faught in the old War ... and [who have] near[ly] starve[d] [doing] thir Duty in trying to support Both the army and thir family and these men [the militia officers] that has remained at home ever since the war commenced are taking them up and keeping them under gard without a Mouthfull to eat for several days and taking up the women and keeping them under gard and Boxing thir jaws and nocking them a bout as if they ware Bruts and Keping them from thir little children that they hav almost wareout thir lives in trying to Make Support for them and some of thes women is in no fix to leave homes and others have little suckling infants not more than 2 Months old and they also have [been] taking up little children and Hange them untill they turn Black in the face trying to Make them tell whear their fathers is when the little children knows nothing atall a bout thir fathers[.] [T]hir plea is they hav orders from the governer to do this and they also say that they hav orders from the governer to Burn up the Barns and houses and Destroy all that they have

> got to live on Becaus they hav a poor wore out son or husband that has served in the army some of them for 2 or 3 years and is almost wore out and starved to Death and has come home to try to take a little rest and are Doing no Body any harm and are eating thir own Rations and these men that has Remained at home ever sence the ware comenced will take thir guns and go out in the woods and shoot them down without Halting [warning] them as if they war Bruts or Murders and these men [the militia officers] will also pilfer and plunder and steel.[131]

In her devastating indictment exposing the barbarities wrought by certain overzealous and cruel militia officers, she continued:

> As for my self i am a young Lady that has Neather Husband son father no[r] Brother in the woods. But i always like to [see] peple have jestes and i think if thes Most powerfull fighting men [militia officers] that has all ways remained at home Would go and fight the enemy and let thes poore wore out soldiers Remain at [home] a little while and take a little rest that we would hav Better times[.] But they say that if they [the militia officers] are called to go [that is, drafted] they Will Lie in the Woods until they Rot Before they will go to the War and now why Should thes men hav the power to Punish men for ... a crime that they would Be guilty of ... so i will close By Requesting you to answer this note if you pleas and answer it Amediatly.[132]

Phebe Crook's letter to the governor presents a powerful exhibition of the class resentments caused by the Confederate government granting deferments from military service to militia officers and other county and state officials so they could hunt and capture deserters and draft-dodgers and force them to serve in the Confederate army. Phebe was a sister of Clarinda Hulin, who had married into a family of Wesleyan Methodist abolitionist, living in the Lovejoy community in north-central Montgomery County.[133]

From Thomasville, a community in northeastern Davidson County, a mother of five wrote the governor that while she was away from her home on business, troops had come by the house to arrest her and, not finding her there, had left word with her terrified children that they would soon return. She claimed that her son (either a deserter or draft-dodger) had not been home in nearly a year, yet the authorities continued to torment her about him as if he were still there. Indignantly she wrote: "Now Gov. in the name of a widowed Mother and four orphan daughters I implore your protection against such indignities as are practiced by these men ordered to hunt deserters. The destruction of property when we need all that we can make and sowe and the shameful treatment of women too indecent to express and now in the midst of gathering in my crops and attending to household matters I must be dragged off to the Camp to endure the torments of merciless men and leave my daughters alone without any protection." She begged Vance to intervene; he endorsed her letter with the following statement: "Say that she shall not be disturbed etc."[134]

In a letter to the editor labeled "Arrests of Women" published on September 29, the Salem *People's Press* noted that the Home Guards had arrested several women and incarcerated them in the county jail in Forsyth County as hostages until their deserter sons or husbands surrendered to military authorities. The writer continued: "In other counties a similar course has been pursued by this arm of the military service, and I learn from credible authority that some of the women arrested in these counties, were roped around their necks and hung as to extort from them the whereabouts of their husbands, sons and relatives, who it was said deserted from the army; and that others were forced to undergo the pains of having their fingers put under the joints of heavy rail fences and squeezed until they told where their friends etc., were, if they could so." The writer noted that "an impression prevails with some" that Governor Vance ordered his troops to commit these atrocities. The writer did not think it "reasonable" that the governor would order the arrest and incarceration of women. He laid the blame for the actions on the county court officials for not bringing charges against the military men who perpetrated these crimes.

Mrs. B.S. Hedrick in Washington, D.C., wrote an interesting commentary upon events that were taking place in the Randolph area at this time. She got the information from two refugees from Randolph County who had recently visited her and her husband. She told their story this way:

> The refugees tell some hard stories of conscription officers in the western part of the state[.] [H]ouses were pulled down & wives and children marched off to the Rebel camp, locked up and fed on bread & water till the husband and father came in and gave them-selves up. One of the men had five guns discharged at him at once but escaped free.... They mention several conscript officers who were killed one man fell with fifty-two bullet holes in him. [Probably a reference to the assassination of Peter Gardner].... These men are well to do & own house and land well stocked and had no notion of fighting for Jeff. Davis's kingdom. They gave them-selves up to save mother sisters wife and child[,] remained in the ary [army] about three weeks when an opportunity of taking French leave occurred and they filed away to the Union lines, they have been trying to get employment here[.] I do not know how they will succeed.

Reflecting the hatred engendered by this ordeal, she wrote: "You neednt think there is no bitterness against their persecutors in their hearts[.] [W]oe unto them if ever it shall ... be in the power of such men to take the sword of vengeance in their own hands."[135]

Congressman J.M. Leach, on September 18, wrote Vance that scores of citizens "have appealed to me, to know whether the instances of gross insult & most brutal & inhuman treatment ... toward the relations of Deserters, were committed by your authority." Having defended the good name of the governor, Leach informed Vance that "I indignantly answered 'NO' in every case recited." Leach continued: "Why Governor, some of the *arresting* soldiers themselves — men of property character & intelligence have detailed to me instances of hor-ror & brutality that *they were made to participate in*— that no decent man can contemplate without *burning indignation*."[136] Then Leach gave several examples of the abhorrent treatment to which he was referring:

> the choking & dragging some hundred yards on the ground of an old lady, skinning her knees [and] hips till they bleed — & she a respectable and respected woman, — insulting delicate women with children at their breast, cursing them & their little ones for asking for bread after having been arrested & held for days out in camp — following women of admitted respectability in obeying the calls of nature taunting them hissing obscene language seizing another & dragging her by the arms & head etc etc — eating up & wasting & destroying the little that a deserter's wife or child or mother may have etc etc — arresting & taking to camp & insulting the sister of one of our merchants of this place who is also a magistrate & tax assessor for this county & a *terribly strong Vance man.*[137]

Leach urged Vance "for humanity's sake" to restrain his officers and men within proper and legitimate bounds in the future.[138] Suggesting that he was as concerned about his political career as he was about humanity, Leach warned Vance that a "malignant" political enemy — Colonel Jesse Hargrave — threatened to write to the governor in an effort to secure his (Leach's) arrest.[139]

Thomas Settle,[140] a noted lawyer, wealthy planter, and state solicitor, told Vance that his orders granting military authorities the power to arrest anyone suspected of aiding and abetting deserters lacked proper legal sanctions.[141] Settle interwove his arguments among examples of the atrocities that had been committed:

> Allow me Governor ... to call to your attention a matter in which you certainly must be misunderstood although your orders on their face bear the interpretation which your officers give to them. I found in Chatham, Randolph and Davidson that some fifty women in each County & some of them in delicate health and far advanced in pregnancy were rudly (in some instances) draged from their homes & put under close guard & there kept for some weeks. The consequences in some instances have been shocking. Women have been frightened into abortions almost under the eyes of their terrifiers. This matter has been called to the attention of Judge French and in his charges to the grand jury, he forcibly and at length instructs them that all such proceedings are against law, and that unless a magistrate first issues a warrant there is not and cannot be any authority for such arrests.
>
> ...
>
> I know that your Excellency never has intended by any order to justify torture & yet in many cases where the treatment has been equally as bad as it was in the Owens Case [Bill Owens's wife], the officers boldly avow their conduct & say that they understand your orders to be a full justification.
>
> Last week in Randolph I tried a man who had actually hung his neighbor until he was senseless, in order to extort confessions from him.[142]

On September 30, an article appeared in the Greensboro *Citizen* that described the hanging of a man named Jones in Randolph County until he was "senseless" by a man named Robert C. Grey. Perhaps this is the same situation that Settle refers to above. According to the report, Grey and his squad of militia suspected Jones of harboring his son, a deserter. Grey and his men "tied him [Jones] and a small son not liable to service and carried them several miles, where they separated them and tied a rope round the father's neck; that they called upon him to pray as his end was nigh at hand, ..., and then tied him to a tree and hung him until he was senseless; that he lay for sometime like he was lifeless." The militia then carried Jones to Asheboro and turned him over to the court officials for prosecution. The court released Jones because he had broken no law. Jones then sued Grey. The jury convicted Grey, and the judge sentenced him to six months in jail.[143]

Before he had received word on the matter from Settle, Vance became concerned about the possible negative legal repercussions of his orders. On September 27 he ordered his Home Guard commanders to "without delay make and forward to this Office a full report of all arrests made by them giving the names of the persons[,] the cause of the arrest and the length of time the parties were detained."[144] Eleven days later, the adjutant general sent a circular to Home Guard commanders in ten counties revoking their authority "to arrest persons suspected of aiding and assisting deserters ... as it was designed that such authority should not extend beyond the time the several commands were operating in the field under existing Special Orders."[145] Both Thomas Settle, a "Holdenite," and J.M. Leach, a peace advocate and Confederate congressman, were at the time on the opposite side of the political fence from Vance; however, there is no reason to believe that either fabricated or even grossly exaggerated the situation in their reports to the governor about the excesses and atrocities of the military.

The Peace Conservative press also excoriated Governor Vance for his extralegal and brutal treatment of the wives, parents, and children of outliers. On September 30, the Raleigh *Daily Progress* published an article titled "Civil Liberty Gone." The author, "Veritas," wrote that the militia and Home Guards, under the orders of Governor Vance, had been hunting deserters for the past month in Randolph and surrounding counties. In the process, they arrested, imprisoned, and in many instances tortured women — some of them pregnant — to force them to disclose the whereabouts of their deserter husbands, brothers, sons, or sweethearts. "In some instances thirty or forty [women] ... have been huddled together in an old school house and kept guarded for several days."[146] The troops claimed they were acting under the orders of Governor Vance, who had promised "to stand between them and all damages."[147] "Veritas" conceded that harboring deserters was a crime, but not "one of those great State crimes [in] which ... torture was used ... in England and Scotland several centuries ago." Governor Vance, continued "Veritas," should have addressed his order to arrest aiders and abettors of deserters "*to his civil and not his military officers.*" The editor of the *Daily Progress* denounced the "arrest and penning of women and children, by the Home Guard officers now engaged in deserter hunting," as "high handed proceedings" that had "no parallel in the history of this war." "There is no law to authorise it and it is an unmitigated outrage."[148]

An account of the violent acts committed by Confederate troops against civilians in Randolph County made it into the pages of the *New York Times* in October. One of their reporters working in the Norfolk area interviewed some "stampeders" who had recently fled to the Union lines from central North Carolina. They reported that old men between 60 and 80 years of age had been arrested by military authorities and tortured to try to force them to tell where their sons where hiding. In one case, a woman was tied up by her waist for three hours to force information from her about her husband's whereabouts. She was so severely injured by this ordeal that she died soon after she was cut down.[149]

On October 5, the editor of the Greensboro *Citizen* released his denunciation of the excesses perpetrated by state troops against the people in the Randolph area. Indignantly, he related that "the most illegal orders have been issued by superiors and carried ruthlessly into effect by inferiors. Houses have been leveled with the ground, persons entirely innocent of any violation of the law have been restrained of their liberty, some have been hanged dead, and others have been shot in cold blood without a court marital or any investigation of the case before a civil tribunal." He warned that, though done by men acting under orders, they "have laid themselves liable to be sued for damages and to be prosecuted in our Courts for these violations of the criminal law." He concluded: "No excuse, or pretext can justify or palliate such gross and wicked violations of law."[150]

Holden noted in his *Weekly Standard* that the outrages referred to in the *Citizen* "have been perpetrated under color of orders issued to the officers of the Home Guards by Gov. Vance, through Adjutant General Gatlin." Through his newspaper, Holden earlier had asked the governor to publish his orders to the Home Guard commanders that led to their arresting and detaining citizens, especially in the Randolph County area, suspected of aiding and abetting deserters. Citizens then could judge for themselves whether the orders sanctioned such conduct by his subordinates. Vance refused. In response, Holden wrote: "We must, therefore, conclude that such an order has been issued, and that Gov. Vance is himself primarily responsible for these gross, palpable, and cruel violations of the civil law."[151] Then, getting at the nub of his argument, Holden asked, "Can it be possible that the people of Randolph County have been thus scourged on account of the way they voted at the last election?" Randolph had been one of only three counties — Johnston and Wilkes being the other two — to give Holden a majority in the 1864 gubernatorial election. Taking a shot at his political nemesis, Holden asked: "But what *must* be thought of an Executive under whose orders such outrages as the above are perpetrated?"[152]

Lieutenant Colonel Jesse Hargrave presented a much different picture of the situation. He was the commander of the Davidson County Home Guards who had led the Home Guard forces in the deserter hunt in Randolph County in September 1864. Greatly disturbed by threatened legal action against him and his men, he exclaimed to the governor: "After seeing you in Raleigh and getting a copy of your letter instructing me to arrest these parties and after you yourself telling me to 'go ahead — *that you would stand between me and all damages*' I returned to Randolph and immediately began acting in accordance *strickly* with those orders — and it had a very happy effect. We caught several deserters or at least induced them to surrender and there was nobody hurt." Just when Hargrave began to get the deserter situation under control, J.M. Leach denounced his tactics as inhumane. Leach went so far as to "order" his major to immediately release all prisoners held on charges of aiding and abetting deserters or face indictments in the courts for illegal seizure of citizens. Hargraves's men became so intimidated that he could no longer get them to arrest any more deserters. As a consequence, the disloyal became bold and defiant and dared his men to arrest them because, according to "General" Leach, such proceedings were illegal.[153] Hargrave said that were it not for the political position of Leach, he certainly would have him arrested. Leach, he said, had thrown more obstacles in the way of arresting deserters than had any man in the county. He added: "If such men are permitted to go on in their present course, I must say to you — it will be out of my power as Commander of the H. Guard — to keep the County clear of Deserters — They will be sure to Crowd a County where they receive so much 'aid and comfort.'"[154] The colonel claimed that if his men committed any outrages, they did them in direct violation of his orders. He discounted the report that his men had frightened a pregnant woman into aborting as a fabrication of the disloyal for their own purposes. Stating that the courts had indicted some of his men in seven or eight different legal actions, he asked Vance to help him get them out of their difficulties. In closing, he demanded: "I desire specific instructions from you which will not only protect me, and my men from indictment, but which will be evidence in any Civil suit which may be brought against us."[155]

The Aftermath

By October 1, the army had stifled the uprising and the crisis was over. The military had returned captured deserters to the army. Those deserters who had eluded capture were deep in the woods lying low. Commanders had disbanded and sent home the Home Guards and Senior Reserves.[156] According to an article printed in the Greensboro *Patriot* in December, the militia and Home Guards over the past four months had returned to the army 1,289 deserters and draft-dodgers, 421 of whom had been apprehended, the rest surrendered.[157] Those who suffered most were not the intended victims — the deserters and draft-dodgers — but rather the women, children, and the elderly. A strong-willed governor unafraid to act decisively even if it meant bending the rules had thwarted a rebellion at its inception. Though one might argue that Governor Vance tarnished his image as a "Champion of Personal Freedom" by his conduct in this campaign against deserters and draft-dodgers, one could counter by noting that the governor was caught in a dilemma wherein only draconian measures could overcome the exigencies he faced.[158] Certainly Holden viewed as flawed the claim that Vance was a defender of individual liberty: "His friends claim that he is, *par excellence*, the champion of civil liberty — yet these proceedings are a most outrageous violation of the civil law, and in fact establish the supremacy of the military over it."[159]

In January 1865, Joel Ashworth — peace advocate, schoolteacher, and Wesleyan abolitionist minister elected to the House of Commons from Randolph County in 1864 — introduced resolutions in the House advocating an investigation of the outrages committed by Vance and his troops against the civilian population in his home county during the deserter hunt in the summer of 1864. Ashworth charged that military authorities under the orders of Governor Vance arrested and imprisoned persons of all ages without due process of law "on mere suspicion that they were harboring, or otherwise aiding and abetting deserters, with a view of *torturing* them into a disclosure of their whereabouts." Ashworth asked that a House committee be appointed to investigate these charges, ascertain their truth, report to the House the extent of these outrages and whether Governor Vance authorized them, and what action should be taken by the House. In its investigation, the House committee should be sure to inspect Governor Vance's Letter Books.[160]

Holden printed a statement in his newspaper supporting this House investigation of Governor Vance. According to Holden, Vance ordered these outrages to punish the people of Randolph County because they elected all Holden candidates in the elections last August. As part of their chastisement, "hundreds of detailed men and hundreds of soldiers" from Randolph County "were sent to the front to be slaughtered, because they voted last August against Gov. Vance and the Destructive candidates. This was nothing more nor less than murder for opinion's sake. The wrath of the people will yet burn after and consume the authors of these outrages." The House rejected Ashworth's resolutions.[161]

The *Conservative*, the political organ of Governor Vance, printed a letter, purportedly from a Quaker living in the Holly Springs community of southwestern Randolph County, belittling Ashworth's call for an investigation of the governor. The writer complained that while Ashworth decried the atrocities made by Vance's Home Guards in Randolph County, he said not a word about enquiring "into the hundreds of robberies and thefts, to say nothing of the numerous murders committed by the deserters." Ashworth, concluded the "Quaker," must be an ally of the deserters since he only looks at one side of the issue. Surely, Ashworth was aware that there have been "several murders and innumerable robberies, more than one hundred in that part of the county where he has been a school teacher for the last twenty years. Why, since he has been in Raleigh aunt Aley Cox, an old widow, and Sarah Henly, both exemplary Friends, have been robbed of the most of their years' supply of meal. Other Friends, and innumerable persons not Friends, have shared the same fate."[162]

The issue of the maltreatment of civilians by state and Confederate troops in the Quaker Belt during the war reemerged in postwar politics. In 1872, when Collett Leventhorpe was running for state auditor on the Democratic ticket, his opponents accused him of being the "Bull-Pen Man" for his role as commander of the state Home Guards in its late summer 1864 deserter hunt in the Randolph County area.[163] According to them, General Leventhorpe was guilty of the "inhumane torture" of forty-two Randolph women his troops had arrested and confined to a "bull-pen" because their husbands, fathers, or sons refused "to fire on the old flag, or fight against the Union. In that bull-pen these women were subjected to all the barbarities that the most inhumane mind could suggest. They were not allowed to attend the calls of nature without being attended by an armed male guard." Further, under Leventhorpe's command, troops shot and killed a young Unionist by the name of Northcote only because "he would not raise his arm to fight against the Union." What is more, the former Home Guard commandant belonged to the Democratic Party, the party that murdered William Owens, and "that put his wife's fingers between fence rails in order to compel her to tell where her husband was, he then being in the woods to keep from being conscripted." Referring to the Democratic Party, the accusers quizzed: "What party penned women and hunted and shot down Union men like wild beasts, plundered the women and children at home and roped and handcuffed the men and marched them to the front to fight and die in the slaveholder's rebellion?"[164] The general denied all the charges levied by his political enemies of cruelty against civilians while commander of the Home Guards in the Randolph County area during the war. He disclaimed having any role in the torture of women and children or the murder of William Owens or any other Unionist. Nonetheless, Leventhrope's reputation as the "Bull-Pen Man" dogged him for the rest of his life.[165]

In the gubernatorial election of 1876, when Democrat Zeb Vance opposed Republican Thomas Settle, the latter charged that the arrest, imprisonment, and at times torture of women, children, and the elderly in the deserter hunt in the late summer of 1864 by Confederate and state troops under the direct orders of Governor Vance was despotic, inhumane, and illegal. Settle put particular emphasis on the atrocities committed by state forces in Randolph County. Vance replied that state law bound the governor of North Carolina to protect his citizens against illegal activities of disloyalists and deserters; he was only doing his duty. He noted that overzealous subordinates might have gone too far in some instances, but that he as governor never sanctioned torture.[166]

Civilians in the South suffered repression and atrocities by both Federal and Confederate forces during the war. However, it is unlikely that any discrete body of white Southerners of comparable size suffered more at the hands of Confederate and state authorities during the war than did the militant Unionists, deserters, and draft-dodgers and their families in the Quaker Belt of North Carolina in September 1864. While the pro–Union citizens of the Quaker Belt suffered severely at the hands of state and Confederate authorities, according to John Pool, leader of the peace faction in the General Assembly from late 1864 until the end of the war, Unionists throughout the state during the war underwent brutal treatment by military and local authorities. Much of the suppression of Unionism was

> left to the neighborhood scouts and authorized bands of guerrilla robbers [such as Peter Garner and Adam Brewer in Randolph], not only unrestrained but encouraged in lawless violence and outrage to suspected Unionists, their wives and children. In remote places, upon the public highways, in the public dwellings of the poor and around the family hearth, from which the husband and father had been dragged in chains to the army and prison, or driven to the mountain caves and forests, scenes were enacted that can never be described, and, if told, would not be credited as possible in a Christian age.

In what seemed to be a veiled charge of widespread rape of deserters' wives by troops, Pool exclaimed: "For the crime of not betraying husbands or sons to death, the virtues and claims of womanhood were set to naught." Pool then described the imprisonment of the wives of Unionists in Randolph County, many of whom were pregnant, until their sons or husbands surrendered to authorities. He also detailed the torture of the wife of William Owens in front of two of her children until, screaming with pain, she consigned her husband to death by telling her tormentors where her husband was hiding. Pool continued:

> The Polk county murders, the "Laurel massacre," the horrible murder, by guerrillas, of Thaddeus Cox, and his wife and children, in Pasquotank [County], and the shocking atrocities in Buncombe, Haywood, Ashe, Wilkes, and Alleghany are but isolated instances of what was done in almost every county. They can be truthfully multiplied by hundreds. These things were done by authorized parties, in uniform and under officers. Add to this the want and mourning that sat in every humble household, and even then but an inadequate conception can be formed of the terrible condition to which we were reduced.[167]

CHAPTER EIGHT

The Last Hunt and the Conclusion of the Inner Civil War

Governor Vance's resort to severe repressive measures against the dissidents in the Quaker Belt in the late summer of 1864 had the effect desired. Hundreds of deserters, rather than see Confederate authorities abuse their wives, children, parents, or siblings or suffer troops to pilfer and destroy their homes and farms, surrendered and returned to the ranks. However, as part of the gradual disintegration of Lee's army at Petersburg in the winter of 1865, many of the victims of the Vance repression deserted for home once again. By February, the absconders had arrived in the Quaker Belt in large numbers. They linked up with the dissidents who had successfully eluded Vance's dragnet the previous September and organized themselves into marauding bands that spread terror through the loyalist community. As the disloyalists robbed, murdered, and assailed their former tormentors, violence and anarchy gripped the Quaker Belt as never before.

Fort Fisher and the Reorganization of the Senior Reserves and Home Guards

By the fall of 1864, the Confederacy was in its death throes: Atlanta had fallen, and Sherman was making his march to the sea. Lee's army was hopelessly pinned in the trenches around Petersburg, and the Federal forces, long entrenched in the sound region of tidewater North Carolina, threatened to take Fort Fisher below Wilmington and march into the interior of the state. Fort Fisher, located near the mouth of the Cape Fear River, defended Wilmington, the last major seaport in the Confederacy by late 1864 that still maintained a lively trade with the outside world via a fleet of blockade runners. Wilmington, with its rail connections to Virginia, became famous in the last year of the war as "the lifeline of the Confederacy."[1] In September 1864, Federal military commanders began assembling naval and army forces for an assault on Fort Fisher. The next month, Union forces in the sound region initiated a campaign that led to their recapture of the small towns of Plymouth and Washington.[2]

To help the Confederate army meet the threat posed by Union military forces in the eastern part of the state, Vance ordered a reorganization of the Guard for Home Defense that made it possible for one-third of the state troops to be kept in the field at all times. The adjutant general instructed the Home Guard commanders in Surry, Yadkin, Rowan, Cabarrus, Lincoln, Cleveland and all the counties lying east of them to divide their commands into three equal parts — referred to as the first, second, and third classes — to be called up for duty in rotation when less than the whole was needed. He ordered the first class selected, equipped, and sent immediately to Goldsboro in the eastern part of the state.[3] A few weeks later, state military leaders consolidated the counties of Surry, Wilkes, Iredell, Catawba, Rutherford, and all counties lying west of them into the Western District of North Carolina, and placed them under the command of Brigadier General J.G. Martin. They divided these Home Guard battalions into three classes and ordered them to defend the Tar Heel State from attack by the Federals from the west.[4]

At the same time that the state reorganized its military command to meet the anticipated assault on Fort Fisher and the impending arrival of Sherman's army from South Carolina, the War Department ordered the Senior Reserves to organize into combat units on a statewide basis.[5] The Confederacy also utilized the men detailed from the army as another source of troops at this time.[6] The Confederate Conscript Bureau had detailed these men subject to Confederate service to special duty making weapons, ammunition, and supplies for the Confederacy, or providing special services such as maintaining and operating the railroads and mines.[7] The Conscript Bureau organized them into companies.

The Stampeders

This call of auxiliary state and Confederate military forces to defend the state against regular Union troops precipitated a "stampede" to the Union lines in Tennessee of Home Guardsmen, militia officers, justices of the peace, and other civil officials who had been until now exempted from the draft.[8] Most of the "stampeders" were covert militant Unionists who had used their office as a shield from the draft so that they could remain at home and care for their families. Their military obligations had been limited mostly to service in their home and surrounding counties in half-hearted attempts at catching deserters and draft-dodgers. Rather than allow Confederate authorities to coerce them into the ranks to fight the United States, these men chose to flee to the Union lines in East Tennessee. Once within Union lines, they could either join the Federal forces or receive free transportation to go to live with relatives or friends residing in the North.

Most of the stampeders came from the highly disaffected counties of Randolph, Guilford, Forsyth, and Davidson. One observer speculated that they numbered between two and four hundred men.[9] In October, the Home Guard commanders of Forsyth, Yadkin, Surry, Stokes, and Wilkes counties ordered their troops to patrol the roads and ferry crossings in their districts to intercept the stampeders as they fled to East Tennessee.[10] Home Guardsmen arrested twenty-three mounted stampeders, most of whom were from Guilford, at Love's Meeting House in Forsyth.[11] Guardsmen captured many other stampeders and sent their detainees either to Castle Thunder in Richmond or to Camp Stokes in Guilford County.[12] Numerous stampeders, however, made it through the lines to safety. Jesse Wheeler, describing the stampeder influx into his area of Indiana in November 1864, wrote that in that month over one hundred Tar Heel deserters and draft-dodgers, mostly from the counties of Forsyth, Davidson, and Guilford, had made it through the lines.[13]

The numerous stampeders passing through the western part of the Quaker Belt stimulated the deserters and draft-dodgers in that area into action. By November, deserter bands were robbing and intimidating loyalists in the counties of Surry, Alleghany, Ashe, Watauga, and Wilkes. In the latter county alone, where "rape, murder and robbery, is the order of the day," four deserter bands ravaged the countryside.[14] An observer complained: "The tories of this county have formed themselves into about four squads. One in the Brushy Mountains is under the command of the Youngers — one on Roaring river is under the Shoemstes — one on Mulberry is under Jennings — one in the Flat Woods six miles from town is under your friend Harrison Church." The informant then listed the names of individuals who fell victim to the deserters: "McGrady, Lovett, McGrady, Mason Brown, Brown again, Abscher, Wyatt, Col. Eller, Jas. Eller, Frank McNeil, Wm. McNeil, Jas. McNeil, Jos. Gray who lives three miles from town. Pretty large sums of money were taken from several of them besides everything that the robbers wanted. These squads are formed from robbers of every part of the Confederacy and some from the Yankee army." He concluded his narrative with "A good many of our best citizens have been driven from their homes and have moved their property and some have been killed in the attempt to move."[15] According to another report, deserters in Wilkes "set fire to a Mr. Russell's house and robbed him of his guns and other property. The fire was extinguished by the inmates, and the perpetrators left and set fire to the dwelling of a Mr. Laws and destroyed it."[16]

Michael Williams of Wilkes County wrote a letter to the editor of *The Daily Conservative* in November in which he denied reports that his two daughters had been raped by deserters. He then gave an account of a group of five deserters coming to his house "demanding my guns and ammunition, but finding the guns of poor quality they left them. I offered no resistance to the demand, feeling that an old man could not withstand such a number. This was 11 o'clock at night, we were all a bed, two of the deserters had gone to the fire place and struck a light, leaving two or three at the doors. When they satisfied themselves about the guns they left without offering any insult or violence." In conclusion, Williams noted that "one of them returned to say to me that if I reported them they would burn me out. Next morning my wife found they had entered her kitchen and taken the knives and forks and a crock of milk, which was all we missed."[17]

Peace Conservatives, anxious to downplay the accounts of disloyalty and mayhem in Wilkes County as exaggerations of the War Conservative press designed to impugn the integrity and loyalty of counties that strongly supported Holden in the 1864 gubernatorial election, denied that rape, arson, and murder were widespread in Wilkes, or that robbery was as frequent as claimed.[18] One observer, while admitting deserters had recently robbed about a half dozen persons in the north part of the county, declared that on the whole, the deserter gangs in the county were no great threat: "They go in gangs of about a dozen and intimidate by their numbers, but seldom show fight. The gangs are composed of the worst of our own citizens, and deserters from other parts, but they are not armed only as they seize the weapons of citizens, and cannot cope with the Home Guard. A regiment of regulars would fail to find them. It is only by 'still hunting' that they can be taken."[19]

In mid–November, a Wilkes County Home Guard patrol ambushed a band of about thirty deserters at a location about seven miles from Wilkesboro, wounding and capturing

Harrison Church, the dissidents' leader.[20] An account of this skirmish stated that a Lieutenant Johnson "was in search of deserters, and happened to come upon this band. He secreted his men near the road, and waited until Church's party came within range, then let them have a volley. Church ordered a charge, and when again within thirty yards, the Guards delivered another fire, in which Church was severely wounded.... No one else was hurt."[21] The guardsmen declared Church was wearing a "Yankee Uniform" and carrying "a Yankee [officer's] commission in his pocket." Treated as a traitor rather than a Union officer, Confederates incarcerated Church in Castle Thunder in Richmond.[22]

Lawlessness was also rife in neighboring Ashe, Alleghany, and Surry counties. On November 12, the adjutant general ordered the Home Guard battalions in those counties to hunt deserters who were "committing robberies and depredations."[23] A band of deserters in Surry County robbed several citizens of "money, clothing and almost everything that could be carried off." The callous desperados took a shroud from "a very aged lady" who had made it in preparation for her burial. They hanged a captured Home Guard trooper. As they fled to the safety of the Blue Ridge Mountains of neighboring Alleghany County, the dissidents threatened to return to Surry and burn its courthouse.[24]

The troubles precipitated in the western part of the Quaker Belt by the stampeders came to a head on November 3 in Watauga County, where a band of deserters ambushed Major H. Bingham's Home Guard patrol. "Bingham's command formed in the woods and as the fog cleared away fired into the enemy. The fight was kept up from sunrise to about ten o'clock, A.M. in a regular Indian style. We had one man mortally wounded, who died the next day; another severely wounded and 2 slightly." When the guards ran low on ammunition, they fell back. Jim Hartley commanded the bushwhackers, which included men from both armies. Bingham's men killed eight of the deserters and wounded several more.[25]

Fort Fisher Falls

On December 22, 1864, Governor Vance delivered his annual message to the General Assembly. He complained that deserters infested the swamps and mountains in the interior of the state where the desperadoes were "stealing, plundering and in many instances murdering the inhabitants." "In some places," he added, "they muster in such force as to almost amount to a suspension of the civil authority, aided and protected as they are by their relatives and friends."[26] Even though the defeat of the Confederacy was imminent, Vance's detestation for the deserters and draft-dodgers remained unabated. He told the North Carolina lawmakers: "I see no remedy for the evil, but to outlaw them and drive them from the State by the strong hand." Vance urged the General Assembly to pass laws that would give him greater control over the militia, to make it easier to convict those who harbored or aided and abetted deserters, and to require all civil as well as military officers to assist in the arrest of deserters "under such penalties as will enforce obedience." Had he but the legal power to do so, Vance asserted, "I am confident I could easily rid the community of this pest."[27] The General Assembly, many of whose members were Peace Conservatives and covert reunionists, paid little heed to the governor's pleas. They were more concerned about making a peace with the Federals short of subjugation than they were with pursuing the failed, and by then hopeless, policy of containing the deserters and draft-dodgers.

The rapid build up of Union military strength along coastal North Carolina in late 1864 lay behind Vance's efforts to exterminate the armed dissidents in the central part of the state. He needed to put in the field every able-bodied man of military age in the state to check the Federal forces that were jockeying into position for a combined naval and land assault on Fort Fisher. The governor simply could not muster a force sufficient to help the Richmond authorities defend the "lifeline of the Confederacy" if a large portion of his state troops had to be used to police his interior counties against marauding deserters. Just three days before he delivered his speech to the General Assembly, he ordered his first class Home Guard battalions to Kinston as part of the Confederate defense network against the impending Federal assault on Fort Fisher.[28] The Federals launched an attack on the fort on December 22 that lasted three days.[29] The attack failed, and Vance ordered his Home Guard troops home on January 4, 1865.[30] In mid–January, the Federal navy reassembled its fleet at the mouth of the Cape Fear River below Wilmington to make a second attempt at taking Fort Fisher. Prompted by this emergency, Vance once again called up and ordered his Home Guard battalions to Goldsboro.[31] Fort Fisher fell to the Federals on the 15th, and Vance sent the Home Guards home on the 27th.[32]

All Hell Breaks Loose in Randolph, Chatham, Moore, and Montgomery Counties

After the disbanding of the Senior Reserves and the Home Guards in late September 1864, matters remained quiet for a short time in the eastern part of the Quaker Belt.[33] However, the peace was short-lived. In late October, the enrolling officer for Randolph County reported to his superior the existence of about 150 deserters in the county, including 90 Senior Reservists who refused to obey orders to go to the eastern part of the state.[34] On November 5, the adjutant general ordered the Randolph and Montgomery County Home Guard battalions into the field to rid the area of some "bad men."[35] Over the next several weeks, the guardsmen captured a few outliers.[36] Despite their efforts, deserters continued pillaging and robbing loyal citizens into the New Year.[37] For example, in November, a band of lawless men in Montgomery County robbed the house of Col. John F. Cotton "of a gun and a repeater, blankets, hats, clothing, etc."[38]

As the New Year unfolded, conditions began to worsen rapidly in the Randolph area, especially along the Randolph, Moore, Montgomery border. In early January a band of deserters "went to William Luck's house for the purpose of shooting him, and, his wife, in endeavoring to assist him, was shot by one of the deserters and is said to be severely wounded.... Luck ... shot one of the men dead.... They visited quite a number of other residences and pilfered them."[39] Two days later, a notice appeared in a newspaper describing the depredations of deserters in Randolph County who were probably involved in the incident described above regarding William Luck and his wife: "Four of the most substantial citizens robbed in the space of as many hours, and one lady wounded, supposed to be mortally, by bands of deserters who declared themselves the friends of Holden and Lincoln last summer, and that they would go to the polls and vote for Holden or die."[40]

On January 10, a loyal citizen wrote the governor that there were about 400 deserters in Randolph County committing robberies against the patriotic community, but letting the

Red Strings alone. The deserters, just as their strident Confederate counterparts, were no respecters of the elderly or Victorian womanhood. For example, the correspondent told Vance of "two heartrending cases. Mrs. C. Staly near 90 years old had to leave her home old Mrs. Lane near 75 years old lately robbed and many others burning & distroying fences & they seem to do pretty much as they please if something is not spedily done numbers are bound to be ruined & some ruined already."[41] Because of the renewed daring of the deserters in the area, the adjutant general in late January exempted the Randolph Home Guard battalion from serving in the eastern part of the state. Instead, he ordered them to hunt, capture, and destroy deserters in Randolph and adjoining counties reported to be murdering and robbing citizens.[42]

Not all of the trumps, however, were in the hands of the outliers and deserters at this time. On January 28, some hunters caught four draft-dodgers lying out on Dark Mountain in Montgomery County.[43] Three of the captives were the Hulin brothers — Jesse, John, and William. They were militant Unionists and Wesleyan abolitionists.[44] According to Hiram Hulin, the father of the brothers, Home Guard troops "while on their way to the pretended prison ... deliberately shot and beat to death with guns and rocks my three sons and Atkins while tied with their hands and hand-cuffed together."[45] Another account of the incident described the capture and execution of the Hulin brothers this way: "In January of 1865 [the Hulin brothers] were captured by Confederate and Home Guard troops who were looking for outliers. They were imprisoned in Beans' Mill on Barns' Creek in Montgomery County, tried in a meeting held without their presence and sentenced to death. The following morning, on 28 January 1865, they were marched about two miles to a place near Buck Mountain where they were lined up and shot. A messenger was sent to their family to tell them where to find their bodies."[46]

The Hulin brothers' mass grave at the Lovejoy Methodist Church cemetery in north-central Montgomery County bears the following epitaph carved in stone: "Murdered." In a letter to the editor of the *Standard*, a person writing from Troy commented on the murder of the Hulin brothers: "Since I commenced writing this, a man has come in and says they have just shot four deserters without trial. I expect some of them were bad men, but they ought to have had a trial. Times are bad here, and growing worse."[47] In another incident, a black "hunter" reportedly killed a deserter on Dark Mountain. If true, this event adds an ironic twist to the Civil War history of the area — an armed black "bounty hunter" sent out to hunt and kill anti–Confederate and possibly antislavery or even abolitionist deserters and draft-dodgers.[48]

By mid–February, the position of the loyal element in the Randolph area had become desperate. The deserters, encouraged by Sherman's approach from South Carolina and greatly increased in number by new arrivals from Lee's army, boldly asserted themselves and terrorized the local Confederate and state officials and loyal citizens into abject submission.[49] On February 11, a Confederate officer passing through Asheboro recorded: "The whole country is in a furor about deserters 400 of whom now infest Randolph County & are burning and robbing every thing before them."[50] A few weeks later, a clerk in the Confederate War Department in Richmond noted in his diary that "there are 800 [deserters] in Randolph County [North Carolina] committing depredations on the *rich* farmers, etc."[51] One Randolph native who, as a small child, witnessed this reign of terror by the deserters in the winter of 1865 wrote: "More dreadful in those last days was the havoc wrought by 'deserters' from our armies hiding by day and roaming the country by night. Many a time our trembling family, roused by a sky lit with flames from some house which had been robbed and burned, watched in terror, afraid to go back to bed again."[52]

The marauders were mostly former Holdenite deserters and draft-dodgers whom Confederate authorities forced to surrender during the deserter hunt in the late summer of 1864 in order to secure the release of their arrested wives, children, and parents. Their feelings were less than cordial towards their loyal Confederate neighbors who had supported Vance in his cruel campaign against them. Revenge was in order. As one observer noted, "[The] Deserters have banded together and swear vengeance on all who sympathise with the confederacy."[53] A witness to the deserter retribution wrote the following:

> It is reported that the most of the men in General Lee's Army from the County [Randolph] have deserted and come home and they are traveling in different squads in different parts of the county with waggons and horses as many as two waggons in company and hauling our meet and corn a way from us and robbing the loyal citizens of all their money, that they come in dead time of knight four or five guard the man with their guns pointed at him ... while the others are plundering the house and when they cant carry off all I am told they brake and distroy in some mens houses all most all his furniture.[54]

A victim of the deserters living in the Why Not community in south-central Randolph County vented his rage at what was happening: "The many robberies, thefts, murders, and outrages that are inflicted on the people of this county is incredible to believe, but it is so; men are beaten, maimed and murdered on every side, some have had to fly from their homes and take refuge elsewhere. I, for one, am in that position, and am now a refugee from home, and still those traitorous blood-hounds pursue me." He left his son, a wounded soldier, with his wife and two children at home. He then described the ensuing plunder and wreckage of his home by a gang of vengeful deserters:

> The devils went to my house, fifteen in number, all armed, and robbed them of ... all of our provisions. They then went to breaking and destroying the house and other property with the butts of their guns. They broke mirrors, engravings in frames, the glass windows of the house, and with axes tore up the floors. In fact, they demolished everything; even bursting the grind stone in the yard; took the clothing, bedding &c. I cannot enumerate all they did. My son, coming to the house at the time was fired on three times.— He had to run for his life. They threatened to kill the negro boys, and took a chunk of fire to burn the house. My son's wife begged hard, and they desisted.[55]

Lamenting the perilous predicament of the loyal Confederates in the Randolph area, the correspondent continued: "In the name of God, can not something be done to relieve us. There is more than twenty worse cases than mine, that I could name; but it is only necessary to show my own. I have not been beaten or abused in my person, as yet; but others have. Threats against my life are daily made.— Three thousand dollars would not replace the damage done me. It is said that the deserters have procured legal advice, and they now take day light for their work."[56]

Both hunters and deserters scored victories in Chatham County at this time. A band of about eight deserters entered the house of Thomas C. Dixon of the Cane Creek community. At the time, Dixon was a soldier in the army. The marauders "carried off a large quantity of bed clothing, leather, jewelry and other valuables."[57] A group of hunters in the Mount Vernon Springs neighborhood turned the tables against some deserters when they went after a band of absconders who had been robbing people in their area. "In the course of the night they came upon a party of five, who had just robbed the home of a Mrs. Dark, whose husband is in the service and who had no man at her house to protect her. The five were found sitting before a fire dividing their plunder. They were fired upon and two, ___ Hall and Solomon Dunn were mortally wounded; the other three were captured without resistance, and carried to Pittsboro Jail." The three captives were Louisiana cavalrymen.[58]

J.M. Worth wrote to his brother Jonathan in Raleigh from Asheboro of the anarchy and chaos caused by the avenging Red Strings: "There is no spot upon this earth more completely subjugated than Randolph County. There is not a day or night passes but what some one is robbed of all the parties can carry away. They are in bands in nearly all parts of the County unless it is stopped we shall be utterly used up." Noting that the deserters had a well-organized intelligence network, Worth stated: "The deserters ... have friends that visit this [Asheboro] and all other places and keep them informed on all subjects at all times."[59] On February 16, a citizen from the northeast Randolph community of Troy's Store complained that the "Holdenites or Toryes," which included many militia officers, was "mutch the larger party" in Randolph. He noted that those Home Guard members who had been loyal enough to go to the eastern part of the state when ordered to do so have had their houses plundered and families abused while away. He also reported that "one man was murdered last week by a Deserter and others threaten[ed] but those that are true dare not interfer." He concluded with: "Worse than all som[e] Yankeys are her[e] a mong us and those people who harbor them I think should be swung up and let hang.... I had better close as they have threatened my life & if this gets out I expect nothing else but to go up."[60] A citizen writing from Hillsborough (seat of Orange County), after recounting several instances of deserters robbing and wantonly destroying property in Randolph and western Chatham, added that they "most unmercifully" beat "those who have heretofore—been engaged in taking up deserters." Suggesting the paradox that loyal soldiers became deserters in order to protect their families from deserters, he stated: "I understand many soldiers who have heretofore shown themselves true to the Cause are now at home—(not skulking in the woods) but say they intend to protect their families—if they can—or die with them."[61]

Reports also came from Montgomery and Chatham counties decrying the perilous predicament of the loyal citizens. From Montgomery came word that the advent of Sherman into South Carolina emboldened the deserters. The writer warned, "Unless checked, the destruction of the property of the loyal men of Montgomery will be equally as great as if visited by the Enemy's Army."[62] A loyalists in Chatham County lamented that the deserters have been robbing in places "too numerous to mention." Indicating that the hated Yankee was not anathema to all Southerners, the writer exclaimed that "100 of them [deserters] met at Nat Newlines the other day and elected a Yankee prisoner who ran away from Salisbury Captain[.] [T]hey are 50 to 75 in number in squads."[63]

At the small northern Randolph community of Julian's Cross Roads, a squad of cavalry guarded a quantity of goods deposited there by the Confederate tax agents who had been enforcing the unpopular tax-in-kind law. On February 24, deserters attacked them. The Confederates suffered three casualties.[64] According to J.M. Worth in Asheboro, a Supporting Force unit under the command of a Captain Lilly "on hearing of the battle at Julian ran off from here without orders and left about 100 guns without any protection."[65] The vestige of respect and authority the Confederacy commanded in Randolph County at this time vanished with Captain Lilly and his men. Confederates suffered further humiliation in Randolph when "A band of deserters captured Gen. Hardee's engineer corps in Randolph County, last week, stripping them of their clothing, and robbing them of all the money in their possession."[66] Hundreds of Confederate troops passed through Randolph and Guilford counties at this time on their way toward Durham, where they would mass to form a front against Sherman's army.

On February 9, the adjutant general ordered the Home Guard battalions to reorganize into just two classes: the first class, made up of all able-bodied men liable for service beyond the limits of their counties, and the second class, comprised of those exempt from duty except within the limits of their counties.[67] On the 19th, commanders ordered the battalions east of the Blue Ridge to send their first class men to Raleigh.[68] Due to "the defenseless condition of the County against the robbers and deserters," the governor excused the Randolph Home Guards from going to Raleigh, provided they "will immediately reorganize — and all the efficient officers go to work with determined resolution to suppress the disturbances."[69]

As part of a strategy to divide and conquer the deserter bands in Randolph County, J.M. Worth made the novel suggestion that the "better class of deserters" — that is, those who had taken no part in robbing or plundering — be granted pardon if they would organize and help drive out those committing depredations.[70] The governor responded that "he will authorize any person you [J.M. Worth] may design to form a company of the better class of deserters to drive the robbers from the country or to exterminate them as you suggest."[71] Worth apparently believed that companies composed of the "better class of deserters" would have a surer chance of capturing "robbers," because the deserters knew the location of the caves and hideouts frequented by the delinquents, whereas his son-in-law's regular troops did not.

In at least one instance, Confederate authorities did try "to organize the citizens and inoffensive deserters into a company to put an end to the robberies going on in the county." They attempted the stratagem in the Little River district of south-central Randolph. At the public meeting called for the purpose, Private William F. Walters, a scout from Sherman's army who had become a leader in the local deserter-guerrilla band, stepped forward and "said ... that if they [i.e., members of the crowd] would follow him to Asheboro, they would get arms and drive the deserter hunters out of the county." George Auman, a witness to the meeting, testified that Walters added: "If there were any in the crowd who were willing to serve under him as first Lieutenant they should step aside." Some ten or fifteen men did so.[72] Next, Lewis Parks, militant Unionist, addressed the assembly. He said, "that they (the deserters) must forage upon the secessionists of the country and that when the hunters became too numerous they must get to their dens — if they could not drive them out."[73]

The preceding testimony depicts a situation indicative of Randolph's estrangement from the Confederacy. A group of its citizens assembled to consider a proposal that they aid Confederate authority in ridding the area of "desperadoes" reacted by denouncing "secessionists" and "hunters" and, on the part of some, offered to form a guerrilla unit to defy Confederate power commanded by a Yankee soldier. After this fiasco, Confederates in the Randolph County area abandoned the idea of soliciting the aid of the "better class" of deserters in their cause.

Problems in Wilkes, Forsyth, and Alexander Counties

Loyal citizens in other parts of the Quaker Belt fared little better at the hands of the disaffected and disloyal than did those in the Randolph area. A group of patriots from Forsyth County petitioned Governor Vance to protect them from a band of 50 to 60 deserters and draft-dodgers who had "formed themselves in to companies and squads and have and are going to the Residences of Loyal citizens at the dead hour of night," robbing them of guns, ammunition, clothes, food, and money. What they did not take, the deserters often destroyed or burned. The deserter bands, complained the petitioners, "picket the public roads all the time and watch for loyal citizens to put them to death[.] [T]hey caught the Hon A. Waugh and beat and wallowed him in the mud and other wise injured him."[74] On March 9, the *People's Press* reported that five residences in Forsyth had been robbed of guns, ammunition, and other articles during the past few days.[75]

An Alexander County soldier serving in the trenches at Petersburg received word from home that the old Union flag "waves avery day." (Alexander County, while not in the Quaker Belt, adjoins both Wilkes and Iredell counties.) The soldier, V.S. Cavin, responded, "I wish I was there[.] I hope it [that is, the United States flag] will Wave over me bee fore long[.]" Cavin was considering deserting for home, but he was warned by family members that "it wont do to come home," because "the [home] gard was killing every body the[y] Could[.]" Rather than desert for home and risk death at the hands of the Home Guards, Cavin's relatives urged him to "cross the lines," that is, desert to the Yankees, which Cavin agreed to try to do.[76]

In February a citizen wrote Governor Vance that a state of anarchy existed in the Wilkes County area: "I have nothing charey to write you[.] [I]t is shoot and hang[,] rob[,] steal and the like thing is of daily occurance[.]"[77] The Wilkes loyalists found a champion in a Confederate soldier named Price who was home on leave from Lee's army. Price agreed "without parchment or commission" to "clean out" the deserters if authorities placed a sufficient force under his command. Forty men volunteered to serve under him, and within fifteen days, Pierce's recruits had hanged or shot 55 deserters.[78] Someone reporting from Wilkes County to the *Standard* about the actions of an "independent company" of Confederates that may well have been "Pierce's force" wrote: "The Home Guard and a kind of independent company professing to put down robbery, have hung women till nearly dead (some of them pregnant) to make them tell on deserters in this County. They have done nearly everything an unbridled soldiery could do."[79]

Lieutenant-Colonel Alexander C. McAlister and the Last Deserter Hunt

Confederate authorities in Richmond agonized over the challenge to Confederate power in their underside. The anarchy in the Quaker Belt threatened the security of Confederate supply depots in Greensboro, High Point, and other railheads in the area.[80] Moreover, it threatened the railroad system that ran west to east across North Carolina from the base of the mountains to the coastal plain. Especially endangered was the Piedmont Railroad, which ran from Greensboro to Danville, Virginia. It provided an escape route into central North

Worth/McAlister house, built by John M. Worth in the mid–1850s, later became the residence of Worth's son-in-law, Lt. Col. Alexander Cary McAlister. It was the finest residence in Asheboro at the time of the Civil War (courtesy Randolph County Public Library's Historical Photograph Collection).

Carolina, where the hard-pressed Army of Northern Virginia and a fleeing Confederate government might join up with Joseph Johnston's army to make a last stand against the Yankee invaders. To secure the area from threats by local pro–Union guerrillas and from possible raids from Sherman's army (which was about fifty miles south of Greensboro) or Union forces in East Tennessee, General Lee ordered two regiments and ten companies detached from Cook's and Lane's Brigades into the Quaker Belt south and west of Greensboro.[81] Thus began the seventh and final drive by Confederate and state forces against armed dissidents in the area since the summer of 1861. Vance's state forces, which were by then in disarray, played only a small role in the action.

Confederates ordered half of the Twenty-third Regiment North Carolina Troops led by a Captain Wall into Forsyth, Yadkin, and Davidson counties; they sent the other half of the regiment commanded by Lieutenant P.P. Leach into Moore, Montgomery, and Richmond counties.[82] The Seventh Regiment North Carolina Troops and the ten companies detached from several different regiments — about six hundred troops commanded by Lieutenant-Colonel Alexander Carey McAlister (1836–1916) — marched into Randolph, Moore, and Chatham counties to hunt down the deserter bands there.[83] State authorities ordered the second class Home Guards into the field in all counties entered by Confederate troops to assist in the search.[84] The adjutant general ordered Major Noah Rush, commander of Randolph County's Fifth Battalion Home Guards, to take advantage of the force that had been sent into Randolph "to destroy the marauders there" and reorganize his battalion and return it to duty.[85]

Lieutenant-Colonel McAlister was the son of a wealthy Cumberland County planter. He married a daughter of J.M. Worth and settled in Asheboro, where he died in 1916. Before coming to the Quaker Belt as commanding officer of the troops ordered there by General Lee, he had served as commandant of the Forty-sixth Regiment North Carolina Troops.[86] Major General H. Hith ordered McAlister into the Randolph, Chatham, Moore area, because "it is believed organized bands of deserters are collected in those counties to a greater extent than any other portion of the state."[87] The lieutenant-colonel arrived in Greensboro on March 2, and two days later marched from High Point toward Asheboro with six hundred men. His troops — officially referred to as a "Detachment of Cooke's and Lane's Brigades" — encamped in Asheboro on the fifth.[88] McAlister gave little thought to the niceties of the civil law. He ordered his subordinate Major J. Waddell, "to any who may resist your authority or who may have resisted the authority of the Govt, no quarter will be shown. They will be shot down wherever found."[89] Troops were not to countenance aiders and abettors of deserters. "You are authorized to arrest and hold while in the county any and all persons who may hinder you in the discharge of your duties by giving aid to deserters by the blowing of horns, ringing of bells or by the giving of any other signal or who in any way may assist in their escape."[90] Knowing that he would have great difficulty in finding loyal persons to guide his troops, McAlister ordered his officers to force citizens to serve the army as guides in hunting deserters. If anyone refused, he ordered his officers to "inflict such punishment as you may think necessary to protect you from betrayal."[91]

On March 7, McAlister sent a report of his operations to the chief of staff of General Joseph E. Johnston's army, which was concentrating near Raleigh to make one last stand against the approaching Union hordes under Sherman. McAlister reported that Randolph County had six hundred deserters — two hundred organized into well-armed bands. He charged that they were "active sympathizers with the enemy & should a raiding party or other force come within convenient distance they would doubtless cooperate with it." To prove his point, he said that deserters had set fire to a bridge on the Fayetteville and Western Plank Road to prevent the passage of Confederate wagon trains then en route to supply Johnston's army. Further, he lamented, they had recently robbed a Confederate officer within ten miles of Asheboro traveling from Cheraw, South Carolina, to Greensboro. McAlister concluded, "The only speedy and

Lt. Col. Alexander Cary McAlister (1836–1916) about 1860. Asheboro resident and commander of the Forty-Sixth Regiment North Carolina troops, he led three regiments into the Randolph County area in March 1865 to quell an insurrection of deserters (courtesy Randolph County Public Library's Historical Photograph Collection).

effectual cure for it is a summary punishment of such of those bands as may fall into my hands." To do this, he requested that he be "authorized to appoint a Genl Court Martial into power to confirm sentence for the trial of such of these robbers as may be apprehended." Failing that, authorities should assign someone with such power to him.[92]

On March 15, McAlister issued a report to General Lee's headquarters summarizing his accomplishments to date. A lack of reliable guides and information, he noted, hampered his first week's operations. To gain the cooperation of the citizens of Randolph, he issued a printed circular asking for their assistance; however, he observed, "the call has not been responded to."[93] Indicating that the same problems plagued him that beset his predecessors in hunting deserters in the Randolph area, the colonel wrote: "The armed bands who have been committing most outrageous robberies on citizens and travelers fled from the county upon our approach, or have disbanded or so concealed themselves that all efforts to discover their hiding places have thus far proved unsuccessful." McAlister added: "The mountainous portions of this section afford good cover for them, and they possess so generally the sympathy of the inhabitants that we are laboring under great difficulties."[94] Not all had been in vain, however, for McAlister reported that "40 deserters have been arrested — one of them was severely wounded, and one killed."[95]

While McAlister's six hundred Confederate veterans hunted the militant Randolph deserters, elements of Sherman's cavalry wrought havoc in the lower part of the Seventh Congressional District. As early as March 2, a detachment of Federal cavalry pillaged Wadesboro (seat of Anson County).[96] On the seventh, skirmishes occurred near Rockingham — only about fifty miles below Asheboro — between Confederate cavalry under Generals Hampton and Wheeler and Union foragers.[97] On the eighth, Sherman, who was marching toward Fayetteville, camped the bulk of his army a few miles below Rockingham at Laurel Hill.[98] A minor battle occurred on the tenth at the Cumberland County community of Monroe's Crossroads between General Kilpatrick — the Union cavalry commander — and Hampton and Wheeler's troops. A Confederate surprise attack routed the Union forces.[99] On the eleventh, Sherman occupied Fayetteville, and on the twelfth, a detachment of Federal troops occupied Carthage, the seat of Moore County.[100]

Finding themselves participants in one of the dramatic closing scenes in the fall of the Confederacy, the citizens of the Randolph area were in a quandary. Whichever way their sympathies lay, they stood to lose. Loyal Confederates faced death, robbery, and pillage by deserters and their disloyal sympathizers, and stood in dread of the imminent arrival of Sherman's army. Militant Unionists and deserters, whose predicament became critical as the area swelled with hundreds of troops sent in to hunt them down and to reinforce General Johnston's army, faced death, capture, and plunder at the hands of vengeful Confederate troops. Describing the turmoil and confusion of those days, J.M. Worth wrote: "The county is full of all sorts of folks moving from Sherman and we are being swallowed up.... I am bothered with all sorts of trouble sick, wounded and hungry, robbers and dangers and every other sort of trouble."[101] Another Asheboro resident wrote, "a large number of cavalry and wagons, etc. have passed here on their way to Raleigh. You ought to have seen us hiding meat, corn, etc. the other day. We heard that 4000 Cavalry were to pass here and we knew if they did we would be eaten out.... We expected a train of 150 wagons a day or two ago and they ... went to Franklinsville, and yesterday 100 cavalry and 100 wagons passed here and they went to the same place.... Pittsboro is full to overflowing with refugees from Fayetteville." Purporting to express a widespread sentiment, the correspondent concluded: "Peace now would be more acceptable to the people than all the wealth of the world even a peace on Lincoln's terms."¹⁰²

The presence of McAlister's troops in Randolph had a negative effect upon the citizens of Guilford — especially those in the southeastern part of the county — for many deserters in escaping them fled into that area and began wreaking their vengeance upon its loyal citizens. One witness wrote: "I have not the language to express how we are treated in the South East Corner of Guilford.... The Deserters have taken ever good gunn in the neighbourhood[.]"¹⁰³ Another wrote from Greensboro: "We seem to be on the eve of a reign of terror." He noted that fifty "scoundrels" raided residences within two and one-half miles of town.¹⁰⁴ One victim was a "lone widow woman" who the deserters suspected had a large amount of money hidden in her house. When she refused to disclose the location of her money, "they tortured her severely pulling her hair, scratching her face and abusing her in many ways." Only when "they tied a rope around her neck and told her that they would hang her till she was dead" did she give in.¹⁰⁵ In addition to the deserters, Guilford residents suffered from depredations by elements of Wheeler's Cavalry (Confederate) then in the county. Lamenting this double plague, one man wrote, "We have all forgotten our scare at the Yankees from these new and unexpected troubles."¹⁰⁶ From Forsyth County came the report that the deserters who "have had things quite their own way, ... Stealing and burning," were being pressed hard by the army troops ordered into the area by General Lee.¹⁰⁷ According to one source, the Confederate regulars, who captured "quite a number of men" in Forsyth and Yadkin counties, summarily executed several deserters rather than send them back into the ranks.¹⁰⁸ A Forsyth loyalist, who "hate[d] the idea of subjugation," lamented that "many around us are rejoicing at the thought of their [the Yankees] coming."¹⁰⁹

In Randolph County, the deserters "visited the widow [of] I.H. Foust and robbed her of a great deal of specie and other monies and pillaged her house carrying off such things as they wanted, regardless of all she could say." Colonel Foust died in December. He had been an owner of a cotton mill, a magistrate, a member of the House of Commons, and commander of the Randolph County Home Guards. The deserters who pillaged Foust's house treated wealthy secessionists likewise throughout Randolph and Guilford counties. For example, "they went to a aged citizen's house in Randolph, a Mr. Lutterlough, pillaged his house [and] burned all his valuable papers, set his house on fire several times, but he begged the Captain of the thieves to have it put out, and they put it out."¹¹⁰ A week later, about one hundred deserters attacked a Lieutenant Bass and his detachment of twenty-two of McAlister's troops while they crossed Bear Creek at a point near the Randolph-Moore border.¹¹¹ A trooper in the Seventh Regiment Senior Reserves wrote his wife from Asheboro about this incident: "In Moore County the deserters fired into Cooks men & wounded one & captured one prisoner & 5 guns Cooks men run like wild men."¹¹²

Meanwhile, soldiers cornered and attacked some deserters in "the neighborhood of old Goleyhorns."¹¹³ The Confederates captured two men: Alpheus Gollihorn, a Confederate deserter, and private William F. Walters of Company L, Third Indiana Cavalry.¹¹⁴ A third man, Milton Gollihorn, escaped.¹¹⁵ The soldiers carried the two prisoners to the detachment's headquarters near Page's Toll Gate (present-day Seagrove) on the plank road. After a "drum head" court-martial, the Confederates staked and shot Alpheus Gollihorn; they sent the Indiana cavalryman to Lieutenant-Colonel McAlister.¹¹⁶ Accounting for his execution of

Gollihorn, Captain D.C. Green explained: "He fired upon two of our men with the intention no doubt of killing them while they ... were moving upon him in his fortified position. If I had been present when he was first taken he would not have been brought to camp. But such not being the case he was brought before me. I gave him the benefit of a Drum head court martial which condemned him to be shot to death with musketry on the 22d day march 1865 at 4 P.M."[117] About Private Walters, Green noted: "He admits that he was engaged in the robbery of Randall Presnell he also had with him a double barrel shot gun but did not offer to use it. He made no attempt to fight whatever."[118] Captain Green spared Walter's life either because he feared future revenge at the hands of the conquering Federals or felt the soldier deserved leniency for not resisting. Lieutenant-Colonel McAlister, disappointed at his subordinate's forbearance with private Walters, wrote "but for the misinterpretation of my orders, he would not have been taken alive." McAlister wrote Governor Vance seeking permission to try Walters by general court-martial. He felt that the Indiana private should be executed as a warning to all "desperadoes" that a similar fate awaited them if they fell into his hands. As further justification for executing Walters, McAlister claimed: "He is recognized as an officer of an armed band of deserters, and is a notoriously audacious robber, is suspected of having participated in two murders recently committed in the county & is one of a party that fired upon my men."[119] The governor granted McAlister's request for a court-martial of private Walters; it convened in Asheboro on March 28, 1865. The military court found Private Walters "guilty of robbery and of associating with armed bands of deserters and robbers — of resisting military authority of the Confederate States and of being a leader and counsellor of such armed resistance[.]" The court ordered that the Indiana soldier be "shot to death with musketry," which was carried out on April 1, 1865, in Asheboro.[120]

On the day a firing squad executed Private Walters, the army ordered McAlister's troops to Salisbury to prepare a defense against Stoneman's raiders reportedly threatening the area.[121] Two days earlier, the lieutenant-colonel issued a report to General Lee's headquarters stating that since the 16th, his men had arrested sixty-one deserters. They killed one and wounded one.[122] Thus, in 25 days of continuous operations, McAlister's 600 troops netted only about 100 deserters out of 600 believed to be in the area. On the departure of McAlister's troops from the Randolph area on April 1, the deserters emerged from their hiding places and resumed their depredations on the loyal citizens. As one observer put it, the area, especially Montgomery and Moore counties, was "terribly infested by deserters, who were by day and night committing robberies and outrages upon the citizens. In fact the citizens were subjugated and terror stricken."[123]

Stoneman's Raiders

Stoneman's raiders rode into the Wilkes County area from East Tennessee in the last two days of March 1865. Instead of heading directly to Salisbury and Greensboro as planned, the Union cavalrymen moved up into southwestern Virginia to block a possible retreat of Lee's army into the area. Once Lee was safely contained, Stoneman rode back into North Carolina and occupied Salem in Forsyth County, where "old men wept like children and prominent citizens took off their hats and bowed to it [the United States flag]."[124] The

Federal raiders burned the railroad bridges around Greensboro and High Point, and then headed for Salisbury.[125] Before Stoneman arrived in Salisbury, the Confederates evacuated the Federal prisoners. Since Confederate commanders ordered their main force at Salisbury to the defense of Greensboro, the Federals easily took the town and burned the prison, government factories, and nearby railroad bridges. The Yankee raiders then headed back to Tennessee via Statesville, Morganton, and Asheville.[126]

Much of Stoneman's foray into North Carolina took place in the Quaker Belt. Ina W. Van Noppen, the historian who first chronicled the incursion of the Yankee cavalrymen into the Tar Heel State, noted that the presence of the blue-clad raiders unleashed a civil war between Southerners of neighbor against neighbor. Stoneman's Raiders included Kirk's regiment of North Carolina Mounted Infantry, as well as hundreds of other troops recruited from Tennessee and North Carolina. Local militant Unionists, in conjunction with their relatives and friends clad in blue, took every opportunity to get revenge on their secesh neighbors while they had the upper hand.[127]

After Stoneman's cavalry left the area, new bands of bushwhackers appeared in western Wilkes County. One group specialized in stealing horses and transporting them to Tennessee where they sold them.[128] S.A. Sharp, the former commander of the Iredell County Home Guards, organized a force of men from the surrounding counties to hunt down the thieves. Several weeks after the war ended Sharp's troops surrounded and captured the last of the bushwhackers in Wilkes at their hideout called Fort Hamby. Sharp's troopers staked and shot four of the captives.[129]

Quaker Belt Militant Unionists Celebrate Victory in Mass Meetings

The Civil War formally ended in North Carolina when Confederate general Johnston surrendered his army to Sherman at Durham's Station on April 26, 1865. After two and one-half years of state and Confederate military forces hunting them like wild animals, the outliers in the Quaker Belt were free to abandon their caves and hideouts, return to their homes and families, and resume a normal existence. The pro–Confederate element could likewise relax and rejoice at having the reign of terror lifted under which they had suffered so long. The "inner civil war," however, continued. A deep bitterness lingered in the hearts of many Unionists and Confederates for months afterward. Each faction committed many brutal acts of revenge upon the other to settle wartime grudges.[130] A magistrate in Asheboro related to a traveler in September that "he could count more than a hundred houses owned by secessionists which had been broken into and robbed within the past few months."[131]

Following the assassination of President Lincoln, the militant Unionists in the Quaker Belt held public meetings at which they "assembled, after years of oppression and tyranny, to enjoy once more the sacred right of freedom of speech, and to give expression to our unchanged affection for the Federal Union."[132] They passed resolutions condemning the murder of President Lincoln and rejoicing at the reestablishment of United States rule in the Tar Heel State. One assembly of Union enthusiasts in Davidson County rhapsodized: "We throw to the breeze the Star Spangled Banner—the emblem of freedom, and pledge ourselves forever to defend it." They added: "That the manly, magnanimous bearing of the

Federal army now in our midst, commands our warmest admiration and esteem."[133] These former outliers, deserters, draft-dodgers, and militant Unionists resolved to support the new president of the United States, Andrew Johnson, and the newly appointed provisional governor of North Carolina, William Woods Holden. They embraced the Constitution of the United States as the supreme law of the land and accepted the abolition of slavery as "an inevitable result of the rebellion."[134]

From Randolph County came a resolution offering sympathy to the "bereaved widows, mothers, orphans and maimed," and to the Confederate soldiers from the Quaker Belt killed in action — the vast majority of whom opposed secession and the war — "who were driven to the slaughter pen like wild swine of the forest."[135] The Randolph Unionists boldly declared the former deserters, draft-dodgers, and militant Unionists to be true heroes of America: "We recognize in all men who fled from their homes and families rather than stain their hands in brothers blood, and fight against their government, the principle of true patriotism, and cordially invite them to return to their homes."[136]

At the Union meetings, the Peace Conservatives, deserters, draft-dodgers, and Red Strings, said little that would heal the wounds between themselves and their wartime antagonists and oppressors, the secessionists and War Conservatives. Rather, they demanded that the Federals punish the leaders of the rebellion.[137] In a resolution that served as an opening salvo in the political war during Reconstruction between Scalawags and Redeemers, the militant Unionists asserted "that we will support no man for any office of trust, profit or honor, who has willingly aided or abetted in the late Rebellion."[138]

At a public meeting in Graham, the seat of Alamance County, a Colonel Jordan — commander of the Federal occupation troops — gave a well-received speech to the assembled Southern Unionists. A Union army band enlivened the gathering with music.[139] In retrospect, this meeting seems ironical, because the town of Graham and Alamance County three years later became the scene of some of the bloodiest Klan activity in the Reconstruction South.[140] The band of the One-hundred-twelfth Illinois Regiment entertained an assembly of Unionists at Jamestown in Guilford County. After denouncing the former Confederacy and all its supporters, and reaffirming their allegiance to the old Union, the crowd passed a resolution guaranteed to rattle their former Confederate antagonists to the marrow. It read: "That we tender our heartfelt gratitude to the authorities of the United States government, and to the brave officers and men of the Union army who have defended, protected, and perpetuated our rights and liberties, as free and loyal citizens of the United States."[141]

At a Union meeting in at Mt. Airy in Surry County over 3,000 people assembled, including citizens from Alleghany, Yadkin, and Stokes counties. The Unionists claimed that North Carolina never would have seceded had the question of secession been put to a popular vote. They asserted their loyalty to the Union, expressed sorrow over the assassination of President Lincoln, and pledged support for President Andrew Johnson. They accepted the abolition of slavery as an inevitable result of secession.[142]

A Unionist meeting at Pleasant Union Church in Guilford County passed several strongly worded resolutions. One motion stated: "That as citizens of the United States who have been for four years deprived of civil rights — who have had a State Government forced upon us by fraud and violence — whose lives and property have been in constant danger — who have been branded with every mark of ignominy, and who have been cut off from our fellow-citizens of the loyal states — we hail the advent of the United States forces as our deliverers and hail in our national Flag as again unfurled over us, the assurance of our freedom and protection." They rejoiced at the end of slavery and vowed to "support no man for any office who advocated secession — who was in favor of the Conscription act — who favored the repeal of the Bill of Rights — who used the authority of any office to become the supple tools of our tyrants, to insult, to harass, oppress and murder loyal men — who upheld the rebellion — who urged the prosecution of the war to starvation and extermination." In conclusion, the Unionists expressed profound class resentments against the slave-owning landed aristocracy that had promoted secession and the war. They recommended the establishment of a "true" Union newspaper in Greensboro that will "advocate all measures that will make North Carolina intelligent and prosperous, that will seek to elevate the great body of the people until their shadow shall wither the Cotton and slave aristocracy of the South, and make our country what God and nature designed it to be."[143]

The Salem Brass Band entertained a crowd of citizens at the Forsyth County courthouse in Winston assembled to celebrate the raising of "the Union flag, which had during four years of tyranny, under a bogus government, been prohibited to float from the dome of the Court House." The flag represented "the second advent of freedom and liberty" to the people of North Carolina. The officers and men of the Tenth Ohio Regiment of Cavalry marched around the flag saluting the audience. An observer of the occasion described it in rapturous terms: "The joy was so overwhelming, that many of the old and young shed tears freely, as cheer after cheer went up in honor of the occasion. It was the proudest day in the history of Forsyth County."[144] On the day that the Unionists held their meeting in Forsyth, three members of the Twelfth Ohio and Tenth Michigan Regiments published a card in the *People's Press* thanking the citizens of Winston and Salem for the kind treatment the people of the communities extended to them while they convalesced from wounds received in battle: "We were left here among entire strangers, and, now, after a stay of four weeks, during which time we have made many friends and become much attached to the place, we are again fit for duty, but cannot leave here without expressing to the citizens our warmest thanks for the kind attentions and many acts of kindness shown us during our stay among them."[145]

The resolutions passed by the militant Unionists at public meetings held in the Quaker Belt in May and June of 1865 stand as a witness to their long, heroic, and unheralded struggle on behalf of the United States of America during the war.[146] They lend credence to historian Carl Degler's "Other South" thesis and reveals that the nineteenth-century South was not a monolithic polity that thought, spoke, and fought in unison. There were many Souths; there are many Souths. The Union meetings by wartime militant Unionists in the spring and summer of 1865 endorsing the Radical Republicans in Congress and denouncing former secessionists demonstrate that passions between former Confederates and Unionists remained unabated from what they had been during the war. Indicating that the two camps remained divided into hostile divisions in the community, Provisional Governor William Woods Holden in September 1865 admonished Randolph County authorities about continuing internal conflict in their community: "Complaints have been made to me that there is a disposition on the part of a portion of the citizens of Randolph County to take the law into their own hands and to inflict punishment on certain persons for real or supposed past injuries." The war is now over and peace must be preserved, chided Holden. He warned that "no man can be permitted to redress his own wrongs by his own Strong hand.... Citizens must Seek a redress for their injuries before the loyal tribunals of the county." Holden expressed sympathy for "the ultra Union men" who had been harshly and unjustly treated during the war for their loyalty to the United States. But the president has proclaimed a general amnesty and pardon that applies to most of the populace, and everyone must submit to the law. "Wrongs and grievances must be redressed in the Courts and by the Constituted authorities. Every citizen must appeal to them only for justice."[147]

The hostile factions in Randolph County took the governor's advice and began fighting their battles in the courts. A resident of the New Salem community reported in April 1866 that there were about 2,000 criminal cases in the Randolph courts, and that many citizens were going west, especially the antislavery component.[148] On April 6, the Greensboro *Patriot* printed an article entitled "Randolph Superior Court" that vividly described the legal strife in the county: "The old citizens and such as were called loyal during the days of the Confederacy are prosecuting the Bushwhackers [outliers] and robbers; and, on the other hand, the Bushwhackers who now set themselves up as *par excellence* Union citizens, are indicting the Militia officers and such as acted under their orders for assaults and batteries, forcible trespasses, false imprisonment and murder. The spirit of retaliation has just begun to move them, and it is difficult to tell how far and to what extremes it may impel them."[149]

Severe unrest between the wartime Unionists and the diehard Confederates continued into 1867. In August of that year, Major W.S. Worth, commander of the U.S. Army post in Greensboro, issued a letter to be read before the Randolph County Court of Pleas and Quarter Sessions in Asheboro. In the letter he expressed alarm at the continued reports of Randolph citizens refusing to obey the laws and defying civil authorities. He warned that military force will be used if necessary to protect the sheriff, constables, and other officials in enforcing the laws. The major declared it illegal to carry a deadly weapon in Randolph County.[150]

Clearly, the wartime discord between loyal Confederates and loyal Americans — that is, militant Unionists, deserters, and draft-dodgers of the Heroes of America stripe — continued for years after the war ended under the new appellations of Redeemers and Scalawags — but that is another story.

Summary and Conclusions

During the American Civil war, an inner civil war on the home front raged in many parts of the Confederacy between Southerners. Nowhere was it more vicious or cruel than the one between the secessionists and the militant Unionists and their deserter and draft-dodger allies in the Quaker Belt of Confederate North Carolina. (Militant Unionists were anti-secession Unionists who remained loyal to the United States after secession.) It began in the spring of 1861 when Wesleyan abolitionists, antislavery Quakers and Moravians, and anti-secession Whigs refused to accept disunion and went underground to form a guerrilla front to oppose Confederate power and to try to effect a reunion with the United States. John Hilton of the Thomasville area of Davidson County emerged as their leader. Observers reported that the Hilton band contained about five hundred recruits who mustered under the United States flag and schemed to make a "strike for the old Union" that would soon make certain secessionists "feel the rope." Abolitionists, Lincolnites, and anti-secession Whigs fleshed out their ranks.

The militant Unionists who flocked to support Hilton reflected the unique historical development of central North Carolina from the Revolution to secession. Quakers and Moravians, who early on widely settled in the part of the central piedmont referred to here as the "Quaker Belt," initiated an antipathy to slavery that diffused throughout the region as the decades progressed. With the advent of the Wesleyan Methodist abolitionists and the publication of Hinton Helper's *Impending Crisis*, the section developed a renewed antislavery impulse in the decade before Fort Sumter. Those who opposed slavery on principle formed the bedrock of the opposition to the Confederacy in the Quaker Belt.

Another cause of antipathy to the Confederacy in the Quaker Belt was persistent Whiggery. The great majority of the counties in the region were Whig to the core and formed the largest Whig community in the state. The Whigs favored a progressive state government that encouraged economic development, railroads, public roads, public schools, asylums, and other civic improvements. They bitterly opposed secession as foolhardy and unnecessary. In February 1861, over ninety percent of the electorate in the region voted against holding a convention to consider secession. During the war, area old Whig leaders such as Bryan Tyson, Lewis Hanes, J.M. Leach, Calvin Cowles, and Samuel H. Christian emerged to direct the reunionist peace and convention movements of 1863 and 1864.

The Quaker Belt was located largely outside the commercial plantation economy of the Old South. While slaveholding was common, the region contained few large plantations with huge slave populations. Indeed, the nonslaveholding, subsistent yeoman farmer was typical of the constituency. In addition, a large number of artisans, mechanics, tenant farmers, and laborers infused the population — about thirty percent in all. This rural working class had little incentive to fight or die for the right to own slaves — a right few of them ever expected to exercise. Composed of only fifteen of the eighty-nine counties in Confederate North Carolina in 1861, the Quaker Belt contained about 25 percent of the state's white population. This translated into a powerful voting block and into one-fourth of the state's manpower for the army. The decision of many in the area to not support the Confederacy and, in the case of lots of others, to oppose the Confederacy led to an inner civil war in the Quaker Belt between the secessionist and the anti–Confederate and pro–Union factions that was endemic in the area from the summer of 1861 until war's end.

The insurrection of militant Unionists under John Hilton provoked Confederate commanders to send over 150 troops into Davidson, Randolph, and Guilford counties in August 1861 to assist local authorities in making arrests. This was the first of seven times that Confederate and state military commanders ordered troops into the Quaker Belt during the war to repress rebellion. The suppression of the Hilton disloyalists marked the beginning of an inner civil war in the district. Thus, a war of neighbor against neighbor waxed hot in the Quaker Belt before the war against the Yankee invaders had seriously gotten underway elsewhere.

With many of their leaders captured and imprisoned or forced into the army, the militant Unionists remained relatively quiet until Governor Clark, in March 1862, drafted one-third of the state militia to fight against the Federal forces ensconced in the sound region of the commonwealth. The state draft precipitated a crisis in Randolph and Davidson counties. Persistent Unionists held "peace meetings" at Kennedy Schoolhouse near Thomasville in Davidson County and at Scott's Old Field in western Randolph County in which supporters opposed the state draft and advocated peace and reunion with the United States. These meetings marked the first organized manifestation of peace sentiment in the Confederacy; by 1863, peace movements similar to the one in North Carolina appeared in many areas of the South.[1] Confederate military authorities ordered hundreds of troops into the area and quickly suppressed the peace insurgents. They rounded up the leaders and sent them without trial to prisons in Richmond and Salisbury. The activities of the Hilton band in 1861 and the peace demonstrators in 1862 prove that reunion sentiment was strong in the Quaker Belt before the appearance of the sources of disloyalty historians usually mention: the Confederate conscription acts with their exemptions for planters and provisions for hiring substitutes, rampant inflation, food and clothing shortages, class antagonisms, and defeatism. Thus, in the first year of the war reconstruction-oriented Unionism was a spontaneous "home-grown" phenomenon in the Quaker Belt. It grew out of political, religious, and cultural opposition to the creation of the Confederacy and not out of reactions to wartime hardships or out of class resentments precipitated by the Confederate draft laws.

In April 1862, Congress passed its first national conscription act making white males between 18 and 35 liable to the draft; in October, a second law upped the age to 45. In February 1864, all men between the ages of 17 and 50 became liable for the draft. These laws forced many men, who hitherto reluctantly or passively had accepted the Confederacy or had tried to remain neutral, to ally themselves with the militant Unionists underground.

They may have been willing to tolerate the Confederacy, but they were unwilling to fight or die for it. This attitude was especially marked among the old-line, anti-secession Whigs in the Quaker Belt. They were at best reluctant Confederates. They viewed the conscript laws as unconstitutional and despotic measures forced on the body politic by their former political enemies, the Democrats.

Many men who wanted to avoid the draft took to the woods and became "outliers." Others, who submitted to conscription, often deserted at the first opportunity and returned home to join the draft-dodgers in the bushes. The draft laws forced volunteers serving in the army to remain there for the duration of the war. Many of the twelve-month volunteers believed that they had already shouldered their fair share of the burden of the war. They deserted for home at the expiration of their enlistments in the summer of 1862 and joined the ranks of the outliers.

In the late summer and early fall of 1862, the inner civil war metamorphosed from a minor skirmish into a major conflict that became increasingly bloody and cruel as time went by. The main cause of this development was the merger of deserters, draft-dodgers, and militant Unionists in the Quaker Belt into one powerful anti–Confederate guerrilla force that presented a formidable challenge to Confederate authority, especially to militia and Confederate troops ordered to hunt, capture, and return them to the ranks or prison. The militant Unionists provided the ideological and organizational core of the deserter bands that infested the Quaker Belt during the war. After secession they remained loyal to the United States and formed the underground guerrilla organization called the Heroes of America or, alternately, the Red Strings. They came from all classes of society: Bryan Tyson of Moore County and William F. Henderson of Davidson County, both owners of slaves and businesses, were from the commercial middle class. The brothers Z.F. and Noah Rush, who were respectively the sheriff and the commander of Randolph County's Home Guard Battalion, and whose father was the leader of the Heroes of America in Randolph County, came from the prosperous yeoman farmer class. Enos T. Blair, a Quaker farmer, and Joel Ashworth, a schoolteacher and Wesleyan abolitionist minister, who were elected to the state legislature from Randolph County in 1864, were from the rural professional and middle class. Colonel William B. Richardson, merchant, slave owner, and commander of the county militia, came from the upper social strata of Moore County. Lewis Hanes of Davidson County—a slave owner, farmer, and newspaper editor—and Dr. J.L. Johnson, a dentist who lived in Forsyth County, came from the professional class. The two well-known leaders of powerful deserter bands—John Quincy Adams Bryan of Wilkes and William Owens of Montgomery—were farmers (a tenant in the case of Owens) of marginal economic means. During the war, Bryan became a captain in the Union army and during Reconstruction a major general in the state militia. Owens, like so many of the militant Unionist deserter leaders during the war, was murdered by vengeful captors.

Not all of the draft-dodgers and deserters became militant Unionists. While most of them had been against secession, the main sources of their alienation from the Confederacy were the draft laws and difficult economic times back home. When the Confederacy proved itself incapable of warding off the starvation and destitution of their families, they felt it their duty to desert and go home and provide for their loved ones.[2] If they did not care for them, no one else would. When they arrived home they fell under the influence of the Red String organization, which offered them a well-planned system of self-defense from state and Confederate troops sent in to hunt them down and return them to the army. Most of them opted to remain in the woods as outliers so they could care for their families and protect their wives and daughters from marauding gangs of men roaming the countryside during the night. In order to survive, they stole food and provisions from secessionist neighbors to feed and clothe their families.

Many outliers chose not to ally themselves with pillaging bands of deserters. Their wives and children could tend crops while they concealed themselves from the hunters. They could fish and hunt and trap small game. Many of these "non offensive" deserters, as J.M. Worth called them, were ambivalent in their political leanings; they were neither ardent Unionists nor eager Confederates. They simply wanted the war to stop and to be left alone to resume tending their farms and raising their families.[3]

The new governor-elect Zeb Vance, though a strong anti-secession Whig before the war, spoke plainly with the dissidents when he took the reins of power in August 1862. He issued a proclamation denouncing disloyalty and ordered his militia forces to arrest deserters and draft-dodgers and return them to the ranks. Governor Vance's rhetoric denouncing deserters as criminal marauders and his unflagging determination to hunt them down, arrest them, and return them to the ranks or prison augmented the intensity of the inner civil war. Soon conflict led to bloodshed, and the populace in every community squared off into pro- and anti–Confederate factions. From that point on the inner civil war waxed red-hot as neighbor fought neighbor and brother opposed brother.

The passage of the October 1862 conscription act exacerbated the internal war. It created a host of new exemptions that aroused class resentments across the South. The most controversial exemption pertained to the owners of twenty or more slaves. The nonslaveholding yeomanry of western North Carolina, already angered by the substitution clause, which allowed the "better sort" to buy their way out of the army, was infuriated at the exemption of planters. Critics complained that the draft laws made the war for Confederate independence "a rich man's war and a poor man's fight." Soldiers from the yeoman class knew that the families of planters would never starve from food shortages brought on by a lack of labor to put in, tend, and harvest crops. Yet due to their absence from home, their own wives and children not only confronted hunger, they faced destitution. By the fall of 1862, the rampant inflation and material destruction caused by the war had impoverished the lower classes across the land.[4] With their fathers and older brothers in the army, few yeoman and artisan families had the labor or financial resources to ward off food shortages and penury. Though they tried to provide necessities to the families of soldiers, the state governments proved incapable of preventing widespread scarcity and want. Moreover, planters became infamous for their refusal to forestall the production of cotton, tobacco, and other commercial crops in favor of growing food crops desperately needed to feed the soldiers in the field and their families and farm animals back home.[5]

Prompted by the Heroes of America, wives and other relatives wrote to soldiers in the army imploring them to come home and take care of their families. They promised that the Unionist faction in the community would aid and abet them in case the authorities began pressing too hard in search of them. Many soldiers responded and deserted, especially after the failure of Lee's first invasion of the North with his bloody standoff at Sharpsburg. The deserters united with the draft-dodgers and militant Unionists to form guerrilla bands that terrorized their loyal neighbors through larceny, assault, arson, death threats, and murder. Unable to earn a livelihood through ordinary means, they robbed and plundered their pro–Confederate neighbors for provisions and supplies. Confederate authorities and loyal citizens alike considered the guerrilla bands to be desperadoes, outlaws, highway robbers, murderers, and house burners. This depiction of the anti–Confederate dissidents as "criminals," which has survived largely to the present day, was unjust and biased. Had they been mere "criminals," they would have aimed their depredations at rich, poor, pro–Confederate, pro–Union, and neutral citizens alike. The facts do not support this contention. As numerous examples in the text attest, the dissidents directed their wrath with but very few exceptions at the pro–Confederate citizens, especially those who actively assisted state and Confederate authorities to hunt them down. Most of the deserters studied in this narrative viewed their criminal activities against secessionists as legitimate acts of guerrilla warfare conducted on behalf of the United States of America. The depiction of them as "criminals" by Confederate authorities and the loyal citizenry was patently hypocritical. Confederate and state troops often engaged in illegal acts such as torture, rape, woman and child abuse, stealing, pillaging, house demolition, and other atrocities directed toward the dissident population. Both the deserter gangs and the Confederate and state troops routinely committed criminal acts, the deserters mostly out of necessity, the troops typically out of malice.

This study presents several accounts of sexual assault on the wives of deserters by national and state troops.[6] John Pool — Peace Party leader, U.S. senator during Reconstruction, and Whig candidate for governor in 1860 — implied in a postwar essay that militia, Home Guard, and Confederate troops often raped deserters' wives during the war.[7] No reports of the rape of the wives and daughters of loyal citizens by deserters have been found by this study, but that does not mean that none occurred. One observer wrote that rampaging deserters committed rape in the Wilkes County area, but he failed to note whether their victims were Unionists or secessionists or both.[8] The evidence of rape presented in this study suggests that the long-held belief that the American Civil War was a "low rape" or "no rape" conflict to be invalid.[9]

In the late summer and early fall of 1862, Bryan Tyson issued his *A Ray of Light* and reunion circular. He implored Southerners to abandon the Confederate cause and seek a compromise on the basis offered by the Northern Peace Democrats that would return the Southern states to the Union with slavery protected by the Constitution. Tyson warned Southern leaders that approximately one-half of the Confederacy was already in the hands of Union forces and the South had little hope of retaking its lost provinces. Furthermore, inflation, high food prices, shortages of salt, cloth and other necessities would lead to hunger and destitution among the families of soldiers. The prescient Tyson warned Confederate leaders that to keep the sons and fathers of yeoman farmer families in the ranks for the duration of the war surely would result soon in a cessation of food production, starvation, and a collapse of the economy across the land. Rather than continue a war that no reasonable person believed they could win, Tyson urged Confederate leaders — while they still had a powerful army in the field to give them credibility — to negotiate a peace with the North along lines advocated by the Northern Peace Democrats and return to the Union. Tyson proved to be an accurate prognosticator. In less than a year after he issued his warnings, shortages of food, salt, cloth, grain, and other necessities had rendered the families of soldiers — who were already in dire economic straits when he disseminated his publications —

destitute. The defeats suffered by Confederates at Gettysburg and Vicksburg in July 1863 made it clear that the South could never win independence through military means alone.

According to his own testimony, Tyson issued copies of his publications to Confederate political leaders in Richmond and Raleigh. Beyond that, it is unclear whether Tyson widely distributed his political writings in North Carolina. Since he published his works in Raleigh, it is likely that the Unionist community there, which was considerable in numbers and power, knew of them.[10] It seems reasonable to assume that the Heroes of America, with its underground network, distributed copies of his works in the Quaker Belt, especially in Randolph and adjoining counties, but there is no extensive proof of that happening.[11] What is clear is that Tyson anticipated by almost a year the peace movement that swept across the state in the summer of 1863 with its demands for an armistice and a negotiated peace with the North—preferably one along the lines offered by the Northern Peace Democrats—before the Confederacy became too weak militarily to exact an honorable peace. His writings no doubt influenced the leaders of that movement.

In late September 1862, Governor Vance's militia force, in conjunction with Major Peter Mallett's battalion of troops who manned the Confederate Conscript Bureau's Camp of Instruction at Camp Holmes in Raleigh, launched a campaign against disloyalists and rampaging deserters in the Quaker Belt. This action wound down in December, and commanders ordered most of the troops back to base in this third effort by Confederate forces to subdue rebellion in the Quaker district. By January 1863, the insurgency had recommenced and spread all across the region. Confederate authorities ordered a regiment of infantry and a squadron of cavalry into the area to help Vance's militia and Mallett's Battalion quash the uprising. In this wide-ranging operation, troops hunted defiant deserters across the Quaker Belt from Wilkes in the west to Orange County in the east and into Montgomery and Moore counties to the south. This was the fourth time during the war in which Confederate and state forces rushed into the Quaker Belt to suppress revolt. The Yadkin County schoolhouse affray occurred during this campaign. Militia troops assaulted a band of about 25 deserters and draft-dodgers hold up in a school building located near Yadkinville. The deserters shot two militia officers dead while suffering two fatalities themselves. The militia captured three of the deserters, but the remainder escaped.[12]

Confederate authorities never effectively routed the dissidents who stationed their neighbors and family members as sentinels to give warning in case troops approached. In addition, in many instances disloyal members of the militia and Home Guards informed the outliers in advance of any plans by the state forces to capture them. When warned, the dissidents took to the woods and their caves until the hunters left their communities. Then they emerged from their hiding places and plundered the families and farms of the officers and men who had hunted them. If the hunters killed or wounded an outlier or injured a family member or destroyed their property, the dissidents exacted revenge on an eye-for-an-eye basis on the offenders.

The extensive campaigns by state and national forces against dissidents in the Quaker Belt between September 1862 and March 1863 failed to stay the problem. A new wave of desertion of Tar Heel troops occurred in the spring of 1863 when Chief Justice Richmond Pearson ruled that Governor Vance had no legal authority to arrest deserters or draft-dodgers with his militia. Along with Pearson's ruling, the passage of the unpopular tax-in-kind and impressment laws in the early spring of 1863, and the high casualties suffered by Tar Heel troops at the battles of Fredericksburg (December 1862) and Chancellorsville (March 1863), the North Carolina yeomanry fled the ranks for home at ever-increasing rates.

In January 1863, the Northern Peace Democrats, led by Clement Vallandigham of Ohio, launched their bid in Congress for an "honorable peace" with the South. Advocating an armistice followed by a peace convention of all the states North and South to hammer out a final settlement that would return the Confederate states to the Union with the constitutional guarantee of slavery preserved, the Peace Democrats — also referred to as "Copperheads" — clamored for "the Constitution as it is, and the Union as it was." The Northern peace movement triggered a Southern peace movement.

In May 1863, Dr. J.T. Leach, in a letter published in William Holden's *Standard*, advocated a return to the Union on the basis offered by the Northern Peace Democrats. Leach was the first person in the state since Bryan Tyson issued his *A Ray of Light* and reunion circular in August and September the previous year to promote reunion on the basis offered by the Northern Copperheads. Six months later, Leach, a wealthy planter from Johnston County, won a seat in the Confederate Congress on a peace platform.

Shortly after the defeats at Gettysburg and Vicksburg, Holden, Leach, and their Peace Conservative supporters — following the lead of the Northern Peace Democrats — launched their movement for an "honorable peace." The peace men denounced the Davis administration as a "central military despotism" for ignoring the decisions of Tar Heel courts pertaining to the draft laws and for enforcing the conscription, tax-in-kind, and impressment laws in North Carolina more harshly than elsewhere. More importantly, advocates passed resolutions at several Peace Party rallies calling for a return to the Union on the Copperhead basis. The Quaker Belt, which hosted more than half of the peace meetings while composed of only fifteen of the state's eighty-nine counties, formed the focal point of the peace movement.

Holden's 1863 peace movement had its roots in the Quaker Belt peace activists of March 1862 at Kennedy's Schoolhouse (Davidson County) and Scott's Old Field (Randolph County). Other important factors influencing the peace crusade included the writings of Bryan Tyson, the Northern Copperheads and their peace movement, the recent devastating defeats at Gettysburg and Vicksburg, the futility of continuing a war for independence that clearly could not be won, the hunger and destitution engulfing the population of the state due to the war, the refusal of Confederate authorities to obey the rulings of the North Carolina courts, the centralizing measures of the Richmond government such as the draft and tax laws that the yeomanry felt unfairly burdened them, the desire to preserve slavery and prevent emancipation and the social turmoil it would entail, and the unleashing in the summer of 1863 of long-held, pent-up resentments by the anti-secession Whigs against their old political enemies — the secessionists — in which they opted to replace the Confederacy with a new Copperhead America.

Many among the Peace Conservative leadership — especially the old-line Whigs — enjoyed the economic, social, and educational advantages common to the gentry. They advocated the Copperhead plan for reunion to end the war and to preserve the institution of slavery and the old social order. They feared that the emancipation of hundreds of thousands of illiterate and propertyless freedmen into society would lead to unmanageable social problems that might dovetail into a race war Armageddon. At the same time, a lot of the rural rank-and-file Peace Conservatives — especially members of deserter bands — who were usually less affluent, educated, and socially refined than their leaders, supported the Lincoln plan for reunion with emancipation and social transformation. The ablest among them either fled to the Federal lines and joined the Union army, migrated via the Underground Railroad to a Northern state to live, deserted to the enemy, or took the oath of allegiance to the United States after capture. Others joined deserter bands where many fell victim to military authorities who captured and imprisoned or shot them. The gentry feared the influence of the many deserters and militant Unionists who favored the Lincoln plan of reunion, who, if they gained enough power, might pull off an agrarian revolution that would disestablish traditional Conservative rule in North Carolina.

Those favoring reunion on the Lincoln basis included most Quakers, Moravians, Wesleyans, and Heroes of America, but by the 1860s, they, while influential, composed a minority of the population of the Quaker district. It was paradoxical to witness the majority of the population in the area in 1863 and 1864 support the Copperhead plan of reunion that sought to preserve slavery, when it was the antislavery Moravians, Quakers, Wesleyans, and Red Strings who had originated and championed the anti–Confederate and pro-peace cause in the district in 1861 and 1862. The Democrat-hating old Whigs formed a majority of the population during the war, and they led the Copperhead crusade for reunion in the Quaker Belt.

In July 1863, Holden published Lewis Hanes's Copperhead Manifesto in the *Standard*. In it, Hanes expressed the political views common among the Whig gentry and most of the Peace Conservatives. He denounced the secessionist leaders as the political tyrants the old Whigs had predicted they would be. Under Davis and the Democrats, they had led the once prosperous South into poverty and desolation. The Confederacy had no hope of help from outside powers or of winning independence through military means. King Cotton had proved to be a failure. The only way left open to stop the bloodletting and preserve slavery was to negotiate promptly an honorable peace with the North through a convention of the states from both sections on the basis of the Constitution in which slavery would be protected. In other words, a peace as advocated by the Northern Copperheads.

Meanwhile, Bryan Tyson in his *Institution of Slavery* encouraged Northerners to cooperate with the Southern peace advocates in returning the southern states to the Union. He also issued his Day-Star Circular, in which he advised Tar Heel peace activists to "pluck" North Carolina from the Confederacy and, by example, lead the other Southern states back into the Union. Tyson, himself a self-confessed "Holdenite" who supported the editor's peace and convention movements, also worked closely with many of the leading Copperhead leaders of the Northern Democratic Party to implement their goal of peace and reunion under the banner of "the Constitution as it is, the Union as it was." Tyson's efforts on behalf of the Tar Heel peace agitators lend credence to the charge that Holden and his followers were themselves Copperheads.

Holden favored the Copperhead wing of the Peace Conservatives. He had warned that the fight for independence would only lead to defeat and emancipation. The only way to save slavery and avoid the racial and social turmoil that emancipation would entail was to arrange an armistice and negotiate a peace before the Confederacy was defeated or too weak to demand favorable peace terms. What Holden could not afford to state, because he would have been arrested for treason had he done so, was that reunion on the Copperhead basis, other than the defeat of United States military forces—a feat no one deemed possible—

was the only avenue open to save slavery. Everyone at the time knew that. And that is why Davis was so alarmed at the peace activists in North Carolina, and why Holden's political enemies constantly called him a traitor. In fact, Holden was a covert Copperhead. In an editorial in the *Weekly Standard* on August 25, 1863, Holden tacitly revealed his Copperhead proclivities when he boldly called for a "restoration of the old government ... with all our rights guaranteed." Again, in the winter of 1865 he wrote that slavery could have been saved by a "restoration of the old government" if Governor Vance had supported his 1863 peace movement.[13]

One is forced to ask why, if the people of the Quaker Belt were so pro–Union and anti–Confederate, were they not better able to counter or overthrow Confederate power during the war? Bryan Tyson asked the same question. Tyson concluded that all the power in society lay in the hands of the Confederate authorities in Raleigh and Richmond who controlled the army, militia, Home Guards, and the national, state, and local governments. No grassroots opposition movement had a chance of overcoming such a power advantage. As Tyson put it, "But when the law gets against the people they can't do much. For an organized force can swallow up and make subservient one unorganized many times larger."[14] The rural, relatively poor, and socially unsophisticated population of North Carolina — who were the strongest advocates of reunion — had little chance of pulling off a successful rebellion against strong military forces led by the wealthier, comparatively better educated, socially refined gentry of the state who mostly supported the Confederacy. There seemed to be a town and country divide between secessionists and Unionists. Bryan Tyson observed that "city people were more inclined to be secessionists than country people."[15] As an observer of the peace movement in Randolph County noted: "The opposition to propositions for peace I find mostly in the towns and villages."[16]

The yeoman farmer majority in the Quaker Belt — indeed throughout the piedmont and mountain sections of western North Carolina — by the summer of 1863 had had enough of the Confederacy and the war. Secession and war, along with inflation and the impressment, tax-in-kind, and draft laws, had led to death, impoverishment, and ruin. To them, Confederate independence offered no attraction. They preferred to return to the old Union where they had been happy and content with things as they were. The Copperhead plan of reunion offered citizens of the Quaker Belt and western North Carolina a means to return to the halcyon days of the antebellum era by ending the war and achieving reunion without suffering the humiliation of defeat or the social turmoil of emancipation.

Excited by the peace agitation provoked by Holden's Peace Party rallies, armed bands of deserters — numbering in the hundreds in Randolph, Yadkin, Wilkes, Iredell, Montgomery, Chatham, and Moore counties — organized across the Quaker Belt. In several instances, they mustered under the United States flag and vowed to fight for the Union. The two most successful guerrilla units appeared in areas remote from cities and railheads: Wilkes and Montgomery counties. John Quincy Adams Bryan of Trap Hill led the Wilkes area rebels and William Owens of Auman's Hill headed the Montgomery vicinity dissenters. Numerous local small bands of deserters appeared from time to time in the Quaker Belt during the war, but none gained the power or influence that Bryan and Owens did.

By August 1863, a wave of anarchy and violence engulfed the Quaker Belt. The state's militia officers, magistrates, sheriffs, and constables were powerless to enforce the laws or protect the lives and property of loyal citizens. In desperation, Governor Vance wired the secretary of war for troops. Lee sent two regiments of infantry and a squadron of cavalry under the command of Brigadier General Robert F. Hoke to the governor's aid. Mallett's Battalion (the Raleigh Guards), Vance's newly organized Home Guards, and miscellaneous detachments of Confederates sent into the area to assist in the hunt from time to time, reinforced Hoke's troops. Soon after Hoke's arrival in North Carolina, Vance issued a proclamation denouncing the peace meetings as disloyal. Confederate soldiers mobbed Holden's newspaper office, destroying much of his equipment. Thus did the 1863 phase of the peace movement end in a wave of military repression.

Troops scoured the Quaker Belt from the base of the Blue Ridge in Wilkes County to the Haw River in Orange County in this fifth wartime sweep into the Quaker Belt by national and state forces. General Hoke's troops broke the power of the Bryan deserter army in Wilkes County in the late summer of 1863. Bryan and many of his followers fled to the Union lines and joined the Federal army. In one of the largest and longest hunts for dissidents in the Confederacy, Confederate forces apprehended over three thousand deserters and draft-dodgers over a five-month period.

In December 1863, Lincoln issued his ten percent plan for reconstruction. As a carrot to Southern proslavery Unionists, the president hinted that perhaps the Supreme Court might declare the Emancipation Proclamation unconstitutional, or an act of Congress might overrule it. Northern Peace Democrats argued that Congress should readmit any Southern state with all its constitutional rights guaranteed (including the right to own slaves) that announced — through a state convention or other means — its desire to return to the Union.

Encouraged by the overtures to Southern reunionists made by Lincoln and Copperhead congressional leaders and by the election of six North Carolina peace men to the Confederate House in November, Holden renewed his peace agitation in January 1864. Peace rallies passed resolutions calling for a state convention and/or a convention of all the Southern states to convene and negotiate a peace with the North. The peace leaders rarely mentioned Confederate independence. As its opponents charged, the convention movement, like the peace movement the year before, was a scheme by Peace Conservatives to bypass the Confederate authorities in Richmond and negotiate a return to the Union. The Peace Conservative leaders did not look to Lincoln and the Republicans for a peace founded on emancipation as their War Conservative and Confederate Party opponents charged. Rather, as many of their counterparts had done in the summer of 1863, they hoped to link up with the Copperheads and conservative Republicans in the North and vie for reunion based on the "the Constitution as it is, and the Union as it was." To be brusque, they wanted to annul the blunder of secession and return to the pristine world that, in their eyes, existed before Fort Sumter. The Copperhead plan of reunion provided the perfect blueprint to achieve that goal.

Alarmed by the resurrection of the peace movement, Vance and the War Conservatives fell in behind Jefferson Davis and pledged to support the cause of Confederate independence. In February 1864, Davis, who feared that Holden's convention movement was a conspiracy of Tar Heel Copperheads, prompted the Confederate Congress to suspend the writ of habeas corpus as a countermeasure against their growing influence. He feared a collapse of the Confederate war effort if the Tar Heel peace activists linked up with the Copperheads in the North. Holden countered by opposing Vance for the governorship on a peace platform in the August election. (It is interesting to speculate on what would have happened had

Holden been successful and his Copperhead crusade had spread through the Confederacy and Southerners demanded to return to the Union on the Copperhead basis. Would a war have broken out between Northern and Southern Copperheads on the one hand, and Republicans on the other?)

Vance preempted Holden in the contest by running on the peace issue himself. However, Vance's peace had to include Confederate independence and be made by the duly constituted authorities in Richmond. Vance injected the specter of race conflict when he warned that a victory by Holden and his convention supporters would lead to secession from the Confederacy, a Lincoln reconstruction based on emancipation, and an unthinkable revolution in race relations in the South. The incumbent threatened the electorate that any attempt to achieve a peace through a state convention or a convention of the Southern states would be disloyal. He warned that Confederate authorities would react with overwhelming military force to any attempt to secede from the Confederacy, or to make a separate state peace with the North. Such actions would culminate in a bloody civil war in the state between Confederate troops and convention advocates. Vance discredited Holden by constantly charging him with being a Lincolnite who supported emancipation. The sensational expose of the Heroes of America a month before the gubernatorial election in which the War Conservative and Confederate press accused Holden of being a member and leader, convinced many people that Vance and the pro–Confederate press were accurate in their charges that Holden was a radical pro–Lincoln reconstructionist.

In an election marred by voting irregularities and voter intimidation, Vance won by a landslide. The suspension of the writ of habeas corpus made it impossible for Holden and his convention followers to freely express their political opinions. If they openly admitted Copperhead proclivities, they faced being charged with treason followed by arrest and imprisonment without any recourse to the law. In addition, the men deferred and detailed from the army feared that if it became known that they supported Holden, their military exemptions would be revoked, and they would be forced into the ranks. Due to the use of different colored ballots, how each man voted quickly became public knowledge. For that reason, most pro–Holden men, to prevent the revocation of their exemptions, voted for Vance. Likewise, enlisted men in the army faced ridicule and unpleasant and hazardous duties if they professed sympathy for Holden. Another cause for Holden's defeat was his lack of a well-organized political machine in the counties. Most of the old Whig leadership, along with the Democrats, sided with Vance. Thus, Vance was backed by an experienced political machine with numerous operatives in every county. In general, the Peace Party managers lacked leadership experience and political savvy.[17]

Infuriated by the intimidation of legitimate pro–Holden voters and by the glaring irregularities at the polling stations, the outliers rebelled once again when their champion Holden met defeat at the polls in August 1864. Another cause of disorder at this time was the reorganization of Home Guard battalions and the mustering into service of the Junior and Senior Reserves — forces created by the conscription act passed in February 1864, which upped the enlistment age to 50 — into combat units to fight the Union forces threatening the eastern part of the state. Augmented by a new wave of deserters from the army and Home Guards, and from "stampeders" avoiding service in the Reserves, the dissident bands rearmed and reorganized themselves and once again spread terror through the loyal community.

Reinforced by the Raleigh Guards, the Senior Reserves, and at least one regiment of Confederate regulars, Vance ordered his Home Guard battalions into the field to put down the deserter uprising in the Quaker Belt in August 1864 — the sixth time Confederate and state military forces rushed into the area during the war to quell insurrection. Emboldened by his landslide victory over Holden and pressed by the need to use his scarce state forces against the Yankee invader rather than squander them in wasteful police action against dissidents, Vance decided to break precedent and initiate extreme repressive measures against the insurrectionists. By doing so, he could quickly overcome the rebellion and free his state troops for combat duty against the enemy forces in the eastern part of the state, especially at Fort Fisher near Wilmington.

The governor ordered his troops to ignore the civil law of the state and arrest anyone suspected of aiding and abetting deserters and draft-dodgers and imprison them until the hunt was over. This amounted to a suspension of the writ of habeas corpus and the imposition of marital law, powers not conferred on Vance by law. Troops arrested women, children, and the elderly suspected of aiding the outliers and transported them to makeshift prisons (usually churches, barns, or schoolhouses), where they detained them for days. Guards often abused, insulted, or tortured their detainees, who frequently lacked proper sanitation facilities or adequate food and water supplies. The prisoners — many of whom were women with suckling infants or in advanced stages of pregnancy — suffered unnecessary physical harm and personal indignities. Nevertheless, Vance's tactics worked. Hundreds of outliers surrendered to save their property and secure the release of their wives and children and elderly parents from makeshift prisons. The outliers who survived the hunt retreated to the safety of their caves and hideouts. This turn of events freed the bulk of the governor's state forces to go to the defense of Fort Fisher as the year ended.

Vance's strong-armed tactics against the dissidents in the Randolph area elicited an angry response from Joel Ashworth, Wesleyan abolitionist elected to the House of Commons in 1864. Ashworth submitted a proposal in the Commons calling for a House investigation of Vance's actions against the families of deserters and draft dodgers in the Quaker Belt in September 1864, with a recommendation that charges be brought against the governor for his illegal actions. In his newspaper, Holden supported Ashworth in his indictment against the governor. Nevertheless, the House refused to act on the matter.

As 1864 came to a close, Holdenite peace activists John Pool, Leander Q. Sharpe, and Dr. J.T. Leach introduced peace resolutions: Leach into the Confederate House calling for a negotiated peace on the Copperhead basis, Sharpe (from Iredell County) into the state House of Commons demanding that the sovereign states make a peace without consulting with President Davis, Pool into the House of Commons suggesting that commissioners from the Confederate states meet together and hammer out a peace. In January 1865, Lewis Hanes (from Davidson County) proposed resolutions in the North Carolina House of Commons advocating a convention of all the Confederate states to arrange a peace with the North on the Copperhead basis. Jefferson Davis was to have no role in the negotiations. All four efforts failed to pass, and thus ended the last belated labors by Peace Conservatives to make a peace based on the Copperhead doctrine of "The Constitution as It Is, The Union as It Was." It was ironic to witness these politicians advocate reunion on the Copperhead basis after the reelection of Lincoln rendered that strategy futile.

Bryan Tyson, bitter at the defeat of Holden in the 1864 gubernatorial campaign and the failure of the convention movement, issued his *Object of the Adminstration* accusing Lincoln and the Radical Republicans of deliberately sabotaging the efforts of Southern peace activists to return their states to the Union, because they tended to be proslavery. Tyson felt that the better plan would have been to first end the bloodletting, reunite the country, and then address the problem of slavery. (After the war, Tyson supported the adoption of the Fourteenth Amendment, Black suffrage, equal rights before the law for Blacks, woman suffrage, and the Populist crusade.) In *Object of the Administration* Tyson stated that he was a Holdenite and had been working with Holden and the Peace Conservatives in North Carolina to help bring the state back into the Union on the Copperhead basis.

Bryan Tyson's labors in the North during the war with Copperhead leaders to win Northern support for Tar Heel and Southern Unionists provides evidence of contact between the peace movement in North Carolina and the Copperheads. While no paper trail has been produced to connect Holden with the Northern Copperheads, many of his strongest supporters — such as Lewis Hanes, Samuel H. Christian, Dr. J.T. Leach, and Bryan Tyson, to name a few — looked to the Copperheads for salvation from the war and from the perceived racial problems associated with emancipation. Some, who did not support him, such as Jonathan Worth, did likewise. A groundswell of pro–Copperhead sentiment underlay Holden's peace and convention movements.

Vance and the War Conservatives paid dearly for their strong-armed abuse of the outliers' families and kin during the deserter roundup in late 1864. At the first opportunity, hundreds of the captives deserted Lee's army and returned home. By February, they had regrouped in many areas of the Quaker Belt. The deserters then unleashed a war of revenge against the loyal element that had taken part in or had supported Vance's unprecedented repression against them the previous summer. The vengeful deserters terrorized, murdered, and assaulted loyal citizens and burned their homes and barns. Anarchy and violence once again consumed the Quaker Belt. Moreover, Vance was now helpless to do anything about it.

Confederate authorities in Richmond worried about the growing anarchy in central North Carolina. They wanted to keep the railroads between Danville and Greensboro and Charlotte open in case Richmond and Petersburg fell and a retreat into the area became necessary. In addition, Greensboro, High Point, and other piedmont railheads contained important Confederate supply depots. To secure the area from marauding deserter bands, raiding parties from Sherman's army, and invaders from East Tennessee, Lee ordered two regiments of regular army troops plus ten companies detached from various regiments into the region — the seventh time in the war in which Confederate troops were sent into the Quaker Belt. They concentrated their forces in the counties to the west and south of Greensboro. Commanders ordered half of the troops in the Twenty-third Regiment North Carolina Troops into Forsyth, Yadkin, and Davidson counties — the other half into Montgomery, Moore, and Richmond counties. The Seventh Regiment North Carolina Troops plus the ten companies dethatched from several other regiments — about 600 troops in all — ranged over Randolph, Chatham, and Moore counties. These soldiers operated for three weeks in March, giving no quarter to anyone who opposed them with arms. Despite a cavalry raid by Union general Stoneman through the central piedmont, Davis and members of his cabinet were able to ride the rails safely to Greensboro and then escape on to Charlotte and points farther south before being captured.

With the surrender of Johnston's army near Durham's Station in May 1865, the Confederate phase of the inner civil war ended. For four long and bloody years internal war had raged across the North Carolina Quaker Belt. This was primarily a conflict between two groups, the secessionists and the militant Unionists and their deserter and draft-dodger allies. The deserters, draft-dodgers, and militant Unionists were a combination of Whigs, antislavery zealots, and an anti–Confederate faction that had become disenchanted with the plunging economic situation and the centralizing measures adopted by the Davis government such as the draft and tax laws. All shared the common bond of having opposed secession in 1861. This domestic conflict left scores killed and many more wounded, tortured, or injured. It resulted in the pulling down, burning, or otherwise damaging of an untold number of homes, barns, fences and other properties. Agriculture production plummeted and livestock numbers diminished as hunger stalked the land. Thousands of deserters and draft-dodgers took to the woods, thereby denying valuable manpower to the Confederate army. The rampaging bands of deserters in the Quaker Belt forced Confederate commanders to order hundreds of state and regular army troops into the area to hunt them down and to suppress disloyalty and rebellion. The inner civil war proved to be a major drain on the Confederacy in men and materials — resources desperately needed in the struggle against the Yankee invaders. Despite extensive efforts to repress the deserter bands in the Quaker Belt, Confederate authorities were never able to guarantee safety to its loyal citizens in the area.[18] Along with inflation, hunger, desertion, and class resentments, internal war rates as a major factor in the defeat and collapse of the Confederacy.

The hatreds engendered by the inner civil war were too great for the antagonists to lay to rest with a handshake and a smile. Bloody showdowns between former outliers and former Confederate loyalists occurred across the Quaker Belt in the summer months following the cessation of hostilities. During the early years of Reconstruction, the adversaries charged each other in the courts with crimes such as murder, larceny, arson, and assault committed during the war.

During Reconstruction, the inner civil war continued in the political arena.[19] In the months after the war ended, former anti–Confederate dissidents in the Quaker Belt held Unionist political rallies to celebrate the defeat of the Confederacy and the reestablishment of United States rule. They passed resolutions supporting the Reconstruction plans of the Radical Republicans in Congress and vowed to never support any former secessionist for public office. Most of these former peace men became Republicans. Their political opponents pejoratively referred to them as Scalawags. A study of the Reconstruction Era Tar Heel Republicans found that a direct correlation existed between the leadership and electorate of the wartime Peace Party and the leadership and electorate of the post-bellum Republican Party.[20] Based on his research, the author concluded that the North Carolina Republican Party was a native institution that had its origins in the Peace Party founded by Holden in 1863. The wartime Confederate Party and War Conservatives combined forces after the war and called themselves Conservatives, but later adopted the old appellation of Democrat. Marred by extreme political and racial violence, especially on the part of the Ku Klux Klan, North Carolina experienced its historical nadir in the years between 1865 and 1870.[21]

In the summer of 1865, President Johnson appointed William Holden provisional governor of North Carolina; in 1868, the people elected him the state's first Republican governor. For two years, he and the Republican Party had the political ascendancy. The Conservatives

(Democrats) regained the General Assembly in 1870. They impeached Holden and removed him from office the following year for the extralegal measures he adopted to repress Klan activity. (On April 12, 2011, the state senate of North Carolina pardoned William Woods Holden.)[22] In contrast, Vance never had impeachment proceedings initiated against him for the illegal and inhumane measures he used in the suppression of the deserter uprising in the Quaker Belt in the summer of 1864.

The election of 1876 proved to be the most volatile and bitterly contested in the state's history. Republican Thomas Settle, Holdenite and state solicitor from Rockingham County, contested Democrat Zeb Vance for the governor's chair. In the race, Settle brought up the issue of the unusually cruel tactics use by state troops under the orders of Vance against civilians in the Randolph area in September 1864. Notwithstanding these charges, Vance won the election of 1876, and later the state legislature repeatedly reappointed him to the United States Senate until his death in 1894.[23] Meanwhile, Holden spent his last years in disgrace for being the only governor in American history to be impeached and removed from office.

With the Conservative Party victory in 1870 and the successful impeachment of Holden the following year, the inner civil war ceased for the most part in North Carolina. Its last vestiges disappeared when the Democrats won the executive mansion in 1876. Thereafter, with but one exception, Democratic governors ruled North Carolina until the 1970s. Republicanism survived on a local level in many of the Quaker Belt counties — especially in strongly disaffected Randolph, Davidson, Yadkin, Davie, and Wilkes. Today the area is the backbone of a rejuvenated and growing Republican Party in the state.[24] Nonetheless, few Republicans today in North Carolina are aware of their militant Unionist, deserter, draft-dodger, outlier, Heroes of America, Moravian, Quaker, and Wesleyan abolitionist progenitors.

Paradoxically, the vast majority of the descendants of those who defied and cursed the Confederacy — the draft-dodgers, deserters, and militant Unionists — today pay homage to the memory of Robert E. Lee, Jefferson Davis, and Stonewall Jackson and honor the Confederate battle flag. Indeed, most of the progeny of the anti–Confederate participants in the inner civil war have no knowledge or recollection of it; they think their Confederate era ancestors were all selflessly dedicated to The Lost Cause from beginning to end.[25] Southerners suffer from a severe case of collective historical amnesia. Few traumatic episodes in a people's past have been so successfully blocked from the communal memory as has been the fratricidal inner civil war that raged between white Southerners in the Quaker Belt and in many other areas of the South during the War Between the States.

As historian Carlton Beals put it, "The old proslavery leaders, the die-hards of a lost cause, have been glamorized in fact and fiction, even in the North. But the real Southern heroes, those of a war within a war, have had no hearing, have in fact gone unsung and unhonored into the twilight of history."[26] Another voice lamenting the failure to recognize the contributions of Southern Unionists to the Union victory came from Albion W. Tourgee, author of *A Fool's Errand*, who played an active role in the Republican Party in North Carolina during Reconstruction. He also edited *Red String*, the official publication of the Heroes of America published in Greensboro after the war. Disgusted by Northern indifference to the wartime suffering of Southern Unionists and to their contribution to final victory, Tourgee charged that the United States "made no offer of encouragement or reward to those who had stood fast friends of the nation in the hour of its peril. The ingratitude of Republics is the tritest of thoughts, but there never was a more striking illustration of its verity. Perhaps no nation ever before, after the suppression of a rebellion which threatened its life, quite forgot the claims of those who had been its friends in the disaffected region."[27]

Beals and Tourgee were correct. Few citizens of the United States today have ever heard of the Heroes of America or the Red Strings or about the protracted struggle against Confederate power by those who remained loyal Americans in the Tar Heel state after secession. With the almost complete domination of state politics for a century after the 1876 election by the Democratic Party, a romantic vision of the Confederacy as a noble defender of a "Lost Cause" against a crude Yankee behemoth permeated all ranks of society in the Tar Heel state. In that vision there was no room for the Heroes of America, the Red Strings, antislavery Quakers and Moravians, Wesleyan abolitionists, antisecession Whigs, Copperheads, William Owens, the Dial Brothers, Harrison Church, John Quincy Adams Bryan, Lewis Hanes, or Bryan Tyson. As a result, their rebellion against the Confederacy and their championing of the Union cause remain in the historical shadows.

Notes

Introduction

1. See map of the three physiographic regions of North Carolina and the location of the Quaker Belt within them. While the western one-third of Wilkes County is in the Blue Ridge Mountains, the remainder, including the majority of its population and the county seat, lies in the piedmont region. Thus, I treat Wilkes in this study as a piedmont county. For a map of the physiographic regions of North Carolina, see Clay, Orr, and Stuart, *North Carolina Atlas*, 112.

2. The pioneering historians in the subject were Ella Lonn, Georgia Lee Tatum, Frank L. Owsley, and Albert Burton Moore. See Tatum, *Disloyalty in the Confederacy*; Lonn, *Desertion During the Civil War*; Moore, *Conscription and Conflict in the Confederacy*; and Owsley, "Defeatism in the Confederacy."

3. Williams, *Bitterly Divided*. Other accounts on the topic include Ash, *When the Yankees Came*; Durrill, *War of Another Kind*; Fellman, *Inside War: The Guerrilla Conflict in Missouri*; Fisher, *War at Every Door*; Inscoe and Kenzer, *Enemies of the Country*; Inscoe and McKinney, *The Heart of Confederate Appalachia*; Paludan, *Victims*; Sutherland, *Guerrillas, Unionists, and Violence on the Confederate Home Front* and *A Savage Conflict: The Decisive Role of Guerrillas in the American Civil War*; Weity, *More Damning Than Slaughter: Desertion in the Confederate Army*; Williams, *Rich Man's War*; Ash, "Sharks in an Angry Sea: Civilian Resistance and Guerrilla Warfare"; Baker, "Class Conflict and Political Upheaval: The Transformation of North Carolina Politics During the Civil War"; Brown, "North Carolina Ambivalence: Rethinking Loyalty and Disaffection in the Civil War Piedmont"; Brown, *Southern Outcast: Hinton Rowan Helper*; Bynum, *The Free State of Jones*, *Unruly Women*, *The Long Shadow of the Civil War*, "Occupied at Home: Women Confront Confederate Forces in North Carolina's Quaker Belt" and "War Within a War"; Escott, *Many Excellent People* and "The Moral Economy of the Crowd"; Bardolph, "Inconstant Rebels" and "Confederate Dilemma: North Carolina Troops and the Desertion Problem," Part I and Part II; Klingberg, *The Southern Claims Commission*; Degler, *The Other South*; Escott and Crow, "The Social Order and Violent Disorder"; Shanks, "Disloyalty to the Confederacy in Southwestern Virginia"; Ramsdell, *Behind the Lines in the Southern Confederacy*; Auman and Scarboro, "The Heroes of America in Civil War North Carolina"; Auman, "Neighbor Against Neighbor: The Inner Civil War" and "Bryan Tyson: Southern Unionist"; Harris, *William Woods Holden: Firebrand of North Carolina Politics* and "The Southern Unionist Critique"; Reid, "William W. Holden and Disloyalty in the Civil War" and "A Test Case of the 'Crying Evil': Desertion Among North Carolina Troops"; Robbins, "The Confederacy and the Writ of Habeas Corpus"; Van Zant, "Confederate Conscription"; Zuber, "Conscientious Objectors in the Confederacy"; and McKenzie, *Lincolnites and Rebels*.

4. For example, see Williams, *Bitterly Divided*, 1–8; Weitz, *More Damning than Slaughter*, 290; Escott, *Many Excellent People*, Chapter 3, especially pp. 59 and 69; and Auman, "Neighbor Against Neighbor: The Inner Civil War in the Randolph County Area of Confederate North Carolina." For a critique of Williams' *Bitterly Divided* and a discussion of important works in recent Confederate historiography, see Gallagher, "Disaffection, Persistence, and Nation: Some Directions in Recent Scholarship on the Confederacy."

5. Tatum, *Disloyalty in the Confederacy*, 36–44, 54–60, 143–155.

6. Scott et al., eds., *The War of the Rebellion*, III, Series IV, 786, hereinafter cited as *Official Records Army*.

7. Tatum, *Disloyalty in the Confederacy*, 109–110.

8. Sutherland, *A Savage Conflict*, 44–45, 116; Inscoe and McKinney, *The Heart of Confederate Appalachia*, 45–46, 94–95, 106.

9. Manarin, ed., *Guide to Military Organizations and Installations in North Carolina*, Section III, 1.

10. Barrett, *The Civil War in North Carolina*, 30–130.

11. Brown, *Edward Stanly*, 244–248.

12. *Ibid.*, 201–253.

13. Manarin, *Guide to Military Organizations and Installations in North Carolina, 1861–1865*, Section III, 1–2.

14. Barrett, *The Civil War in North Carolina*, 174–177. For detailed accounts of disaffection and disloyalty to the Confederacy in the sound region of eastern North Carolina, see Durrill, *War of Another Kind* and Myers, *Executing Daniel Bright*.

15. Tatum, *Disloyalty in the Confederacy*, 113.

16. The following works by William T. Auman have focused on disaffection in the central piedmont of Confederate North Carolina: "North Carolina's Inner Civil War: Randolph County" (MA thesis); "Neighbor Against

Neighbor: The Inner Civil War in the Central Counties of Confederate North Carolina" (PhD Dissertation); "The Heroes of America in Civil War North Carolina" (coauthored with David D. Scarboro); "Neighbor Against Neighbor: the Inner Civil War in the Randolph County Area of Confederate North Carolina"; and "Bryan Tyson: Southern Unionist and American Patriot." See also Escott, *Many Excellent People*, and Bynum, *Unruly Women, The Long Shadow of the Civil War,* "Occupied at Home: Women Confront Confederate Forces in North Carolina's Quaker Belt," and "War Within a War."

17. See Chapter One for a discussion of the settlement of the Quaker Belt and its religious configuration. A few Catholics and Jews lived in the area.

18. See Chapter Two for a discussion of Whiggery and secession in the Quaker Belt.

19. See Auman and Scarboro, "Heroes of America," and Auman, "Neighbor Against Neighbor."

Chapter One

1. Degler, *The Other South*.
2. Powell, *North Carolina*, 104–111. See also Fischer, *Albion's Seed*, 605–782.
3. For a general discussion of the settlement of the North Carolina piedmont by the Scots-Irish, Moravians, Germans, and English Quakers, see Powell, *North Carolina*, 104–111, 122–126. For a more detailed look at this migration, see Ramsey, *Carolina Cradle*. On the Scots-Irish, see Leyburn, *The Scots-Irish: A Social History*. On the Moravians, see Fries, *The Road to Salem*. Weeks presents a detailed account of the Quakers in *Southern Quakers and Slavery*, 70, 101, 109, 328–344, and map facing page 400. For an account of the early German settlers in piedmont North Carolina, see Welker, "Early German Reformed Settlements in North Carolina," 727–757. In Rouse, *The Great Wagon Road* the migration patters of the Moravians, Germans, and Scots-Irish are discussed.
4. Powell, *North Carolina*, 79–81; Johnson, *Ante-Bellum North Carolina*, 3–19.
5. This was especially true of the counties of Orange, Alamance, Randolph, Chatham, Montgomery, Davidson, and Moore.
6. Powell, *North Carolina*, 146–159.
7. The Regulators were most active in what are now the central Piedmont counties of Davidson, Rowan, Randolph, Chatham, Moore, Montgomery, Alamance, and Guilford.
8. Escott and Crow, "The Social Order and Violent Disorder," 373–402; Powell, *North Carolina*, 189, 207–209. Fanning, *Narrative of Colonel David Fanning*.
9. Powell, *North Carolina*, 73–74, 122; Hilty, *Toward Freedom for All*, 9–10, 16–20.
10. Hilty, *Toward Freedom for All*, 15–26.
11. Sowle, "The North Carolina Manumission Society," 47–69; Wagstaff, *Minutes of the North Carolina Manumission Society*; Hinshaw and Hinshaw, *Carolina Quakers*, 33.
12. Sowle, "The North Carolina Manumission Society," 55. Benjamin Lundy was born in 1789 into a family of Quaker farmers in New Jersey. He moved to Ohio where he became a dedicated anti-slavery activist. In 1821, he founded his abolitionist newspaper *The Genius of Universal Emancipation* which he published in Ohio and Tennessee before moving to Baltimore, Maryland, in 1824. There he co-edited *The Genius* for two years with William Lloyd Garrison before the two antislavery activists went their separate ways. Garrison established *The Liberator* in Boston and Lundy moved his newspaper to Washington, D.C. Lundy died in Illinois in 1839. See Carnes and Garraty, eds., *American National Biography*, XIV, 137–38.

13. General Association of the Manumission Society of North Carolina, *An Address to the People of North Carolina on the Evils of Slavery*.

14. Arnett, *William Swaim*, 2, 56–60, 222–234. Greensboro was spelled Greensborough until 1895, however Greensboro is used throughout.

15. Hinshaw, *Carolina Quakers*, 32; Sowle, "The North Carolina Manumission Society," 63–64; Hilty, *Toward Freedom for All*, 91–96.

16. Johnson, *Ante-Bellum North Carolina*, 499, 515–519.

17. Hinshaw, *Carolina Quakers*, 33; Wagstaff, "Minutes of the North Carolina Manumission Society," 7–8; Sowle, "The North Carolina Manumission Society," 64–66.

18. Sowle, "The North Carolina Manumission Society," 66–67; Johnson, *Ante-Bellum North Carolina*, 356; Hilty, *Toward Freedom for All*, 97–99.

19. Johnson, *Ante-Bellum North Carolina*, 356–357; Anscombe, *I Have Called You Friends*, 235–237.

20. In the state as a whole, the Baptists outnumbered the Methodists by 4000. See Johnson, *Ante-Bellum North Carolina*, 349.

21. Johnson, *Ante-Bellum North Carolina*, 343–348; Mathews, *Religion in the Old South*, 68–69.

22. Johnson, *Ante-Bellum North Carolina*, 347–348; Nicholson, *Wesleyan Methodism in the South*, 26–32; E.W. Crooks, *Life of Rev. A. Crooks*, 13–25.

23. Mathews, *Slavery and Methodism*, 230–233.

24. Nicholson, *Wesleyan Methodism*, 31–36.

25. Crooks, *Life of Rev. A. Crooks*, 25.

26. *Ibid.*, 22.

27. *Ibid.*, 27.

28. Nicholson, *Wesleyan Methodism*, 35–36; Anscombe, *I Have Called You Friends*, 79.

29. Nicholson, *Wesleyan Methodism*, 36.

30. *Ibid.*, 37–43.

31. *True Wesleyan*, April 13, 1850.

32. By 1850, there were five cotton mills situated along the Deep River in Randolph County. See Whatley, *The Architectural History of Randolph County North Carolina*, 17–19. See also Randolph County Historical Society, *Randolph County, 1779–1979*, 76–79.

33. *True Wesleyan*, April 13, 1850.

34. *Ibid.*, July 27, 1850.

35. "Franklinsville Factory," *The Patriot* (Greensboro), May 10, 1851. The author is indebted to Mac Whatley for bringing this article to his attention.

36. Records of the Island Ford Manufacturing Company, semiannual meeting of the stockholders, July 8, 1851. The fired employees were John Burgess, Bethry York, and Nancy Hudson.

37. *True Wesleyan*, November 9, 1850; Johnson, *Ante-Bellum North Carolina*, 575–576; Nicholson, *Wesleyan Methodists*, 46–63.

38. *True Wesleyan*, November 16, 1850.

39. *Ibid.*, June 7, 1851.

40. *Ibid.*, January 11, 1851.

41. *Ibid.*, August 2, 1851.

42. *Ibid.*, May 17 and July 12, 1851.

43. *Ibid.*, August 2, 1851.

44. *Ibid.*, February 8, 1851.

45. Christian was elected as a peace candidate to the Confederate Congress in the 1863 congressional elections.

See "Vote in the Seventh District," *North Carolina Standard* (Raleigh), November 20, 1863. S.H. Christian's real estate was valued in 1860 at $15,000 and his personal estate at $48,000. He owned 42 slaves. See 1860 Federal Census, Population and Slave Schedules, Montgomery County, North Carolina.

46. *True Wesleyan*, August 9, 1851; Crooks, *Life of Rev. A. Crooks*, 76–100.

47. *True Wesleyan*, September 13, 1851.

48. *Ibid.*, September 27 and October 11, 1851. John Gilmer was a successful lawyer and Whig politician from Greensboro; Francis Fries was a wealthy textile manufacturer from Salem. See Powell, ed., *Dictionary of North Carolina Biography*, II, 300–301. On Gilmer, see Ashe, ed., *Biographical History of North Carolina From Colonial Times to the Present*, III, 129–134.

49. *True Wesleyan*, September 27, 1851.

50. Crooks, *Life of Rev. A. Crooks*, 104.

51. *True Wesleyan*, October 11, 1851.

52. *Ibid.*

53. Samuel H. Wiley to C.H. Wiley, August 3, 1851, Calvin H. Wiley Papers, Southern Historical Collection, University of North Carolina at Chapel Hill.

54. *True Wesleyan*, October 11, 1851.

55. Nicholson, *Wesleyan Methodism*, 70.

56. *True Wesleyan*, October 11, 1851.

57. *Ibid.*, June 26, 1851.

58. *Ibid.*, February 21, 1852.

59. Johnson, "Abolitionist Missionary Activities in North Carolina," 301. The 1850 census listed Daniel Wilson, age 34, as a Methodist clergyman and a native of Guilford County, North Carolina. He had a wife and seven children. He owned no real estate. See 1850 Federal Census, Population Schedule, Guilford County, North Carolina. Daniel Wilson did not appear in the 1860 Federal Census of North Carolina.

60. Nicholson, *Wesleyan Methodism*, 32; Johnson, "Abolitionist Missionary Activities in North Carolina," 298. See also Huddle, *North Carolina's Forgotten Abolitionist*, 416–455.

61. *True Wesleyan*, November 6, 1852.

62. Daniel Wilson to S.S. Jocelyn, February 19, 1855, American Missionary Association Archives (microfilm), Amistad Research Center, Fisk University Library, Nashville, Tennessee.

63. Randolph County Historical Society and the Randolph Arts Guild, *Randolph County*, 27, 54, 122.

64. Johnson, "Abolitionist Missionary Activities in North Carolina," 301.

65. Daniel Wilson to George Whipple, August 10, 1852, American Missionary Association Archives.

66. Johnson, "Abolitionist Missionary Activities in North Carolina," 301.

67. Daniel Wilson to George Whipple, June 22, 1852, American Missionary Association Archives.

68. Daniel Wilson to S.S. Jocelyn, November 30, 1853, American Missionary Association Archives.

69. This may have been the John Stafford living in the south division of Guilford County in 1860, age 32, occupation black smith, real estate worth $50 and personal estate $150, with a wife and three young children under six, Post Office Greensboro. See 1860 Federal Census, Population Schedule, Guilford County, North Carolina.

70. Huddle, "Incendiaries in Our Midst," 44–45.

71. Johnson and Porter, *National Party Platforms: 1840–1972*, 16–20. The quotation is from page 18.

72. Gerhke, "Negro Slavery Among the Germans in North Carolina," 308; Boyd and Krummel, "German Tracts Concerning the Lutheran Church in North Carolina During the Eighteenth Century," 81.

73. Hamilton, *Benjamin Sherwood Hedrick*, 14. For an updated account of Hedrick's life, see Smith, *A Traitor and a Scoundrel*. See also Smith's *North Carolina Historical Review* article, "A Traitor and a Scoundrel."

74. Bassett, *Anti-Slavery Leaders of North Carolina*, 30; Smith, *A Traitor and a Scoundrel*, 27, 31–32, 47.

75. Smith, *A Traitor and a Scoundrel*, 68, 73–74.

76. Bassett, *Anti-Slavery Leaders of North Carolina*, 32–38; Smith, *A Traitor and a Scoundrel*, 75–81.

77. Bassett, *Anti-Slavery Leaders of North Carolina*, 43–46; Smith, *A Traitor and a Scoundrel*, 96, 111.

78. Auman, "Bryan Tyson," 279. Hedrick's wartime correspondence includes numerous letters from Tar Heel refugees in the North on political matters and from Confederate prisoners of war with Unionist sympathies seeking aid and advice on how to gain their freedom and United States citizenship. See Benjamin Sherwood Hedrick Papers, Duke Manuscript Department.

79. Bassett, *Anti-Slavery Leaders of North Carolina*, 11–24; Smith, *A Traitor and a Scoundrel*, 10–11, 25–42, 91–127.

80. Bassett, *Anti-Slavery Leaders of North Carolina*, 17–18; Smith, *A Traitor and a Scoundrel*, 137–188.

81. Tolbert, "Daniel Worth," 284–288.

82. Jonathan Worth to Geo. McNeill, March 10, 1860, in Hamilton, *The Correspondence of Jonathan Worth*, I, 110.

83. Tolbert, "Daniel Worth," 287–289.

84. In 1860 Alfred Vestal, age 55, lived in the western division of Chatham County in the community of Mud Lick. He had a wife and five children. He was a farmer that owned $1100 worth of real estate and $900 worth of personal property. See 1860 Federal Census, Population Schedule, Chatham County, North Carolina.

85. Jas. S. Davis to ____, July 27, 1857, and Daniel Worth to the Rev. S.S. Jocelyn, February 9, 1858, American Missionary Association Archives.

86. Tolbert, "Daniel Worth," 288–289.

87. *Ibid.*, 289; Daniel Worth to S.S. Jocelyn, January 1, 1858, American Missionary Association Archives.

88. Daniel Worth to S.S. Jocelyn, January 1, 1858, American Missionary Association Archives.

89. Johnson, "Abolitionist Missionary Activities in North Carolina," 312.

90. In 1860 John T. Harris, age 42, lived in the western division of Randolph County. His Post Office was Asheboro. He had a wife and three children and worked as a farm laborer. He owned no real estate and $500 worth of personal property. See 1860 Federal Census, Population Schedule, Randolph County, North Carolina.

91. Tolbert, *The Papers of John Willis Ellis*, I, 340–341. In 1860, Jacob Briles, age 60, was a farmer worth $2500 in real estate and $700 in personal property. See 1860 Federal Census, Population Schedule, Randolph County, North Carolina.

92. John W. Ellis to John M. Dick, January 4, 1860, in Tolbert, *The Papers of John Willis Ellis*, II, 342–343.

93. John M. Dick to John W. Ellis, January 6, 1860, in Tolbert, *The Papers of John Willis Ellis*, II, 343–345. The 1860 Federal Census lists two Jesse Wheelers living in Guilford County. Both were 54-year-old farmers with 52-year-old wives named "Cinthia." Each has three children of approximately the same ages. One was worth $3500 in real estate and $3000 in personal property; the other $2500 and $1000. See 1860 Federal Census, Population Schedule (pages 69 and 151), Guilford County, North Carolina.

94. Over the decades, Wheeler had been a magistrate, poll worker, county surveyor, tax lister, census taker, president of the Guilford Temperance Society, a member of the Manumission Society, a Whig, a major stockholder in the Randolph Manufacturing Company, and a member of the Unitarian church. See Jesse Wheeler to B.S. Hedrick, August 20, 1859, Benjamin Sherwood Hedrick Papers, Duke Manuscript Collection; O'Brien, *The Legal Fraternity and the Making of a New South Community*, 44–45; *Southern Citizen* (Asheboro), March 3, 1838.

95. Jesse Wheeler to H.R. Helper, September 10, 1859, Henry B. Anthon Letters, New York Public Library; Jesse Wheeler to B.S. Hedrick, August 20, 1859, Duke Manuscript Collection.

96. Tolbert, "Daniel Worth," 291–303.

97. Hamilton, *Benjamin Sherwood Hedrick*, 6.

98. Bassett, *Anti-Slavery Leaders of North Carolina*, 10.

99. Tyson, *Object of the Administration*, 9.

100. Bassett, *Anti-Slavery Leaders of North Carolina*, 10.

101. Bassett did note two antislavery leaders from outside the Quaker Belt: Daniel Reaves Goodloe from Franklin County and Lunsford Lane from Wake County. Both were from piedmont counties. See Bassett, *Anti-Slavery Leaders of North Carolina*, 47, 60.

Chapter Two

1. Powell, *North Carolina*, 282–299; Kruman, *Parties and Politics in North Carolina*, 14, 25–27.

2. Pegg, *The Whig Party in North Carolina*, 91.

3. Lefler and Newsome, *North Carolina*, 357, 376, 386; Kruman, *Parties and Politics in North Carolina*, 14.

4. Powell, *North Carolina*, 300–305, 339–348; Kruman, *Parties and Politics in North Carolina*, 63, 85.

5. Only Alamance, Stokes, Surry, and Forsyth were strongly Democratic. The following voted Whig majorities in every gubernatorial and presidential election between 1836 and 1860: Davidson, Davie, Guilford, Iredell, Montgomery, Randolph, Wilkes, and Yadkin. Cheney, *North Carolina Government*, 1328–1331, 1396–1401; Kruman, *Parties and Politics in North Carolina*, 27.

6. Cheney, *North Carolina Government*, 1328–1331, 1396–1401.

7. Lefler and Newsome, *North Carolina*, 447; Cheney, *North Carolina Government*, 1331, 1401.

8. Surry and Stokes.

9. Cheney, *North Carolina Government*, 1400–1401.

10. Sitterson, *The Secession Movement in North Carolina*, 168–176; Lefler and Newsome, *North Carolina*, 447–448.

11. Surry and Stokes.

12. Cheney, *North Carolina Government*, 1330–1331.

13. Sitterson, *The Secession Movement in North Carolina*, 179–194.

14. Letter to the Editor from S. Wood at Salem Church, Randolph County, *Weekly Standard* (Raleigh), August 19, 1863.

15. "Our Circulation," *Weekly Standard* (Raleigh), May 13, 1863; "Probable 'Change of Base,'" *Weekly Standard* (Raleigh), August 26, 1864; "Gov. Vance's Attempt to Disorganize and Destroy the Conservative Party," *Daily Progress* (Raleigh), June 25, 1864. For a history of the short-lived Union party that spread across the upper South in the early months of 1861, see Crofts, "The Union Party of 1861 and the Secession Crisis," 327–76, and *Reluctant Confederates*. For a pithy discussion of the secession crisis in North Carolina see Harris, *North Carolina and the Coming of the Civil War*, especially pages 26–56.

16. Sitterson, *The Secession Movement in North Carolina*, 182, 193, 197.

17. See also Harris, *North Carolina and the Coming of the Civil War*, 42.

18. Sitterson, *The Secession Movement in North Carolina*, 194, 197–198; Kruman, *Parties and Politics in North Carolina*, 201, 208.

19. "Union Meeting in Randolph County," *Observer* (Fayetteville), January 7, 1861. See also February 18, 1861.

20. "Union Meeting at Bush Hill," *Observer* (Fayetteville), January 28, 1861.

21. McPherson, *Battle Cry of Freedom*, 493–494, 591–595, 692.

22. "Union Meeting in Moore County," *Observer* (Fayetteville), January 17, 1861.

23. "Public Meeting in Wilkes County," January 7, 1861, and "Union Meeting in Wilkes" February 21, 1861, both *Observer* (Fayetteville).

24. Sitterson, *The Secession Movement in North Carolina*, 205–206; Crofts, *Reluctant Confederates*, 131, 133, 145, 147, 154, 159.

25. Sitterson, *The Secession Movement in North Carolina*, 208.

26. They were Alamance, Randolph, Guilford, Orange, Iredell, Wilkes, Davie, Montgomery, Davidson, Yadkin, Moore, and Chatham. See Sitterson, *The Secession Movement in North Carolina*, 208.

27. The ten counties were Hertford, Richmond, Robeson, Tyrrell, Hyde, Rutherford, Beaufort, Camden, Bertie, and Pasquotank. Ibid.

28. Kruman, *Parties and Politics in North Carolina*, 210; Sitterson, *The Secession Movement in North Carolina*, 223.

29. Connor, *A Manual of North Carolina*, 1013–1015.

30. Sitterson, *The Secession Movement in North Carolina*, 11–18; Lefler and Newsome, *North Carolina*, 365–366, 392. The North Carolina Railroad ran from Goldsboro to Charlotte and divided the central counties in half. Railroad stops in the central counties included Durham Station, Hillsboro, Company Shops (Burlington), Greensboro, Jamestown, High Point, Thomasville, and Lexington.

31. Kennedy, *Population of the United States in 1860*, 358–359.

32. Secretary of the Interior, *Statistics of the United States, 1860*, 346–347; Kennedy, *Agriculture of the United States in 1860*, 210.

33. Secretary of the Interior, *Statistics of the United States, 1860*, 346–347.

34. Kennedy, *Agriculture of the United States in 1860*, 210.

35. Bolton, *Poor Whites of the Antebellum South*, 14.

36. Ibid., 12–28.

37. Lefler and Newsome, *North Carolina*, 391–402.

38. Ibid.; Secretary of the Interior, *Manufactures of the United States in 1860*, 420–435.

39. They were Randolph, Chatham, Alamance, Orange, Moore, Cabarrus, Davidson, Davie, Guilford, Rowan, Stanly, and Iredell. See Secretary of the Interior, *Manufactures of the United States in 1860*, 420–435.

40. Between one and three tobacco factories existed in Wilkes, Iredell, Davie, Yadkin, Forsyth, Chatham, and Orange counties, five in Surry, and seventeen in Stokes. See Ibid., 420–435.

41. Secretary of the Interior, *Manufactures of the United States in 1860*, 420–435.

42. Sitterson, *The Secession Movement in North Carolina*, 5, 11, 18.
43. Kennedy, *Population of the United States in 1860*, 358–359.
44. Of the other central counties having Quaker meetinghouses in 1860, Yadkin had two, Alamance one, Chatham three, and Guilford four. Four Quaker meetinghouses were located in the eastern coastal plain. See Secretary of the Interior, *Statistics of the United States in 1860*, 436, 439. On the Wesleyan churches in Randolph County, see Nicholson, *Wesleyan Methodism*, 45, 52.
45. Goff, "The Geographic Origins of North Carolina Enlistments in the War Between the States," 40, 44, 50, 55, 66–67. The direct quotation comes from pages 66–67.
46. Calculated from figures presented in Goff, "The Geographic Origins of North Carolina Enlistments in the War Between the States," 71–73. Alamance had an enlistment rate in 1861 of 23.6 percent, Chatham 17.4 percent, Davidson 9.5 percent, Davie 19.6 percent, Forsyth 16.9 percent, Guilford 11.8 percent, Iredell 22.0 percent, Montgomery 25.4 percent, Moore 20.1 percent, Orange 24.6 percent, Randolph 14.2 percent, Stokes 19.5 percent, Surry 21.9 percent, Wilkes 15.3 percent, and Yadkin 21.4 percent. See *Ibid.*, 31, 71–73.
47. Calculated from figures presented in Goff, "The Geographic Origins of North Carolina Enlistments in the War Between the States," 71–73. The enlistment rate for the war, April 1861 to April 1865, was Alamance 57.6 percent, Chatham 57.8 percent, Davidson 43.2 percent, Davie 66.1 percent, Forsyth 44.0 percent, Guilford 36.8 percent, Iredell 58.0 percent, Montgomery 57.9 percent, Moore 58.9 percent, Orange 61.6 percent, Randolph 39.0 percent, Stokes 56.0 percent, Surry 37.6 percent, Wilkes 45.7 percent, Yadkin 42.1 percent. See *Ibid.*, 33, 71–73. Keep in mind that after April 1862, many, if not most enlistees were conscripts, and that many of them deserted, some of them multiple times.
48. See the next paragraph for a discussion of the rate of conscription of troops from the Quaker Belt.
49. "Exempts in North-Carolina," *Semi-Weekly Standard*, November 20, 1863; Connor, *A Manual of North Carolina*, 360–361.
50. Reid, "A Test Case of the 'Crying Evil,'" 234. In his 1981 study, Richard M. Reid concluded that the desertion rate of North Carolina troops had been overestimated by previous historians. Reid calculated that Tar Heel troops deserted at the rate of 12.2 percent for the war. He estimated the desertion rate for the "Guilford area" as only 9 percent. This figure stands in marked contrast to the desertion rate of 22.8 percent for Randolph County troops arrived at by William Auman in his article on disaffection in the Randolph County area. See Auman, "The Inner Civil War in the Randolph County Area of Confederate North Carolina," 69.
51. Weitz, *More Damning than Slaughter*, ix-xi, xvi-xvii.
52. Reid, "A Test Case of the 'Crying Evil,'" 253–254; Lonn, *Desertion During the Civil War*, 231.
53. Jesse Wheeler to [B.S. Hedrick], May 6, 1861, Benjamin Hedrick Papers, Duke Manuscript Department.
54. Hamilton, *Reconstruction in North Carolina*, 44.
55. Jim to his brother, April 17, 1861, Lilly Collection, North Carolina State Archives. See Chapter 8 for an account of the capture and execution of the three Hulin brothers.
56. Tolbert, ed., *The Papers of John Willis Ellis*, II, 662–664.

57. "Statement of C.J. Cowles connected with & illustrating his loyalty" (rough and incomplete), ca. 1865–1866, Calvin J. Cowles Papers, North Carolina State Archives. Obidiah Sprinkle, age 36 in 1860, had real estate worth $2000 and personal property worth $2000. He owned three slaves. Milton Speaks, age 23, lived with him. See 1860 Federal Census, Population and Slave Schedules, Wilkes County, North Carolina.
58. Entry for May 4, 1861, in Diary of J. Gwyn, 1852 to 1877, in Thurman Chatham Papers, North Carolina State Archives.
59. "The Home Guards," *People's Press* (Salem), May 17, 1861.
60. B.V. Smith to Ralph Gorrell, May 4, 1861, Ralph Gorrell Papers, Southern Historical Collection.
61. Bolton, *Poor Whites of the Antebellum South*, 149.
62. John S. Fogleman, J.P. Aldridge, and Leander York to John W. Ellis, in Tolbert, *Ellis Papers*, II, 867–868.
63. In 1860 John Hilton, aged 32, lived at Rich Fork. He owned a 62-acre farm. His real estate was worth $450, his personal estate $250. He was married and had three children. See 1860 Federal Census, Population and Agriculture Schedules, Davidson County, North Carolina. The census taker misspelled his name Helton.
64. Jas. H. Moore to H.T. Clark, July 18, 1861, Henry T. Clark Letter Book, North Carolina State Archives.
65. Poteat, "'A Modest Estimate of His Own Abilities': Governor Henry Toole Clark and the Early Civil War Leadership of North Carolina," Part 2, 134, and *Henry Toole Clark: Civil War Governor of North Carolina*, 106–107.
66. David Schenck Books, Diary (May 25, 1861–December 15, 1861), entry for Tuesday, August 6, 1861, entitled "Disturbance in Davidson County," Southern Historical Collection. Information gathered from typed copy of original available in the search room; Poteat, "A Modest Estimate of His Own Abilities," 132–137. See also Steward, *David Schenck and the Contours of Confederate Identity*.
67. J.F. [Shaffner] to "My Dear Miss Carrie," July 31, 1861, Shaffner Diary and Papers, North Carolina State Archives.
68. "Arrests," *Observer* (Fayetteville), August 5, 1861.
69. In 1860, Braxton Craven, age 36, owned $2,200 in real estate and had a personal estate worth $21,000. He had a wife and three children and owned three slaves. See Population and Slave Schedules, 1860 Federal Census, Randolph County, North Carolina.
70. Chaffin, *Trinity College 1839–1892: The Beginnings of Duke University*, 217–239; Brooks, "Captain Craven and the Trinity Guard," 172–173.
71. Braxton Craven to Henry T. Clark, August 5, 1861, quoted in Chaffin, *Trinity College*, 223–224.
72. Marinda [Branson] to her mother, August 25, 1861, Branson Family Papers, North Carolina State Archives.
73. "State vs. Thomas Dougan for using language in favor of Federal Government, 1861," Randolph County Civil War Records, North Carolina State Archives. Thomas Dougan, age 21 in 1860, was a farmer who owned $600 worth of real estate and had a personal estate worth $350. See 1860 Federal Census, Population Schedule, Randolph County, North Carolina, North Carolina State Archives.
74. "An Action Against Martine Wilson for 'Treasonable Talk,' 1861," in Chatham County Miscellaneous Records, 1772–1956, North Carolina State Archives.
75. "The Demand for Vigilance," *Patriot* (Greensboro), January 16, 1862. Reprinted from the *Richmond Examiner*.
76. William [Scott] to McLean, January 30, 1862,

William Lafayette Scott Papers, Duke Manuscript Department.

77. William K. Ruffin to Thomas Ruffin, February 14, 1862, in Hamilton, ed., *The Papers of Thomas Ruffin*, III, 215–216.

78. J.F. Graves to H.T. Clark, February 18, 1862, Governors Papers, Henry T. Clark, North Carolina State Archives.

79. Clark, *Histories of the Several Regiments and Battalions from North Carolina in the Great War 1861–65*, I, 8–9.

80. Tyson, *Object of the Administration in Prosecuting the War*, 7.

81. J.G. Martin to Capt. Murchinson, March 22, 1862, and J.G. Martin to Sergeant Thomas R. Long, March 24, 1862, Adjutant General Letter Book, December 1861 to April 1862, North Carolina State Archives. The quotation comes from the letter to Murchinson.

82. A.G. Martin to Col. Amos A. Sharpe, April 11, 1862; Jno. C. Winder to Col. G.A. McCraw, June 3, 1862; J.G. Martin to Col. D. Coble, April 17, 1862; Militia Letter Book, 1862 to 1864, Adjutant General Papers (AG 44), North Carolina State Archives; I.F. Graves to H.T. Clark, March 27, 1862, Governors Papers, Henry Toole Clark, North Carolina State Archives.

83. P.L. Paterson to his uncle, March 1862, Edmund Walter Jones Papers, Southern Historical Collection; R. L. Patterson to his father, March 5, 1862, Jones and Patterson Family Papers, Southern Historical Collection.

84. Elvira Worth Jackson to Fannie Long, March 15, 1862, in Hamilton, *The Correspondence of Jonathan Worth*, I, 163–164.

85. See Roberts, "The Peace Movement in North Carolina," 195, and Coulter, *The Confederate States of America*, 534.

86. Proclamation against disaffection and disloyalty in Randolph County, March 4, 1862, Governors Letter Books, Henry Toole Clark, North Carolina State Archives.

87. *Ibid.*; H.T. Clark to Spier Whitaker, March 6, 1862, Governors Letter Books, Henry Toole Clark, North Carolina State Archives.

88. Auman and Scarboro, "The Heroes of America in Civil War North Carolina," 327–363.

89. Ledford, *Reminiscences of the Civil War*, 22–25.

90. "Union Meeting—Celebration," *Tri-Weekly Standard* (Raleigh), March 19, 1867. The Kennedy Schoolhouse was located at the northeast corner of the intersection of Hasty School Road and Joe Moore Road across from the Hasty Baptist Church in Davidson County just a few miles north of the center of Thomasville.

91. Henry T. Clark to Col. Spier Whitaker, March 6, 1862, Henry T. Clark Letter Book, North Carolina State Archives.

92. J.G. Martin to Major E.A. Ross, March 8, 1862, Adjutant General's Letter Book, December 1861–April 1862, North Carolina State Archives.

93. S. Whitaker to [Governor Clark], March 14, 1862, Governors Papers, Henry T. Clark, North Carolina State Archives.

94. In the 1890 Federal Census for North Carolina, Special Schedules, Union Veterans and Widows of Union Veterans, Nancy I. Hilton is listed as the widow of John W. Hilton of Thomasville, Davidson County, North Carolina; Petition of citizens of Davidson County on behalf of "Captain John Hilton," addressed to Governor W.W. Holden, November 16, 1865, Governors Papers, William Woods Holden, North Carolina State Archives.

95. S. Whitaker to [Governor Clark], March 14, 1862, Governors Papers, Henry T. Clark, North Carolina State Archives.

96. B. Craven to Governor Clark, March 13, 1862, Governors Papers, Henry T. Clark, North Carolina State Archives.

97. H.T.C. to a Southerner, March 14, 1862, Henry T. Clark Letter Book, North Carolina State Archives.

98. Milton D. Raper to Capt. Lewis, April 2, 1862, Governors Papers, Henry T. Clark, North Carolina State Archives.

99. Lt. J.A.M. Coble to Henry T. Clark, July 14, 1862, Governors Papers, Henry T. Clark, North Carolina State Archives.

Chapter Three

1. Ashe, *History of North Carolina*, II, 749, 788; Coulter, *The Confederate States of American*, 314, 315, 326, 327; Lefler and Newsome, *North Carolina*, 470.

2. Ashe, *History of North Carolina*, II, 749; Lefler and Newsome, *North Carolina*, 471.

3. Martha Coletrane to Governor Vance, November 18, 1862, Governors Papers, Zebulon Baird Vance, North Carolina State Archives.

4. "The Crops—Conscription, etc," *Semi-Weekly Standard* (Raleigh), July 12, 1862.

5. "Corn and Wheat for the Poor," *Weekly Standard* (Raleigh), September 14, 1864.

6. "How to Stop Desertion," *People's Press* (Salem), October 16, 1863.

7. "Meeting of Orange Conscripts," *Semi-Weekly Standard* (Raleigh), July 23, 1862.

8. Moser, "Reaction in North Carolina to the Emancipation Proclamation," 54, 56, 61.

9. Tyson, *Object of the Administration*, 7.

10. Jonathan Worth to Z.B. Vance, September 16, 1862, in Hamilton, *The Correspondence of Jonathan Worth*, I, 187–188; Escott, *Many Excellent People*, 72, and *Military Necessity*, 81.

11. Joshua Boner to "Respected Sir," January 16, 1862, Governors Papers, Henry Toole Clark, North Carolina State Archives. See also "Traveller,—Sentinel,—Citizen," *People's Press* (Salem), January 31, 1862.

12. J. Elliott to Benj. [Elliott], September 5, 1862, Benjamin Elliott Papers, Duke Manuscript Department.

13. Others receiving exemptions included blacksmiths (588), county and state officers (282), details (1913), disability (7868), factory employees (155), millers (668), millwrights (123), mail carriers (72), overseers (120), preachers (156), physicians (264), policemen (84), printers (54), railroad employees (533), shoemakers (651), salt makers (627), school teachers (139), substitutes (2040), state ordinance employees (258), tanners (174), wagon makers (219), plus miscellaneous occupations each involving a small number of individuals. See "Exempts in North-Carolina," *Semi-Weekly Standard* (Raleigh), November 20, 1863.

14. Moore, *Conscription and Conflict in the Confederacy*, 27, 53, 67, 68.

15. *Ibid.*, 27; Lefler and Newsome, *North Carolina*, 466, 467, 470, 471; Raper, "William W. Holden and the Peace Movement in North Carolina," 497; Moser, "Reaction in North Carolina to the Emancipation Proclamation," 55, 61, 70.

16. Lefler and Newsome, *North Carolina*, 465–468; Kruman, *Parties and Politics in North Carolina*, 236.

17. Kruman, *Parties and Politics in North Carolina*, 232–233.
18. *Ibid.*, 237–238. The election figures used here are from Cheney, *North Carolina Government*, 1401.
19. The seven counties were Chatham, Guilford, Iredell, Montgomery, Randolph, Wilkes, and Yadkin. See Cheney, *North Carolina Government*, 1400–1401.
20. Statistics calculated from Cheney, *North Carolina Government*, 1400–1401.
21. C.J. Cowles to W.W. Holden, July 12, 1862, Letterpress Book J, 843, Calvin J.C. Cowles Papers, North Carolina State Archives.
22. Lefler and Newsome, *North Carolina*, 467–468; Hamilton, *Reconstruction in North Carolina*, 40–44.
23. Letter from "Virginius," *Landmark* (Norfolk, Virginia), January 15, 1885, quoted in Tucker, *Zeb Vance*, 156.
24. Z.B. Vance to Major Peter Mallett, September 11, 1862, Governors Papers, Zeb Vance Letter Book, North Carolina State Archives; Major [Peter Mallett] to Capt. Jas. C. McRae, September 10, 1862, Letter Book, June 23, 1862, to January 27, 1863, Peter Mallett Papers, Southern Historical Collection; J.G. Martin to Col. J.M. Worth, October 1, 1862, Adjutant General Papers, Militia Letter Book, 1862 to 1864, North Carolina State Archives.
25. Clark, *Histories of the North Carolina Regiments*, IV, 645–647.
26. Moore, *Conscription and Conflict in the Confederacy*, 68; *An Account of the Sufferings of Friends of North Carolina*, 7.
27. Edward Needles Wright, *Conscientious Objectors in the Civil War*, 188; Zuber, "Conscientious Objectors in the Confederacy," 1–19.
28. J.M. Worth was a merchant living in Asheboro, the seat of Randolph County. His real property was valued at $8,000 and his personal property at $25,850. He owned nine slaves. See 1860 Federal Census, Population and Slave Schedules, Randolph County, North Carolina.
29. Henry T. Clark to Col. J.M. Worth, March 10, 1862, Governors Papers, Henry Toole Clark, Letter Book, North Carolina State Archives.
30. See Auman and Scarboro, "The Heroes of America in Civil War North Carolina," 361; Zuber, *Jonathan Worth*, 174–177; "List of Men Drafted from State Salt Works" and "List of Hands Employed at State Salt Works near Wilmington, N.C.," n.d., Governors Papers, Zebulon Baird Vance, North Carolina State Archives.
31. *An Account of the Sufferings of Friends of North Carolina*, 8; Cartland, *Southern Heroes*, 201, *et passim*; Weeks, *Southern Quakers and Slavery*, 307.
32. "A Genuine Calumet," *The Daily Standard* (Raleigh), June 7, 1865.
33. Escott, *Many Excellent People*, 52–58.
34. Ashe, *History of North Carolina*, II, 775–776.
35. "Old Hubbie" to his wife, April 24, 1862, John Thomas Conrad Papers, North Carolina State Archives.
36. Bonnie [Kinyoun] to her husband, June 29, 1862, John Hindricks Kinyoun Papers, Duke Manuscript Department.
37. Daniel McIntosh to A.S. Caddell, September 4, 1862, Artemus S. Caddell Papers, Duke Manuscript Department.
38. Proclamation Against Deserters in Randolph County, August 4, 1862, Governors Papers, Henry Toole Clark, Letter Book, 1861–1862, North Carolina State Archives.
39. *Official Records Army*, Series I, Vol. XVIII, 753–754.
40. Peter Mallett was the son of a Fayetteville, North Carolina, banker and planter. Before the war, Mallett was a wholesale merchant in New York City. After the war, he returned to New York and resumed his business career. See biographical sketch of Mallett in the Peter Mallett Papers, Southern Historical Collection. See also Moore, *Roster of North Carolina Troops*, IV, 452.
41. [Peter Mallett] to Geo. W. Randolph, August 6, 1862, Letter Book, June 1862–January 1863, Peter Mallett Papers, Southern Historical Collection.
42. See 1850 Federal Census, Population and Slave Schedules, Randolph County, North Carolina. In the population schedule of the 1850 census, the polltaker erroneously listed Aaron Tyson's last name as Brown. See also Will of Aaron Tyson, January 16, 1852, Randolph County Wills, Book 9, 377, Randolph County Courthouse, Asheboro, North Carolina (hereinafter cited as Will of Aaron Tyson), and Hinshaw, *Encyclopedia of American Quaker Genealogy*, I, 424. The author is indebted to Mr. and Mrs. Claude Billy Tyson of Monroe, North Carolina, for sharing with him the genealogical information and memorabilia that they have collected on the Tyson family.
43. On the career and writings of Bryan Tyson see Auman, "Bryan Tyson—Southern Unionist," 257–292, and Larry Tise and William T. Auman, "Bryan Tyson" in Powell, *Dictionary of North Carolina Biography*, V, 71–73.
44. Bryan Tyson, *A Ray of Light*, 97.
45. 1860 Federal Census, Population, Slave, and Manufacturing Schedules, Moore County, North Carolina; Will of Aaron Tyson. The Gold Region was located north of the present-day town of Robbins along Bear Creek as it flowed northward to the Deep River. The area was also known as Carter's Mills.
46. Tyson, *A Ray of Light*, 142–143; "Union Meeting in Moore County," in *North Carolina Standard* (Raleigh), January 31, 1861; Bryan Tyson, *Object of the Administration*, 6.
47. Tyson, *Object of the Administration*, 6.
48. Bryan Tyson to the Editor of the *National Republican* (Washington, D.C.), July 3, 1869; a clipping of this letter is in the Robert and Newton D. Woody Papers, Duke Manuscript Department, hereinafter cited as Woody Papers; and in the Bryan Tyson Papers, Miscellaneous Collection, Manuscript Division, Library of Congress, Washington, D.C., hereinafter cited as Tyson Papers, Library of Congress. The Woody Papers also contain a printed copy of the same letter as sent "To the Editor of the Chronicle," July 2, 1869. The letter will hereinafter be cited as Tyson, "To the Editor of the Chronicle," July 2, 1869. It contains valuable biographical information about Tyson not found elsewhere.
49. Tyson, *A Ray of Light*, 100–135.
50. *Ibid.*, 14–16, 30–33. Tyson was essentially correct in his statement that the electorate did not establish the Confederacy with a popular vote. Only three states—Texas, Virginia, and Tennessee—had made provisions for a popular vote to approve their secession ordinances. However, in each case these plebiscites were held after the state legislature had ratified a military alliance with the Confederacy, and in Virginia and Tennessee, the popular votes came well after the Fort Sumter crisis and Lincoln's call for troops. See Randall and Donald, *The Civil War and Reconstruction*, 141, 187n; Howe, *Political History of Secession*, 456–458.
51. Tyson, *A Ray of Light*, 80–83, 94–95, 138–140.
52. "Copperheads," Kutler, ed., *Dictionary of American History: Third Edition*, II, 44. For accounts of the political

activities of the Democrats in the North during the Civil War, see Weber, *Copperheads*; Klements, *The Copperheads in the Middle West, The limits of Dissent, Dark Lanterns,* and *Clement L. Vallandigham and the Civil War*; Dell, *Lincoln and the War Democrats*; Silbey, *A Respectable Minority*; Zornow, *Lincoln and the Party Divided*; Baker, *Affairs of Party*; Baker, "A Loyal Opposition"; Curry, "The Union as It Was" and "Congressional Democrats, 1861–1863"; Sears, *George B. McClellan: The Young Napoleon*; Smith, *No Party Now: Politics in the Civil War North*.

53. Weber, *Copperheads*, 1–3; Silbey, *A Respectable Minority*, xi–xiii, 56–59, 100–105; Curry, "Congressional Democrats," 213–229, and "The Union as It Was," 25–39.

54. Weber, *Copperheads*, 1.

55. Tyson, *A Ray of Light*, 94–95, 138–139.

56. Tyson, "To the Editor of the Chronicle," July 2, 1869; Bryan Tyson, printed circular (no title), Brower's Mills, North Carolina, September 24, 1862, hereinafter cited as Tyson, reunion circular. On arrival in the North in 1863, Tyson had more copies of this circular printed and distributed. In a handwritten statement dated February 10, 1885, attached to a copy of this circular in the Rare Book Room, Library of Congress (hereinafter cited as Tyson Statement, February 15, 1885), Tyson noted that its main points were basically a synthesis of the arguments made by him in letters sent to Zebulon Baird Vance, Jefferson Davis, and Alexander H. Stephens.

57. Tyson Statement, February 10, 1885.

58. Tyson, "To the Editor of the Chronicle," July 2, 1869.

59. *Ibid.*

60. *Ibid.*

61. Tyson, *The Institution of Slavery*, 57.

62. Tyson, "To the Editor of the Chronicle," July 2, 1869; Tyson Statement, February 10, 1885; Bryan Tyson to Horace Greeley, March 21, 1864, Horace Greeley Papers, Library of Congress, hereinafter cited as Greeley Papers.

63. Tyson, *The Institution of Slavery*, 57.

64. Tyson, "To the Editor of the Chronicle," July 2, 1869. The 1860 census lists Joshua Moon, age 57, as a "trader" living in Mud Lick in the western division of Chatham County. He had a wife and three young children. A poor man, his real estate was worth $10 and his personal estate $110. Mud Lick was located in northwestern Chatham County about four miles east of Randolph County and about six miles south of Alamance County.

65. "Interesting from North Carolina," *New York Times*, May 1, 1863.

66. *Ibid.*; Tyson, "To the Editor of the Chronicle," July 2, 1869.

67. Bryan Tyson to Benjamin Sherwood Hedrick, April 5, 1865, Benjamin Sherwood Hedrick Papers, Duke Manuscript Department; Hamilton, *Benjamin Sherwood Hedrick*, 41.

68. Tyson, "To the Editor of the Chronicle," July 2, 1869.

69. Tyson, "To the Editor of the Chronicle," July 2, 1869; Bryan Tyson to the Secretary of War, April 22, 1863, Letters Received, Records of the United States Secretary of War, Main Series, 1801–1870, Record Group 107, National Archives, Washington, D.C., Microfilm Publication M 222, Reel 224; Bryan Tyson to Jonathan Worth, December 16, 1867, Private Collections, Jonathan Worth Papers, North Carolina State Archives.

70. Bryan Tyson to Abraham Lincoln, April 30 and May 1, 1863, Abraham Lincoln Papers (microfilm), Library of Congress.

71. Auman and Scarboro, "The Heroes of America," 340–341.

72. Auman, "North Carolina's Inner Civil War: Randolph County," 234–245.

73. Peter Mallett to Governor Vance, September 11, 1862, Governors Letter Books, Zebulon Baird Vance, North Carolina State Archives.

74. Governor Vance to Major Peter Mallett, September 11, 1862, Governors Letter Books, Zebulon Baird Vance, North Carolina State Archives.

75. Major [Peter Mallett] to General S. G. French, October 16, 1862, Letter Book, June 1862–January 1863, Peter Mallett Papers, Southern Historical Collection.

76. Col. [Peter Mallett] to Genl. S. Cooper, December 4, 1862, Letter Book, June 23, 1862–January 27, 1863, Peter Mallett Papers, Southern Historical Collection.

77. Clark, *The Histories of the North Carolina Regiments*, IV, 407–408; Moore, *Roster of North Carolina Troops in the War Between the States*, 452–454.

78. Hilderman, *Confederate Conscription in North Carolina*, 25–56.

79. *Ibid.*, 140, 160, 195.

80. J.G. Martin to Col. J.F. Revis, September 22, 1862, Adjutant General Papers, Militia Letter Book, 1862–1864, North Carolina State Archives.

81. J.G. Martin to Col. J.M. Worth, October 1, 1862, Adjutant General Papers, Letter Book, 1862–1864, North Carolina State Archives.

82. J.G. Martin to Col. James F. Revis, October 24, 1862, Adjutant General Papers, Letter Book, 1862–1864, North Carolina State Archives.

83. Major [Peter Mallett] to General S. Cooper, November 8, 1862, Letter Book, June 1862–January 1863, Peter Mallett Papers, Southern Historical Collection.

84. Capt. [McRae?] to Lieut. Thos. S. Robards, November 3, 1862, Letter Book, June 1862–January 1863, Peter Mallett Papers, Southern Historical Collection.

85. J.M. Worth to Gov. Z.B. Vance, November 4, 1862, Governors Papers, Zebulon Baird Vance, North Carolina State Archives.

86. Colonel [Peter Mallett] to Capt. J.C. McRae, November 24, 1862, Letter Book, June 1862–January 1863, Peter Mallett Papers, Southern Historical Collection. The army promoted Major Peter Mallett to Colonel on November 14, 1862. See Colonel Peter Mallett to General S. Cooper, November 20, 1862, Letter Book, June 1862–January 1863, Peter Mallett Papers, Southern Historical Collection.

87. *Ibid.*

88. C.J. Cowles to W.W. Holden [July 5, 1862], Letterpress Book J, 841, Calvin J. Cowles Papers, North Carolina State Archives.

89. C.J. Cowles to W.W. Holden, Letterpress Book J, 888, Calvin J. Cowles Papers, North Carolina State Archives.

90. John A. Burnett to A.C. Myers, October 6, 1862, A. C. Myers Papers, North Carolina State Archives.

91. Z.B. Vance to The Honorable General Assembly, November 17, 1862, *Official Records Army*, Series IV, Vol. II, 186.

92. H.W. Ayer to Governor Vance, November 10, 1862, Governors Papers, Zebulon Baird Vance, North Carolina State Archives.

93. John A. Craven to Governor Vance, October 21, 1862, Governors Papers, Zebulon Baird Vance, North Carolina State Archives.

94. H.W. Ayers to Governor Vance, October 25, 1862, Governors Papers, Zebulon Baird Vance, North Carolina

State Archives. For another report on barn-burning in Randolph by outliers, see J. Elliott to Benj., January 14, 1863, Benjamin Elliott Papers, Duke Manuscript Department.

95. "State vs. Thomas Brown, Tabithia Brown, Elizabeth Brown, and Adeline Boling," Randolph County Civil War Records, North Carolina State Archives.

96. Capt. B.B. Marley to Governor Vance, January 15 and 25, 1863, Governors Papers, Zebulon Baird Vance, North Carolina State Archives.

97. Col. [Peter Mallett] to Genl. W.H.C. Whiting, December 5, 1862, Letter Book, June 1862–January 1863, Peter Mallett Papers, Southern Historical Collection.

98. G.B. Jordan (Sgt. 26 N.C. Regt.) to the Editor of the *Journal* [December 1862], Governors Papers, Zebulon Baird Vance, North Carolina State Archives.

99. Adjutant General's Roll of Honor, Regiments 49–55, 1861–1865, North Carolina State Archives.

100. For a history of the Why Not community, see Auman and Stuart, *Why Not, North Carolina*.

101. Jas. S. Dunn to E.J. Hale & Sons, January 8, 1863, Governors Papers, Zebulon Baird Vance, North Carolina State Archives; Bynum, *The Long Shadow of the Civil War*, 29.

102. Jas. S. Dunn to E.J. Hale & Sons, January 8, 1863, Governors Papers, Zebulon Baird Vance, North Carolina State Archives.

103. Private interview and field trip in which Buren Garner showed the author the home places of William Owens, John Latham, William Gollihorn, Alfred Brower, and Bryan Tyson. Subsequent research has revealed that the home place Garner identified as that of the deserter leader William Owens was probably the farm of one William B. Owens. The author held the interview on November 13, 1977, at Garner's home located beside North Carolina Highway 705 at the Randolph/Moore line. The Garner home is located only about a quarter mile from the Owens and Gollihorn home sites. This interview will hereinafter be cited as the Garner interview.

104. William Auman, age 45, farmer and merchant, had a wife and two sons. His real estate was worth $350 and his personal estate $700. The census taker failed to list his post office which was Auman's Hill—the location of both a Confederate and a United States Post Office during the mid-nineteenth century. He lived in the Diffies Captain's District. A Dr. Reuben Gatlin roomed at his house. See 1860 Federal Census, Population Schedule, Montgomery County, North Carolina.

105. Asbury is located off Exit 41 of Interstate 73–74 at the intersection of Black Ankle Road and Old U.S. 220. The Auman's Hill Post Office was located across Black Ankle Road from present-day Asbury Baptist Church in northeastern Montgomery County. The William Owens farm would have been located within about a mile radius of the Asbury Baptist Church. It is probable that Owens lived east of the church near the point where Randolph, Montgomery, and Moore counties intersected. The William Owens deserter band used this area as their base during the war.

106. William Owens, farmer, owned no real estate and $75 worth of personal property. See 1860 Federal census, Population Schedule, Montgomery County, North Carolina, and Bynum, *The Long Shadow of the Civil War*, 21, and footnote 3 on page 153.

107. So far I have not been able to ascertain the exact location of the Good Spring community; however, the fact that the census taker for 1860 listed households on the same day in both the Gold Region and Good Spring neighborhoods indicates that the latter community probably was situated in the region of Moore County on the waters of Bear Creek north of present-day Robbins where the Gold Region is known to have existed in the nineteenth century.

108. See 1870 Federal census, Population Schedule, Moore County, North Carolina, and Bynum, *The Long Shadow of the Civil War*, 21, and footnote 3 on page 153.

109. John Harper to J.L. Stuart, November 26, 1862, John Lane Stuart Papers, Duke Manuscript Department.

110. The hanging occurred at Buffalo Ford in the east-central part of Randolph. See Ralph Bulla, "Civil War Hanging Recalled," *Courier-Tribune* (Asheboro), June 2, 1974.

111. J.R. McLean to William [Scott], January 27, 1863, William Lafayette Scott Papers, Duke Manuscript Department.

112. [Adjutant General to officers in charge of soldiers sent to arrest deserters and conscripts], January 6, 1863, Adjutant Generals Letter Book, 1862–1864, Adjutant Generals Papers, North Carolina State Archives.

113. *Ibid*.

114. *Ibid*.

115. Mary A. Harper to J.L. Stuart, January 12, 1863, John Lane Stuart Papers, and Sue to "Dear June," January 20, 1863, Nathan G. Hunt Papers, Duke Manuscript Department; John W. Graham to William A. Graham, January 13, 1863, in Williams and Hamilton (eds.), *The Papers of William Alexander Graham*, V, 441–443.

116. "Special Message from Gov. Vance," *Semi-Weekly Standard* (Raleigh), January 23, 1863.

117. *Official Records Army*, Series I, Vol. XVIII, 860–861.

118. *Ibid*.

119. Petition from Iredell, Wilkes, and Yadkin counties to Governor Vance, January 27, 1863, Governors Papers, Zebulon Baird Vance, North Carolina State Archives.

120. Williams, *Bitterly Divided*, 76–82; Weitz, *More Damning than Slaughter*, 284–285; Escott, "Poverty and Governmental Aid for the Poor in Confederate North Carolina," 464, and *passim*.

121. Tyson, *A Ray of Light*, 140–141.

122. R.P. Buxton to Z.B. Vance, January 21, 1863, Governors Papers, Zebulon Baird Vance, North Carolina State Archives. Buxton graduated from the University of North Carolina in 1845, and later settled in Fayetteville to practice law. In 1861, he was a Whig and an anti-secessionist. After the war, he became a Republican. See Dowd, *Sketches of Prominent Living North Carolinians*, 120–127.

123. R.P. Buxton to Z.B. Vance, January 21, 1863, Governors Papers, Zebulon Baird Vance, North Carolina State Archives.

124. *Ibid*.

125. *Ibid*.

126. See "List of Warrants placed in the hands of Shff of Moore County on 20th Jan. 1863," Governors Papers, Zebulon Baird Vance, North Carolina State Archives. The members of the Owens gang were Mark A. Spivey, Josiah Spivey, Temple Spivey, Asa Owen, Riley Cagell, William Owen, Emsley Owen, Henry Cagell, James R. Phillips, Kisey Williams, Jesse Jordan, Enoch Jordan, and John Dunlop, Jr.

127. Pugh served as Adjutant of the Twelfth Battalion North Carolina Cavalry in 1863. In 1864, the Army promoted him to Captain and made him assistant Quartermaster. See Manarin, *North Carolina Troops*, II, 624.

128. J.G. Martin to Col. Henry L. Steed, January 29, 1863, Adjutant General Papers, Militia Letter Book, 1862–1864, North Carolina State Archives.
129. Lt. Wm. A. Pugh to Maj. Archer Anderson, July 1, 1863, Governors Papers, Zebulon Baird Vance, North Carolina State Archives.
130. *Ibid.* For a report on cavalry troops taking horses from deserters' families in Moore County, see Mary A. Harper to J. L. Stuart, February 20, 1863, John Lane Stuart Papers, Duke Manuscript Department.
131. Danl. G. Fowle to Col H.L. Steed, March 14, 1863, Adjutant General Papers, Militia Letter Book, 1862–1864, North Carolina State Archives.
132. M.A. Harper to J.L. Stuart, March 22, 1863, John Lane Stuart Papers, Duke Manuscript Department.
133. John W. Hunt to Governor Vance, March 6, 1863, Governors Papers, Zebulon Baird Vance, North Carolina State Archives.
134. *Ibid.*
135. *Ibid.*
136. *Ibid.*
137. Jeremiah Phillips to Gov. Vance, April 14, 1863, Governors Papers, Zebulon Baird Vance, North Carolina State Archives.
138. Chesley Jones to Z.B. Vance, June 24, 1863, Governors Papers, Zebulon Baird Vance, North Carolina state Archives.
139. "Many Citizens" to Gov. Vance, April 18, 1863, Governors Papers, Zebulon Baird Vance, North Carolina State Archives. The 1860 federal census records for Montgomery county records no family in the Auman's Hill (Diffies Captain's District) community with anywhere close to 16 children.
140. Mary L. Harrison to Gov. Vance, June 15, 1863, Governors Papers, Zebulon Baird Vance, North Carolina State Archives.
141. "The Contrast," *Weekly Standard* (Raleigh), July 20, 1864. For a close look at the role women played in the inner civil war as breadwinners and defenders of the family while the husband and elderly sons were away from home, see Bynum, "'War Within a War': Women's Participation in the Revolt of the North Carolina Piedmont, 1863–1865."
142. N.W. Ayers to Gov. Vance, March 10, 1863, Governors Papers, North Carolina State Archives.
143. *Ibid.*
144. I.H. Foust to Z.B. Vance, March 17, 1863, Governors Papers, North Carolina State Archives.
145. "Randolph County," *Observer* (Fayetteville), January 5, 1863.
146. I.H. Foust to Gov. Z.B. Vance, March 17, 1863, Governors Papers, Zebulon Baird Vance, North Carolina State Archives.
147. Z.B. Vance to Genl. D.H. Hill, April 22, 1863, Governors Papers, Zebulon Baird Vance, North Carolina State Archives.
148. Lt. Wm. A. Pugh to Maj. Archer Anderson, July 1, 1863, Governors Papers, Zebulon Baird Vance, North Carolina State Archives.
149. *Ibid.*
150. *Ibid.*
151. *Official Records Army*, Series I, Vol. XVIII, 880–881. Other members of the gang included Thomas Adams, Enoch Brown, Jack Douglas, Anderson Douglas, Sanford Douglas, Hugh Sprinkle, and Horace Allgood.
152. "Confederate Friends" to Governor Vance, February 17, 1863, Governors Papers, Zebulon Baird Vance, North Carolina State Archives.
153. See Kennedy, *Preliminary Report on the Eighth Census*, 1860, 275.
154. *Official Records Army*, Series I, Vol. XVIII, 886–887.
155. *Ibid.*
156. Z.B. Vance to President Davis, May 13, 1863, *Official Records Army*, Series I, Vol. LI, Pt. II, 709–710.
157. Mitchell, *Legal Aspects of Conscription and Exemption in North Carolina, 1861–1865*, 38.
158. Lefler and Newsome, *North Carolina*, 470–471; Zeb Vance to James A. Seddon, May 25, 1863, *Official Records Army*, Series I, Vol. LI, Pt. II, 715–716.
159. *Ibid.*
160. Adjt. Genl. to Brig. Genl. G.A. McCraw, 18th Brigade North Carolina Militia, Mt. Airy, June 16, 1863, Militia Letter Book, 1862–1864, Adjutant General's Papers, North Carolina State Archives. This law was entitled "An Act to Punish Aiders and Abettors of Deserters." It was inserted just before the index to the published general statutes of North Carolina, adjourned session of 1863. This law was omitted in the published laws of the July 1863 session of the state legislature.
161. Danl. G. Fowle to Colonel John A. Murry, May 21, 1863, and to Captain Daughton, May 18, 1863, Adjutant General Papers, Militia Letter Book, 1862–1864, North Carolina State Archives.
162. Brig. Genl. W.D. Pender to "Major," April 23, 1863, Governors Letter Book, Zebulon Baird Vance, North Carolina State Archives.
163. Letter to the editor from Yadkin County, *Daily Progress* (Raleigh), August 25, 1863.
164. J.R. Lowrey to his mother, April 27, 1863, John Robert Lowrey Papers, Southern Historical Collection.
165. A Proclamation by the governor of North Carolina, May 11, 1863, *Official Records Army*, Series I, Vol. LI, Pt. II, 706–708.
166. R.E. Lee to James A. Seddon, May 21, 1863, Governors Papers, Zebulon Baird Vance, North Carolina State Archives.
167. R. Stred to Gov. Vance, April 10, 1863, Governors Papers, Zebulon Baird Vance, North Carolina State Archives.
168. W.D. King and Wiley M. Smith to Gov. Holden, December 9, 1868, W.W. Holden Papers, Duke Manuscript Department.
169. Miss Emily Branson to Gov. Vance, April 21, 1863, Governors Papers, Zebulon Barid Vance, North Carolina State Archives.
170. R. Stred to Gov. Vance, April 10, 1863, Governors Papers, Zebulon Baird Vance, Private Collections, North Carolina State Archives.
171. *Ibid.*
172. *Ibid.* The governor wrote the request on the back of Stred's letter.
173. *Ibid.* The general endorsed his reply to Vance on the back of Stred's letter.
174. O.S. Hanner to Z.B. Vance, April 17, 1863, Governors Papers, Zebulon Baird Vance, North Carolina State Archives. For additional testimony stating that the deserters had become more audacious than before, see John Harper to J.L. Stuart, April 26, 1863, John Lane Stuart Papers, Duke Manuscript Department.
175. O.S. Hanner to Z.B. Vance, April 17, 1863, Governors Papers, Zebulon Baird Vance, North Carolina State Archives.
176. R.W. Freeman, Harrison Freeman, & A.J. Parnell to Gov. Vance, July 15, 1863, Governors Papers, Zebulon Baird Vance, North Carolina State Archives.

177. Ibid.
178. A.H. Neill to Gov. Vance, May 5, 1863, Governors Papers, Zebulon Baird Vance, North Carolina State Archives.
179. A.D. Caddell et al. to Gov. Vance, July 18, 1863, Governors Papers, Zebulon Baird Vance, North Carolina State Archives.
180. "D of Co. I, 17th N.C.T." to the editor, *Weekly Standard* (Asheboro), May 20, 1863.
181. Beyer, *North Carolina: The Years Before Man*, 168. Other landmarks in the piedmont dating to this period are King's Mountain, Crowder's Mountain, Pilot Mountain, and Hanging Rock.
182. The Charlotte and Rutherford Railroad ran from Rutherfordton at the base of the mountains eastward to Wilmington on the Atlantic coast. It passed through Mecklenburg, Union, Anson, and Richmond — counties that bordered the Quaker Belt on the south. A good map showing the location and names of the railroads in North Carolina during the Civil War is located inside the covers of Barrett, *Civil War in North Carolina*.
183. See Chapters I and II.
184. [Account of two Randolph County, North Carolina, Unionists written by Mrs. B.S. Hedrick, Washington, D.C.], February 1865, Benjamin Sherwood Hedrick Papers, Duke Manuscript Department.
185. *Ibid.*
186. Dodge, "The Cave-Dwellers of the Confederacy," 516. David Dodge was a pseudonym used by Oscar Williams Blacknall who was born in 1852 and raised in the Vance County community of Kittrell (which, during the Civil War, was in Granville County). His father, Colonel C.C. Blacknall of the Twenty-third North Carolina Regiment, died in the Battle of Winchester in 1864. For more biographical information on the Blacknalls, see "Biographical Sketches" in Charles Leonard Van Noppen Papers, Duke Manuscript Department, and Powell, *Dictionary of North Carolina Biography*, I, 168.
187. Dodge, "Cave-Dwellers of the Confederacy," 517.
188. *Ibid.*, 516. See also Cox, *Hoot Owls, Honeysuckle and Halleluyah*, 82–83.
189. Jesse Wheeler to B.S. Hedrick, January 12, 1864, Benjamin Sherwood Hedrick Papers, Duke Manuscript Department. See also Lt. Col. McAlister to Major Jno. U. Waddell, March 6, 1865, Alexander Carey McAlister Papers, Southern Historical Collection.
190. A. Brower to Z.B. Vance, January 10, 1865, Governors Papers, Zebulon Baird Vance, North Carolina State Archives. For additional evidence of cave-dwelling in Randolph County and central North Carolina, see Cox, *Hoot Owls, Honeysuckle and Halleluyah*, 84; Cartland, *Southern Heroes*, 143, 117; Weeks, *Southern Quakers and Slavery*, 284; Clark, *The Histories of North Carolina Regiments*, IV, 101; E.T. Tompson to B.S. Hedrick, May [1865], B.S. Hedrick Papers, Duke Manuscript Department.; Spencer, *The Last Ninety Days of the War in North Carolina*, 243.
191. John Harper to John Stuart, n.d., John Lane Stuart Papers, Duke Manuscript Department.
192. Carter, *Memorial of John Carter* (pamphlet), extracted from the Minutes of Cottonwood Quarterly Meeting, Cottonwood, Kansas, Ninth Month, 19th, 1903. From a copy in the John B. Crenshaw Papers, Quaker Collection, Guilford College, Greensboro, North Carolina.
193. Jesse Wheeler to B.S. Hedrick, Nov. 16, 1862, Benjamin Sherwood Hedrick Papers, Duke Manuscript Department. See also Inscoe and McKinney, *The Heart of Confederate Appalachia*, 124.

194. James W. Savage, "The Loyal Element of North Carolina During The War" (paper read before the Nebraska Commandery of the Military Order of the Loyal Legion of the United States, May 5, 1886), Omaha, Nebraska, 1886, 45. For other examples of the existence of the Underground Railroad in central North Carolina during the Civil War, see Cartland, *Southern Heroes*, 181, 396 and Burson, *A Race for Liberty*, 64–73.
195. Van Noppen, "The Significance of Stoneman's Last Raid," Part I, 33.
196. Jesse Wheeler to B.S. Hedrick, January 20, 1862, Benjamin Sherwood Hedrick Papers, Duke Manuscript Department.
197. Jesse Wheeler to B.S. Hedrick, December 4, 1863, Benjamin Sherwood Hedrick Papers, Duke Manuscript Department.
198. Jesse Wheeler to B.S. Hedrick, May 2, 1864, Benjamin Sherwood Hedrick Papers, Duke Manuscript Department.
199. Jesse Wheeler to B.S. Hedrick, November 27, 1864, Benjamin Sherwood Hedrick Papers, Duke Manuscript Department.
200. *Ibid.*
201. *Ibid.*
202. Massah Trogdon to M.S. Robins, September 25, 1864, Marmaduke S. Robins Papers, Southern Historical Collection.
203. Jesse A. Miller to his aunt and uncle, July 18, 1864, James Patterson Papers, Duke Manuscript Department.
204. *Ibid.* Miller wrote "Hero of America" in the margin of this letter.
205. Numerous examples are in the Bryan Tyson Papers and the Benjamin Sherwood Hedrick Papers, in 1863 and 1864, Duke Manuscript Department.
206. Case of George Clark, Claim No. 43,444, settlement No. 2,708, depositions taken at Lexington, North Carolina, May 14, 1875, in Southern Claims Commission Records for Davidson County, North Carolina, National Archives, Washington, D.C. I thank Michael Honey for bringing this case to my attention. George Clark, age 47, had a wife and eight children. He lived in the Rich Fork community and was a blacksmith by trade. He owned no real estate and held $500 in personal property. See 1860 Federal Census, Population Schedule, Davidson County, North Carolina.
207. Kate E.L. Virdein to Vance, February 23, 1865, Zebulon Baird Vance Papers, Private Collections, North Carolina State Archives.
208. J.H. Haughton to [Vance], August 9, 1864, Zebulon Baird Vance Papers, Private Collections, North Carolina State Archives.
209. State vs Jane Deaton, Minute Docket, Montgomery County Superior Court, Spring Term (February 28, 1864), North Carolina State Archives.
210. "Your Brother Lewis" to "Dear sister Marinda," January 8, 1863, Branson Family Papers, North Carolina State Archives.

Chapter Four

1. For accounts of the peace movement in Confederate North Carolina, see Raper, "William W. Holden and the Peace Movement in North Carolina," 493–526; Roberts, "The Peace Movement in North Carolina," 190–199; Yates, "Governor Vance and the Peace Movement," Parts I and II, 1–25 and 89–113; Reid, "William W.

Holden and 'Disloyalty' in the Civil War," 23–44; Zuber, *Jonathan Worth*, 177–183; Hamilton, *Reconstruction in North Carolina*, 50–68; Scarboro, "An Honourable Peace: The Peace Movement in Civil War North Carolina" (unpublished dissertation); Kruman, *Parties and Politics in North Carolina*, 241–270; McKinney, *Zeb Vance*, 168–230; Harris, *William Woods Holden*, 127–155.

2. On the slogan of the Copperheads, see Klement, *The Limits of Dissent*, 90, 97, 130.

3. Klement, *The Limits of Dissent*, 130.

4. On defeatism and the Copperhead peace movement in the first half of 1863 in the North, see Klement, *The Copperheads of the Middle West*, 41–125, and Klement, *The Limits of Dissent*, 116–137.

5. In recent years, historians have published three biographies of Holden: Folk and Shaw, *W.W. Holden*; Raper, *William W. Holden*; and Harris, *William Woods Holden*.

6. See "The Way Vance Papers are Made," *Weekly Standard* (Raleigh), June 22, 1864.

7. "From Illinois," *Weekly Standard* (Raleigh), January 28, 1863.

8. *Weekly Standard* (Raleigh), June 17, 1863. For other examples, see "Signs at the North," *Weekly Standard* (Raleigh), February 11, 1863; "The Peace Movements in the North" and "Another Speech from Vallandigham," *People's Press* (Salem), January 30 and March 20, respectively.

9. "Peace by Negotiation," August 13, 1863.

10. "Congress," *Observer* (Fayetteville), March 9, 1864.

11. "Holden's Right Hand Man," *Daily Confederate* (Raleigh), May 11, 1864; Warner and Yearns, *Biographical Register of the Confederate Congress*, 148–149; Escott, "James T. Leach" in Current, *Encyclopedia of the Confederacy*, II, 911–913. In 1860, Dr. Leach was 55 years old and owned $25,000 in real estate and $28,200 in personal property. He owned 47 slaves. See 1860 Federal Census, Population and Slave Schedules, Johnston County, North Carolina.

12. "The Northern Democracy," *Weekly Standard* (Raleigh), May 20, 1863.

13. "The Peace Movement at the North," *Weekly Standard* (Raleigh), June 17, 1863.

14. Between July 22 and October 7, the *Weekly Standard* printed accounts of eighty peace meetings. The proceedings of eight of those were destroyed by rioting Confederate troops before they could be printed. The same account of each meeting was printed in each paper.

15. Yates, "Governor Vance and the Peace Movement," Part I, 5; Powell, *North Carolina*, 369–370; Kruman, *Parties and Politics in North Carolina*, 248; Pool, *Address of the Hon. John Pool*, 2. For specific examples, see resolutions passed at public meetings printed in the *Semi-Weekly Standard* (Raleigh), August 14, 18, 21, 25, 28, 1863.

16. For examples, see "Public Meeting in Randolph County," August 25; "Public Meeting in Iredell County" and "Public Meeting in Wilkes County," September 1; "Public Meeting in Forsyth County" and "Public Meeting in Alamance County," September 4; all in the *Semi-Weekly Standard* (Raleigh), 1863.

17. See Klement, *The Limits of Dissent*, 100, 117–118, 121, 210, 241, 278, 285–286.

18. C. Hampton to "Dear Nephew," August 31, 1863, Caleb Hampton Papers, Duke Manuscript Department. John Fink of Concord, physician, age 44, held $7,493 in real estate and $7,000 in personal estate. John Litaker of Mill Hill, age 42, farmer, held $720 real and $1,000 personal. See 1860 Federal Census, Population Schedule, Cabarrus County, North Carolina.

19. Scarboro, "An Honourable Peace," 104; Kruman, *Parties and Politics in North Carolina*, 249.

20. Yates, "Governor Vance and the Peace Movement," Part I, 9–23.

21. Bartholomew F. Moore (1801–1878) graduated from the University of North Carolina in 1820 and entered the legal profession. He opened a law office in Raleigh where he became one of the state's most famous jurists. Moore, a Democrat, ardently opposed secession and never warmed up to the Confederacy. During Reconstruction, he considered William Holden to be a corrupt politician. See Powell, *Dictionary of North Carolina Biography*, Vol. 4, 294–295.

22. W.W. Holden to Bartholomew F. Moore, August 2, 1866, Moore and Gatling Law Firm Papers, Southern Historical Collection. In 1864, Moore defended in court several men accused of belonging to the Heroes of America. See "B.F. Moore, Esq.," *Weekly Standard* (Raleigh), August 3, 1864.

23. "The Asheville *News*..." in *Weekly Standard* (Raleigh), March 1, 1865.

24. "To the Conservatives of North-Carolina," *Semi-Weekly Standard* (Raleigh), May 20, 1864.

25. Editorial, *Weekly Standard* (Raleigh), February 22, 1865. It is unclear what Holden meant by "a temporary separation."

26. *Semi-Weekly Standard*, July 31, 1863. Holden also published this article in his *Weekly Standard*, August 5, 1863.

27. In a footnote on page 53 in *Reconstruction in North Carolina*, J.G. de Roulhac Hamilton did note that Lewis Hanes wrote "a series of ably written articles against secession and the war, signed 'Davidson.'"

28. "To the Voters of the 7th Congressional District," *People's Press* (Salem), October 28, 1865.

29. "Lewis Hanes, Esq., &c, &c.," *Weekly Confederate* (Raleigh), July 6, 1864.

30. See obituary notice of Lewis Hanes in Lewis Hanes Papers, Southern Historical Collection.

31. Hamilton, *Correspondence of Jonathan Worth*, I, 254.

32. [Lewis Hanes], *A Voice from North Carolina*. See Scarboro, "An Honourable Peace," 114–118, and Bryan Tyson to Samuel F.B. Morse, November 15, 1863, Samuel F.B. Morse Papers, Manuscript Collection, Library of Congress.

33. Edward Everett (1794–1865) served as a Whig in the U.S. House and Senate, as governor of Massachusetts, and as secretary of state. A graduate of Harvard, he also served as president of the university. He was the first American to receive a Ph.D. from a German university. In 1860, he was nominated to run as vice-president on the Constitutional Union ticket. See Carnes and Garraty, *American National Biography*, VII, 629–30.

34. "The Influence of the Standard," *Observer* (Fayetteville), January 7, 1864.

35. "Read This," *Daily Conservative* (Raleigh), May 28, 1864.

36. *Ibid.*

37. "A man is known by the company he keeps," *Observer* (Fayetteville), July 14, 1864.

38. "Shameful," *Observer* (Fayetteville), July 14, 1864.

39. "To the Public," *Semi-Weekly Standard* (Raleigh), October 2, 1863.

40. Raper, *William W. Holden*, 49.

41. Proclamation by Governor Vance, *Weekly Standard* (Raleigh), September 7, 1863.

42. Yates, "Governor Vance and the Peace Movement,"

Part I, 3–4, 11–12, 15. See also "Hard Run — More Humbuggery," *Daily Conservative* (Raleigh), June 8, 1864.
43. "The Peace Question," October 16, 1863.
44. "Public Meeting in Surry County," *Semi-Weekly Standard* (Raleigh), August 11, 1863.
45. See the *Semi-Weekly Standard* (Raleigh), September 1 (Rowan and Alamance), 8 (Stanley), 25 (Guilford), and *Weekly Standard* (Raleigh), September 2 (Iredell). See also "Read This," *Daily Conservative* (Raleigh), May 28, 1864.
46. "Read This," *Weekly Conservative* (Raleigh), June 1, 1864.
47. See the editorial about the *Standard*, Holden, and the peace movement in *Observer* (Fayetteville), August 27, 1863.
48. Z.B. Vance to Edward J. Hale, August 11, 1863, Edward Jones Hale Papers, North Carolina State Archives.
49. See the *Semi-Weekly Standard* (Raleigh), August 18 (Wilkes), 21 (Montgomery), 25 (Randolph, Orange, and Alleghany), September 1 (Randolph), 4 (Alamance).
50. "Public Meeting in Wilkes County," *Semi-Weekly Standard* (Raleigh), August 18, 1863.
51. "Public Meeting in Orange County," *Semi-Weekly Standard* (Raleigh), August 25, 1863.
52. "Public Meeting in Montgomery County," *Semi-Weekly Standard* (Raleigh), August 21, 1863; Scarboro, "An Honourable Peace," 126–130. Oliver Dockery owned 41 slaves in 1860. His father, "General" Alfred Dockery, was a prominent Tar Heel Whig politician who served in the state legislature and as a representative in Congress. In 1854, he ran unsuccessfully for governor. Between his estates in North Carolina and Alabama, he owned about 700 slaves and 7000 acres of land. See Scarboro, "An Honourable Peace," 127, footnote 39.
53. *Weekly Standard* (Raleigh), July 22, 1863. Patriota wrote from Guilford County.
54. "Public Meeting in Chatham County," *Semi-Weekly Standard* (Raleigh), September 4, 1863.
55. *Semi-Weekly Standard* (Raleigh), August 11, 1863.
56. *Ibid.*; Curry, *A House Divided: A Study of Statehood Politics and the Copperhead Movement in West Virginia*, 10–11, 109; Curry, *Radicalism, Racism, and Party Realignment: The Border States During Reconstruction*, 42; Folmsbee, Corlew, and Mitchell, *History of Tennessee*, II, 181–82; Hall, *Andrew Johnson*, 139–149; Fleming, "The Peace Movement in Alabama During the Civil War: [Part] I, Party Politics, 1861–1864," *South Atlantic Quarterly*, II (April 1903), 121–123.
57. *Semi-Weekly Standard* (Raleigh), August 25, 1863.
58. On the Northern Democrats calling for a national convention of states, north and south, to settle the war and reconstruct the "Union as it was," see "A Voice from Illinois," *People's Press* (Salem), January 30, 1863; "From Illinois," *Weekly Standard* (Raleigh), January 28, 1863; Klement, *The Copperheads of the Middle West*, 49, 57, 60, 107, 111, 116, 118–120.
59. "Union Meeting at Bush Hill," January 28, 1861, and "Union Meeting in Randolph County," January 7, 1861, both in *Observer* (Fayetteville).
60. "North-Carolina Politics," *Semi-Weekly Standard* (Raleigh), August 25, 1863.
61. *Ibid.*
62. Nelson, *Bullets, Ballots, and Rhetoric*, 28, 131; Scarboro, "The Peace Movement in Civil War North Carolina," 218; *Offical Records Army*, Series IV, III, 67.
63. On the question of a Convention and slavery, see "Gov. Vance and the Convention Question," *Weekly Standard* (Raleigh), July 13, 1864; "Negotiations for Peace," *Weekly Standard* (Raleigh), November 23, 1864, and "The Peace Negotiations," *People's Press* (Salem), September 1, 1864.
64. "The Peace Conventions and Gov. Vance," *Weekly Standard* (Raleigh), September 9, 1863.
65. See Hamilton, *Reconstruction in North Carolina*, 58.
66. "The Peace Conventions and Gov. Vance," *Weekly Standard* (Raleigh), September 9, 1863.
67. *Ibid.*
68. See the *Semi-Weekly Standard* (Raleigh), September 1 (Rowan and Alamance), 8 (Stanley), 25 (Guilford), and *Weekly Standard* (Raleigh), September 2 (Iredell).
69. See the *Semi-Weekly Standard* (Raleigh), August 18 (Wilkes), 21 (Montgomery), 25 (Randolph, Orange, and Alleghany), September 1 (Randolph), 4 (Alamance).
70. "North Carolina Politics," *Observer* (Fayetteville), August 17, 1863. For another claim that deserters and draft-dodgers hiding out in the woods were behind many of the peace meetings, see "Who Compose Some of the So-Called Peace Meetings," *Observer* (Fayetteville), September 10, 1863.
71. Harris Tysor to Gov. Vance, July 6, 1863, Governors Papers, Zebulon Baird Vance, North Carolina State Archives.
72. "Public Meeting in Randolph County," *Weekly Standard* (Raleigh), September 2, 1863.
73. Buren Garner Interview. In 1860, William Gollihorn, age 46, owned real estate valued at $1,000 and a personal estate valued at $650. He had a wife and seven children. See 1860 Federal Census, Population Schedule, Randolph County, North Carolina.
74. Fall Term Superior Court, 1862, in Minute Docket Superior Court, 1855–1865, and May Term, 1862, in Minute Docket County Court, February 1860–October 1866, Randolph County Records, North Carolina State Archives.
75. State vs. William Gollihorn for harboring deserters, Spring Term, 1864, in State Docket Superior Court, 1861–1868, Randolph County Records, North Carolina State Archives. "Bands of Deserters, Renegades Terrorize Families Back Home," *Randolph Guide* (Asheboro), July 21, 1976, 9-B.
76. Roll of Honor, Regiments 49–55, Adjutant Generals Papers, North Carolina State Archives; On March 22, 1865, a company of Confederate troops hunting deserters in southern Randolph County captured, staked, and shot Alpheus Gollihorn. Alpheus had deserted from Company B, Fifty-second Regiment North Carolina Troops. See Capt. D.C. Green to Col. McAlister, March 27, 1865, Alexander Carey McAlister Papers, Southern Historical Collection.
77. "Public Meeting in Moore County," *Semi-Weekly Standard* (Raleigh) February 10, 1864.
78. Roster of the Militia [Officers] of North Carolina, 1861–1862, 1864, page 182, Adjutant General Papers, North Carolina State Archives.
79. In 1860, W. B. Richardson, age 35, was a merchant who lived in or near Carthage (the seat of Moore County). He had $9,000 in real property, $17,500 in personal property, and owned five slaves. See 1860 Federal Census, Population and Slave Schedules, Moore County, North Carolina.
80. Tyson, *Object of the Administration*, 6.
81. E.J. Hale to Governor Vance, August 14, 1863, Zebulon Baird Vance Papers, Private Collections, North Carolina State Archives.
82. J. R. Brown to Gov. W.W. Holden, June 23, 1868, and Thomas H. Ritter to Gov. Holden, June 23, 1868,

W.W. Holden Papers, Private Collections, North Carolina State Archives. The quotations came from the Brown letter.

83. For the claim that deserters and draft-dodgers hiding out in the woods were behind many of the peace meetings, see "Who Compose Some of the So-Called Peace Meetings," *Observer* (Fayetteville), September 10, 1863.

84. See Scarboro, "An Honourable Peace," 228–229, and Sanders, ed., *Maps of North Carolina Congressional Districts, 1789–1960*, 12.

85. The seventh congressional district contained Randolph, Chatham, Davidson, Montgomery, Moore, Anson, and Stanly counties. All of them but Anson and Stanly were in the Quaker Belt. See Sanders, *Maps of North Carolina Congressional Districts*, 12.

86. In 1860, Thomas Ashe, age 47, lawyer, owned $3,000 in real property, $14,575 in personal property, and 17 slaves. See 1860 Federal Census, Population and Slave Schedules, Anson County, North Carolina.

87. Wakelyn, *Biographical Dictionary of the Confederacy*, 80.

88. "Mind Your Own Business," *Daily Progress* (Raleigh), March 17, 1864. S.H. Christian's real estate was valued in 1860 at $15,000 and his personal estate at $48,000. He owned 42 slaves. See 1860 Federal Census, Population and Slave Schedules, Montgomery County, North Carolina.

89. "The 7th Congressional District," *Observer* (Fayetteville), October 12, 1863.

90. Letter to the Editor from S.H. Christian, *Weekly Standard* (Raleigh), August 26, 1863.

91. "Congressional Discussion," *Observer* (Fayetteville), September 7, 1863.

92. "Seventh Congressional District," *Semi-Weekly Standard* (Raleigh), October 9, 1863.

93. On Holden, see "North-Carolina Politics," *Semi-Weekly Standard* (Raleigh), August 25, 1863. On Dr. Leach, see "Congress," *Observer* (Fayetteville), March 9, 1864.

94. Letter to the Editor from S.H. Christian, *Weekly Standard* (Raleigh), August 26, 1863.

95. Letter from S.H. Christian to the *Standard* in *Semi-Weekly Standard*, August 21, 1863. See also "Congressional Canvass," August 17, 1863, and "Congressional Discussion," September 7, 1863, both in the *Observer* (Fayetteville),

96. *Observer* (Fayetteville), September 3, 1863.

97. *Semi-Weekly Standard* (Raleigh), October 23, 1863, and "The war will not last one day longer..." *Semi-Weekly Standard* (Raleigh), October 28, 1863.

98. "Vote in the Seventh District," *North Carolina Standard* (Raleigh), November 20, 1863.

99. *Wilmington Journal*, March 10, 1864.

100. Scarboro, "An Honourable Peace," 107–170, 290, 292.

101. Scarboro, "An Honourable Peace," 126–180 (Alfred and Oliver Dockery), 134–141 (Andrew and Calvin Cowles), 143–146 (Dr. J.T. Leach), 148–150 (Samuel H. Christian), 151–152 (J.M. Leach).

102. On William Owens, see G.B. Jordan (Sgt. 26 N.C. Regt.) to the Editor of the *Journal* [December 1862], Governors Papers, Zebulon Baird Vance, North Carolina State Archives; on John Quincy Adams Bryan and Granville Smoot, see W.W. Hampton to Vance, September 7, 1863, Governors Papers, Zebulon Baird Vance, North Carolina State Archives; on Harrison Church, see "A Fight in Wilkes," *Weekly Conservative* (Raleigh), November 16, 1864, and "A Deserter," *Daily Watchman* (Salisbury), December 21, 1864; on the Dial brothers, see Wilse, James, and Calvin Dial to Capt. Quill Hunter, July 29, 1863, Dial Brothers Letter, Southern Historical Collection. See also Jas. S. Dunn to E.J. Hale & Sons, January 8, 1863, Governors Papers, Zebulon Baird Vance, North Carolina State Archives.

103. For examples, see "North Carolina Politics," *Observer* (Fayetteville), August 17, 1863; "A Citizen," letter to the editor, *Semi-Weekly Standard* (Raleigh), August 14, 1863.

104. Scarboro, "An Honourable Peace," XII, 69–70, 107, 111, 120, 169–170.

105. See "The Peace Conventions and Gov. Vance," *Weekly Standard* (Raliegh), September 9, 1863, for a discussion of the pent-up resentments held by the old anti-secession Tar Heel Unionists against their old secessionist enemies. See also Hamilton, *Reconstruction in North Carolina*, 58.

106. "Union Meeting in Randolph County," January 7, 1861, and "Union Meeting at Bush Hill," January 18, 1861, both in *Observer* (Fayetteville), January 28, 1861—see also article in February 18 issue of the *Observer* on this topic; McPherson, *Battle Cry of Freedom*, 493–494, 591–595, 692.

107. Harris, *William Woods Holden*, 5–10.

108. Escott, "White Republicans and Ku Klux Klan Terror," 4–34; Powell, *North Carolina*, 392–403.

109. A copy of Tyson's Day-Star Circular is in the Jonathan Worth Papers, Private Collections, North Carolina State Archives.

110. Zuber, *Jonathan Worth*, 181.

111. Tyson, *Object of the Administration*, 9, 12–13, and *The Institution of Slavery*, 35–41. In his chapter on Bryan Tyson, historian Jon L. Wakelyn reprints the text of Tyson's *The Institution of Slavery*. See Wakelyn, *Southern Unionist Pamphlets and the Civil War*, 170–202. The pamphlet is also available online at *Documenting the American South*.

112. Tyson, *Object of the Administration*, 2.

113. Tyson, *The Institution of Slavery*, 55–58. The direct quotation is from page 55.

114. Bryan Tyson to Jonathan Worth, December 16, 1867, Jonathan Worth Papers, Private Collections, North Carolina State Archives, and Bryan Tyson's Prospectus for *A Ray of Light* and *The Institution of Slavery in the Southern States, Religiously and Morally Considered in Connection with our Sectional Troubles* in Zebulon Baird Vance Papers, Private Collections, North Carolina State Archives.

Chapter Five

1. Hamilton, *Reconstruction in North Carolina*, 54; Lefler and Newsome, *North Carolina*, 475.

2. Nancy Royal to Gov. Vance, August 9, 1863, Governors Papers, Zebulon Baird Vance, North Carolina State Archives.

3. O.S. Hanner to Governor Vance, August 3, 1863, Governors Papers, Zebulon Baird Vance, North Carolina State Archives.

4. Ibid.

5. Clark, *The Histories of North Carolina Regiments*, IV, 649.

6. Ibid., V, 629.

7. *Public and Private Laws of North Carolina 1863–64*.

8. Capt. J.C. Kirkman to Z.B. Vance, August 27,

1863, Marmaduke S. Robins Papers, Southern Historical Collection.

9. James H. Foote to Lt. Col. S.G. Worth, August 27, 1863, Marmaduke S. Robins Papers, Southern Historical Collection.

10. I.A. Sugg to her husband, September 2, 1863, Lewis O. Sugg Papers, Duke Manuscript Department.

11. _____ to E.J. Hale & Sons, September 21, 1863, Governors Papers, Zebulon Baird Vance, North Carolina State Archives.

12. Lt. Col. S.G. Worth to Gov. Vance, September 3, 1863, Governors Papers, Zebulon Baird Vance, North Carolina State Archives.

13. Special Order No. 6, Enrolling Office, Asheboro, N.C., September 12, 1863, Marmaduke S. Robins Papers, Southern Historical Collection.

14. I.H. Foust to Gov. Vance, August 29, 1863, Governors Papers, Zebulon Baird Vance, North Carolina State Archives.

15. *Ibid.*

16. *Ibid.*

17. David Schenck Diary, entry for June 11, 1863, titled "Gloomy Crisis," Southern Historical Collection.

18. W.H. McNeil to Vance, July 19, 1863, Governors Papers, Zebulon Baird Vance, North Carolina State Archives.

19. Julia P. Gwyn to her uncle, July 25, 1863, James Gwyn Papers, Southern Historical Collection.

20. "Organized for Resistance," *Daily Progress* (Raleigh), September 7, 1863.

21. W.H. Profit to his sister Louisa, August 10, 1863, Profitt Family Papers, Southern Historical Collection.

22. Diary of James Gwyn, Volume IV, entry for September 1, 1863, James Gwyn Papers, Southern Historical Collection.

23. Granville Smoot, aged 39 in 1860, was a farmer with real property worth $500 and personal property worth $500. He had seven children. See 1860 Federal Census, Population Schedule, Wilkes County, North Carolina.

24. The 1860 Federal Census listed John Quincy Adams Bryan as living in the household headed by Thomas Bryan, his future father-in-law. He was 27 years old and worth $500 in real property and $450 in personal property.

25. W.W. Hampton to Vance, September 7, 1863, Governors Papers, Zebulon Baird Vance, North Carolina State Archives.

26. See Federal Census, Population Schedule, Wilkes County, North Carolina for 1870 and 1900.

27. David Schenck Diary, Vol. III, from an entry entitled "Civil War at Home," dated September 11, 1863, Southern Historical Collection.

28. Col. Peter Mallett to Vance (telegram), September 9, 1863, Governors Papers, Zebulon Baird Vance, North Car-olina State Archives.

29. Jacob Fraley, age 49 in 1860, owned a general store, a large tanning business, and three slaves. He was worth $10,113 in personal property and $3680 in real estate. After the war, he became a Republican. He had to flee his home in the middle of the night and take refuge in a nearby county to avoid vengeance at the hands of his political enemies during Reconstruction. The Whig party was dominant in Iredell County before the Civil War. After the war, Republicans (mostly old Whigs) commanded over 40 percent of the vote, but only rarely a majority. See Keever, *Iredell: Piedmont County*, 90, 110, 235, 303–304, 306–307; and 1860 Federal Census, Population and Slave Schedules, Iredell County, North Carolina.

30. J.C. McRae to R.H. Simonton, September 17, 1863, S. A. Sharpe Papers, Southern Historical Collection.

31. "The Trouble in Iredell and Wilkes," copied from the *Iredell Express* in the *People's Press* (Salem), September 24, 1863.

32. See Tomlinson, *Assembly Sketch Book Session 1883 North Carolina*, II, 73; Absher, ed., *The Heritage of Wilkes County*, 49–50, 121; Lancaster, "The Scalawags of North Carolina, 1850–1868," 482; Pension Records for John Quincy Adams Bryan and his wife, Claim No. 673,559 in Records Relating to Pension and Bounty Land Claims, Records of the Veterans Administration, Record Group 15, National Archives.

33. "Bannie" to her husband, September 3, 1863, John Hendricks Kinyoun Papers, Duke Manuscript Department.

34. "Bannie" to her Husband, August 26, 1863, John Hendricks Kinyoun Papers, Duke Manuscript Department.

35. Maj. N.G. Hunt to Capt. J.A. Bitting, October 26, 1863, Jarrett-Puryear Family Papers, Duke Manuscript Department.

36. Wilse, James, and Calvin Dial to Capt. Quill Hunter, July 29, 1863, Dial Brothers Letter, Southern Historical Collection. Wilson (Wilse?) Dial, age 19 in 1860, was a day laborer who lived near Bethania in Forsyth County. He owned no real property and $25 worth of personal property. He was head of a household that included his brothers James and Calvin, ages 15 and 13, respectively. Four women, aged 40, 24, 20, and 11, comprised the remainder of his household. See 1860 Federal Census, Population Schedule, Forsyth County, North Carolina.

37. "Your Affectionate Mother" to "My Dear Son," October 29, 1863, Jarrett-Puryear Family Papers, Duke Manuscript Department.

38. "Deserters Shot," *Daily Conservative* (Raleigh), March 6, 1865. The article was reprinted from the *Winston Sentinel*.

39. *Ibid.*

40. "A Citizen" letter to the editor, *Semi-Weekly Standard* (Raleigh), August 14, 1863.

41. *Semi-Weekly Standard*, September 1, 1863. In 1860, John Templeton, age 42, farmer, owned $655 in real estate and $500 in personal property. Thomas Templeton, age 35, farmer, owned $255 real and $300 personal. See 1860 Federal Census, Population Schedule, Iredell County, North Carolina.

42. S.A. Sharpe to Capt McRae, September 29, 1863, S.A. Sharpe Papers, Southern Historical Collection.

43. J.S. Overcash to his brother, August 28, 1863, Joseph Overcash Papers, Duke Manuscript Department.

44. [T.F. Baggarly] to his wife, August 25, 1863, Tilmon F. Baggarly Papers, Duke Manuscript Department.

45. *Official Records Army*, Series IV, Vol. II, 783–786.

46. *Ibid.*

47. *Ibid.*

48. *Ibid.*

49. *Ibid.*

50. *Ibid.*

51. *Official Records Army*, Series I, XXIX, Part II, 676. See also R.E. Lee to Vance (telegram), September 1, 1863, Governors Papers, Zebulon Baird Vance, North Carolina State Archives. For other accounts of the disorder in western North Carolina at this time, see David Schenck Diary, December 1853–December 1863, entry for August 13, 1863, titled "Civil War at Home," Southern Historical

Collection, and Wilson, *A Brief History of the Cruelties and Atrocities of the Rebellion*, 5, a pamphlet printed by the "Union Congressional Committee." Wilson noted that Bryan Tyson was the source for information in his book describing events in North Carolina.

52. *Official Records Army*, Series I, XXIX, Part II, 676. Only one of the two regiments sent into North Carolina under Hoke's command, the Twenty-first, was from his brigade (the other regiments in his brigade remained in Virginia). The second regiment was the Fifty-sixth North Carolina from Ransom's Brigade. The cavalry squadron came from Jenkins's Brigade. See *Official Records Army*, Series I, Vol. 27, Part III, 1058–1068, and Series I, Vol. 29, Part II, 692.

53. Vance to Hoke, September 7, 1863, Governors Letter Book, Zebulon Baird Vance, North Carolina State Archives. General Robert Frederick Hoke (1837–1912), a native Tar Heel from Lincoln County commanded with distinction a brigade of North Carolina troops in the Army of Northern Virginia during the war. He suffered a severe wound at Chancellorsville that nearly took his life. After the war, he became a successful businessman with interests in railroads and mining. See Boatner, *The Civil War Dictionary*, 404–405.

54. Special Order No. 6, September 7, 1863, listed in General and Special Orders [to the Home Guards], August 18, 1863–April 11, 1865 (AG 35), Adjutant Generals Papers, North Carolina State Archives.

55. Special Order No. 8, September 9, 1863, listed in General and Special Orders [to the Home Guards], August 18, 1863–April 11, 1865 (AG 35), Adjutant General Papers, North Carolina State Archives.

56. Mary to "My dearest Rufus," September 9, 1863, Patterson Collection, Southern Historical Collection.

57. Special Order No. 6, issued by General R.F. Hoke on September 11, 1863, at his headquarters in Yadkinville, North Carolina, Jarrett-Puryear Family Papers, Duke Manu-script Department.

58. Entry for September 15, 1863, in Diary of J. Gwyn, 1852–1877, in Thurmond Chatham Papers, North Carolina State Archives. For an account of General Hoke's deserter hunt in the Wilkes County area, see Barefoot, *General Robert F. Hoke*, 96–104.

59. Cowles to Jas. M. Sanders, September 17, 1863, Letterpress Book K, Calvin J. Cowles Papers, North Carolina State Archives.

60. Cowles to Wm. A. Williams, September 22, 1863, Letterpress Book K, Calvin J. Cowles Papers, North Carolina State Archives. In 1860, Cowles, age 39, was worth $20,000 in real estate and $5,295 in personal property. He owned four slaves. See 1860 Federal Census, Population and Slave Schedules, Wilkes County, North Carolina.

61. Cowles to his father, September 22, 1863, Letterpress Book K, Calvin J. Cowles Papers, North Carolina State Archives.

62. J. Gwyn to his mother, September 25, 1863, Lenior Family Papers, Southern Historical Collection.

63. "Outrages by the Military," *Weekly Standard* (Raleigh), December 23, 1863.

64. "Shameful Treatment," *Weekly Standard* (Raleigh), January 20, 1864.

65. J.J. Cowles to Calvin Cowles, September 12, 1863, Calvin J. Cowles Papers, North Carolina State Archives.

66. Cowles to P.F. Pescud, September 27, 1863, Letterpress Book K, Calvin J. Cowles Papers, North Carolina State Archives.

67. Cowles to Jas. M. Sanders, September 27, 1863, Letterpress Book K, Calvin J. Cowles Papers, North Carolina State Archives.

68. Cowles to Vance, October 9, 1863, Letterpress Book K, Calvin J. Cowles Papers, North Carolina State Archives. Castle Thunder was the name of the Confederate prison in Richmond for political prisoners, spies, and traitors. It had "an unsavory reputation, and its officers were charged with unnecessary brutality and cruelty." See Boatner, *Civil War Dictionary*, 131.

69. See "Public Meeting in Guilford County" and "Public Meeting in Yadkin County," *Semi-Weekly Standard* (Raleigh), September 4 and August 25, respectively, 1863.

70. J.A. Parks to Vance, November 16, 1863, and Rhoda Ledder to Vance, November 29, 1863, Governors Papers, Zebulon Baird Vance, North Carolina State Archives.

71. Pool, *Address of the Hon. John Pool*, 2.

72. Cowles to "Publisher Richmond Examiner," September 18, 1863, Letterpress Book K, Calvin J. Cowles Papers, North Carolina State Archives; General Hoke to Colonel Sharpe, September 25, 1863, S.A. Sharpe Papers, Southern Historical Collection.

73. James H. Foote to Col. Sharpe, September 1, 1863, and R.L. Gatlin to Col. S.A. Sharpe, October 6, 1863, S.A. Sharpe Papers, Southern Historical Collection; Special Order No. 6, September 7, 1863, listed in General and Special Orders [to the Home Guards], August 18, 1863–April 11, 1865 (AG 35), Adjutant Generals Papers, North Carolina State Archives.

74. Col. P.F. Faison to Col. Sharpe, September 22, 1863, S.A. Sharpe Papers, Southern Historical Collection.

75. "More Deserters Coming In," *Observer* (Fayetteville), October 19, 1863.

76. P.F. Faison to Col. [Sharpe], October 21, 1863, S.A. Sharpe Papers, Southern Historical Collection.

77. "Arrest of Deserters, &c," *Observer* (Fayetteville), November 5, 1863.

78. "The 21st Regiment, Hoke's brigade," *The Patriot* (Greensboro), November 19, 1863.

79. Peter W. Hairston Diary, entry for November 23, 1863, Peter Wilson Hairston Papers, Southern Historical Collection.

80. J.A. Parks to Vance, November 16, 1863, Governors Papers, Zebulon Baird Vance, North Carolina State Archives.

81. S.E. Love to his father, November 26, 1863, Mathew N. Love Papers, Duke Manuscript Department.

82. Cowles to W.W. Holden, December 8, 1863, Letterpress Book K, Calvin J. Cowles Papers, North Carolina State Archives.

83. Faison to Vance, January 4, 1864, Governors Papers, Zebulon Baird Vance, North Carolina State Archives.

84. On September 10, 1863, the Fifty-sixth Regiment was on its way to Statesville. See Col. Peter Mallett to Vance (telegram), September 10, 1863, Governors Papers, Zebulon Baird Vance, North Carolina State Archives.

85. Jonathan Worth to B.G. Worth, September 16, 1863, in Hamilton, *The Correspondence of Jonathan Worth*, I, 264–266. For another account of this skirmish, see W.S. Tomlinson to David Jordan, Esq., September 7, 1863, William Henry Snow Papers, Tomlinson Series, Southern Historical Collection.

86. Special Order No. 19, October 3, 1863, listed in General and Special Orders [to the Home Guards], August 18, 1863–April 11, 1865 (AG 35), Adjutant Generals Papers, North Carolina State Archives.

87. "Robbery and Incendiarism," *The Patriot* (Greensboro), October 5, 1863.
88. R.L. Gatlin to Lt. Col. S.G. Worth, October 19, 1863, Home Guard Letter Book, 1863–1865 (AG 52), Adjutant Generals Papers, North Carolina State Archives.
89. "More Deserters Come In," *Observer* (Fayetteville), October 19, 1863.
90. Faison to Vance, January 4, 1864, Governors Papers, Zebulon Baird Vance, North Carolina State Archives.
91. T.B. Carlton to his brother, December 30, 1863, John Washington Carlton Letters, North Carolina State Archives.
92. Dr. John Shaw to Ralph P. Buxton, January 8, 1864, Governors Papers, Zebulon Baird Vance, North Carolina State Archives.
93. "61st North Carolina Infantry," by N. A. Ramsey in *New River Notes* at www.newrivernotes.com/cw-nc/61ncinf.htm.
94. I.H. Foust to Gov. Vance, December 30, 1863, Marmaduke S. Robins Papers, Southern Historical Collection.
95. T.B. Carlton to his brother, December 30, 1863, John Washington Carlton Letters, Duke Manuscript Department.
96. "Incendiarism," *The Patriot* (Greensboro), December 24, 1863.
97. "Supposed Incendiarism," *Observer* (Fayetteville), January 7, 1864.
98. James Harwell to his wife, November 9, 1863, James Harwell Letters, North Carolina State Archives.
99. *Ibid.*, December 11, 1863.
100. *Ibid.*, March 14, 1864.
101. *Ibid.*, April 17, 1864.
102. R.L. Gatlin to Col. Jesse Hargrave, October 6, and December 15, 1863, Home Guard Letter Book, 1863–1865 (AG 52), Adjutant General Papers, North Carolina State Archives.
103. L.S. Wright to B & E Wright, November 27, 1863, Wright Family Papers, Duke Manuscript Department.
104. Captain Graham probably served under the command of Colonel Faison.
105. John W. Graham to William A. Graham, November 21, 1863, in Williams and Hamilton, *The Papers of William Alexander Graham*, V, 539–540.
106. *Ibid*, 539.
107. John W. Graham to Gov. Z.B. Vance, December 6, 1863, Governors Papers, Zebulon Baird Vance, North Carolina State Archives. See also E.B. Cranford to Vance, November 16, 1863, Governors Papers, Zebulon Baird Vance, North Carolina State Archives.
108. Alexander K. Pearce (1842?–?), age 18 in 1860, lived with his father, Thomas, a farmer, his mother and seven siblings in the Brower's Mills community in southern Randolph County. Thomas Pearce owned no real estate and possessed only $325 worth of personal property. Pearce enlisted for the duration of the war in Company I, Fifth Regiment North Carolina Troops, on July 15, 1862. Federals captured him at Sharpsburg, Maryland, in September 1862, and incarcerated in Fort McHenry. Paroled and exchanged in October, he returned to his company but deserted to Federal forces at Morton's Ford, Virginia, in November. Military authorities jailed him in the Old Capitol Prison in Washington, D.C. Pearce took the oath of amnesty and authorities released and sent him to Philadelphia on March 18, 1864. See Manarin and Jordan, *North Carolina Troops*, IV, 240. Pearce joined the Union army in Philadelphia. In March 1865, the army stationed him at Fort Dushane, Virginia, where he became a member of Battery B4, United States Artillery, Fifth Army Corps. See Alexander K. Pearce to Bryan Tyson, March 1, 1865, Bryan Tyson Papers, Duke Manuscript Department, and 1860 Federal Census, Population Schedule, Randolph County, North Carolina.
109. A.K. Pearce to Bryan Tyson, November 25, 1863, Bryan Tyuson Papers, Duke Manuscript Department.
110. *Ibid.*
111. *Ibid.*
112. A.K. Pearce to Bryan Tyson, December 3, 1863, Bryan Tyson Papers, Duke Manuscript Department. The murdered Unionist Benjamin Northens may have been Ben Northcut of Moore County, age 30 in 1860, with a wife and two children. Northcut was a tenant farmer with $100 worth of personal property. See Cole and Foley, *Collett Leventhrope*, 177–78, and footnote 104, p. 268, and 1860 Federal Census, Moore County, North Carolina, Population Schedule. According to Victoria Bynum, Benjamin Northcutt was a relative of William Owens and a member of his deserter gang. See Bynum, *The Long Shadow of the Civil War*, 23, and footnote 6 on page 154.
113. *Ibid.*
114. *Ibid.*
115. A.K. Pearce to Bryan Tyson, May 9, 1864, Bryan Tyson Papers, Duke Manuscript Department.
116. C. Dowd to R.P. Buxton, January 7, 1864, Governors Papers, Zebulon Baird Vance, North Carolina State Archives. The 1860 census listed Peter Garner as "Pete Gardner, Jr," age 27, with a wife and two-year-old daughter and an eight-year-old "mullatto" (bound). He was an "overseer" and his personal and real property was valued each at $500. A miller, age 51, Adam Brewer had a wife and daughter. His real estate was valued at $3,300 and his personal estate at $7,150. He owned six slaves. See 1860 Federal Census, Population and Slave Schedules, Randolph County, North Carolina.
117. Thomas W. Ritter to Governor Z.B. Vance, January 25, 1864, Governors Papers, Zebulon Baird Vance, North Carolina State Archives.
118. Wilson, *A Brief History of the Cruelties and Atrocities of the Rebellion*, 5. Wilson gives another account of this incident in *Sufferings Endured for a Free Government; or a History of the Cruelties and Atrocities of the Rebellion*, 91–92. In both books, Wilson credited Bryan Tyson as the source of information for the incident. In his book, *Object of the Administration in Prosecuting the War*, page 2, Tyson claimed that Wilson exaggerated the circumstances of the killing of McDonald when he stated that neighbors found his body "completely riddled with bullets." Tyson told Wilson that neighbors found McDonald's body three or four days after the atrocity when it looked like six or seven pullets had penetrated the body, but decay made it impossible to be sure just how many. Wilson exaggerated the incident to present the "rebels" in as bad a light as possible for the Republican propaganda document. Of the five men living in Moore County in 1860 carrying the name Neil McDonald, three of them, ages 17, 21, and 27 in 1860, could have been the Neil murdered in this account. All of them were poor with little or no property. See 1860 Federal Census, Population Schedule, Moore County, North Carolina.
119. Alexander K. Pearce to Bryan Tyson, October 24, 1864, Bryan Tyson Papers, Duke Manuscript Department.
120. *Ibid.*
121. State vs. Adam Brewer for distilling, May Term

1864, Minute Docket County Court, February 1860–October 1866, Randolph County Records, North Carolina State Archives.

122. Thos. W. Ritter to Governor Vance, January 1, 1864, Governors Papers, Zebulon Baird Vance, North Carolina State Archives. George Moore, age 37 in 1860, had a wife and 8 young children. He owned no real estate and only $200 worth of personal property. He lived in the "Gold Region" area of the county where Bryan Tyson owned land and a farm implement manufacturing company. See 1860 Federal Census, Moore County, North Carolina.

123. *Ibid.* The 1860 census of Moore County does not include a Thomas W. Ritter. The 1870 census lists him as a farmer, age 42, living near Carthage. He owned $500 in real and $500 in personal property. See 1870 Federal Census, Population Schedule, Moore County, North Carolina.

124. Thos. W. Ritter to Gov. Z.B. Vance, January 25, 1864, Governors Papers, Zebulon Baird Vance, North Carolina State Archives.

125. *Ibid.* The Governor's reply was endorsed on the back of Ritter's letter.

126. Col. Wm. B. Richardson to Ralph P. Buxton, January 11, 1864, Governors Papers, Zebulon Baird Vance, North Carolina State Archives.

127. Five men with the name Enoch Davis lived in Moore, Montgomery, and Randolph counties in 1860. Going mainly by age, the Enoch Davis described in this account was likely the one age 24 living at Pharr's Mills in Moore County. He had a wife and 3 young children, possessed no real estate, and $100 in personal property.

128. Thos. W. Ritter to Gov. Vance, January 1, 1864, Governors Papers, ZebulonBaird Vance, North Carolina State Archives.

129. C. Dowd to R.P. Buxton, January 7, 1864, Governors Papers, Zebulon Baird Vance, North Carolina State Archives.

130. Israel Lowdermilk to Bryan Tyson, October 20, 1864, and Kelly H. Trogden to Bryan Tyson, Novbember 22, 1864, Bryan Tyson Papers, Duke Manuscript Department.

131. Case No. 158: State vs. Adams Brewer — warrant for murder of George Moon, Spring Term, 1866, State Docket Superior Court, 1861–1868, Randolph County Records, North Carolina State Archives.

132. New York: Vantage Press, 1966, 72–86.

133. "Murder, Violence and Treason," *Daily Confederate* (Raleigh), February 27, 1864. In 1860, Pleasant Simons, age 62, was a farmer worth $3,500 in real estate and $4,700 in personal property. He owned four slaves. See 1860 Federal Census, Population and Slave Schedules, Moore County, North Carolina. A Jacob Sanders in his sixties is not listed in the 1860 North Carolina Federal Census.

134. "Murder, Violence and Treason," *Daily Confederate* (Raleigh), February 27, 1864.

135. Bynum, *The Long Shadow of the Civil War*, 29, and footnotes 27 and 28, page 156.

136. J.M. Leach to Governor Holden, April 5, 1869, Governor's Papers, William Woods Holden, North Carolina State Archives. In 1860, Murphy Owens lived in the Auman's Hill community in the northeastern corner of Montgomery County. He was 42 years old, a farmer, with $350 in real estate and $200 in personal property. He had a wife and seven children. See 1860 Federal Census, Population Schedule, Montgomery County, North Carolina.

137. *Ibid.*

138. J.M. Leach to Governor Holden, September 1, 1869, Governor's Papers, William Woods Holden, North Carolina State Archives.

139. "Capture of a Noted Outlaw," *Observer* (Fayetteville), April 28, 1864. The sheriff captured Owens about two miles southeast of the residence of Colonel Jesse D. Cox, a merchant living at Stone Lick in southeastern Randolph County. Stone Lick was near Brower's Mills, the home community of Bryan Tyson and Alexander K. Pearce.

140. The 1860 Census listed Alfred Pike, age 43, and father of nine, as a deputy sheriff. It is likely, though not certain, that he held that position during the war. He lived in or near Franklinsville and owned $1700 in real estate, $2100 in personal property, and three slaves. See 1860 Federal Census, Population and Slave Schedules, Randolph County, North Carolina.

141. Thomas Settle to Z.B. Vance, September 21, 1864, Governors Papers, Zebulon Baird Vance, North Carolina State Archives.

142. Thomas Settle to Z.B. Vance, October 4, 1864, Thomas Settle Letters (1863–1864), North Carolina State Archives. These are photocopies of the originals in the Hampton L. Carson Collection, Rare Book Department of the Free Library of Philadelphia. For a recent interpretation of this event, see Myers, "Dissecting the Torture of Mrs. Owens," 141–159. In this article, historian Barton A. Myers based his identification of the wife of the deserter leader on the erroneous claim advanced in my dissertation that she was Mary B. Owens, wife of William B. Owens of Moore County. In fact, she was Adeline, the wife of William Owens of Montgomery County as listed in the 1860 Federal census. See Myers, "Dissecting the Torture of Mrs. Owens," footnote 1, pages 153–154.

143. "Moore County," *Daily Progress* (Raleigh), September 5, 1864.

144. "Chatham Superior Court," *The Patriot* (Greensboro), September 29, 1864.

145. *Weekly Standard* (Raleigh), May 30, 1866.

146. C.J. Hardin, to Lieut. F.J. Hill, May 23, 1864, Letter Book No. 7, May 19, 1864–July 7, 1864, Peter Mallett Papers, Southern Historical Collection.

147. I.H. Foust to Gov. Vance, February 6, 1864, Governors Papers, Zebulon Baird Vance, North Carolina State Archives.

148. *Ibid.*

149. I.H. Foust to Gov. Vance, December 30, 1863, Marmaduke S. Robins Papers, Southern Historical Collection.

150. *Ibid.*

151. *Ibid.*

152. Jesse Kinley to Gov. Z.B. Vance, October 17, 1863, Governors Papers, Zebulon Baird Vance, North Carolina State Archives.

153. Mary Overman to Gov. Vance, October 27, 1863, Governors Papers, Zebulon Baird Vance, North Carolina State Archives.

154. Clarinda Hulin to Mr. Z.B. Vance, November 20, 1863, Governors Papers, Zebulon Baird Vance, North Carolina State Archives.

155. Bynum, *The Long Shadow of the Civil War*, 47 and footnote 38, page 162.

156. Doctor D. Gorden to Z.B. Vance, December 3, 1863, Governors Papers, Zebulon Baird Vance, North Carolina State Archives.

157. Gilliam Jones to Z.B. Vance, January 2, 1864, Governors Papers, Zebulon Baird Vance, North Carolina

State Archives. This may have been the Gilliam Jones listed in the 1860 Randolph County Federal Census. Gilliam, age 50 in 1860, had a wife and ten children, no real estate, and $200 in personal property. His occupation was farm laborer.

158. Delphina E. Mendenhall to Vance, October 9, 1863, Governors Papers, Zebulon Baird Vance, North Carolina State Archives.

159. D.L. May to Vance, November 13, 1863, Governors Papers, Zebulon Baird Vance, North Carolina State Archives.

160. Cowles to V.P. Caldwell, November 26, 1863, Letterpress Book K, Calvin J. Cowles Papers, North Carolina State Archives. For a feminist perspective on the role of women in the inner civil war in the Quaker Belt see Bynum, "'War Within a War': Women's Participation in the Revolt of the North Carolina Piedmont, 1863–1865."

161. Cowles to his brother, November 23, 1863, Letterpress Book K, Calvin J. Cowles Papers, North Carolina State Archives.

162. For example, see Jesse Kinley to Vance, October 17, 1863; Rebecca Varner to Vance, and E.B. Cranford to Vance, November 16, 1863; W.H. George to Vance, November 21, 1863; Governors Papers, Zebulon Baird Vance, North Carolina State Archives.

163. R.F. Hoke to Dr. Hackett, December 8, 1863, Gaden-Hackett Papers, Southern Historical Collection.

164. C. Dowd to Vance, February 15, 1864, Governors Papers, Zebulon Baird Vance, North Carolina State Archives.

165. Poem by a militant Unionist, probably from Taylorsville, Alexander County, ca. 1862–1864, Governors Papers, Zebulon Baird Vance, North Carolina State Archives.

166. General Gideon J. Pillow conducted the largest deserter hunt in the Confederacy in September and October 1863. Pillow, who claimed that he restored over 17,000 men to the army, was the commandant of the conscript bureau for the states of Alabama, Tennessee, and Mississippi. See Lonn, *Desertion During the Civil War*, 53, 89.

Chapter Six

1. Yates, "Governor Vance and the Peace Movement," Part I, 15–17.

2. "A Dialogue," February 3, 1864; "The Fayetteville Observer and the Proposition to call a State Convention," January 20, 1864; "Governor Vance's Wilkesborough Speech," April 6, 1864 — all in the *Weekly Standard* (Raleigh).

3. Extract from a letter from a citizen from Western North Carolina, January 13, 1864; "A Dialogue," February 3, 1864; "To the Voters of Iredell, Wilkes, and Alexander Counties," June 29, 1864; "Another Falsehood Exposed," June 1, 1864; letter to the Standard from "Pacificus," January 27, 1864 — all in the *Weekly Standard* (Raleigh).

4. Nelson, *Bullets, Ballots, and Rhetoric: Confederate Policy for the United States Presidential Contest of 1864*, 140.

5. *Ibid.*, 131; "If You," *Daily Conservative* (Raleigh), July 28, 1864.

6. W.W. Holden to [Thomas Settle], December 22, 1863, Thomas Settle Papers, Southern Historical Collection.

7. "Gov. Vance and the Convention Question," *Weekly Standard* (Raleigh), July 13, 1864.

8. For Holden's views on the convention question, see: "Another Falsehood Exposed," June 1, 1864; "The Fayetteville Observer and the Proposition to Call a State Convention," January 20, 1864; letter to the *Standard* from "Pacificus," January 27, 1864; "Governor Vance's Wilkesborough Speech," April 6, 1864; "A Dialogue," February 3, 1864; "Gov. Vance and the Convention Question," July 13, 1864 — all in the *Weekly Standard* (Raleigh).

9. Vance to "My Dear Sir," January 2, 1864, Zebulon Baird Vance Papers, Private Collections, North Carolina State Archives.

10. Mobley, "Zeb B. Vance: A Confederate Nationalist in the Gubernatorial Election of 1864," 438–439.

11. Escott, "The Failure of Confederate Nationalism," 18–21, and *After Secession*

12. John Gilmer to Vance, January 5, 1864, Zebulon Baird Vance Papers, Private Collections, North Carolina State Archives.

13. Jefferson Davis to [Zeb Vance], January 8, 1864, Zebulon Baird Vance Papers, Private Collections, North Carolina State Archives.

14. Yates, "Governor Vance and the Peace Movement," Part I, 19, Part II, 98–99; Scarboro, "The Peace Movement in Civil War North Carolina," 229–233; Yates, "Vance as War Governor of North Carolina," 69–70; Folk and Shaw, *W. W. Holden*, 179–182; Raper, *William W. Holden*, 50–51; Harris, *William Woods Holden*, 140–143.

15. Z.B. Vance to Jefferson Davis, December 30, 1863, Zebulon Baird Vance Papers, Private Collections, North Carolina State Archives.

16. On slavery and the constitution, see "Negotiations for Peace," *Weekly Standard* (Raleigh), November 23, 1864, and "The Peace Negotiations," *People's Press* (Salem), September 1, 1864.

17. Sanger, ed., *The Statutes at Large, Treaties, and Proclamations, of the United States of America*. XIII, 738.

18. For Lincoln's discussion of this aspect of his proclamation in his third annual message to Congress, delivered on December 8, 1863, see Richardson, ed., *A Compilation of the Messages and Papers of the Presidents, 1789–1897*, VI, 189.

19. *Ibid.*, 190.

20. *Ibid.*

21. *Ibid.*, 191.

22. *Ibid.*, 190.

23. John C. Rives, ed., *The Congressional Globe: Containing the Debates and Proceedings of the First Session of the Thirty-eighth Congress*, 22.

24. "Public Meeting in Johnston County," *Semi-Weekly Standard* (Raleigh), January 12, 1864.

25. "More Trouble," *Carolina Watchman* (Salisbury), January 25, 1864, copied from the *Western Democrat* (Charlotte).

26. I derived the figure 32 from the accounts of peace meetings printed in *The Patriot* (Greensboro), the *Daily Progress* (Raleigh), and the *North Carolina Standard* (Raleigh) between January and August.

27. "North-Carolina" by "Solus" in *Weekly Standard*, January 20, 1864.

28. Letter to the *Weekly Standard* (Raleigh) from "Pacificus," January 27, 1864.

29. Yates, "Governor Vance and the Peace Movement," Part I, 91–92.

30. Messers. Martin, Starbuck, Lash, Wilson, and Wheeler to Thos. Settle, January 7, 1864, Thomas Settle Papers, Southern Historical Collection.

31. Hamilton, *The Correspondence of Jonathan Worth*, I, 254–58, 282, 284–85, 289, 292, 297; Zuber, *Jonathan Worth*, 179.

32. Worth to S.S. Jackson, January 5, 1864, quoted in Zuber, *Jonathan Worth*, 179.

33. Hamilton, *The Correspondence of Jonathan Worth*, I, 282.

34. *Ibid.*, 284, 289.

35. Robert P. Dick to the editor of *The Patriot* (Greensboro), February 18, 1864; "Another Falsehood Exposed," *Semi-Weekly Standard* (Raleigh), May 29, 1864.

36. Public Meeting in Chatham County, *Daily Progress* (Raleigh), January 13, 1864.

37. Fernando Wood (1812–1881), elected mayor of New York City thrice in the late 1850s, was a leader of Tammany Hall. He was a member of the House of Representatives from New York 1863–1865 and 1867–1881. In early 1863, he joined with Clement L. Vallandigham in organizing the peace Democrats. Malone, ed., *Dictionary of American Biography*, X, 456–457.

38. Rives, *Congressional Globe*, 21.

39. Nelson, *Bullets, Ballots, and Rhetoric*, 28, 131.

40. Scarboro, "The Peace Movement in Civil War North Carolina," 218; *Official Records Army*, Series IV, III, 67.

41. *Weekly Standard* (Raleigh), December 30, 1863. This source is a three sentence statement with no title. It is from the bottom left of page 2 or 3 of the December 30 issue; the title page has been lost.

42. Four large planters are known to have supported Holden: Thomas Settle (Rockingham), Alfred Dockery (Richmond), Dr. J.T. Leach (Johnston), and Samuel H. Christian (Montgomery). Several smaller slaveholders supported him such as Bryan Tyson (Moore), Henderson Adams and Lewis Hanes (Davidson), Andrew C. Cowles (Wilkes), and Colonel William B. Richardson (Moore).

43. For examples, see "Gov. Vance's Wilkesborough Speech," April 6, 1864, "The Fayetteville Observer" and "Rumors — Arrests — Mob Law, &c.," January 27, 1864, all in *Weekly Standard* (Raleigh); "Mr. Holden Among the Yankees," May 23, 1864, "Shameful," July 14, 1864, both in *Observer* (Fayetteville); "Holden's Right Hand Man," May 10, 1864, and "Reconstruction," July 22, 1864, both in *Daily Confederate* (Raleigh); "Read This," *Weekly Conservative* (Raleigh), June 1, 1864.

44. "The Chicago Convention," *The Daily Confederate* (Raleigh), September 3, 1864.

45. "The Chicago Convention," *The Daily Conservative* (Raleigh), September 3, 1864.

46. Nelson, *Bullets, Ballots, and Rhetoric*, 28, 131.

47. "North Carolina Politics," *Observer* (Fayetteville), August 27, 1863.

48. See Scarboro, "An Honourable Peace," 111–113, and Auman, "Bryan Tyson: Southern Unionist," 276–285, and "Neighbor Against Neighbor: The Inner Civil War in the Central Counties of Confederate North Carolina" (doctoral dissertation, 1988), 201–213, 219–222, 305–307, 312, 343–347.

49. Historians Horace W. Rapier, Richard E. Yates, Mark W. Kruman, Richard Reid, and A. Sellew Roberts — the leading chroniclers of the Peace Movement in North Carolina — do not indicate in their writings that the Copperheads significantly influenced the Tar Heel Peace men either in the summer 1863 phase or the 1864 Convention stage of the movement. The same can be said for William C. Harris, Horace W. Rapier, Edgar E. Folk, and Bynum Shaw, the biographers of William Woods Holden. Harris did recognize that the peace sentiment among the northern Democrats swayed Holden's views somewhat on peace (pp. 131, 143). Richard L. Zuber in his biography of Jonathan Worth discussed the peace movement (pp. 177–183) but made no connection between the Tar Heel peace faction and the northern peace Democrats. Gordon B. McKinney in his recent biography of Zeb Vance mentioned attempts at cooperation between North Carolina peace advocates and northern Democrats, but he did not go any further in his analysis (pp. 165, 174–175). See Raper, "William W. Holden and the Peace Movement in North Carolina"; Yates, "Governor Vance and the Peace Movement," Part I & II; Roberts, "The Peace Movement in North Carolina"; Reid, "William W. Holden and 'Disloyalty' in the Civil War," 23–44; Kruman, *Parties and Politics in North Carolina, 1836–1865*; Harris, *William Woods Holden: Firebrand of North Carolina Politics*; Raper, *William W. Holden: North Carolina's Political Enigma*; Folk and Shaw, *W.W. Holden: A Political Biography*; McKinney, *Zeb Vance: North Carolina's Civil War Governor and Gilded Age Political Leader*; Zuber, *Jonathan Worth: A Biography of a Unionist*.

50. Manning, "The Order of Nature Would Be Reversed: Soldiers, Slavery, and the Gubernatorial Election of 1864," 101–119. See also Gallagher, "Disaffection, Persistence, and Nation: Some Directions in Recent Scholarship on the Confederacy," 344–345.

51. Manning, "The Order of Nature Would Be Reversed: Soldiers, Slavery, and the Gubernatorial Election of 1864," 110.

52. "Conservatism," *Daily Conservative* (Raleigh), April 26, 1864.

53. "The Secessionists — their Promises and their Performances — the Condition into which they have brought the Country — the Remedy, etc." *Semi-Weekly Standard* (Raleigh), July 31, 1863.

54. Application for Pardon, J.M. Leach, Lexington, North Carolina, 1865, North Carolina State Archives. (Photocopy of the original in the National Archives.)

55. Letter to the editor, *Weekly Standard* (Raleigh), May 27, 1863.

56. "Hon. J.T. Leach's Resolutions And Remarks," *Semi-Weekly Standard* (Raleigh), December 2, 1864.

57. George B. McClellan, pro-slavery Democrat and commander of the Army of the Potomac during the 1862 Peninsula Campaign, received the nomination for the presidency by the Democrats to run against Lincoln in the fall 1864 election.

58. D.L. Swain to [Z.B. Vance], September 28, 1864, Zebulon Baird Vance Papers, Private Collections, North Carolina State Archives.

59. Worth to S.S. Jackson, January 5, 1864, quoted in Zuber, *Jonathan Worth*, 179.

60. Hamilton, *Correspondence of Jonathan Worth*, I, 254–258, 282, 284–285, 289, 292, 297.

61. Dunbar Rowland, ed., *Jefferson Davis Constitutionalist: His Letters, Papers and Speeches*, VI, 165. See also "Vance on Habeas Corpus," *Weekly Standard* (Raleigh), July 6, 1864, and "Tories and Deserters," *Weekly Standard* (Raleigh), July 27, 1864.

62. Dunbar Rowland, ed., *Jefferson Davis Constitutionalist: His Letters, Papers and Speeches*, VI, 167, 169.

63. Yates, "Governor Vance and the Peace Movement," Part II, 92–93. See also Robbins, "The Confederacy and the Writ of Habeas Corpus," 91–92.

64. D.L. Swain to [Z.B. Vance], September 28, 1864, Zebulon Baird Vance Papers, Private Collections, North Carolina State Archives.

65. "To the People of North-Carolina," *Semi-Weekly Standard* (Raleigh), March 3, 1864; Yates, *The Confederacy and Zeb Vance*, 100.

66. Klement, *The Copperheads in the Middle West*, 112–114.

67. Application for Pardon, J.M. Leach, Lexington, North Carolina, 1865, North Carolina State Archives. (Photocopy of the original in the National Archives.)
68. "The Conservatives and Dr. Leach," *Weekly Standard* (Raleigh), May 25, 1864.
69. "An Honorable Peace," *The Patriot* (Greensboro), September 10, 1863.
70. Extract of a letter to the editor from a soldier in camp at Orange Court House, Virginia, November 14, 1863, *Weekly Standard* (Raleigh), November 27, 1863.
71. Jordan and Manarin, *North Carolina Troops: A Roster*, Vol. VII, 1–132.
72. Christopher Hackett to John C. Hackett & Family, January 15, 1864, John C. Hackett Papers, Duke Manuscript Department.
73. Weitz, *More Damning Than Slaughter*, 287.
74. "F" to _____, January 12, 1864, Shaffner Diary and Papers, North Carolina State Archives.
75. "F" to _____, February 4, 1864, Shaffner Diary and Papers, North Carolina State Archives.
76. "F" to _____, April 30, 1864, Shaffner Diary and Papers, North Carolina State Archives.
77. Hatley and Huffman, *Letters of William F. Wagner: Confederate Soldier*, 57, 65, the quote comes from the latter page. For an account of the regimental meetings of North Carolina troops at Orange Court House in August 1863 to discuss the peace issue and the influence of Holden's newspaper in the ranks, see Harris, *William Woods Holden*, 138–139, and editorial in *Semi-Weekly Standard*, August 21, 1863.
78. *Ibid.*, 68.
79. J. W. Bell to Ike Bell, March 14, 1864, A. W. Bell Papers, Duke Manuscript Department, Duke University, as quoted in Hilderman, *Confederate Conscription in North Carolina*, 147.
80. See Jason C. Harris to Gov. Z.B. Vance, March 8, 1864, and A.G. Foster to Gov. Vance, March 13, 1864, Governors Papers, Zebulon Baird Vance, North Carolina State Archives.
81. For biographical sketches of James Madison Leach, see M. Jewell Sink, "James Madison Brown Leach" in Powell, *Dictionary of North Carolina Biography*, 4, 38–39; Warner and Yearns, *Biographical Register of the Confederate Congress*, 147; Dowd, *Sketches of Prominent Living North Carolinians*, 313–315; "James Madison Leach Served both in U.S. and Confederate Congresses," *Randolph Guide* (Asheboro), July 21, 1976. J.M. Leach, aged 34 in 1860, owned real estate worth $20,000, and personal estate worth $15,000. He was married with three children, and he owned three slaves. See 1860 Federal Census, Davidson County, North Carolina. Leach also owned a plantation in Alabama. See "The War — Hon. J.M. Leach," in *The Patriot* (Greensboro), February 13, 1862.
82. Hamilton, *Reconstruction in North Carolina*, 4.
83. "Mr. Holden's Opinion of a 'Holdenite,'" *Observer* (Fayetteville), April 7, 1864. In this article, the *Observer* inaccurately depicted J.M. Leach as a pro-Holden candidate.
84. J.M. Leach to Governor Vance, March 8, 1864, Zebulon Baird Vance Papers, Private Collections, North Carolina State Archives. Note that there are two letters to Vance on March 8 from Leach. The above quotes are from the letter marked "Private".
85. "To the soldiers of the 7th Congressional District," printed broadside dated April 5, 1864, Governors Papers, Zebulon Baird Vance, North Carolina State Ar-chives.
86. A.G. Foster to Gov. Vance, March 13, 1864, Governors Papers, Zebulon Baird Vance, North Carolina State Archives. Alfred G. Foster in 1860 was 34 years old and had a wife and seven children. The value of his real estate was $9,700 and his personal estate $20,000. He owned 27 slaves. See 1860 Federal Census, Population and Slave Schedules, Randolph County, North Carolina.
87. "From the 7th Congressional District," *Observer* (Fayetteville), April 11, 1864.
88. *Ibid.*
89. J.M. Leach to Vance, April 27, 1864, Zebulon Baird Vance Papers, Private Collections, North Carolina State Archives.
90. Application for Pardon, J.M. Leach, Lexington, North Carolina, 1865, North Carolina State Archives. (Photocopy of the original in the National Archives.) Soon after the war ended, President Johnson appointed Holden provisional governor of North Carolina. Leach's postwar claim that he implied reconstruction in his political discourse during the war does not square with his wartime statements that he supported peace based on Confederate independence. See Paul Escott's essay on James Madison Leach in the *Encyclopedia of the Confederacy*, II, 910–911.
91. "The Meeting in Forsyth," *Weekly Standard* (Raleigh), September 2, 1863.
92. *Weekly Standard* (Raleigh), September 9, 1863.
93. "Pen & Ink" to the editor of the *Daily Progress* (Raleigh), May 14, 1864.
94. Sheriffs of the Several Counties of the 7th Congressional District to Gov. Vance, Ap. 28, 1864, Governors Papers, Zebulon Baird Vance, North Carolina State Archives.
95. Yates, "Vance and the Peace Movement," Part II, 96–107; Lefler and Newsome, *North Carolina*, 476–477.
96. Vance spoke at Wilkesborough on February 22, Fayetteville on April 23, Egypt (on Moore–Chatham line) on April 24, Asheboro on May 3, Carthage on May 6, Pittsboro on May 7, Snow Camp (Alamance County) in mid–May. See Yates, "Vance and the Peace Movement," Part II, 101–102.
97. For Holden's denial that he ever said that he intended to use a convention to secede from the Confederacy, see "Hard Run — More Humbuggery," June 8, 1864, and "Another Falsehood Exposed," June 1, 1864, both in the *Weekly Standard* (Raleigh).
98. "The Holdenites are working...," *Weekly Standard* (Raleigh), July 13, 1864; Yates, "Vance and the Peace Movement," Part II, 107; Lefler and Newsome, *North Carolina*, 476; Manning, "The Order of Nature Would Be Reversed: Soldiers, Slavery, and the Gubernatorial Election of 1864," 101–119; Vance's platform is printed in the *Weekly Conservative* (Raleigh), April 27, 1864.
99. Manning, "The Order of Nature Would Be Reversed: Soldiers, Slavery, and the Gubernatorial Election of 1864," 101–119.
100. The two pro-Holden newspapers other than the *Standard* were the Raleigh *Progress* and the Salem *People's Press*. See Yates, "Vance and the Peace Movement," Part II, 105.
101. About Holden's three prominent supporters, see Hamilton, *Reconstruction in North Carolina*, 61. For Worth's position, see Jonathan Worth to Jos. Newlin, July 12, 1864, in Hamilton, *Worth Correspondence*, 1, 321–322.
102. *Semi-Weekly Standard* (Raleigh), May 20, 1864; Yates, "Governor Vance and the Peace Movement," Part II, 109.
103. Scarboro, "An Honourable Peace," 262–264; Yates, "Governor Vance and the Peace Movement," Part II, 109. See also *Journal of the House of Commons ...*

Adjourned Session, 1864, 52–56; *Public Laws of the State of North Carolina passed by the General Assembly at the Sessions of 1861– '62 – '63 – '64, and One in 1859*, Chapter 11, 28; *Semi-Weekly Standard* (Raleigh), May 31, 1864.

104. Zuber, *Jonathan Worth*, 177–178; Jonathan Worth to Jos. Newlin, July 12, 1864, in Hamilton, *Worth Correspondence*, I, 321–322.

105. Kruman, *Parties and Politics in North Carolina*, 262–263.

106. Scarboro, "An Honourable Peace," 288.

107. Hamilton, "Heroes of America," 11.

108. Scarboro, "An Honourable Peace," 265.

109. "The Great Landslide," *Weekly Conservative* (Raleigh), July 27, 1864.

110. "The Criminal Organization," *Weekly Confederate* (Raleigh), July 20, 1864.

111. Yates "Vance and the Peace Movement," Part II, 110; Hamilton, *Reconstruction in North Carolina*, 64.

112. *Conservative* (Raleigh), July 2, 1864. For biographical information on the Methodist circuit rider, see Auman and Scarboro, "The Heroes of America in Civil War North Carolina," 354. In 1860, Orrin Churchill, age 40, had a wife and five children and owned $312 in real estate and $200 in personal property. See 1860 Federal Census, Population Schedule, Chatham County, North Carolina.

113. July 12, 1864.

114. This was probably the same man as the "Dr. E. Phillips" who was one of the leaders of the "Public Meeting" held in the Little River District of Randolph County as reported in the *Weekly Standard* on September 2, 1863. See Hamilton, "Heroes of America," 13–14.

115. "For the Observer, Troy, N.C., July 18, 1864," *Observer* (Fayetteville), August 1, 1864.

116. Noah Auman to Gov. Z.B. Vance, August 12, 1864, Governors Papers, Zebulon Baird Vance, North Carolina State Archives. In 1860, Noah Auman, age 27, was a farmer worth $175 in real and $300 in personal property. See 1860 Federal Census, Population Schedule, Montgomery County, North Carolina.

117. Soon after the war ended, President Johnson appointed W.W. Holden provisional governor of North Carolina—apparently as a reward for his reputation as the leader of the "Peace Party" which most observers considered to be pro-Union and for reconstruction.

118. Noah Auman to Gov. W.W. Holden, July 5, 1865, Governors Papers, William W. Holden, North Carolina State Archives.

119. See County Court Minutes, July 1858–January 1867, 236, Montgomery County Records, North Carolina State Archives, and W.W. Holden Record Book Relative to the Provisional Government, 1865, 61, North Carolina State Archives.

120. Hamilton, "Heroes of America," 10.

121. Daniel Reaves Goodloe, a native of Louisburg, the seat of Franklin County, turned antislavery in 1832. In 1844, he moved north and became a Republican, a newspaper editor, and an abolitionist activist. He wrote numerous abolitionist tracts and became friends with fellow Tar Heel expatriates Hinton R. Helper, Bryan Tyson, and Benjamin Hedrick. After the war, he returned to North Carolina and played a role in Reconstruction politics. See Smith, *A Traitor and a Scoundrel*, 23, 24, 26, 100, 101, 116, 144, 145, 147–150, 152.

122. On Dr. John Lewis Johnson, see Auman and Scarboro, "The Heroes of America in Civil War North Carolina," 336–341. On William F. Henderson, see Hamilton, *Reconstruction in North Carolina*, 281, 364, 367, 388, 497, 505, 580, 601, and "To The H.O.A. In North-Carolina" in the *Weekly Standard* (Raleigh), February 12, 1868. William F. Henderson, age 42 in 1870, had a wife and two young children. He lived in the town of Lexington and listed his occupation as "Int. Rev. Assessor." See 1870 Federal Census, Population Schedule, Davidson County, North Carolina. On Henderson Adams as a founder of the HOA, see *Weekly Standard* (Raleigh), March 13, 1868. See also "To the Voters of Davidson County," in *Weekly Standard* (Raleigh), August 3, 1864, and H. Walser to Gov. Z.B. Vance, August 15, 1864, Zebulon Baird Vance Papers, Private Collections, North Carolina State Archives. In 1860, Henderson Adams, age 48, was a merchant in Lexington worth $8000 in real estate and $20,775 in personal property. He owned eight slaves. See 1860 Federal Census, Population and Slave Schedules, Davidson County, North Carolina. For additional evidence of the Heroes of America in North Carolina and the Quaker Belt during the war, see *Rituals of the First and Second Degrees, Heroes and United Heroes of America*, 4; Jesse Wheeler to B.S. Hedrick, January 12, 1864, B.S. Hedrick Papers, Duke Manuscript Department; A.B. Chapin to Bryan Tyson, June 14 and 20 [1864], Bryan Tyson Papers, Duke Manuscript Department; T.G. Morton to Ralph Gorrell, March 25, 1864, Ralph Gorrell Papers, Southern Historical Collection.

123. A.G. Foster to Gov. Z.B. Vance, June 23, 1864, Governors Papers, Zebulon Baird Vance, North Carolina State Archives.

124. For information on Brownlow, see Tatum, *Disloyalty in the Confederacy*, 5, 6, 143, 146, 147, 149, 151, 152, and Coulter, *William G. Brownlow, Fighting Parson of the Southern Highlands*.

125. Burson, *A Race for Liberty*, 64–65. A photocopy of this book is available online. I am grateful to Mac Whatley of Franklinville, North Carolina, for directing me to this book.

126. *Ibid.*, 72–73.

127. *Weekly Conservative* (Raleigh), July 20, 1864, and August 3, 1864.

128. Letter to the editor by Jno. C. Merrill, *Daily Conservative* (Raleigh), July 26, 1864.

129. Connor, *North Carolina Manual*, 1913, 1000.

130. "The North-Carolina Standard," *Weekly Standard* (Raleigh), August 17, 1864.

131. *The Institution of Slavery in the Southern States* and *Object of the Administration in Persecuting the War*.

132. Bryan Tyson to Governor Vance, September 1, 1864, Governor's Papers, Zebulon Baird Vance, North Carolina State Archives.

133. Connor, *North Carolina Manual*, 999–1000.

134. For accounts of the election in Randolph County, see *Weekly Conservative* (Raleigh), July 20, 1864, and the *Observer* (Fayetteville), August 8, 18, 1864. In 1860, Joel Ashworth, age 39, was a Common School teacher. His real estate was valued at $600 and his personal estate at $590. Enos T. Blair was a farmer, age 38. His real estate was valued at $1,000 and his personal estate at $1,200. Zebidee Rush, age 67, was a farmer worth $3000 in real property and $4500 in personal property. He owned four slaves. Z.F. Rush (listed as Zebidee), age 22 in 1860, lived with his father. His occupation was farm laborer. See 1860 Federal Census, Population and Slave Schedules, Randolph County, North Carolina. For biographical sketches of M.S. Robins, see "Marmaduke Swaim Robins, Outspoken Critic of Times," *Randolph Guide* (Asheboro), July 21, 1976; Dowd, *Sketches of Prominent Living North Car-*

olinians, 64; see also the Marmaduke S. Robins Papers, Southern Historical Collection.

135. "M.S. Robbins, Esq.," *Weekly Standard* (Raleigh), October 5, 1864.

136. "Montgomery County," *Observer* (Fayetteville), August 15, 1864.

137. For election returns in Chatham, Moore, Montgomery, and Davidson counties, see *Observer* (Fayetteville), August 8, 1864.

138. "To the Voters of Davidson County," *Weekly Standard* (Raleigh), August 3, 1864.

139. H. Walser to Gov. Z.B. Vance, August 15, 1864, Zebulon Baird Vance Papers, Private Collections, North Carolina State Archives.

140. James A. Hague to [Vance], August 10, September 28, 1864, Zebulon Baird Vance Papers, Private Collections, North Carolina State Archives; Cheney, *North Carolina Government*, 1312, 1401.

141. "Guilford Election, 1864," and "Guilford Candidates," *The Patriot* (Greensboro), September 1 and July 3, 1864, respectively; Cheney, *North Carolina Government*, 1152–1153, 1400.

142. Cheney, *North Carolina Government*, 1135, 1400; "Stokes and Forsyth," *Weekly Standard* (Raleigh,) July 6, 1864.

143. J.W. Fries to "Dear brother Rufe," August 21, 1864, Patterson Collection, North Carolina State Archives.

144. A.C. Cowles to Z.B. Vance, August 7, 1864, Zebulon Baird Vance Papers, Private Collections, North Carolina State Archives.

145. Two examples of this line of reasoning are Kruman, *Parties and Politics in North Carolina, 1836–1865*, 241–270, and Reid, "William W. Holden and 'Disloyalty' in the Civil War," 43–44.

146. "Conservatism versus Destructivism," *Semi-Weekly Standard* (Raleigh), June 17, 1864; Robbins, "The Confederacy and the Writ of Habeas Corpus," 91.

147. Moore, *Conscription and Conflict in the Confederacy*, 308–310; Yates, "Governor Vance and the Peace Movement," 112; Editorial, *Daily Standard* (Raleigh), April 28, 1865; "The Recent Elections in this State," *Weekly Standard* (Raleigh), August 26, 1864.

148. "Open Ticket" for the *Standard*, *Semi-Weekly Standard* (Raleigh), July 29, 1864. See also "Pen & Ink" to the editor of the Progress, *Daily Progress* (Raleigh), May 14, 1864.

149. "Militia Officers and Magistrates," *Daily Progress* (Raleigh), July 18, 1864.

150. "Extract from a letter to the Editor, dated Randolph Co., August 11, 1864," *Weekly Standard* (Raleigh), August 24, 1864.

151. Editorial, *The Daily Standard* (Raleigh), April 28, 1865; "The Recent Elections in this State," *Weekly Standard* (Raleigh), August 26, 1864; "Open Ticket" for the *Standard*, *Semi-Weekly Standard* (Raleigh), July 29, 1864; Inscoe and McKinney, *The Heart of Confederate Appalachia*, 163; Yates, "Governor Vance and the Peace Movement," 111.

152. Baker, "Class Conflict and Political Upheaval: The Transformation of North Carolina Politics during the Civil War," 178; "The Recent Elections in this State," August 26, 1864; "The Way It Was Done," August 10, 1864, and extract of a letter to the editor from Randolph County, August 24, 1864, all in the *Weekly Standard* (Raleigh).

153. W.W. Holden to J.W.H., July 29, 1864, William Woods Holden Papers, Private Collections, North Carolina State Archives; editorial, *Daily Standard* (Raleigh), April 28, 1865.

154. "False Statement Corrected," *Semi-Weekly Standard*, August 26, 1864.

155. Lefler and Newsome, *North Carolina*, 476.

156. Editorial, *Semi-Weekly Standard*, December 23, 1864.

157. "Boyce Letter," *Semi-Weekly Standard* (Raleigh), October 25, 1864.

158. "Peace! Peace!" *People's Press* (Salem), October 13, 1864. For another call for southern cooperation with the Copperheads, see "A Western Farmer" to the *Standard*, *Semi-Weekly Standard* (Raleigh), June 3, 1864.

159. John Pool (1826–1884) was born on a plantation near Elizabeth City. He graduated from the University of North Carolina in 1847 and served in the state senate in the 1850s. The Opposition party (Whig) nominated him to run for governor in the 1860 election, which he lost in a close race to Democrat John Ellis. He strongly opposed secession and at first refused to take part in the new Confederate government. In 1864, he joined Holden in the convention movement when he was elected to the state senate from Bertie County. He soon emerged as the leading peace advocate in the General Assembly. After the war, he, along with William Holden, supported the Radical Congressional plan of Reconstruction. He was appointed to the U.S. Senate by the General Assembly and took a leading role in the suppression of the Ku Klux Klan during the Kirk-Holden war. After failing to be reappointed to the Senate in 1873, he remained in Washington, D.C., where he practiced law for the remainder of his life. See Powell, *Dictionary of North Carolina Biography*, Vol. 5: 118–119.

160. Inscoe and McKinney, *The Heart of Confederate Appalachia*, 164; "Hon. J.T. Leach's Resolutions And Remarks," *Semi-Weekly Standard* (Raleigh), December 2, 1864.

161. "Peace Resolutions," *Observer* (Fayetteville), December 8, 1864.

162. "The Two Plans" in *Weekly Standard* (Raleigh), December 7, 1864.

163. Pool, *Address of the Hon. John Pool*, 3.

164. "An Act of Gross Discourtesy—The Davis Destructives and Vance Destructives Refuse to Discuss the Question of Peace" in *Weekly Standard* (Raleigh), December 21, 1864.

165. "House of Commons," *Semi-Weekly Standard* (Raleigh), December 20, 1864; Scarboro, "An Honourable Peace," 289–290.

166. "Mr. Sharpe's Resolutions," *Semi-Weekly Standard* (Raleigh), December 20, 1864.

167. "Peace Movements in the Legislature," *Weekly Standard* (Raleigh), January 25, 1865.

168. "Resolutions on the Subject of a General Convention of the Confederate States" in *Weekly Standard* (Raleigh), January 25, 1865. See also "Speech of Mr. Hanes of Davidson" in *Weekly Standard* (Raleigh), February 1, 1865.

169. Speech of Mr. Hanes, of Davidson," *Semi-Weekly Standard* (Raleigh), January 31, 1865.

170. Pool, *Address of the Hon. John Pool*, 3.

171. Weber, *Copperheads*, 82–83.

172. Bryan Tyson to Manton Marble, October 6, 1864, Manton Marble Papers, Library of Congress; George B. McClellan to Bryan Tyson, August 23, 1866?, Bryan Tyson Papers, Duke Manuscript Collection, Durham, North Carolina; Bryan Tyson to Charles Mason, October 1, 1864, Charles Mason Papers, Iowa State Archives, Des

Moines; Bryan Tyson to Samuel F.B. Morse, November 16, 1863, Samuel F.B. Morse Papers, Library of Congress; Auman, "Bryan Tyson: Southern Unionist," 268, 278, 282; Wubben, "Copperhead Charles Mason," 46–65.

173. On the Republican refusal to cooperate with southern Unionists and the peace movement in the south, see Smith, *A Traitor and a Scoundrel*, 117–118; Auman and Scarboro, "The Heroes of America," 340–341.

174. Tyson, *Object of the Administration*, 9.

175. *Ibid.*, 8.

176. Bryan Tyson to Charles Mason, May 24, 1880, Charles Manson Papers, Iowa State Archives, Des Moines.

177. *Object of the Administration*, 9.

178. "B. Tyson" to the editor, *Weekly Standard* (Raleigh), June 18, 1862.

179. Tyson, "To the Editor of the Chronicle," July 2, 1869. Strother (listed as "T."K. Strother in the 1860 census) owned $1200 in real estate and $1000 in personal property. See 1860 Federal Census for Wake County, North Carolina.

180. Bryan Tyson to Governor Holden, July 7, 1870, Governors Papers, William Woods Holden, North Carolina State Archives.

Chapter Seven

1. Moore, *Conscription and Conflict in the Confederacy*, 308; Clark's *Regiments*, IV, 407–408.

2. D.C. Pearson to Lieut. E.R. Holt, July 2, 1864, Confederate Conscript Office Papers, Seventh North Carolina District, Southern Historical Collection. The seventh congressional district included the Quaker Belt counties of Randolph, Chatham, Moore, Montgomery, and Davidson.

3. D.C. Pearson, Capt. & EO, to E.O. Randolph, June 10, 1864, Confederate Conscript Office Papers, Seventh North Carolina District, Southern Historical Collection.

4. Capt. Jones' Co. (Supporting Force) Compiled Service Records of Confederate Soldiers who Served In Organizations From the State of North Carolina, Roll 578, National Archives Microfilm Publication, Microcopy No. 270 (Washington, D. C., 1960).

5. Major N.G. Hunt to Capt. Jarrett, July 15, 1864, Jarrett-Puryear Papers, Duke Manuscript Department.

6. [R.L. Gatlin] to Maj. A.A. Harbin, July 16, 1864, Home Guard Letter Book, 1863–65, Adjutant Generals Papers (AG 52), North Carolina State Archives.

7. [R.L. Gatlin] to Maj. A.A. Harbin, July 18, 1864, Home Guard Letter Book, 1863–65, Adjutant Generals Papers (AG 52), North Carolina State Archives.

8. Bench Warrant for M.L. Cranfield, executed August 8, 1864, and W.A. Joice and R.F. Armfield to Maj. J.R. McLean, July 30, 1864, Richmond M. Pearson Papers, Duke Manuscript Department. See also "The Threats of Deserters and Tories," *Weekly Conservative* (Raleigh), July 27, 1864.

9. Major J.R. McLean to Hon. R.M. Pearson, August 4, 1864, Richmond M. Pearson Papers, Duke Manuscript Department.

10. Officials named Benjamin and Lee Willard as leaders of the deserter gang involved in the Yadkin schoolhouse shootout. See *Official Records Army*, Series I, Vol. XVIII, 880–881.

11. *Ibid.*

12. "Broke Jail," *Weekly Conservative* (Raleigh), February 1, 1865.

13. C.J. Cowles to W.W. Holden, July 25, 1864, Calvin J. Cowles Papers, North Carolina State Archives.

14. Major J.R. McLean to Hon. R.M. Pearson, August 4, 1864, Richmond M. Pearson Papers, Duke Manuscript Department.

15. L.D. Sugart to Maj. McLean, July 30, 1864, Richmond M. Pearson Papers, Duke Manuscript Department.

16. "Tories Captured," *Daily Conservative* (Raleigh), July 28, 1864; Major J.R. McLean to Hon. R.M. Pearson, August 4, 1864, Richmond M. Pearson Papers, Duke Manuscript Department. The quotation comes from the McLean letter.

17. "Another Murder by Deserters," *Observer* (Fayetteville), July 11, 1864, and "Another Murder by Deserters," *Weekly Confederate* (Raleigh), July 13, 1864. "Jo. Younger" may have been Joseph Younger, age 41 in 1864, farmer with a wife and four young children and $200 in real estate and $400 in personal property. See 1860 Federal Census, Population Schedule, Wilkes County, North Carolina. His Post Office was Wilkesboro.

18. "Murder in Davie," *Daily Conservative* (Raleigh), July 16, 1864.

19. "The Threats of Deserters and Tories," *Weekly Conservative* (Raleigh), July 27, 1864.

20. "Tories Captured," *Weekly Conservative* (Raleigh), August 3, 1864.

21. Major J.R. McLean to Hon. R.M. Pearson, August 4, 1864; Bench Warrant for M.L. Cranfield, executed August 8, 1864; L.D. Sugart to Maj. McLean, July 30, 1864, Richmond M. Pearson Papers, Duke Manuscript Department.

22. Notes of testimony given by witnesses pertaining to M.L. Cranfill [Cranfield] of Yadkin County on examination before Maj. J.R. McLean at Camp Vance prior to the arrest of Cranfill [July or August 1864], Richmond M. Pearson Papers, Duke Manuscript Department.

23. Arthur, *A History of Watauga County, North Carolina*, 168.

24. C.J. Cowles to W.W. Holden, July 25, 1864, Calvin J. Cowles Papers, North Carolina State Archives

25. Barrett, *Civil War in North Carolina*, 233–235.

26. Some observers credited Kirk forces to be nearly 300 strong. *Ibid.*, 233.

27. *Ibid.*

28. *Ibid.*, 235.

29. For a particularly lucid example of this type of yellow journalism, see Jno. C. Merrill's letter to the editor, *Daily Conservative*, July 26, 1864.

30. E.O. for Montgomery Co. to Capt. D.C. Pearson, Chief E.O., June 29, 1864, Confederate Conscript Office Papers, Seventh North Carolina District, Southern Historical Collection.

31. *Ibid.*

32. Thomas H. Houghton to Capt. D.C. Pearson, July 11, 1864, Confederate Conscript Office Papers, Seventh North Carolina District, Southern Historical Collection.

33. Thomas H. Haughton to Capt. D.C. Pearson, July 14, [1864], Confederate Conscript Office Papers, Seventh North Carolina District, Southern Historical Collection.

34. J.A. Little to Capt. Pearson, July 11, 1864, Confederate Conscript Office Papers, Seventh North Carolina District, Southern Historical Collection.

35. Conscription Report for Moore County, for Month of July 1864, Confederate Conscript Office Papers, Seventh North Carolina District, Southern Historical Collection.

36. *Ibid.*

37. Lt. E.R. Holt to Capt. D.C. Pearson, C.E.O. 7th

Dist., July 19, 1864, Confederate Conscript Office Papers, Seventh North Carolina District, Southern Historical Collection.

38. "Disturbance at Camp Holmes," *Daily Conservative* (Raleigh), July 13, 1864.

39. "'Heroes' in Chatham," *Weekly Conservative* (Raleigh), August 3, 1864. See also John A. Hanks to Gov. Vance, July 20, 1864, Governors Papers, Zebulon Baird Vance, North Carolina State Archives.

40. "Look Out for the Deserters and Robbers," *Observer* (Fayetteville), July 18, 1864.

41. "More Warnings," *Daily Confederate* (Raleigh), July 20, 1864.

42. Adjt. Genl. to Lt. Col. I.H. Foust, July 25, 1864, Home Guard Letter Book, 1863–65 (AG 52), Adjutant Generals Papers, North Carolina State Archives.

43. *Ibid*.

44. Adjt. Genl. to Lt. Col. E.L. Yellowly, July 27, 1864, Adjutant General Letter Book, 1864–1865, Adjutant Generals Papers, North Carolina State Archives.

45. Capt. Pearson to En. Off. Randolph Co., July 29, 1864, Confederate Conscript Office Papers, Seventh North Carolina District, Southern Historical Collection.

46. "Deserters Voting at the Election," *Observer* (Fayetteville), August 15, 1864. See also P.H. Williamson to Capt. D.C. Pearson, August 1, 1864, Confederate Conscript Office Papers, Seventh North Carolina District, Southern Historical Collection.

47. E. Garner to Z.B. Vance, August 19, 1864, Governors Papers, Zebulon Baird Vance, North Carolina State Archives.

48. C.D. Caddell to A.S. Caddell, August 2, 1864, Artemus S. Caddell Papers, Duke Manuscript Department.

49. "Outrages in Moore County," *Observer* (Fayetteville), August 11, 1864. The article stated that witnesses saw armed bands of deserters up to 900 in number. This was probably a misprint, 90 having been the intended number.

50. Mrs. L.J. Dowd, "Reminiscences from Moore County," *Morning Post* (Raleigh), August 17, 1905.

51. A.M. Dunlap to A.S. Caddell, August 22, September 16, 1864, Artemus S. Caddell Papers, Duke Manuscript Department. Quotations are from the August letter.

52. P.H. Williamson to Capt. D.C. Pearson, Aug. 1, 1864, Confederate Conscript Office Papers, Seventh North Carolina District, Southern Historical Collection.

53. Wellman, *The County of Moore 1847–1947*, 58.

54. Shields, *Country Doctor for a Half Century*, 27. The members of the Supporting Force killed by the deserters were D.R. Rush of Randolph, and J.C. Dodd and John Howard of Chatham. E. Womble of Chatham was the one mortally wounded. See "Outrages in Moore County," *Observer* (Fayetteville), August 11, 1864, and "Deserters Attack the Home Guard," *Daily Watchman* (Salisbury), August 15, 1864.

55. "Deserters Attack the Home Guard," *Daily Watchman* (Salisbury), August 15, 1864.

56. Shields, *Country Doctor for a Half Century*, 27.

57. *Ibid*. Wellman, *County of Moore*, 59.

58. Jane to her brother, August 8, 1864, Lewis O. Sugg Letters, Duke Manuscript Department.

59. "A Raid on Troy," *People's Press* (Salem), August 18, 1864.

60. H.J. Haughton to [Gov. Vance], August 9, 1864, Governors Papers, Zebulon Baird Vance, North Carolina State Archives.

61. *Ibid*.

62. J.M. Worth to Gov. Z.B. Vance, August 9, 1864, Governors Papers, Zebulon Baird Vance, North Carolina State Archives.

63. *Ibid*.

64. A.G. Foster to Gov. Vance, August 27, 1864, Zebulon Baird Vance Papers, Private Collections, North Carolina State Archives. For proof that Zebedee Rush (age 67 in 1860) was the father of Z.F. Rush (the sheriff elect) and Noah Rush (the commander of Randolph's Fifth Battalion Home Guards), see "Will of Zebedee Rush of Randolph County, North Carolina," Will Book 15, p. 85, Randolph County Courthouse, Asheboro, North Carolina. In 1860, Zebidee Rush, age 67, was a farmer worth $3000 in real property and $4500 in personal property. He owned four slaves. Z.F. Rush (listed as Zebidee), age 22 in 1860, lived with his father. His occupation was farm laborer. See 1860 Federal Census, Population and Slave Schedules, Randolph County, North Carolina.

65. J.M. Worth to Gov. Z.B. Vance, August 9, 1864, Governors Papers, Zebulon Baird Vance, North Carolina State Archives.

66. Noah Rush, age 37 in 1860, was a farmer with a wife and five children. He had $2500 in real property and $800 in personal property. See 1860 Federal Census, Population Schedule, Randolph County, North Carolina.

67. See Richard Anderson to Gov. Vance, September 19, 1864, Zebulon Baird Vance Papers, Private Collections, North Carolina State Archives.

68. The other three times had been in the fall of 1862, in the winter of 1863, and in the summer, fall, and winter of 1863–1864. See above, chapters three and five.

69. Special Orders No. 74, August 13, 1864, General and Special Orders to the Home Guard, 1863–1865, Adjutant Generals Papers (AG 35), North Carolina State Archives. The local Home Guard Battalions already in each county are included in these figures.

70. Josiah Jones to Capt. Pearson, August 11, 1864, Confederate Conscript Office Papers, Seventh North Carolina District, Southern Historical Collection.

71. Lewis Waynick to Sarah Waynick, August 22, 1864, Capus M. Waynick Collection, North Carolina State Archives.

72. Thomas Miller to Gov. Vance, August 22, 1864, Governors Papers, Zebulon Baird Vance, North Carolina State Archives.

73. A.M. Dunlap to A.S. Caddell, August 22, 1864, Artemus S. Caddell Papers, Duke Manuscript Department.

74. Josiah Cowles to C.J. Cowles, August 1, 1864, Calvin J. Cowles Papers, North Carolina State Archives.

75. Special Orders No. 71, August 9, 1864, General and Special Orders to the Home Guard, 1863–1865, Adjutant Generals Papers (AG 35), North Carolina State Archives.

76. "Deserters in the West," *Observer* (Fayetteville), August 18, 1864, and "Trouble in Wilkes," *People's Press* (Salem), August 18, 1864. In September 1864, Wilkes County officials claimed deserters in the county killed only one Confederate soldier in August. See "Public Meeting in Wilkes County," *Weekly Conservative* (Raleigh), September 14, 1864.

77. "Outrages in Moore County," *Observer* (Fayetteville), August 11, 1864.

78. Quoted in the *Daily Watchman* (Salisbury), August 19, 1864. See also "Outrages of Deserters and Tories," *Western Democrat* (Charlotte), August 23, 1864.

79. Special Order No. 78, August 20, 1864, Special

Order No. 80, August 24, 1864, and Special Order No. 82, August 27, 1864. General and Special Orders to the Home Guard, 1863–1865, Adjutant Generals Papers (AG 35), North Carolina State Archives; [R. L. Gatlin] to Maj. J. Masten, August 20, 1864, Home Guard Letter Book, 1863–65, Adjutant Generals Papers (AG 52), North Carolina State Archives.

80. Special Order No. 91, Home Guard Letter Book, 1863–65, Adjutant Generals Papers (AG 52), North Carolina State Archives. For an account of the Lowery band, a Robeson County Lumbee Indian guerrilla group, see Evans, *To Die Game*, 3–53.

81. Special Order No. 78, August 20, 1864, Special Order No. 80, August 24, 1864, and Special Order No. 82, August 27, 1864. General and Special Orders to the Home Guard, 1863–1865, Adjutant Generals Papers (AG 35), North Carolina State Archives; [R. L. Gatlin] to Maj. J. Masten, August 20, 1864, Home Guard Letter Book, 1863–65, Adjutant Generals Papers (AG 52), North Carolina State Archives.

82. Entry for September 5, 1864, in Diary of J. Gwyn, 1852–1877, in Thurmond Chatham Papers, North Carolina State Archives.

83. [R.L. Gatlin] to Maj. J. Masten, August 20, 1864, Home Guard Letter Book, 1863–65, Adjutant Generals Papers (AG 52), North Carolina State Archives.

84. [R.L. Gatlin] to J.H. Alspaugh, August 22, 1864, Home Guard Letter Book, 1863–65, Adjutant Generals Papers (AG 52), North Carolina State Archives.

85. [R.L. Gatlin] to Maj. A.A. Harbin, August 26, 1864, Home Guard Letter Book, 1863–65, Adjutant Generals Papers (AG 52), North Carolina State Archives; H.D. Low to R.L. Patterson, August 22, 1864, Patterson Collection, North Carolina State Archives.

86. *Official Records Army*, Series I, Vol. LI, Part II, 1038–1039.

87. J.L. Wright to his father, September 2, 1864, John Wright Family Papers, North Carolina State Archives.

88. Entry for September 23, 1864, John F. Flintoff Diary, North Carolina State Archives.

89. Entry for May 1, 1865, John F. Flintoff Diary, North Carolina State Archives.

90. "Outrages by Tories and Others," *Weekly Standard* (Raleigh), January 25, 1865.

91. Adjt. Genl. to Maj. W.D. Barringer, August 26, 1864, Home Guard Letter Book, 1863–65, Adjutant Generals Papers (AG 52), North Carolina State Archives. For similar orders to a Davie County officer, see [R.L. Gatlin] to Maj. A.A. Harbin, July 18, 1864, Home Guard Letter Book, 1863–65, Adjutant Generals Papers (AG 52), North Carolina State Archives.

92. A. G. Foster to Gov. Vance, August 27, 1864, Zebulon Baird Vance Papers, Private Collections, North Carolina State Archives.

93. The 1860 Census lists a Jesse Hargrave, age 22, as living at Jackson Hill. His real estate was valued at $15,000 and personal estate at $46,363. He owned 60 slaves. See 1860 Federal Census, Population and Slave Schedules, Davidson County, North Carolina.

94. A.G. Foster to Gov. Vance, August 27, 1864, Zebulon Baird Vance Papers, Private Collections, North Carolina State Archives.

95. See also [R.L. Gatlin] to Maj. A.A. Harbin, July 18, 1864, Home Guard Letter Book, 1863–65, Adjutant Generals Papers (AG 52), North Carolina State Archives.

96. Adjt. Genl. to Lt. Col. J. Hargrave, Aug. 29, 1864, Home Guard Letter Book, 1863–65, Adjutant Generals Papers (AG 52), North Carolina State Archives.

97. *Ibid.*

98. Adjt. Genl. to Col. S.A. Sharpe, August 30, 1864, Home Guard Letter Book, 1863–65, Adjutant Generals Papers (AG 52), North Carolina State Archives.

99. "Have We Civil Liberty?" November 9, 1864, and "Have We Any Civil Law In North-Carolina," October 5, 1864, both in *Weekly Standard* (Raleigh).

100. Lewis Waynick to Sally Waynick, August 29, 1864, Capus M. Waynick Collection, North Carolina State Archives.

101. Lewis Waynick to his wife, August 30, 1864, Capus M. Waynick Collection, North Carolina State Archives.

102. W.S. Cavness to Carrie Jackson, August 24, 1864, Carrie Jackson Papers, Southern Historical Papers.

103. A.M. Dunlap to A.S. Caddell, Esq., September 6, 1864, Artemus S. Caddell Papers, Duke Manuscript Department.

104. Rany G. Caddell to A.S. Caddell, September 22, 1864, Artemus S. Caddell Papers, Duke Manuscript Department.

105. Wm. Lindly to Gov. Vance [Sept. 1864?], Governors Papers, Zebulon Baird Vance, North Carolina State Archives.

106. *Ibid.*

107. In 1860, Isham Wallace, farmer, lived in Caledonia, Moore County, with a wife and five children. His four sons were ages 17, 14, 12, and 10. His real estate was worth $5000 and personal property $1000. See 1860 Federal Census, Moore County, North Carolina.

108. Tyson, *Object of the Administration*, 7. Tyson did not give a date for this incident.

109. *Ibid.*, 8. Tyson did not give a date for this incident.

110. Burson, *Race for Liberty*, 70.

111. *Ibid.*

112. *Ibid.*, 71–72.

113. "A letter to the Editors of the *Confederate* from Stokes county," *Daily Watchman* (Salisbury), August 26, 1864.

114. "Deserters," *People's Press* (Salem), September 8, 1864.

115. "A letter to the Editors of the *Confederate* from Stokes county," *Daily Watchman* (Salisbury), August 26, 1864.

116. For a detailed account of this action, see "Tories Captured in Watauga County," *Daily Conservative*, August 30, 1864.

117. Collett Leventhorpe (1816–1889), a native of Exmouth, England, was an author, physician, and soldier. He resigned his captaincy in the Fourteenth Regiment of Foot of the British army in 1842, and settled in North Carolina about 1847. After service as a colonel in the Eleventh Regiment North Carolina Troops, he resigned his commission for reasons of health. He had been wounded at Gettysburg, captured, imprisoned, and exchanged. In September 1864, he accepted a commission from Governor Vance as brigadier general in the Home Guards. He died in Happy Valley, Caldwell County. See Manarin and Jordan, *North Carolina Troops*, V, 6, and Cole and Foley, *Collett Leventhorpe: The English Confederate*.

118. Special Order No. 86, September 1, 1864, General and Special Orders to the Home Guard, 1863–1865, Adjutant Generals Papers (AG 35), North Carolina State Archives.

119. Adjt. Genl. to Brig. Genl. C. Leventhorpe, Comdg. H. G. Asheboro, N. C., September 14, 1864,

Home Guard Letter Book, 1863–65, Adjutant Generals Papers (AG 52), North Carolina State Archives.

120. "Deserters," September 8, 1864.

121. "Deserters Coming In," *Observer* (Fayetteville), September 19, 1864.

122. "Deserters Surrendered and Taken," *Observer* (Fayetteville), September 24, 1864.

123. Massah Trogdon to M.S. Robins, September 25, 1864, Marmaduke S. Robins Papers, Southern Historical Collection.

124. A.C. Allen to N.H. Brown, September 12, 1864, Hamilton Brown Papers, Southern Historical Collection.

125. Arthur, *A History of Watauga County*, 168. It was likely that Granville was a close relative of Gideon Smoot, who along with John Quincey Adams Bryan led the deserter uprising in Wilkes County in the late summer of 1863. In 1860, Granville Smoot was a thirty-nine-year-old farmer living at Trap Hill. He had a wife and seven children. His real and personal property each were worth $500. See 1860 Federal census, population schedule, Wilkes County, North Carolina.

126. "Stokes County," *Weekly Standard* (Raleigh), September 21, 1864.

127. "Another Barn Burnt," *Observer* (Fayetteville), September 19, 1864. The Raper barn incident is in the *People's Press* (Salem), September 8, 1864.

128. Adjt. Genl. to Brig. Genl. C. Leventhorpe, Sept. 19, 1864, Home Guard Letter Book, 1863–65, Adjutant Generals Papers (AG 52), North Carolina State Archives.

129. Adjt. Genl. to Col. W. Draughan, Sept. 27, 1864, Home Guard Letter Book, 1863–65, Adjutant Generals Papers (AG 52), North Carolina State Archives.

130. *Ibid*; Charity Robins to M.S. Robins, October 1, 1864, Marmadude S. Robins Papers, Southern Historical Collection.

131. Phebe Crook to Mr. Vance, September 15, 1864, Governors Papers, Zebulon Baird Vance, North Carolina State Archives.

132. *Ibid*.

133. Bynum, *The Long Shadow of the Civil War*, 47–48.

134. Martha Hough to Gov. Vance, September 28, 1864, Governors Papers, Zebulon Baird Vance, North Carolina State Archives.

135. [Mrs. B.S. Hedrick?] to "Dear brother John," n.d., n.p., Benjamin Sherwood Hedrick Papers, Duke Manuscript Department. Though the correspondence is undated, the content of the letter suggests that the author wrote it in late 1864 or early 1865 in Washington, D.C., where the Hedricks were living during the war.

136. J.M. Leach to Gov. Vance, September 18, 1864, Zebulon Baird Vance Papers, Private Collections, North Carolina State Archives.

137. *Ibid*.

138. *Ibid*.

139. *Ibid*.

140. Thomas Settle, a wealthy planter from Rockingham County who owned 26 slaves, was a state solicitor during the war. He was a staunch peace man. After the war, he was a leading Republican in the state. In 1876, his defeat by Vance in the gubernatorial contest marked the end of the Reconstruction Era in North Carolina. See Lefler and Newsome, *North Carolina*, 485, 488, 501. It is interesting to note that Thomas Settle's plantation house, though unoccupied, is still standing a few miles northwest of Wentworth, the seat of Rockingham County. The house and grounds should be preserved as a state historical site.

141. Thomas Settle to Z.B. Vance, October 4, 1864, Thomas Settle Letters (1863–1864), North Carolina State Archives. These letters are photocopies of the originals in the Hampton L. Carson Collection, Rare Book Department of the Free Library of Philadelphia.

142. *Ibid*.

143. "Arbitrary Power—Mob Law," *Semi-Weekly Standard* (Raleigh), October 7, 1864.

144. "Circular" September 27, 1864, Home Guard Letter Book, 1863–65, Adjutant Generals Papers (AG 52), North Carolina State Archives.

145. R.L. Gatlin to Col. S.A. Sharpe, October 8, 1864, Home Guard Letter Book, 1863–65, Adjutant Generals Papers (AG 52), North Carolina State Archives. The ten counties were Cumberland, Mecklenburg, Chatham, Davie, Montgomery, Wayne, Edgecombe, Iredell, Wilson, and Forsyth.

146. September 30, 1864.

147. Lt. Col. Jesse Hargrave—commander of the Davidson County Home Guard battalion, and the senior Home Guard officer who led the deserter hunt in the Randolph County area in the summer of 1864—in a letter to Governor Vance, verified that the Governor used precisely that language. See Lt. Col. Jesse Hargrave to Z.B. Vance, October 5, 1864, Zebulon Baird Vance Papers, Private Collections, North Carolina State Archives.

148. "Have We any Civil Law in North Carolina?" *Daily Progress* (Raleigh), September 30, 1864.

149. October 24, 1864. I am indebeted to Mac Whatley for bringing this article to my attention.

150. Quoted in article titled "Arbitrary Power—Mob Law," *Weekly Standard* (Raleigh), October 12, 1864.

151. *Ibid*.

152. *Ibid*. For other articles denouncing the repressive measures taken by Vance against the deserter uprising in the aftermath of the 1864 election, see "'Citizen' Again," *People's Press* (Salem), December 8, 1864; "Have We Civil Liberty," *Weekly Standard* (Raleigh), November 9, 1864; "Outrages by Tories and Others," *Weekly Standard* (Raleigh), January 25, 1865; Editorial, *Daily Standard* (Raleigh), April 28, 1865.

153. Lt. Col. Jesse Hargrave to Z.B. Vance, October 5, 1864, Zebulon Baird Vance Papers, Private Collections, North Carolina State Archives.

154. *Ibid*.

155. *Ibid*.

156. Z. B. Vance to Genl. Whiting, September 28, 1864, Governors Letter Books, Zebulon Baird Vance, North Car-olina State Archives.

157. "Militia and Home Guards," *The Patriot* (Greensboro), December 8, 1864.

158. Viewing Governor Vance as a "Champion of Personal Freedom" is the underlying theme of Glenn Tucker's biog-raphy of Vance entitled *Zeb Vance: Champion of Personal Freedom*.

159. "Have We Any Civil Law In North-Carolina," *Weekly Standard* (Raleigh), October 5, 1864.

160. "House of Commons" and "Resolutions Introduced by Mr. Ashworth" in *Weekly Standard* (Raleigh), February 1, 1865.

161. See Editorial, *Daily Standard* (Raleigh), April 28, 1865, and "The Outrages in Randolph" *Weekly Standard* (Raleigh), February 3, 1865. See also "Outrages in Randolph and Other Counties" in *Ibid.*, February 1, 1865.

162. Letter from "A Quaker" to the editor of the *Conservative* printed in the *Semi-Weekly Standard* (Raleigh), February 14, 1865. See also the editorial on Governor Vance, *The Daily Standard* (Raleigh), April 28, 1865.

163. Cole and Foley, *Collett Leventhrope*, 139.

164. *Read and Circulate! The elections in August imposed upon the people of North Carolina....* (North Carolina, 1872). Available online through the University of North Carolina's "Documenting the American South."

165. Cole and Foley, *Collett Leventhrope*, 139–40, 177–78.

166. On the 1876 gubernatorial contest in North Carolina and the issue of wartime abuses of civilians by Governor Vance, see McKinney, "Zebulon Vance and the Reconstruction of the Civil War in North Carolina," 78–80, 83, and Crow, "Thomas Settle, Jr., Reconstruction, and the Memory of the Civil War," 696–698, 715–719, 724, 726.

167. Pool, *Address of the Hon. John Pool*, 2, 3. For an account of the "Laural Massacre," where over a dozen captured Unionists were hung by Confederate authorities, see Paludan, *Victims*.

Chapter Eight

1. Barrett, *The Civil War in North Carolina*, 244–261.

2. *Ibid.*, 231, 262–263.

3. General Orders No. 24, October 4, 1864, General and Special Orders to the Home Guard, 1863–65, Adjutant Generals Papers (AG 35), North Carolina State Archives.

4. *Ibid.*, and General Orders No. 27, October 29, 1864, General and Special Orders to the Home Guard, 1863–65, Adjutant Generals Papers, North Carolina State Archives.

5. Jno. W. Hinsdale to Capt. D. C. Pearson, October 7, 1864, Confederate Conscript Office Papers, Seventh North Carolina District, Southern Historical Collection; "6th Regiment Reserves," *Observer* (Fayetteville), December 19, 1864. The Sixth Regiment North Carolina Senior Reserves was also denoted as the Seventy-sixth Regiment North Carolina Troops. See Clark, *The Histories of North Carolina Regiments*, IV, 4.

6. Capt. D.C. Pearson, District EO, Circular No. 27, September 30, 1864, Confederate Conscript Office Papers, Seventh North Carolina District, Southern Historical Collection.

7. Clark, *The Histories of North Carolina Regiments*, IV, 652.

8. "Disloyalty in Forsyth," *People's Press* (Salem), October 27, 1864.

9. *Ibid.*

10. [R.L. Gatlin] to Maj. W. Vannoy, October 27, 1864, and [R.L. Gatlin] to Maj. J. Mastin, October 28, 1864, Home Guard Letter Book, 1863–65, Adjutant Generals Papers (AG 52), North Carolina State Archives.

11. Editorial, *Daily Watchman* (Salisbury), October 24, 1864; "The Forsyth Home Guards," *Weekly Standard* (Raleigh), October 26, 1864.

12. "Arrested," *People's Press* (Salem), November 3, 1864. Camp Stokes, a Confederate Camp of Instruction for draftees, was established near Greensboro in October 1864. It replaced Camp Vance near Morganton, which authorities had disbanded. See "Camp Vance," *People's Press* (Salem), October 27, 1864.

13. Jesse Wheeler to B.S. Hedrick, November 27, 1864, Benjamin Sherwood Hedrick Papers, Duke Manuscript Department.

14. "Several days ago," *Daily Conservative* (Raleigh), November 4, 1864.

15. *Ibid.*

16. "The Deserters in Wilkes County," *Daily Conservative* (Raleigh), November 18, 1864.

17. "Are Highly Gratified," *Daily Conservative*, November 14, 1864. In 1860, Michael Williams, age 60, had a wife and eight children between the ages of four and seventeen. He was a farmer living in the upper division of Wilkes County. His real estate was worth $3000, his personal estate $6000. See 1860 Federal Census for Wilkes County, North Carolina.

18. For example, see "To Governor Vance," *Weekly Standard* (Raleigh), December 14, 1864.

19. "To Governor Vance," *Semi-Weekly Standard* (Raleigh), November 25, 1864.

20. In 1860, Harrison Church, age 24, was a farmer living in the Perlier's Creek community. He had a wife and two young children. He was worth $300 in real and $200 in personal property. See 1860 Federal Census, Population Schedule, Wilkes County, North Carolina.

21. "A Fight in Wilkes," *Weekly Conservative* (Raleigh), November 16, 1864.

22. "A Deserter," *Daily Watchman* (Salisbury), December 21, 1864.

23. Special Orders No. 140, November 12, 1864, General and Special Orders to the Home Guard, 1863–65, Adjutant Generals Papers, North Carolina State Archives.

24. "Outrages in Surry County," *Observer* (Fayetteville), December 15, 1864.

25. "A Fight in Watauga," *People's Press* (Salem), November 24, 1864; "The Home Guard of Watauga County," *Daily Conservative* (Raleigh), November 18, 1864.

26. Document No. 1, Session 1864–1865 in *Legislative Documents, 1864–1865, 1865–1866*, 2.

27. *Ibid.*

28. Special Orders No. 171, December 19, 1864, General and Special Orders to the Home Guard, 1863–65, Adjutant Generals Papers, North Carolina State Archives.

29. Barrett, *Civil War in North Carolina*, 266–270.

30. Special Orders No. 2, January 4, 1865, General and Special Orders to the Home Guard, 1863–65, Adjutant Generals Papers, North Carolina State Archives.

31. Special Orders No. 6, January 13, 1865, General and Special Orders to the Home Guard, 1863–65, Adjutant Generals Papers (AG 35), North Carolina State Archives.

32. Special Orders No. [left blank], January 27, 1865, General and Special Orders to the Home Guard, 1863–65, Adjutant Generals Papers (AG 35), North Carolina State Archives.

33. George A. Foust to M.S. Robins, October 6, 1864, and J.M. Odell to Capt. M.S. Robins, October 17, 1864, Marmaduke S. Robins Papers, Southern Historical Collection.

34. J.H. Welborn to Maj. M. Lane, October 24, 1864, Confederate Conscript Office Papers, Seventh North Carolina District, Southern Historical Collection.

35. Adjutant General to Lt. Col. I.H. Foust, November 5, 1864, Home Guard Letter Book, 1863–65, Adjutant Generals Papers (AG 52), North Carolina State Archives.

36. John Staley to John W. Staley, November 29, 1864, John W. Staley Papers, Duke Manuscript Department.

37. "Outrages of Deserters, etc.," *Observer* (Fayetteville), November 28, 1864; Elizabeth Staley to John W. Staley, December 7, 1864, and Milton R. Fox to John W. Staley, December 25, 1864, John W. Staley Papers, Duke Manuscript Department.

38. "Outrages of Deserters," *Observer* (Fayetteville), November 28, 1864.

39. D. Curtis to M.S. Robins, January 9, 1865, Marmaduke S. Robins Papers, Southern Historical Collection. In this letter, Curtis congratulates Robins on his appointment as editor of the Raleigh *Conservative*—Vance's personal political organ representing the pro-Confederate faction of the Conservative party.
William Luck, farmer, age 48, in 1860 had a wife and seven children. His real estate was valued at $1,000 and his personal estate at $6,700. He owned seven slaves. 1860 Federal Census, Population and Slave Schedules, Randolph County, North Carolina.
40. "All quiet in Randolph," *Daily Conservative* (Raleigh), January 11, 1865.
41. A. Brower to Z.B. Vance, January 10, 1865, Governors Papers, Zebulon Baird Vance, North Carolina State Archives.
42. Special Orders No. 15, January 23, 1865, General and Special Orders to the Home Guard, 1863-65, Adjutant Generals Papers (AG 35), North Carolina State Archives.
43. Moffitt, *An Afternoon Hike into the Past*, 101.
44. Nicholson, *Wesleyan Methodism in the South*, 111. According to Nicholson, the Hulins were close friends and supporters of Crooks when he was in Montgomery County. The other captive was one James Atkins.
45. Hiram Hulin to Col. M. Cogwell, September 28, 1867, printed in McPherson, "Letters from North Carolina to Andrew Johnson," 118-119. In 1860, Hiram Hulin, age 53, was a farmer with a wife and six children. John, 20, and William, 19, were "farm hands" living with their father. Hiram owned no real estate and only $25 worth of personal property. Jesse L. Hulin, age 26, farmer, had a wife and two children. He owned $130 in real and $100 in personal property. See 1860 Federal Census, Population Schedule, Montgomery County, North Carolina.
46. Jarrell, *The Randolph Hornets in the Civil War*, 97-98.
47. Extract from a letter to the editor from Troy, *Semi-Weekly Standard* (Raleigh), February 3, 1865.
48. Moffitt, *An Afternoon Hike into the Past*, 101-102.
49. J.M. McCorkle to Gov. Vance, February 24, 1865, and Robert M. Stinson to Gov. Z.B. Vance, March 5, 1865, Zebulon Baird Vance Papers, Private Collections, North Carolina State Archives.
50. Entry for Saturday, February 11, 1865, Tench Tilghman Diary (microfilm), Southern Historical Collection.
51. Jones, *A Rebel War Clerks' Diary*, II, 444.
52. Long, *High Time to Tell It*, 5.
53. Mrs. Kate E.L. Virdein to Governor Vance, February 23, 1865, Zebulon Baird Vance Papers, Private Collections, North Carolina State Archives.
54. Robert M. Stinson to Gov. Z.B. Vance, March 5, 1865, Zebulon Baird Vance Papers, Private Collections, North Carolina State Archives.
55. "Affairs in Randolph," *Daily Conservative*," March 14, 1865. This letter is dated March 6, 1865.
56. *Ibid*.
57. "Outrage in Chatham," *Weekly Conservative* (Raleigh), February 15, 1865.
58. "Two Deserters Killed," *Observer* (Fayetteville), March 9, 1865.
59. J.M. Worth to Jonathan Worth, February 16, 1865, in Hamilton. *The Correspondence of Jonathan Worth*, I, 348-349.
60. M.M. McMasters to Mr. Editor, February 16, 1865, Marmaduke S. Robins Papers, Southern Historical Collection. The Yankees referred to were probably escapees from the Salisbury prison though some may have been deserters from Sherman's Army.
61. A.C. Murdock to Gov. Vance, March 6, 1865, Zebulon Baird Vance Papers, Private Collections, North Carolina State Archives.
62. J.M. Corkle to Gov. Vance, February 24, 1865, Zebulon Baird Vance Papers, Private Collections, North Carolina State Archives.
63. "Several Citizens" to Gov. Vance, March 3, 1865, Zebulon Baird Vance Papers, Private Collections, North Carolina State Archives.
64. Charity Robins to Brother Marmaduke, February 26, 1865, Marmaduke S. Robins Papers, Southern Historical Collection; David [Dick] to Brother Bob [R.P. Dick], February 28, 1865, Marmaduke S. Robins Papers, Southern Historical Collection.
65. John M. Worth to Jonathan Worth, February 28, 1865, in Hamilton, *The Correspondence of Jonathan Worth*, I, 357-358.
66. "A band of deserters...," *Daily Conservative*, March 15, 1865.
67. General Orders No. 2, February 9, 1865, General and Special Orders to the Home Guard, 1863-65, Adjutant Gen-erals Papers, North Carolina State Archives.
68. Special Orders No. 32, February 19, 1865, and Special Orders No. 33, February 20, 1865, General and Special Orders to the Home Guard, 1863-65, Adjutant Generals Pa-pers, North Carolina State Archives.
69. See Jonathan Worth to John M. Worth, February 20, 1865, in Hamilton, *The Correspondence of Jonathan Worth*, I, 354.
70. J.M. Worth to Jonathan Worth, February 16, 1865, Ibid., 348-349.
71. Jonathan Worth to John M. Worth, February 20, March 6 and 9, 1865, Ibid., 354, 363-364.
72. Testimony of George Auman in "Proceedings of a Military Court Convened at Ashboro by Virtue of Special Order No. 11," pp. 13-15, March 28, 1865, Alexander Carey McAlister Papers, Southern Historical Collection. In 1860, George Auman, age 44, was a farmer with a wife and eight children. He lived in the Auman's Crossroads community in south central Randolph and owned $700 in real estate and $760 in personal property. See 1860 Federal Census, Population Schedule, Randolph County, North Carolina.
73. Testimony of Lewis Parks in "Proceedings of a Military Court Convened at Ashboro by Virtue of Special Order No. 11," pp. 13-15, March 28, 1865, Alexander Carey McAlister Papers, Southern Historical Collection. In 1860, Lewis Parks, age 47, was a farmer with a wife and seven children. He held $1500 in real and $1580 in personal property. See 1860 Federal Census, Population Schedule, Randolph County, North Carolina.
74. William Welbourne and others to Z. B. Vance, March 3, 1865, Zebulon Baird Vance Papers, Private Collections, North Carolina State Archives.
75. "Robberies."
76. V.S. Cavin to William Cavin, March 2, 1865, Patterson-Cavin Papers, Duke Manuscript Department. In 1860, Virgil S. Cavin, age 16, was a farm laborer living with his father, W. H. Cavin, age 45, farmer, worth $650 in real and $200 in personal property. See 1860 Federal Census, Population Schedule, Alexander County, North Carolina. Private Cavin did not desert to the enemy. Rather, he remained in Confederate service until April 3, 1865, when the Yankees at Amelia Court House, Virginia captured him. He served in Company G, Thirty-eighth

Regiment North Carolina Troops. See Jordan and Manarin, *North Carolina Troops*, X, 69.

77. A. Carmichael to Vance, February 21, 1865, Zebulon Baird Vance Papers, Private Collections, North Carolina State Archives.

78. "Deserters in Wilkes," *Daily Conservative* (Raleigh) February 21, 1865.

79. Extract from a letter to the editor from Wilkes County, *Semi-Weekly Standard* (Raleigh), February 10, 1865.

80. Clark, *The Histories of North Carolina Regiments*, III, 78–79.

81. Major General H. Hith to Lt. Col. A.C. McAllester, February 27, 1865, Alexander Carey McAlister Papers, Southern Historical Collection; Z.B. Vance to R.E. Lee, March 2, 1865, Governors Papers, Zebulon Baird Vance Letter Book, North Carolina State Archives; R.E. Lee to Z.B. Vance, March 9, 1865, Governors Papers, Zebulon Baird Vance, North Carolina State Archives; R.E. Lee to Z.B. Vance, February 24, 1865, *Official Records Army*, Series I, Vol. XLVII, Part II, 1270–1271.

82. Special Orders No. 44, March 8, 1865, General and Special Orders to the Home Guard, 1863–65, Adjutant Gen-erals Papers, North Carolina State Archives.

83. Major General H. Hith to Lt. Col. A.C. McAllester, February 27, 1865, Alexander Carey McAlister Papers, Southern Historical Collection; Clark, *The Histories of North Carolina Regiments*, III, 78–79.

84. Special Orders No. 38, March 1, 1865; Special Orders No. 40, March 3, 1865; Special Orders No. 41, March 4, 1865; Special Orders No. 44, March 8, 1865; General and Special Orders to the Home Guard, 1863–65, Adjutant Generals Papers, North Carolina State Archives.

85. Adjutant General to Major Noah Rush, Asheboro, March 4, 1865, General and Special Orders to the Home Guard, 1863–65, Adjutant Generals Papers, North Carolina State Archives.

86. Major General H. Hith to Lt. Col. A.C. McAllester, February 27, 1865, Alexander Carey McAlister Papers, Southern Historical Collection. A.C. McAlister was born in Cumberland County in 1836 and was the son of a wealthy planter. His parents named him after his grandfather who was a member of the Provincial Congress at Halifax and Hillsborough. In 1853, he graduated from the University of North Carolina. In May 1861, he married Adelaide Worth, daughter of J.M. Worth. He died in 1916 in Asheboro. See "Col. A.C. McAlister: Soldier, Statesman," *Randolph Guide* (Asheboro), July 21, 1976. See also Grant, *Alumni History of the University of North Carolina*, 381. In 1860, Alexander C. McAlister, age 21, was a farmer worth $3,150 in real and $24,645 in personal property. He lived in Bladen County in the Dezerett community and owned 26 slaves. See 1860 Federal Census, Population and Slave Schedules, Bladen County, North Carolina.

87. Major General H. Hith to Lt. Col. A.C. McAllester, February 27, 1865, Alexander Carey McAlister Papers, Southern Historical Collection.

88. A.C. McAlester, Report made to Gen. J.E. Johnson's Chief of Staff, March 7, 1865, Alexander Carey McAlister Papers, Southern Historical Collection.

89. Lt. Col. McAlister to Major Jno. U. Waddell, March 6, 1865, Alexander Carey McAlister Papers, Southern Historical Collection. See also Major General H. Hith to Lt. Col. A.C. McAllester, February 27, 1865, Alexander Carey McAlister Papers, Southern Historical Collection.

90. Lt. Col. McAlister to Major Jno. U. Waddell, March 6, 1865, Alexander Carey McAlister Papers, Southern Historical Collection.

91. *Ibid*.

92. A.C. McAlester, Report made to Gen. J.E. Johnson's Chief of Staff, March 7, 1865, Alexander Carey McAlister Papers, Southern Historical Collection.

93. "Report made to General Lee…, " March 15, 1865, Alexander Carey McAlister Papers, Southern Historical Collection.

94. *Ibid*.

95. *Ibid*.

96. Barrett, *Civil War in North Carolina*, 296.

97. *Ibid*, 297.

98. *Ibid*., 300.

99. *Ibid*, 311.

100. J.J. Jackson to Jonathan Worth, March 12, 1865, in Hamilton, *The Correspondence of Jonathan Worth*, I, 365–366.

101. J.M. Worth to Jonathan Worth, March 9, 1865, Ibid., 364.

102. Elvira Worth to Mrs. Jonathan Worth, March 16, 1865, Ibid., 368–369.

103. D. Coble to Z.B. Vance [March 1865], Zebulon Baird Vance Papers, Private Collections, North Carolina State Archives.

104. C.H. Wiley to M.S. Robins, March 20, 1865, Marmaduke S. Robins Papers, Southern Historical Collection.

105. Letter to the editor from "Guilford," *The Conservative* (Raleigh), March 15, 1865.

106. *Ibid*.

107. Beverly Jones to Alexander C. Jones, March 12, 1865, Jones Family Papers, Southern Historical Collection.

108. "Your Mother" to "My dear Alex," March 19, 1865, Jones Family Papers, Southern Historical Collection.

109. *Ibid*.

110. Letter to the editor from "Guilford," *The Conservative* (Raleigh), March 15, 1865. On the death of Foust, see "Death of Esq. Foust," *Daily Conservative* (Raleigh), December 10, 1864.

111. D.C. Green to Col. McAlister, March 22, 1865, Alexander Carey McAlister Papers, Southern Historical Collection.

112. Peter Gross to his wife and children, March 26, 1865, John Wright Family Letters, North Carolina State Archives.

113. D.E. Green to Col. McAlister, March 22, 1865, Alexander Carey McAlister Papers, Southern Historical Collection.

114. *Ibid*. Private Walters was nineteen years old and from a working-class family in Indiana. While serving with General Judson Kirkpatrick's chief of scouts, Confederates captured him while "on the march to the sea" and sent him to Andersonville. He escaped, returned to duty, and "while in line of discharge of his duty as a scout was captured by the rebel authorities, tied to a tree and shot." See depositions by General W. McCain, J.S. Thompson, and Fount Robertson in the military pension application by Walter's mother, Julia A. Carroll, April 11, 1884, file no. 314609, Records Relating to Pension and Bounty Land Claims, 1773–1942, in Records of the Veterans Administration, Record Group 15, National Archives.

115. D.E. Green to Col. McAlister, March 22, 1865, Alexander Carey McAlister Papers, Southern Historical Collection. Milton and Alpheus were sons of militant

Unionist William Gollihorn. Alpheus was a deserter from company B, 52 Regiment North Carolina Troops. See Jordan, *North Carolina Troops*, XII, 431 (here, Gollihorn is spelled "Gallahorn").

116. *Ibid.*

117. Capt. D.C. Green to Col. McAlister, March 27, 1865, Alexander Carey McAlister Papers, Southern Historical Collection. Local residents named the springs located behind present-day Seagrove Elementary School "Gollihorn Springs," as it was near there that Confederate troops staked and shot Alpheus Gollihorn.

118. D.C. Green to Col. McAlister, March 22, 1865, Alexander Carey McAlister Papers, Southern Historical Collection.

119. [Lt. Col. A.C. McAlister] to Z.B. Vance, March 1865, Alexander Carey McAlister Papers, Southern Historical Collection. This letter is in the form of a penciled rough draft with a note attached to Lt. Jno. Waddell to copy it, and take it to High Point with the probable intention of sending it by telegraph.

120. "Proceedings of a Military Court Convened at Ashboro by Virtue of Special Order No. 11," March 28, 1865, 17–18, Alexander Carey McAlister Papers, Southern Historical Collection. See also Genl. Orders No. 3, March 30, 1865, Alexander Carey McAlister Papers, Southern Historical Collection.

121. Clark, *The Histories of North Carolina Regiments*, I, 386. See Hartley, *Stoneman's Raid* for a full account of the raid.

122. Lt. Col. A.C. [McAlister's] Report to Gen. Lee, March 30, 1865, Alexander Carey McAlister Papers, Southern Historical Collection.

123. "The Sufferings of the People," *Daily Confederate* (Raleigh), April 11, 1865.

124. Kirk, ed., *History of the Fifteenth Pennsylvania Volunteer Cavalry*, 501, quoted in Van Noppen, "The Significance of Stoneman's's Last Raid," Part II, 165; Hartley, *Stoneman's Raid*, 67–188.

125. Van Noppen, "The Significance of Stoneman's's Last Raid," Part II, 167–171; Hartley, *Stoneman's Raid*, 189–221.

126. Van Noppen, "The Significance of Stoneman's Last Raid," Part III, 341–361, and Part IV, 500–526; Hartley, *Stoneman's Raid*, 222–372.

127. *Ibid.*, Part I, 20.

128. S.F. Patterson to his son, June 2, 1865, Patterson Collection, North Carolina State Archives.

129. S.F. Patterson to his son, June 2, 1865, Patterson Collection, North Carolina State Archives; H.A. Eller to his brother, September 21, 1931, Jay Broadus Hubbell Papers, Duke Manuscript Department; H.A. Eller, "Recollection of Bushwhacker Rule in Western North Carolina, 1864–1865," in Paul E. Hubbell Paper, North Carolina State Archives.

130. For some interesting accounts of this showdown, see Dennett, *The South As It Is*, 141–145, and Andrews, *The South since the War*, 112–114, 116.

131. Dennett, *The South As It Is*, 145.

132. "Public Meeting of the Citizens of Alamance and Guilford, Held at Boon Station," *Daily Standard* (Raleigh), May 31, 1865.

133. "Union Meeting in Davidson County," *Daily Standard* (Raleigh), June 8, 1865.

134. "Great Union Mass Meeting in Alamance County," *Ibid.*, June 7, 1865.

135. "Public Meeting in Randolph County," *Ibid.*, June 10, 1865.

136. *Ibid.*

137. "Public Meeting of the Citizens of Alamance and Guilford, Held at Boon Station," *Ibid.*, May 31, 1865.

138. "Union Meeting at Bloomington, N.C.," *Ibid.*, June 14, 1865 (Bloomington was in Guilford County); "Public Meeting in Randolph County," *Ibid.*, June 10, 1865; "Public Meeting of the Citizens of Alamance and Guilford, Held at Boon Station," *Ibid.*, May 31, 1865; "Union Meeting at Jamestown," *Ibid.*, June 10, 1865.

139. "Great Union Mass Meeting in Alamance County," *Ibid.*, June 7, 1865.

140. See Lefler and Newsome, *North Carolina*, 495–498; Nelson, "Red Strings and Half Brothers," 37–53.

141. "Union Meeting at Jamestown," *Daily Standard* (Raleigh), June 10, 1865.

142. Escott, *Many Excellent People*, 87.

143. "Union Meeting in Guilford County," *Ibid.*, June 12, 1865.

144. "Raising of the Stars and Strips," *People's Press* (Salem), May 27, 1865.

145. "A Card," *Ibid.*

146. Unionist also held meetings in the eastern counties of Lenoir and Johnston. See *Daily Standard* (Raleigh), May 4 and 16, 1865.

147. W.W. Holden to the Sheriff and Justices of the Peace, Randolph County, September 16, 1865, Governors Papers, Holden, North Carolina State Archives.

148. J. Elliott to his son, April 15, 1866, Benjamin P. Elliott Papers, Duke Manuscript Department.

149. For other accounts Of political strife in Randolph and other Quaker Belt counties, see, James Jones to his father, April 21, 1866, Jones Family Papers, Southern Historical Collection; "State vs. Reuben E. Wilson," *People's Press* (Salem), December 23, 1865; "Forsyth Superior Court," *People's Press* (Salem), April 21, 1866.

150. "Randolph County — Letter From Maj. Worth, and Remarks of Mr. Dick," *Weekly Standard* (Raleigh), October 2, 1867.

Summary and Conclusions

1. McPherson, *Battle Cry of Freedom*, 613; Escott, *The Confederacy*, 101–102.

2. Escott, *Many Excellent People*, 53–58.

3. Brown, "North Carolinian Ambivalence," 7–31, and Escott, *Many Excellent People*, 73, 83.

4. Escott, *Many Excellent People*, 52–58.

5. Weitz, *More Damning Than Slaughter*, 115.

6. See John W. Hunt to Governor Vance, March 6, 1863, and Wm. Lindly to Gov. Vance [Sept. 1864?], Governors Papers, Zebulon Baird Vance, North Carolina State Archives; Pool, *Address of the Hon. John Pool*, 2, 3; "Several days ago," *Daily Conservative* (Raleigh), November 4, 1864.

7. Pool, *Address of the Hon. John Pool*, 2, 3.

8. "Several days ago," *Daily Conservative* (Raleigh), November 4, 1864. For accounts denying that rape by deserters was widespread in Wilkes, see "Are Highly Gratified," *Daily Conservative*, November 14, 1864; "To Governor Vance," *Weekly Standard* (Raleigh), December 14, 1864.

9. Barber and Ritter, "Physical Abuse ... and Rough Handling," 51.

10. "The Criminal Combination," *Weekly Confederate* (Raleigh), July 6, 1864.

11. Since postal authorities banned Tyson's book from circulation through the mails, it was difficult for him to distribute it. The only evidence that I have found

indicating that *A Ray of Light* was distributed in the Quaker Belt was presented in a letter from A.K. Pearce. See A.K. Pearce to Bryan Tyson, November 25, 1863, Bryan Tyson Papers, Duke Manuscript Department.

12. *Official Records Army*, Series I, Vol. XVIII, 880–881.

13. Editorial in the *Weekly Standard* (Raleigh), February 22, 1865. See also "The Asheville *News*..." in *Weekly Standard* (Raleigh), March 1, 1865, and W.W. Holden to Bartholomew F. Moore, August 2, 1866, Moore and Gatling Law Firm Papers, Southern Historical Collection.

14. Tyson, *The Institution of Slavery*, 46.

15. Tyson, *Object of the Administration*, 6.

16. Letter to the Editor from Long's Mills, Randolph County, *Semi-Weekly Standard* (Raleigh), July 21, 1863.

17. Raper, *William W. Holden*, 53.

18. Weitz, *More Damning Than Slaughter*, 290.

19. For accounts of Reconstruction in North Carolina, see Olsen, *Carpetbagger's Crusade: The Life of Albion Wingear Tourgee*; and Hamilton, *Reconstruction in North Carolina*.

20. See Lancaster, "The Scalawags of North Carolina, 1850–1868" (unpublished doctoral dissertation), 39, 46, 50, 55, 94, 148, 155, 162, 214, 216, 217, 231, 232, 289, 290, 362, 371, 394, 405.

21. Escott, "White Republicanism and Ku Klux Klan Terror," 4–34.

22. "State Senate Votes to Pardon Ousted Governor," *News and Observer* (Raleigh), April 13, 2011.

23. McKinney, *Zeb Vance*, 321, 345, 368.

24. Escott, "White Republicanism and Ku Klux Klan Terror," 34, and Clay, Orr, and Stuart, *North Carolina Atlas*, 76–77.

25. See Harris, "The Southern Unionist Critique of the Civil War," 55–56.

26. Beals, *War within a War*, 161.

27. Tourgee, *A Fool's Errand*, 144.

Bibliography

Primary Sources

MANUSCRIPTS

Department of Cultural Resources, Division of Archives and History, Raleigh, North Carolina.

Adjutant Generals Papers. General and Special Orders [to the Home Guard], August 1863–April 1865.
Adjutant Generals Papers, Home Guard Letter Book, 1863–65.
Adjutant Generals Papers, Adjutant General Letter Book, 1861–1862.
Adjutant Generals Papers, Adjutant General Letter Book, 1862–1864.
Adjutant Generals Papers, Adjutant General Letter Book, 1864–1865.
Adjutant Generals Papers, Militia Letter Book, 1862–1864.
Adjutant Generals Papers, Militia Letter Book, 1864–65.
Adjutant Generals Papers, Roll of Honor.
Adjutant Generals Papers, Roster of Militia [Officers] of North Carolina, 1861–1862, 1864.
Applications for Pardon, 1865 (photocopies).
Branson Family Papers.
John Washington Carlton Letters.
Thurman Chatham Papers.
Henry Toole Clark, Governors Papers, Correspondence, Letter Book.
Compiled Service Records of Confederate Soldiers Who Served In Organizations from the State of North Carolina. Washington, D.C.: National Archives Microfilm Publications, 1960.
John Thomas Conrad Papers.
County Court Minutes, July 1858-January 1867, County Records, Montgomery County.
Calvin J. Cowles Papers.
E.J. Hale Papers.
James Harwell Letters.
William Woods Holden, Governors Papers, Correspondence, Private Collections, Record Book Relative to the Provisional Government, 1865.
Paul E. Hubbell Papers.
John R. Lowry Papers
Minute Docket County Court, February 1860-Octobe, 1866. County Records, Randolph County.
Minute Docket Superior Court 1855–1865, County Records, Randolph County.
A.C. Myers Papers.
Patterson Collection.
Randolph County Civil War Records.
Randolph County Miscellaneous Records.
Roster of the Militia [Officers] of North Carolina (1861–1862, 1864).
Thomas Settle Letters.
Shaffner Diary and Papers.
State Docket Superior Court, 1861–1868, County Records, Randolph County.
U.S. Bureau of Census. Eighth Census of the United States, 1860, Davidson County, North Carolina.
U.S. Bureau of Census. Eighth Census of the United States, 1860, Montgomery County, North Carolina.
U.S. Bureau of Census. Eighth Census of the United States, 1860, Moore County, North Carolina.
U.S. Bureau of Census. Eighth Census of the United Statess, 1860, Randolph County, North Carolina.
U.S. Bureau of Census. Eighth Census of the United Statess, 1860, Wake County, North Carolina.
U.S. Bureau of Census. Eleventh Census of the United States, 1890, Special Schedules, North Carolina, Union Veterans and Widows of Union Veterans (Microfilm).
U.S. Bureau of Census. Seventh Census of the United States, 1850, Randolph-County, North Carolina.
Zebulon Baird Vance, Governors Papers, Correspondence, Letter Book, Private Collections.
Capus M. Waynick Collection.
Jonathan Worth Papers, Private Collections.
John Wright Family Papers.

Duke Manuscript Collection, Perkins Library, Duke University, Durham, North Carolina

Joseph Allred Papers.
Tilmon F. Baggarly Papers.
Artemus S. Caddell Papers.

Enoch Clark Papers.
Benjamin Elliott Papers.
Caleb Hampton Papers.
Benjamin Sherwood Hedrick Papers.
William Woods Holden Papers.
Jay Broadus Hubbell Papers.
Nathan G. Hunt Papers.
Jarrett-Puryear Papers.
John Hindricks Kinyoun Papers.
Henry Lewallen Papers.
Mathew N. Love Papers.
Joseph Overcash Papers.
James Patterson Papers.
Richmond M. Pearson Papers.
Scarborough Family Papers.
William Lafayette Scott Papers.
John W. Staley Papers.
John Lane Stuart Papers.
Lewis O. Sugg Papers.
Bryan Tyson Papers.
Charles Leonard Van Noppen Papers.
Robert and Newton D. Woody Papers.
Wright Family Papers.

Library of Congress, Washington, D.C.
Horace Greeley Papers.
Abraham Lincoln Papers (Microfilm).
Manton Marble Papers.
Samuel F. B. Morse Papers.
Bryan Tyson Papers.

Iowa State Archives, Des Moines.
Charles Mason Papers.
Quaker Collection, Guilford College, Greensboro, North Carolina.
John B. Crenshaw Papers.

Amistad Research Center, Fisk University Library, Nashville, Tennessee.
American Missionary Association Archives (Microfilm).

Southern Historical Collection, University of North Carolina at Chapel Hill.
Confederate Conscript Office Papers.
Dial Brothers Letter.
Gaden-Hackett Papers.
Ralph Gorrell Papers.
James Gwyn Papers.
Peter Wilson Hairston Papers.
Carrie Jackson Papers.
Jones Family Papers.
Jones and Patterson Family Papers.
Lenior Family Papers.
John Robert Lowrey Papers
Peter Mallett Papers.
Alexander Carey McAlister Papers.
Moore and Gatling Law Firm Papers.
Patterson Collection.
Christian Thomas Pfohl Papers.
Profitt Family Papers.
Marmaduke S. Robins Papers.
David Schenck Books.

S.A. Sharpe Papers.
William Henry Snow Papers, Tomlinson Series.
Tench Tilghman Diary.
Calvin H. Wiley Papers.
Daniel Worth Papers.

National Archives, Washington, D.C.
Compiled Service Records of Confederate Soldiers Who Served in Organizations from the State of North Carolina (Microfilm).
Letters Received, Records of the United States Secretary of War, Main Series, 1801–1870, Record Group 107 (Microfilm).
Pension and Bounty Land Claims in Records of the Veterans Administration.
Southern Claims Commission Papers.

Privately Held Manuscripts

Records of the Island Ford Manufacturing Company, organized February 27, 1847, Franklinsville, North Carolina, These records are owned by Mac Whatley of Franklinville, North Carolina, who generously allowed me to use them.

Pamphlets, Broadsides and Miscellaneous

An Account of the Sufferings of Friends of North Carolina Yearly Meeting in Support of their Testimony Against War from 1861 to 1865, 2d ed. The Peace Association of Friends in America, 1868. Quaker Collection, Guilford College.
An Address to the People of North Carolina on the Evils of Slavery. The General Association of the Manumission Society of North Carolina, 1830. William Swaim is the reputed author of the tract.
Carter, Jacob V. *Memorial of John Carter*. Pamphlet extracted from the Minutes of Cottonwood Quarterly Meeting, Cottonwood, Kansas, Ninth Month, 19th, 1903. Privately printed by Jacob V. Carter of Garden City, Kansas.
[Clark, Walter.] *Address by Walter Clark about Randolph County Soldiers in the Great War 1861–1865*. [191?]. Randolph Room, Randolph Public Library, Asheboro, North Carolina.
Eller, H.A. "Recollections of Bushwhacker Rule in Western North Carolina, 1864–1865." Eight-page typescript in Paul E. Hubbell Papers, North Carolina State Archives.
General Association of the Manumission Society of North Carolina. *An Address to the People of North Carolina on the Evils of Slavery*. Greensobro, N.C.: William Swaim, Printer, 1830. Reprinted on microfiche, Louisville, KY: Lost Cause Press, 1973.
[Hanes, Lewis]. *A Voice from North Carolina. The Secessionists: Their Promises and Performances: The Condition into which they have brought the Country: The Remedy, Etc*. New York: Anson D. F. Randolph, 1863.
Harriss, H. J. "To the Voters of Randolph County." Political Poster. North Carolina Collection, University of North Carolina at Chapel Hill.

Legislative Documents, 1864–1865, 1865–1866. Raleigh: John B. Neathery, Printer to the State, [1866].
Memorial of John Carter. Garden City, KS: Privately printed by Jacob Carter, 1903. Quaker Collection, Guilford College, rev. ed. Asheboro: Randolph County Historical Society, 1976.
"Record Book of the Camp of the Senior Reserves, September, 1864-January, 1865." Randolph Room, Randolph Public Library, Asheboro, North Carolina.
Rituals of the First and Second Degrees, Heroes and United Heroes of America. Charleston, WV: Moore and Brothers, Printers, 1864.
Savage, James W. "The Loyal Element of North Carolina During The War." Omaha, Nebraska, 1886. Pamphlet Collection, Perkins Library, Duke University.
Tyson, Bryan. Printed circular [no title]. Brower's Mills, N.C., September 24, 1862. North Carolina Collection, University of North Carolina at Chapel Hill.
———. "To the People of Virginia, North Carolina, …, and Texas." Washington, D. C., July 5, 1866. Broadside Collection, Rare Book Room, Perkins Library, Duke University.
Walker, David. *Appeal in Four Articles.* New York: Hill & Wang, 1965.
Wilson, Thos. L. *A Brief History of the Cruelties and Atrocities of the Rebellion: Compiled from the Most Authentic Sources.* Printed by McGill & Witherow for the Union Congressional Committee, n.d. North Carolina Collection, University of North Carolina at Chapel Hill.

Documents

Cheney, John L., ed. *North Carolina Government, 1585–1979: A Narrative and Statistical History.* Raleigh: North Carolina Department of the Secretary of State, 1981.
Clay, James W., Douglas M. Orr, Jr., Alfred W. Stuart, eds. *North Carolina Atlas: Portrait of a Changing Southern State.* Chapel Hill: University of North Carolina Press, 1975.
Connor, R.D.W., comp. and ed. *A Manual of North Carolina.* Raleigh: E.M. Uzzell, 1913.
Deed Books, Randolph County Courthouse.
Johnson, Donald Bruce, and Kirk H. Porter, eds. *National Party Platforms: 1840–1972*, 5th ed. Urbana: University of Illinois Press, 1975.
Journal of the House of Commons … Adjourned Session, 1864. Raleigh: W.W. Holden, Printer to the State, 1864.
Kennedy, Joseph C. G. *Agriculture of the United States in 1860.* Washington, D.C.: Government Printing Office, 1864.
———. *Population of the United States in 1860.* Washington, D.C.: Government Printing Office, 1864.
———. *Preliminary Report on the Eighth Census, 1860.* Washington, D.C.: Government Printing Office, 1862.
Legislative Documents, 1864–1865, 1865–1866. [Raleigh]: John B. Neathery, Printer to the State.
Manarin, Louis H., ed. *Guide to Military Organizations and Installations in North Carolina, 1861–1865.* Raleigh: North Carolina Confederate Centennial Commission, [1961].
Public Laws of the State of North Carolina passed by the General Assembly at the Sessions of 1861– '62 – '63 – '64, and One in 1859. Raleigh: Wm. E. Pell, Printer to the State, 1866.
Public and Private Laws of North Carolina 1863–64.
Rives, John C., ed. *The Congressional Globe: Containing the Debates and Proceedings of the First Session of the Thirty-eighth Congress.* Washington, D.C.: Congressional Globe Office, 1864.
Richardson James D., ed. *A Compilation of the Messages and Papers of the Presidents, 1789–1897.* Washington, D.C.: Government Printing Office, 1897.
Rowland, Dunbar, ed. *Jefferson Davis Constitutionalist: His Letters, Papers and Speeches.* Jackson: Mississippi Department of Archives and History, 1923.
Sanders, John L. *Maps of North Carolina Congressional Districts and State Senatorial Districts and Apportionment of State Representatives 1776–1960.* Chapel Hill: Institute of Government, 1961.
Sanger, George P., ed. *The Statutes at Large, Treaties, and Proclamations, of the United States of America.* Boston: Little, Brown, 1863–1869.
Scott, R.N., et al., eds. *The War of the Rebellion: A Compilation of the Official Records of the Union and Confederate Armies*, 70 vols. (127 books, atlases, and index). Washington, D.C.: Government Printing Office, 1880–1901.
Secretary of the Interior. *Manufactures of the United States in 1860.* Washington, D.C.: Government Printing Office, 1865.
———. *Statistics of the United States, 1860.* Washington, D.C.: Government Printing Office, 1864.
Simpson, J. Arnold, comp. *1860 Census, Randolph County, North Carolina.*
Will Books, Randolph County Courthouse, Asheboro, North Carolina.

Newspapers

Conservative (Raleigh).
Courier-Tribune (Asheboro).
Daily Confederate (Raleigh).
Daily Watchman (Salisbury)
Observer (Fayetteville)
The Patriot (Greensboro)
Morning Post (Raleigh)
National Republican (Washington, D.C.)
New York Times
North Carolina Standard (Raleigh)
People's Press (Salem)
Randolph Guide (Asheboro)
Semi-Weekly Patriot (Greensboro)
Semi-Weekly Standard (Raleigh)
Southern Citizen (Asheboro)
Times (Hendersonville)
Tri-Weekly Standard (Raleigh)
True Wesleyan
Weekly Conservative (Raleigh)
Western Democrat (Charlotte)
Wilmington Journal

Secondary Sources

BOOKS

Absher, W.O., ed. *The Heritage of Wilkes County.* Winston-Salem: Hunter, 1982.

Ashe, Samual A'Court. *History of North Carolina,* 2 vols. Raleigh: Edwards and Broughton Printing Company, 1925. Reprinted Spartanburg, S.C.: The Reprint Company, 1971.

Andrews, Sidney. *The South Since the War.* Boston: Tickonor & Fields, 1866; New York: Arno Press and New York Times, 1969.

Anscombe, Francis Charles. *I Have Called You Friends: The Story of Quakerism in North Carolina.* Boston: Christopher, 1959.

Arnett, Ethel Stephens. *William Swaim, Fighting Editor: The Story of O. Henry's Grandfather.* Greensboro: Piedmont Press, 1963.

Arthur, John Preston. *A History of Watauga County, North Carolina with Sketches of Prominent Families.* Richmond: Everett Waddey, 1915.

Ash, Stephen V. *When the Yankees Came: Conflict and Chaos in the Occupied South, 1861–1865.* Chapel Hill: University of North Carolina Press, 1995.

Ashe, Samuel A., ed. *Biographical History of North Carolina from Colonial Times to the Present,* 8 vols. Greensboro: Charles L. Van Noppen, 1906.

Auman, William T., and Minnie S. Stuart. *Why Not, North Carolina: A History of the Why Not Academy, the Why Not Memorial Association, the Why Not Community, and the Fair Grove Methodist Church.* Why Not: The Why Not Memorial Association, 1986.

Bailey, Hugh C. *Hinton Rowan Helper: Abolitionist Racist.* Tuscaloosa: University of Alabama Press, 1967.

Baker, Jean H. *Affairs of Party: The Political Culture of Northern Democrats in the Mid-Nineteenth Century.* Ithaca: Cornell University Press, 1983.

Barefoot, Daniel W. *General Robert F. Hoke: Lee's Modest Warrior.* Winston-Salem: John F. Blair, 1996.

Barney, William L. *Flawed Victory: A New Perspective on the Civil War.* Lanham, MD: University Press of America, 1980.

_____. *The Passage of the Republic: An Interdisciplinary History of Nineteenth-Century America.* Lexington, MA: D.C. Heath, 1987.

_____. *The Secession Impulse: Alabama and Mississippi in 1860.* Princeton: Princeton University Press, 1974.

Barrett, John G. *The Civil War in North Carolina.* Chapel Hill: University of North Carolina Press, 1963.

Basset, John Spencer. *Anti-Slavery Leaders of North Carolina.* Series XVI, No. 6 of Johns Hopkins University Studies in Historical and Political Science. Edited by Herbert B. Adams. Baltimore: Johns Hopkins Press, 1898.

Beals, Carlton. *War Within a War: The Confederacy Against Itself.* Philadelphia: Chilton, 1965.

Beyer, Fred. *North Carolina: The Years Before Man, a Geologic History.* Durham: Carolina Academic Press, 1991.

Boatner, III, Mark M. *Civil War Dictionary.* New York: David McKay, 1959.

Bolton, Charles C. *Poor Whites of the Antebellum South: Tenants and Laborers in Central North Carolina and Northeast Mississippi.* Durham: Duke University Press, 1994.

Brown, David. *Southern Outcast: Hinton Rowan Helper and The Impending Crisis of the South.* Baton Rogue: Louisiana State University Press, 2006.

Brown, Louis A. *The Salisbury Prison: A Case Study of Confederate Military Prisons, 1861–1865.* Wendell, N.C.: Avera Press, 1980.

Brown, Norman D. *Edward Stanly: Whiggery's Tarheel "Conqueror."* Tuscaloosa: University of Alabama Press, 1974.

Burson, William. *A Race for Liberty; Or, My Capture, Imprisonment, and Escape.* Wellsville, OH: W.G. Foster, Printer, 1867.

Bynum, Victoria E. *The Free State of Jones: Mississippi's Longest Civil War.* Chapel Hill: University of North Carolina Press, 2001.

_____. *The Long Shadow of the Civil War: Southern Dissent and Its Legacies.* Chapel Hill: University of North Carolina Press 2010.

_____. *Unruly Women: The Politics of Social and Sexual Control in the Old South.* Chapel Hill: University of North Carolina Press, 1992.

Carnes, Mark C., and John A. Garraty, eds. *American National Biography,* 24 vols. Oxford: Oxford University Press, 1999.

Cartland, Fernando G. *Southern Heroes or the Friends in War Time,* 3d ed. Poughkeepsie, N.Y.: Fernando G. Cartland, 1897.

Cecil-Fronsman, Bill. *Common Whites: Class and Culture in Antebellum North Carolina.* Lexington: University Press of Kentucky, 1992.

Chaffin, Nora Campbell. *Trinity College 1839–1892: The Beginnings of Duke University.* Durham: Duke University Press, 1950.

Clark, Walter, ed. *Histories of the Several Regiments and Battalions from North Carolina in the Great War 1861–65,* 5 vols. Raleigh: E. M. Uzzell, 1901.

Coulter, E. Merton. *The Confederate States of America, 1861–1865.* Vol. VII of *A History of the South.* Edited by Wendell Holmes Stephenson and E. Merton Coulter. Baton Rouge: Louisiana State University Press, 1950.

_____. *William G. Brownlow, Fighting Parson of the Southern Highlands.* Chapel Hill: University of North Carolina Press, 1937.

Cox, C. Waldo. *Hoot Owls, Honeysuckle and Halleluyah.* New York,: Vantage, 1966.

Crofts, Daniel W. *Reluctant Confederates: Upper South Unionists in the Secession Crisis.* Chapel Hill: University of North Carolina Press, 1989.

Crooks, E.W. *Life of Rev. A. Crooks, A.M.* Syracuse: D.S. Kenny, Wesleyan Methodist Publishing House, 1875.

Crowe, Jeffrey J., Paul D. Escott, and Charles L. Flynn, Jr. *Race, Class, and Politics in Southern History: Essays in Honor of Robert F. Durden.* Baton Rogue: Louisiana State University Press, 1989.

Current, Richard Nelson. *Lincoln's Loyalists: Union Soldiers from the Confederacy.* Boston: Northeastern University Press, 1992.

_____, ed. in chief. *Encyclopedia of the Confederacy*, 4 vols. New York: Simon & Schuster, 1993.

Cyclopedia of Eminent and Representative Men of the Carolinas of the Nineteenth Century, vols. Madison, WI: Brant and Muller, 1892.

Degler, Carl N. *The Other South: Southern Dissenters in the Nineteenth Century*. New York: Harper & Row, 1974.

Dell, Christopher. *Lincoln and the War Democrats: The Grand Erosion of Conservative Tradition*. Rutherford, N.J.: Fairleigh Dickenson University Press, 1970.

Dennett, John Richard. *The South as It Is: 1865–1866*. New York: Viking, 1965.

Dowd, Jerome. *Sketches of Prominent Living North Carolinians*. Raleigh: Edwards & Broughton, 1888.

Durrill, Wayne K. *War of Another Kind: A Southern Community in the Great Rebellion*. New York: Oxford University Press, 1990.

Escott, Paul D. *After Secession: Jefferson Davis and the Failure of Confederate Nationalism*. Baton Rouge: Lousiana State University Press, 1978.

_____. *The Confederacy: The Slaveholder's Failed Venture*. Santa Barbara: Praeger, 2010.

_____. *Many Excellent People: Power and Privilege in North Carolina, 1850–1900*. Chapel Hill: University of North Carolina Press, 1985.

_____. *Military Necessity: Civil-Military Relations in the Confederacy*. Westport, CT: Praeger, 2006.

Evans, W. McKee. *To Die Game: The Story of the Lowry Band, Indian Guerrillas of Reconstruction*. Baton Rogue: Louisiana State University Press, 1971.

Fanning, David. *Narrative of Colonel David Fanning*. Spartanburg, S.C.: Reprint Company, 1973.

Fellman, Michael. *Inside War: The Guerrilla Conflict in Missouri during the American Civil War*. New York: Oxford University Press, 1989.

Fischer, David Hackett. *Albion's Seed: Four British Folkways in America*. New York: Oxford University Press, 1989.

Fisher, Noel C. *War at Every Door: Partisan Politics and Guerrilla Violence in East Tennessee, 1860–1869*. Chapel Hill: University of North Carolina Press, 1997.

Folk, Edgar E., and Bynum Shaw. *W.W. Holden: A Political Biography*. Winston-Salem: John F. Blair, 1982.

Foster, Gaines M. *Ghosts of the Confederacy: Defeat, the Lost Cause, and the Emergence of the New South, 1865–1913*. New York: Oxford University Press, 1987.

Fries, Adelaide. *The Road to Salem*. Winston-Salem: John F. Blair, 1993.

Gara, Larry. *The Liberty Line: The Legend of the Underground Railroad*. Lexington: University of Kentucky Press, 1961.

Grant, Daniel Lindsey. *Alumni History of the University of North Carolina*. Durham: Christian & King Printing, 1924.

Hamilton, J.G. de Roulhac. *Benjamin Sherwood Hedrick*. Vol. 10, No. 1 of *The James Sprunt Historical Publications*. Chapel Hill: University of North Carolina Press, 1910.

_____, ed. *The Papers of Thomas Ruffin*, 4 vols. Raleigh: Edwards & Broughton Printing, 1920.

Hamilton, J.G. de Roulhac. *Reconstruction in North Carolina*. New York: Columbia University Press, 1914.

_____, comp. and ed. *The Correspondence of Jonathan Worth*, 2 vols. Raleigh: Edwards & Broughton Printing, 1909.

Harris, William C. *North Carolina and the Coming of the Civil War*. Raleigh: Division of Archives and History, 1988.

_____. *William Woods Holden: Firebrand of North Carolina Politics*. Baton Rouge: Louisiana State University Press, 1987.

Hartley, Chris J. *Stoneman's Raid 1865*. Winston-Salem: John F. Blair, 2010.

Hatley, Joe A., and Linda B. Huffman, eds. *Letters of William F. Wagner*. Wendell, N.C.: Broadfoot, 1983.

Hilderman, Walter C. *They Went into the Fight Cheering: Confederate Conscription in North Carolina*. Boone, N.C.: Parkway, 2005.

Hilty, Hiram H. *Toward Freedom For All: North Carolina Quakers and Slavery*. Richmond, IN: Friends United Press, 1984.

Hinshaw, Seth B., and Mary E. Hinshaw, eds. *Carolina Quakers: Our Heritage Our Hope*. Greensboro: North Carolina Yearly Meeting, 1972.

Hinshaw, William Wade. *Encyclopedia of American Quaker Genealogy*, 4 vols. Baltimore: Genealogical Publishing, 1969.

Howe, Daniel Wait. *Political History of Secession*. New York: G. P. Putnam's Sons, 1914.

Inscoe, John C., and Robert C. Kenzer, eds. *Enemies of the Country: New Perspectives on Unionists in the Civil War South*. Athens: University of Georgia Press, 2001.

Inscoe, John C., and Gordon B. McKinney, eds. *The Heart of Confederate Appalachia: Western North Carolina in the Civil War*. Chapel Hill: University of North Carolina Press, 2000.

Jarrell, Wallace E. *The Randolph Hornets in the Civil War: A History and Roster of Company M, 22nd North Carolina Regiment*. Jefferson, N.C.: McFarland, 2004.

Jeffrey, Thomas E. *State Parties and National Politics: North Carolina, 1815–1861*. Athens: University of Georgia Press, 1989.

Johnson, Guion Griffis. *Ante-Bellum North Carolina: A Social History*. Chapel Hill: University of North Carolina Press, 1937.

Jones, Alexander H. *Knocking at the Door: His Course Before the War, During the War, and After the War*. Washington, D.C.: McGill and Witherow, 1966.

Jones, J.B. *A Rebel War Clerk's Diary*, 2 vols. New York: Old Hickory Bookshop, 1935.

Jordan, W.T., Jr., and L.H. Manarin. *North Carolina Troops: A Roster*, 15 Vols. Raleigh: Division of Archives and History, 1966–2003.

Keever, Homer M. *Iredell: Piedmont County*. Statesville, N.C.: Iredell County Bicentennial Commission, 1976.

Kirk, Charles H., ed. *History of the Fifteenth Pennsylvania Volunteer Cavalry*. Philadelphia: Historical Committee of the Society of the Fifteenth Pennsylvania Cavalry, 1906.

Klement, Frank L. *The Copperheads in the Middle West.* Chicago: University of Chicago Press, 1960.
———. *Dark Lanterns: Secret Political Societies, Conspiracies, and Treason Trials in the Civil War.* Baton Rouge: Louisiana State University Press, 1984.
———. *The Limits of Dissent: Clement L. Vallandigham & the Civil War.* Lexington: University Press of Kentucky, 1970.
———. *Lincoln's Critics: The Copperheads of the North.* Shippensburg, PA: White Maine Books, 1999.
Klingberg, Frank W. *The Southern Claims Commission.* Berkeley: University of California Press, 1955.
Kruman, Marc W. *Parties and Politics in North Carolina, 1836–1865.* Baton Rouge: Louisiana State University Press, 1983.
Kutler, Stanley I. *Dictionary of American History*, 3d ed., 10 vols. New York: Charles Scribner's Sons, 2003.
Ledford, Preston Lafayette. *Reminiscences of the Civil War 1861–65.* Thomasville, N.C., 1909.
Lefler, Hugh T. *Hinton Rowan Helper Advocate of a "White America."* In *Southern Sketches, No. 1.* Charlottesville, VA: Historical Publishing, 1935.
Lefler, Hugh T., and Albert Ray Newsome. *The History of a Southern State: North Carolina*, 3d ed. Chapel Hill: University of North Carolina Press, 1973.
Leyburn, James G. *The Scots-Irish: A Social History.* Chapel Hill: University of North Carolina Press, 1962.
Long, Mary Alves. *High Time to Tell It.* Durham: Duke University Press, 1950.
Lonn, Ella. *Desertion During the Civil War.* New York: The Century Co., 1928.
Malone, Dumas, ed. *Dictionary of American Biography.* New York: Charles Scribner's and Sons, 1936.
Mathews, Donald G. *Religion in the Old South.* Chicago: University of Chicago Press, 1977.
———. *Slavery and Methodism: A Chapter in American Morality.* Westport, CT: Greenwood Press, 1978; PrincetoN: Princeton University Press, 1965.
McKenzie, Robert Tracy. *Lincolnites and Rebels: A Divided Town in the American Civil War.* New York: Oxford University Press, 2006.
McKiever, Charles F. *Slavery and tho Emigration of North Carolina Friends.* Murfresboro, N.C.: Johnson Publishing, 1970.
McKinney, Gordon B. *Zeb Vance: North Carolina's Civil War Governor and Gilded Age Political Leader.* Chapel Hill: University of North Carolina Press, 2004.
McPherson, James M. *Battle Cry of Freedom.* New York: Oxford University Press, 1988.
Mitchell, Memory F. *Legal Aspects of Conscription and Exemption in North Carolina, 1861–1865.* Chapel Hill: University of North Carolina Press, 1965.
Mobley, Joe A. *War Governor of the South: North Carolina's Zeb Vance in the Confederacy.* Gainesville: University Press of Florida, 2005.
———. *Weary of War: Life on the Confederate Home Front.* Westport, CT: Praeger, 2008.
Moffitt, Joseph T. *An Afternoon Hike into the Past.* Joseph T. Moffitt, 1975.
Moore, Albert Burton. *Conscription and Conflict in the Confederacy.* New York: Macmillan, 1924.
Moore, John W. *Roster of North Carolina Troops in the War Between the States*, 4 vols. Raleigh: State of North Carolina, 1882.
Myers, Barton A. *Executing Daniel Bright: Race, Loyalty, and Guerrilla Violence in a Coastal Carolina Community, 1861–1865.* Baton Rouge: Louisiana State University Press, 2009.
Nelson, Larry E. *Bullets, Ballots, and Rhetoric: Confederate Policy for the United States Presidential Contest of 1864.* Tuscaloosa: University of Alabama Press, 1980.
Nicholson, Roy S. *Wesleyan Methodism in the South.* Syracuse: Wesleyan Methodist Publishing House, 1933.
Nor, Kenneth W. *Reluctant Rebels: The Confederates Who Joined the Army after 1861.* Chapel Hill: University of North Carolina Press, 2010.
O'Brien, Gail Williams. *The Legal Fraternity and the Making of a New South Community, 1848–1882.* Athens: University of Georgia Press, 1986.
Olsen, Otto H. *Carpetbagger's Crusade: The Life of Albion Winegar Tourgee.* Baltimore: Johns Hopkins University Press, 1965.
Paludan, Phillip Shaw. *Victims: A True Story of the Civil War.* Knoxville: University of Tennessee Press, 1981.
Pegg, Herbert Dale. *The Whig Party in North Carolina.* Chapel Hill: The Colonial Press, n.d.
Pool, John. *Address of the Hon. John Pool to the People of North Carolina.* Raleigh: Standard Book and Job Office Print, 1867.
Poteat, R. Matthew. *Henry Toole Clark: Civil War Governor of North Carolina.* Jefferson, N.C.: McFarland, 2009.
Powell, William S. *North Carolina Through Four Centuries.* Chapel Hill: University of North Carolina Press, 1989.
Powell, William S., ed. *Dictionary of North Carolina Biography*, 6 vols. Chapel Hill: University of North Carolina Press, 1979–1996.
Ramsdell, Charles W. *Behind the Lines in the Southern Confederacy.* Baton Rouge: Louisiana State University Press, 1944.
Ramsey, Robert W. *Carolina Cradle: Settlement of the Northwest Carolina Frontier, 1747–1762.* Chapel Hill: University of North Carolina Press, 1987.
Randall, J.G., and David Donald. *The Civil War and Reconstruction*, 2d ed. Boston: D.C. Heath, 1961.
Randolph County Historical Society and the Randolph Arts Guild. *Randolph County, 1779–1979.* Winston Salem: Hunter Publishing, 1980.
Raper, Horace W. *William W. Holden: North Carolina's Political Enigma.* Chapel Hill: University of North Carolina Press, 1985.
Rouse, Parke. *The Great Wagon Road: From Philadelphia to the South.* Richmond, VA: Deitz Press, 2004.
Sears, Stephen W. *George B. McClellan: The Young Napoleon.* New York: Ticknor & Fields, 1988.
Sharpe, Bill. *A New Geography of North Carolina*, 4 vols. Raleigh: Sharpe Publishing, 1954–1965.
Shields, H.B. *Country Doctor for a Half Century.* N.p.: Katherine Shields Melvin, 1975.
Silbey, Joel H. *A Respectable Minority: The Democratic Party in the Civil War Era, 1860–1868.* New York: W. W. Norton, 1977.

Sitterson, Joseph Caryle. *The Secession Movement in North Carolina.* Chapel Hill: University of North Carolina Press, 1939.
Smith, Adam I.P. *No Party Now: Politics in the Civil War North.* Oxford: Oxford University Press, 2006.
Smith, Michael Thomas. *A Traitor and a Scoundrel: Benjamin Hedrick and the Cost of Dissent.* Newark: University of Delaware Press, 2003.
Spencer, Cornelia Phillips. *The Last Ninety Days of the War in North Carolina.* New York: Watchman, 1866.
Steward, Rodney. *David Schenck and the Contours of Confederate Identity.* Knoxville: University of Tennessee Press, 2012.
Sutherland, Daniel E. *A Savage Conflict: The Decisive Role of Guerrillas in the American Civil War.* Chapel Hill: University of North Carolina Press, 2009.
_____, ed. *Guerrillas, Unionists, and Violence on the Confederate Home Front.* Fayetteville: University of Arkansas Press, 1999.
Tatum, Georgia Lee. *Disloyalty in the Confederacy.* Chapel Hill: University of North Carolina Press, 1934.
Tolbert, Noble J., ed. *The Papers of John Willis Ellis*, 2 vols. Raleigh: State Department of Archives and History, 1964.
Tomlinson, J.S. *Assembly Sketch Book Session 1883 North Carolina.* Raleigh: Edwards, Broughton, 1883.
Tourgee, Albion W. *A Fools Errand: A Novel of the South During Reconstruction.* Introd. George M. Frederickson. New York: Fords, Howard, and Hulbert, 1879; New York: Harper & Row, 1966.
Trotter, William R. *Silk Flags and Cold Steel: The Piedmont.* Winston-Salem: John F. Blair, 1988.
Tucker, Glenn. *Zeb Vance: Champion of Personal Freedom.* Indianapolis: Bobbs-Merrill, 1965.
Tyson, Bryan. *The Institution of Slavery in the Southern States, Religiously and Morally Considered in Connection with Our Sectional Troubles.* Washington, D.C.: H. Polkinhorn, 1863.
_____. *Object of the Administration in Prosecuting the War.* Washington, D. C.: McGill & Witherow, 1864, 1869. The two editions of the pamphlet are identical except for the introduction on page 2.
_____. *A Ray of Light; or, A Treatise on the Sectional Troubles Religiously and Morally Considered.* Brower's Mills, N.C.: Privately printed by the author, 1862.
Wagstaff, Henry M., ed. *Minutes of the North Carolina Manumission Society, 1816–1834.* Chapel Hill: University of North Carolina Press, 1934.
Wakelyn, Jon L. *Biographical Dictionary of the Confederacy.* Westport, CT: Greenwood Press, 1977.
_____, ed. *Southern Unionists Pamphlets and the Civil War.* Columbia: University of Missouri Press, 1999.
Warner, Ezra J., and W.B. Yearns. *Biographical Register of the Confederate Congress.* Baton Rouge: Louisiana State University Press, 1975.
Watson, Harry L. *Jacksonian Politics and Community Conflict: The Emergence of the Second American Party System in Cumberland County, North Carolina.* Baton Rouge: Louisiana State University Press, 1981.
Webber, Jennifer L. *Copperheads: The Rise and Fall of Lincoln's Opponents in the North.* Oxford: Oxford University Press, 2006.
Weeks, Stephen B. *Southern Quakers and Slavery.* Baltimore: John Hopkins University Press, 1896.
Weitz, Mark A. *More Damning Than Slaughter: Desertion in the Confederate Army.* Lincoln: University of Nebraska Press, 2005.
Wellman, Manly Wade. *The County of Moore, 1847–1947.* Southern Pines, N.C.: Moore County Historical Association, 1962.
Whatley, Jr., Lowell McKay, et al. *The Architectural History of Randolph County North Carolina.* Raleigh: North Carolina Division of Archives and History, 1985.
Whites, LeeAnn, and Alecia P. Long. *Occupied Women: Military Occupation and the American Civil War.* Baton Rouge: Louisiana State University Press, 2009.
Williams, David. *Bitterly Divided: the South's Inner Civil War.* New York: The New Press, 2008.
Williams, David. *Rich Man's War: Class, Cast, and Confederate Defeat in the Lower Chattahoochee Valley.* Athens: University of Georgia Press, 1998.
Williams, Mark R., and J.G. deRoulhac Hamilton, eds. *The Papers of William Alexander Graham*, 5 vols., Raleigh: North Carolina Office of Archives and History, 1973.
Wilson, Thos. A. *A Brief History of the Cruelties and Atrocities of the Rebellion.* Washington, D.C.: Union Congressional Committee, 1864.
_____. *Sufferings Endured for a Free Government; or a History of the Cruelties and Atrocities of the Rebellion.* Philadelphia: King & Baird, 1865.
Wright, Edward Needles. *Conscientious Objectors in the Civil War.* Philadelphia: University of Pennsylvania Press, 1931.
Yates, Richard E. *The Confederacy and Zeb Vance.* Tuscaloosa: Confederate Publishing, 1958.
Yearns, W. Buck, and John G. Barrett, eds. *North Carolina Civil War Documentary.* Chapel Hill: University of North Carolina Press, 1980.
Zornow, William Frank. *Lincoln and the Party Divided.* Norman: University of Oklahoma Press, 1954.
Zuber, Richard L. *Jonathan Worth: A Biography of a Unionist.* Chapel Hill: University of North Carolina Press, 1965.

Articles

Ambrose, Stephen E. "Yeoman Discontent in the Confederacy." *Civil War History*, VIII (September 1962), 259–268.
Ash, Stephen V. "Sharks in an Angry Sea: Civilian Resistance and Guerrilla Warfare in Occupied Middle Tennessee, 1862–1865." *Tennessee Historical Quarterly*, XLV (Fall 1986), 217–229.
Auman, William T. "Bryan Tyson: Southern Unionist and American Patriot." *North Carolina Historical Review*, LXII (July 1985), 257–292.
Auman, William T. "Neighbor Against Neighbor: The Inner Civil War in the Randolph County Area of Confederate North Carolina." *North Carolina Historical Review*, LXI (January 1984), 59–92.
Auman, William T., and David D. Scarboro. "The Heroes of America in Civil War North Carolina."

North Carolina Historical Review, LVIII (October 1981), 327–363.
Baker, Jean H. "A Loyal Opposition: Northern Democrats in the Thirty-seventh Congress." *Civil War History*, XXV (June,1979), 139–155.
Baker, Robin E. "Class Conflict and Political Upheaval: The Transformation of North Carolina Politics during the Civil War." *North Carolina Historical Review*, LXIX (Apri 1992), 148–178.
Barber, E. Susan, and Charles F. Ritter. "'Physical Abuse ... and Rough Handling': Race, Gender, and Sexual Justice in the Occupied South," 49–64 in LeeAnn Whites and Alecia P. Long, *Occupied Women: Military Occupation and the American Civil War*. Baton Rouge: Louisiana State University Press, 2009.
Bardolph, Richard. "Confederate Dilemma: North Carolina Troops and the Desertion Problem." *North Carolina Historical Review*, Part I and Part II, LXVI (January 1989), 61–86, and (April 1989), 178–210
_____. "Inconstant Rebels: Desertion of North Carolina Troops in the Civil War." *North Carolina Historical Review*, XLI (April 1964), 163–189.
Boyd, William K., and Charles A. Krummel. "German Tracts Concerning the Lutheran Church in North Carolina During the Eighteenth Century." *North Carolina Historical Review*, VII (January 1930), 79–147.
Brooks, E.C. "Captain Craven and the Trinity Guard." *Trinity Alumni Register*, III (October 1917), 169–185.
Brown, David. "North Carolina Ambivalence: Rethinking Loyalty and Disaffection in the Civil War Piedmont," 7–36 in Paul D. Escott, *North Carolinians in the Era of the Civil War and Reconstruction*. Chapel Hill: University of North Carolina Press, 2008.
Brumgardt, John R. "Alexander H. Stephens and the State Convention Movement in Georgia: A Reappraisal." *Georgia Historical Quarterly*, LIX (Spring 1975), 38–49.
Bynum, Victoria. "Occupied at Home: Women Confront Confederate Forces in North Carolina's Quaker Belt," 155–170 in Lee Ann Whites and Alecia P. Long, *Occupied Women: Military Occupation and the American Civil War*. Baton Rouge: Louisiana State University Press, 2009.
_____. "'War Within a War': Women's Participation in the Revolt of the North Carolina Piedmont, 1863–1865." *Frontiers*, IX, No. 3, 1987.
Cardoso, Jack J. "Southern Reaction to *The Impending Crisis*." *Civil War History*, XVI (March 1970), 5–17.
Cox, Monty W. "Freedom During the Fremont Campaign: The Fate of One North Carolina Republican in 1856." *North Carolina Historical Review*, XLV (Autumn 1968), 357–383.
Crofts, Daniel W. "The Union Party of 1861 and the Secession Crisis," 327–76 in Donald Fleming, ed., *Perspectives in American History*, IX (1977–1978), published by The Charles Warren Center for Studies in American History, Harvard University.
Crow, Jeffrey J. "Thomas Settle, Jr., Reconstruction, and the Memory of the Civil War." *The Journal of Southern History*, LXII (November 1996), 689–726.

Curry, Leonard P. "Congressional Democrats, 1861–1863." *Civil War History*, XII (September 1966), 213–229.
Curry, Richard O. "The Union as It Was: A Critique of Recent Interpretations of the 'Copperheads.'" *Civil War History*, XIII (March 1967), 25–39.
Dodge, David. [Oscar Williams Blacknall.] "The Cave-Dwellers of the Confederacy." *Atlantic Monthly*, LXVIII (October 1891), 514–521.
Dorris, Jonathan Truman. "Pardoning North Carolinians." *North Carolina Historical Review*, XXIII (July 1946), 360–401.
Escott, Paul D. "The Failure of Confederate Nationalism: The Old South's Class System and the Crucible of War," 15–28 in Harry P. Owens and James J. Cooke, eds., *The Old South in the Crucible of War*. Jackson: University Press of Mississippi, 1983.
Escott, Paul D. "Joseph E. Brown, Jefferson Davis, and the Problem of Poverty in the Confederacy." *Georgia Historical Quarterly*, LXI (Spring 1977), 59–71.
Escott, Paul D. "The Moral Economy of the Crowd in Confederate North Carolina." *The Maryland Historian*, XIII (Spring/Summer 1982), 1–17.
Escott, Paul D. "Poverty and Governmental Aid for the Poor in Confederate North Carolina." *North Carolina Historical Review*, LXI (October 1984), 462–480.
Escott, Paul D. "White Republicanism and Ku Klux Klan Terror: The North Carolina Piedmont During Reconstruction," in Jeffrey J. Crowe, Paul D. Escott, and Charles L. Flynn, Jr. *Race, Class, and Politics in Southern History: Essays in Honor of Robert F. Durden*. Baton Rogue: Louisiana State University Press, 1989.
Escott, Paul D., and Jeffrey J. Crow. "The Social Order and Violent Disorder: An Analysis of North Carolina in the Revolution and the Civil War." *Journal of Southern History* LII (August 1986), 373–402.
Fleming, Walter L. "The Peace Movement in Alabama During the Civil War: [Part] I, Party Politics, 1861–1864." *South Atlantic Quarterly*, II (April (1903), 114–124.
Gallagher, Gary W. "Disaffection, Persistence, and Nation: Some Directions in Recent Scholarship on the Confederacy." *Civil War History*, LV, no. 3 (2009), 329–353.
Gehrke, William Herman. "Negro Slavery among the Germans in North Carolina." *North Carolina Historical Review*, XIV (October 1937), 307–324.
Hall, Clifton R. *Andrew Johnson: Military Governor of Tennessee*. Princeton: Princeton University Press, 1916.
Hall, Mark. "Alexander H. Stephens and Joseph E. Brown and the Georgia Resolutions for Peace." *Georgia Historical Quarterly*, LXIV (Spring 1980), 50–63.
Hamilton, J.G. deRoulhac. "Heroes of America," 10–19 in vol. XI of Colyer Merriwether, ed., *Publications of the Southern History Association*. Washington, D.C.: The Association, 1907.
_____. "The North Carolina Courts and the Confederacy." *North Carolina Historical Review*, IV (October 1927), 366–403.

Harris, William C. "The Southern Unionist Critique of the Civil War." *Civil War History*, XXXI (March 1985), 39–56.

Honey, Michael K. "The War within the Confederacy: White Unionists of North Carolina." *Prologue*, XVIII (Summer 1986), 75–93.

Huddle, Mary Andrew. "North Carolina's Forgotten Abolitionist: The American Missionary Association Correspondence of Daniel Wilson." *North Carolina Historical Review*, LXXII (October, 1995), 416–455.

Johnson, Clifton H. "Abolitionist Missionary Activities in North Carolina." *North Carolina Historical Review*, XL (Summer 1963), 295–320.

Johnston, Frontis W. "Zebulon Baird Vance: A Personality Sketch." *North Carolina Historical Review*, XXX (April 1953), 178–190.

Kruman, Marc W. "Dissent in the Confederacy: The North Carolina Experience." *Civil War History*, XXVII (1981), 293–313.

McKinney, Gordon B. "Zebulon Vance and His Reconstruction of the Civil War in North Carolina." *North Carolina Historical Review*, LXXV (January 1998), 69–85.

McPherson, Elizabeth Gregory. "Letters from North Carolina to Andrew Johnson." *North Carolina Historical Review*, XXIX (January 1952), 104–119.

Mobley, Joe A. "Zeb B. Vance: A Confederate Nationalist in the North Carolina Gubernatorial Election of 1864." *North Carolina Historical Review*, LXXVII (October, 2000), 434–454.

Moore, John Hammond. "Sherman's 'Fifth Column': A Guide to Unionist Activities in Georgia." *Georgia Historical Quarterly*, LXVIII (Fall 1984), 382–409.

Moser, Harold D. "Reaction in North Carolina to the Emancipation Proclamation." *North Carolina Historical Review*, XLIV (Winter 1967), 53–71.

Myers, Barton A. "Dissecting the Torture of Mrs. Owens: The Story of a Civil War Atrocity," 141–159 in Stephen Berry, ed., *Weirding the War: Stories from the Civil War's Ragged Edges*. Athens: University of Georgia Press, 2011.

Nelson, Scott Reynolds. "Red Strings and Half Brothers: Civil Wars in Alamance County, North Carolina, 1861–1871," 37–53 in John C. Inscoe and Robert C. Kenzer, *Enemies of the Country: New Perspectives on Unionists in the Civil War South*. Athens: University of Georgia Press, 2001.

Opper, Peter Kent. "North Carolina Quakers: Reluctant Slaveholders." *North Carolina Historical Review*, LII (January 1975), 37–58.

Owsley, Frank L. "Defeatism in the Confederacy." *North Carolina Historical Review*, III (July 1926), 446–454.

Poteat, R. Matthew. "'A Modest Estimate of His Own Abilities': Governor Henry Toole Clark and the Early Civil War Leadership of North Carolina, Part 2." *North Carolina Historical Review*, 84 (April 2007), 127–155.

Raper, Horace W. "William W. Holden and the Peace Movement in North Carolina." *North Carolina Historical Review*, XXXI (October 1954), 493–526.

Reid, Richard. "A Test Case of the 'Crying Evil': Desertion among North Carolina Troops during the Civil War." *North Carolina Historical Review*, LVIII (July 1981), 234–262.

Reid, Richard. "Civil Liberties in the Confederacy: The Test Case of North Carolina." *Canadian Journal of History*, XIV (August 1979), 173–197.

_____. "William W. Holden and 'Disloyalty' in the Civil War." *Canadian Journal of History*, XX (April 1985), 23–44.

Roberts, A. Sellow. "The Peace Movement in North Carolina." *Mississippi Valley Historical Review*, XI (September 1924), 190–199.

Robbins, John B. "The Confederacy and the Writ of Habeas Corpus." *Georgia Historical Quarterly*, LV (Spring 1971), 91–92.

St. Clair, Kenneth E. "Judicial Machinery in North Carolina." *North Carolina Historical Review*, XXX (July 1953), 415–439.

Scarboro, David D. "North Carolina and the Confederacy: The Weakness of States' Rights during the Civil War." *North Carolina Historical Review*, LVI (April 1979), 133–149.

Shanks, Henry T. "Disloyalty to the Confederacy in Southwestern Virginia, 1861–1865." *North Carolina Historical Review*, XXI (April 1944), 118–135.

Smith, Michael Thomas. "'A Traitor and a Scoundrel': Benjamin S. Hedrick and the Making of a Dissenter in the Old South." *North Carolina Historical Review*, LXXVI (July 1981), 316–336.

Sowle, Patrick. "The North Carolina Manumission Society, 1816–1834." *North Carolina Historical Review*, XLII (January 1965), 47–69.

Tolbert, Noble J. "Daniel Worth: Tar Heel Abolitionist." *North Carolina Historical Review*, XXXIX (Summer 1962), 284–304.

Van Noppen, Ina W. "The Significance of Stoneman's Last Raid, Part I." *North Carolina Historical Review*, XXXVIII (January 1961), 19–44.

_____. "The Significance of Stoneman's Last Raid, Part II." *North Carolina Historical Review*, XXXVIII (January 1961).

_____. "The Significance of Stoneman's Last Raid, Part III." *North Carolina Historical Review*, XXXVIII (October 1961).

_____. "The Significance of Stoneman's Last Raid, Part IV." *North Carolina Historical Review*, XXXVIII (October 1961).

Van Zant, Jennifer. "Confederate Conscription and the North Carolina Supreme Court." *North Carolina Historical Review*, LXXII (January 1995), 54–75.

Welker, G. William. "Early German Reformed Settlements in North Carolina," in vol. VIII of William L. Saunders, ed., *Colonial Records of North Carolina*. Raleigh: Josephus Daniels, 1890.

Wubben, H.H. "Copperhead Charles Mason: A Question of Loyalty." *Civil War History*, XXIV (March 1978), 46–65.

Yates, Richard E. "Governor Vance and the End of the War in North Carolina." *North Carolina Historical Review*, XVIII (October 1941), 315–338.

_____. "Governor Vance and the Peace Movement, Part I." *North Carolina Historical Review*, XVII (January 1940), 1–25.

_____. "Governor Vance and the Peace Movement,

Part II." *North Carolina Historical Review*, XVII (April 1940), 89–113.

Yearns, Wilfred B. "North Carolina in the Confederate Congress." *North Carolina Historical Review*, XXIX (July 1952), 359–378.

———. "The Peace Movement in the Confederate Congress." *Georgia Historical Quarterly*, XLI, (March 1957), 1–18.

Zuber, Richard L. "Conscientious Objectors in the Confederacy: The Quakers of North Carolina." *Quaker History*, LXVII (Spring 1978), 1–19.

UNPUBLISHED WORKS

Auman, William T. "Neighbor Against Neighbor: The Inner Civil War in the Central Counties of Confederate North Carolina." Doctoral dissertation, University of North Carolina at Chapel Hill, 1988.

———. "North Carolina's Inner Civil war: Randolph County." Master's thesis, University of North Carolina at Greensboro, 1978.

Briggs, Martha T. "Mill Workers in an Antebellum North Carolina County." Master's thesis, University of North Carolina at Chapel Hill, 1975.

Cecil-Fronsman, Bill. "The Common Whites: Class and Culture in Antebellum North Carolina." Doctoral dissertation, University of North Carolina at Chapel Hill, 1983.

Durrill, Wayne K. "Uncivil War: A Southern Community in the Great Rebellion." Doctoral dissertation, University of North Carolina at Chapel Hill, 1987.

Goff, Jerry Charishopher. "The Geographic Origins of North Carolina Enlistments in the War Between the States." Master's thesis, 1987.

Huddle, Mark Andrew. "Incendiaries in Our Midst: Wesleyan Methodist Abolitionist in North Carolina, 1847–1860." Master's thesis, Western Carolina University, 1995.

Lancaster, James Lawrence. "The Scalawags of North Carolina, 1850–1868." Doctoral dissertation, Princeton University, 1974.

Reid, Richard M. "Protest and Dissent in Civil War North Carolina." Doctoral dissertation, University of Toronto, 1976.

Scarboro, David D. "An Honourable Peace: The Peace Movement in Civil War North Carolina." Doctoral dissertation, Cambridge University, 1981.

Shay, John Michael. "The Antislavery Movement in North Carolina." Doctoral dissertation, Princeton University, 1971.

Whittenburg, James P. "Colonial North Carolina's 'Burntover District': The Pattern of Backcountry Settlement, 1740–1770." paper presented at the annual meeting of the Southern Historical Association, November 13, 1986, Charlotte, North Carolina.

INTERVIEWS

Interview with Buren Garner of Seagrove, N.C., on November 13, 1977, about the militant Unionists of the southern Randolph border area, especially William or "Bill" Owens.

Interview with Mrs. Hollis Sink of Winston-Salem, N.C., on November 28, 1977, about Dr. J.L. Johnson.

Index

Numbers in ***bold italics*** indicate pages with photographs.

abolition 7, 11, 12, 13, 15, 16, 17, 27, 29, 34, 35, 36, 52, 57, 73, 79, 83, 90, 95, 100, 136, 141, 147, 148, 152, 163, 171, 177, 185, 196, 199, 201, 210, 214; *see also* antislavery movement; emancipation
Abscher (victim of deserters) 182
"an Act to Punish Aiders and Abettors of Deserters" (law) 104
Adams, Henderson 145, 148, 234n42
An Address to the People of North Carolina on the Evils of Slavery (document) 11
Africa 11
African Americans 7, 13, 21, 35, 57, 76, 79, 92, 100, 101, 134, 142, 185, 211; *see also* abolition; emancipation; Emancipation Proclamation; freedmen; Preliminary Emancipation Proclamation; slavery; slaves
agrarians 99
Alabama 6, 90, 92, 94, 163
Alamance County, N.C. 5, 10, 11, 14, 16, 22, 30, 32, 38, 55, 56, 60, 75, 81, 91, 95, 100, 114, 115, 131, 154, 196
alcohol 13, 65, 108, 118, 123, 124
Alexander County, N.C. 69, 72, 123, 157, 189
Alexander County Home Guard 112
Alleghany County, N.C. 81, 91, 179, 182, 183, 196
Allen, Samuel 122–123
Allred, Alson 60
American Missionary Association 18, 22
American Party 27
American Revolution 10, 12, 199
American System 12

ammunition 56, 109, 157, 159, 189; *see also* arms; gunpowder
Anderson, Richard 163
Anson County, N.C. 33, 54, 97, 192
Anti-Slavery Leaders of North Carolina (book) 23
antislavery movement 1, 7, 30, 47, 74, 75, 83, 117, 129, 130, 141, 185, 199, 212, 214; in N.C. Quaker Belt 9–25; *see also* abolition; emancipation; Emancipation Proclamation
Anti-Slavery Society of Indiana 21
Appalachian Mountains 6, 72, 158
Appeal in Four Articles (tract) 12
Archdale, John 10
Arkansas 6, 88
Arkins (killed by Home Guard) 185
Armfield, R.F. 67
arms 40, 43, 44, 58, 70, 71, 76, 85, 104, 108, 109, 110, 119, 132, 150, 157, 159, 160, 161, 162–163, 189, 198; *see also* ammunition; gunpowder
Army of Northern Virginia 8, 78, 105, 137, 138, 155, 186, 190
Army of the Rappahannock 67
"Arrests of Women" (letter to editor) 172–173
arsenals 58
artisans 9, 10, 19, 26, 31, 43, 61, 67, 82, 99, 100, 200, 202
Asbury, N.C. 59
Asbury Baptist Church 59
Ashe, Thomas 97
Ashe County, N.C. 111, 179, 182, 183
Asheboro, N.C. 28, 63, 71, 89, 103, 104, 114, 116–117, 120, 140, 163, 164, 166, 167, 168, 169, 170, 171, 174, 185, 187, 190, 191, 192, 193, 194, 195, 198

Asheville, N.C. 195
Ashworth, Joel 147, 177, 201, 210
Atlanta, Ga. 180
Auman, George 188
Auman, Noah 144
Auman's Hill, N.C. 58, 59, 64, 144, 207
Auman's precinct 148

backcountry 11
Bacon, Jarvis C. 15, 17, 18, 19, 22, 24, 141
Baltimore, Md. 12
banks 12, 26, 29
Baptists 7, 13
Barns' Creek 185
Barrett, J.A. 96
Barrett, Joseph 144
Barrett, S.C. 96
Barringer, Major (Home Guard) 170
Bass, Lieutenant (attacked by deserters) 193
Bassett, John Spencer 24
Battle of Alamance 10
Battle of Antietam 202
Battle of Chancellorsville 79, 205
Battle of Franklin 107
Battle of Fredericksburg 79, 205
Battle of Gettysburg 85, 87, 89, 103, 117, 139, 166, 204, 205
Battle of Malvern Hill 70
Battle of New Bern 70
Battle of Sharpsburg *see* Battle of Antietam
Battle of Vicksburg 85, 87, 92, 103, 204, 205
Beals, Carlton 213–214
Beans' Mill 185
Bean's precinct 148
Bear Creek 193
Bell, John 27
Belmont, August 153

257

Bertie County, N.C. 151
Bethel, N.C. 115
Bethel Methodist Church 115
the Bible 22
the Bill of Rights 11, 197
Bingham, H. (Home Guard) 183
Bitting, Joe 107
Black Republicans 20, 27, 133
Blair, Enos T. 147, *148*, 201
blockade 87, 155, 180
Blue Ridge Mountains 72, 105, 157, 159, 182, 188, 208
Bohanan, Cabal 34
Boon, Col. (sheriff) 23, 114
Boyce, William W. 150, 151
Breckenridge, John C. 27
Brewer (outlier) 119
Brewer, Adam 117, 118, 178
Briles, Jacob 22
Brooks (deserter) 171
Brower, Alfred 65
Brower's Mills, N.C. 48, 74, 116, 117, 168
Brown (deserter) 171
Brown, Enoch 157
Brown, John 20, 21, 22, 23
Brown, Mason (victim of deserters) 182
Brown, Thomas 96
Brownlow, William Gannaway ("Parson") 145
Brushy Mountains 72, 182
Bryan, America 106
Bryan, John Grant 106
Bryan, John Quincey Adams 99, 106, 107, 111, 201, 207, 208, 214, 241n125
Bryan, Martha Ann 106
Bryan, Thomas 106
Bryan, Thomas Sherman 106
Buck Mountain 185
Buell, Don Carlos 153–154
buffaloes (armed bands) 7
Buncombe County, N.C. 44, 81, 179
Burke County, N.C. 55, 158, 161
Burlington, N.C. 72
Burson, William 76, 145–146
Bush Hill, N.C. 29
bushwhackers 106, 161, 183, 195, 198
Butler, Benjamin 154
Buxton, Ralph P. 62
Bynum, Victoria E. 59

Cabarrus County, N.C. 10, 81, 83; *see also* Cabarrus County Home Guards
Cabarrus County Home Guards 181
Cagle (arson victim) 65
Cagle, Riley 120
Cagle Road 62
Caldwell, David F. 149
Caldwell County, N.C. 72
Caldwell Institute 139
Calhoun, John C. 87
California 20

Calloway, A.S. "Tip" 149
Calvinists 9
Cambridge, Mass. 20
Camp Bethel 55, 115
Camp Hill 54
Camp Holmes 43, 54, 55, 63, 156, 159, 160, 170, 204
Camp Stokes 55, 170, 181
Camp Vance 55, 157, 159, 164
Campbell, B.G. 64
Camps of Instruction 32–33, 44, 55, 56, 94, 106, 110, 159
Cane Creek, N.C. 186; *see also* Cane Creek Meetinghouse
Cane Creek Meetinghouse 14
Cape Fear River 46, 73, 180, 184; *see also* Cape Fear Valley
Cape Fear Valley 10; *see also* Cape Fear River
Captain's District 38
Caraway, N.C. 57; *see also* Caraway Wesleyan Church
Caraway Wesleyan Church 18
Carbonton, N.C. 104
The Carolinian (Fayetteville newspaper) 167–168
Carter, John 74
Carthage, N.C. 48, 51, 52, 58, 71, 96, 161–162, 167, 192
Castle Thunder prison 112, 181, 183
Caswell Cavalry 166
Caswell County, N.C. 33, 100, 154, 165; *see also* Caswell Cavalry
Catawba County, N.C. 109, 139, 181
"Cave-Dwellers of the Confederacy" (essay) 74
Cavin, V.S. 189
Centre, N.C. 11, 21, 34, 46
Chamberlain, L.L. 158
Charleston, S.C. 29
Charlotte, N.C. 16, 72, 159, 211
Chatham County, N.C. 30, 31, 32, 139, 148, 162; anti-Confederate sentiment in 36, 37, 53, 75, 116; antislavery sentiment in 11, 14, 16, 19, 22; as a center of anti-Confederate unrest 7; conscription and draft in 33, 38, 54, 123; desertion and its impact in 55, 56, 60, 62, 63, 64, 69, 70, 76, 104, 114, 159, 163–164; 174, 186–187, 190, 191, 207, 211; Heroes of America in 121, 144, 146; one of strongest Quaker counties 10; peace rallies in 81, 131, 133; Wesleyanism in 16, 18, 21; *see also* Chatham County Home Guards
Chatham County Home Guards 114, 161, 167, 168, 170
Chatham Superior Court 121
Cheraw, S.C. 191
Chicago platform 150
children 1–2, 28, 45, 56, 59, 61, 64, 65, 70, 73, 88, 89, 91, 103, 111, 120–121, 122, 123, 124–125,
138–139, 168, 169, 170, 171, 172, 173, 174–175, 176, 178–179, 186, 202, 203, 210
Christian, Samuel H. 16, 97, 98, 99, 139, 140, 199, 211, 234n42
Christian Union, N.C. 58, 96, 114
Christianity 7, 107, 178
Church, Harrison 99, 182, 183, 214
Churchill, Orrin 144
Cincinnati, Ohio 12
Citizen (Greensboro newspaper) 174, 175
"a Citizen" (pen name) 108
civil liberties 12, 33, 44, 60, 68, 70, 79, 82, 94, 134, 142, 143, 166, 167, 177, 195, 196
"Civil Liberty Gone" (newspaper article) 174–175
Clapp, Abraham 149
Clark, George 76
Clark, Henry Toole 34, 35, 36, 38, 40, 48, 50, 96, 200
Clay, Henry 12
clergy 43, 98, 201
Cleveland County Home Guards 181
coastal plain region 6, 9, 24, 26, 27, 29, 32, 34, 81, 82, 164–165, 189
Coble, Lieutenant (reports Union meetings) 40–41
Coffin, Levi 12
Coffin, Vestal 12
the Colberts (guerrillas) 107
Cole, Widow (guerrilla victim) 59
colonization 11
Columbia Manufacturing Company *14*
Columbus, Miss. 92
Company Shops, N.C. 72
Concord, N.C. 83
Confederate Adjutant General's Department 38, 55, 56, 60, 63, 68, 112, 114, 122, 149, 156, 160–161, 163, 165, 175, 181, 183, 184, 185, 188
Confederate army 31, 36, 65, 69, 73, 103, 104, 105, 124, 140, 162, 188, 200, 204, 209; depredations of 64, 70, 90, 108, 111, 116, 122–123, 124, 125, 177–180, 203; and deserters and draft-dodgers 42, 47, 55, 60, 62–63, 74, 75, 77, 102, 107, 109, 110, 112, 114, 117, 138, 157, 163, 164–165, 166, 169, 176, 180–181, 185, 189, 190–191, 193, 202, 208, 210, 211; Heroes of America protects members from 39, 47; hesitancy to volunteer for 33, 34, 3839; men detailed away from service in 46, 149–150; and prisoners of war in Salisbury 159, 195; *see also* names of individual Confederate army units
Confederate Congress 38, 41, 42, 43, 53, 60, 68, 82, 86, 96, 97–

98, 100, 126, 128, 136, 137, 139–142, 143, 146, 151, 155, 164, 201, 205, 208
Confederate Conscript Bureau 45, 48, 54, 104–105, 156, 159, 181, 204
Confederate Constitution 68, 93, 127, 128–129
Confederate House of Representatives 80, 146, 151, 208, 210
Confederate Party 45, 83, 92, 134, 143, 208, 212
Confederate Quartermaster's Department 66
Confederate Senate 143, 146
Confederate Supreme Court 68, 141
Confederate War Department 169, 181, 185
conscription acts for 5, 38, 41, 42, 45, 47, 54, 56, 63, 67, 82, 104, 107, 149, 155, 169, 200, 201, 202, 205; Bryan Tyson's stance on 50, 52; endangers families' livelihood 42–43; military enforcement of 45, 54–60, 60–66, 68, 104; peace supporters' stance on 46, 90, 130, 196; rate of, in Quaker Belt 32–33; requires Home Guard service 105; *see also* deferments (military); draft; draft-dodgers; exemptions (military); substitution (military)
The Conservative (Raleigh newspaper) 143, 144, 147, 148, 177
Conservative Party 71, 89, 127, 128, 129, 154, 155, 196, 211; "Central Confederacy" of states supporting 29; class concerns of 99–101; and convention movement and Copperheads 131–136, 208, 210; and 1864 gubernatorial election 146, 147, 149, 158, 174, 182; and 1862 gubernatorial election 45; formation of 28, 44; Hanes articulates views of peace wing of 87; members become Democrats 212; and N.C. General Assembly 18, 183, 213; and peace movement 151–153, 205, 206; secessionists' mistreatment of 94, 95; splits into war and peace wings 83; Vance and war members of, deem Holden a traitor to the South 90, 91, 92; war members of, support Foster 139–140; *see also* Union Party
Constitutional Union Party 7, 27
convention movement 25, 29, 30, 40, 54, 86, 88, 94, 96, 97, 98, 108, 126–153, 205, 208, 209
Cook, Philip 190, 191, 193
Cook's Brigade 190, 191, 193
Cooly, Lieutenant (menaces woman) 123
the Cooper Union 20
Copperhead Manifesto 84, 86–90, 93, 136, 206; *see also* Copperheads
Copperheads 2, 3, 5, 8, 25, 28, 29, 45, 49, 50, 51–52, 54, 78–102, 126–153, 205, 206–207, 208–209, 210, 211, 214; *see also* Copperhead Manifesto
Corrikier, D. (combatant) 83
cotton 15, 31–32, 62, 65, 145, 197, 202, 206
Cotton, John F. 184
Courts of Oyer and Terminer 71
Covington meeting house 106
Cowles, Andrew C. 99, 149, 234n42
Cowles, Calvin J. 29, 99, 111, 124, 149, 158, 199
Cowles, Josiah 111, 165
Cox, Aley 177
Cox, C. Waldo 119
Cox, J.D. 96
Cox, Thaddeus 179
Craven, Braxton 36, 37, 40
Craven, Jacob 65
Crook, Phebe 171–172
Crooks, Adams 13–18, 19, 22, 24, 58, 141
Cumberland County, N.C. 72, 165, 191; conscription rate in 33

Daily Confederate (Raleigh newspaper) 144, 160, 164
Daily Conservative (Raleigh newspaper) 89, 134, 135–136, 146, 182
Daily Progress (Raleigh newspaper) 79, 133, 174–175
Danville, Va. 72, 189, 211
Dark, Mrs. (victim of deserters) 187
Dark Mountain 185
Davidson (pen name) *see* Hanes, Lewis
Davidson, N.C. 64, 148
Davidson County, N.C. 5, 7, 9, 19, 20, 31, 72, 76, 86, 139, 141, 145, 152; antislavery sentiment in 11, 23; deserters in 75, 104, 115, 190; enlistment rate in Quaker Belt 32; enrolling officer in 54; Heroes of America in 144, 201; militant Unionism in 34, 35, 36, 37, 40, 199–201; military abuses in 123, 171–172, 174; objection to draft in 38, 41; peace activism in 8, 39, 41, 81, 94, 131, 205, 210; "stampeders" from 181–182; support for Holden in 148; support for Republican Party in 213; Union meetings in 29, 195; *see also* Davidson County Home Guards
Davidson County Home Guards 115, 166, 176
Davie County, N.C. 5, 9, 20, 21, 36, 37, 81, 138, 156–158, 165, 213; *see also* Davie County Home Guards

Davie County Home Guards 167
Davis, Enoch 119
Davis, James 123
Davis, Jefferson 2, 6, 42, 44, 46, 53, 80, 81, 82, 83, 84, 85, 93, 94, 116, 112, 126, 127, 128, 129, 133, 134–135, 136–137, 141, 142, 143, 147, 149, 150, 151, 152, 164, 165, 169, 173, 205, 206, 207, 208, 210, 211, 212, 213
Davis, Sam 107
Day-Star Circular 101, 136, 206
the Declaration of Independence 11
Deep Creek 11, 67
Deep River 10, 14
deferments (military) 43, 172, 209; *see also* exemptions (military)
Degler, Carl 9, 197
Delaware 87
"The Demand for Vigilance" (newspaper article) 36
Democratic Party 20, 26, 81, 86, 87, 102, 140, 141, 152, 153, 177, 178, 206, 214; *see also* Democrats
Democratic Resident Executive Committee 153
Democrats 28, 29, 34, 44, 131, 143, 152, 206; Bryan Tyson and 53, 153, 203; Chicago platform of northern 150; and Conservative Party 44, 87, 212; draft Whig enemies 43–44; geographic strongholds of 26–27; and peace agitation 80, 82, 88–89, 94–95, 137; regain N.C. General Assembly 213; and reunion plans 51, 91, 93, 100, 108, 128, 130, 132, 133, 134, 135, 137, 153, 203, 205, 208; split into factions 27, 51; support Vance 209; and views on slavery 51, 53, 128, 130; 132, 133, 134, 135, 137, 153, 203, 205, 208; *see also* Copperheads; Democratic Party
Department of North Carolina and Virginia 154
deserters 77, 78, 96, 97, 99, 142, 178, 199, 203, 207, 213; habeas corpus suspended for 136–137; and Heroes of America 47, 201–202; support Holden and peace movement 95, 137–139, 144, 146, 148–149, 154; use of caves and Underground Railroad 73–76; Vance's hunt for and repression of Confederate 43–44, 54–70, 103–125, 131, 155–198, 201–202, 204, 208, 209–210, 211, 212; *see also* desertion; guerrillas
desertion 1, 2, 6, 8, 24, 32, 33, 39, 43, 44–45, 46, 47–48, 52, 69, 138; *see also* deserters
Dial brothers (deserter leaders) 99, 107–108, 214
Dick, John M. 23

Dick, Robert P. 133, 143, 149
disloyalists 1, 2, 3, 5, 6, 7, 8, 34, 35–38, 39–40, 42, 45, 48, 50, 54, 56, 60, 62, 95–97, 104, 107, 108, 109, 117, 127, 133, 136, 137, 142, 146, 149, 150, 156, 158, 160, 163, 165–166, 178, 192, 200, 202, 204; *see also* Unionists
Dixon, Albright, & Co. (shops burned) 114
Dixon, Thomas C. 186
Dobbins, Jesse 66
Dobbins, William 66
Dockery, Alfred 99, 143, 234n42
Dockery, Oliver H. 91, 99
Dodd, J.C. 234n49
Dodge, David 74
Donnell, R.S. 89
Dougan, Thomas 36
Douglas, Stephen A. 27
draft 1, 2, 5, 8, 24, 34, 38–41, 42, 45, 47–48, 50, 64, 69, 79, 96, 126, 136–137, 145, 147–148, 149, 200, 201, 205, 207, 212; *see also* conscription; deferments (military); draft-dodgers; exemptions (military); substitutions (military)
draft-dodgers 1, 8, 24, 34, 39, 47, 52, 77, 142, 154, 199, 201, 202, 213; Vance represses insurrection among 155–179; Vance's hunt for 43–45, 48, 54–70, 73–74, 103–125, 180–198, 210; *see also* guerrillas
Dublin, Indiana 75
Duke University 139
Dunlop, Cornelius 96
Dunn, Solomon 187
Durham, N.C. 72, 188
Durham County, N.C. 56
Durham's Station, N.C. 56, 72, 195, 212

East Bend, N.C. 107
Eden, N.C. 22
Edgecombe County Home Guards 167
education 11, 12, 43, 65, 98, 199, 201, 205–206
the elderly 2, 45, 122, 124, 173, 175, 176, 182, 185, 193, 194, 210
Election Day 150, 159, 160
Eller, Col. (victim of deserters) 182
Eller, Jas. (victim of deserters) 182
Ellis, F. (deserter) 169
Ellis, John Willis 22, 23, 26, 27, 28, 35
emancipation 2, 7, 11, 12, 13, 54, 83, 85, 89, 91, 92, 94, 101, 102, 128, 129, 132, 134, 135, 142, 151, 153, 206, 207, 208, 211; *see also* abolition; antislavery movement; Emancipation Proclamation; Preliminary Emancipation Proclamation
Emancipation Proclamation 51, 79, 153; *see also* Preliminary Emancipation Proclamation
England 53, 87, 175
English (language) 9
enrolling officers 54–55, 156, 159, 160, 161, 164
Episcopals 7
espionage 39, 135
Europe 53
Everett, Edward 89
executions 137–139, 171, 193–194
exemptions (military) 43, 44, 46–47, 52, 64, 99, 112, 149, 150, 165, 181, 200, 202, 209

factories *see* manufacturing; mills
Fair Haven, N.C. 95, 114
Fair View College 107
Faison, Colonel (opposes deserters) 113, 114, 115, 122
Fann (killed by Dial brother) 108
farmers 9, 10, 19, 20, 26, 42, 43, 48, 61–62, 67, 73, 99, 100, 148, 168, 185, 199, 201, 202, 203, 207; *see also* farming; plantations; planters; tenants
farming 9, 31, 47, 52, 61–62, 65, 70, 103, 202, 212; *see also* cotton; farmers; plantations; planters; tobacco
Fayetteville, N.C. 58, 62, 72–73, 192–193
Fayetteville and Western Plank Road 59, 191
Fifth Battalion Home Guards 104, 163, 167, 190
Fiftieth Regiment North Carolina Militia 55
Fifty-eighth Battalion Home Guards 163
Fifty-first Regiment North Carolina Militia 96
Fifty-second Regiment North Carolina Troops 58
Fifty-seventh Regiment North Carolina Troops 139
Fifty-sixth Regiment North Carolina Troops 60, 112, 115
Fink, Doc 83
Fire-Eaters 27, 29
First Congressional District 44
First Manassas 140
Flat Woods 182
Flint Hill 14
Florence, S.C. 76, 145
Folk, Edgar E. 234n49
A Fool's Errand (book) 213
foothill region 6
Forsyth County, N.C. 5, 7, 10, 32, 34, 36, 37, 56, 72, 149, 194, 201; antislavery sentiment in 15, 17; conscription and draft in 33, 38, 43; deserters' depredations in 107, 171, 189, 193; Heroes of America in 144, 145; and peace activism 81, 131, 141; and petitions for state convention 132; "stampeders" from 181–182; troops hunt deserters in 112–113, 138, 157, 164–165, 169, 190, 211; Unionism in 75, 197; *see also* Forsyth County Home Guards
Forsyth County Home Guards 164, 169, 181
Fort Caswell 34
Fort Fisher 155, 180, 181, 183–184, 210
Fort Hamby 195
Fort Sumter 30, 199, 208
Fortner, Elizabeth 123
Forty-ninth North Carolina Regiments 115
Forty-second Regiment North Carolina Troops 115, 123
Forty-sixth Regiment North Carolina Troops 191
Foster, Alfred G. 139, 140, 141, 142, 145, 166
Fourteenth Amendment 211
Fourth Regiment North Carolina Troops 138
Foust, Issac H. 65, 66, 105, 122–123, 160, 164, 193
Fraley, Jacob 106, 112
France 87
Franklinsville, N.C. 15, 35, 122–123, 145–146, 161, 169, 192
Free Democratic Party *see* Free Soil Party
Free Methodist Church 13
Free Soil Party 15, 16, 18–19, 24
freedmen 11, 12, 13, 31, 34, 67, 76, 142, 170
Freedom's Hill 14
French, Judge (consulted about military authorities' abuse) 174
Friends *see* Quakers; Society of Friends
Fries, Francis 17
Fugitive Slave Law 19
Fulp, William 171
Fultin, Joel 171
furlough system 61, 150

Gardner, Peter 173
Garner, Buren 59
Garner, John 116
Garner, Peter 117, 118, 119, 120, 178
Garrison, William Lloyd 11
Gaston County, N.C. 81
Gatlin, Adjutant General 175
"General Amnesty in this State" (newspaper article) 122
General Association of the Manumission Society of North Carolina 11
The Genius of Universal Emancipation (book) 11
gentry 98–99, 205, 206
Georgia 6, 47
German (language) 9, 10
German Reformed Church 7
Germans 19, 20; *see also* German (language); German Reformed Church; Palatine Germans
Germantown, N.C. 56

Index

the Gettysburg Address 89
Gilded Age 9
Gilmer, John A. 17, 97, 128
Gladesboro, N.C. 40
Glasscock, Mr. (Home Guard) 157
gold 32
Gold Region (Moore County, N.C.) 48, 50
Goldsboro, N.C. 181, 184
Goldston, A.J. 160
Goldston, J.J., Sr. 160
Goldston, T.J. 160
Gollihorn, Alpheus 96, 193–194
Gollihorn, Milton 96, 193
Gollihorn, William 96, 97
Good Springs, N.C. 59
Goodloe, Daniel R. 144, 145
Governor's Council 89
Graham, John W. 115
Graham, William A. 20
Graham, N.C. 196
Grant, Ulysses S. 145
Gray, Jos. (victim of deserters) 182
Grayson County, Va. 15
the Great Wagon Road 9
Greek (language) 48
Green, D.C. 194
Greene County, N.C. 81
Greensboro, N.C. 23, 37, 55, 60, 72, 128, 137, 139, 159, 165–166, 170, 189, 190, 191, 193, 194, 195, 197, 198, 211, 213
Grey, Robert C. 174
Guard for Home Defense 103–104, 169, 170, 180–181
guerrillas 42, 58–60, 67, 71, 107, 161, 178, 179, 180, 186, 190, 199, 201, 202–203, 207
Guilford Circuit 15
Guilford College 10, 11
Guilford County, N.C. 5, 7, 9, 10, 12, 13, 31, 46, 55, 138, 143, 149; antislavery sentiment in 16–19, 21–24, 74; deserters' depredations 104, 114, 123; enlistment and conscription rates in 32–33; hunt for deserters and draft-dodgers in 38, 56, 60, 144, 165, 193; peace activism in 81, 91, 97, 112, 131, 133; "stampeders" from 181–182; Unionism in 30, 29, 34, 36, 37, 40, 74, 75, 196–197, 200; *see also* Guilford College; Guilford County Militia
Guilford County Militia 41
Gulf, N.C. 160
gunpowder 40, 56, 65

habeas corpus 2, 44, 67, 82, 96, 126, 131, 136–137, 149, 167, 168–169, 209
Hackett, Dr. (investigates troops) 124
Haiti 11
Hale, John P. 19
Hall (deserter) 187
Hamilton, J.G. de Roulhac 23, 24, 144

Hamlin and Hoover Hotels 63
Hampton, Wade 192
Hamptonville, N.C. 111
Hanes, Lewis 2, 3, 78, 84, 86–90, 93, 98, 99, 135, 136, 145, 148, 152, 199, 201, 206, 210, 211, 214, 234n42
Harbin, A.A. 156
Hardee, General (head of engineer corps) 188
Hargrave, Jesse 166, 167, 173, 176
Harnett County, N.C. 81
Harpers Ferry, Va. 20, 21, 22, 23
Harris, John T. 22
Harris, Mrs. (guerrilla victim) 59
Harris, William C. 234n49
Hartley, Jim 183
Harvard University 20
Haughton, H.J. 162–163
Haw River 10, 208
Haywood County, N.C. 179
Healing Springs, N.C. 115
Hedrick, Benjamin Sherwood *19*–20, 23, 24, 53, 54, 76, 141, 144
Hedrick, Mrs. Benjamin Sherwood 73–74, 173
Helper, Hinton Rowan 19, 20–*21*, 22, 23, 24, 141, 199
Henderson, William F. 145, 201
Henderson County, N.C. 81; *see also* Henderson County Home Guards
Henderson County Home Guards 161
Hendricks, Solomon 65
Henly, Sarah 177
Herald (New York newspaper) 151
"Heroes in Chatham" (newspaper article) 160
Heroes of America 1, 7, 8, 24, 39, 46, 47, 52, 73, 76, 83, 109, 121, 124, 138, 143–146, 147, 148, 160, 163, 164, 185, 187, 196, 198, 201, 202, 204, 206, 209, 213, 21; *see also* Hilton, John
High Point, N.C. 36, 40, 72, 104, 113, 159, 189, 191, 195, 211
Highland Scots 10
Hill (dissident) 40
Hill, Daniel Harvey 66, 70, 108
Hill, John C. 39, 109
Hill, William H. 17
Hill's Store, N.C. 15
Hillsborough, N.C. 72, 186
Hilton, John 7, 8, 32, 35–36, 37, 40, 94, 109, 144, 199, 200; *see also* Heroes of America
Hith, H. (Confederate general) 191
Hock, Captain (Twelfth New York Cavalry) 75
Hoke, Colonel (leads Thirty-third Regiment) 40
Hoke, Robert F. *78*, 103–125, 208
Holden, William Woods 97, 109, 148, 149, 153, 160, 174, 211; Bryan Tyson and 154; and Conservative Party 44, 159, 182; and convention movement 126–129, 130, 131, 133, 134, 152; criticizes Vance 175–177, 210; deserters and draft dodgers support 122, 137–139, 161, 162, 164–165, 169, 184, 186; and 1864 gubernatorial campaign 1, 89–91, 135, 142–143, 144, 146, 149–150, 208–209, 155; as governor of N.C. 100–101, 120, 196, 197–198; 212, 213; and Heroes of America 144, 145, 209; J.M. Leach and 140–141; and peace movement 2, 3, 8, 47, 49, 50, 51, 78, 79–86, *80*, 88, 96, 98, 99, 132, 134, 147, 152, 205–207, 208; supports secession 20; supports slavery 22, 92–95, 101; and Unionism 28; *see also* North Carolina Standard
Holly Springs, N.C. 177
Holt, E.R. 160
Holton, A.S. 149
Holy Scriptures 11
home front 2, 38, 62, 131
Home Guards (local forces) 122, 149, 207; abuses of 166, 168, 174, 175, 176, 178, 203; and deserters and draft-dodgers 35, 104–107, 110–112, 124, 125, 156, 157, 159, 160–161, 163, 165, 171, 181, 182, 183, 184, 187, 189, 190–191, 204, 208, 209; *see also* Home Guards (state forces); names of individual Home Guard units
Home Guards (state forces) 1, 8, 39, 55, 103, 104, 169; *see also* Home Guards (local forces); names of individual Home Guard units
Hoot Owls, Honeysuckle, and Halleluyah (book) 119
Hoover Hill, N.C. 64
Horton, Phineas T. 149
Houghton, T.H. 159–160
Howard, John 234n49
Hulin, Clarinda 123, 172
Hulin, Hiram 34, 148, 185
Hulin, Jesse 185
Hulin, John 185
Hulin, Nelson 123
Hulin, William 185
hunger 2, 5, 6, 42, 47, 61–62, 65, 71, 91, 103, 111, 112, 116, 124, 169, 171–172, 173, 197, 201, 202, 205, 210, 212
Hunnicut, Private (executed) 138
Hunt, John W. 64
Hunter, Quill 107
Husband, Herman 10

Ihrie, Lieutenant Colonel (Chatham County Home Guard) 168
Illinois 27, 51, 79
illiteracy 101
immigrants 9–10
The Impending Crisis of the South:

How to Meet It (book) 20–21, 22, 23, 199
impressments 82, 115, 122, 124, 130, 160, 162, 167, 204, 205, 207
Indiana 12, 21, 23, 51, 54, 74, 75, 76, 158, 170, 181, 194
Indiana Conference (Wesleyan) 21
Indians *see* Native Americans
inflation 5, 6, 42, 43, 47, 200, 202, 203, 212
The Institution of Slavery in the Southern States, Religiously and Morally Considered in Connection with Our Sectional Troubles (book) 101–102, 136, 206
insurrection *see* rebellion
Iowa 153
Iredell County, N.C. 5, 7, 9; 30, 32, 33, 38, 54, 61, 72, 81, 91, 95, 105, 106, 108, 109, 112, 123, 131, 138, 151, 164–165, 181, 189, 207, 210; *see also* Iredell County Home Guards
Iredell County Home Guards 108, 112, 161, 195
Iredell Express (newspaper) 106
iron works 32
Isam (slave) 161–162
Island Ford Manufacturing Company 15

Jackson, Andrew 168
Jackson, Stonewall 105, 213
Jamestown, N.C. 13, 15, 17, 19, 23, 40, 72, 123, 196
Jefferson, Thomas 87
Jennings (deserter) 182
Jenning's Mill 108
Johnson, Alexander 156, 158
Johnson, Andrew 40, 145, 196, 212
Johnson, John Lewis 33, 54, 145, 201
Johnson, Lieutenant (present at capture of Harrison Church) 183
Johnston, Joseph E. 190, 191, 192, 195, 212
Johnston, William L. 44
Johnston County, N.C. 33, 81, 97, 127, 130, 131, 147, 161, 165, 175–176, 205
Jones (hanging victim) 174
Jordan, G.B. 57
Jordan, John 170
Julian's Cross Roads 187
Junior Reserves 55, 155–156, 159, 169, 170, 209
justices of the peace 64, 98–99, 144, 149, 165, 181

Kennedy's School House 39, 40, 200, 205
Kentucky 10, 12, 27, 74, 87, 88
Kindly (dissident) 40
King, Private (executed) 138
Kinston, N.C. 184
Kirkman, Robert 138

Know-Nothing Party: former Whigs' allegiance to 27
Kruman, Mark W. 234n49
Ku Klux Klan 80, 100, 145, 154, 196, 212, 213

labor 7, 31, 42, 43, 47, 51, 61, 99, 200, 202
land 9, 26, 28, 31, 99; *see also* landholders
landholders 31, 35, 99, 197; *see also* land
Lane, James Henry 190
Lane, Mrs. (victim of deserters) 185
Lane's Brigade 190
"The Last Desperate Game" (newspaper article) 146
Latham, John 120
Latin 48
Laws, Mr. (victim of deserters) 182
Lawson (deserter) 169
Lay, George W. 108–109
Leach, James M. 99, 120, 137, 139–142, 171, 173, 174, 176, 211
Leach, J.T. 80–81, 97, 98, 99, 127, 130, 131, 136, 146–147, 151, 205, 210, 234n42
Leach, P.P. 190
Lee, Robert E. 8, 69, 78, 110, 162, 180, 185, 186, 190, 191, 192, 193, 194, 202, 211, 213; *see also* Army of Northern Virginia
Leonard, Lindsay 76
"Let Us Have a Peace Convention" (letter to editor) 91
Leventhorpe, Collett 169–171, **170**, 177–178
Lexington, N.C. 54, 72, 139, 145, 159
Lilly, Captain (Supporting Force) 187–188
Lincoln, Abraham 2, 7, 27, 28, 30, 34, 35, 36, 51, 52, 53–54, 57, 58, 59, 64, 75, 79, 80, 83, 86, 87; 88, 90, 91, 92, 93, 94, 99, 102, 105, 128, 129, 130, 132, 134, 135, 140, 142, 145, 146, 147, 150, 151, 153, 154, 159, 184, 193, 195, 196, 199, 206, 208, 210, 211
Lincoln County, N.C. 81; *see also* Lincoln County Home Guards
Lincoln County Home Guards 181
Little, J.A. 160
Little River Captain's District 95, 188
Logan, George W. 97
London, England 53
the Lost Cause 213, 214
Louisiana 88, 154, 187
Louisville, Ky. 80
Love, S.E. 113
Lovejoy, N.C. 16, 171
Lovejoy Methodist Church 185
Love's Meeting House 181
Lovett (victim of deserters) 182
Luck, William 184

lumber 31, 32
Lundy, Benjamin 2, 12
Lutherans 7, 9
Lutterlough, Mr. (victim of deserters) 193

Macon, Thomas 168
Mallett, Peter 48, 54, 55, 56, 69, 159, 169, 204; *see also* Mallett's Battalion
Mallett's Battalion 54, 55, 115, 117, 122–123, 204, 208; *see also* Mallett, Peter
Manning, Chandra 135
manufacturing 14, 15, 26, 31, 32, 43, 52, 97; *see also* mills
Marble, Manton 153
Marlborough Friends Meetinghouse 12, 18
Marley, B.B. 57
Marley's Mill, N.C. 123
Maroney, Lieutenant (leads depredations in Yadkin County) 108
martial law 2, 33, 85, 126, 134, 156, 167
Martin, J.G. 55, 181
Maryland 9, 73, 87
Mason, Charles 152–153
Massachusetts 9, 45, 149
McAlister, Alexander C. 189–194, **191**
McBane, Sarah 168
McBane, William 168
McBride, Jesse 15, 16, 18, 19, 21, 22, 24, 58, 141
McClellan, George 134–135, 136, 150, 153–154
McDaniel, Private (executed) 138
McDonald, Neil 116, 117, 118
McGrady (victim of deserters) 182
McKinney, Gordon B. 234n49
McLean, John K. 96
McLean, J.R. 60, 157
McMasters, W.R. 57
McNeil, Frank (victim of deserters) 182
McNeil, Jas. (victim of deserters) 182
McNeil, Wm. (victim of deserters) 182
McRae, John 56
mechanics 3, 200
Mecklenberg County, N.C. 33, 165; *see also* Mecklenberg County Home Guards
Mecklenberg County Home Guards 167
men 31, 44
Mendenhall, Richard 13
Methodist Episcopal Church 13
Methodist Episcopal Church, South 13
Methodist Protestants 7
Methodists 13, 36, 37, 107; *see also* Methodist Protestants; Wesleyan Methodists
Mexican War 19

Military Reconstruction Act of 1867 100
militia 8, 13, 28, 41, 198, 201, 207; abuses of 123, 171–172, 175, 203; and antislavery sentiment 17; and deserters and draft-dodgers 38, 43, 45, 54–70, 103, 106, 110, 159, 163, 168–169, 202, 204; disobedience and disloyalty of 38, 105, 107, 110, 149–150, 160, 183; draft imposed upon 39, 96; and exemptions 43–44, 97, 98, 99, 108, 149–150, 165, 181; members vote for Holden 161; and peace agitation 108, 129; *see also* names of individual militia units
Miller, Jesse A. 76
mills 14, 15, 32, 65, 145, 193
Mills, Lieutenant (commands Supporting Force) 162
Miocene Epoch 72
missionaries 13–18, 21–23
Mississippi 88, 93, 126
Missouri 87, 88
Mocksville, N.C. 157s
Monday, B.J. 123
Montgomery County, N.C. 5, 97; antislavery sentiment in 15, 16; deserters in 54–56, 58–60, 62–63, 69–72, 75–76, 104, 115, 119–120, 159, 162, 163, 164, 166, 170, 184–185, 187, 201, 204, 207, 211; and 1864 gubernatorial election 146, 148, 211; Heroes of America in 144; military depredations in 64, 123; and peace movement 81, 91, 98; Unionism in 30, 32, 34, 36; *see also* Montgomery County Home Guards
Montgomery County Home Guards 114, 161, 162, 167, 170, 184
Moon, George 119
Moon, Joshua 53
Moore, Albert Burton 215n2
Moore, Bartholomew F. 83, 84
Moore, George 118
Moore, J.H. 35
Moore County, N.C. 30, 32, 43, 148, 192, 201; deserters and draft-dodgers in 38, 47, 48, 50, 54–60, 62, 63, 69–72, 75, 103–104, 115, 119, 121–122, 156, 159, 160, 161–165; 167–168, 170, 184, 190, 193, 204, 207, 211; military depredations in 64, 66; and peace movement 52, 81, 95–97, 131, 207; Unionism in 28–29, 34, 40, 191; *see also* Moore County Home Guards
Moore County Home Guards 114, 119, 161, 167, 170, 171
Moravians 1, 7, 9, 10, 73, 83, 199, 206, 213, 214
Morganton, N.C. 55, 158, 159, 161, 195
Morse, Samuel F.B. 152

Moses, T.C. 28
Mt. Airy, N.C. 196
Mount Vernon Springs (neighborhood) 186–187
mountain region 6, 24, 26, 27, 81, 82, 97, 112, 138, 189
Mrs. Hoover's Hotel 65
Mulberry, N.C. 106, 182
Murrow, A.C. 35

Nantucket Island, Mass. 11
Nash County, N.C. 165
National Almanac 20
Native Americans 9
"Negotiations for Peace" (article) 128–129
New Bern, N.C. 38, 53, 70
New England 29, 100
New Garden, N.C. 10; *see also* New Garden Boarding School
New Garden Boarding School 74
New Hampshire 19
New Hanover County, N.C. 33
New Jersey 9, 51
New Market, N.C. 18
New Salem, N.C. 11, 21, 22, 198
New Year 184
New York 18, 20, 51, 89, 133, 170
New York City, N.Y. 53, 80
New York Times 175
Newlines, Nat 187
Newport, Ind. 12
Norfolk, Va. 175
Norman, Calvin 107
North America 23
North Carolina Constitution 11
North Carolina General Assembly 53, 61, 143, 151, 152, 178, 183–184, 213
North Carolina House of Commons 65, 86, 89, 96, 118, 147, 148, 149, 151, 152, 177, 193, 210
North Carolina Manumission Society 11, 12, 13, 23
North Carolina Militia 107
North Carolina Mounted Infantry 195
"North-Carolina Politics" (editorial) 85, 93
North Carolina Railroad 31, 72, 141
North Carolina Standard (newspaper) 2, 20, 22, 42, 43, 47, 71, 79, 84–85, 89, 90, 91, 98, 100, 108, 109, 126, 127, 131–132, 136, 137, 138, 140, 142, 144, 146, 147, 148, 150, 166, 185, 189, 205, 206
North Carolina State Legislature 35, 68, 86, 87, 91, 96, 103, 107, 129, 131, 139–140, 147, 149, 201, 213
North Carolina State Senate 97, 148, 151, 213
North Carolina State Treasury Department 28, 46, 132
North Carolina Supreme Court 67, 68, 96, 157
North Carolina Yearly Meeting (Quaker) 11

Northcote (Unionist) 178
Northens, Benjamin 117
nullification 87

Oak Grove Church 167
Oath of Allegiance 76
Object of the Administration in Prosecuting the War (book) 136, 152–154, *153*, 211
Observer (Fayetteville newspaper) 36, 58–59, 89–90, 91, 95, 96, 97, 112, 119, 135, 140, 141, 144, 148, 151, 161, 164–165, 170
"Observer" (pen name) 131
Ohio 12, 13, 51, 75, 145, 205
Ohio River Valley 29
Old Capitol prison 54, 116
Old Gap Road 62
"Old Main" (building) *37*
The Old North State (newpaper) 86–87
Old Northwest Territory 19, 29
One-hundred-twelfth Illinois Regiment 196
Opposition Party *see* Whigs
Orange County, N.C. 5, 10, 11, 19, 32, 33, 43, 56, 60, 81, 91, 100, 186, 204, 208
Orange Court House (Va.) 108, 138, 139
outliers 72–76, 114, 115, 117, 119, 120, 124, 162, 167, 169, 185, 196, 201, 204, 209, 210, 212, 213; *see also* deserters; draft-dodgers
Overcash, Wilson 83
Owens, Adeline 59, 174, 179
Owens, Bailey 59
Owens, Murphy 120
Owens, William 58–60, 62, 63, 70, 99, 109, 119–122, 144, 148, 160, 178, 201, 207, 214
Owens, William B. 59
Owsley, Frank L. 215n2

pacifism 1, 7, 10, 11, 12, 46, 47; *see also* peace movement; Peace Party
"Pacifus" (pen name) 131–132
Page's Toll Gate 193
Palatine Germans 9
paramilitary units 35
Paris, France 53
Parks, Lewis 188
Pasquotank County, N.C. 179
Patriot (Greensboro newspaper) 12, 37, 121, 146, 176, 198
Patriota (pen name) 91
peace movement 25, 77, 174, 178, 204, 205–208; and Bryan Tyson 48, 49, 51, 54, 153, 154, 210–211; and convention movement 126–134, 139; and Copperheads 2, 29, 150–152; and 1864 gubernatorial election 146, 148, 149, 209; and election for Seventh Congressional District 140–143; meetings and demonstrations supporting 38, 39, 40, 41, 108,

109, 112; and plans for reunion 135–137, 139; *see also* pacifism; Peace Party
Peace Party 33, 39, 45, 51, 78, 82, 91, 98, 126, 128, 130, 133, 140, 141, 203, 205, 209, 212
"Peace — When Shall We Have Peace!" (editorial) 84
Pearce, Alexander K. 76, 116, 147, 118
Pearson, D.C. 156, 159, 160, 161, 169
Pearson, Richmond M. 67, 68, 136, 158, 204
Peddlar's Hill, N.C. 56
Pender, W.D. 68
Pennsylvania 9, 10, 11, 51
the People's Party 9
People's Press (Salem newspaper) 43, 80, 90, 150–151, 170, 171, 172–173, 197
Petersburg, Va. 8, 180, 189, 211
Pharr's Mill, N.C. 69, 70
Phillips (gunshot victim) 116
Phillips (Heroes of America member) 144
Phillips (militia victim) 64
Phillips, E. (peace meeting leader) 96
Phillips, Jeremiah 64
Piedmont Railroad 189–190
Pike, Alfred 120, 121
Pittsboro, N.C. 55, 104, 121, 162, 164, 192; *see also* Pittsboro Jail
Pittsboro Jail 186
plantations 26, 30, 31, 32, 67, 81, 199–200; *see also* planters
planters 10, 11, 26, 43, 61–62, 82, 98, 99, 120, 134, 166, 202; *see also* plantations
Pleasant Union Church 196
plebiscite 51
Plymouth, N.C. 180
Point Lookout prison 54, 73
Polk County, N.C. 179
polling irregularities 150, 154, 156, 157–158, 159, 160, 161, 209; *see also* voter intimidation
Pool, John 27, 112, 151, 152, 178–179, 203, 210
Populists 211
Pounds, James 122–123
poverty 20, 42, 43, 47, 61–62, 88, 99, 100, 124, 149, 164, 201, 202, 205, 207
Precambrian Epoch 72
Preliminary Emancipation Proclamation 53
Presbyterians 7, 168
Presnell, Randall 194
Pressly, Captain (guerrilla victim) 59
Price (Confederate soldier) 189
prisoners 34, 39, 58, 67, 75, 112, 121, 149, 156–157, 161, 166, 167, 170, 171, 172–173, 177, 178, 187, 195, 209, 210; *see also* prisoners of war; prisons

prisoners of war 34, 54, 65, 73, 75, 76, 116, 145, 158, 159, 169; *see also* prisons
prisons 2, 12, 23, 36, 39, 40, 45, 52, 53, 54, 55, 71, 75, 76, 94, 104, 112, 121, 124, 145, 156–157, 158, 149, 167, 168, 169, 170, 178, 195, 200, 202; *see also* names of individual prisons; prisoners; prisoners of war
professional class 26, 201
proletariat 99
Prosperity, N.C. 70, 103, 161
Protestants 9, 13
Provo, Major (leads shooting party) 56
Pugh, William A. 63, 65–66, 69, 115

Quakers 1, 7, 9, 10–13, 19, 21, 32, 35, 36, 37, 46–47, 53, 73, 74, 76, 83, 101, 115, 132, 145, 147, 148, 168, 170, 177, 199, 201, 206, 213; *see also* Society of Friends

race 2, 11, 67, 92, 93, 99, 102, 128, 135, 209, 211
Radical Reconstruction 112
Radical Republicans 197, 211, 212
railroads 12, 26, 29, 43, 44, 72, 158, 159, 161, 165, 180, 189, 195, 199, 207, 211; *see also* North Carolina Railroad; Piedmont Railroad
Raleigh, N.C. 33, 40, 43, 44, 50, 52, 53, 54, 55, 56, 58, 63, 72, 79, 83, 84, 89, 94, 100, 106, 126, 132, 134, 136, 139, 143, 147, 149, 151, 154, 156, 159, 165, 170, 177, 187, 188, 191, 192, 204, 207; *see also* Raleigh Guards
The Raleigh Era (newspaper) 87
Raleigh Guards 54, 55, 56, 60, 69, 104, 106, 122, 208, 210
Ramseur, N.C. 14, 65
Ramsey, George G. 97
Ramsey, N.A. 114, 115, 118, 119, 139, 142
Randolph, Anson D.F. 89
Randolph County, N.C. 5, 7, 9, 10, 13, 31, 46, 122, 138, 148, 201, 205; antislavery sentiment in 11, 12, 15–16, 18, 21–24, 141; conscription rate in 33; deserters and draft-dodgers in 36, 39, 41, 42–43, 44, 48, 54–66, 69–74, 103, 104, 105, 109, 113–115, 116–117, 119–120, 144, 146, 157, 159–161, 162, 163, 165, 166, 167–170, 173–174, 176, 184–188, 190, 191, 192, 193, 194, 201, 210; and 1864 gubernatorial election 147, 150; Heroes of America in 144, 145, 146; Home Guard in 35, 105, 163–164, 190–191; military's depredations in 63–66, 123, 175, 177–179, 213; and peace movement 2, 8, 41, 81, 91, 93–96, 131,

207; "stampeders" from 181; support for Republican Party in 213; Unionism in 28–29, 30, 32, 34, 37, 38, 40, 75, 76, 196, 197–198, 211; *see also* Randolph County Home Guards
Randolph County Court of Pleas and Quarter Sessions 96, 198
Randolph County Courts 36
Randolph County Home Guards 114, 167, 184, 185, 188, 193, 201
Randolph County Superior Court 96
Randolph Manufacturing Company 15
Randolph Public Library 170
Randolph Superior Court 119
"Randolph Superior Court" (newspaper article) 198
Ransom, General (Seventeenth Regiment North Carolina Troops) 71
rape 64, 168, 178, 182, 203
Raper, Jasper 171
Rapier, Horace W. 234n49
A Ray of Light; or, a Treatise on the Sectional Troubles Religiously and Morally Considered (book) 2, 49–54, **50**, 62, 79, 86, 88, 101, 116, 132, 136, 154, 203–204, 205
rebellion 2, 21, 22, 23, 24, 44, 56, 104, 155–179
reconstruction 5, 40, 83, 85, 86, 89, 90, 91, 92, 94, 95, 98, 99, 102, 129, 130, 132, 134, 135, 136, 137, 141, 142, 152, 200, 208, 209
Reconstruction era 8, 9, 4, 97, 100, 112, 145, 196, 201, 203, 212, 213
Recorder (Hillsborough newspaper) 100
Red String (publication) 213
Red Strings *see* Heroes of America
Redeemers 196
Reed Creek, N.C. 65
reenlistment 47–48
Reformed faith 9
Regulators 10
Reid, Richard 234n49
Republican Party 20, 21, 27, 35, 40, 51, 52, 53, 80, 87, 96, 97, 100, 112, 117, 134, 144, 178, 212, 213; *see also* Republicans
republicanism 33, 129
Republicans 9; 28, 40, 51, 53, 86, 87, 88, 91, 92, 100, 102, 107, 134, 144, 152, 153, 154, 197, 208, 209, 211, 212; *see also* Black Republicans; Republican Party
Reunionist Manifesto 145, 148, 152
reunionists *see* Unionists
Revis, J.F. 55, 56
revolt *see* rebellion
Revolutionary War *see* American Revolution
Richardson, W.B. 96, 97
Richardson, William A. 79

Richardson, William B. 55, 234n42
Richmond, Ind. 23
Richmond, Va. 5, 29, 45, 48, 53, 54, 79, 84, 88, 97, 100, 108, 110, 112, 113, 126, 128, 132, 134, 142, 143, 147, 156, 181, 183, 185, 189, 200, 204, 205, 207, 208, 209, 211
Richmond County, N.C. 91, 143, 144, 161, 164, 211; *see also* Richmond County Home Guards
Richmond County Home Guards 170
Richmond Examiner (newspaper) 36
Ritter, Thomas W. 96, 118, 119
Roanoke Island, N.C. 7, 38
Roaring River, N.C. 106, 182
Robards, Robert S. 106
Robards, T.S. 56
Roberts, A. Sellew 234n49
Robeson County, N.C. 165
Robins, M.S. 147–148
Rockingham, N.C. 191
Rockingham County, N.C. 143, 213
Ross, Captain (aids Randolph County sheriff) 40
Rowan County, N.C. 9, 27, 31, 81, 91, 95, 97, 158; *see also* Rowan County Home Guards
Rowan County Home Guards 181
Rush (dissident) 40
Rush, D.R. 238n54
Rush, Noah 163, 190–191, 201
Rush, Zebedee 147, 163
Rush, Z.F. 147, 163, 201
Russell, Mr. (victim of deserters) 182
Rutherford County, N.C. 81, 97, 132, 181

sabotage 39
Salem, N.C. 36, 37, 43, 72, 149, 194, 197
Salem Brass Band 197
Salem Church, N.C. 64, 66
Salisbury, N.C. 72, 75, 86, 94, 112, 158, 159, 186, 194, 195, 200
salt 43, 46, 71, 170, 203
Sanders, Jacob 119–120
Sandy Creek, N.C. 10
Sandy Ridge Wesleyan Church 16
Satterthwaite, F.D. 89
Sauratown Mountains 72
Scalawags 8, 40, 145, 196
Scarboro, David D. 98, 99, 100
Schooley peneplain 72
Scotland 175
Scots-Irish 9
Scott, W.L. 37
Scott's Old Field 38, 39, 200, 205
Seagrove, N.C. 193
Seawell, A.A. 96
Seawell, S.W. 96
secession 1, 36, 44, 38, 45, 81, 82, 83, 144, 149, 199, 200, 201, 205, 212, 214; conventions 7, 30, 33, 131; deserters and insurgents target supporters of 58, 59, 70, 107, 108, 119–120, 164, 188, 193, 2; Hanes on 86–88; Holden and 20, 95, 134, 140–141, 154, 164, 209; and Home Guards 35; illegality of 51; and peace movement 95–96, 99–100, 127, 132; Unionism and 28–29, 32, 197; Vance and 202, 209; widespread opposition to 27, 196
"The Secessionists — their Promises and their Performances — the Condition into which they have brought the Country — the Remedy, etc." (tract) 86
Seckler, A. Henry (combatant) 83
Seddon, John 109–110
sedition 35, 37
Semi-Weekly Standard (newspaper) 2, 82, 85, 146, 154
Senior Reserves 1, 55, 149, 155–156, 159, 161, 162, 164, 165, 169, 170, 176, 181, 184, 209, 210
Settle, Thomas 120, 143, 171, 173–174, 178, 213, 234n42,59
Seventeenth Regiment North Carolina Troops 71
Seventh Congressional District 86, 139–142, 156, 159, 161, 164, 192
Seventh Regiment North Carolina Troops 211
Seventh Regiment Senior Reserves 193
Shaffner, J.F. 138
Shamburger, Peter 58
Sharpe, Leander Q. 151, 210
Sharpe, S.A. 112, 195
Shaw, Bynum 234n49
Sheffield Township, N.C. 59
Shenandoah Valley 9
Sherman, William T. 40, 121, 151, 155, 180, 181, 185, 187, 188, 190, 191, 192, 211
Shoemstes (deserter) 182
Silver Valley, N.C. 115
Simons, Pleasant 58, 119, 120
Sixty-eighth Regiment North Carolina Troops 161
Sixty-first North Carolina Regiment 114
Sixty-fourth Militia Regiment 64
Sixty-third Militia Regiment 63
slaveholders 11, 13, 14, 15, 16, 21, 24, 27, 43, 44, 101, 133, 134, 140, 197, 200, 201, 202
slavery 9, 11, 15, 16, 19, 20–21, 22, 23–24, 25, 28, 29, 31, 32, 54, 87, 88, 94, 95, 101, 117, 126, 131, 136, 141, 152, 153–154, 196, 197, 199; plans for peace and reunion that protect 8, 49, 51, 79, 82, 84–86, 92, 93, 99, 101, 102, 127, 128, 129–130, 132, 133–134, 135, 137, 141, 157, 203, 205, 206–207, 211; *see also* abolition; anti-slavery movement; emancipation; Emancipation Proclamation; Preliminary Emancipation Proclamation; slaveholders; slaves
slaves 7, 10, 27, 28, 31, 32, 42, 43, 44, 48, 51, 52, 53, 58, 61, 67, 73, 74, 76, 85, 87, 88, 89, 94, 95, 97, 99, 129, 130, 132, 134, 145, 151, 156, 161–163, 200, 201, 208; 89; *see also* abolition; anti-slavery movement; emancipation; Emancipation Proclamation; Preliminary Emancipation Proclamation; slaveholders; slavery
Smith, W.M. 96
Smoot, Gideon 241n125
Smoot, Granville 99, 106, 111, 171
Snow Camp, N.C. 14, 53, 55, 114, 115
Society for the Diffusion of Political Knowledge 152
Society of Friends 11, 12, 14, 46, 47, 48; *see also* Quakers
"Solus" (pen name) 131
sound region 7, 27, 89, 151, 180
South Carolina 6, 10, 29, 150, 181, 185, 187
Southampton County, Va. 12
Speaks, Milton 34
speculation 43
Spencer, Clark 65
spies *see* espionage
Spring Town, Ind. 75
Sprinkle, Lindsey 34
Sprinkle, O. (Unionist) 34
squirearchy 98, 99, 100
Stafford, John 19
Stafford, Thomas 41
Stage Road 104
Staly, C. (victim of deserters) 185
Stanly County, N.C. 9, 15, 16, 72, 81, 91, 95
starvation *see* hunger
states' rights 5, 51, 68, 82, 87, 96, 134, 142, 143
Statesville, N.C. 54, 106, 112, 195
steamships 73
Steed, Henry 63
Stephens, Alexander H. 53, 149, 154
Stevens, Thaddeus 40
Stipe, W.B. 149
Stokes County, N.C. 5, 10, 11, 16, 33, 56, 138, 169, 171, 181, 196
Stokes County Home Guards 181
Stone, Mr. (Wesleyan minister) 17
Stoneman, George 76, 194–195, 211
Strother, F.K. 50, 154
substitutions (military) 43, 44, 200
suffrage *see* voting rights
sugar 62
Supporting Force 156, 159, 160, 161, 164, 187
Surry County, N.C. 5, 10, 11, 19, 32, 38, 72, 81, 85, 90–91; 138,

181, 182, 183, 196, 200; *see also* Surry County Home Guards
Surry County Home Guards 157, 161, 181
Swaim, Benjamin 11
Swaim, William 11, 12
Swain, David L. 20, 136, 137

Tabernacle Township, N.C. 38
Tatum, Georgia Lee 7, 215n2
tax laws 2, 82, 87, 90, 96, 130, 187, 204, 205, 207, 212
telegraph 152, 159
Templeton, John 99, 108
Templeton, Thomas 108
The Ten Commandments (tract) 15
tenants 26, 31, 43, 47, 73, 200
Tennessee 6, 10, 27, 40, 75, 85, 88, 92, 107, 126, 145, 146, 151, 157, 158, 159, 160, 169, 171, 181, 190, 194, 195, 211
Tenth Michigan Regiment 197
Tenth Ohio Regiment of Cavalry 197
Tenth Tennessee Cavalry 107
Texas 88
Third Indiana Cavalry 193
Third North Carolina Mounted Infantry Volunteers 158
Thirty-third Regiment North Carolina troops 40
Thomas (militiaman) 64
Thomasville, N.C. 36, 39, 40, 141, 171, 199, 200
tidewater 11, 180
Times (Hendersonville newspaper) 79
"To the Soldiers of the 7th Congressional District" (circular) 140
tobacco 13, 31, 32, 62, 65, 108, 202
Tom (company commander) 47
Tories 10, 24, 33, 69, 76, 103, 107, 113, 157, 158, 160, 166, 182, 187; *see also* Unionists
Tourgee, Albion W. 213–214
Trap Hill, N.C. 105, 106, 107, 111, 161, 164, 207
Trap Hill Seminary (Methodist) 107
"A Traveler" (pen name) 36–37
treason 34, 35, 40, 58, 69, 90, 91, 93, 128, 134, 137, 144, 149, 206, 209
Trinity, N.C. 29, 139
Trinity College 36, 37; *see also* Trinity Guards
Trinity Guards 36, **37**, 40
Troy, N.C. 16, 98, 148, 162, 166–167, 170
Troy's Store, N.C. 187
Tryon, William 10
Turner, Josiah, Jr. 97
turpentine 31–32
Twelfth New York Cavalry 75
Twelfth Ohio Regiment 197
Twenty-first Regiment North Carolina Troops 113, 115, 138

Twenty-fourth Regiment North Carolina Troops 68
Twenty-second Regiment North Carolina Troops 137–138
Twenty-sixth Regiment North Carolina Troops 44, 57, 70
Twenty-third Regiment North Carolina Troops 190, 211
Tyson, Aaron 48
Tyson, Bryan 43, 62, 201, 214; and *Object of the Administration in Prosecuting the War* 152–154, 210–211; and peace movement 2–3, 78, 88, 98, 109, 203–204, 234n42; and slavery 24, 76, 101–102, 135; Unionist and reunionist sentiments of 8, 29, 47–54, **49**, 79, 88, 99, 126, 132, 135–136, 147, 205, 207
Tysor, Harris 114

Ulster 9
Underground Railroad 1, 12, 39, 53, 74–76, 145–146, 169, 205
Union County, N.C. 165
Union Institute Academy 139; *see also* Trinity College
Union Meetinghouse 17, 18
Union Party 28, 45, 117; *see also* Conservative Party; Unionists
"A Union War Democrat" (pen name) *see* Tyson, Bryan
Unionists 1, 5, 6, 7–8, 24–25, 30, 47–48, 53, 55, 73, 77, 87, 95, 99–100, 102, 112, 144, 145, 163, 178, 207, 208, 213; Bryan Tyson and 116, 153–154; 199–202; flee the Confederacy 74–76, 181; harsh treatment of, by political and military enemies 82, 112, 192; Lincoln fails to assist southern 54; meetings and demonstrations of 40, 93, 96, 106–107, 111, 116, 117, 195–198, 211, 212; organize in early days of war, 33–38; *see also* Constitutional Union Party; disloyalists; Heroes of America; Tories; Union Party
United States Army 7, 38, 39, 40, 44, 50, 52, 57, 73, 74, 75, 76, 79, 84, 85, 89, 93, 97, 101, 103, 107, 116, 117, 121, 129, 130, 143, 146, 149, 151, 153–154, 155, 158–, 169, 171, 175, 178, 180, 181, 184, 189, 190, 192, 195, 196, 198, 200, 201, 203, 206, 210; and Confederate deserters 54, 157, 158, 182, 183, 188, 208
United States Congress 27, 40, 44, 81, 86, 87, 93, 100, 128, 129, 130, 140, 152, 197, 205, 208, 212
United States Constitution 2, 8, 11, 17, 27, 29, 49, 51, 52, 68, 79, 80, 82, 88, 89, 91, 95, 98, 102, 108, 129, 130, 132, 133, 135, 137, 140, 147, 151, 152, 153, 154, 196, 203, 205, 206, 208, 210

United States House of Representatives 21, 81, 86, 130, 139
United States Military Academy 139
United States Navy 7, 20, 46, 51, 52, 180, 184
United States of America 7, 12, 13, 29, 30, 35, 49, 52, 53, 54, 71, 73, 75, 76, 80, 87, 105, 106, 107, 121, 125, 126, 127, 129, 130, 133, 134, 151, 152, 181, 195–196, 197, 198, 199, 203, 212, 213, 214
United States Patent Office 19, 20, 53, 153
United States Regulars 107
United States Senate 213
United States Supreme Court 87, 129, 130
United States Treasury Department 53
University of North Carolina 19, 20, 87, 136, 137
Uwharrie Mountains 72

Vallandigham, Clement L. 79, 82, 205
Van Buren, Martin 19
Vance, Zebulon Baird 42, 85, 89, 91, 136, 144–145, 147–148, 151, 180–181; and deserters' and Confederates' depredations 69–70, 115, 118–119, 120, 122, 123, 188, 189, 207–208; and 1876 gubernatorial election 213; and 1864 gubernatorial campaign 139, 142–143, 146, 147, 149–150, 208–209; and peace movement 53, 83, 84, 90, 91–92, 94–97, 126, 127, 128–129, 131, 134–135, 140, 141, 208; rumored assassination of 146; and suppression of draft-dodgers, deserters, and disloyalists 1–2, 44–**45**, 47–48, 54–60, 60–70, 74, 76–77, 78, 103–105, 109–113, 155–180, 183–184, 190, 194, 202, 204, 210, 211;
Van Noppen, Ina W. 195
"Veritas" (pen name) 174–175
Vestal, Alfred 21
vigilance committee 34
vigilantism 16–17, 59
Virginia 6, 9, 10, 12, 18, 108, 138, 142, 151, 158, 180, 194
A Voice from North Carolina (tract) 89
volunteers (military) 33, 34, 36, 38, 39, 40
voter intimidation 149–150, 209; *see also* polling irregularities
"Voting in the Woods" (newspaper article) 146
voting rights 211

Waddell, J. (Confederate soldier) 191
Wadesboro, N.C. 54, 192
Wagner, William F. 139
Wake County, N.C. 33, 81, 131

Walker, David 12
Wall, Captain (Twenty-third Regiment North Carolina Troops) 190
Wallace, Isham 168
Walters, William F. 188, 193, 194
War Democrats 51
War of 1812 168
Warren's Bridge (gathering place for deserters) 106–107
Washington, D.C. 19, 53, 54, 87, 88, 89, 116, 131, 140, 147, 152, 153, 154, 173
Washington, N.C. 180
Watauga County, N.C. 157, 158, 169, 171, 182, 183
Watauga County Home Guards 169, 171, 183
Watson, B.N. 160
Waugh, A. (beaten by deserters) 189
Wayne County, Ind. 75
Wayne County Home Guards (N.C.) 167
Weekly Conservative (Raleigh newspaper) 121, 146, 157, 160
Weekly Standard (newspaper) 80, 94, 137, 175, 207
Weldon, N.C. 114
Wesley, Charles 13
Wesley, John 13
Wesleyan Methodist Church 13, 21
Wesleyan Methodist Connection 13
Wesleyan Methodists 7, 10, 13–18, 123, 172, 199; *see also* Wesleyan Methodist Church
Wesleyans 18–19, 32, 34, 73, 83, 141, 147, 148, 177, 185, 199, 201, 206, 210, 213, 214; *see also* Worth, Daniel
West, James 66
West Virginia 92
Western District of North Carolina 181
Western North Carolina Railroad 72
Wheeler, B.F. 160
Wheeler, Jesse 23, 24, 74, 75, 181–182
Wheeler, Joseph 192, 193
Wheeler, William H. 149
Wheeler's Cavalry 193

Whigs 1, 2, 5, 7, 10, 12, 19, 26, 27, 28, 29, 30, 34, 43–44, 45, 46, 49, 73, 81, 82, 83, 86, 87, 94, 99, 100, 112, 115, 132, 137, 139, 140, 141, 143, 199, 201, 202, 203, 205, 206, 209, 212, 214
Whisky Rebellion 10
Whitaker, Spier 39, 40
whites 7, 9, 11, 16, 21, 23, 31, 33, 34, 35, 44, 65, 67, 91, 100, 101, 153, 178, 200, 201
Whiting, William Henry Chase 46, 114
Why Not, N.C. 58, 186
Wilkes County, N.C. 5, 7, 33, 55–56, 61, 107, 108, 181, 194, 213; deserters, draft-dodgers, and disloyalists in 69, 72, 75, 109, 110–113, 124, 138–139, 157, 164–165, 169, 179, 182, 189, 195, 201, 203, 204, 207, 208; and peace agitation 81, 91, 105, 114, 131, 149; support for Holden in 247, 161, 175–176; Unionism in 28, 29, 30, 32, 34, 36, 37, 106; *see also* Wilkes County Home Guards
Wilkes County Home Guards 113, 161, 167, 169, 181, 182–183
Wilkesboro, N.C. 29, 34, 106, 111, 112, 114, 142, 157, 165
Willard, Benjamin 66, 156–157
Willard, Elkanah 156
Willard, Lee 66, 156–157
Willard, William 157
Williams, Captain (killer of Dial brother) 108
Williams, David 5, 7
Williams, John 66
Williams, Loton 65
Williams, Michael 182
Williamson, Noah 170
Wilmington, N.C. 12, 46, 73, 132, 136, 155, 180, 184, 210
Wilson, Daniel 17, 18–19, 21, 22
Wilson, Martine 36
Wilson County, N.C. 165; *see also* Wilson County Home Guards
Wilson County Home Guards 167
Winston, N.C. 37, 197
Womble, E. (killed by Supporting Force) 234n49
women 56, 61, 67, 111, 115, 162, 166, 202, 203; abuse of, by deserters and military 1–2, 45, 59, 64–65, 118, 120–122, 123–125; 168, 169, 170, 171–173, 174, 175, 178, 179, 185, 189, 193; assist and encourage deserters, draft-dodgers, and disloyalists 73, 105, 106, 139
Wood, Fernando 133, 153
Woodward, J. F. 157
World (New York newspaper) 153
Worth, Daniel 19, 21–22, 24, 58, 141
Worth, John Milton 28–29, **46**, 55, 56, 88–89, 147, 163, 187, 188, 190, 191, 192, 202
Worth, Jonathan 21, **28**–29, 46, 65, 88, 101, 132, 133, 136, 143, 147, 187, 211
Worth/McAlister house **190**
Worth, Shubal G. 104, 122
Worth, W.S. 198
Wyatt (victim of deserters) 182

Yadkin County, N.C. 5, 7, 10, 61, 149, 111, 213; antislavery sentiment in 11; Confederate depredations in 108; deserters, draft-dodgers, and disloyalists in 38, 47, 55, 57, 72, 105, 106, 107, 112, 156–158, 161, 164–165, 169, 190, 193, 207; and peace agitation 81, 131, 207; schoolhouse shootout in 66–69, 157, 204; Unionism in 30, 34, 36, 37, 196; *see also* Yadkin County Home Guards
Yadkin County Home Guards 107, 161, 181
Yadkin River 75, 112, 158
Yadkinville, N.C. 67, 156, 157, 204
Yates, Richard E. 234n49
Yellowly, E.L. 161
yeomen 9, 10, 19, 24, 26, 31, 43, 61, 73, 82, 83, 99, 200, 201, 202, 203, 205, 207
Yonkers, N.Y. 89
York, Harris 65
Younger, Jo. 157
Youngers (deserters) 182

Zuber, Richard L. 101

www.ingramcontent.com/pod-product-compliance
Ingram Content Group UK Ltd.
Pitfield, Milton Keynes, MK11 3LW, UK
UKHW050538150426
5217IPUK00026B/1986